Ancient Texts *for* New Testament Studies

Ancient Texts *for* New Testament Studies

A Guide to the Background Literature

CRAIG A. EVANS

HENDRICKSON PUBLISHERS

© 2005 by Hendrickson Publishers, Inc.
P. O. Box 3473
Peabody, Massachusetts 01961-3473

ISBN 1-56563-409-8

Ancient Texts for New Testament Studies: A Guide to the Background Literature is a major expansion and revision of an earlier work by Craig A. Evans, *Noncanonical Writings and New Testament Intepretation* (Peabody, Mass.: Hendrickson, 1992).

Printed in the United States of America

First Printing — November 2005

Cover Art: The cover photograph is of a third-century Christian sarcophagus depicting the deceased reading his testament to his heirs. Museu i Necròpolis Paleocristians, Tarragona, Spain. Photograph by James H. Charlesworth.

Library of Congress Cataloging-in-Publication Data

Evans, Craig A.
    Ancient texts for New Testament studies : a guide to the background literature / Craig A. Evans.
        p. cm.
    Includes bibliographical references and index.
    ISBN 1-56563-409-8 (alk. paper)
    1. Bible. N.T.—Study and teaching. 2. Literature, Ancient—History and criticism. 3. Intertextuality in the Bible—Study and teaching. 4. Literature, Ancient—Bibliography. I. Title.
    BS2530.E93 2005
    225'.066—dc22

                                                        2005023156

For James A. Sanders
Scholar, Mentor, Colleague

Contents

Preface

Ancient Texts for New Testament Studies is an introduction to the diverse bodies of literatures that are in various ways cognate to biblical literature, especially to the New Testament. It has been written to serve the needs of students who aspire to become New Testament interpreters. Although it has been prepared primarily for the student, veterans of academy and church will find it useful as well.

The last generation has witnessed the discovery and publication of a remarkable amount of ancient literature that in various ways is relevant to New Testament interpretation. Scholarly research has made it abundantly clear that much of this material proves to be exegetically helpful. But the sheer magnitude and diversity of this material have also proven to be intimidating to many students. Indeed, there are many teachers of biblical literature who are not sure exactly what makes up this literature, how it is relevant, and how it is to be accessed. The purpose of this book is to arrange these diverse literatures into a comprehensible and manageable format. Not only will the various components of these literatures be listed and briefly described, specific examples will be offered to illustrate how they contribute to New Testament exegesis. Brief bibliographies will also be included with each section. A selected number of the major primary and secondary works will be cited. An index to the titles and authors of these writings will make it possible for the non-specialist to find them quickly.

A word of thanks is due Matthew Walsh and Danny Zacharias for their assistance in the preparation of the indexes.

Because this book is a tool designed to encourage students to make better use of the various primary literatures that are cognate to the writings of the Bible, I think that it is entirely fitting that it should be dedicated to James A. Sanders, Emeritus Professor of Biblical Studies at Claremont School of Theology and retired president of the Ancient Biblical Manuscript Center for Preservation and Research. From him I have learned much about Scripture and the communities of faith that studied and transmitted it.

C. A. Evans
Acadia Divinity College

Abbreviations

General Abbreviations

B.C.E.	before the Common Era
ca.	circa
C.E.	Common Era
cf.	*confer*, compare
ch(s).	chapter(s)
cm	centimeter(s)
col(s).	column(s)
ed(s).	editor(s), edited by
e.g.	*exempli gratia*, for example
Eng.	English
esp.	especially
ET	English translation
et al.	*et alii*, and others
etc.	*et cetera*, and the rest
exp.	expanded
fasc.	fascicle(s)
fig.	figurative, figuratively
frg.	fragment
FS	Festschrift
Gk.	Greek, referring to lexical forms, not translation
Heb.	Hebrew
i.e.	*id est*, that is
lit.	literally
LXX	Septuagint (the Greek OT)
MS(S)	manuscript(s)
MT	Masoretic Text (of the OT)
NASB	New American Standard Bible
NB	*nota bene*, note carefully

NEB	New English Bible
n.p.	no place; no publisher; no page
NHC	Nag Hammadi Codex
no(s).	number(s)
NRSV	New Revised Standard Version
NS	new series
NT	New Testament
OT	Old Testament
p(p).	page(s)
par.	parallel (use to indicate textual parallels, e.g., Matt 25:14–30 par. Luke 19:11–27)
pl(s).	plural; plate
praef.	*praefatio*, preface
repr.	reprinted
rev.	revised (by)
RSV	Revised Standard Version
sg.	singular
SP	Samaritan Pentateuch
trans.	translator, translated by; transitive
v(v).	verse(s)
viz.	*videlicet*, namely
vol(s).	volume(s)

Old Testament Pseudepigrapha

Apoc. Ab.	*Apocalypse of Abraham*
Apoc. El. (C)	Coptic *Apocalypse of Elijah*
Apoc. Ezek.	Use *Apocr. Ezek.*
Apoc. Mos.	*Apocalypse of Moses*
Apoc. Sedr.	*Apocalypse of Sedrach*
Apoc. Zeph.	*Apocalypse of Zephaniah*
Apocr. Ezek.	*Apocryphon of Ezekiel*
As. Mos.	*Assumption of Moses*
Ascen. Isa.	*Mart. Ascen. Isa.* 6–11
2 Bar.	*2 Baruch (Syriac Apocalypse)*
3 Bar.	*3 Baruch (Greek Apocalypse)*
4 Bar.	*4 Baruch (Paraleipomena Jeremiou)*
1 En.	*1 Enoch (Ethiopic Apocalypse)*
2 En.	*2 Enoch (Slavonic Apocalypse)*
3 En.	*3 Enoch (Hebrew Apocalypse)*
Hist. Rech.	*History of the Rechabites*
Jos. Asen.	*Joseph and Aseneth*
Jub.	*Jubilees*

L.A.B.	*Liber antiquitatum biblicarum* (Pseudo-Philo)
L.A.E.	*Life of Adam and Eve*
Let. Aris.	*Letter of Aristeas*
Liv. Pro.	*Lives of the Prophets*
Mart. Ascen. Isa.	*Martyrdom and Ascension of Isaiah*
Mart. Isa.	*Mart. Ascen. Isa.* 1–5
Pr. Jos.	*Prayer of Joseph*
Pss. Sol.	*Psalms of Solomon*
Sib. Or.	*Sibylline Oracles*
Syr. Men.	*Sentences of the Syriac Menander*
T. Ab.	*Testament of Abraham*
T. Ash.	*Testament of Asher*
T. Benj.	*Testament of Benjamin*
T. Dan	*Testament of Dan*
T. Gad	*Testament of Gad*
T. Isaac	*Testament of Isaac*
T. Iss.	*Testament of Issachar*
T. Job	*Testament of Job*
T. Jos.	*Testament of Joseph*
T. Jud.	*Testament of Judah*
T. Levi	*Testament of Levi*
T. Mos.	*Testament of Moses*
T. Naph.	*Testament of Naphtali*
T. Reu.	*Testament of Reuben*
T. Sim.	*Testament of Simeon*
T. Sol.	*Testament of Solomon*
T. Zeb.	*Testament of Zebulun*

Dead Sea Scrolls and Related Texts

For the abbreviations of the many texts from the area of the Dead Sea, see chapter 3.

Ḥev	Naḥal Ḥever
Ḥev/Se	Used for documents earlier attributed to Seiyal
Mas	Masada
Mird	Khirbet Mird
Mish	Naḥal Mishmar
Mur	Murabbaʿat
Q	Qumran
Sdeir	Wadi Sdeir
Ṣe	Naḥal Ṣeʾelim

Philo

Alleg. Interp. 1, 2, 3	*Allegorical Interpretation* 1, 2, 3
Cherubim	*On the Cherubim*
Confusion	*On the Confusion of Tongues*
Creation	*On the Creation of the World*
Decalogue	*On the Decalogue*
Dreams 1, 2	*On Dreams* 1, 2
Embassy	*On the Embassy to Gaius*
Flaccus	*Against Flaccus*
Flight	*On Flight and Finding*
Giants	*On Giants*
Good Person	*That Every Good Person Is Free*
Heir	*Who Is the Heir?*
Migration	*On the Migration of Abraham*
Moses 1, 2	*On the Life of Moses* 1, 2
Posterity	*On the Posterity of Cain*
Providence 1, 2	*On Providence* 1, 2
QE 1, 2	*Questions and Answers on Exodus* 1, 2
QG 1, 2, 3, 4	*Questions and Answers on Genesis* 1, 2, 3, 4
Rewards	*On Rewards and Punishments*
Sacrifices	*On the Sacrifices of Cain and Abel*
Sobriety	*On Sobriety*
Spec. Laws 1, 2, 3, 4	*On the Special Laws* 1, 2, 3, 4
Virtues	*On the Virtues*
Worse	*That the Worse Attacks the Better*

Josephus

Ag. Ap.	*Against Apion*
Ant.	*Jewish Antiquities*
J.W.	*Jewish War*
Life	*The Life*

Mishnah, Talmud, and Related Literature

b.	Babylonian Talmud
m.	Mishna
t.	Tosefta
y.	Jerusalem Talmud

ʿAbod. Zar.	ʿAbodah Zarah	Avodah Zarah
ʿArak.	ʿArakin	Arakhin
B. Bat.	Baba Batra	Bava Batra
B. Meṣiʿa	Baba Meṣiʿa	Bava Metziʾa
B. Qam.	Baba Qamma	Bava Qamma
Bek.	Bekorot	Bekhorot
Ber.	Berakot	Berakhot
Bik.	Bikkurim	Bikkurim
ʿEd.	ʿEduyyot	Eduyyot
ʿErub.	ʿErubin	Eruvin
Giṭ.	Giṭṭin	Gittin
Ḥag.	Ḥagigah	Ḥagigah
Hor.	Horayot	Horayot
Ḥul.	Ḥullin	Hullin
Ker.	Kerithot	Keritot
Ketub.	Ketubbot	Ketubbot
Mak.	Makkot	Makkot
Meg.	Megillah	Megillah
Meʿil.	Meʿilah	Meʾilah
Menaḥ.	Menaḥot	Menahot
Moʾed Qaṭ.	Moʾed Qaṭan	Moʾed Qatan
Naz.	Nazir	Nazir
Ned.	Nedarim	Nedarim
Neg.	Negaʿim	Negaʾim
Nid.	Niddah	Niddah
Pesaḥ.	Pesaḥim	Pesahim
Qidd.	Qiddušin	Qiddushin
Roš Haš.	Roš Haššanah	Rosh HaShanah
Šabb.	Šabbat	Shabbat
Sanh.	Sanhedrin	Sanhedrin
Šeb.	Šebiʾit	Sheviʾit
Šebu.	Šebuʿot	Shevuʾot
Šeqal.	Šeqalim	Sheqalim
Taʿan.	Taʿanit	Taʾanit
Ṭohor.	Ṭohorot	Tohorot
Yad.	Yadayim	Yadayim
Yebam.	Yebamot	Yevamot
Zebaḥ.	Zebaḥim	Zevahim

Targumic Texts

C.Tg.	Cairo (Geniza) Targum
Frg. Tg.	Fragmentary Targum

Sam. Tg.	Samaritan Targum	
Tg. Esth. I, II	First or Second Targum of Esther	
Tg. Isa.	Targum Isaiah	
Tg. Onq.	Targum Onqelos	
Tg. Neof.	Targum Neofiti	
Tg. Ps.-J.	Targum Pseudo-Jonathan	

Other Rabbinic Works

ʾAbot R. Nat.	ʾAbot de Rabbi Nathan	Avot of Rabbi Nathan
Der. Er. Rab.	Derek Ereṣ Rabbah	Derekh Eretz Rabbah
Kallah Rab.	Kallah Rabbati	Kallah Rabbati
Mek.	Mekilta	Mekilta
Mek. R. Sim. Yoh.	Mekilta de Rabbi Simeon ben Yohai	
Midr.	Midrash I (+ biblical book)	Midrash
Pesiq. Rab.	Pesiqta Rabbati	Pesiqta Rabbati
Pesiq. Rab Kah.	Pesiqta de Rab Kahana	Pesiqta of Rab Kahana
Pirqe R. El.	Pirqe Rabbi Eliezer	Pirqe Rabbi Eliezer
Rab. (e.g., Gen. Rab. = Genesis Rabbah)	Rabbah (+ biblical book)	Rabbah
S. Eli. Rab.	Seder Eliyahu Rabbah	Seder Eliyahu Rabbah
Sem.	Semaḥot	Semahot
Tanḥ.	Tanḥuma	Tanhuma

Apostolic Fathers

Barn.	Barnabas
1–2 Clem.	1–2 Clement
Did.	Didache
Herm. Vis.	Shepherd Hermas, Vision
Ign. Rom.	Ignatius, To the Romans
Pol. Phil.	Polycarp, To the Philippians

Nag Hammadi Codices

Nag Hammadi Codices (=NHC) are identified by the codex number (I) followed by treatise number (1).

Ap. Jas.	I,2 Apocryphon of James
Treat. Res.	I,4 Treatise on the Resurrection
Ap. John	II,1 Apocryphon of John

Gos. Phil.	II,*3 Gospel of Philip*
Dial. Sav.	III,*5 Dialogue of the Savior*
Acts Pet. 12 Apos.	VI,*1 Acts of Peter and the Twelve Apostles*
Apoc. Pet.	VII,*3 Apocalypse of Peter*
Ep. Pet. Phil.	VIII,*2 Letter of Peter to Philip*
Testim. Truth	IX,*3 Testimony of Truth*
Interp. Know.	XI,*1 Interpretation of Knowledge*
Sent. Sextus	XII,*1 Sentences of Sextus*

New Testament Apocrypha and Pseudepigrapha

Acts Pil.	*Acts of Pilate*
Apos. Con.	*Apostolic Constitutions and Canons*
Gos. Eb.	*Gospel of the Ebionites*
Gos. Eg.	*Gospel of the Egyptians*
Gos. Heb.	*Gospel of the Hebrews*
Gos. Naz.	*Gospel of the Nazarenes*
Gos. Pet.	*Gospel of Peter*
Gos. Thom.	*Gospel of Thomas*
Inf. Gos. Thom.	*Infancy Gospel of Thomas*
Prot. Jas.	*Protevangelium of James*
Ps.-Clem.	*Pseudo-Clementines*

Ancient Christian Writings

Clement of Alexandria

Exc.	*Excerpta ex Theodoto*	
Paed.	*Paedagogus*	
Strom.	*Stromata*	

Epiphanius

Pan.	*Panarion (Adversus haereses)*

Eusebius

Hist. eccl.	*Historia ecclesiastica*
Praep. ev.	*Praeparatio evangelica*
Theoph.	*Theophania*

Hippolytus

Haaer.	*Refutatio omnium haeresium (Philosophoumena)*	*Refutation of All Heresies*

Irenaeus

Haer.	*Adversus haereses*

Jerome
  Comm. Eph.   *Commentariorum in Epistulam*
                    ad Ephesios libri III
  Comm. Isa.   *Commentariorum in Isaiam*
                    libri XVIII
  Comm. Matt.   *Commentariorum in Mattheum*
                    libri IV
  Pelag.   *Adversus Pelagianos dialogi III*   Against the Pelagians
  Vir. ill.   *De viris illustribus*   On Men of Distinction
Justin Martyr
  1 Apol.   *First Apology*
  Dial.   *Dialogue with Trypho*
Lactantius
  Inst.   *Divinarum institutionum*   Divine Institutes
                    libri VII

Origen
  Cels.   *Contra Celsum*   Against Celsus
  Comm. Jo.   *Commentarii in evangelium*   Commentary on John
                    Johannis
  Comm. Matt.   *Commentarium in*   Commentary on Matthew
                    evangelium Matthei
  Hom. Jer.   *Homiliae in Jeremiam*
Philostorgius
  Hist. eccl.   *Historia ecclesiastica*
  Marc.   *Adversus Marcionem*
Tertullian
  Bapt.   *De baptismo*
  Marc.   *Adversus Marcionem*

Ancient Non-Christian Writings

Aelian
  Hist. var.   *Historia varia*
Aelius Aristides
  Or.   *Orationes*
Aeschylus
  Ag.   *Agamemnon*
  Pers.   *Persae*   Persians
  Prom.   *Prometheus vinctus*   Prometheus Bound
  Sept.   *Septem contra Thebas*   Seven against Thebes
  Suppl.   *Supplices*   Suppliant Women
Aetius
  Plac. phil.   *De placita philosophorum*

Ammianus Marcellinus
   Res gest.   *Res gestae*
Anthologia palatina
   Anth. pal.   *Anthologia palatina*
Appian
   Bell. civ.   *Bella civilia*   *Civil Wars*
   Hist. rom.   *Historia romana*   *Roman History*
Apuleius
   Metam.   *Metamorphoses*
Aratus
   Phaen.   *Phaenomena*
Aristotle
   Cael.   *De caelo*   *Heavens*
   Eth. eud.   *Ethica eudemia*   *Eudemian Ethics*
   Eth. nic.   *Ethica nichomachea*   *Nicomachean Ethics*
   Pol.   *Politica*   *Politics*
   Rhet.   *Rhetorica*   *Rhetoric*
Arrian
   Anab.   *Anabasis*
Caesar
   Bell. gall.   *Bellum gallicum*   *Gallic War*
Callimachus
   Hymn. Cer.   *Hymnus in Cererem*   *Hymn to Ceres or Demeter*
Cebetis Tabula
   Ceb. Tab.   *Cebetis Tabula*
Cicero
   Fam.   *Epistulae ad familiares*
   Fin.   *De finibus*
   Nat. d.   *De natura deorum*
   Off.   *De officiis*
   Rosc. Amer.   *Pro Roscio Amerino Sexto*
   Sen.   *De senectute*
   Tusc.   *Tusculanae disputationes*
Corpus hermeticum
   Corp. herm.   *Corpus hermeticum*
Crates
   Ep.   *Epistulae*
Digesta
   Dig.   *Digesta*
Dio Cassius
   Hist. rom.   *Historia romana*
Dio Chrysostom
   Disc.   *Discourses*
Diodorus Siculus
   Bib. hist.   *Bibliotheca hist.*   *Library of History*

Diogenes
   Ep.   *Epistulae*
Diogenes Laertius
   Vit. phil.   *Vitae philosophorum*   *Lives of Eminent*
                                                  Philosophers
Epictetus
   Diatr.   *Diatribai (Dissertationnes)*
   Ench.   *Encheiridion*
Euripides
   Bacch.   *Bacchae*
   Hipp.   *Hippolytus*
   Orest.   *Orestes*
   Rhes.   *Rhesus*
Gaius
   Inst.   *Institutiones*
Galen
   Plac. Hip.   *De placitis Hippocratis et*   *On the Opinions of*
      Plat.   *Platonis*   *Hippocrates and Plato*
Heliodorus
   Aeth.   *Aethiopica*
Herodotus
   Hist.   *Historiae*   *Histories*
Hesiod
   Op.   *Opera et dies*   *Works and Days*
   Theog.   *Theogonia*   *Theogony*
Homer
   Il.   *Ilias*   *Iliad*
   Od.   *Odyssea*   *Odyssey*
Horace
   Ars   *Ars poetica*
   Carm.   *Carmina*   *Odes*
   Ep.   *Epistulae*
   Sat.   *Satirae*   *Satires*
Isocrates
   Aeginet.   *Aegineticus (Or. 19)*
   Demon.   *Ad Demonicum (Or. 1)*
   Ad Nic.   *Ad Nicoclem (Or. 2)*
Juvenal
   Sat.   *Satirae*   *Satires*
Lucian
   Alex.   *Alexander Pseudomantis*   *Alexander the False Prophet*
   Imag.   *Imagines*   *Lessons in Portraiture*
   Men.   *Menippus (Necyomantia)*
   Peregr.   *De morte Peregrini*   *The Passing of Peregrinus*
   Philops.   *Philopseudes*   *The Lover of Lies*

Macrobius
  Sat.   *Saturnalia*
Marcus Aurelius
  Med.   *Meditationes*
Martial
  Epigr.   *Epigrammaton libri XII*   *Epigrams*
Maximus of Tyre
  Diss.   *Dissertationes (Dialexeis)*
Menander
  Sent.   *Sententiae*
Ovid
  Am.   *Amores*
  Metam.   *Metamorphoses*
Pausanias
  Descr.   *Graeciae descriptio*   *Description of Greece*
Petronius
  Sat.   *Satyrica*
Philostratus
  Vit. Apoll. *Vita Apollonii*   *Life of Apollonius of Tyana*
Pindar
  Nem.   *Nemeonikai*   *Nemean Odes*
  Ol.   *Olympionikai*   *Olympian Odes*
  Pyth.   *Pythionikai*   *Pythian Odes*
Plato
  Apol.   *Apologia*   *Apology of Socrates*
  [Ax.]   *Axiochus*
  Ep.   *Epistulae*
  Gorg.   *Gorgias*
  Phaedr.   *Phaedrus*
  Resp.   *Respublica*   *Republic*
  Soph.   *Sophista*   *Sophist*
  Symp.   *Symposium*
  Theaet.   *Theaetetus*
  Tim.   *Timaeus*
Pliny the Elder
  Nat.   *Naturalis historia*
Pliny the Younger
  Ep.   *Epistulae*   *Epistles*
  Pan.   *Panegyricus*
Plutarch
  Alex. fort. *De Alexandri magni fortuna*   *On the Fortune or the*
                 aut virtute   *Virtue of Alexander*
  An vit.   *An vitiositas ad infelicitatem* *Whether Vice is Sufficient*
                 sufficiat   *to Cause Unhappiness*
  [Apoph. lac.] *Apophthegmata laconica*   *Sayings of Spartans*

Conj. praec.	*Conjugalia praecepta*	*Advice to Bride and Groom*
[Cons. Apoll.]	*Consolatio ad Apollonium*	*Letter of Condolence to Apollonius*
Def. orac.	*De defectu oraculorum*	*On the Obsolescence of Oracles*
Fort. Rom.	*De fortuna Romanorum*	*On the Fortune of the Romans*
Inim. util.	*De capienda ex imimicis utilitate*	*How to Profit by One's Enemies*
Is. Os.	*De Iside et Osiride*	*Isis and Osiris*
[Lib. ed.]	*De liberis educandis*	*On the Education of Children*
Mor.	*Moralia*	
Quaest. conv.	*Quaestionum convivialium libri IX*	*Table-Talk*
Sept. sap. conv.	*Septem sapientium convivium*	*Dinner of the Seven Wise Men*
Sera	*De sera numinis vindicta*	*On the Delays of Divine Vengeance*
Superst.	*On Superstition*	

Polybius
Hist.	*Historiae*	

Ps.-Phocylides
Sent.	*Sententiae*	

Ps.-Quintilian
Decl.	*Declamationes*	

Publilius Syrus
Sent.	*Sententiae*	

Seneca
Ag.	*Agamemnon*	
Ben.	*De beneficiis*	*On Benefits*
Brev. vit.	*De brevitate vitae*	
Ep.	*Epistulae morales*	*Moral Epistles*
Ira	*De ira*	*On Anger*
Lucil.	*Ad Lucilium*	
Marc.	*Ad Marciam de consolatione*	*To Marcia, on Consolation*
Nat.	*Naturales quaestiones*	
Ot.	*De otio*	*On Leisure*
Polyb.	*Ad Polybium de consolatione*	*To Polybius, on Consolation*
Tranq.	*De tranquillitate animi*	
Vit. beat.	*De vita beata*	*On the Happy Life*

Sophocles
Ant.	*Antigone*	
Oed. col.	*Oedipus coloneus*	
Oed. tyr.	*Oedipus tyrannus*	

Stobaeus
    Anth.   *Anthologium*
    Ecl.   *Eclogae*
    Flor.   *Florilegium*
Strabo
    Geogr.   *Geographica*
Suetonius
    Aug.   *Divus Augustus*
    Cal.   *Gaius Caligula*
    Claud.   *Divus Claudius*
    Dom.   *Domitianus*
    Vesp.   *Vespasianus*
Tacitus
    Ann.   *Annales*   *Annals*
    Hist.   *Historiae*   *Histories*
Theocritus
    Id.   *Idylls*
Theophrastus (*see* Diogenes Laertius)
Valerius Maximus
    Fact. dict.   *Factorum ac dictorum memorabilium libri XI*
Xenophon
    Cyr.   *Cyropaedia*
    Lac.   *Respublica Lacedaemoniorum*
    Mem.   *Memorabilia*
    Oec.   *Oeconomicus*
Virgil
    Aen.   *Aeneid*
    Ecl.   *Eclogae*   *Ecloges*
Zosimus
    Hist.   *Historia nova*

Abbreviations of Papyrus, Inscription, and Ostraca Collections

O.Amst.   Amsterdam ostraca
O.Berl.   Berlin ostraca
O.Bodl.   Bodleian Library ostraca
O.Florida   Florida ostraca
O.L.Bat.   Lugduno-Batavia ostraca
O.Leid.   National Museum of Antiquities at Leiden ostraca
O.Mich.   University of Michigan ostraca
O.Ont.Mus.   Royal Ontario Museum ostraca
O.Stras.   Strassburg ostraca
O.Theb.   Theban ostraca
O.Wilck.   Ulirch Wilcken ostraca

P.Amh.   Amherst papyri
P.Ant   Antinoopolis papyri
P.Cairo   Cairo papyri
P.Cair.Zen   Zenon papyri in the Cairo Museum
P.Colon.   Coloniensia papyri; see P.Köln
P.Dur.   Dura-Europos papyri
P.Edg.   C. C. Edgar papyri
P.Fay.   Fayûm papyri
P.Flor.   Florence papyri
P.Hib.   Hibeh papyri
P.Köln   Kölner (or Cologne) papyri
P.Lond.   London papyri
P.Louvre   Louvre Museum papyri
P.Merton   Merton papyri
P.Mich.   Michigan University papyri
P.Oxy.   Oxyrhynchus papyri
P.Tebt.   Tebtunis papyri

Secondary Sources

AASOR   Annual of the American Schools of Oriental Research
AB   Anchor Bible
ABRL   Anchor Bible Reference Library
AbrN   *Abr-Nahrain*
AGJU   Arbeiten zur Geschichte des antiken Judentums und des
              Urchristentums
AJP   *American Journal of Philology*
AJSL   *American Journal of Semitic Languages and Literature*
ALGHJ   Arbeiten zur Literatur und Geschichte des hellenistischen
              Judentums
AnBib   Analecta biblica
AnOx   Anecdota oxoniensia
ANRW   *Aufstieg und Niedergang der römischen Welt: Geschichte und
              Kultur Roms im Spiegel der neueren Forschung.* Edited by
              H. Temporini and W. Haase. Part 2. Berlin: de Gruyter, 1972–
ANT   *The Apocryphal New Testament: A Collection of Apocryphal
              Christian Literature in an English Translation Based on M. R.
              James.* Edited by J. K. Elliott. Oxford: Clarendon, 1993
Anuario   *Anuario de filología*
AOS   American Oriental Series
AOT   *The Apocryphal Old Testament.* Edited by H. F. D. Sparks. Ox-
              ford: Clarendon, 1984

APAMS 1	American Philosophical Association Monograph Series: Philological Monographs 1
APOT	*The Apocrypha and Pseudepigrapha of the Old Testament.* Edited by R. H. Charles. 2 vols. Oxford: Clarendon, 1913
AramSt	*Aramaic Studies*
ArBib	The Aramaic Bible
ASNU	Acta seminarii neotestamentici Upsaliensis
ASP	American Studies in Papyrology
ASTI	*Annual of the Swedish Theological Institute*
ATD	Das Alte Testament Deutsch
ATDan	Acta theologica danica
ATLA	American Theological Library Association
AThR	*Anglican Theological Review*
BA	*Biblical Archaeologist*
BASOR	*Bulletin of the American Schools of Oriental Research*
BASORSup	Bulletin of the American Schools of Oriental Research: Supplement Studies
BASPSup	Bulletin of the American Society of Papyrologists: Supplement
BBR	*Bulletin for Biblical Research*
BCNH	Bibliothèque copte de Nag Hammadi
BE	*The Books of Enoch: Aramaic Fragments of Qumrân Cave 4.* Edited by J. T. Milik with Matthew Black. Oxford: Clarendon, 1976
BEATAJ	Beiträge zur Erforschung des Alten Testaments und des antiken Judentums
BeO	*Bibbia e oriente*
BETL	Bibliotheca ephemeridum theologicarum lovaniensium
BFCT	Beiträge zur Förderung christlicher Theologie
BGU	Ägyptische Urkunden aus den Staatlichen [Königlichen] Museen zu Berlin, Griechische Urkunden. 18 vols. Berlin: Staatliche Museen zu Berlin, 1895–2000
Bib	*Biblica*
BibInt	*Biblical Interpretation*
BibOr	Biblica et orientalia
BIOSCS	*Bulletin of the International Organization for Septuagint and Cognate Studies*
BIS	Biblical Interpretation Series
BJRL	*Bulletin of the John Rylands University Library of Manchester*
BJS	Brown Judaic Studies
BN	*Biblische Notizen*
BPR	*A Bibliography of Pseudepigrapha Research, 1850–1999.* By L. DiTommaso. JSPSup 39. Sheffield: Sheffield Academic Press, 2001
BR	*Biblical Research*
BRev	*Bible Review*
BST	Basel Studies in Theology

BTB	*Biblical Theology Bulletin*
BZ	*Biblische Zeitschrift*
BZAW	Beihefte zur Zeitschrift für die alttestamentliche Wissenschaft
CBC	Cambridge Bible Commentary
CBET	Contributions to Biblical Exegesis and Theology
CBQ	*Catholic Biblical Quarterly*
CBQMS	Catholic Biblical Quarterly Monograph Series
CBS	Catalogue of Babylonian Section, University of Pennsylvania
CCHS	*A Catholic Commentary on Holy Scripture.* Edited by B. Orchard et al. New York: Thomas Nelson, 1953
CCSA	Corpus Christianorum: Series apocryphorum. Turnhout, 1983–
CCWJCW	Cambridge Commentaries on the Writings of the Jewish and Christian World, 200 B.C. to A.D. 200
CEJL	Commentaries on Early Jewish Literature
CG	*The Complete Gospels.* Edited by R. J. Miller. Sonoma, Calif.: Polebridge, 1992
CGPAT	*Concordance grecque des pseudépigraphes d'Ancien Testament.* By A.-M. Denis. Leuven: Peeters, 1987
CH	Corpus hermeticum
ChrEg	*Chronique d'Egypte*
CIA	*Corpus inscriptionum atticarum.* Edited by W. Dittenberger, A. Kirchhoff, and U. L. Koehler. 4 vols. Berlin: G. Reimer, 1873–1902.
CIG	*Corpus inscriptionum graecarum.* Edited by A. Boeckh. 4 vols. Berlin, 1828–1877. Repr., Hildesheim: Georg Olms, 1977
CII	*Corpus inscriptionum iudaicarum.* Edited by J. B. Frey. 2 vols. Rome: Pontificio Istituto di Archeologia Cristiana, 1936–1952
CIL	*Corpus inscriptionum latinarum.* 17 vols. Berlin: G. Reimer, 1862–
CJAS	Christianity and Judaism in Antiquity Series
CJO	*A Catalogue of Jewish Ossuaries in the Collections of the State of Israel.* By L. Y. Rahmani. Jerusalem: Israel Antiquities Authority, 1994
CLE	*Carmina latina epigraphica.* Edited by F. Buecheler and E. Lommatzch. 3 vols. Leipzig: Teubner, 1895–1926
CLPAT	*Concordance latine des pseudépigraphes d'Ancien Testament.* By A.-M. Denis. Corpus Christianorum: Thesaurus patrum latinorum Supplement. Turnhout: Brepols, 1993
ConBOT	Coniectanea biblica: Old Testament Series
CPJ	*Corpus papyrorum judaicarum.* Edited by V. Tcherikover. 3 vols. Cambridge: Harvard University Press, 1957–1964
CREJ	Collection de la Revue des études juives
CRHPR	Cahiers de la Revue d'histoire et de philosophie religieuses
CRINT	Compendia rerum iudaicarum ad Novum Testamentum
CSCO	Corpus scriptorum christianorum orientalium

CSEL	Corpus scriptorum ecclesiasticorum latinorum
CTM	*Concordia Theological Monthly*
CurBS	*Currents in Research: Biblical Studies*
DBAT	*Dielheimer Blätter zum Alten Testament und seiner Rezeption in der Alten Kirche*
DJD	Discoveries in the Judaean Desert
DJDJ	Discoveries in the Judaean Desert of Jordan
DMOA	Documenta et monumenta orientis antiqui
DNTB	*Dictionary of New Testament Background.* Edited by Craig A. Evans and Stanley E. Porter. Downers Grove, Ill.: InterVarsity, 2000
DSD	*Dead Sea Discoveries*
DSS	*The Dead Sea Scrolls: Major Publications and Tools for Study.* By Joseph A. Fitzmyer. Rev. ed. SBLRBS 20. Atlanta: Scholars Press, 1990
DSSP	*The Dead Sea Scrolls: Hebrew, Aramaic, and Greek Texts with English Translations.* Edited by J. H. Charlesworth et al. Princeton Theological Seminary Dead Sea Scrolls Project. Louisville: Westminster John Knox, 1994–
ECB	*Eerdmans Commentary on the Bible.* Edited by J. D. G. Dunn and J. W. Rogerson. Grand Rapids: Eerdmans, 2003
ECDSS	Eerdmans Commentaries on the Dead Sea Scrolls
EDSS	*Encyclopedia of the Dead Sea Scrolls.* Edited by L. H. Schiffman and J. C. VanderKam. 2 vols. Oxford: Oxford University Press, 2000
EG	G. Kaibel, *Epigrammata graeca.* Berlin: G. Reimer, 1878
EJMI	*Early Judaism and Its Modern Interpreters.* Edited by R. A. Kraft and G. W. E. Nickelsburg. Atlanta: Scholars Press, 1986
EncJud	*Encyclopaedia judaica.* 16 vols. Jerusalem: Encyclopaedia Judaica, 1972
EPRO	Études preliminaires aux religions orientales dans l'Empire romain (continued by RGRW)
ERW	*Early Rabbinic Writings.* By H. Maccoby. CCWJCW 3. Cambridge: Cambridge University Press, 1988
ESBNT	*Essays on the Semitic Background of the New Testament.* J. A. Fitzmyer. Missoula, Mont.: Scholars Press, 1974
EstBib	*Estudios bíblicos*
EvT	*Evangelische Theologie*
ExpTim	*Expository Times*
FB	Forschung zur Bibel
FCB	Feminist Companion to the Bible
FF	Foundations and Facets
FO	*Folia orientalia*
FPSG	*Fragmenta pseudepigraphorum quae supersunt graeca.* Edited by A.-M. Denis. PVTG 3. Leiden: Brill, 1970

GAP	Guides to Apocrypha and Pseudepigrapha
GCS	Die griechische christliche Schriftsteller der ersten [drei] Jahrhunderte
GNS	Good News Studies
GRR	Graeco-Roman Religion
HBC	*Harper's Bible Commentary.* Edited by J. L. Mays et al. San Francisco: Harper & Row, 1988
HBD	*Harper's Bible Dictionary.* Edited by P. J. Achtemeier. San Francisco: Harper & Row, 1985
HCS	Hellenistic Culture and Society
HDR	Harvard Dissertations in Religion
Hen	*Henoch*
HeyJ	*Heythrop Journal*
HibJ	*Hibbert Journal*
HSCP	*Harvard Studies in Classical Philology*
HSM	Harvard Semitic Monographs
HSS	Harvard Semitic Studies
HTKAT	Herders theologischer Kommentar zum Alten Testament
HTR	*Harvard Theological Review*
HTS	Harvard Theological Studies
HUCA	*Hebrew Union College Annual*
IA	*An Introduction to the Apocrypha.* By Bruce M. Metzger. New York: Oxford University Press, 1957
IAMCS	*Introducing the Apocrypha: Message, Context, and Significance.* By David A. deSilva. Grand Rapids: Baker, 2002
IBA	*An Introduction to the Books of the Apocrypha.* By W. O. E. Oesterley. London: SPCK, 1953
IBC	*The International Bible Commentary: A Catholic and Ecumenical Commentary for the Twenty-First Century.* Edited by W. R. Farmer et al. Collegeville, Minn.: Liturgical Press, 1998
IBS	*Irish Biblical Studies*
IDBSup	*Interpreter's Dictionary of the Bible: Supplementary Volume.* Edited by K. Crim. Nashville: Abingdon, 1976
IEJ	*Israel Exploration Journal*
IEph	*Die Inschriften von Ephesos.* Edited by H. Wankel et al. 8 vols. in 10. Inschriften griechischer Städte aus Kleinasien 11–17. Bonn: Habelt, 1979–1984
IG	*Inscriptiones graecae.* Deutsche Akademie der Wissenschaften zu Berlin. Berlin: G. Reimer, 1873–
IGA	*Inscriptiones graecae antiquissimae praeter Atticas in Attica repertas.* Edited by H. Roehl. Berlin: G. Reimer, 1882
IGR	*Inscriptiones graecae ad res romanas pertinentes.* Edited by R. Cagnat et al. 4 vols. (vol. 2 unpublished). Paris: Leroux, 1911–1927. Repr., Rome: L'Erma, 1964
IJA	*International Journal of Apocrypha*

ILS	*Inscriptiones latinae selectae.* Edited by H. Dessau. 3 vols. in 5. Berlin: Weidmann, 1892–1916
IMJ	*Israel Museum Journal*
Imm	*Immanuel*
Int	*Interpretation*
INT	*Introduction to the New Testament.* By H. Koester. 2 vols. Rev. ed. New York: de Gruyter, 1995–2000
InvA	*Invitation to the Apocrypha.* By Daniel J. Harrington. Grand Rapids: Eerdmans, 1999
IOS	*Israel Oriental Society*
IRL	*Introduction to Rabbinic Literature,* By J. Neusner. ABRL 8. New York: Doubleday, 1994
ISBE	*International Standard Bible Encyclopedia.* Edited by G. W. Bromiley. 4 vols. Grand Rapids: Eerdmans, 1979–1988
ITM	*Introduction to the Talmud and Midrash.* By H. L. Strack and G. Stemberger. Translated by M. Bockmuehl. Minneapolis: Fortress, 1992
JA	*Journal asiatique*
JAB	*Journal for the Aramaic Bible* (continued as *Aramaic Studies*)
JAL	Jewish Apocryphal Literature
JAOS	*Journal of the American Oriental Society*
JBL	*Journal of Biblical Literature*
JBLMS	Journal of Biblical Literature Monograph Series
JBR	*Journal of Bible and Religion*
JDS	Judean Desert Studies
JE	*The Jewish Encyclopedia.* Edited by I. Singer. 12 vols. New York, 1925
JECS	*Journal of Early Christian Studies*
JETS	*Journal of the Evangelical Theological Society*
JHebS	*Journal of Hebraic Studies*
JJ	*Jesus within Judaism.* By James H. Charlesworth. ABRL. New York: Doubleday, 1988
JJS	*Journal of Jewish Studies*
JLBM	*Jewish Literature between the Bible and the Mishnah.* By G. W. E. Nickelsburg. Philadelphia: Fortress, 1981
JNES	*Journal of Near Eastern Studies*
JPOS	*Journal of the Palestine Oriental Society*
JQR	*Jewish Quarterly Review*
JQRMS	Jewish Quarterly Review Monograph Series
JR	*Journal of Religion*
JRS	*Journal of Roman Studies*
JSHRZ	*Jüdische Schriften aus hellenistisch-römischer Zeit.* Edited by W. G. Kümmel et al. 6 vols. Gütersloh: G. Mohn, 1973–2001
JSJ	*Journal for the Study of Judaism in the Persian, Hellenistic, and Roman Periods*

JSJSup	Supplements to the Journal for the Study of Judaism
JSNT	*Journal for the Study of the New Testament*
JSNTSup	Journal for the Study of the New Testament: Supplement Series
JSOT	*Journal for the Study of the Old Testament*
JSOTSup	Journal for the Study of the Old Testament: Supplement Series
JSP	*Journal for the Study of the Pseudepigrapha*
JSPSup	Journal for the Study of the Pseudepigrapha: Supplement Series
JSQ	*Jewish Studies Quarterly*
JSS	*Journal of Semitic Studies*
JTS	*Journal of Theological Studies*
JWSTP	*Jewish Writings of the Second Temple Period: Apocrypha, Pseud-epigrapha, Qumran Sectarian Writings, Philo, Josephus.* Edited by M. E. Stone. CRINT 2.2. Philadelphia: Fortress, 1984
JZWL	*Jüdische Zeitschrift für Wissenschaft und Leben*
LAOT	*The Lost Apocrypha of the Old Testament: Their Titles and Fragments.* By M. R. James. TED I: Palestinian Jewish Texts 14. London: SPCK, 1920
LCC	Library of Christian Classics
LCL	Loeb Classical Library
LEC	Library of Early Christianity
LS	*The Literature of the Sages.* Part 1. Edited by S. Safrai. Philadel-phia: Fortress, 1987
MAMA	*Monumenta Asiae Minoris antiqua.* Manchester: Manchester University Press; London: Longmans, Green, 1928–1993
MdB	Le monde de la Bible
MGWJ	*Monatschrift für Geschichte und Wissenschaft des Judentums*
MHUC	Monographs of the Hebrew Union College
Mikra	*Mikra: Text, Translation, Reading, and Interpretation of the He-brew Bible in Ancient Judaism and Early Christianity.* Edited by M. J. Mulder. Philadelphia: Fortress, 1988
MTS	Marburger theologische Studien
Mus	*Muséon: Revue d'études orientales*
NCHSA	*A New Commentary on Holy Scripture, Including the Apocry-pha.* Edited by C. Gore et al. 2 vols. London: SPCK, 1929
NewDocs	*New Documents Illustrating Early Christianity.* Edited by G. H. R. Horsley and S. Llewelyn. Vols. 1–7, North Ryde, N.S.W.: Macquarie University Press; vols. 8–9, Grand Rapids: Eerdmans, 1981–
NGS	New Gospel Studies
NHC	Nag Hammadi Codices
NHL	*Nag Hammadi Library in English.* Edited by J. M. Robinson. 3d ed. San Francisco: Harper & Row, 1988
NHS	Nag Hammadi Studies
NIB	*The New Interpreter's Bible*
NIBC	New International Biblical Commentary

NovT	*Novum Testamentum*
NovTSup	Novum Testamentum Supplements
NTAbh	Neutestamentliche Abhandlungen
NTAP	*New Testament Apocrypha and Pseudepigrapha: A Guide to Publications, with Excursuses on Apocalypses.* By James H. Charlesworth with J. R. Mueller. ATLA Bibliography Series 17. [Chicago]: American Theological Library Association, 1987
NTApoc	*New Testament Apocrypha.* Edited by Edgar Hennecke and Wilhelm Schneemelcher. 2 vols. Philadelphia: Westminster, 1963–1965
NTApoc²	*New Testament Apocrypha.* Edited by W. Schneemelcher. 2 vols. Rev. ed. Louisville: Westminster John Knox, 1991–1992
NTL	New Testament Library
NTOA	Novum Testamentum et orbis antiquus
NTS	*New Testament Studies*
NTTS	New Testament Tools and Studies
OAA	*Oxford Annotated Apocrypha: The Apocrypha of the Old Testament, Revised Standard Version.* Edited by B. M. Metzger. New York: Oxford University Press, 1977
OBO	Orbis biblicus et orientalis
ODCC	*The Oxford Dictionary of the Christian Church.* Edited by F. L. Cross and E. A. Livingstone. 3d ed. New York: Oxford University Press, 1997
OG	*The Other Gospels: Non-canonical Gospel Texts.* Edited by R. Cameron. Philadelphia: Westminster, 1982
OGIS	*Orientis graeci inscriptiones selectae.* Edited by W. Dittenberger. 2 vols. Leipzig: S. Hirzel, 1903–1905. Repr., Hildesheim, Ger.: Olms, 1960
OOT	*Outside the Old Testament.* Edited by M. de Jonge. Cambridge: Cambridge University Press, 1985
OrChrAn	Orientalia christiana analecta
OTApo	*Old Testament Apocrypha.* By Otto Kaiser. Peabody, Mass.: Hendrickson, 2004.
OTM	Old Testament Message
OTP	*Old Testament Pseudepigrapha.* Edited by J. H. Charlesworth. 2 vols. New York: Doubleday, 1983
OTS	Old Testament Studies
OtSt	*Oudtestamentische Studiën*
PDM	*Papyri demoticae magicae.* Demotic texts in the *PGM* corpus as collated in vol. 1 of H. D. Betz, ed. *The Greek Magical Papyri in Translation, Including the Demotic Spells.* 2d ed. Chicago: University of Chicago Press, 1996–
PEFQS	*Palestine Exploration Fund Quarterly Statement*
PEQ	*Palestine Exploration Quarterly*

PEUDSS   *A Preliminary Edition of the Unpublished Dead Sea Scrolls: The*
                Hebrew and Aramaic Texts from Cave Four. By B. Z.
                Wacholder and M. G. Abegg Jr. Washington, D.C.: Biblical
                Archaeology Society, 1991–
PGM   *Papyri graecae magicae: Die griechischen Zauberpapyri.* Edited
                by K. Preisendanz. 3 vols. Berlin: Teubner, 1928–1941. 2d ed.,
                2 vols. Stuttgart: Teubner, 1973–1974. (Selections edited and
                translated in vol. 1 of H. D. Betz., ed., *The Greek Magical Pa-*
                pyri in Translation, Including the Demotic Spells. 2d ed. Chi-
                cago: University of Chicago Press, 1996–[*PDM*])
PIASH   *Proceedings of the Israel Academy of Sciences and Humanities*
PIBA   *Proceedings of the Irish Biblical Association*
PL   Patrologia latina [= Patrologiae cursus completus: Series
                latina]. Edited by J.-P. Migne. 217 vols. Paris, 1844–1864
PMR   *The Pseudepigrapha and Modern Research: With a Supplement.*
                By J. H. Charlesworth. SBLSCS 7. 2d ed. Chico, Calif.: Schol-
                ars Press, 1981
PRSt   *Perspectives in Religious Studies*
PSI   *Publicazioni della Società italiana per la Ricerca dei Papiri greci*
                e latini en Egitto: Papiri greci e latini. Edited by G. Vitelli et al.
                15 vols. Florence: Felice le Monnier [and other publishers],
                1912–1979
PVTG   Pseudepigrapha Veteris Testamenti graece
Qad   *Qadmoniot*
QC   *Qumran Chronicle*
QDAP   *Quarterly of the Department of Antiquities in Palestine*
RAr   *Revue archéologique*
RB   *Revue biblique*
RBén   *Revue bénédictine*
RCB   *Revista de cultura biblica*
REJ   *Revue des études juives*
RelSRev   *Religious Studies Review*
RenIL   *Rendiconti dell'Istituto lombardo*
RevQ   *Revue de Qumran*
RGRW   Religion in the Graeco-Roman World (continues EPRO)
RH   *Revue historique*
RHPR   *Revue d'histoire et de philosophie religieuses*
RILP   Roehampton Institute London Papers
RSR   *Recherches de science religieuse*
RTP   *Revue de théologie et de philosophie*
SAC   Studies in Antiquity and Christianity
SB   *Sammelbuch griechischer Urkunde aus Ägypten.* Edited by
                F. Preisigke. 5 vols. Strassburg: K. J. Trübner, 1915–1955
SBB   Stuttgarter biblische Beiträge
SBF   Studium biblicum franciscanum

SBL	Society of Biblical Literature
SBLAS	Society of Biblical Literature Aramaic Studies
SBLDS	Society of Biblical Literature Dissertation Series
SBLEJL	Society of Biblical Literature Early Judaism and Its Literature
SBLHS	*The SBL Handbook of Style: For Ancient Near Eastern, Biblical, and Early Christian Studies.* Edited by P. H. Alexander et al. Peabody, Mass.: Hendrickson, 1999
SBLMS	Society of Biblical Literature Monograph Series
SBLRBS	Society of Biblical Literature Resources for Biblical Studies
SBLSCS	Society of Biblical Literature Septuagint and Cognate Studies
SBLSP	*Society of Biblical Literature Seminar Papers*
SBLTT	Society of Biblical Literature Texts and Translations
SBS	Stuttgarter Bibelstudien
SBT	Studies in Biblical Theology
SC	Sources chrétiennes. Paris: Cerf, 1943–
SCHNT	Studia ad corpus hellenisticum Novi Testamenti
SCI	*Scripta classica israelica*
ScrAeth	Scriptores aethiopici
ScrHier	Scripta hierosolymitana
ScrSyr	Scriptores syri
SCS	Septuagint and Cognate Studies
SD	Studies and Documents
SE	*Studia evangelica I, II, III* (= TU 73 [1959], 87 [1964], 88 [1964], etc.)
SEAug	Studia ephemeridis Augustinianum
SecCent	*Second Century*
Sef	*Sefarad*
SEG	*Supplementum epigraphicum graecum.* Leiden and Amsterdam: J. C. Gieben, 1923–
SFACS	South Florida Academic Commentary Series
SFSHJ	South Florida Studies in the History of Judaism
SGM	Sources gnostiques et manichéennes
SHR	Studies in the History of Religions (supplement to *Numen*)
SIG	*Sylloge inscriptionum graecarum.* Edited by W. Dittenberger. 4 vols. 3d ed. Leipzig: Hirzel, 1915–1924
SJLA	Studies in Judaism in Late Antiquity
SJT	*Scottish Journal of Theology*
SNTSMS	Society for New Testament Studies Monograph Series
SPB	Studia postbiblica
SPhilo	*Studia philonica*
SR	*Studies in Religion/Sciences religieuses* (continues Canadian *Journal of Theology*)
SSEJC	Studies in Scripture in Early Judaism and Christianity
SSN	Studia semitica neerlandica
SSS	Semitic Study Series

ST	*Studia theologica*
STAC	Studien und Texte zu Antike und Christentum
STDJ	Studies on the Texts of the Desert of Judah
StPatr	*Studia Patristica*
STR-T	Studia theologica rheno-traiectina
SubBi	Subsidia biblica
SUNT	Studien zum Umwelt des Neuen Testaments
SVTP	Studia in Veteris Testamenti pseudepigrapha
TBC	Torch Bible Commentaries
TED	Translations of Early Documents
Text	*Textus*
ThT	*Theologisch tijdschrift*
TQum	*Les textes de Qumran.* Translated and annotated by J. Carmignac et al. 2 vols. Paris: Letouzey et Ané, 1961–1963
TS	*Theological Studies*
TSAJ	Texte und Studien zum antiken Judentum
TSJTS	Texts and Studies of the Jewish Theological Seminary of America
TU	Texte und Untersuchungen
TUAT	*Texte aus der Umwelt des Alten Testaments.* Edited by Otto Kaiser et al. 4 vols. in 19. Gütersloh: G. Mohn, 1982–2001
TUGAL	Texte und Untersuchungen zur Geschichte der altchristlichen Literatur
TZ	*Theologische Zeitschrift*
UCOP	University of Cambridge Oriental Publications
UNT	Untersuchungen zum Neuen Testament
VC	*Vigiliae christianae*
VCSup	Supplements to Vigiliae christianae
VT	*Vetus Testamentum*
VTS	Vetus Testamentum syriace
VTSup	Supplements to Vetus Testamentum
WBC	Word Biblical Commentary
WUNT	Wissenschaftliche Untersuchungen zum Neuen Testament
YJS	Yale Judaica
YOSR	Yale Oriental Series, Researches
ZAC	*Zeitschrift für antikes Christentum/Journal of Ancient Christianity*
ZAH	*Zeitschrift für Althebräistik*
ZAW	*Zeitschrift für die alttestamentliche Wissenschaft*
ZDMG	*Zeitschrift der deutschen morgenländischen Gesellschaft*
ZNW	*Zeitschrift für die neutestamentliche Wissenschaft und die Kunde der älteren Kirche*
ZPE	*Zeitschrift für Papyrologie und Epigraphik*

Introduction

There are two principal difficulties that those who aspire to NT exegesis must face: learning the biblical languages and becoming familiar with the myriad of cognate literatures. The first difficulty is overcome through the study of Hebrew, Aramaic, and Greek. But the second difficulty is not so easily dealt with. Because these cognate literatures are so diverse and involve numerous difficulties of their own, many students and even a surprising number of teachers and professors are acquainted with very few of them. Perhaps another factor is knowing that there are scholars who have made it their lives' work to master certain of these literatures. It is understandable then that a beginning NT interpreter often hesitates to plunge into the Talmud or the Dead Sea Scrolls or some other body of writings.

Nevertheless, if one is to do competent NT exegesis, one must know something of these writings and of their relevance for the NT. Some of these writings are vital for understanding the NT, some much less so. But all are referred to by the major scholars. Thus, intelligent reading of the best of NT scholarship requires familiarity with these writings (just as it is necessary to know the biblical languages), if for no other reason.

An Overview of the Writings

1. *The Old Testament Apocrypha.* All of the writings of the OT Apocrypha (or deuterocanonical books, as some call them) predate the NT (with the exception of portions of 2 Esdras). Most of these writings were written one or two centuries before the NT era. Most, if not all, were known to early Christians and to the writers of the NT. The OT Apocrypha forms, then, an indispensable bridge linking the worlds of the OT and the NT.

2. *The Old Testament Pseudepigrapha.* Many of the writings of the OT Pseudepigrapha, which represent the most diverse collection considered in this book, predate the NT; some are contemporaneous, and some postdate the NT.

Many contain themes that are represented in the NT. In a few instances NT authors even quote pseudepigraphal writings.

3. *The Dead Sea Scrolls.* The Dead Sea Scrolls probably represent the most sensational twentieth-century archaeological and literary discovery in biblical studies. These writings, mostly in Hebrew, though some are in Aramaic and Greek, either predate the NT or are contemporaneous with the earliest NT writings (e.g., Paul's letters and perhaps one or two of the Synoptic Gospels). The authors of these writings (i.e., those found near Qumran) were probably members of the group that Josephus called the Essenes. They lived throughout Palestine, not just in the Dead Sea area where the caves are located, in which the scrolls were discovered. The scrolls provide significant parallels to NT vocabulary and ideas.

4. *Versions of the Old Testament.* The Greek OT, called the Septuagint (LXX), is also central for researching the NT for the simple reason that more than one half of the NT's quotations of the OT are from the Septuagint and not from the Hebrew. Three recensions of the Septuagint need to be mentioned. This chapter will also treat the Masoretic Text (MT), the Old Latin, the Vulgate, and the Peshitta. The Aramaic tradition is treated in a chapter of its own.

5. *Philo and Josephus.* Two of the most noteworthy non-Christian Jewish authors of the first century are Philo and Josephus. Philo, who was born during the reign of Herod the Great, wrote several volumes in which he interprets various passages, institutions, and characters of the OT (primarily the Torah) in an allegorical manner. His allegorical interpretation parallels NT interpretation in a few places. Josephus, who lived a generation later, was raised in Palestine and became a participant in the Jews' bloody rebellion against Rome (66–70 C.E.). Befriended by the Roman conquerors, he wrote several works that describe the Jewish conflict and the biblical history of the Jewish people. His writings provide excellent background for NT interpretation, especially for the Gospels.

6. *The Targumim.* The Targumim are Aramaic paraphrases of the Hebrew Bible. They originated in the synagogue, though how early is debated. Some targumic tradition can be traced to the first century and some of it is clearly relevant to certain NT passages.

7. *Rabbinic Literature.* The sayings and traditions of some of the Tannaic rabbis may be traced back to the first century and may clarify certain aspects and passages of the NT. Here will be considered the Mishnah, Tosefta, and the early midrashim. Although not from the early period, but containing some Tannaic material, the Babylonian and Palestinian Talmuds and some of the later midrashim will also be briefly discussed.

8. *The New Testament Pseudepigrapha.* The NT Pseudepigrapha (or Apocrypha) is made up of numerous pseudonymous gospels, books of acts, epistles, and apocalypses. Although most of this material is of no use for NT interpretation, there are some scholars who maintain that in a few instances (esp. in certain gospels) tradition has been preserved that may derive from the NT period and shed light on what is obscure in the NT itself.

9. *Early Church Fathers.* In addition to examining the so-called Apostolic Fathers (Ignatius, Polycarp, Clement of Rome, etc.) this chapter will survey some

of the church's earliest exegetes and theologians, such as Origen, Clement of Alexandria, Tertullian, Cyprian, Eusebius, Jerome, and Augustine. Some of these writings may preserve traditions that derive from the NT period that could aid in exegesis.

10. *Gnostic Writings.* The Coptic Gnostic Codices from Nag Hammadi, Egypt, provide us with most of our gnostic primary materials. Many of these fourth-century Coptic writings are based on much earlier Greek writings that in some cases might date from the late first and early second centuries. Some scholars claim that they may even contain sayings of Jesus that are either authentic or at least more primitive than their counterparts in the Gospels of the NT. Some think that Johannine and Pauline Christology may owe its origin to ideas preserved in the gnostic writings. A few other gnostic writings will also be considered.

11. *Other Writings.* In the final chapter the Hermetic and Samaritan writings, among others, will be reviewed briefly. The former have been compared to Johannine theology, while the latter contain traditions that cohere with distinctive elements in Luke-Acts. A few of the most relevant pagan authors will be included. The chapter will conclude with a survey of the most important papyri, inscriptions, coins, and ostraca. Although the items in this category do not constitute literature as such, they do offer text, even if quite brief, that is very important for NT study. Papyri are the most obvious in their importance, for they provide us with our oldest samples of the writings of the Bible itself. The non-literary papyri provide us with a wealth of everyday correspondence, such as personal letters, contracts, memoranda, agenda, receipts, and the like. The papyri assist us in identifying and defining with greater precision and nuance the semantic range of the Hebrew, Aramaic, and Greek vocabularies of the biblical literature. Inscriptions and coins provide us with important insight into a variety of public declarations (such as imperial propaganda), and the ostraca, like the personal papyri, provide examples of names, receipts, and such. Thus these materials lend important background color to everyday life in the NT period.

The Value

How is NT exegesis facilitated by studying these writings? These writings clarify the following areas of exegetical concern:

1. *The meaning of words.* In older commentaries the meaning of words is often defined by appeal to the classics (usually Greek, though sometimes Latin). It is not clear, however, how relevant these parallels are. (Is the way that Plato used a word in fourth-century B.C.E. Greece germane to the way the same word is used in the Gospel of Mark?) Perhaps in some cases, but parallels that are closer in time (first century B.C.E. to first century C.E.) and location (Palestine, eastern Mediterranean world) are more likely to be relevant. Appeal to the LXX, which contains the Apocrypha, is therefore quite appropriate. Although written mostly

in Hebrew, Qumran documents often can be helpful in determining the meaning of certain words in the NT. Some of the pseudepigrapha circulating in Palestine and the eastern Mediterranean can therefore be helpful in determining the meaning of words used in the NT. As an example, consider the word *episkopē* ("visitation"), which occurs a few times in the NT (Luke 19:44; 1 Pet 2:12; for the verb form, see Luke 1:68, 78; 7:16; Acts 15:14). The NT's connotation of judgment, either for reward or for punishment, is clarified by OT usage (*episkopē* in the LXX, *pequddah* in the Hebrew; cf. Isa 10:3; Jer 8:12; 23:12; 50:27), not classical. Other words are not found in the Greek or Hebrew OT, but derive from the Targum (e.g., "Gehenna"; cf. Mark 9:47–48; *Tg. Isa.* 66:24) or from pseudepigraphal writings (e.g., "Tartarus"; cf. 2 Pet 2:4; *L.A.B.* 60:3).

2. *Syntax.* The grammar of the NT is Koine, not classical. It is also heavily influenced by the Semitic style of the LXX. This is seen by the NT's frequent use of *egeneto de* or *kai egeneto* ("and it came to pass"). This expression comes right out of the LXX. To "set one's face" and to go "before one's face" (cf. Luke 9:51–53) are idioms that derive from the LXX and whose meanings are clarified by the Greek OT. Other grammatical expressions reflect the Aramaic language of Palestine ("in truth" [Luke 4:25; 1QapGen^ar 2:5]; "he was seen," meaning "he appeared" [Luke 24:34; 1QapGen^ar 22:27]). Some of the NT's syntax seems to reflect Hebrew (preposition *en* with the articular infinitive meaning "while doing" [Luke 1:21; 2:6; 5:1]).

3. *The meaning of concepts.* When Jesus tells his disciples that they have been given authority to "tread upon serpents [*ophis*] and scorpions" and that "the spirits are subject" to them (Luke 10:19–20), he may have alluded to Ps 91:13 ("You will tread upon lion and the adder, young lion and the serpent you will trample under foot"). Psalm 91 has nothing to do with Satan; but Jesus' words do (cf. Luke 10:17–18). Would a reference to treading upon serpents have been understood in first-century Palestine as a reference to Satan and demons? Very much so. Consider this eschatological hope expressed in one of the *Testaments of the Twelve Patriarchs:* "And Beliar [i.e., Satan] shall be bound by him [i.e., an agent of salvation on whom the Spirit of God shall rest; Isa 11:2]. And he shall grant to his children the authority to trample on wicked spirits" (*T. Levi* 18:12; cf. *T. Sim.* 6:6; *T. Zeb.* 9:8). Since Satan is represented as a serpent (*ophis*) in Gen 3:1–15 and the righteous will trample serpents under foot it is not too difficult to see how the language of Psalm 91 could be adopted and applied to Satan and evil spirits as we find it in Luke 10 and *T. Levi* 18. The targumic tradition also links serpents and scorpions with Satan and evil spirits (and Gen 3:15, which speaks of the woman's seed crushing the serpent's head, is understood in a messianic sense in the Targumim).

4. *History.* Some of the writings that will be considered in this book contribute to what we know about the intertestamental and NT periods. First and second Maccabees are invaluable sources for our knowledge of the Jewish revolt against Antiochus IV in 167 B.C.E. Josephus's *Jewish War* and *Jewish Antiquities* reveal helpful information about Jewish politics and history at the turn of the era,

especially with reference to Herod the Great and his family, and the time of Jesus and his earliest followers.

5. *Historical, social, and religious context (i.e.,* Sitz im Leben). Following the death of Herod the Great Palestine went through a period of political instability and upheaval. Josephus cynically remarks, "Anyone might make himself a king" (*Ant.* 17.10.8 §285). Josephus has no sympathy for Jewish nationalists and would-be-liberators, calling them "brigands" (*lēstēs*). This is the very word that is used when Jesus is arrested and crucified (Mark 14:48; 15:27). In view of Josephus's description of these kingly claimants as *lestai,* some of whom may very well have thought of themselves as messiahs, it is possible that when *lēstēs* is used of Jesus, it meant "insurrectionist." Josephus also tells of false prophets who deluded the people by promising signs of deliverance, sometimes urging them to withdraw to the desert. The language that he uses (*Ant.* 17.10.7 §§278–284; 20.8.6 §168; 20.8.10 §188; *J.W.* 2.13.5 §§261–263; 6.5.4 §315) parallels, at places quite closely, the warnings that we read in the Gospels (cf. Matt 24:26; Mark 13:21–22).

6. *Exegetical context.* Of major importance is the fact that the noncanonical writings quite often shed light on the interpretation of the OT passages quoted or alluded to in the NT. For example, parts of 2 Sam 7:12–16, the "Davidic covenant," are quoted (Heb 1:5) or alluded to (Luke 1:32–33) in the NT as fulfilled in Jesus. Since Nathan's oracle originally spoke of Solomon the son of David, one wonders if early Christian interpretation would have been understood or accepted. Qumran has made it clear, however, that this oracle was interpreted in an eschatological sense, at least in some circles. The eschatological deliverer will be God's Son (4QFlor 1:11–12; 4Q246 1:6–9; 2:1–4) and he will be seated on the throne of David (4Q252 5), thus fulfilling the promise of 2 Samuel 7 in a way that Solomon and his descendants did not. As another example, the presentation of Jesus in the Prologue of the Fourth Gospel as the Logos ("word") is illumined by Philo and possibly by the Targumim. Philo describes the Logos as "God's first-born, the Word" (*Confusion* 28 §146), through whom God created the world (*Cherubim* 35 §127). The Targumim say that God created humanity through the Memra ("word"): "The Memra of the Lord created man in his own image" (*Tg. Neof.* Gen 1:27; cf. *Tg. Isa.* 45:12). The presence of "Word" as agent of creation in Genesis 1 is highly suggestive, since John 1 ("In the beginning . . .") echoes the language of the creation account.

7. *Hermeneutical context (i.e., how Scripture could be interpreted, how it could be applied, adapted).* The literatures surveyed in this book help us understand how biblical literature was interpreted and what role it played in the life of the Jewish and Christian communities of faith. Qumran affords us with examples of pesher interpretation whereby various prophetic details of Scripture were applied to contemporary events and events felt to be imminent. Rabbinic writings provide us with numerous examples in midrashic interpretation whereby Scripture was searched in an effort to find answers to the questions relating to how God's people should live and how they should understand their sacred tradition. Philo's writings illustrate allegorical interpretation. Do the details of Scripture point to meanings beyond the obvious and literal? The Targumim and some of the pseud-

epigraphal writings show how the biblical story can be paraphrased, expanded, and enriched. But perhaps more importantly, these various literatures aid us in understanding what role Scripture played in the life of the believing community. All of this sheds light on how early Christians understood their own sacred tradition.

8. *Canonical context (i.e., what was regarded as Scripture and why).* The literatures surveyed in this book also help us understand what it meant to regard certain writings as authoritative. By what criteria were certain writings preserved and treated with reverence and respect not accorded to other writings? What was the understanding of the relationship between the OT and NT? In what sense is the NT part of the Bible? (And from a Christian point of view: In what sense is the OT part of the Bible?) In what sense did the "canonical" writings possess authority? What does the author of 2 Esdras mean when he says that whereas both the worthy and unworthy may read the twenty-four books (i.e., the OT), only the wise should be permitted to read the "seventy" books (i.e., the Apocrypha/Pseudepigrapha) that were written last (14:44–47; cf. 12:37–38)? The literatures surveyed in this book do not definitely answer these and related questions, but they provide much of the raw data that must be processed before we can begin to answer them responsibly.

The Method

How are these writings put to use in doing NT exegesis? This is the principal concern of the present book. Comparative study of these writings constitutes an important step in the exegetical process.

In order to understand a given passage one must reconstruct as much as possible the world of thought in which the NT writer lived. Since the NT frequently quotes the OT (hundreds of times) or alludes to it (thousands of times) and everywhere presupposes its language, concepts, and theology, exegesis should be particularly sensitive to its presence and careful to reconstruct the exegetical-theological context of which a given OT quotation or allusion may have been a part. A comparative approach is essential. How was the OT passage quoted or alluded to understood by early Christians and Jews? To answer this question the interpreter should examine every occurrence of the passage. This involves studying the ancient versions and cognate literatures, the very writings treated in this book.

To assess properly the function of the OT in the NT the following questions must be raised:

(1) What OT text(s) is(are) being cited? Two or more passages may be conflated, and each may contribute insight.

(2) Which text-type is being followed (Hebrew, Greek, Aramaic)? What are the respective meanings of these versions? (Each may have an interpretive tradition of its own.) How does the version that the NT has followed contribute to the meaning of the quotation?

(3) Is the OT quotation part of a wider tradition or theology in the OT? If it is, the quotation may be alluding to a context much wider than the specific passage from which it has been taken.

(4) How did various Jewish and Christian groups and interpreters understand the passage? This question is vital, for often the greatest help comes from comparing the function of the OT in these sources.

(5) In what ways does the NT citation agree or disagree with the interpretations found in the versions and other ancient exegeses? Has the Jesus/Christian tradition distinctively shaped the OT quotation and its interpretation, or does the NT exegesis reflect interpretation current in pre-Christian Judaism?

(6) How does the function of the quotation compare to the function of other quotations in the NT writing under consideration. Has a different text-type been used? Has the OT been followed more closely or less so?

(7) Finally, how does the quotation contribute to the argument of the NT passage in which it is found?

If these questions are carefully considered, one's exegesis will be in large measure complete. Although the above steps have been applied to passages where the OT is present, either explicitly or implicitly, most of these steps are relevant for exegesis of any passage, for it is indeed a rare passage that alludes to or parallels no other. (For treatments concerned with other questions of exegesis consult the works listed in the bibliography below.)

In the chapters that follow the various literatures will be surveyed with the questions just considered kept in mind. In the final chapter a selection of passages from the NT will be studied and offered as examples of the benefits to be derived from addressing these questions and taking into account the various literatures of the biblical period.

General Bibliography

C. K. BARRETT, ed., *The New Testament Background: Writings from Ancient Greece and the Roman Empire That Illuminate Christian Origins* (rev. ed.; San Francisco: HarperCollins, 1989); J. BARTON, ed., *The Cambridge Companion to Biblical Interpretation* (Cambridge: Cambridge University Press, 1998); R. BECKWITH, *The Old Testament Canon of the New Testament Church and Its Background in Early Judaism* (Grand Rapids: Eerdmans, 1985); H. CONZELMANN and A. LINDEMANN, *Interpreting the New Testament: An Introduction to the Principles and Methods of N.T. Exegesis* (Peabody, Mass.: Hendrickson, 1988); E. J. EPP and G. W. MACRAE, eds., *The New Testament and Its Modern Interpreters* (Atlanta: Scholars Press, 1989) (for backgrounds, see esp. pp. 1–71); C. A. EVANS and S. E. PORTER, eds., *DNTB;* G. D. FEE, *New Testament Exegesis: A Handbook for Students and Pastors* (3d ed.; Louisville: Westminster John Knox, 2002); K. FROEHLICH, *Biblical Interpretation in the Early Church* (Philadelphia: Fortress, 1984); D. J. HARRINGTON, *Interpreting the New Testament: A Practical Guide* (Wilmington, Del.: Glazier,

1979); J. H. HAYES and C. R. HOLLADAY, *Biblical Exegesis: A Beginner's Handbook* (Atlanta: John Knox, 1982); O. KAISER and W. G. KÜMMEL, *Exegetical Method: A Student's Handbook* (New York: Seabury, 1981); H. KOESTER, *INT;* J. L. KUGEL and R. A. GREER, *Early Biblical Interpretation* (Philadelphia: Westminster, 1986); I. H. MARSHALL, ed., *New Testament Interpretation: Essays on Principles and Methods* (Grand Rapids: Eerdmans, 1977); L. M. MCDONALD, *The Formation of the Christian Biblical Canon* (rev. and exp. ed.; Peabody, Mass.: Hendrickson, 1995); L. M. MCDONALD and J. A. SANDERS, eds., *The Canon Debate* (Peabody, Mass.: Hendrickson, 2002); S. MCKNIGHT, ed., *Introducing New Testament Interpretation* (Guides to New Testament Exegesis 1; Grand Rapids: Baker, 1989); B. M. METZGER, *The Canon of the New Testament: Its Origin, Development, and Significance* (Oxford: Clarendon, 1987); S. E. PORTER, ed., *Handbook to Exegesis of the New Testament* (NTTS 25; Leiden: Brill, 1997); J. A. SANDERS, *Canon and Community* (Philadelphia: Fortress, 1984).

CHAPTER ONE

The Old Testament Apocrypha

OLD TESTAMENT APOCRYPHA

1 Esdras	Susanna
2 Esdras	Bel and the Dragon
Tobit	Prayer of Manasseh
Judith	1 Maccabees
Additions to Esther	2 Maccabees
Wisdom of Solomon	3 Maccabees (see Old Testament
Ecclesiasticus (Sirach)	Pseudepigrapha)
Baruch	4 Maccabees (see Old Testament
Epistle of Jeremiah	Pseudepigrapha)
Prayer of Azariah and the Song of the	Psalm 151 (see Old Testament
Three Children	Pseudepigrapha)

Fifteen books make up the OT Apocrypha. Some editions of the Bible incorporate the Epistle of Jeremiah into Baruch as its sixth and final chapter. These editions, therefore, have fourteen books. Whereas Protestants do not regard the books of the Apocrypha as inspired or as canonical, the Roman Catholic, Greek Orthodox, Russian Orthodox, and Coptic Churches accept most of them. (For a listing of their respective canons of the Apocrypha, see appendix 1.)

The word "apocrypha" is a Greek word literally meaning "hidden away." Why "hidden"? Over the centuries those who appreciated and approved of these books as authoritative thought of them as hidden from the uninitiated and simple. They were reserved for the wise and learned. On the other hand, those who viewed these books as spurious and as possessing no authority have understood them as hidden because of perceived heretical tendencies. It is probably for this reason that the word "apocrypha" has come to mean "false." For example, when a story about a well-known person is suspected of being untrue we say that it is "apocryphal."

The Apocrypha (the word is actually plural—the singular is apocryphon—but people often think of it as singular) represent several types of writing. Some of the writings are historical (e.g., 1 Esdras, 1 and 2 Maccabees), some are romantic (e.g., Tobit, Judith, Susanna, Additions to Esther), some are didactic (e.g., Wisdom of Solomon, Ecclesiasticus), some are moralistic (e.g., Baruch, Epistle of Jeremiah, Bel and the Dragon), and some are devotional (e.g., Prayer of Azariah and the Song of the Three Young Men, Prayer of Manasseh). One is apocalyptic (2 Esdras).

The Greek text of the Apocrypha is found in the LXX (see ch. 4). The best English translation is B. M. Metzger, *OAA*. This edition contains several helpful notes and tables. Metzger has also edited *A Concordance to the Apocryphal/ Deuterocanonical Books of the Revised Standard Version* (Grand Rapids: Eerdmans, 1983). See also the English translation edition of the Apocrypha in the *New Revised Standard Version* (New York: Oxford, 1989). For current introductions, see D. A. deSilva, *IAMCS*, and D. J. Harrington, *InvA*. For current one-volume commentaries on the Apocrypha, see J. L. Mays et al., eds., *HBC*, W. R. Farmer et al., eds., *IBC*, and O. Kaiser, *OTApo*.

Summaries

1 Esdras. First Esdras is not accepted as canonical by the Roman Catholic Church. (It was rejected by the Council of Trent, 8 April 1546.) The Roman Catholic Bible includes it in an appendix. (In the Vulgate it is called 3 Esdras.) It is, however, accepted by the Greek Orthodox and Russian Orthodox Churches. It is a historical writing based upon 2 Chr 35:1–36:23, Ezra, and Neh 7:38–8:12 (see the table below). However, the story of the three men in the court of Darius (3:1–5:6), which has no parallel in the OT, may represent the author's chief concern (Metzger, *IA* 18), perhaps to encourage the renewal of God's people (Harrington, *InvA* 153) and to highlight the qualities of Zerubbabel (deSilva, *IAMCS* 286–87). The book follows neither the MT nor the LXX. The unknown author apparently intended to emphasize the religious reforms of Josiah (1:1–24), Zerubbabel (5:47–6:34), and Ezra (8:1–9:55). It was written probably in the second century B.C.E. First Esdras relates to biblical literature as follows (Klein, 769):

1 Esdr 1:1–22	=	2 Chr 35:1–19
1 Esdr 1:23–24	=	(no parallel)
1 Esdr 1:25–58	=	2 Chr 35:20–36:21
1 Esdr 2:1–5a	=	2 Chr 36:22–23/Ezra 1:1–3a
1 Esdr 2:5b–15	=	Ezra 1:3b–11
1 Esdr 2:16–30	=	Ezra 4:7–24
1 Esdr 3:1–5:6	=	(no parallel)
1 Esdr 5:7–73	=	Ezra 2:1–4:5
1 Esdr 6:1–9:36	=	Ezra 5:1–10:44
1 Esdr 9:37–55	=	Neh 7:73–8:13a

Text: R. HANHART, *Esdrae liber 1* (Septuaginta 8/1; Göttingen: Vandenhoeck & Ruprecht, 1974). **Survey:** H. W. ATTRIDGE, "Historiography," *JWSTP* 157–60; D. A. DESILVA, *IAMCS*

280–95; D. J. HARRINGTON, *InvA* 152–65; O. KAISER, *OTApo* 24–29; B. M. METZGER, *IA* 11–19; G. W. E. NICKELSBURG, "Stories of Biblical and Early Post-biblical Times," *JWSTP* 131–35; W. O. E. OESTERLEY, *IBA* 133–41; Z. TALSHIR, "1 Esdras," *DNTB* 341–42. **Commentary:** R. J. COGGINS and M. A. KNIBB, *The First and Second Books of Esdras*, 4–75; S. A. COOK, "I Esdras," *APOT* 1:1–58; J. C. H. HOW, "I. Esdras," *NCHSA* 2:30–32; R. W. KLEIN, "1 Esdras," *HBC* 769–75; J. M. MYERS, *I and II Esdras*, 1–104; Z. TALSHIR, *1 Esdras: A Text Critical Commentary* (SBLSCS 50; Atlanta: Society of Biblical Literature, 2000); H. G. M. WILLIAMSON, "1 Esdras," *ECB* 851–58. **Critical Study:** T. C. ESKENAZI, "The Chronicler and the Composition of 1 Esdras," *CBQ* 48 (1986): 39–61; A. E. GARDENER, "The Purpose and Date of I Esdras," *JJS* 37 (1986): 18–27; Z. TALSHIR, *1 Esdras: From Origin to Translation* (SBLSCS 47; Atlanta: Scholars Press, 1999).

2 Esdras. Second Esdras is not accepted by the Roman Catholic Church either, although it is included in a form of the Latin Vulgate with 1 Esdras. It is, however, accepted by the Russian Orthodox Church. In the Vulgate it is 4 Esdras. (Part of 2 Esdras is also known as 4 Ezra and is sometimes included in the OT Pseudepigrapha. On the confusing Esdras-Ezra nomenclature, see the tables below.) Second Esdras does not resume the historical narrative of 1 Esdras, as one might suppose, but is called "2 Esdras" because of the opening verse: "The second book of the prophet Ezra. . . ." The book is an apocalypse consisting largely of seven revelations (3:1–5:20; 5:21–6:34; 6:35–9:25; 9:38–10:59; 11:1–12:51; 13:1–58; 14:1–48) which are primarily concerned with moral themes. Apparently, at least three authors are responsible for 2 Esdras. The original author was probably a first-century Palestinian Jew who, writing in Aramaic or Hebrew, produced chapters 3–14 (the original 4 Ezra). It was subsequently translated into Greek. A second-century Christian added a Greek introduction (chs. 1–2, also called 5 Ezra). Finally, a third-century Christian added the last two chapters (15–16, also called 6 Ezra) in Greek. The Semitic original is lost, and only a fragment of the Greek has survived (15:57–59). The purpose of the original author was to show that God is just, despite the evil of the Rome of his day and the calamities that had befallen Jerusalem (Metzger, *IA* 30).

TABLE OF ESDRAS NOMENCLATURE

Hebrew Bible	Septuagint	Vulgate	English Apocrypha
Ezra		1 Esdras	
Nehemiah		2 Esdras	
	1 Esdras	3 Esdras	1 Esdras
	4 Esdras	2 Esdras	

TABLE OF EZRA NOMENCLATURE

1 Ezra	Ezra-Nehemiah of the Hebrew Bible
2 Ezra	4 Esdras (Vulgate) = 2 Esdras (English Apocrypha) chaps. 1–2
3 Ezra	1 Esdras (Septuagint) = 3 Esdras (Vulgate) = 1 Esdras (English Apocrypha)
4 Ezra	4 Esdras (Vulgate) = 2 Esdras (English Apocrypha) chaps. 3–14
5 Ezra	4 Esdras (Vulgate) = 2 Esdras (English Apocrypha) chaps. 15–16

(adapted from H. W. Attridge, "Historiography," *JWSTP*, 158)

Text: R. L. BENSLY, *The Fourth Book of Ezra, the Latin Version Edited from the MSS* (Texts and Studies 3/2; Cambridge: Cambridge University Press, 1895); B. VIOLET, *Die Über-lieferung,* vol. 1 of *Die Esra-Apokalypse (IV. Ezra)* (GCS 18; Leipzig: Hinrich, 1910). *Survey:* D. A. DESILVA, *IAMCS* 323–51; D. J. HARRINGTON, *InvA* 185–206; R. A. KRAFT, "Ezra Materials in Judaism and Christianity," *ANRW* 19.1:119–36; B. W. LONGENECKER, *2 Esdras* (GAP; Sheffield: Sheffield, 1995); B. M. METZGER, *IA* 21–30; W. O. E. OESTERLEY, *IBA* 142–60; M. E. STONE, "Apocalyptic Literature," *SJWSTP* 412–14; J. E. WRIGHT, "Ezra, Books of," *DNTB* 337–40. *Commentary:* R. J. COGGINS and M. A. KNIBB, *The First and Second Books of Esdras,* 76–305; J. M. MYERS, *I and II Esdras,* 107–354; W. O. E. OESTERLEY, *II Esdras (The Ezra Apocalypse)* (London: Methuen, 1933); IDEM, "II. (IV.) Esdras," *NCHSA* 2:32–42; J. J. SCHMITT, "2 Esdras," *ECB* 876–87; M. E. STONE and T. A. BERGREN, "2 Esdras," *HBC* 776–90. *Critical Study:* G. K. BEALE, "The Problem of the Man from the Sea in IV Ezra 13 and Its Relation to the Messianic Concept in John's Apocalypse," *NovT* 25 (1983): 182–88; T. A. BERGREN, *Fifth Ezra: The Text, Origin, and Early History* (SBLSCS 25; Atlanta: Scholars Press, 1990); IDEM, *Sixth Ezra: The Text and Origin* (Oxford: Oxford University Press, 1998); E. BREECH, "These Fragments I Have Shored against My Ruins: The Form and Function of 4 Ezra," *JBL* 92 (1973): 267–74; G. N. STANTON, "5 Ezra and Matthean Christianity in the Second Century," *JTS* 28 (1997): 67–83. See bibliography on 4 Ezra in chapter 2.

Tobit. Tobit is accepted by the Roman Catholic, Greek Orthodox, and Russian Orthodox Churches. The book of Tobit is a romance (deSilva, *IAMCS* 70; Harrington, *InvA* 11) relating a moralistic story of the adventures of Tobit and his son Tobias in Nineveh shortly after the exile of the northern kingdom (2 Kgs 17:1–6). It was originally written in Aramaic or Hebrew—as attested by the Dead Sea Scrolls (i.e., 4Q196–200; cf. Fitzmyer)—sometime in the second century B.C.E. by an unknown author. Subsequently it was translated into Greek. Tobit emphasizes piety (such as attending to the burial of the dead) in the face of paganism. Tobit's prophecy of the rebuilding of the temple (14:5–7) has received attention in recent scholarship concerned with the place of the temple in first-century eschatological expectations.

Text: R. HANHART, *Tobit* (Septuaginta 8/5; Göttingen: Vandenhoeck & Ruprecht, 1983). *Survey:* D. A. DESILVA, *IAMCS* 63–84; R. DORAN, "Narrative Literature," *EJMI* 296–99; D. J. HARRINGTON, *InvA* 10–26; L. R. HELYER, "Tobit," *DNTB* 1238–41; O. KAISER, *OTApo* 30–39; B. M. METZGER, *IA* 31–41; C. A. MOORE, "Tobit, Book of," *ABD* 6:585–94; G. W. E. NICKELSBURG, "Stories of Biblical and Early Post-biblical Times," *SJWSTP* 40–46; W. O. E. OESTERLEY, *IBA* 161–71. *Commentary:* J. CRAGHAN, *Esther, Judith, Tobit, Jonah, Ruth,* 127–62; C. F. DEVINE, "Tobias," *CCHS* 393–402; J. A. FITZMYER, *Tobit* (CEJL; New York: de Gruyter, 2003); L. L. GRABBE, "Tobit," *ECB* 736–47; C. A. MOORE, *Tobit* (AB 40A; New York: Doubleday, 1996); G. W. E. NICKELSBURG, "Tobit," *HBC* 791–803; I. NOWELL, "The Book of Tobit," *NIB* 973–1071; IDEM, "Tobit," *IBC* 687–95; H. SCHÜNGEL-STRAUMANN, *Tobit* (HTKAT; Freiburg in Breisgau: Herder, 2000); D. C. SIMPSON, "The Book of Tobit," *APOT* 1:174–241; H. St. J. THACKERAY, "Tobit," *NCHSA* 2:42–58; F. ZIMMERMANN, *The Book of Tobit* (JAL; New York: Harper, 1958); E. ZENGER, *Judit und Tobit.* *Critical Study:* A. DI LELLA, "The Deuteronomic Background of the Farewell Discourse in Tobit 14:3–11," *CBQ* 41 (1979): 380–89; J. A. FITZMYER, "The Aramaic and Hebrew Fragments of Tobit from Cave 4," *CBQ* 57 (1995): 655–75; D. MCCRACKEN, "Narration and Comedy in the

Book of Tobit," *JBL* 114 (1995): 401–18; C. A. MOORE, "Scholarly Issues in the Book of Tobit before Qumran and After: An Assessment," *JSP* 5 (1989): 65–81; A. PORTIER-YOUNG, "Alleviation of Suffering in the Book of Tobit: Comedy, Community, and Happy Endings," *CBQ* 63 (2001): 35–54; W. SOLL, "The Family as Scriptural and Social Construct in Tobit," in *The Function of Scripture in Early Jewish and Christian Tradition* (ed. C. A. Evans and J. A. Sanders; JSNTSup 154; SSEJC 6; Sheffield: Sheffield, 1998), 166–75; IDEM, "Misfortune and Exile in Tobit: The Juncture of a Fairy Tale Source and Deuteronomic Theology," *CBQ* 51 (1989): 209–31; R. A. SPENCER, "The Book of Tobit in Recent Research," *CurBS* 7 (1999): 147–80.

Judith. Judith is accepted by the Roman Catholic, Greek Orthodox, and Russian Orthodox Churches. Notwithstanding several serious anachronisms and historical blunders, the book tells a heroic tale of the beautiful Judith whose courage and faith in God saved her village from destruction at the hands of one of Nebuchadnezzar's generals. In many ways the book stands in the tradition of the heroes in Judges (see 4:4–22). Originally a second-century B.C.E. Hebrew composition, probably reflecting the tensions and fears of the Maccabean struggle (Metzger, *IA* 43; though see the cautions in deSilva, *IAMCS* 93–95), the work survives in Greek, Latin, Syriac, and several later Hebrew recensions. Nothing is known of the author.

Text: R. HANHART, *Iudith* (Septuaginta 8/4; Göttingen: Vandenhoeck & Ruprecht, 1979). *Survey:* D. A. DESILVA, *IAMCS* 85–109; R. DORAN, "Narrative Literature," *EJMI* 302–4; D. J. HARRINGTON, *InvA* 27–43; L. R. HELYER, "Judith," *DNTB* 624–27; O. KAISER, *OTApo* 39–45; B. M. METZGER, *IA* 43–53; C. A. MOORE, "Judith, Book of," *ABD* 3:1117–25; G. W. E. NICKELSBURG, "Stories of Biblical and Early Post-biblical Times," *SJWSTP* 46–52; W. O. E. OESTERLEY, *IBA* 172–82. *Commentary:* L. ALONSO-SCHÖKEL, "Judith," *HBC* 804–14; N. D. COLEMAN, "Judith," *NCHSA* 2:58–62; A. E. COWLEY, "The Book of Judith," *APOT* 1:242–67; J. CRAGHAN, *Esther, Judith, Tobit, Jonah, Ruth,* 64–126; A.-M. DUBARLE, *Judith* (2 vols.; AnBib 24; Rome: Pontifical Biblical Institute, 1966); M. LEAHY, "Judith," *CCHS* 403–7; C. A. MOORE, *Judith* (AB 40; Garden City, N.Y.: Doubleday, 1985); R. J. RAJA, "Judith," *IBC* 696–706; G. WEST, "Judith," *ECB* 748–57; L. M. WILLS, "The Book of Judith," *NIB* 1073–1183; E. ZENGER, *Judit und Tobit.* *Critical Study:* T. S. CRAVEN, *Artistry and Faith in the Book of Judith* (SBLDS 70; Chico, Calif.: Scholars Press, 1983); M. S. ENSLIN and S. ZEITLIN, *The Book of Judith* (JAL 7; Leiden: Brill, 1972); R. HARRIS, "A Quotation from Judith in the Pauline Epistles," *ExpTim* 27 (1915–1916): 13–15; J. W. VAN HENTEN, "Judith as a Female Moses: Judith 7–13 in the Light of Exodus 17, Numbers 20, and Deuteronomy 33:8–11," in *Reflections on Theology and Gender* (ed. F. van Dijk-Hemmes and A. Brenner; Kampen, Neth.: Kok Pharos, 1994), 33–48; P. J. MILNE, "What Shall We Do with Judith? A Feminist Reassessment of a Biblical 'Heroine,'" *Semeia* 62 (1993): 37–58; P. W. SKEHAN, "The Hand of Judith," *CBQ* 25 (1963): 94–109; IDEM, "Why Leave Out Judith?" *CBQ* 24 (1962): 147–54; J. C. VANDERKAM, ed., *"No One Spoke Ill of Her": Essays on Judith* (SBLEJL 2; Atlanta: Scholars Press, 1992); L. M. WILLS, "The Jewish Novellas," in *Greek Fiction: The Greek Novel in Context* (New York: Routledge, 1994), 223–38.

Additions to Esther. Six additions to Esther, comprising 107 verses, have been accepted by the Roman Catholic, Greek Orthodox, and Russian Orthodox Churches. When translating the Hebrew, Jerome collected these additions, which are found only in the Greek version (the LXX), and placed them at the end of the original Hebrew Esther as 10:4–16:24 (which is followed by the Rheims and Douay edition), thus confusing the chronological sequence. The order of the LXX, which contains the translation of the original Hebrew, as well as the Greek additions, is as follows: (1) Addition 1 (11:2–12:6); (2) Hebrew 1:1–3:13; (3) Addition 2 (13:1–7); (4) Hebrew 3:14–4:17; (5) Addition 3 (13:8–14:19); (6) Hebrew 5:1–2 (= Addition 4 [15:1–2]); (7) Addition 4 (15:1–16); (8) Hebrew 5:3–8:12; (9) Addition 5 (16:1–24); (10) Hebrew 8:13–10:3; (11) Addition 6 (10:4–11:1). Esther may have been translated into Greek by "Lysimachus the son of Ptolemy" (11:1), who claims that the entire document—additions and all—is genuine. The purpose of the additions is to introduce God and religion into a book which originally did not once mention the name of God.

Text: R. HANHART, *Esther* (2 ed.; Septuaginta 8/3; Göttingen: Vandenhoeck & Ruprecht, 1983). *Survey:* D. A. DESILVA, *IAMCS* 110–26; D. J. HARRINGTON, *InvA* 44–54; J. JARICK, "Daniel, Esther, and Jeremiah, Additions to," *DNTB* 250–52; O. KAISER, *OTApo* 45–48; B. M. METZGER, *IA* 55–63; G. W. E. NICKELSBURG, "The Bible Rewritten and Expanded," *SJWSTP* 135–38, 155; W. O. E. OESTERLEY, *IBA* 183–95; J. C. VANDERKAM, *An Introduction to Early Judaism* (Grand Rapids: Eerdmans, 2001), 85–88. *Commentary:* C. M. BECHTEL, *Esther* (Interpretation; Louisville: John Knox, 2002); D. J. A. CLINES, "The Additions to Esther," *HBC* 815–19; S. W. CRAWFORD, "The Additions to Esther," *NIB* 943–72; J. A. F. GREGG, "The Additions to Esther," *APOT* 1:665–84; J. C. H. HOW, "The Rest of the Chapters of the Book of Esther," *NCHSA* 2:63–64; J. JARICK "Greek Esther," *ECB* 758–62; C. A. MOORE, *Daniel, Esther, and Jeremiah,* 153–252; S. PAGÁN, "Esther," *IBC* 707–21; O. H. STECK, *Das Buch Baruch, der Brief des Jeremia, Zusatze zu Ester und Daniel.* *Critical Study:* W. H. BROWNLEE, "Le livre grec d'Esther et la royauté divine: Corrections orthodoxes au livre d'Esther," *RB* 73 (1966): 161–85; D. J. A. CLINES, *The Esther Scroll: The Story of the Story* (JSOTSup 30; Sheffield: Sheffield, 1995); L. DAY, *Three Faces of a Queen: Characterization in the Books of Esther* (JSOTSup 186; Sheffield, Eng.: Sheffield Academic Press, 1995); M. V. FOX, *The Redaction of the Books of Esther* (SBLMS 40; Atlanta: Scholars Press, 1991).

Wisdom of Solomon. The Wisdom of Solomon is accepted by the Roman Catholic, Greek Orthodox, and Russian Orthodox Churches. It is a pseudepigraphon that claims to have been written by Israel's celebrated monarch (see 7:1–14; 8:17–9:18; compare 1 Kgs 3:6–9; 2 Chr 1:8–10). This book is part of the late wisdom tradition and is comparable to Sirach (see below) and parts of Proverbs. It was originally written in Greek and probably derives from Alexandria of the first century B.C.E. It warns the wicked, praises wisdom, provides examples of God's mighty acts in history, and ridicules idolatry. It also exhorts the Jewish people to remain faithful to its religious heritage, eschewing the enticements of paganism. At some points there are close parallels to Paul's thought. Bruce Metzger (*IA* 163) remarks that "there can be little doubt that the Apostle had at one time made a close study of" the book of Wisdom.

Text: J. ZIEGLER, *Sapientia Salomonis* (2d ed.; Septuaginta 12/1; Göttingen: Vandenhoeck & Ruprecht, 1980). *Survey:* D. A. DESILVA, *IAMCS* 127–52; M. GILBERT, "Wisdom Literature," *SJWSTP* 301–13; L. L. GRABBE, *Wisdom of Solomon* (GAP; Sheffield, Eng.: Sheffield, 1997); D. J. HARRINGTON, *InvA* 55–77; O. KAISER, *OTApo* 104–25; B. L. MACK and R. E. MURPHY, "Wisdom Literature," *EJMI* 380–87; B. M. METZGER, *IA* 65–76; W. O. E. OESTERLEY, *IBA* 196–221; D. WINSTON, "Solomon, Wisdom of," *ABD* 6:120–27. **Commentary:** E. G. CLARK, *The Wisdom of Solomon* (CBC; Cambridge: Cambridge University Press, 1973); W. J. DEANE, ΣΟΦΙΑ ΣΑΛΩΜΩΝ, *The Book of Wisdom: The Greek Text, the Latin Vulgate and the Authorised English Version* (Oxford: Clarendon, 1881); J. GEYER, *The Wisdom of Solomon* (TBC; London: SCM Press, 1963); A. T. S. GOODRICK, *The Book of Wisdom, with Introduction and Notes* (Oxford Church Bible Commentary; London: Rivingtons, 1913); J. A. F. GREGG, *The Wisdom of Solomon* (Cambridge Bible for Schools; Cambridge: Cambridge University Press, 1909); C. HARRIS, "The Wisdom of Solomon," *NCHSA* 2:64–78; A. P. HAYMAN, "The Wisdom of Solomon," *ECB* 763–78; S. HOLMES, "The Wisdom of Solomon," *APOT* 1:518–68; H. HÜBNER, *Die Weisheit Salomons: Liber sapientiae Salomonis* (ATD: Apokryphen 4; Göttingen: Vandenhoeck & Ruprecht, 1999); M. KOLARCIK, "The Book of Wisdom," *NIB* 5:435–600; C. LATTEY, "The Book of Wisdom," *CCHS* 504–11; W. O. E. OESTERLEY, *The Wisdom of Solomon* (TED II: Hellenistic Jewish Texts 1; London: SPCK, 1918); J. M. REESE, "Wisdom of Solomon," *HBC* 820–35; J. REIDER, *The Book of Wisdom* (JAL; New York: Harper, 1957); J. VÍLCHEZ, "Wisdom," *IBC* 908–22; D. WINSTON, *The Wisdom of Solomon* (AB 43; Garden City, N.Y.: Doubleday, 1979). **Critical Study:** S. CHEON, *The Exodus Story in the Wisdom of Solomon* (JSPSup 23; Sheffield, Eng.: Sheffield Academic Press, 1997); P. E. ENNS, *Exodus Retold: Ancient Exegesis of the Departure from Egypt in Wis 15–21 and 19:1–9* (HSM 57; Atlanta: Scholars Press, 1997); IDEM, "A Retelling of the Song of the Sea in Wisdom 10.20–21," in *The Function of Scripture in Early Jewish and Christian Tradition* (ed. C. A. Evans and J. A. Sanders; JSNTSup 154; SSEJC 6; Sheffield, Eng.: Sheffield Academic Press, 1998), 142–65; M. KOLARCIK, *The Ambiguity of Death in the Book of Wisdom 1–6* (AnBib 127; Rome: Pontifical Biblical Institute, 1991); S. LANGE, "The Wisdom of Solomon and Philo," *JBL* 55 (1936): 293–306; J. M. REESE, *Hellenistic Influence on the Book of Wisdom and Its Consequences* (AnBib 41; Rome: Pontifical Biblical Institute, 1970); R. T. SIEBENECK, "The Midrash of Wisdom 10–19," *CBQ* 22 (1960): 176–82; J. P. WEISENGOFF, "Death and Immortality in the Book of Wisdom," *CBQ* 3 (1941): 104–33; IDEM, "The Impious in Wisdom 2," *CBQ* 11 (1949): 40–65; A. G. WRIGHT, "The Structure of the Book of Wisdom," *Bib* 48 (1967): 165–84; IDEM, "The Structure of Wisdom 11–19," *CBQ* 27 (1965): 28–34.

Ecclesiasticus. Commonly called (Jesus ben) Sira, or the Wisdom of Jesus the son of Sirach, though in the Latin tradition it is known as Ecclesiasticus (i.e., the "church book"). Sirach is accepted by the Roman Catholic, Greek Orthodox, and Russian Orthodox Churches. The original document was written in Hebrew by Joshua ben Sira (ca. 180 B.C.E.) and was later introduced and translated into Greek by his grandson around 132 B.C.E. Only fragments of the Hebrew text remain, most of which date from the Middle Ages, though fragments have been recovered from the region of the Dead Sea (see Yadin). These include 2QSir (or 2Q18), which preserves portions of chapters 1 and 6; MasSir, which preserves portions of chapters 39–44; and 11QPs^a, which preserves a portion of the poem in chapter 51. Sirach is probably intended to be two volumes, consisting of chapters 1–23 and 24–51, with each volume beginning with an encomium on wisdom (see 1:1–10; 24:1–34). In many respects the book resembles Proverbs. It is, as

Bruce Metzger has remarked, "the first specimen of that form of Judaism which subsequently developed into the rabbinical schools of the Pharisees and the Sadducees" (*OAA* 128). The nature of theodicy in Sirach remains a topic of debate (see deSilva, *IAMCS* 187–92). Sirach 24 is of special interest for the interpretation of John 1:1–18.

Text: P. C. BEENTJES, *The Book of Ben Sira in Hebrew* (VTSup 68; Leiden: Brill, 1997); I. LÉVI, *The Hebrew Text of the Book of Ecclesiasticus* (SSS 3; Leiden: Brill, 1904); M. SEGAL, *Book of Ben Sira, Complete* (Jerusalem: Mosad Bialik, 1953) (pointed Hebrew text); Y. YADIN, *The Ben Sira Scroll from Masada, with Introduction, Emendations, and Commentary* (Jerusalem: Israel Exploration Society and Shrine of the Book, 1965) (Hebrew); J. ZIEGLER, *Sapientia Iesu filii Sirach* (2d ed.; Septuaginta 12/2; Göttingen: Vandenhoeck & Ruprecht, 1980) (Greek). *Survey:* R. J. COGGINS, *Sirach* (GAP; Sheffield: Sheffield, 1998); D. A. DESILVA, "Sirach," *DNTB* 1116–24; IDEM, *IAMCS* 153–97; A. A. DI LELLA, "Wisdom of Ben Sira," *ABD* 6:931–45; M. GILBERT, "Wisdom Literature," *SJWSTP* 290–301; D. J. HARRINGTON, *InvA* 78–91; O. KAISER, *OTA* 88–104; B. L. MACK and R. E. MURPHY, "Wisdom Literature," *EJMI* 373–77; B. M. METZGER, *IA* 77–88; W. O. E. OESTERLEY, *IBA* 222–55. *Commentary:* G. H. BOX and W. O. E. OESTERLEY, "The Book of Sirach," *APOT* 1:268–517; J. L. CRENSHAW, "The Book of Sirach," *NIB* 5:601–867; IDEM, "Sirach," *HBC* 836–54; D. J. HARRINGTON, "Sirach," *IBC* 923–50; C. J. KEARNS, "Ecclesiasticus," *CCHS* 512–26; W. O. E. OESTERLEY, *The Wisdom of Ben-Sira* (TED I: Palestinian Jewish Texts 2; London: SPCK, 1916); IDEM, "The Wisdom of Jesus, the Son of Sirach, or Ecclesiasticus," *NCHSA* 2:79–102; G. SAUER, *Jesus Sirah, Ben Sira* (ATD: Apokryphen 1; Göttingen: Vandenhoeck & Ruprecht, 2000); P. W. SKEHAN and A. A. DI LELLA, *The Wisdom of Ben Sira* (AB 39; New York: Doubleday, 1987); J. G. SNAITH, *Ecclesiasticus* (CBC; Cambridge: Cambridge University Press, 1974); IDEM, "Sirach," *ECB* 779–798; Y. YADIN, *The Ben Sira Scroll from Masada, with Introduction, Emendations, and Commentary* (Jerusalem: Israel Exploration Society, 1965). *Critical Study:* J. BLENKINSOPP, *Wisdom and Law in the Old Testament* (Oxford: Oxford University Press, 1995), 151–82; J. L. CRENSHAW, "The Problem of Theodicy in Sirach: On Human Bondage," *JBL* 94 (1975): 47–64; D. A. DESILVA, "The Wisdom of Ben Sira: Honor, Shame, and the Maintenance of the Values of a Minority Culture," *CBQ* 58 (1996): 433–55; A. A. DI LELLA, "Conservative and Progressive Theology: Sirach and Wisdom," *CBQ* 28 (1966): 139–54; R. EGGER-WENZEL, ed., *Ben Sira's God: Proceedings of the International Ben Sira Conference* (BZAW 321; New York: de Gruyter, 2002); E. JACOB, "Wisdom and Religion in Sirach," in *Israelite Wisdom: Theological and Literary Essays in Honor of Samuel Terrien* (ed. J. Gammie et al.; Homage 3; Missoula, Mont.: Scholars Press, 1978), 247–60; T. R. LEE, *Studies in the Form of Sirach 44–50* (SBLDS 75; Atlanta: Scholars Press, 1986); B. L. MACK, *Wisdom and the Hebrew Epic: Ben Sira's Hymn in Praise of the Fathers* (Chicago: University of Chicago Press, 1985); H. MCKEATING, "Jesus ben Sira's Attitude to Women," *ExpTim* 85 (1973–1974): 85–87; O. MULDER, *Simon the High Priest in Sirach 50: An Exegetical Study of the Significance to the Praise of the Fathers in Ben Sira's Concept of the History of Israel* (JSJSup 78; Leiden: Brill, 2003); J. T. SANDERS, *Ben Sira and Demotic Wisdom* (SBLMS 28; Chico, Calif.: Scholars Press, 1983); E. J. SCHNABEL, *Law and Wisdom from Ben Sira to Paul* (WUNT 2.16; Tübingen: Vandenhoeck & Ruprecht, 1985), esp. 8–92; R. T. SIEBENECK, "May Their Bones Return to Life! Sirach's Praise of the Fathers," *CBQ* 21 (1959): 411–28; W. C. TRENCHARD, *Ben Sira's View of Women: A Literary Analysis* (BJS 38; Chico, Calif.: Scholars Press, 1982); B. G. WRIGHT, *No Small Difference: Sirach's Relationship to Its Hebrew Parent Text* (SBLSCS 26; Atlanta: Scholars Press, 1989).

Baruch. Baruch, or 1 Baruch, purports to be the work of Baruch, friend and secretary of the prophet Jeremiah (see Jer 32:12; 36:4). Originally a Hebrew writing, it has survived in Greek, Latin, Syriac, and other languages of the Mediterranean. It appears to have at least two parts, the first consisting of prose (1:1–3:8), the second poetry (3:9–5:9). The purpose of the first part is to bring an awareness of sin and the need for repentance, while the purpose of the second part is to offer praise to wisdom and comfort to an oppressed Jerusalem. The two parts were probably brought together about 100 B.C.E.

Text: J. ZIEGLER, *Jeremias, Baruch, Threni, Epistula Jeremiae.* **Survey:** D. A. DESILVA, *IAMCS* 198–213; D. J. HARRINGTON, *InvA* 92–102; O. KAISER, *OTA* 54–62; B. L. MACK and R. E. MURPHY, "Wisdom Literature," *EJMI* 377–78 (on Bar 3:9–4:4); METZGER, *IA* 89–94; G. W. E. NICKELSBURG, "The Bible Rewritten and Expanded," *SJWSTP* 140–46; W. O. E. OESTERLEY, *IBA* 256–67; J. E. WRIGHT, "Baruch, Books of," *DNTB* 148–51. **Commentary:** D. J. HARRINGTON, "Baruch," *HBC* 855–60; L. HERIBERTO RIVAS, "Baruch," *IBC* 1043–47; C. A. MOORE, *Daniel, Esther, and Jeremiah,* 255–316; A. J. SALDARINI, "The Book of Baruch," *NIB* 927–82; P. P. SAYDON, "Baruch," *CCHS* 596–99; J. J. SCHMITT, "Baruch," *ECB* 799–802; O. H. STECK, *Das Buch Baruch, der Brief des Jeremia, Zusatze zu Ester und Daniel;* H. St. J. THACKERAY, "Baruch," *NCHSA* 2:102–11; O. C. WHITEHOUSE, "I Baruch," *APOT* 1:569–95. **Critical Study:** D. G. BURKE, *The Poetry of Baruch: A Reconstruction and Analysis of the Original Hebrew Text of Baruch 3:9–5:9* (SBLSCS 10; Chico, Calif.: Scholars Press, 1982); W. HARRELSON, "Wisdom Hidden and Revealed according to Baruch (Baruch 3.9–4.4)," in *Priests, Prophets, and Scribes: Essays on the Formation and Heritage of Second Temple Judaism in Honour of Joseph Blenkinsopp* (ed. E. Ulrich; JSOTSup 149; Sheffield: JSOT Press, 1992), 158–71; R. R. HARWELL, *The Principal Versions of Baruch* (New Haven: Yale University Press, 1915); J. R. LUNDBOM, "Baruch, Seraich, and Expanded Colophons in the Book of Jeremiah," *JSOT* 36 (1986): 89–114; C. A. MOORE, "Toward the Dating of the Book of Baruch," *CBQ* 36 (1974): 312–20; E. TOV, *The Book of Baruch also called 1 Baruch* (SBLTT 8; Pseudepigrapha 6; Missoula, Mont.: Scholars Press, 1975) (on Bar 1:1–3:8); IDEM, *The Septuagint Translation of Jeremiah and Baruch: A Discussion of an Early Revision of Jeremiah 29–52 and Baruch 1:1–3:8* (HSM 8; Missoula, Mont.: Scholars Press, 1976); J. E. WRIGHT, "Baruch: His Evolution from Scribe to Apocalyptic Seer," in *Biblical Figures outside the Bible* (ed. M. E. Stone and T. A. Bergren; Harrisburg, Pa.: Trinity Press International, 1998), 264–89.

Epistle of Jeremiah. The Epistle of Jeremiah (or Jeremy) appears as chapter 6 of Baruch in the LXX, which is followed by the Vulgate (and the Rheims and Douay version). The letter is accepted by the Roman Catholic, Greek Orthodox, and Russian Orthodox Churches. The document purports to be a letter from the prophet Jeremiah, exhorting the Jewish exiles to eschew idolatry. The apocryphal letter may have been inspired by Jer 10:11, an Aramaic verse that reads: "The gods who did not make the heavens and the earth shall perish from the earth and from under the heavens" (Oesterley, *IBA* 269; Metzger, *IA* 96). But this is disputed (deSilva, *IAMCS* 218 n. 6). Several OT passages have been drawn upon (Isa 40:18–20; 41:6–7; Jer 10:3–9, 14; Ps 115:4–8). The letter was probably originally written in Greek, perhaps as early as 300 B.C.E. A small Greek portion (vv. 43–44) has been found at Qumran (i.e., 7QpapEpJer gr).

Text: J. ZIEGLER, *Jeremias, Baruch, Threni, Epistula Jeremiae.* **Survey:** D. A. DESILVA, *IAMCS* 214–21; D. J. HARRINGTON, *InvA* 103–8; J. JARICK, "Daniel, Esther, and Jeremiah, Additions to," *DNTB* 250–52; O. KAISER, *OTA* 62–64; B. M. METZGER, *IA* 95–98; G. W. E. NICKELSBURG, "The Bible Rewritten and Expanded," *SJWSTP* 146–49, 156; W. O. E. OESTERLEY, *IBA* 268–71. **Commentary:** C. J. BALL, "Epistle of Jeremy," *APOT* 1:596–611; D. J. HARRINGTON, "Letter of Jeremiah," *HBC* 861–62; L. HERIBERTO RIVAS, "Letter of Jeremiah," *IBC* 1048–49; C. A. MOORE, *Daniel, Esther, and Jeremiah,* 317–58; A. J. SALDARINI, "The Letter of Jeremiah," *NIB* 983–1010; P. P. SAYDON, "Baruch," *CCHS* 599–600; J. J. SCHMITT, "Baruch," *ECB* 802; O. H. STECK, *Das Buch Baruch, der Brief des Jeremia, Zusatze zu Ester und Daniel;* H. St. J. THACKERAY, "The Epistle of Jeremy," *NCHSA* 2:111–16. **Critical Study:** G. M. LEE, "Apocryphal Cats: Baruch 6:21," *VT* 18 (1968): 488–93; W. NAUMANN, *Untersuchungen über den apokryphen Jeremiasbrief* (Giessen: Töpelmann, 1913).

Prayer of Azariah and the Song of the Three Children. The Prayer of Azariah and the Song of the Three Children is an addition inserted between Dan 3:23 and 3:24. It is accepted by the Roman Catholic, Greek Orthodox, and Russian Orthodox Churches. There are several additions to Daniel, the three major ones being the Prayer of Azariah and the Song of the Three Children (or Young Men), Susanna, and Bel and the Dragon. These additions were probably composed in Greek, although Aramaic is possible. In the case of the addition under consideration, the original language of composition may have been Hebrew. The Prayer of Azariah and the Song of the Three Children itself probably represents a combination of two additions. The Prayer of Azariah is uttered by one of the young men in the furnace (i.e., Abednego; cf. Dan 1:7). It confesses Israel's sin and petitions God that Israel's enemies be put to shame. It is followed by a song of praise and exhortation to praise. It owes much of its inspiration to Ps 148:1–2, 7–12 (Metzger, *IA* 103).

Text: J. ZIEGLER, *Susanna, Daniel, Bel et Draco.* **Survey:** D. A. DESILVA, *IAMCS* 225–31; D. J. HARRINGTON, *InvA* 109–13; J. JARICK, "Daniel, Esther, and Jeremiah, Additions to," *DNTB* 250–52; O. KAISER, *OTA* 48–53; B. M. METZGER, *IA* 99–105; G. W. E. NICKELSBURG, "The Bible Rewritten and Expanded," *SJWSTP* 149–52; W. O. E. OESTERLEY, *IBA* 272–79. **Commentary:** W. H. BENNETT, "Prayer of Azariah and Song of the Three Children," *APOT* 1:625–37; N. D. COLEMAN, "Additions to the Book of Daniel," *NCHSA* 2:117–23; A. LACOCQUE, "Daniel," *IBC* 1094–95; C. A. MOORE, *Daniel, Esther, and Jeremiah,* 39–76; J. W. ROGERSON, "Additions to Daniel," *ECB* 803–4; P. P. SAYDON, "Daniel," *CCHS* 642–43; D. L. SMITH-CHRISTOPHER, "The Prayer of Azariah and the Song of the Three Jews," *NIB* 158–70; O. H. STECK, *Das Buch Baruch, der Brief des Jeremia, Zusatze zu Ester und Daniel.* **Critical Study:** E. HAAG, "Die drei Männer im Feuer nach Dan. 3:1–30," in *Die Entstehung der jüdischen Martyrologie* (ed. J. W. van Henten; SPB 38; Leiden: Brill, 1989), 20–50; J. W. VAN HENTEN and F. AVEMARIE, *Martyrdom and Noble Death,* 59–62; C. KUHL, *Die drei Männer im Feuer (Daniel, Kapitel 3 und seine Zusätze): Ein Beitrag zur israelitisch-jüdischen Literaturgeschichte* (BZAW 55; Giessen: Töpelmann, 1930).

Susanna. Susanna is accepted by the Roman Catholic, Greek Orthodox, and Russian Orthodox Churches. In the LXX and Vulgate Susanna is chapter 13 of Daniel. In other versions, however, Susanna appears as an introduction to chapter 1 (perhaps because in v. 45 Daniel is referred to as a "young lad" and according to v. 64 it was "from that day onward" that Daniel enjoyed a great reputation). Susanna is the story of a beautiful woman who is pursued by two lustful elders. When wrongly accused, she is defended by the wise Daniel. The lesson of Susanna is that virtue and faith will ultimately be vindicated. It is likely that the story was origi- nally composed in Greek, as is especially seen in the Greek word-plays in verses 54–59 (Metzger, *IA* 110–11).

Text: J. ZIEGLER, *Susanna, Daniel, Bel et Draco.* **Survey:** D. A. DESILVA, *IAMCS* 231–36; R. DORAN, "Narrative Literature," *EJMI* 299–301; D. J. HARRINGTON, *InvA* 113–16; J. JAR- ICK, "Daniel, Esther, and Jeremiah, Additions to," *DNTB* 250–52; O. KAISER, *OTA* 48–53; B. M. METZGER, *IA* 107–13; G. W. E. NICKELSBURG, "Stories of Biblical and Early Post- biblical Times," *SJWSTP* 37–38; W. O. E. OESTERLEY, *IBA* 280–86. **Commentary:** N. D. COLEMAN, "Additions to the Book of Daniel," *NCHSA* 2:117–23; D. M. KAY, "Susanna," *APOT* 1:638–51; A. LACOCQUE, "Daniel," *IBC* 1106–7; C. A. MOORE, *Daniel, Esther, and Jeremiah,* 77–116; J. W. ROGERSON, "Additions to Daniel," *ECB* 804–5; P. P. SAYDON, "Daniel," *CCHS* 642–43; D. L. SMITH-CHRISTOPHER, "The Prayer of Azariah and the Song of the Three Jews," *NIB* 171–84; O. H. STECK, *Das Buch Baruch, der Brief des Jeremia, Zusatze zu Ester und Daniel.* **Critical Study:** B. BOHN, "Rape and the Gendered Gaze: Susanna and the Elders in Early Modern Bologna," *BibInt* 9 (2001): 259–86; D. W. CLANTON, "(Re)dating the Story of Susanna: A Proposal," *JSJ* (2003): 121–40; J. A. GLANCY, "The Accused: Susanna and Her Readers," in *A Feminist Companion to Esther, Ju- dith, and Susanna* (ed. A. Brenner; FCB 7; Sheffield: Sheffield, 1995), 288–302; A.-J. LEVINE, " 'Hemmed In on Every Side': Jews and Women in the Book of Susanna," in *Social Location and Biblical Interpretation in the United States* (vol. 1 of *Reading from This Place;* ed. F. F. Segovia and M. A. Tolbert; Minneapolis: Fortress, 1996), 175–90; C. A. MOORE, "Susanna: A Case of Sexual Harassment in Ancient Babylon," *BRev* 8, no. 3 (1992): 20–29, 52; E. SPOLSKY, ed., *The Judgment of Susanna: Authority and Witness* (SBLEJL 11; Atlanta: Scholars Press, 1996); F. ZIMMERMANN, "The Story of Susanna and Its Original Lan- guage," *JQR* 48 (1957–58): 236–41.

Bel and the Dragon. Bel and the Dragon is accepted by the Roman Catholic, Greek Orthodox, and Russian Orthodox Churches. This addition is made up of two sto- ries designed to demonstrate the foolishness of idolatry and the dishonesty of the heathen priesthood. Like the other additions to Daniel, these stories teach that God's people will persevere if they have faith. It may have been inspired by bibli- cal traditions that speak of God's slaying Leviathan (Metzger, *IA* 120). In the LXX, Bel and the Dragon is added to Daniel 12, while in the Vulgate it makes up chapter 14.

Text: J. ZIEGLER, *Susanna, Daniel, Bel et Draco.* **Survey:** D. A. DESILVA, *IAMCS* 237–43; R. DORAN, "Narrative Literature," *EJMI* 301–2; D. J. HARRINGTON, *InvA* 116–21; J. JAR- ICK, "Daniel, Esther, and Jeremiah, Additions to," *DNTB* 250–52; O. KAISER, *OTA* 48–53; B. M. METZGER, *IA* 115–22; G. W. E. NICKELSBURG, "Stories of Biblical and Early Post- biblical Times," *SJWSTP* 38–40; W. O. E. OESTERLEY, *IBA* 287–93. **Commentary:** N. D. COLEMAN, "Additions to the Book of Daniel," *NCHSA* 2:117–23; W. DAVIES, "Bel and the Dragon," *APOT* 1:652–64; A. LACOCQUE, "Daniel," *IBC* 1099; C. A. MOORE, *Daniel, Esther, and Jeremiah,* 117–49; J. W. ROGERSON, "Additions to Daniel," *ECB* 805–6;

P. P. SAYDON, "Daniel," *CCHS* 642–43; D. L. SMITH-CHRISTOPHER, "The Prayer of Azariah and the Song of the Three Jews," *NIB* 185–94; O. H. STECK, *Das Buch Baruch, der Brief des Jeremia, Zusatze zu Ester und Daniel*. **Critical Study:** J. J. COLLINS, " 'The King Has Become a Jew': The Perspective on the Gentile World in Bel and the Snake," in *Diaspora Jews and Judaism: Essays in Honor of, and in Dialogue with, A. Thomas Kraabel* (ed. J. A. Overman and R. S. MacLennan; SFSHJ 41; Atlanta: Scholars Press, 1992), 335–45; A. WYSNY, *Die Erzählungen von Bel und dem Drachen: Untersuchung zu Dan 14* (SBB 33; Stuttgart: Katholisches Bibelwerk, 1996); F. ZIMMERMANN, "Bel and the Dragon," *VT* 8 (1958): 438–40.

Prayer of Manasseh. The Prayer of Manasseh is accepted by the Greek Orthodox Church. Inspired by 2 Chr 33:11–13, this document purports to be King Manasseh's prayer of repentance after being exiled. Moreover, the reference to two works that contain Manasseh's prayer (2 Chr 33:18–20), which are lost, may very well have prompted our unknown writer to compose this piece (Metzger, *IA* 124–25). According to R. Hvalvik, the prayer consists of (1) invocation (v. 1), (2) ascription of praise to God (vv. 2–7), (3) confession of sin (vv. 8–10), (4) petition for forgiveness (vv. 11–15a), and (5) doxology (v. 15b). See further comments in chapter 2.

Text: A. RAHLFS, *Psalmi cum Odis* (2d ed.; Septuaginta 10; Göttingen: Vandenhoeck & Ruprecht, 1979). **Survey:** D. A. DESILVA, *IAMCS* 296–300; D. FLUSSER, "Psalms, Hymns, and Prayers," *SJWSTP* 555; D. J. HARRINGTON, *InvA* 166–69; R. HVALVIK, "Prayer of Manasseh," *DNTB* 821–22; O. KAISER, *OTA* 75–78; B. M. METZGER, *IA* 123–28; W. O. E. OESTERLEY, *IBA* 294–99. **Commentary:** J. H. CHARLESWORTH, "Prayer of Manasseh," *OTP* 2:625–37; N. D. COLEMAN, "The Prayer of Manasses," *NCHSA* 2:124–26; J. C. DANCY, "The Prayer of Manasseh," in J. C. Dancy et al., *The Shorter Books of the Apocrypha* (CBC; Cambridge: Cambridge University Press, 1972), 242–48; P. R. DAVIES, "The Prayer of Manasseh," *ECB* 859–61; D. J. HARRINGTON, "Prayer of Manasseh," *HBC* 872–74; H. E. RYLE, "Prayer of Manasses," *APOT* 1:612–24. **Critical Study:** W. BAARS and H. SCHNEIDER, "Prayer of Manasseh," in *The Old Testament in Syriac according to the Peshitta Version* (VTS 4/6; Leiden: Brill, 1972), i–vii, 1–9; P.-M. BOGAERT, "La légende de Manassé," in *Apocalypse de Baruch* (SC 144; Paris: Cerf, 1969), 296–319; H. N. BREAM, "Manasseh and His Prayer," *Lutheran Theological Seminary Bulletin* 66 (1986): 5–47.

1 Maccabees. First Maccabees is accepted by the Roman Catholic, Greek Orthodox, and Russian Orthodox Churches. The book tells of the events surrounding the Jewish uprising against Antiochus IV Epiphanes. First Maccabees describes the courage of Mattathias the priest and his sons, especially Judas Maccabeus, after whom the book and the period of time are named. The book is probably an apology for the Hasmonean dynasty which, not too many years after Israel had regained its independence, had fallen into disfavor among many of the strictest observers of Judaism. Originally written in Hebrew, probably sometime late in the second century B.C.E. (though some scholars place chs. 14–16 after 70 C.E.), the history of 1 Maccabees is for the most part trustworthy (though at times it is at variance with 2 Maccabees—and it is not always certain which account is to be preferred). Unlike 2 Maccabees, 1 Maccabees contains no miraculous accounts. Solomon Zeitlin thinks that the book which the *Yosippon* (see ch. 5) refers to as

Sepher Bet Hasmanaim ("The Book of the House of the Hasmoneans") is the Hebrew 1 Maccabees.

Text: W. KAPPLER, *Maccabaeorum liber I* (Septuaginta 9/1; Göttingen: Vandenhoeck & Ruprecht, 1967). *Survey:* H. W. ATTRIDGE, "Historiography," *SJWSTP* 171–76; IDEM, "Jewish Historiography," *EJMI* 316–23; J. R. BARTLETT, *1 Maccabees* (GAP; Sheffield: Sheffield, 1998); D. A. DESILVA, *IAMCS* 244–65; T. FISCHER, "Maccabees, Books of," *ABD* 4:439–50, esp. 439–42; L. L. GRABBE, "1 and 2 Maccabees," *DNTB* 657–61; D. J. HARRINGTON, *InvA* 122–36; O. KAISER, *OTA* 13–17; B. M. METZGER, *IA* 129–37; W. O. E. OESTERLEY, *IBA* 300–314. *Commentary:* J. R. BARTLETT, "1 Maccabees," *ECB* 807–30; IDEM, *The First and Second Books of Maccabees* (CBC; Cambridge: Cambridge University Press, 1973), 14–214; T. CORBISHLEY, "1 & 2 Maccabees," *CCHS* 706–17; J. C. DANCY, *A Commentary on I Maccabees* (Oxford: Basil Blackwell, 1954); R. DORAN, "The First Book of Maccabees," *NIB* 4:1–178; W. FAIRWEATHER and J. S. BLACK, *The First Book of Maccabees* (Cambridge Bible for Schools and Colleges; Cambridge: Cambridge University Press, 1897); H. A. FISCHEL, *The First Book of Maccabees: A Commentary* (New York: Schocken Books, 1948); J. A. GOLDSTEIN, *I Maccabees* (AB 41; Garden City, N.Y.: Doubleday, 1976); J. W. HUNKIN, "I. and II. Maccabees," *NCHSA* 2:126–46; H. G. JIMÉNEZ, "1 Maccabees," *IBC* 722–38; H. LICHTENBERGER, *Die Makkabäerbücher;* W. O. E. OESTERLEY, "The First Book of Maccabees," *APOT* 1:59–124; L. H. SCHIFFMAN, "1 Maccabees," *HBC* 875–897; S. TEDESCHE and S. ZEITLIN, *The First Book of Maccabees* (JAL; New York: Harper, 1950). *Critical Study:* J. A. GOLDSTEIN, "How the Authors of 1 and 2 Maccabees Treated the 'Messianic' Promises"; D. J. HARRINGTON, *The Maccabean Revolt,* 57–86; J. W. VAN HENTEN and F. AVEMARIE, *Martyrdom and Noble Death,* 62–63; G. O. NEUHAUS, "Quellen im 1. Makkabäerbuch?" *JSJ* 5 (1974): 162–75; S. SCHWARTZ, "Israel and the Nations Roundabout: 1 Maccabees and the Hasmonean Expansion," *JJS* 42 (1991): 16–38; D. S. WILLIAMS, *The Structure of 1 Maccabees* (CBQMS 31; Washington, D.C.: Catholic Biblical Association, 1999); S. ZEITLIN, "Josippon," *JQR* 53 (1962–1963): 277–97, esp. 290.

2 Maccabees. Second Maccabees is accepted by the Roman Catholic, Greek Orthodox, and Russian Orthodox Churches. The book is not a sequel to 1 Maccabees; rather it covers approximately the same events and period of time (=1 Macc 1:10–7:50). According to 2:23–28, 2 Maccabees is an abridgment of a five-volume work by one "Jason of Cyrene." This larger history is now lost. Most suspect that 2 Maccabees is historically less trustworthy. Its purpose is to enhance the theological dimensions of the Jerusalem temple and the Jewish struggle for independence. See also its seventh chapter for a defense of the resurrection. Second Maccabees was probably written originally in Greek in the first century B.C.E.

Text: R. HANHART, *Maccabaeorum liber II* (Septuaginta 9/2; Göttingen: Vandenhoeck & Ruprecht, 1959). *Survey:* H. W. ATTRIDGE, "Historiography," *SJWSTP* 176–83; IDEM, "Jewish Historiography," *EJMI* 316–23; D. A. DESILVA, *IAMCS* 266–79; T. FISCHER, "Maccabees, Books of," *ABD* 4:439–50, esp. 442–47; L. L. GRABBE, "1 and 2 Maccabees," *DNTB* 657–61; D. J. HARRINGTON, *InvA* 137–51; O. KAISER, *OTA* 17–24; B. M. METZGER, *IA* 129–37; W. O. E. OESTERLEY, *IBA* 300–314. *Commentary:* G. ARANDA PÉREZ, "2 Maccabees," *IBC* 739–50; J. R. BARTLETT, *The First and Second Books of Maccabees* (CBC; Cambridge: Cambridge University Press, 1973), 215–344; IDEM, "2 Maccabees," *ECB* 831–50; T. CORBISHLEY, "1 & 2 Maccabees," *CCHS* 706–7, 717–23; R. DORAN, "The Second Book of Maccabees," *NIB* 4:179–299; J. A. GOLDSTEIN, *II Maccabees* (AB 41A; Garden City, N.Y.: Doubleday, 1983); J. W. HUNKIN, "I. and II. Maccabees," *NCHSA* 2:126–28, 146–58; H. LICHTENBERGER, *Die Makkabäerbücher;* J. MOFFATT, "The Second Book of Maccabees," *APOT* 1:125–54; L. H. SCHIFFMAN, "2 Maccabees," *HBC* 898–915; S. ZEITLIN and S. TEDESCHE, *The Second Book of Maccabees* (JAL; New York: Harper, 1954). **Critical Study:** R. DORAN, "2 Maccabees and 'Tragic History,'" *HUCA* 50 (1979): 107–14; IDEM, *Temple Propaganda: The Purpose and Character of 2 Maccabees* (CBQMS 12; Washington, D.C.: Catholic Biblical Association, 1981); J. A. GOLDSTEIN, "How the Authors of 1 and 2 Maccabees Treated the 'Messianic' Promises"; D. J. HARRINGTON, *The Maccabean Revolt,* 36–56; J. W. VAN HENTEN, *The Maccabean Martyrs as Saviours of the Jewish People: A Study of 2 and 4 Maccabees* (JSJSup 57; Leiden: Brill, 1997); J. W. VAN HENTEN and F. AVEMARIE, *Martyrdom and Noble Death,* 64–72; A. OPPENHEIMER, "Oral Law in the Books of the Maccabees," *Imm* 6 (1976): 34–42.

Themes

The writings that make up the OT Apocrypha contribute much to NT background. There are several political and theological themes that may be reviewed briefly.

God. Second Maccabees 7:28 may be the first to teach that God created the universe out of nothing. In Sir 43:27 God is called "the All." God is called "Father" (Tob 13:4), "Judge" (Sir 17:15–24), and "King" (Jdt 9:12; 2 Macc 7:9). Wisdom 11:22–12:2 teaches that God's love is universal. God is all-knowing and all-powerful (Sir 42:15–25).

Piety and Martyrdom. In 1 Esdr 4:13–47 the pious wisdom of Zerubbabel is cited as an important factor in reminding the Persian king Darius of his vow to have Jerusalem and the temple rebuilt. The wickedness of God's people is cited in 2 Esdras as the major cause of Israel's misfortunes. The book of Tobit revolves around the piety of Tobit and his son Tobias. Tobit tithed, kept the dietary laws, gave food and clothing to the poor, and greatest of all, buried the dead. (According to Sir 3:30; 7:10, almsgiving atones for sin.) The book of Judith tells the story of a beautiful woman who risked her life, but kept herself from being dishonored by Holofernes. In 9:1 she humbles herself and prays. In Add Esth 14:1–19 Queen Esther humbles herself (v. 2) and prays fervently to God. In Bar 1:5–14 the penitent weep, fast, pray, and send money to Jerusalem to reestablish worship in Jerusalem. The Prayer of Azariah and the Song of the Three Young Men greatly enhances the theme of piety found in Daniel. In Susanna the piety of Susanna and the wisdom of the young man Daniel are vindicated. The Prayer of Manasseh is a classic in pious penitence. Perhaps the greatest example of piety in the face of persecution occurs in 2 Maccabees 7 where a mother and her seven sons are put to death for refusing to eat pork (v. 1; cf. 4 Macc 8–17; *b. Giṭ.* 57b; *Lam. Rab.* 1:16 §50).

Salvation History. A frequent theme is that of Israel's obduracy (1 Esdr 1:47–52; 2 Esdr 3:20–22; 4:30; Tob 1:5; Jdt 5:17–21; Bar 1:15–2:10; Add Esth

14:6–7; PrAzar 4–7, 14; Sus 52–53; Pr Man 9–10, 12) and return from the exile (1 Esdr 2:1–15; Bar 5:1–9).

Zionism. Much of 2 Esdras is concerned with the fate of "Zion" (i.e., Jerusalem). In 13:29–50 the Messiah is seen standing on the top of Mount Zion (v. 35), with Zion now sitting in judgment upon the nations (vv. 36–38). In Tob 14:5b the aged Tobit prophesies that Jerusalem and the temple, having been destroyed, will be rebuilt "in splendor." Sirach recounts the recent glories of the temple (Sir 49:11–13; 50:1–21). Baruch 1:10–14 is concerned with the reestablishment of worship in Jerusalem.

Defense of Hasmonean dynasty. First Maccabees probably affords the best examples (14:25–15:9; 16:1–3; 2 Macc 15:7–24; see also Sir 50:1–24 [praise of Simon]).

Messiah. The Messiah is kept by the Most High until the last days (2 Esdr 12:32; 13:26; 14:9). He will judge the wicked and rescue God's remnant (12:33–35). He is described in terms of Dan 7:13 (cf. Mark 14:62). The Messiah will set up a kingdom that will last 400 years (2 Esdr 7:26–30), after which time he and all people will die. After seven days of silence there will be a general resurrection and judgment (7:31–44). Elsewhere hope is expressed that a prophet will arise (1 Macc 4:46; 9:27; 14:41). This hope is probably based on Deut 18:15–18.

Resurrection. According to 2 Macc 7:9: "The King of the universe will raise us up to an everlasting renewal of life, because we have died for his laws" (see vv. 11, 14, 23, 29). Also, in 2 Macc 12:44 we read: " . . . those who had fallen would rise again. . . ." (see also 14:46). Also, in 2 Esdr 7:32: "And the earth shall give up those who are asleep in it, and the dust those who dwell silently in it; and the chambers shall give up the souls which have been committed to them." Wisdom 3:1–9 teaches immortality, if not resurrection (see also 6:17–20).

Eschatology. "Signs of the End" include terror, unrighteousness, the sun shining at night, the moon during the day, blood dripping from wood, talking stones, and falling stars (2 Esdr 5:1–13; see also 6:21–24; 15:12–27). The End will involve salvation for the righteous and judgment for the wicked (2 Esdr 5:56–6:6, 25–28; 7:26–44; 8:63–9:13).

Intercession of the Saints. According to 2 Macc 15:11–16, dead saints intercede for the living. (Onias the high priest and Jeremiah the prophet intercede for Judas.) Furthermore, according to 12:43–45, the living may pray and offer sacrifices for the dead (does this relate to 1 Cor 15:29?).

The Canon of Scripture. In Sir 39:1 the OT is referred to as "law" and "prophecies." In 2 Esdr 14:44 "ninety-four" books are mentioned. The reference is to the "twenty-four books" of the OT (v. 45) and, most likely, the seventy of the Apocrypha and Pseudepigrapha. Both the seventy and the twenty-four are restored miraculously by Ezra and five others (vv. 37–48), a legend that parallels the translation of the LXX (*Let. Aris.* §307b). Whereas the twenty-four are to be read by all, the seventy are to be read only by the wise (2 Esdr 14:45–46). There are at least fifty-one apocryphal writings among the scrolls and fragments of Qumran (M. J. McNamara, *Palestinian Judaism and the New Testament* [GNS 4; Wilmington, Del.: Glazier, 1983], 121–24). More than sixty writings are found in

J. H. Charlesworth, *OTP.* The OT itself refers to books which are now lost: Book of the Wars of Yahweh (Num 21:14), Book of Jasher (Josh 10:13; 2 Sam 1:18), Book of the Acts of Solomon (1 Kgs 11:41), Book of the Annals of the Kings of Israel (1 Kgs 14:19; 2 Chr 33:18), Book of the Annals of the Kings of Judah (1 Kgs 14:29; 15:7), Annals of Samuel the Seer and Annals of Gad the Seer (1 Chr 29:29), Words of Nathan the Prophet (2 Chr 9:29), Prophecy of Ahijah the Shilonite (2 Chr 9:29), Annals of Shemaiah the Prophet and of Iddo the Seer (2 Chr 12:15), Annals of Jehu son of Hanani (2 Chr 20:34), an untitled writing of Isaiah (2 Chr 26:22), Annals of Hozai (2 Chr 33:18), a lament for Josiah by Jeremiah (2 Chr 35:25). First Maccabees 16:24 refers to the Annals of John Hyrcanus. Various lost writings are mentioned in the Pseudepigrapha (*T. Job* 40:14 ["Omissions"]; 41:6 ["Omissions of Eliphas"]; 49:3 ["Hymns of Kasia"]; 50:3 ["The Prayers of Amaltheia's Horn"]). In *Hist. eccl.* 6.13.6 Eusebius refers to several "disputed books" (*antilegomena*): Sirach and Wisdom of Solomon (of the OT Apocrypha), Hebrews and Jude (of the NT), and Barnabas and Clement (of the Apostolic Fathers).

General Bibliography

Text: A. RAHLFS, *Septuaginta* (2 vols.; Stuttgart: Württembergische Bibelanstalt, 1935); J. ZIEGLER, *Jeremias, Baruch, Threni, Epistula Jeremiae* (2d ed.; Septuaginta 15; Göttingen: Vandenhoeck & Ruprecht, 1976); IDEM, *Susanna, Daniel, Bel et Draco* (Septuaginta 16/2; Göttingen: Vandenhoeck & Ruprecht, 1954); J. ZIEGLER et al., *Septuaginta: Vetus Testamentum graecum* (16 vols.; Göttingen: Vandenhoeck & Ruprecht, 1939–). **Translation:** E. J. GOODSPEED, *The Apocrypha: An American Translation* (Chicago: University of Chicago Press, 1938); B. M. METZGER, ed., *OAA.* **Introduction, Commentary, Critical study:** G. W. ANDERSON, "Canonical and Non-canonical," in *The Cambridge History of the Bible* (ed. P. R. Ackroyd and C. F. Evans; 3 vols.; Cambridge: Cambridge University Press, 1963–1970), 1:113–59; R. H. CHARLES, *APOT,* vol. 1; J. H. CHARLESWORTH, "The Interpretation of the Tanak in the Jewish Apocrypha and Pseudepigrapha," in *The Ancient Period* (vol. 1 of *A History of Biblical Interpretation;* ed. A. J. Hauser and D. F. Watson; Grand Rapids: Eerdmans, 2003), 253–82 (very helpful bibliography); R. J. COGGINS and M. A. KNIBB, *The First and Second Books of Esdras* (CBC; Cambridge: Cambridge University Press, 1979); J. CRAGHAN, *Esther, Judith, Tobit, Jonah, Ruth* (OTM 16; Wilmington, Del.: Glazier, 1982); N. DE LANGE, *Apocrypha: Jewish Literature of the Hellenistic Age* (New York: Viking, 1978); D. A. DESILVA, *IAMCS;* J. A. GOLDSTEIN, "How the Authors of 1 and 2 Maccabees Treated the 'Messianic' Promises," in *Judaisms and Their Messiahs at the Turn of the Christian Era* (ed. J. Neusner; Cambridge: Cambridge University Press, 1987), 69–96; D. J. HARRINGTON, *InvA;* IDEM, *The Maccabean Revolt: Anatomy of a Biblical Revolution* (OTS 1; Wilmington, Del.: Glazier, 1988); J. W. VAN HENTEN and F. AVEMARIE, *Martyrdom and Noble Death: Selected Texts from Graeco-Roman,*

Jewish, and Christian Antiquity (New York: Routledge, 2002); H. LICHTENBERGER, *Die Makkabäerbücher* (ATD: Apokryphen 2; Göttingen: Vandenhoeck & Ruprecht, 2001); B. M. METZGER, *IA;* C. A. MOORE, *Daniel, Esther, and Jeremiah: The Additions* (AB 44; Garden City, N.Y.: Doubleday, 1987); J. M. MYERS, *I and II Esdras* (AB 42; Garden City, N.Y.: Doubleday, 1964); G. W. E. NICKELSBURG, *Faith and Piety in Early Judaism: Texts and Documents* (Philadelphia: Fortress, 1983); IDEM, *Jewish Literature between the Bible and the Mishnah* (Philadelphia: Fortress, 1981); W. O. E. OESTERLEY, *IBA;* L. ROST, *Judaism outside the Hebrew Canon: An Introduction to the Documents* (Nashville: Abingdon, 1976), 21–99; H. F. D. SPARKS, *AOT;* O. H. STECK, *Das Buch Baruch, der Brief des Jeremia, Zusatze zu Ester und Daniel* (ATD: Apokryphen 5; Göttingen: Vandenhoeck & Ruprecht, 1998); M. E. STONE, ed., *SJWSTP* 33–184, 283–324, 412–14; D. W. SUTER, "Old Testament Apocrypha," *HBD* 36–38; C. C. TORREY, *The Apocryphal Literature: A Brief Introduction* (New Haven: Yale University Press, 1945); L. T. WHITELOCKE, ed., *An Analytical Concordance of the Books of the Apocrypha* (Washington, D.C.: University Press of America Press, 1978); H. ZENGER, *Judit und Tobit* (ATD: Apokryphen 3; Göttingen: Vandenhoeck & Ruprecht, 2001).

CHAPTER TWO

The Old Testament Pseudepigrapha

(continued on next page)

OLD TESTAMENT PSEUDEPIGRAPHA, CONT'D.

Jannes and Jambres	Philo the Epic Poet
History of the Rechabites	Theodotus
Eldad and Modad	Orphica
History of Joseph	Ezekiel the Tragedian
Ahiqar	Fragments of Pseudo-Greek Poets
3 Maccabees	Pseudo-Hesiod
4 Maccabees	Pseudo-Pythagoras
Pseudo-Phocylides	Pseudo-Aeschylus
The Sentences of the Syriac Menander	Pseudo-Sophocles
More Psalms of David	Pseudo-Euripides
Psalm 151 (see OT Apocrypha)	Pseudo-Philemon
Psalm 152	Pseudo-Diphilus
Psalm 153	Pseudo-Menander
Psalm 154	Aristobulus
Psalm 155	Demetrius the Chronographer
Prayer of Manasseh (see OT	Aristeas the Exegete
Apocrypha)	Eupolemus
Psalms of Solomon	Pseudo-Eupolemus
Hellenistic Synagogal Prayers	Cleodemus Malchus
Prayer of Joseph	Artapanus
Prayer of Jacob	Pseudo-Hecataeus
Odes of Solomon	5 Maccabees

The writings of the OT Pseudepigrapha are numerous and diverse. Several literary genres are represented in this amorphous collection. Their dates of composition also cover a broad period of time, with *Ahiqar* being the oldest at about seventh or sixth century B.C.E. and the Apocalypse of Daniel the youngest at about ninth century C.E. Many of these books were among those to which 4 Ezra refers: "Ninety-four books were written. And . . . the Most High spoke to me, saying, 'Make public the twenty-four books that you wrote first and let the worthy and unworthy read them; but keep the seventy that were written last, in order to give them to the wise among your people. For in them is the spring of understanding, the fountain of wisdom, and the river of knowledge'" (14:44–47). The "twenty-four" books are the books that make up the Jewish Bible or what Christians call the OT. The seventy books are the books of the Apocrypha (see ch. 1) and the books of the Pseudepigrapha. The author of 4 Ezra was probably very close to the truth. In addition to the sixty-six books treated in this chapter (many of which did not exist when 4 Ezra was written) some fifty more apocryphal and pseudepigraphal writings were found among the scrolls of Qumran (see ch. 3). Thus, in the time of the writing of 4 Ezra there were probably more than seventy books in this category of those "written last."

The word *pseudepigrapha* is a Greek word meaning "falsely superscribed," or what we moderns might call writing under a pen name. The classification, "OT

Pseudepigrapha," is a label that scholars have given to these writings. Although some of them have been grouped together or associated in one way or another, most never had any connection to one another. James Charlesworth and a team of scholars wrestled for a decade or longer with the definition of this category called "Pseudepigrapha." They decided to retain the word because of its widespread and long-time usage, but they have carefully defined what the word means and what the criteria are for inclusion in this category. According to Charlesworth:

> The present description of the Pseudepigrapha is as follows: Those writings 1) that, with the exception of *Ahiqar*, are Jewish or Christian; 2) that are often attributed to ideal figures in Israel's past; 3) that customarily claim to contain God's word or message; 4) that frequently build upon ideas and narratives present in the OT; 5) and that almost always were composed either during the period 200 B.C. to A.D. 200 or, though late, apparently preserve, albeit in an edited form, Jewish traditions that date from that period. (Charlesworth, *OTP* 1:xxv)

Charlesworth further notes that the following pseudepigraphal items were not included "because they were far removed from the Old Testament in date and character" (*OTP* 1:xxvi):

Vision of Daniel
Death of Abraham
Hebrew Apocalypse of Elijah
Book of Jasher
Conflict of Adam and Eve with Satan
Cave of Treasures
Book of the Rolls
Sin of Solomon
Pirqe de Rabbi Eliezer (see ch. 8)
Syriac Apocalypse of Ezra
Book of the Bee
Questions Addressed by the Queen [of Sheba], and Answers Given by Solomon

The line that divides the OT Apocrypha from the OT Pseudepigrapha is not clearly drawn. Two writings found in the Apocrypha, the Prayer of Manasseh and 4 Ezra (contained within 2 Esdras), belong in the Pseudepigrapha. Three writings found in the Pseudepigrapha, 3 Maccabees, 4 Maccabees, and Psalm 151, appear in some canons of Scripture as part of the Apocrypha (see appendix 1).

The OT Pseudepigrapha greatly enhance our study into the background of early Judaism and Christianity. These writings shed light on various doctrines, including how Scripture was interpreted. For bibliography, see the dated but still useful J. H. Charlesworth, *PMR*, and the more current L. DiTommaso, *BPR*.

Summaries

To simplify reference to the following summaries the pseudepigraphal books have been subdivided according to the categories and order found in *OTP*:

(1) Apocalyptic Literature, (2) Testaments, (3) Old Testament Expansions, (4) Wisdom and Philosophical Literature, (5) Prayers, Psalms, and Odes, and (6) Fragments, with an appendix.

Part One: Apocalyptic Literature

1 Enoch. First *Enoch,* also known as the *Ethiopic Apocalypse of Enoch,* is the oldest of the three pseudepigraphal books attributed to Enoch, the man who apparently did not die, but was taken up to heaven (Gen 5:24). The book was originally written in either Hebrew or Aramaic, perhaps both, but it survives in complete form only in Ethiopic (*Ge'ez*), and in fragmentary form in Aramaic, Greek (1:1–32:6; 6:1–10:14; 15:8–16:1; 89:42–49; 97:6–104), and Latin (106:1–18). As it now stands, *1 Enoch* appears to consist of the following five major divisions: (1) The Book of the Watchers (chs. 1–36); (2) The Book of the Similitudes (chs. 37–71); (3) The Book of Astronomical Writings (chs. 72–82); (4) The Book of Dream Visions (chs. 83–90); and (5) The Book of the Epistle of Enoch (chs. 91–107). The materials in *1 Enoch* range in date from 200 B.C.E. to 50 C.E. *First Enoch* contributes much to intertestamental views of angels, heaven, judgment, resurrection, and the Messiah. This book has left its stamp upon many of the NT writers, especially the author of Revelation. *First Enoch's* "Son of Man" is important for Jesus research.

Text: M. BLACK, *Apocalypsis Henochi graece* (PVTG 3; Leiden: Brill, 1970); C. BONNER, *The Last Chapters of Enoch in Greek* (SD 8; London: Christophers, 1937); S. BROCK, "A Fragment of Enoch in Syriac," *JTS* 19 (1968): 626–31; R. H. CHARLES, *The Ethiopic Version of the Book of Enoch: Edited from Twenty-Three MSS, Together with the Fragmentary Greek and Latin Versions* (AnOx 11; Oxford: Clarendon, 1906), 3–75 (Ethiopic), 175–77 (Greek), 219–22 (Latin); A.-M. DENIS, *CGPAT* 818–24; M. A. KNIBB, *The Ethiopic Book of Enoch: A New Edition in the Light of the Dead Sea Fragments* (Oxford: Clarendon, 1978); J. T. MILIK, *BE* 81–82 (Coptic); IDEM, "Fragments grecs du livre d'Hénoch," *ChrEg* 40 (1971): 321–43; H. B. SWETE, *The Psalms of Solomon with the Greek Fragments of the Book of Enoch* (vol. 3 of *The Old Testament in Greek;* Cambridge: Cambridge University Press, 1899), 25–45. *Survey:* J. H. CHARLESWORTH, *PMR* 98–103; J. J. COLLINS, *The Apocalyptic Imagination,* 43–84, 177–93; IDEM, "Enoch, Books of," *DNTB* 313–18, esp. 314–16; L. DITOMMASO, *BPR* 355–430; M. A. KNIBB, "The Ethiopic Book of Enoch," *OOT* 26–55; G. W. E. NICKELSBURG, "Enoch, First Book of," *ABD* 2:508–16; IDEM, *JLBM* 47–55, 90–94, 145–51, 214–23; M. E. STONE, "Apocalyptic Literature," *SJWSTP* 395–406; IDEM, "The Bible Rewritten and Expanded," *SJWSTP* 90–97; J. C. VANDERKAM, *An Introduction to Early Judaism,* 88–94, 103–7, 110–12, 119–21. *Commentary and Critical Study:* R. A. ARGALL, *1 Enoch and Sirach: A Comparative Literary and Conceptual Analysis of the Themes of Revelation, Creation, and Judgment* (SBLEJL 8; Atlanta: Scholars Press, 1995); G. BAMPFYLDE, "The Similitudes of Enoch: Historical Allusions," *JSJ* 15 (1984): 9–31; K. C. BAUTCH, *A Study of the Geography of 1 Enoch 17–19: "No One Has Seen What I Have Seen"* (JSJSup 81; Leiden: Brill, 2003); M. BLACK, "The Messianism of the Parables of Enoch: Their Date and Contribution to Christological Origins," in *The Messiah* (ed. J. H. Charlesworth; Minneapolis: Fortress, 1992), 145–68; M. BLACK and O. NEUGEBAUER, in consultation with J. C. VanderKam, *The Book of Enoch, or I Enoch: A New English Edition with Commentary and Textual Notes* (SVTP 7; Brill: Leiden, 1985); R. H. CHARLES, "Book of Enoch," *APOT*

2:163–281; IDEM, with introduction by W. O. E. Oesterley, *The Book of Enoch* (TED I: Palestinian Jewish Texts 3; London: SPCK, 1917); IDEM, *The Book of Enoch, or 1 Enoch* (Oxford: Clarendon, 1912); M. J. DAVIDSON, *Angels at Qumran: A Comparative Study of 1 Enoch 1–36, 72–108 and Sectarian Writings from Qumran* (JSPSup 11; Sheffield: JSOT Press, 1992); J. C. GREENFIELD and M. STONE, "The Enochic Pentateuch and the Date of the Similitudes," *HTR* 70 (1977): 51–65; E. ISAAC, "1 (Ethiopic Apocalypse of) Enoch," *OTP* 1:5–89; M. A. KNIBB, "1 Enoch," *AOT* 169–319; L. KREITZER, "Luke 16:19–31 and 1 Enoch 22," *ExpTim* 103 (1992): 139–42; G. W. E. NICKELSBURG, *1 Enoch: A Commentary on the Book of 1 Enoch, Chapters 1–36, 81–108* (Hermeneia; Minneapolis: Fortress, 2001); D. C. OLSON, "1 Enoch," *ECB* 904–41; C. D. OSBURN, "The Christological Use of 1 Enoch I.9 in Jude 14, 15," *NTS* 23 (1977): 334–41; IDEM, "1 Enoch 80:2–8 (67:5–7) and Jude 12–13," *CBQ* 47 (1985): 296–303; D. W. SUTER, "Weighed in the Balance: The Similitudes of Enoch in Recent Research," *RelSRev* 7 (1981): 217–21; P. A. TILLER, *A Commentary on the Animal Apocalypse of I Enoch* (SBLEJL 4; Atlanta: Scholars Press, 1993); J. C. VANDER-KAM, *Enoch and the Growth of an Apocalyptic Tradition* (CBQMS 16; Washington, D.C.: Catholic Biblical Association, 1984).

2 Enoch. Second Enoch, or the *Slavonic Apocalypse of Enoch,* was written late in the first century C.E. in Egypt by a Jew. It survives only in late Old Slavonic manuscripts. It may have been composed originally in Aramaic or Hebrew, later being translated into Greek, and later still being translated into Old Slavonic. It is an amplification of Gen 5:21–32 (from Enoch to the Flood). Major theological themes include: (1) God created the world "out of nothing" (24:2); (2) seven heavens (30:2–3) and angelic hosts; (3) God created the souls of men before the foundation of the earth (23:5); (4) abodes of heaven and hell are already prepared for righteous and sinners; and (5) ethical teachings, which at times parallel those of the NT and Proverbs.

Text: A. VAILLANT, *Le livre des sécrets d'Hénoch: Texte slave et traduction française* (Paris: Institut d'Études Slaves, 1952). *Survey:* F. I. ANDERSEN, "Enoch, Second Book of," *ABD* 2:516–22; C. BÖTTRICH, "Recent Studies in the Slavonic Book of Enoch," *JSP* 9 (1991): 35–42; J. H. CHARLESWORTH, *PMR* 103–6; J. J. COLLINS, *The Apocalyptic Imagination,* 243–47; IDEM, "Enoch, Books of," *DNTB* 313–18, esp. 316–7; L. DITOMMASO, *BPR* 431–49; G. W. E. NICKELSBURG, *JLBM* 185–88; M. E. STONE, "Apocalyptic Literature," *SJWSTP* 406–8. *Commentary and Critical Study:* F. I. ANDERSEN, "2 (Slavonic Apocalypse of) Enoch," *OTP* 1:91–221; C. BÖTTRICH, *Weltweisheit–Menschheitsethik–Urkult: Studien zum slavischen Henochbuch* (WUNT 2.50; Tübingen: Mohr [Siebeck], 1992); R. H. CHARLES with W. R. MORFILL, *The Book of the Secrets of Enoch* (Oxford: Clarendon, 1896); N. FORBES and R. H. CHARLES, "The Book of the Secrets of Enoch," *APOT* 2:425–69; C. A. GIESCHEN, "The Different Functions of a Similar Melchizedek Tradition in *2 Enoch* and the Epistle to the Hebrews," in *Early Christian Interpretation of the Scriptures of Israel: Investigations and Proposals* (ed. C. A. Evans and J. A. Sanders; JSNTSup 148; SSEJC 5; Sheffield: Sheffield, 1997), 364–79; A. PENNINGTON, "2 Enoch," *AOT* 321–62; S. PINES, "Eschatology and the Concept of Time in the Slavonic Book of Enoch," in *Types of Redemption* (ed. R. J. Z. Werblowsky and C. J. Bleeker; SHR 18; Leiden: Brill, 1970), 72–87; A. L. RUBINSTEIN, "Observations on the Slavonic Book of Enoch," *JJS* 13 (1962): 1–21; G. G. STROUMSA, "Form(s) of God: Some Notes on Metatron and Christ," *HTR* 76 (1983): 269–88.

3 Enoch. Third Enoch, or the *Hebrew Apocalypse of Enoch,* was supposedly written by Rabbi Ishmael the "high priest" after his visionary ascension into heaven (d. 132 C.E.). Although it contains a few Greek and Latin loan words, there is no reason to suspect that the original language of *3 Enoch* was anything other than Hebrew. Whereas some of the traditions of *3 Enoch* may be traced back to the time of Rabbi Ishmael, and even earlier, the date of composition is probably closer to the fifth or sixth centuries. It was probably written in or near Babylon. The book may be divided into the following four major parts: (1) The ascension of Ishmael (chs. 1–2); (2) Ishmael meets the exalted Enoch (chs. 3–16); (3) a description of the heavenly household (chs. 17–40); and (4) the marvels of heaven (chs. 41–48). *Third Enoch* sheds some light on Merkabah mysticism. In the book there appears to be present a tendency to minimize the powers of Metatron (= Enoch).

Text: A. JELLINEK, "Henoch-Buch," in *Bet ha-Midrasch,* 5:170–90; H. ODEBERG, *3 Enoch, or the Hebrew Book of Enoch,* part 3. **Survey:** P. S. ALEXANDER, "Enoch, Third Book of," *ABD* 2:522–26; J. H. CHARLESWORTH, *PMR* 107–7; J. J. COLLINS, "Enoch, Books of," *DNTB* 313–18, esp. 317; L. DiTOMMASO, *BPR* 451–56. **Commentary and Critical Study:** P. S. ALEXANDER, "3 Enoch and the Talmud," *JSJ* 18 (1987): 40–68; IDEM, "3 (Hebrew Apocalypse of) Enoch," *OTP* 1:223–315; IDEM, "The Historical Setting of the Hebrew Book of Enoch," *JJS* 28 (1977): 156–80; R. J. BAUCKHAM, "The Throne of God and the Worship of Jesus," in *The Jewish Roots of Christological Monotheism* (ed. Newman et al.), 43–69; J. R. DAVILA, "Of Methodology, Monotheism, and Metatron: Introductory Reflections on Divine Mediators and the Origins of the Worship of Jesus," in *The Jewish Roots of Christological Monotheism* (ed. Newman et al.), 3–18, esp. 12–17; J. C. GREENFIELD and M. E. STONE, "The Books of Enoch and the Traditions of Enoch," *Numen* 26 (1979): 89–103, esp. 98–102; H. ODEBERG, *3 Enoch, or the Hebrew Book of Enoch,* parts 1–2.

Sibylline Oracles. Called the *Sibylline Oracles* because of an association with the legendary Sibyls of antiquity, who were aged women who uttered prophecies in poetic form. Scholars are unsure if there ever really was a Sibyl who inaugurated this tradition. Collections of Sibylline oracles appeared in a variety of centers in the ancient world. These collections enjoyed considerable prestige in the Roman Empire and allowed Jews and Christians to communicate their religious views. These oracles, consisting of fourteen books, range in date from the second century B.C.E. to the seventh century C.E. Both Jews and Christians contributed to the collection that now makes up part of the Pseudepigrapha. For NT study, *Sib. Or.* 3–5 is the most significant. The oldest Jewish oracles are found in book 3, portions of which date to the second century B.C.E. and concern the Ptolemaic dynasty. Later additions to this book refer obliquely to Nero.

Text: A.-M. DENIS, *CGPAT* 893–900; J. GEFFCKEN, *Die Oracula sibyllina* (GCS 8; Leipzig: Heinrichs, 1902), 46–129; A. M. KURFESS, *Sibyllinische Weissagungen: Urtext und Übersetzung* (Munich: Heimeren, 1951). **Survey:** J. H. CHARLESWORTH, *PMR* 184–88; J. J. COLLINS, "The Development of the Sibylline Tradition," *ANRW* 21.1:421–59; IDEM, "Sibylline Oracles," *ABD* 6:2–6; IDEM, "Sibylline Oracles," *DNTB* 1107–12; IDEM, "The Sibylline Oracles," *SJWSTP* 357–81; L. DiTOMMASO, *BPR* 795–849; G. W. E. NICKELSBURG, *JLBM* 162–65; J. C. VANDERKAM, *An Introduction to Early Judaism,* 107–10. **Commentary**

and Critical Study: J. R. BARTLETT, "The Sibylline Oracles," in *Jews in the Hellenistic World: Josephus, Aristeas, the Sibylline Oracles, Eupolemus* (CCWJCW 1/1; Cambridge: Cambridge University Press, 1985), 35–55; H. N. BATE, *The Sibylline Oracles (Books iii–v)* (TED II: Hellenistic Jewish Texts 2; London: SPCK, 1918); R. BUITENWERF, *Book III of the Sibylline Oracles and Its Social Setting: With an Introduction, Translation, and Commentary* (SVTP 17; Leiden: Brill, 2003); J. J. COLLINS, "The Jewish Transformation of Sibylline Oracles," in *Seers, Sybils, and Sages in Hellenistic-Roman Judaism* (JSJSup 54; Leiden: Brill, 1997), 181–97; IDEM, "Sibylline Oracles," *OTP* 1:317–472; IDEM, *The Sibylline Oracles of Egyptian Judaism* (SBLDS 13; Missoula, Mont.: Scholars Press, 1974) (*Sib. Or.* 3–5); S. FELDER, "What Is the Fifth Sibylline Oracle?" *JSJ* 33 (2002): 363–85; J. GEFFCKEN, *Komposition und Entstehungszeit der Oracula sibyllina* (TU 8/1; Leipzig: Hinrichs, 1902); J. W. VAN HENTEN, " 'Nero redivivus' Demolished: The Coherence of the Nero Traditions in the Sibylline Oracles," *JSP* 21 (2000): 3–17; L. KREITZER, "Sibylline Oracles 8, the Roman Imperial Adventus Coinage, and the Apocalypse of John," *JSP* 4 (1989): 69–85; H. C. O. LANCHESTER, "The Sibylline Oracles," *APOT* 2:368–406; V. NIKIPROWETZKY, *La troisième Sibylle* (Études juives 9; Paris: Mouton, 1970); D. S. POTTER, *Prophecy and History in the Crisis of the Roman Empire: A Historical Commentary on the Thirteenth Sibylline Oracle* (Oxford: Oxford University Press, 1990); A. RZACH, *Analekta zur Kritik und Exegese der Sibyllinischen Orakel* (Sitzungsberichte der kai. Akademie der Wissenschaften in Wien: Philosophisch-Historische Klasse 156; Vienna: Alfred Hölder, 1907).

Treatise of Shem. The *Treatise of Shem* was originally written in the first century B.C.E. in either Hebrew or Aramaic, but is now preserved in a fifteenth-century Syriac manuscript. It comprises twelve chapters that correspond to the twelve signs of the zodiac, with the last two, due to a scribal error, in reverse order. The interest in stars in this book may shed some light on Matt 2:1–12. The book was written in the aftermath of Octavian's defeat of Cleopatra and Marc Antony at Actium in 31 B.C.E. Jewish interest in astrology is attested at Qumran in 4Q186 and 4Q318 and probably explains the appearance of the Zodiac on the floors of synagogues (e.g., in Hammath Tiberias and Sepphoris).

Text: J. H. CHARLESWORTH, with J. R. MUELLER, "Die 'Schrift des Sem': Einführung, Text, und Übersetzung," *ANRW* 20.2:951–87; A. MINGANA, "The Book of Shem Son of Noah," *BJRL* 4 (1917–1918): 59–118, esp. 76–85, 108–16; repr. in *Some Early Judaeo-Christian Documents in the John Rylands Library: Syriac Texts* (Manchester, Eng.: Manchester University Press, 1917), esp. 52–59. *Survey:* J. H. CHARLESWORTH, *PMR* 182–84; IDEM, "Shem, Treatise of," *ABD* 5:1196–97; IDEM, "Treatise of Shem," *DNTB* 1250–51; L. DiTOMMASO, *BPR* 793–94. *Commentary and Critical Study:* J. H. CHARLESWORTH, "Jewish Astrology in the Talmud, Pseudepigrapha, Dead Sea Scrolls, and Early Palestinian Synagogues," *HTR* 70 (1977): 183–200; IDEM, "Jewish Interest in Astrology during the Hellenistic and Roman Period," *ANRW* 20.2:926–50 and pls. I–VI; IDEM, "Rylands Syriac MS 44 and a New Addition to the Pseudepigrapha: The Treatise of Shem," *BJRL* 60 (1978): 376–403; IDEM, "Treatise of Shem," *OTP* 1:473–86.

Apocryphon of Ezekiel. The *Apocryphon of Ezekiel* was probably written in either Hebrew or Greek between 50 B.C.E. and 50 C.E. The text survives in fragmentary form only (chiefly in the form of quotations) in Greek, Latin, and Hebrew. Current scholarship identifies five fragments. Fragment 1 is preserved in Epiphanius

(*Pan.* 64.70.5–17), and in rabbinic literature (*b. Sanh.* 91a–b; *Mek.* on Exod 15:1 [*Shirata'* §2]; *Lev. Rab.* 4.5 [on Lev 4:2]). Fragment 2 is preserved in *1 Clem* 8:2–3, in Clement of Alexandria (*Paed.* 1.10), and in Nag Hammadi's *Exegesis of the Soul* (NHC II,6). Fragment 3 is preserved in Clement of Alexandria (*Strom.* 7.16), in Tertullian (*De carne Christi* 23), in Epiphanius (*Pan.* 30.30), in Gregory of Nyssa (*Against the Jews* 3), and in *Acts of Peter* 24. Fragment 4 is preserved in more than thirty sources, the oldest of which include Justin Martyr (*Dial.* 47.5) and Ps.-Clement of Alexandria (*Who Is the Rich Man That Is Being Saved?* 40); for a full list of sources, see A. Resch, *Agrapha: Aussercanonische Schriftfragmente* (TU 15/3–4; Leipzig: Hinrichs, 1906), 102, 322–24. Fragment 5 is preserved in Clement of Alexandria (*Paed.* 1.9) and in Origen (*Hom. Jer.* 18.9). Although the original document was of Jewish origin, there is evidence of Christian redaction. Its main contribution concerns the doctrines of resurrection and final judgment. Best known is the parable of the lame and blind man, which constitutes the first fragment (see Bauckham; Bregman).

Text: A.-M. DENIS, *CGPAT* 906; IDEM, *CLPAT* 121–28; IDEM, *FPSG* 121–28. *Survey:* J. H. CHARLESWORTH, *PMR* 109–10; L. DiTOMMASO, *BPR* 457–67. **Commentary and Critical Study:** R. J. BAUCKHAM, "The Parable of the Royal Wedding Feast (Matthew 22:1–14) and the Parable of the Lame Man and the Blind Man (*Apocryphon of Ezekiel*)," *JBL* 115 (1996): 471–88; M. BREGMAN, "The Parable of the Lame and the Blind: Epiphanius' Quotation from an Apocryphon of Ezekiel," *JTS* 42 (1991): 125–38; K.-G. ECKART, "Das Apokryphon Ezechiel," *JSHRZ* 5/1 (1974) 45–54; M. R. JAMES, "The Apocryphal Ezekiel," *JTS* 15 (1913–1914): 236–43; IDEM, *LAOT* 64–68; J. R. MUELLER, *The Five Fragments of the "Apocryphon of Ezekiel": A Critical Study* (JSPSup 5; Sheffield: Sheffield, 1994); J. R. MUELLER and S. E. ROBINSON, "Apocryphon of Ezekiel," *OTP* 1:487–95; L. WALLACH, "The Parable of the Blind and the Lame: A Study of Comparative Literature," *JBL* 62 (1943): 333–39.

Apocalypse of Zephaniah. The *Apocalypse of Zephaniah,* originally composed in Greek sometime between 100 B.C.E. and 70 C.E., survives in a Greek quotation by Clement of Alexandria (*Strom.* 5.11.77) and in twenty pages of Sahidic and Akhmimic Coptic (Copte 135 [Paris] and P 1862 [Berlin]). One scholar conjectures that three-quarters of the original document are lost. This book is typical of the heavenly journey theme in which the seer witnesses the judgment and punishment of sinners and the vindication of the righteous. The *Apocalypse of Paul* may have made use of this work.

Text: U. BOURIANT, "Les papyrus d'Akhmim," in *Mémoires publiées par les membres de la mission archéologique française au Caire* 1 (4 vols.; Paris: Ernest Leroux, 1884–1889), 2:242–304, esp. 260–79; A.-M. DENIS, *CGPAT* 907 (Greek); IDEM, *FPSG* 129 (Greek); G. STEINDORFF, *Die Apokalypse des Elias, eine unbekannte Apokalypse, und Bruchstücke der Sophonias-Apokalypse,* 110–44 (Sahidic), 34–65 (Akhmimic). *Survey:* J. H. CHARLESWORTH, *PMR* 220–23; L. DiTOMMASO, *BPR* 977–82; M. R. JAMES, *LAOT* 72–74. **Commentary and Critical Study:** M. HIMMELFARB, *Tours of Hell: An Apocalyptic Form in Jewish and Christian Literature* (Philadelphia: University of Pennsylvania Press, 1983), 13–16, 147–58; K. H. KUHN, "The Apocalypse of Zephaniah and an Anonymous Apocalypse," *AOT*

915–25; P. LACAU, "Remarques sur le manuscrit akhmimique des apocalypses de Sophonie et d'Élie," *JA* 254 (1966): 169–95; O. S. WINTERMUTE, "Apocalypse of Zephaniah," *OTP* 1:497–515.

Fourth Book of Ezra. Fourth Ezra comprises chapters 3–14 of an expanded book that is part of the Apocrypha and is known as 2 Esdras. Fourth Ezra, a late first-century Jewish writing, contains seven visions that God gave to Ezra the scribe/prophet. The Christian Greek additions (chs. 1–2 and 15–16, also known as 5 Ezra and 6 Ezra, respectively) were added in the second and third centuries. The purpose of 4 Ezra is to denounce the evil of Rome and to lament the misfortunes of Jerusalem. See 2 Esdras in chapter 1.

Text: R. L. BENSLY, with introduction by M. R. James, *The Fourth Book of Ezra, the Latin Version Edited from the MSS* (Texts and Studies 3/2; Cambridge: Cambridge University Press, 1895). *Survey:* J. H. CHARLESWORTH, *PMR* 111–16, 284–86; L. DiTOMMASO, *BPR* 469–513; G. W. E. NICKELSBURG, *JLBM* 287–94; M. E. STONE, "Apocalyptic Literature," *SJWSTP* 412–14. *Commentary and Critical Study:* G. H. BOX, "4 Ezra," *APOT* 2:542–624; IDEM, *The Apocalypse of Ezra (II Esdras III–XIV)* (TED I: Palestinian Jewish Texts 8; London: SPCK, 1917); IDEM, *The Ezra-Apocalypse, Being Chapters 3–14 of the Book Commonly Known as 4 Ezra (or II Esdras)* (London: Sir Isaac Pitman & Sons, 1912); M. A. KNIBB, "Apocalyptic and Wisdom in 4 Ezra," *JSJ* 13 (1982): 56–74; B. M. METZGER, "The Fourth Book of Ezra," *OTP* 1:516–79; M. E. STONE, "Coherence and Inconsistency in the Apocalypses: The Case of 'the End' in 4 Ezra," *JBL* 102 (1983): 229–43; IDEM, *Features of Eschatology of IV Ezra* (HSS 35; Atlanta: Scholars Press, 1989); IDEM, *Fourth Ezra: A Commentary on the Book of Fourth Ezra* (Hermeneia; Minneapolis: Fortress, 1990); IDEM, "The Question of the Messiah in 4 Ezra," in *Judaisms and Their Messiahs at the Turn of the Christian Era* (ed. J. Neusner; Cambridge: Cambridge University Press, 1987), 209–24; A. L. THOMPSON, *Responsibility for Evil in the Theodicy of IV Ezra* (SBLDS 29; Missoula, Mont.: Scholars Press, 1977); T. W. WILLETT, *Eschatology in the Theodicies of 2 Baruch and 4 Ezra.* See bibliography on 2 Esdras in chapter 1.

Greek Apocalypse of Ezra. The *Greek Apocalypse of Ezra* depicts a vision that Ezra received concerning sin and the punishment of the wicked. Ezra descends into hell where he sees Herod and other infamous characters tormented for their sin. The book was likely written in Greek by a Christian sometime between the second and ninth centuries.

Text: A.-M. DENIS, *CGPAT* 871–73; C. TISCHENDORF, *Apocalypses apocryphae Mosis, Esdrae, Pauli, Joannis, item Mariae dormitio* (Leipzig: H. Mendelsohn, 1866), 24–33; O. WAHL, *Apocalypsis Esdrae, Apocalypsis Sedrach, Visio beati Esdrae,* 25–34. *Survey:* J. H. CHARLESWORTH, *PMR* 116–17; L. DiTOMMASO, *BPR* 513–16; M. E. STONE, "Ezra, Greek Apocalypse of," *ABD* 2:728–29. *Commentary and Critical Study:* E. G. CHAZON, "Moses' Struggle for His Soul," esp. 158–62; U. MÜLLER, "Die griechische Ezra-Apokalypse," *JSHRZ* 5/2 (1976) 85–102; F. G. NUVOLONE, "Apocalypse d'Esdras grecque et latine, rapports et rhétorique," *Apocrypha* 7 (1996): 81–108; R. J. H. SHUTT, "The Apocalypse of Esdras," *AOT* 927–41; M. E. STONE, "Greek Apocalypse of Ezra," *OTP* 1:561–79; IDEM, "The Metamorphosis of Ezra: Jewish Apocalypse and Medieval Vision," *JTS* 33 (1982): 1–18; O. WAHL, *Apocalypsis Esdrae, Apocalypsis Sedrach, Visio beati Esdrae.*

Vision of Ezra. The *Vision of Ezra* is an account of Ezra's journey into the regions of hell to witness the punishment of the wicked. Whereas the righteous are able to pass by the gates of hell untouched, the wicked are ripped apart by dogs (or lions) and are burned. After descending into the deeper regions of hell, Ezra witnesses the torture of various types of sinners (e.g., "the angels of hell were pricking their eyes with thorns" [40]). The book was originally written in Greek by a Christian between the fourth and seventh centuries, but survives only in Latin.

Text: A.-M. DENIS, *CLPAT* 617–19; O. WAHL, *Apocalypsis Esdrae, Apocalypsis Sedrach, Visio beati Esdrae,* 49–61. *Survey:* J. H. CHARLESWORTH, *PMR* 119, 287; L. DiTOMMASO, *BPR* 519–21; M. E. STONE, "Ezra, Vision of," *ABD* 2:730–31. *Commentary and Critical Study:* P.-M. BOGAERT, "Une vision longue inédite de la 'Visio beati Esdra' dans la légendier de Teano (Barberini lat. 2318)," *RBén* 94 (1984): 50–70; J. R. MUELLER and G. A. ROBBINS, "Vision of Ezra," *OTP* 1:581–90; R. H. J. SHUTT, "The Vision of Esdras," *AOT* 943–51; O. WAHL, *Apocalypsis Esdrae, Apocalypsis Sedrach, Visio beati Esdrae;* IDEM, "Vier neue Textzeugen der 'Visio beati Esdrae,'" *Salesianum* 40 (1978): 583–89.

Questions of Ezra. The *Questions of Ezra* is extant in Armenian (in two recensions—A and B), but scholars are uncertain if it originated in that language. Beyond the fact that the book is Christian and is modeled on Jewish apocalyptic, nothing can be said with certainty about its date or place of writing. Like the Ezra writings above, the *Questions of Ezra* is concerned with the fate of the righteous and the wicked.

Text: S. JOSEPHEANZ, *Uncanonical Books of the Old Testament* (Venice: Armenian Typography of San Lazzaro, 1896), 300–303; *Translation:* J. ISSAVERDENS, *The Uncanonical Writings of the Old Testament* (Venice: Armenian Typography of San Lazzaro, 1901; repr., 1934), 505–9 (Armenian, recension A); M. E. STONE, "Two New Discoveries concerning the Uncanonical Ezra Books," *Sion* 52 (1978): 54–60 (Armenian, recension B). *Survey:* J. H. CHARLESWORTH, *PMR* 117–18; L. DiTOMMASO, *BPR* 521–23; M. E. STONE, "The Apocryphal Literature in the Armenian Tradition," *PIASH* 4 (1971): 59–77, 371–72; IDEM, "Ezra, Questions of," *ABD* 2:729–30. *Commentary and Critical Study:* M. E. STONE, "A New Edition and Translation of the Questions of Ezra," in *Solving Riddles and Untying Knots: Biblical, Epigraphic, and Semitic Studies in Honor of Jonas C. Greenfield* (ed. Z. Zavit; Winona Lake, Ind.: Eisenbrauns, 1995), 293–316; IDEM, "Questions of Ezra," *OTP* 1:591–99.

Revelation of Ezra. The *Revelation of Ezra* was probably originally written in Latin by a Christian sometime before the ninth century (though how much earlier is unknown). This pseudepigraphon comprises only seven verses. "The author believed that the nature of the year was predetermined by the day of the week on which it began" (Fiensy, *OTP* 1:603).

Text: G. MERCATI, *Note di letteratura biblica e christiana antica,* 74–79. *Survey:* J. H. CHARLESWORTH, *PMR* 118–19; L. DiTOMMASO, *BPR* 523–24. *Commentary and Critical Study:* D. DE BRUYNE, "Fragments d'une apocalypse perdue," *RBén* 33 (1921): 97–109, esp. 105–9; D. A. FIENSY, "Revelation of Ezra," *OTP* 1:601–4; E. A. MATTER, "The 'Revelatio Esdrae' in Latin and English Traditions," *RBén* 92 (1982): 379–87; G. MERCATI, *Note di letteratura biblica e christiana antica,* 61–81.

Apocalypse of Sedrach. The *Apocalypse of Sedrach,* a Christian writing, is an account of one Sedrach, who, after the delivery of a sermon, is taken up into heaven where he questions the Lord concerning the fate of sinners. He begs the Lord to be more lenient with the wicked. When finally satisfied, he allows the Lord to take his soul to Paradise. The text was originally written in Greek sometime between the second and fifth centuries and now survives in a fifteenth-century manuscript.

Text: A.-M. DENIS, *CGPAT* 873–74; O. WAHL, *Apocalypsis Esdrae, Apocalypsis Sedrach, Visio beati Esdrae,* 37–48. *Survey:* J. H. CHARLESWORTH, *PMR* 178–82, 300; IDEM, "Sedrach, Apocalypse of," *ABD* 5:1066–67; L. DITOMMASO, *BPR* 516–19. *Commentary and Critical Study:* S. AGOURIDES, "Apocalypse of Sedrach," *OTP* 1:605–13; E. G. CHAZON, "Moses' Struggle for His Soul," esp. 162–63; G. MERCATI, "The Apocalypse of Sedrach," *JTS* 11 (1909–1910): 572–73; R. J. H. SHUTT, "The Apocalypse of Sedrach," *AOT* 953–66; O. WAHL, *Apocalypsis Esdrae, Apocalypsis Sedrach, Visio beati Esdrae.*

2 Baruch (Syriac Apocalypse). Second Baruch, or the *Syriac Apocalypse of Baruch,* was composed early in the second century C.E. by a Jew who wished to encourage fellow Jews in the Dispersion. Originally written in Hebrew, the document was later translated into Greek and still later into Syriac, Latin, and Arabic. Only a fragment of the Greek survives (see Denis, *CGPAT* 905). Critical discussion has traditionally focused on the Syriac version, as preserved in Bibliotheca Ambrosiana B. 21 Inf. folios 257a–265b, though in recent years the Arabic version has received attention. The theme of the book revolves around the end of the age and the appearance of the Messiah. Although the book ostensibly is concerned with the first destruction of Jerusalem, its real concern is with Jerusalem's second destruction in 70 C.E.

Text: A.M. CERIANI, *Opuscula et fragmenta miscella magnam partem apocrypha* (Monumenta sacra et profana 5; Milan: J. B. Pogliani, 1868), 112–80 (Syriac); A.-M. DENIS, *CGPAT* 905 (Greek); IDEM, *CLPAT* 631 (Latin); A. F. J. KLIJN and G. H. J. GELDER, *The Arabic Text of the Apocalypse of Baruch: Edited and Translated with a Parallel Translation of the Syriac Text* (Leiden: Brill, 1986). *Survey:* P. S. ALEXANDER, "Epistolary Literature," *SJWSTP* 579–96, esp. 593–94; J. H. CHARLESWORTH, "Baruch, Book of 2 (Syriac)," *ABD* 1:620–21; IDEM, *PMR* 83–86, 275; L. DITOMMASO, *BPR* 259–82; G. W. E. NICKELSBURG, *JLBM* 281–87; M. E. STONE, "Apocalyptic Literature," *SJWSTP* 408–10; J. E. WRIGHT, "Baruch, Books of," *DNTB* 148–51. *Commentary and Critical Study:* P.-M. BOGAERT, *Apocalypse de Baruch: Introduction, traduction du Syriac, et commentaire* (2 vols.; SC 144–145; Paris: Cerf, 1969); L. H. BROCKINGTON, "The Syriac Apocalypse of Baruch," *AOT* 835–95; R. H. CHARLES, *The Apocalypse of Baruch Translated from the Syriac* (London: Adam and Charles Black, 1896); IDEM, "II Baruch," *APOT* 2:470–526; IDEM, with introduction by W. O. E. Oesterley, *The Apocalypse of Baruch* (TED I: Palestinian Jewish Texts 9; London: SPCK, 1917); S. DEDERING, *Apocalypse of Baruch* (VTS 4/3; Leiden: Brill, 1973), 1–50; A. F. J. KLIJN, "The Sources and the Redaction of the Syriac Apocalypse of Baruch," *JSJ* 1 (1970): 65–76; IDEM, "2 (Syriac Apocalypse of) Baruch," *OTP* 1:615–52; IDEM, "The Syriac Apocalypse of Baruch," *OOT* 193–212; IDEM, "Die syrische Baruch-Apokalypse," *JSHRZ* 5/2 (1976) 103–91; G. B. SAYLER, *Have the Promises Failed? A Literary Analysis of 2 Baruch* (SBLDS 72; Chico, Calif.: Scholars Press, 1984); T. W. WILLETT, *Eschatology in the*

Theodicies of 2 Baruch and 4 Ezra; J. E. WRIGHT, "The Social Setting of the Syriac Apocalypse of Baruch," *JSP* 16 (1997): 83–98.

3 Baruch (Greek Apocalypse). Third Baruch, or the *Greek Apocalypse of Baruch,* was composed sometime between the first and third centuries in Greek and today survives in Greek and Slavonic. The book may originally have been a Jewish writing that has undergone Christian redaction, or it may have been a Christian writing that relied heavily upon Jewish traditions. The account tells of a weeping Baruch, secretary of the prophet Jeremiah, who by an angel of the Lord is told the "mysteries" of what has happened and what will happen.

Text: A.-M. DENIS, *CGPAT* 866–68; M. R. JAMES, *Apocrypha anecdota: Second Series,* 84–94; J.-C. PICARD, ed., *Apocalypsis Baruchi graece* (PVTG 2; Leiden: Brill, 1967), 61–96. *Survey:* J. H. CHARLESWORTH, "Baruch, Book of 3 (Greek)," *ABD* 1:621–22; IDEM, *PMR* 86–87, 275; L. DiTOMMASO, *BPR* 283–91; G. W. E. NICKELSBURG, *JLBM* 299–303; M. E. STONE, "Apocalyptic Literature," *SJWSTP* 410–12; J. E. WRIGHT, "Baruch, Books of," *DNTB* 148–51. *Commentary and Critical Study:* A. W. ARGYLE, "The Greek Apocalypse of Baruch," *AOT* 897–914; G. BOHAK, "Greek-Hebrew Gematrias in 3 Baruch and in Revelation," *JSP* 7 (1990): 119–21; H. E. GAYLORD, "3 (Greek Apocalypse of) Baruch," *OTP* 1:653–79; IDEM, "How Satanael Lost His '-el,'" *JJS* 33 (1982): 303–9; W. HAGE, "Die griechische Baruch-Apokalypse," *JSHRZ* 5/1 (1974) 15–44; D. C. HARLOW, *The Greek Apocalypse of Baruch (3 Baruch) in Hellenistic Judaism and Early Christianity* (SVTP 12; Leiden: Brill, 1996); H. M. HUGHES, "The Greek Apocalypse of Baruch," *APOT* 2:527–41; J.-C. PICARD, *Apocalypsis Baruchi graeca* (PVTG 2; Leiden: Brill, 1967); J. E. WRIGHT, "Baruch: His Evolution from Scribe to Apocalyptic Seer," in *Biblical Figures outside the Bible* (ed. Stone and Bergren), 264–89, esp. 277–79.

Apocalypse of Abraham. The *Apocalypse of Abraham* was composed by a Jew sometime in the first or second centuries C.E., possibly in Hebrew, but it now survives only in a few Old Slavonic MSS (for a summary of MSS and published editions, see R. Rubinkiewicz, *OTP* 1:681–82). If originally Hebrew (and the evidence for Hebrew is suggestive), then in all probability the *Apocalypse* was composed in Palestine. Although a Jewish work, there are some Christian and gnostic interpolations. The book tells of Abraham's rejection of idolatry, of his request to know the true, living God (chs. 1–8), and of Abraham's journey to heaven, where heaven and the future of the world are revealed to him (chs. 9–32).

Text: N. S. TIKHONRAVOV, *Pamjatniki otrecennoj russkoj literatury,* 1:32–53 (MS S), 54–77 (MS A). *Survey:* J. H. CHARLESWORTH, *PMR* 68–72, 269–70; J. J. COLLINS, *The Apocalyptic Imagination,* 225–32; L. DiTOMMASO, *BPR* 135–44; G. W. E. NICKELSBURG, *JLBM* 294–99; S. E. ROBINSON, "Apocalypse of Abraham," *DNTB* 37–38; R. RUBINKIEWICZ, "Abraham, Apocalypse of," *ABD* 1:41–43; M. E. STONE, "Apocalyptic Literature," *SJWSTP* 415–18. *Commentary and Critical Study:* G. H. BOX and J. I. LANDSMAN, *The Apocalypse of Abraham* (TED I: Palestinian Jewish Texts 10; New York: Macmillan, 1919); R. G. HALL, "The 'Christian Interpolation' in the Apocalypse of Abraham," *JBL* 107 (1988): 107–12; J. R. MUELLER, "The Apocalypse of Abraham and the Destruction of the Second Jewish Temple," *SBLSP* 21 (1982): 341–49; G. W. E. NICKELSBURG, *JLBM* 294–99; A. PENNINGTON, "The Apocalypse of Abraham," *AOT* 363–91; B. PHILONENKO-SAYAR and M. PHILONENKO, "Die

Apokalypse Abrahams," *JSHRZ* 5/5 (1982) 413–60; C. ROWLAND, "The Visions of God in Apocalyptic Literature," *JSJ* 10 (1979): 137–54, esp. 150–54; R. RUBINKIEWICZ, "Les sémitismes dans l'Apocalypse d'Abraham," *FO* 21 (1980): 141–48; IDEM, "La vision de l'histoire dans l'Apocalypse d'Abraham," *ANRW* 19.1:137–51; R. RUBINKIEWICZ and H. G. LUNT, "Apocalypse of Abraham," *OTP* 1:681–705; A. RUBINSTEIN, "Hebraisms in the 'Apocalypse of Abraham,'" *JJS* 5 (1954): 132–35; IDEM, "Hebraisms in the Slavonic 'Apocalypse of Abraham,'" *JJS* 4 (1953): 108–15; IDEM, "A Problematic passage in the Apocalypse of Abraham," *JJS* 8 (1957): 45–50; E. TURDEANU, "*L'Apocalypse d'Abraham* en slave," *JSJ* 3 (1972): 153–80; IDEM, *Apocryphes slaves et roumains de l'Ancien Testament* (SVTP 5; Leiden: Brill, 1981).

Apocalypse of Adam. The *Apocalypse of Adam* is a gnostic revelation that dates from sometime between the first and fourth centuries C.E. It is preserved in Sahidic Coptic as tractate five in Codex V (64.1–85.32) of the Nag Hammadi library (see ch. 11 below). It is likely that the original document was Greek. Although clearly dependent upon Genesis, the *Apocalypse* never quotes this biblical book in its retelling of the creation story. The document purports to be a revelation of Adam to his son Seth. It draws upon Jewish tradition and presents a redeemer myth that some claim (e.g., Hedrick) is not dependent upon Christianity. But there do appear to be a few obvious allusions to Christianity (see Yamauchi). For example, "they will punish the flesh of the man upon whom the Holy Spirit came" (77.16–18) seems to be an unmistakable reference to the baptism of Jesus and his later passion. "The virgin became pregnant and gave birth to the child" in the wilderness (79.11–12) alludes to the infancy narratives of Matthew and Luke and to the symbolic depiction of the woman in the wilderness in Revelation 12.

Text: G. W. MACRAE, "The Apocalypse of Adam V, 5: 64,1–85,32," in *Nag Hammadi Codices V, 2–5 and VI with Papyrus Berolinensis 8502,1 and 4* (ed. Parrott), 151–95; J. M. ROBINSON, ed., *The Facsimile Edition of the Nag Hammadi Codices: Codex V* (Leiden: Brill, 1975), 74–96. *Survey:* J. H. CHARLESWORTH, *PMR* 72–74, 271–72; L. DiTOMMASO, *BPR* 197–203; C. W. HEDRICK, "Adam, Apocalypse of," *ABD* 1:66–68; D. SCHOLER, *Nag Hammadi Bibliography, 1970–1994* (NHS 32; Leiden: Brill, 1994), 394–99. **Commentary and Critical Study:** S. T. CARROLL, "The *Apocalypse of Adam* and Pre-Christian Gnosticism," *VC* 44 (1990): 263–79; C. W. HEDRICK, *The Apocalypse of Adam* (SBLDS 46; Chico, Calif.: Scholars Press, 1980); IDEM, "The Apocalypse of Adam: A Literary and Source Analysis," *SBLSP* 2 (1972): 581–90; G. W. MACRAE, "The Apocalypse of Adam," in *Nag Hammadi Codices V, 2–5 with Papyrus Berolinensis 8502, 1 and 4* (ed. Parrott), 151–95; IDEM, "Apocalypse of Adam," *OTP* 1:707–19; IDEM, "The Apocalypse of Adam Reconsidered," *SBLSP* 2 (1972): 573–79; G. W. E. NICKELSBURG, "Some Related Traditions in the *Apocalypse of Adam,* the Books of Adam and Eve, and *1 Enoch,*" in *The Rediscovery of Gnosticism* (ed. B. Layton; 2 vols.; SHR 41; Leiden: Brill, 1980), 2:515–39, esp. 533–38; D. M. PARROTT, "The Thirteen Kingdoms of the Apocalypse of Adam: Origin, Meaning, and Significance," *NovT* 31 (1989): 67–87; B. A. PEARSON, "Jewish Sources in Gnostic Literature," *SJWSTP* 470–74; P. PERKINS, "Apocalypse of Adam: The Genre and Function of a Gnostic Apocalypse," *CBQ* 39 (1977): 382–95; E. M. YAMAUCHI, "The Apocalypse of Adam, Mithraism, and Pre-Christian Gnosticism," in *Études mithriaques* (Leiden: Brill, 1978), 537–63.

Apocalypse of Elijah. The *Apocalypse of Elijah,* a Christian writing from sometime between the first and fourth centuries, is an eschatological work that describes the coming of the Antichrist, martyrdom of the righteous, and the coming of Christ and the establishment of the millennial kingdom. The *Apocalypse* survives in Coptic (Akhmimic and Sahidic), in Hebrew, and in a Greek fragment. In all likelihood the original language was Greek. (For a convenient assemblage of fragments from diverse "Elijah" sources, see Stone and Strugnell.) According to Origen (*Comm. Matt.* 5.29 [on Matt 27:9]), Paul's curious quotation in 1 Cor 2:9 derives from the *Apocalypse of Elijah* (see Prigent; Ruwet).

Text: A.-M. DENIS, *CGPAT* 904 (Greek); A. JELLINEK, *Bet ha-Midrasch,* 3:65–68 (Hebrew); A. PIETERSMA, S. T. COMSTOCK, and H. W. ATTRIDGE, *The Apocalypse of Elijah: Based on Pap. Chester Beatty 2018* (SBLTT 19; Pseudepigrapha Series 9; Chico, Calif.: Scholars Press, 1981), 20–64 (Coptic), 69–90 (Coptic plates), 92–94 (Greek and Greek plates). *Survey:* J. H. CHARLESWORTH, *PMR* 95–98, 277–78; L. DiTOMMASO, *BPR* 341–54; O. S. WINTERMUTE, "Elijah, Apocalypse of," *ABD* 2:466–69. *Commentary and Critical Study:* M. BLACK, "The 'Two Witnesses' of Rev. 11:3f. in Jewish and Christian Apocalyptic Tradition," in *Donum gentilicium: New Testament Studies in Honour of David Daube* (ed. C. K. Barrett; Oxford: Clarendon, 1978), 227–37; M. BUTTENWIESER, *Die hebraische Elias-Apokalypse und ihre Stellung in der apokalyptischen Literatur des rabbinischen Schrifttums und der Kirche* (Leipzig: Eduard Pfeiffer, 1897); K. H. KUHN, "The Apocalypse of Elijah," *AOT* 753–73; P. PRIGENT, "Ce que l'oeil n'a pas vu, I Cor. 2,9," *TZ* 14 (1958): 416–29, esp. 421–24; J.-M. ROSENSTIEHL, *L'Apocalypse d'Élie: Introduction, traduction, et notes* (Paris: Geuthner, 1972); J. RUWET, "Origène et l'Apocalypse d'Élie à propos de 1 Cor 2:9," *Bib* 30 (1949): 517–19; W. SCHRAGE, "Die Elia-Apokalypse," *JSHRZ* 5/3 (1980) 193–288; G. STEINDORFF, *Die Apokalypse des Elias, eine unbekannte Apokalypse, und Bruchstücke der Sophonias-Apokalypse;* M. E. STONE and J. STRUGNELL, *The Books of Elijah, Parts 1–2* (SBLTT 18; Pseudepigrapha Series 8; Missoula, Mont.: Scholars Press, 1979); O. S. WINTERMUTE, "Apocalypse of Elijah," *OTP* 1:721–53.

Apocalypse of Daniel. The *Apocalypse of Daniel* is a ninth-century Christian apocalypse in which Daniel is purported to have predicted the Byzantine-Arab wars of the eighth century (chs. 1–7). In the second half of the *Apocalypse* (chs. 8–14) Daniel describes the end of the age, the Antichrist, the day of judgment, and the appearance of Christ. Although the book depends on Revelation, it appears to have made use of earlier apocalyptic materials. The *Apocalypse of Daniel* survives in Greek, the language in which it was originally written. There are other late, medieval apocalypses linked to Daniel. These include the *Last Vision of Daniel,* the *Vision of the Monk Daniel on the Seven Hills,* the *Vision of Daniel on the Isle of Cyprus,* and the *Vision of Daniel on the Last Times and the End of the World,* all of which are in Greek. There are also Danielic apocalypses and visions in Syriac (see Henze), Persian, Arabic, Coptic, Slavonic, Armenian, and Hebrew (from the Cairo Genizah; on this text, see Ginzberg).

Text: K. BERGER, *Die griechische Daniel-Diegesis,* 8–23 (Greek); M. HENZE, *The Syriac Apocalypse of Daniel,* 33–63 (Syriac text), 132–43 (Syriac plates). *Survey:* J. H. CHARLESWORTH, *PMR* 180–82, 276–77; L. DiTOMMASO, *BPR* 320–21; G. T. ZERVOS, "Daniel,

Apocalypse of," *ABD* 2:28–29. **Commentary and Critical Study:** K. BERGER, *Die griechische Daniel-Diegesis;* L. GINZBERG, "Vision of Daniel," in *Genizah Studies in Memory of Solomon Schechter* (3 vols.; TSJTS 7–9; New York: Jewish Theological Seminary of America, 1928–1929), 1:313–23 (Hebrew); M. HENZE, *The Syriac Apocalypse of Daniel;* F. MACLER, *Les apocalypses apocryphes de Daniel* (Paris: C. Noblet, 1895); G. T. ZERVOS, "Apocalypse of Daniel," *OTP* 1:755–70.

Part Two: Testaments

Testaments of the Twelve Patriarchs. The *Testaments of the Twelve Patriarchs* were written between 109 and 106 B.C.E. by a Pharisee who greatly admired John Hyrcanus at the zenith of the Maccabean (or Hasmonean) dynasty. The conviction was that Hyrcanus and his Levite family constituted the messianic line. Later revisions condemn the apostate Hasmonean line and expect Messiah to come from the tribe of Judah. The *Testaments* are inspired by Jacob's testament in Genesis 49 and typically follow this form: (1) Introduction in which scene is set; (2) narrative from patriarch's life; (3) ethical exhortation; (4) prediction of future; (5) second exhortation; and (6) patriarch's burial. Major theological themes would include: (1) forgiveness and grace, freely given to those of contrite spirit; (2) exhortation to love God and neighbor (*T. Dan* 5:3; Mark 12:30–31); (3) ethical teachings that frequently parallel the NT; (4) universalism, even Gentiles can be saved through Israel (*T. Levi* 14:4; *T. Benj.* 9:2); (5) Messiah (alternating between Levi and Judah) is free from sin; he is righteous, establishes new priesthood, mediator for Gentiles; (6) resurrection; and (7) demonology and doctrines about Antichrist. Although some scholars have argued for Aramaic as the original language of the *Testaments* (as the evidence from Qumran may suggest), it is more likely that Greek, one of the languages in which the *Testaments* have survived, was the original. Besides the Greek, all or some of the *Testaments* are extant in Armenian, Slavonic, and Hebrew.

At one time Marinus de Jonge argued that the *Testaments* are wholly Christian in origin (though he admitted that some Jewish testamentary material may have been used). More recently, however—mainly because of the evidence of Qumran—he acknowledges that the *Testaments* may in fact have had a Jewish origin, though later thoroughly reworked by a Christian. Most scholars remain convinced that the *Testaments* are Jewish in origin, notwithstanding the Christian interpolations (most of which are obvious; see Charles, *Greek Versions*, xlviii–li; and Marc Philonenko and Howard Kee, who think the interpolations are relatively few in number). These interpolations include *T. Sim.* 6:5, 7; 7:2; *T. Levi* 4:1, 4; 10:2; 14:1, 2; 16:3; 17:2; 18:7, 9; *T. Jud.* 24:4; *T. Iss.* 7:7; *T. Zeb.* 9:8; *T. Dan* 5:10, 13; 6:7, 9; *T. Naph.* 8:2, 3; *T. Gad* 8:2; *T. Ash.* 7:3; *T. Jos.* 19:8, 11; *T. Benj.* 3:8; 9:3–5; 10:7, 8, 9. On the whole question of the origin of the *Testaments*, see Dixon Slingerland's survey.

The testamentary genre is well attested at Qumran (mostly in Aramaic), and in some cases there is overlap with the Greek *Testaments of the Twelve Patriarchs.* Although these Qumran documents do not settle the issue of the origin of the Greek pseudepigraphon, they provide important evidence of the antiquity and function of the genre. We have the *Testament of Levi* (i.e., 1QTLevi ar = 1Q21; 4QTLevi ar^a-f = 4Q213, 4Q213a, 4Q213b, 4Q214, 4Q214a, 4Q214b), which is also attested among the materials retrieved from the Cairo Genizah (i.e., CTLevi ar; see Charles, *APOT* 2:364–67; idem, *Greek Versions*, 245–56). J. T. Milik and Émile Puech have suggested that portions of the *Testament of Levi* are also preserved in the fragmentary 4Q458 and 4Q540–541. Other *Testaments* from Qumran include, or may include, *Judah* (i.e., 3QTJud? = 3Q7; 4Q538), *Joseph* (i.e., 4Q539), *Jacob* (i.e., 4Q537), *Qahat* (or *Kohath*, i.e., 4Q542), and *Amram* (i.e., 4Q543–548). Of special interest is the Hebrew *Testament of Naphtali*, which is preserved in medieval MSS (see Gaster; Wertheimer and Wertheimer; also Charles, *APOT* 2:361–63; idem, *Greek Versions*, li–lvii, 239–44) and may be linked in some way to a Naphtali apocryphon found at Qumran (i.e., 4QTNaph = 4Q215). It is not clear, however, that this document is in fact a testament (see the summary of the discussion in Kugler, "Naphtali"). Some scholars think the medieval Hebrew *Testament of Naphtali* and the earlier Greek *Testament of Naphtali* depend on an earlier Semitic (probably Aramaic) prototype. There may also be fragments of a Hebrew *Testament of Judah* preserved in late rabbinic works (see Jellinek, 3:1–3; Charles, *Greek Versions*, 235–38).

The *Testaments of the Twelve Patriarchs* are very important for NT studies as they appear to have had an influence upon the NT at many points (e.g., see the tabulation in Charles, *APOT* 2:291–92; Charles 1908, lxxviii–xcii; Charles 1917, xx–xxiii).

Text: R. H. CHARLES, *The Greek Versions of the Testaments of the Twelve Patriarchs*, 1–233; A.-M. DENIS, *CGPAT* 832–50. **Survey:** J. H. CHARLESWORTH, *PMR* 211–20, 305–7; J. J. COLLINS, "Testaments," *SJWSTP* 331–44; IDEM, "The Testamentary Literature in Recent Scholarship," *EJMI* 268–76; L. DITOMMASO, *BPR* 919–75; M. DE JONGE, "Patriarchs, Testaments of the Twelve," *ABD* 5:181–86; IDEM, *The Testaments of the Twelve Patriarchs: A Critical Edition of the Greek Text* (PVTG 1; Leiden: Brill, 1978), 1–180; H. C. KEE, "Testaments of the Twelve Patriarchs," *DNTB* 1200–1205; R. A. KUGLER, "Naphtali, Testament of," *EDSS* 2:602–3; IDEM, "Testaments," *EDSS* 2:933–36; IDEM, "Twelve Patriarchs, Testaments of the," *EDSS* 2:952–53; G. W. E. NICKELSBURG, *JLBM* 231–41; H. D. SLINGERLAND, *The Testaments of the Twelve Patriarchs: A Critical History of Research* (SBLMS 21; Missoula, Mont.: Scholars Press, 1977); M. E. STONE, "Levi, Aramaic," *EDSS* 1:486–88; J. C. VANDERKAM, *An Introduction to Early Judaism*, 94–97 (Aramaic Levi), 100–102. **Commentary and Critical Study:** R. H. CHARLES, *The Greek Versions of the Testaments of the Twelve Patriarchs;* IDEM, "The Testaments of the Twelve Patriarchs," *APOT* 2:282–367; IDEM, *The Testaments of the Twelve Patriarchs* (London: Adam and Charles Black, 1908); IDEM, with an introduction by W. O. E. Oesterley, *The Testaments of the Twelve Patriarchs* (TED I: Palestinian Jewish Texts 5; London: SPCK, 1917); B. N. FISK, "One Good Story Deserves Another: The Hermeneutics of Invoking Secondary Biblical Episodes in the Narratives of *Pseudo-Philo* and the *Testaments of the Twelve Patriarchs*," in *The Interpretation of Scripture in Early Judaism and Christianity* (ed. Evans), 217–38; M. GASTER, "The Hebrew Text of One of the Testaments of the Twelve Patriarchs," *Society of Biblical Archaeology: Proceedings* 16–17 (1894): 33–49 (first version of Hebrew *Testament of Naphtali*); M. DE JONGE, ed., *Studies on the Testaments of the Twelve Patriarchs: Text and Interpretation* (SVTP 3;

Leiden: Brill, 1975); IDEM, *The Testaments of the Twelve Patriarchs* (Assen: Van Gorcum, 1953); IDEM, "The Testaments of the Twelve Patriarchs and the NT," *SE* 1 (1957): 546–56; H. W. HOLLANDER, "The Testament of the Twelve Patriarchs," *AOT* 505–600; IDEM, "The Testaments of the Twelve Patriarchs," *OOT* 71–91; H. C. KEE, "The Ethical Dimensions of the Testaments of the XII as a Clue to Provenance," *NTS* 24 (1977–1978): 259–70; IDEM, "Testaments of the Twelve Patriarchs," *OTP* 1:775–828; R. A. KUGLER, *From Patriarch to Priest: The Levi-Priestly Tradition from Aramaic Levi to* Testament of Levi (SBLEJL 9; Atlanta: Scholars Press, 1996); J. T. MILIK, "Le Testament de Lévi in araméen: Fragment de la grotte 4 de Qumrân," *RB* 62 (1955): 398–406; G. W. E. NICKELSBURG, ed., *Studies on the Testament of Joseph* (SCS 5; Missoula, Mont.: Scholars Press, 1975); M. PHILONENKO, *Les interpolations chrétiennes des Testaments des douze patriarches et les manuscrits de Qumrân* (CRHPR 35; Paris: Presses Universitaires de France, 1960); É. PUECH, "Fragments d'un apocryphe de Lévi et le personnage eschatologique, 4QTestLévi^{c-d} (?) et 4QAJa," in *The Madrid Qumran Congress: Proceedings of the International Congress on the Dead Sea Scrolls, Madrid, 18–21 March, 1991* (ed. J. Trebolle Barrera and L. Vegas Montaner; 2 vols.; STDJ 11; Leiden: Brill, 1992), 2:449–501; M. STONE, "Testament of Naphtali," *JJS* 47 (1996): 311–21; S. A. WERTHEIMER and A. J. WERTHEIMER, *Batei Midrashot* (Jerusalem, 1890; repr., 2 vols.; Jerusalem: Mosad ha-Rab, 1950–1953), 1:199–203 (second version of Hebrew *Testament of Naphtali*).

Testament of Job. The *Testament of Job* is an embellishment of the biblical book of Job, originally written in Greek, perhaps as early as the first century B.C.E., but no later than the first century C.E. The book contributes much to our knowledge of early Jewish and Christian beliefs about Satan. The *Testament of Job,* which is concerned with the contrast between heavenly and earthly realities, emphasizes Job's piety (seen especially in his rejection of idolatry) and patient endurance. There are points of coherence between this *Testament* and Hebrews 10–12.

Text: A.-M. DENIS, *CGPAT* 875–79; M. R. JAMES, *Apocrypha anecdota: Second Series,* 104–37; R. A. KRAFT et al., *The Testament of Job* (SBLTT 5; Pseudepigrapha Series 4; Missoula, Mont.: Scholars Press, 1974). *Survey:* J. H. CHARLESWORTH, *PMR* 134–36, 291; J. J. COLLINS, "The Testamentary Literature in Recent Scholarship," *EJMI* 276–77; IDEM, "Testaments," *SJWSTP* 349–54; L. DITOMMASO, *BPR* 565–74; G. W. E. NICKELSBURG, *JLBM* 241–48; R. P. SPITTLER, "The Testament of Job," *DNTB* 1189–92; IDEM, "The Testament of Job: A History of Research and Interpretation," in *Studies on the Testament of Job* (ed. Knibb and van der Horst), 7–32. *Commentary and Critical Study:* C. T. BEGG, "Comparing Characters: The Book of Job and the *Testament of Job,*" in *The Book of Job* (ed. W. A. M. Beuken; BETL 114; Leuven: Peeters, 1994), 435–45; S. P. BROCK, *Testamentum Iobi* (PVTG 2; Leiden: Brill, 1967); J. J. COLLINS, "Structure and Meaning in the Testament of Job," *SBLSP* 13 (1974): 1:35–52; S. R. GARRETT, "The Weaker Sex in the Testament of Job," *JBL* 112 (1993): 55–70; H. C. KEE, "Satan, Magic, and Salvation in the Testament of Job," *SBLSP* 13 (1974): 1:53–76; M. A. KNIBB and P. W. VAN DER HORST, *Studies on the Testament of Job;* R. P. SPITTLER, "Job, Testament of," *ABD* 3:869–71; IDEM, "The Testament of Job," *OOT* 231–47; IDEM, "Testament of Job," *OTP* 1:829–68; R. THORNHILL, "The Testament of Job," *AOT* 617–48.

Testaments of the Three Patriarchs. The *Testaments of the Three Patriarchs* (Abraham, Isaac, and Jacob) probably derive from an original first-century Greek

Testament of Abraham (which is extant in two major recensions), which later was expanded (second to third century) to include the *Testament of Isaac* and the *Testament of Jacob*. The expanded version was eventually adopted by the church and was read with great interest. Christian interpolations occur chiefly in the *Testament of Isaac* and the *Testament of Jacob*. The *Testament of Abraham* is extant in Greek and in several versions (including Coptic, Slavonic, Arabic, and Ethiopic). The *Testament of Isaac* and the *Testament of Jacob* are extant in Coptic, Arabic, and Ethiopic (and the *Testament of Jacob* in Armenian as well). The *Testaments* greatly embellish details in the lives of the patriarchs and describe the judgment of humanity. The latter element is in keeping with rabbinic traditions of afterlife and judgment, in which the great patriarchs are sometimes depicted as gate-keepers, directing the righteous (who almost always are Torah-observant Jews) to paradise and the wicked (Gentiles and sometimes apostate Jews) to Gehenna.

Text: A.-M. DENIS, *CGPAT* 825–29 (Greek *Abraham,* longer recension A), 830–32 (Greek *Abraham,* shorter recension B); M. R. JAMES, *The Testament of Abraham,* 77–104 (recension A), 105–19 (recension B), repr. in *The Testament of Abraham: The Greek Recensions* (ed. Stone), 2–87 (with English translation). *Survey:* J. H. CHARLESWORTH, *PMR* 70–72, 270–71 (Abraham), 123–25, 289–90 (Isaac), 131–33, 290–91 (Jacob); J. J. COLLINS, "The Testamentary Literature in Recent Scholarship," *EJMI* 277–78; L. DiTOMMASO, *BPR* 145–57 (Abraham), 158–61 (Isaac and Jacob); R. DORAN, "Narrative Literature," *EJMI* 287–89; J. M. KNIGHT, "Testament of Abraham," *DNTB* 1188–89; J. R. MUELLER, "Abraham, Testament of," *ABD* 1:43–44; G. W. E. NICKELSBURG, *JLBM* 248–53; IDEM, "Stories of Biblical and Early Post-biblical Times," *SJWSTP* 60–64; M. E. STONE, "Apocalyptic Literature," *SJWSTP* 420–21. *Commentary and Critical Study:* D. C. ALLISON, *Testament of Abraham* (CEJL; New York: de Gruyter, 2003); G. H. BOX, *The Testament of Abraham* (London: Macmillan, 1927); M. DELCOR, *Le Testament d'Abraham: Introduction, traduction du texte grec, et commentaire de la recension grecque longe, suivie de la traduction des Testaments d'Abraham, d'Isaac et de Jacob d'après les versions orientales* (SVTP 2; Leiden: Brill, 1973); M. R. JAMES, *The Testament of Abraham* (see pp. 140–61 for appendixes on the *Testament of Isaac* and *Testament of Jacob;* K. H. KUHN, "The Testament of Isaac," *AOT* 423–39; IDEM, "The Testament of Jacob," *AOT* 441–52; G. W. E. NICKELSBURG, ed., *Studies on the Testament of Abraham* (rev. ed.; SCS 6; Missoula, Mont.: Scholars Press, 1976); E. P. SANDERS, "The Testament of Abraham," *OOT* 56–70; IDEM, "Testament of Abraham," *OTP* 1:871–902; W. F. STINESPRING, "Testament of Isaac," *OTP* 1:903–11 (translation is based on the Arabic [ninth century?], with some help from the Coptic and Ethiopic); IDEM, "Testament of Jacob," *OTP* 1:913–18 (again following the Arabic, with input from the Coptic and Ethiopic); M. E. STONE, *The Testament of Abraham: The Greek Recensions;* N. TURNER, "The Testament of Abraham," *AOT* 393–421.

Testament (Assumption) of Moses. The *Testament* (or *Assumption*) *of Moses* was composed by a Jew in the first century C.E. in either Aramaic or Hebrew. The original author may have been a Pharisee or an Essene. The only extant manuscript is in Latin and apparently is a translation of a Greek version. At least one-third of the original work is lost. Some scholars assume that part of the lost portion is the so-called *Assumption of Moses* to which Jude 9 apparently refers. R. H. Charles thought that originally there were two books, a *Testament* and an *Assumption,* that were later combined (*APOT* 2.208). The book tells of the prophecy that Moses gave to Joshua before the former died. This is a highly useful writing for NT studies. Chapters 5–7 inveigh against Israel's religious leadership (esp. ch. 7, which probably has the ruling priests in view). The criticisms here, which cohere with criticisms found in the Dead Sea Scrolls, may clarify aspects of Jesus' complaints against temple authorities. The idea in chapter 9 that death of the righteous Taxo and his sons will bring deliverance to Israel and (in ch. 10) inaugurate the appearance of the kingdom of God and the demise of the devil is especially pertinent for the study of Jesus. The actual language, "then his kingdom will appear . . . and then the devil will have an end" (10:1), echoes Jesus' reply to his critics, "If Satan has risen up against himself and is divided, he cannot stand, but his end has come" (Mark 3:26).

Text: R. H. CHARLES, *The Assumption of Moses,* 53–101 (Latin), 105–10 (Greek); A.-M. DENIS, *CGPAT* 901; IDEM, *FPSG* 63–67 (Greek); J. TROMP, *The Assumption of Moses,* 5–25 (Latin, with facing English translation), 271–81 (Greek). *Survey:* J. H. CHARLESWORTH, *PMR* 163–66, 296; J. J. COLLINS, "The Testament (Assumption) of Moses," *OOT* 145–58; IDEM, "The Testamentary Literature in Recent Scholarship," *EJMI* 277; IDEM, "Testaments," *SJWSTP* 344–49; D. A. DESILVA, "The Testament of Moses," *DNTB* 1192–99; L. DITOMMASO, *BPR* 731–53; G. W. E. NICKELSBURG, *JLBM* 80–83, 212–14; J. C. VANDER-KAM, *An Introduction to Early Judaism,* 113–15. *Commentary and Critical Study:* D. C. CARLSON, "Vengeance and Angelic Mediation in *Testament of Moses* 9 and 10," *JBL* 101 (1982): 85–95; R. H. CHARLES, *The Assumption of Moses;* N. J. HOFMANN, *Die Assumptio Mosis: Studien zur Rezeption massgültiger Überlieferung* (JSJSup 67; Leiden: Brill, 2000); C. J. LATTEY, "The Messianic Expectation in the 'The Assumption of Moses,'" *CBQ* 4 (1942): 9–21; G. W. E. NICKELSBURG, ed., *Studies on the Testament of Moses* (SCS 4; Cambridge: Society of Biblical Literature, 1973); J. F. PRIEST, "Some Reflections on the Assumption of Moses," *PRSt* 4 (1977): 92–111; IDEM, "Testament of Moses," *OTP* 1:919–34; H. H. ROWLEY, "The Figure of 'Taxo' in *The Assumption of Moses,*" *JBL* 64 (1945): 141–43; A. SCHALIT, *Untersuchungen zur Assumptio Mosis* (ALGHJ 17; Leiden: Brill, 1989); J. P. SWEET, "The Assumption of Moses," *AOT* 601–16; J. TROMP, *The Assumption of Moses;* D. H. WALLACE, "The Semitic Origin of the Assumption of Moses," *TZ* 11 (1955): 321–28; S. K. WILLIAMS, "The Death of the Righteous Ones in Assumption of Moses," in *Jesus' Death as Saving Event: The Background and Origin of a Concept* (HDR 2; Missoula, Mont.: Scholars Press, 1975), 66–70.

Testament of Solomon. The *Testament of Solomon* was composed in Greek sometime between the first and third centuries by a Christian. The MS tradition is complicated, with at least six recensions identified (i.e., recensions A, B, C, D, E, and N; summarized in DiTommaso, *BPR* 895–96). The book "is a haggadic-type folktale about Solomon's building the temple of Jerusalem combined with ancient lore about magic, astrology, angelology, demonology, and primitive medicine" (Duling, *OTP* 1:935). The book stresses God's power over the demons, by whom humankind is often oppressed, links demonology with astrology (i.e., demons reside in the stars), and is keenly interested in medicine. The reference to Beelzebul as "prince of the demons" (*T. Sol.* 2:9; 3:3–6; 6:1–11) recalls this epithet in Mark 3:22 (and par.). Compare also the blind beggar's petition, "Son of David, have mercy on me" (Mark

10:47), with the similar appeal to Solomon in *T. Sol.* 20:1–2 (see Charlesworth 1996). Moreover, the description of the respective evil tasks of the various demons encountered by Solomon may also shed light on the maladies described in the Gospels. See the discussion concerning Eleazar the exorcist in appendix 5.

Text: C. C. McCOWN, *The Testament of Solomon*, 5–97. *Survey:* J. H. CHARLESWORTH, *PMR* 197–202, 304; L. DiTOMMASO, *BPR* 895–900; D. C. DULING, "Solomon, Testament of," *ABD* 6:117–19. *Commentary and Critical Study:* J. H. CHARLESWORTH, "Solomon and Jesus: The Son of David in Ante-Markan Traditions (Mk 10.47)," in *Biblical and Humane* (ed. L. B. Elder et al.; J. F. Priest FS; Homage 20; Atlanta: Scholars Press, 1996), 125–51; IDEM, "The Son of David: Solomon and Jesus," in *The New Testament and Hellenistic Judaism* (ed. P. Borgen and S. Giverson; Aarhus, Den.: Aarhus University Press, 1995), 72–87, esp. 79–84; F. C. CONYBEARE, "The Testament of Solomon," *JQR* 11 (1898): 1–45; D. C. DULING, "The Eleazar Miracle and Solomon's Magical Wisdom in Flavius Josephus' *Antiquitates judaicae* 8.42–49," *HTR* 78 (1985): 1–25; IDEM, "Solomon, Exorcism, and the Son of David," *HTR* 68 (1975): 235–52; IDEM, "Testament of Solomon," *OTP* 1:935–87; IDEM, "The Testament of Solomon: Retrospect and Prospect," *JSP* 2 (1988): 87–112; S. GIVERSEN, "Solomon und die Dämonen," in *Essays on the Nag Hammadi Texts in Honor of Alexander Böhlig* (ed. M. Krause; NHS 3; Leiden: Brill, 1972), 16–21; C. C. McCOWN, "The Christian Tradition as to the Magical Wisdom of Solomon," *JPOS* 2 (1922): 1–24; IDEM, *The Testament of Solomon;* M. WHITTAKER, "The Testament of Solomon," *AOT* 733–51.

Testament of Adam. The *Testament of Adam* was composed sometime between the second and fifth centuries by a Jew, although it now contains several Christian additions. It exists in several languages, and Hebrew, Greek, and Syriac have all been proposed as the original. It seems likely, however, that since virtually no evidence exists for a Hebrew original, and since the Greek appears to be dependent on the Syriac, the book was originally written in Syriac. The book teaches that God originally intended Adam to evolve into a god (3:2, 4), but because of the Fall this did not take place. The book, which is related to the *Cave of Treasures,* is also interested in angelology.

Text: M. R. JAMES, *Apocrypha anecdota: A Collection of Thirteen Apocryphal Books and Fragments,* 138–45 (Greek); S. E. ROBINSON, *The Testament of Adam: An Examination of the Syriac and Greek Traditions* (SBLDS 52; Chico, Calif.: Scholars Press, 1982), 45–104 (Syriac), 110–27 (Greek). *Survey:* J. H. CHARLESWORTH, *PMR* 91–92, 272–73; L. DiTOMMASO, *BPR* 205–20; S. E. ROBINSON, "Adam, the Testament of," *ABD* 1:68. *Commentary and Critical Study:* S. E. ROBINSON, "Testament of Adam," *OTP* 1:990–95; IDEM, *The Testament of Adam: An Examination of the Syriac and Greek Traditions* (SBLDS 52; Chico, Calif.: Scholars Press, 1982); IDEM, "The Testament of Adam and the Angelic Liturgy," *RevQ* 12 (1985–1987): 105–10.

Part Three: Old Testament Expansions

Letter of Aristeas. The *Letter* (or *Epistle*) *of Aristeas* claims to be an eyewitness account of Aristeas, an officer of the court of Ptolemy Philadelphus (285–247 B.C.E.), written to brother Philocrates. It purports to explain the translation of the LXX (see §§10–11), and to defend Alexandrian Judaism (Jewish wisdom, moral insight, value of Torah, political rights). Several historical blunders suggest that it is pseudonymous. Written in Greek, probably between 130 and 70 B.C.E., with additions as late as first century C.E., *Aristeas* was used by Josephus (*Ant.* 12.2.1 §11–12.2.15 §118).

Text: A.-M. DENIS, *CGPAT* 880–92; H. St. J. THACKERAY, in H. B. Swete, *An Introduction to the Old Testament in Greek* (2d ed.; Cambridge: Cambridge University Press, 1914; repr., Peabody, Mass.: Hendrickson, 1989), 551–606. *Survey:* C. C. CARAGOUNIS, "Aristeas, Epistle of," *DNTB* 114–18; J. H. CHARLESWORTH, *PMR* 78–80, 274; L. DiTOMMASO, *BPR* 239–58; B. L. MACK, "Wisdom Literature," *EJMI* 378–79; G. W. E. NICKELSBURG, *JLBM* 165–69; IDEM, "Stories of Biblical and Early Post-biblical Times," *SJWSTP* 75–80; R. J. H. SHUTT, "Aristeas, Letter of," *ABD* 1:380–82; J. C. VANDERKAM, *An Introduction to Early Judaism*, 81–85. *Commentary and Critical Study:* M. HADAS, *Aristeas to Philocrates* (JAL; New York: Harper, 1951); S. JELLICOE, "The Occasion and Purpose of the Letter of Aristeas: a Re-examination," *NTS* 12 (1964): 144–50; H. G. MEECHAM, *The Letter of Aristeas: A Linguistic Study with Special Reference to the Greek Bible* (Publications of the University of Manchester 241; Manchester, Eng.: Manchester University Press, 1935); IDEM, *The Oldest Version of the Bible—"Aristeas" on Its Traditional Origin: A Study in Early Apologetic* (Hartley Lectures 32; London: Holborn, 1932); R. J. H. SHUTT, "Letter of Aristeas," *OTP* 2:7–34; IDEM, "Notes on the Letter of Aristeas," *BIOSCS* 10 (1977): 22–30; H. St. J. THACKERAY, *The Letter of Aristeas, Translated, with an Appendix of Ancient Evidence on the Origin of the Septuagint* (TED II: Hellenistic Jewish Texts 3; London: SPCK, 1917).

Jubilees. Written in Hebrew by a Pharisee between 135 and 105 B.C.E., *Jubilees* is a midrashic rewriting of Genesis-Exodus, from creation to the giving of the law on Sinai, given to Moses while on the Mount (Exod 24:12). The "author has freely condensed (e.g., the story of plagues on Pharaoh, Ex 7–10 = Jub 48:4–11), omitted (e.g. the blessing of Ephraim and Manasseh, Gen 48:1–20), expurgated (e.g., the notice of Abraham's presenting his wife to foreign rulers as his sister, Gen 12:10–20; 20:2–7), explained (e.g., Reuben's apparent incest, Gen 35:22 = Jub 33:2–20), supplemented (e.g., tales of Abraham's youth, Jub 12:1–9, 12f., 16–21, 25–27), and sometimes radically recast the biblical episodes (e.g., Isaac's covenant with Abimelech, Gen 26:23–33 = Jub 24:21–33)" (Wintermute, *OTP* 2:35).

Jubilees may be outlined: (1) Introduction (ch. 1); (2) Creation and Adam stories (chs. 2–4); (3) Noah stories (chs. 5–10); (4) Abraham stories (chs. 11–23); (5) Jacob and his family (chs. 24–45); and (5) Moses stories (chs. 46–50). The purpose of *Jubilees* is to call the Jewish reader to a more faithful obedience to the law. The author is interested in the question of evil. He believes that evil derives from the demonic world and that Adam is not to be blamed for its continuing effects. Whereas the author believes that God will be gracious and forgiving toward Israel, he entertains no hope for Gentiles. Only the Ethiopic version is complete (or nearly so), with a few Greek, Latin, Syriac, and Hebrew (cf. Qumran, caves 1, 2, 3, 4, and 11) fragments extant. Because of the latter, it is believed that *Jubilees* was originally written in Hebrew. Studying the method in which *Jubilees* retells biblical narratives, embellishing respective episodes with otherwise unrelated biblical texts, is very helpful for understanding early biblical interpretation.

Text: R. H. CHARLES, *The Ethiopic Version of the Hebrew Book of Jubilees* (Oxford: Clarendon, 1895) (Ethiopic, Hebrew, Syriac, Greek, and Latin); A.-M. DENIS, *CGPAT* 902–3 (Greek); IDEM, *FPSG* 70–102 (Greek); J. C. VANDERKAM, *The Book of Jubilees* (critical Ethiopic text, followed by surviving versions); J. C. VANDERKAM and J. T. MILIK, "Jubilees," in *Qumran Cave 4: VIII Parabiblical Texts, Part I* (ed. H. Attridge et al.; DJD 13; Oxford: Oxford University Press, 1994), 1–185 (Hebrew). *Survey:* G. W. E. NICKELSBURG, "The Bible Rewritten and Expanded," *SJWSTP* 97–104; J. C. VANDERKAM, "The Book of Jubilees," *OOT* 111–44; IDEM, *An Introduction to Early Judaism*, 97–100; IDEM, "Jubilees, Book of," *EDSS* 434–38. *Commentary and Critical Study:* K. BERGER, "Das Buch der Jubiläen," *JSHRZ* 2/3 (1981) 273–575; R. H. CHARLES, *The Book of Jubilees, or the Little Genesis: Translated from the Editor's Ethiopic Text and Edited with Introduction, Notes, and Indices* (London: Adam and Charles Black, 1902); IDEM, with introduction by G. H. Box, *The Book of Jubilees, or the Little Genesis* (TED I: Palestinian Jewish Texts 4; New York: Macmillan, 1917); G. L. DAVENPORT, *The Eschatology of the Book of Jubilees* (SPB 20; Leiden: Brill, 1971); J. C. ENDRES, *Biblical Interpretation in the Book of Jubilees* (CBQMS 18; Washington, D.C.: Catholic Biblical Association, 1987); B. HALPERN-AMARU, *The Empowerment of Women in the Book of Jubilees* (JSJSup 60; Leiden: Brill, 1999); C. RABIN, "Jubilees," *AOT* 1–139; J. M. SCOTT, *Geography in Early Judaism and Christianity: The Book of Jubilees* (SNTSMS 113; Cambridge: Cambridge University Press, 2002); J. C. VANDERKAM, *The Book of Jubilees* (textual commentary); IDEM, "Das chronologische Konzept des Jubiläenbuches," *ZAW* 107 (1995): 80–100; IDEM, "Genesis 1 in Jubilees 2," *DSD* 1 (1994): 300–321; IDEM, "Jubilees' Exegetical Creation of Levi the Priest," *RevQ* 17 (1996): 359–73; IDEM, *Textual and Historical Studies in the Book of Jubilees* (HSM 14; Missoula, Mont.: Scholars Press, 1977) (Hebrew fragments); O. S. WINTERMUTE, "Jubilees," *OTP* 2:35–142.

Martyrdom and Ascension of Isaiah. The *Martyrdom and Ascension of Isaiah* is made up of two documents: (1) the *Martyrdom* (chs. 1–5) and (2) the *Ascension* (chs. 6–11). The first part perhaps should be further subdivided into the *Martyrdom* (1:1–3:12; 5:1–16) and the *Testament of Hezekiah* (3:13–4:22). The first half of the first part (1:1–3:12; 5:1–16) is a Jewish work that tells of the prophet's martyrdom by order of Manasseh and is probably to be dated to the second century B.C.E. It was probably written in Hebrew. In 5:12–14 we are told that Isaiah was sawed in two. The Babylonian Talmud (*Yebam.* 49b) tells of Isaiah being swallowed up by a cedar, which Manasseh ordered cut in two. According to the Palestinian Talmud (*Sanh.* 10.2), Isaiah attempted to flee from Manasseh by hiding in a cedar. Unfortunately the hem of his garment betrayed the prophet's hiding place, so Manasseh ordered the tree cut down. This tradition is probably echoed in Heb 11:37, where the author tells us that the righteous have been stoned and "sawed in two." *Martyrdom and Ascension of Isaiah* 3:13–4:22 is a later Christian addition, sometimes called the Testament of Hezekiah; it describes Isaiah's vision. The second half of the book (chs. 6–11) is also a Christian addition describing Isaiah's visionary ascension into heaven. The Christian additions were originally composed in Greek and may date as late as the fourth century.

Text: R. H. CHARLES, *The Ascension of Isaiah* (London: Adam and Charles Black, 1900), 83–148 (Ethiopic, Greek, and Latin synopses); A.-M. DENIS, *CGPAT* 904; IDEM, *CLPAT* 630–31 (Latin); IDEM, *FPSG* 105–14 (Greek); B. P. GRENFELL and A. S. HUNT, *The Ascension of Isaiah and Other Theological Fragments* (vol. 1 of *The Amherst Papyri;* London: Henry Frowde, 1900), 1–22, esp. 4–10 (Greek). *Survey:* R. DORAN, "Narrative Literature," *EJMI* 293–94; G. W. E. NICKELSBURG, "Stories of Biblical and Early Post-biblical Times," *SJWSTP* 52–56. *Commentary and Critical Study:* J.M.T. BARTON, "The Ascension of - Isaiah," *AOT* 775–812; R. H. CHARLES, *The Ascension of Isaiah* (London: Adam and Charles Black, 1900); IDEM, "The Martyrdom of Isaiah," *APOT* 2:155–62; A. K. HELMBOLD, "Gnostic Elements in the 'Ascension of Isaiah,'" *NTS* 18 (1972): 222–27; M. A. KNIBB, "Martyrdom and Ascension of Isaiah," *OTP* 2:143–76; IDEM, "The Martyrdom of Isaiah," *OOT* 178–92; E. NORELLI, *Ascension du prophète Isaïe* (Apocryphes 2; Turnhout: Brepols, 1993); IDEM, *Commentarius* (vol. 2 of E. Norelli et al., *Ascensio Isaiae;* CCSA 8; Turnhout: Brepols, 1995).

Joseph and Aseneth. Joseph and Aseneth was composed in Greek (though one scholar has suggested Hebrew), probably in Egypt sometime between the first century B.C.E. and early second century C.E. The work survives in at least four Greek recensions and in several translations (including Latin, Syriac, Ethiopic, Slavonic, and Armenian). Although Jewish in origin, the book contains a few Christian interpolations. The book attempts to explain how it was that Joseph, the most righteous of all of the sons of Jacob, married Aseneth, the daughter of a heathen priest (cf. Gen 41:45). The reason that this book gives is that Aseneth rejected the idolatry of her father and people and came to place her faith in the God of the Hebrews. This aspect of *Joseph and Aseneth* sheds important light on views of proselyting in late antiquity. It moreover contains advocacy for forgiving one's enemies (cf. 28:12). The book narrates an exciting story of intrigue and adventure. After Pharaoh's son dies in an unsuccessful coup attempt (in which he had solicited the support of Dan and Gad), from which Pharaoh himself dies out of grief, Joseph becomes the ruler of Egypt and reigns 48 years.

Text: C. BURCHARD, "Ein vorläufiger griechischer Text von Joseph und Aseneth," *DBAT* 14 (1979): 4–19; 16 (1982): 37–39; A.-M. DENIS, *CGPAT* 851–59. *Survey:* C. BURCHARD, "Joseph und Aseneth," *JSHRZ* 2/4 (1983) 577–735; J. H. CHARLESWORTH, *PMR* 137–40, 291–92; R. D. CHESNUTT, "Joseph and Aseneth," *ABD* 3:969–71; L. DiTOMMASO, *BPR* 575–607; R. DORAN, "Narrative Literature," *EJMI* 290–93; W. KLASSEN, "Joseph and Aseneth," *DNTB* 588–89; G. W. E. NICKELSBURG, *JLBM* 258–63; IDEM, "Stories of Biblical and Early Post-biblical Times," *SJWSTP* 65–71; G. A. YEE, "Aseneth," *ABD* 1:476. *Commentary and Critical Study:* G. BOHAK, *Joseph and Aseneth and the Jewish Temple in Heliopolis* (SBLEJL 10; Atlanta: Scholars Press, 1996); C. BURCHARD, *Gesammelte Studien zu Joseph und Aseneth* (SVTP 13; New York: Brill, 1996); IDEM, "The Importance of Joseph and Aseneth for the Study of the New Testament," *NTS* 33 (1987): 102–34; IDEM, "Joseph and Aseneth," *OOT* 92–110; IDEM, "Joseph and Aseneth," *OTP* 2:177–247; IDEM, *Untersuchungen zu Joseph und Aseneth* (WUNT 8; Tübingen: Mohr [Siebeck], 1965); R. D. CHESNUTT, "The Social Setting and Purpose of Joseph and Aseneth," *JSP* 2 (1988): 21–48; D. COOK, "Joseph and Aseneth," *AOT* 465–503; T. HOLTZ, "Christliche Interpolationen in JA," *NTS* 14 (1967–1968): 482–97; E. M. HUMPHREY, *The Ladies and the Cities: Transformation and Apocalyptic Identity in Joseph and Aseneth* (JSPSup 17; Sheffield: Sheffield,

1995); H. C. KEE, "The Social-Cultural Setting of Joseph and Aseneth," *NTS* 29 (1983): 394–413; M. PHILONENKO, *Joseph et Asénath: Introduction, texte critique, traduction, et notes* (SPB 13; Leiden: Brill, 1968).

Life of Adam and Eve. The *Life of Adam and Eve* was composed in all probability in Hebrew, from which a Greek "Apocalypse of Moses" and a Latin "Life" were translated. These two versions contain differing materials and so probably should be understood as products of independent development. Since the so-called *Apocalypse of Moses* is really an account of the life of Adam and Eve, it is printed along with the Latin "Life" in *OTP*. The original Hebrew probably dates from first century B.C.E. or C.E., while the Greek and Latin versions derive from sometime between the second and fourth centuries.

Text: A.-M. DENIS, *CGPAT* 815–18 (Greek); IDEM, *CLPAT* 545–52 (Latin); W. MEYER, *Vita Adae et Evae* (Abhandlungen der königlich bayerischen Akademie der Wissenschaften: Philosophisch-philologisch Klasse 14; Munich: Verlag der königlich bayerischen Akademie der Wissenschaften, 1878), 221–50 (Latin). *Survey:* G. A. ANDERSON and M. E. STONE, *A Synopsis of the Books of Adam and Eve* (SBLEJL 17; Atlanta: Scholars Press, 1999); G. A. ANDERSON, M. E. STONE, and J. TROMP, *Literature on Adam and Eve* (SVTP 15; Leiden: Brill, 2000); J. H. CHARLESWORTH, *PMR* 74–75, 159–60, 273, 296; L. DITOMMASO, *BPR* 163–203; M. DE JONGE and J. TROMP, *The Life of Adam and Eve and Related Literature* (GAP; Sheffield: Sheffield, 1997); J. R. LEVISON, "Adam and Eve, Life of," *ABD* 1:64–66; IDEM, "Adam and Eve, Literature concerning," *DNTB* 1–6. **Commentary and Critical Study:** G. A. ANDERSON, "Adam and Eve in the 'Life of Adam and Eve,'" in *Biblical Figures outside the Bible* (ed. Stone and Bergren), 7–32; F. C. CONYBEARE, "On the Apocalypse of Moses," *JQR* 7 (1894–1895): 216–35; M. D. JOHNSON, "Life of Adam and Eve," *OTP* 2:249–95; S. T. LACHS, "Some Textual Observations on the Apocalypsis Mosis and the Vita Adae et Evae," *JSJ* 13 (1982): 172–76; J. R. LEVISON, "The Exoneration of Eve in the Apocalypse of Moses 15–30," *JSJ* 20 (1989): 135–30; O. MERK and M. MEISER, "Das Leben Adams und Evas," *JSHRZ* 2/5 (1998) 739–870; G. W. E. NICKELSBURG, "The Bible Rewritten and Expanded," *SJWSTP* 107–18; IDEM, *JLBM* 256–57; R. NIR, "The Aromatic Fragrances of Paradise in the *Greek Life of Adam and Eve* and the Christian Origin of the Composition," *NovT* 46 (2004): 20–45; J. L. SHARP, "The Second Adam in the Apocalypse of Moses," *CBQ* 35 (1973): 35–46 (draws comparisons between Paul and *Apocalypse of Moses*); L. S. A. WELLS, "The Books of Adam and Eve," *APOT* 2:123–54; M. WHITTAKER, "The Life of Adam and Eve," *AOT* 141–67.

Pseudo-Philo. Pseudo-Philo's *Liber antiquitatum biblicarum (Biblical Antiquities)* is a midrashic retelling of biblical history from Adam to David. Probably originally composed in Hebrew and later translated into Greek, the text survives in several Latin manuscripts. Pseudo-Philo may have been written as early as the first or even second century B.C.E., but most scholars favor a date toward the end of the first century C.E. Somewhere along the line this book came to be assigned to Philo Judaeus of Alexandria (see ch. 5), but there is little chance that he was its author; hence the title, "Pseudo-Philo." As with most haggadic midrash, Ps.-Philo, which bears an uncertain relation to the pseudepigraphal *Chronicles of Jerahmeel,* attempts to answer questions raised in the biblical narratives and to take the opportunities to put the various doctrines of early Judaism into the mouths of ancient biblical worthies. Comparing the author's method in retelling the biblical narratives is important for NT studies, particularly in Gospel studies.

Text: A.-M. DENIS, *CLPAT* 565–98; M. R. JAMES, *Apocrypha anecdota: A Collection of Thirteen Apocryphal Books and Fragments,* 164–85 (fragments). **Survey:** J. H. CHARLESWORTH, *PMR* 163, 170–73, 298; L. DiTOMMASO, *BPR* 765–84; L. H. FELDMAN, "Epilogomenon to Pseudo-Philo's *Liber antiquitatum biblicarum,*" *JJS* 25 (1974): 305–12; D. J. HARRINGTON, "Pseudo-Philo," *ABD* 5:344–45; IDEM, "Pseudo-Philo," *DNTB* 864–68; G. W. E. NICKELSBURG, "The Bible Rewritten and Expanded," *SJWSTP* 107–10; IDEM, *JLBM* 265–68. **Commentary and Critical Study:** R. J. BAUCKHAM, "The *Liber antiquitatum biblicarum* of Pseudo-Philo and the Gospels as 'Midrash,'" in *Studies in Midrash and Historiography* (ed. R. T. France and D. Wenham; Gospel Perspectives 3; Sheffield: JSOT Press, 1983), 33–76; C. DIETZFELBINGER, "Pseudo-Philo: Antiquitates biblicae," *JSHRZ* 2/2 (1975) 91–271; B. N. FISK, "One Good Story Deserves Another: The Hermeneutics of Invoking Secondary Biblical Episodes in the Narratives of *Pseudo-Philo* and the *Testaments of the Twelve Patriarchs,*" in *The Interpretation of Scripture in Early Judaism and Christianity* (ed. Evans), 217–38; D. J. HARRINGTON, "The Biblical Text of Pseudo-Philo's Liber antiquitatum biblicarum," *CBQ* 33 (1971): 1–17; IDEM, *The Hebrew Fragments of Pseudo-Philo's Liber antiquitatum biblicarum Preserved in the Chronicles of Jerahmeel* (SBLTT 3; Pseudepigrapha Series 3; Missoula and Cambridge: Society of Biblical Literature, 1974); IDEM, "Pseudo-Philo," *OTP* 2:297–377; IDEM, "Pseudo-Philo, *Liber antiquitatum biblicarum,*" *OOT* 6–25; D. J. HARRINGTON et al., *Pseudo-Philon: Les Antiquités bibliques;* SC 229; Paris: Cerf, 1976): vol. 1, *Introduction et texte critiques, traduction,* vol. 2, *Introduction littéraire, commentaire, et index;* H. JACOBSON, *A Commentary on Pseudo-Philo's Liber antiquitatum biblicarum, with Latin Text and English Translation* (2 vols.; AGJU 31; Leiden: Brill, 1996); F. J. MURPHY, *Pseudo-Philo: Rewriting the Bible* (Oxford: Oxford University Press, 1993); E. REINMUTH, *Pseudo-Philo und Lukas: Studien zum Liber antiquitatum biblicarum und seiner Bedeutung für die Interpretation des lukanischen Doppelwerkes* (WUNT 74; Tübingen: Mohr [Siebeck], 1994).

Lives of the Prophets. The *Lives of the Prophets* (or *Vitae prophetarum*) is a first-century C.E. document that summarizes the key teachings and events in the lives of most of Israel's prophets: Isaiah, Jeremiah, Ezekiel, Daniel, Hosea, Micah, Amos, Joel, Obadiah, Jonah, Nahum, Habakkuk, Zephaniah, Haggai, Zechariah, Malachi, Nathan (2 Sam 7, 11), Ahijah (1 Kgs 11–12), Joad (1 Kgs 13), Azariah (2 Chr 15), Elijah (1 Kgs 17; 2 Kgs 1–2), Elisha (1 Kgs 19; 2 Kgs 2, 4–6, 13), Zechariah (2 Chr 24). The four "major prophets" receive the greatest attention, while Jonah (who is the youth saved by Elijah!), Habakkuk (cf. Bel 33–39), Elijah, and Elisha also figure prominently. Much of the material is legendary and midrashic in nature. Although many once believed that *Lives* was originally composed in Hebrew, the evidence now seems to point to Greek. There are also Latin, Syriac, Ethiopic, Armenian, and Arabic versions. The designation of Moses as "God's chosen one" (2:14) could be significant, for that is a messianic designation in Luke (23:35) as well.

Text: E. A. W. BUDGE, *The Book of the Bee* (AnOx: Semitic Series 1/2; Oxford: Clarendon, 1886), 69–79 (Syriac); A.-M. DENIS, *CGPAT* 868–71 (Greek); I. GUIDI, E. W. BROOKS, and

I.-B. CHABOT, *Chronica minora II* (6 vols.; CSCO 1–6; ScrSyr 3; Paris: E Typographeo Reipublicae, 1904; repr., Leuven: Peeters, 1965), 160–65 (Latin); E. NESTLE, "Die dem Epiphanius zugeschriebenen Vitae prophetarum in doppelter griechischer Rezension," in *Marginalien und Materialen* (2 vols.; Tübingen: J. J. Heckenhauer, 1893), 2:1–64 (Greek); T. SCHERMANN, *Prophetarum vitae fabulosae: Indices apostolorum discipulorumque Domini, Dorotheo, Epiphanio, Hippolyto aliisque vindicata* (Leipzig: Teubner, 1907) (Greek); C. C. TORREY, *The Lives of the Prophets*, 20–32. *Survey:* J. H. CHARLESWORTH, *PMR* 175–77, 299; L. DiTOMMASO, *BPR* 755–63; D. R. A. HARE, "The Lives of the Prophets," *DNTB* 652–54; IDEM, "Prophets, Lives of," *ABD* 5:502–3; D. SATRAN, "Lives of the Prophets," *SJWSTP* 56–60. *Commentary and Critical Study:* D. R. A. HARE, "The Lives of the Prophets," *OTP* 2:379–99; D. SATRAN, *Biblical Prophets in Byzantine Palestine: Reassessing the "Lives of the Prophets"* (SVTP 11; Leiden: Brill, 1995); A. M. SCHWEMER, *Studien zu den frühjüdischen Prophetenlegenden: Vitae prophetarum* (2 vols.; TSAJ 49–50; Tübingen: Mohr [Siebeck], 1995–96); IDEM, "Vitae prophetarum," *JSHRZ* 1/7 (1997) 539–658; C. C. TORREY, *The Lives of the Prophets*.

Ladder of Jacob. The *Ladder of Jacob* was composed by a Jew in the first century C.E., but now survives only in Slavonic (unless the Hebrew *Prayer of Jacob* is related). It is possible that it was originally Hebrew, but it is more likely that it was written in Greek by a Jew who also knew Hebrew and assumed that readers would also know Hebrew. The purpose of the book is to emphasize the sovereignty of God. The story has been inspired by Gen 28:12–14, especially verse 13.

Text: R. LEICHT, "*Qedushah* and Prayer to Helios: A New Hebrew Version of an Apocryphal Prayer of Jacob," *JSQ* 6 (1999): 140–76; I. PORFIRIJEV, *Apokrificheskiia skazaniia o vetkhosavietnykh litsakh* (St. Petersburg: St. Petersburg University Press, 1877), 138–49 (Slavonic); P. SCHÄFER and S. SHAKED, *Magische Texte aus der Kairoer Geniza* (TSAJ 64; Tübingen: Mohr [Siebeck], 1997), 27–78 (Hebrew version of *Prayer of Jacob*); N. S. TIKHONRAVOV, *Pamiatniki otrechennoi russkoi literatury*, 1:91–95 (Slavonic). *Survey:* J. H. CHARLESWORTH, "Jacob, Ladder of," *ABD* 3:609; IDEM, *PMR* 130–31, 290; A. Y. COLLINS, "Christian Apocalypses," *Semeia* 14 (1979): 61–121, esp. 69–70; L. DiTOMMASO, *BPR* 553–56. *Commentary and Critical Study:* J. KUGEL, "The Ladder of Jacob," *HTR* 88 (1995): 209–27; H. G. LUNT, "Ladder of Jacob," *OTP* 2:401–11; A. PENNINGTON, "The Ladder of Jacob," *AOT* 453–63.

4 Baruch. Fourth Baruch, or *Paraleipomena Jeremiou (Omissions of Jeremiah),* was composed in either the final years of the first century or in the early second century C.E. Extant in several versions (including Greek, Ethiopic, Slavonic, and Armenian), *4 Baruch* is dependent on *2 Baruch* and probably was originally composed in Hebrew. The original author was Jewish, but the text contains at least one lengthy Christian interpolation (8:12–9:32). Other interpolations probably include 6:7, 13, 25. In the story the righteous Abimelech falls asleep after gathering figs. Upon waking (a feature that the author interprets as evidence for the resurrection) he discovers that 66 years have elapsed. Babylon has destroyed Jerusalem and has carried off its inhabitants into captivity. He learns, however, that soon God's people will be able to return. *Fourth Baruch* teaches that the holy vessels from the temple survived the temple's destruction and that someday they will be used again when the temple is restored. The *Apocryphon Jeremiae,* which concerns the Babylonian captivity, is "a later modification of 4 Baruch" (Charlesworth, *PMR* 89).

Text: A.-M. DENIS, *CGPAT* 863–65 (Greek); J. R. HARRIS, *The Rest of the Words of Baruch: A Christian Apocalypse of the Year 136 A.D.* (Haverford College Studies 2; Cambridge: Cambridge University Press, 1889) (Greek); R. A. KRAFT and A.-E. PURINTUN, *Paraleipomena Jeremiou,* 12–48 (Greek). ***Survey:*** J. H. CHARLESWORTH, *PMR* 88–91, 275–76; L. DITOMMASO, *BPR* 557–58; R. DORAN, "Narrative Literature," *EJMI* 294–96; R. A. KRAFT and A.-E. PURINTUN, *Paraleipomena Jeremiou,* 7–10 (annotated bibliography); G. W. E. NICKELSBURG, *JLBM* 313–16; IDEM, "Stories of Biblical and Early Post-biblical Times," *SJWSTP* 72–75; S. E. ROBINSON, "Baruch, Book of 4," *ABD* 1:622. ***Commentary and Critical Study:*** J. HERZER, "Direction in Difficult Times: How God Is Understood in the Paralipomena Jeremiae," *JSP* 22 (2000): 9–30; IDEM, *Die Paralipomena Jeremiae: Studien zu Tradition und Redaktion einer Haggada des frühen Judentums* (TSAJ 43; Tübingen: Mohr [Siebeck], 1994); G. W. E. NICKELSBURG, "Narrative Traditions in the Paralipomena of Jeremiah and 2 Baruch," *CBQ* 35 (1973): 60–68; J. RIAUD, "The Figure of Jeremiah in the Paralipomena Jeremiae prophetae: His originality, His 'Christianization' by the Christian Author of the Conclusion (9.10–32)," *JSP* 22 (2000): 31–44; IDEM, "*Paralipomena Jeremiou,*" *OOT* 213–30; S. E. ROBINSON, "4 Baruch," *OTP* 2:413–25; B. SCHALLER, "Is the Greek Version of the Paralipomena Jeremiou Original or a Translation?" *JSP* 22 (2000): 51–89; IDEM, "Paralipomena Jeremiou," *JSHRZ* 1/8 (1998) 661–777; IDEM, "Paralipomena Jeremiou: Annotated Bibliography in Historical Order," *JSP* 22 (2000): 91–118; R. THORNHILL, "The Paraleipomena of Jeremiah," *AOT* 813–33.

Jannes and Jambres. *Jannes and Jambres* was composed in Greek by a Jew sometime in the first or second century. A brief quotation of this work is found in Philostorgius, *Hist. eccl.* 9.2. The legendary figures Jannes and Jambres were thought to have been two of Pharaoh's magicians who opposed Moses. This tradition is alluded to in 2 Tim 3:8–9. In *Targum Pseudo-Jonathan* they interpret a dream of Pharaoh in which Moses' birth is predicted (*Tg. Ps.-J.* Exod 1:15), and they later reappear as Balaam's helpers (*Tg. Ps.-J.* Num 22:22). In his commentary on Matthew (on Matt 27:9) Origen (third century) refers to an apocryphal book entitled the *Book of Jannes and Jambres.* Other ancient authors knew of these magicians. It seems clear that there was such a book in late antiquity, but only Greek and Latin fragments of it have survived. Of interest is Jannes's return from the dead through necromancy to warn his brother Jambres of the consequences of evil.

Text: A.-M. DENIS, *CGPAT* 902; IDEM, *FPSG* 69; M. R. JAMES, "A Fragment of the 'Penitence of Jannes and Jambres,'" *JTS* 2 (1900–1901): 572–77. ***Survey:*** J. H. CHARLESWORTH, *PMR* 133–34, 291; L. DITOMMASO, *BPR* 559–63; A. PIETERSMA, "Jannes and Jambres," *ABD* 3:638–40. ***Commentary and Critical Study:*** S. GERO, "Parerga to 'The Book of Jannes and Jambres,'" *JSP* 9 (1991): 67–85; L. L. GRABBE, "The Jannes/Jambrews Tradition in Targum Pseudo-Jonathan and Its Date," *JBL* 98 (1979): 393–401; P. MARAVAL, "Fragments grecs du Livre de Jannès et Jambré (Pap. Vindob. 29456 et 29828 Verso)," *ZPE* 25 (1977): 199–207; M. MCNAMARA, *The New Testament and the Palestinian Targum to the Pentateuch,* 82–96; A. PIETERSMA, "The Apocryphon of Jannes and Jambres," in *Congress Volume: Leuven, 1989* (ed. J. A. Emerton; VTSup 43; Leiden: Brill, 1991), 383–95; IDEM,

The Apocryphon of Jannes and Jambres the Magicians: P. Chester Beatty XVI (with New Editions of Papyrus Vindoonensis Greek inv. 29456 + 29828 verso and British Library Cotton Tiberius B v.f. 87) Edited, with Introduction, Translation, and Commentary (RGRW 119; Leiden: Brill, 1994); A. PIETERSMA and R. T. LUTZ, "Jannes and Jambres," *OTP* 2:427–36.

History of the Rechabites. The *History of the Rechabites* (variously titled *Narrative of Zosimus, Apocalypse of Zosimus, Testament of Zosimus, Abode of the Blessed, History of the Son of Jonadab,* and *Son of Rechab*) was probably composed in Hebrew or Aramaic, with Greek being the oldest translation. The original author was probably Jewish, writing (chs. 3–15) sometime in the first or second centuries, while later Christians added to it (chs. 1–2, 16, 19–23) in the third and fourth (and possibly later) centuries. The book is a story of a righteous man named Zosimus whose request to visit the abode of the "Blessed Ones" is finally granted. He is transported over the ocean to an island that resembles Paradise where the Blessed Ones live. They identify themselves as the Rechabites who had left Jerusalem in the time of Jeremiah (Jer 35) and describe to the visitor the secrets of death and soul ascent. The comment that "the Spirit of God is greater than wine" (*Hist. Rech.* 1:4) might be compared to Eph 5:18 ("Do not get drunk with wine . . . but be filled with the Spirit").

Text: J. H. CHARLESWORTH, *The Greek Recension,* 14–106; M. R. JAMES, *Apocrypha anecdota: A Collection of Thirteen Apocryphal Books and Fragments,* 96–108 (Greek). *Survey:* J. H. CHARLESWORTH, *PMR* 223–26, 299–300; IDEM, "Rechabites, History of," *ABD* 5:632–33; L. DiTOMMASO, *BPR* 982–93; C. H. KNIGHTS, "A Century of Research into the Story/Apocalypse of Zosimus and/or the History of the Rechabites," *JSP* 15 (1997): 53–66. *Commentary and Critical Study:* J. H. CHARLESWORTH, "Greek, Persian, Roman, Syrian, and Egyptian Influences in Early Jewish Theology: A Study of the History of the Rechabites," in *Hellenica et judaica: Hommage à Valentin Nikiprowetzky* (ed. A. Caquot et al.; CREJ 3; Leuven: Peeters, 1986), 219–43; IDEM, *The Greek Recension,* 1–10; IDEM, "History of the Rechabites," *OTP* 2:443–61; C. H. KNIGHTS, "The *Abode of the Blessed:* A Source of the *Story of Zosimus*?" *JSP* 17 (1998): 79–93; IDEM, "The History of the Rechabites—an Initial Commentary," *JSJ* 28 (1997): 413–36; IDEM, "'The Story of Zosimus' or 'The History of the Rechabites'?" *JSJ* 24 (1993): 235–45; IDEM, "Towards a Critical Introduction to 'The History of the Rechabites,'" *JSJ* 26 (1995): 324–42; IDEM, "Who were the Rechabites?" *ExpTim* 107 (1996): 137–40; B. MCNEIL, "The Narrative of Zosimus," *JSJ* 9 (1978): 68–82.

Eldad and Modad. Eldad and Modad (or *Medad)* was probably composed in either Hebrew or Greek before the writing of the Shepherd of Hermas (second century C.E.). Whether it is Jewish or Christian is impossible to determine. All that survives is one sentence, quoted in Hermas (Herm. *Vis.* 2.3.4; cf. Lake): "'The Lord is near to those who turn [to him],' as it is written in the [book of] Eldad and Modad, who prophesied in the desert to the people." The book apparently was based on Num 11:26–29 which tells of two prophets, Eldad and Medad. "According to rabbinic sources, the contents of the Book of Eldad and Modad apparently contained references to Gog and Magog, the end of time, and the coming of a royal Messiah" (Martin, *OTP* 2:463). This is certainly the case in the *Fragmentary Targum* to Num 11:26, in which the prophecy of Eldad and Modad is recast as an apocalypse predicting Messiah's victory at the end of time: "At the end of days Gog and Magog will ascend against Jerusalem and by the hands of Messiah they will fall."

Text: A.-M. DENIS, *FPSG* 68; IDEM, *CGPAT* 901–2; K. LAKE, *The Apostolic Fathers* (2 vols.; LCL 24–25; Cambridge: Harvard University Press, 1912–1913), 2:22–23. *Survey:* J. H. CHARLESWORTH, "Eldad and Modad," *ABD* 2:431; IDEM, *PMR* 94–95, 277; L. DITOMMASO, *BPR* 337–39. *Commentary and Critical Study:* V. BARTLETT, "The Prophecy of Eldad and Modad, and the Legend of Jannes and Jambres," *IJA* 45 (1916): 22–24; F. BÖHL, "Demut und Prophetie: Eldad und Medad nach der frühen rabbinischen Überlieferung," in *Ich bewirke das Heil und erschaffe das Unheil (Jesaja 45,7): Studien zur Botschaft der Propheten* (ed. F. Diedrich and B. Willmes; FB 88; Würzburg: Echter, 1998), 15–30; R. LE DÉAUT, *Nombres* (vol. 3 of *Targum du Pentateuque;* SC 261; Paris: Cerf, 1979), 110–11; S. Z. LEIMAN, "Inverted *nuns* at Numbers 10:35–36 and the Book of Eldad and Medad," *JBL* 93 (1974): 348–55; E. G. MARTIN, "Eldad and Modad," *OTP* 2:463–65; M. MCNAMARA, *The New Testament and the Palestinian Targum to the Pentateuch,* 235–37.

History of Joseph. The *History of Joseph* was composed originally in Greek, probably before 400 C.E., and seems to be a midrashic expansion of Gen 41:39–42:36. The text is preserved only in fragments. There are also Ethiopic, Arabic, and Coptic versions. As in *Joseph and Aseneth* (29:9), Joseph is referred to as "king" of Egypt.

Text: A.-M. DENIS, *CGPAT* 924; IDEM, *FPSG* 235–36; F. G. KENYON et al., eds., *Greek Papyri in the British Museum* (7 vols.; London: British Museum, 1893–1974), 1:225–27; H. J. M. MILNE, *Catalogue of the Literary Papyri in the British Museum* (London: British Museum, 1927), 127–30. *Survey:* J. H. CHARLESWORTH, *PMR* 138, 293; L. DITOMMASO, *BPR* 609–10; G. T. ZERVOS, "History of Joseph," *ABD* 3:973–74. *Commentary and Critical Study:* J. DOCHHORN and A. K. PETERSEN, "Narratio Ioseph: A Coptic-Joseph Apocryphon," *JSJ* 30 (1999): 431–63; E. ISAAC, "The Ethiopic History of Joseph: Translation with Introduction and Notes," *JSP* 6 (1990): 3–125; G. T. ZERVOS, "History of Joseph," *OTP* 2:467–75.

Part Four: Wisdom and Philosophical Literature

Ahiqar. The story (or "Words") of *Ahiqar* was composed originally in Aramaic sometime in the seventh or sixth century B.C.E. Thus it is by far the oldest item in the Pseudepigrapha. It is extant in several other languages, including Egyptian Demotic, Syriac, Armenian, Arabic, Ethiopic, Slavonic, and Turkish. *Ahiqar* is an instance of the wisdom genre and teaches that the guilty will be found out and the righteous will be vindicated. The story tells of Ahiqar the sage who adopts his nephew Nadin and raises him as his own son. When Nadin succeeds his adopted father as counselor to King Esarhaddon, the young man falsely accuses the aged sage of a plot to overthrow the king. Nadin's scheme, however, is foiled, Ahiqar is reconciled to the king, and Nadin is put in irons and sternly lectured, after which he swells up and bursts.

Text: A. E. COWLEY, *Aramaic Papyri of the Fifth Century B.C.* (Oxford: Clarendon, 1923), 204–48 (Aramaic); A.-M. DENIS, *CGPAT* 907–8; IDEM, *FPSG* 133–48 (Greek); J. R. HARRIS, F. C. CONYBEARE, and A. S. LEWIS, *The Story of Ahikar* (2d ed.; Cambridge: Cambridge

University Press, 1913) (Syriac, Armenian, Aramaic, Old Turkish; parallels with Aesop). *Survey:* J. H. CHARLESWORTH, *PMR* 75–77, 273; L. DiTOMMASO, *BPR* 220–37; J. A. LUND, "Ahiqar," *DNTB* 18–19; J. C. VANDERKAM, "Ahikar/Ahiqar," *ABD* 1:113–15. *Commentary and Critical Study:* J. C. GREENFIELD, "Ahiqar in the Book of Tobit," in *De la Tôrah au Messie* (ed. M. Carrez et al.; Paris: Desclée, 1981), 329–36; J. R. HARRIS et al., "The Story of Ahiqar," *APOT* 2:715–84; I. KOTTSIEPER, "Die Geschichte und die Sprüche des weisen Achiqar," *TUAT* 3/2 (1991): 320–47; IDEM, *Die Sprache der Ahiqarsprüche* (BZAW 194; New York: de Gruyter, 1990); J. M. LINDENBERGER, "Ahiqar," *OTP* 2:479–507; IDEM, *The Aramaic Proverbs of Ahiqar* (Baltimore: Johns Hopkins University Press, 1983).

3 Maccabees. Third Maccabees was written originally in Greek in the first century C.E. It is also extant in Syriac and Armenian. It is a Jewish composition that tells of Ptolemy IV Philopator's (221–204 B.C.E.) persecution of the Jews in Alexandria (out of anger of his being refused entry into the Holy Place of the temple of Jerusalem), a persecution that is thwarted by divine intervention. The prayers of the devout Eleazar finally bring about a change in the king, who now orders an end to the persecutions and a seven-day feast of celebration at his expense. Since the book has nothing to do with the Maccabean period, its title is really a misnomer. The purpose of the writing is probably to encourage Jews to remain faithful to their religious customs.

Text: R. HANHART, *Maccabaeorum liber III* (Septuaginta 9/3; Göttingen: Vandenhoeck & Ruprecht, 1960). *Survey:* H. ANDERSON, "Maccabees, Books of: Third Maccabees," *ABD* 4:450–52; J. H. CHARLESWORTH, *PMR* 149–51, 295; D. A. DESILVA, "3 and 4 Maccabees," *DNTB* 661–66; IDEM, *IAMCS* 304–22; L. DiTOMMASO, *BPR* 673–91; D. J. HARRINGTON, *InvA* 173–84; G. W. E. NICKELSBURG, *JLBM* 169–72; IDEM, "Stories of Biblical and Early Post-biblical Times," *SJWSTP* 80–84; J. C. VANDERKAM, *An Introduction to Early Judaism,* 78–81. *Commentary and Critical Study:* P. S. ALEXANDER, "3 Maccabees," *ECB* 865–75; H. ANDERSON, "3 Maccabees," *OTP* 2:509–29; J. J. COLLINS, "3 Maccabees," *HBC* 916–21; C. W. EMMET, "The Third Book of Maccabees," *APOT* 1:156–73; M. HADAS, *The Third and Fourth Books of Maccabees* (JAL; New York: Harper, 1953), 1–85; B. M. METZGER, "The Third Book of the Maccabees," *OAA* 294–308; J. TROMP, "The Formation of the Third Book of Maccabees," *Hen* 17 (1995): 311–28; D. S. WILLIAMS, "3 Maccabees: A Defense of Diaspora Judaism?" *JSP* 13 (1995): 17–29.

4 Maccabees. Fourth Maccabees was composed originally in Greek in the first century C.E. Like 3 Maccabees, its name is a misnomer, for it has nothing to do with the Maccabean period (though reference to the martyrdoms of Eleazar and the seven sons and their mother [2 Macc 6:18–7:42] is no doubt what gave the book its title). Instead, it is a philosophical treatise that attempts to show in terms of Greek philosophy that the Jewish faith is the true religion. The book teaches that martyrdom is a substitutionary atonement that expiates the sins of the nation (1:11; 6:27–29 ["Make my blood their purification, and take my life in exchange for theirs"]; 17:21; 18:14).

Text: A. RAHLFS, ed., *Septuaginta* (2 vols.; Stuttgart: Wüttembergische Bibelanstalt, 1935; repr., 1971), 1:1157–84. *Survey:* H. ANDERSON, "Maccabees, Books of: Fourth Maccabees,"

ABD 4:452–54; J. H. CHARLESWORTH, *PMR* 151–53, 295–96; D. A. DESILVA, "3 and 4 Maccabees," *DNTB* 661–66; IDEM, *4 Maccabees* (GAP; Sheffield: Sheffield, 1998); IDEM, *IAMCS* 352–79; L. DITOMMASO, *BPR* 693–715; D. J. HARRINGTON, *InvA* 207–18; B. L. MACK, "Wisdom Literature," *EJMI* 396–98; G. W. E. NICKELSBURG, *JLBM* 223–27. *Commentary and Critical Study:* H. ANDERSON, "4 Maccabees," *OTP* 2:531–64; D. E. AUNE, "Mastery of the Passions: Philo, 4 Maccabees, and Earliest Christianity," in *Hellenization Revisited: Shaping a Christian Response within the Greco-Roman World* (ed. W. E. Helleman; Lanham, Md.: University Press of America, 1994), 125–58; D. A. DESILVA, "4 Maccabees," *ECB* 888–901; IDEM, "The Noble Contest: Honor, Shame, and the Rhetorical Strategy of 4 Maccabees," *JSP* 13 (1995): 31–57; M. GILBERT, "Wisdom Literature," *SJWSTP* 316–19; M. HADAS, *The Third and Fourth Books of Maccabees* (New York: Harper, 1953), 91–243; H.-J. KLAUCK, "Brotherly Love in Plutarch and in 4 Maccabees," in *Greeks, Romans, and Christians: Essays in honor of Abraham J. Malherbe* (ed. D. L. Balch et al.; Minneapolis: Fortress, 1990), 144–56; B. M. METZGER, "The Fourth Book of the Maccabees," *OAA* 309–29; S. D. MOORE and J. C. ANDERSON, "Taking It like a Man: Masculinity in 4 Maccabees," *JBL* 117 (1998): 249–73; P. D. REDDITT, "The Concept of *nomos* in Fourth Maccabees," *CBQ* 45 (1983): 249–70; S. K. STOWERS, "4 Maccabees," *HBC* 922–34; J. W. VAN HENTEN, *The Maccabean Martyrs as Saviours of the Jewish People: A Study of 2 and 4 Maccabees* (JSJSup 57; Leiden: Brill, 1997).

Pseudo-Phocylides. Pseudo-Phocylides was originally composed in Greek sometime in the first century B.C.E. The author of this poem claims to be Phocylides, an Ionic poet who lived in Miletus in the sixth century B.C.E. The real author was likely a Jew who wished to show that Jewish ethics had been taught long ago by a respected gentile ethicist.

Text: A.-M. DENIS, *CGPAT* 909–10; IDEM, *FPSG* 149–56; D. YOUNG AND E. DIEHL, eds., *Theognis, Pseudo-Pythagorus, Pseudo-Phocylides, Chares, Anonymi aulodia, fragmentum teliambicum* (Leipzig: Teubner, 1961), 95–112. *Survey:* J. H. CHARLESWORTH, *PMR* 173–75, 298–99; K. D. CLARK, "Pseudo-Phocylides," *DNTB* 868–69; L. DITOMMASO, *BPR* 785–91; M. GILBERT, "Wisdom Literature," *SJWSTP* 313–16; P. W. VAN DER HORST, "Phocylides, Pseudo-," *ABD* 5:347–48; B. L. MACK, "Wisdom Literature," *EJMI* 395–96. *Commentary and Critical Study:* J. J. COLLINS, *Jewish Wisdom in the Hellenistic Age* (Louisville: Westminster John Knox, 1997), 158–77; P. DERRON, *Les sentences du Pseudo-Phocylide: Texte, traduction, commentaire* (Paris: Les Belles Lettres, 1986); P. W. VAN DER HORST, "Pseudo-Phocylides," *OTP* 2:565–82; IDEM, "Pseudo-Phocylides and the New Testament," *ZNW* 69 (1978): 187–202; IDEM, "Pseudo-Phocylides Revisited," *JSP* 3 (1988): 3–30; IDEM, *The Sentences of Pseudo-Phocylides: Introduction, Translation, and Commentary* (SVTP 4; Leiden: Brill, 1978); J. THOMAS, *Der jüdische Phokylides: Formgeschichtliche Zugänge zu Pseudo-Phokylides und Vergleich mit der neutestamentlichen Paränese* (NTOA 23; Göttingen: Vandenhoeck & Ruprecht, 1992); N. WALTER, "Pseudepigraphische jüdisch-hellenistische Dichtung," 173–276, esp. 182–216.

The Sentences of the Syriac Menander. The *Sentences of the Syriac Menander* was originally composed in Syriac in the third century C.E. However, it is quite likely that the author availed himself of a Greek anthology of sayings. It is a wisdom work that seeks to give people practical guidance for living. The author holds to a high view of God and is thus a monotheist, possibly a Jew.

Text: J. P. N. LAND, *Anecdota syriaca* (4 vols.; Leiden: Brill, 1862), vol. 1, 64.21–73.18; E. SACHAU, *Inedita syriaca: Eine Sammlung syrischer Übersetzungen von Schriften griechischer Profanliteratur* (Vienna: K. K. Hof-und Staatsdruckerei, 1870), 80.1–81.10. *Survey:* T. BAARDA, "Syriac Menander," *ABD* 6:281–82; J. H. CHARLESWORTH, *PMR* 158–59, 296; L. DiTOMMASO, *BPR* 727–29. *Commentary and Critical Study:* T. BAARDA, "The Sentences of the Syriac Menander," *OTP* 2:583–606; A. KIRK, "The Composed Life of the *Syriac Menander*," *SR* 26 (1997): 169–83; K. TREU, "Aspekte Menanders," *Kairos* 19 (1977): 22–34.

Part Five: Prayers, Psalms, and Odes

More Psalms of David. There are extant five Syriac psalms beyond the 150 of the MT (for Syriac texts, see Baars). Thanks to the discovery of the Dead Sea Scrolls, we now have another six psalms. Psalm 151 was originally written in Hebrew, possibly at Qumran (=11QPs^a). There are two versions of this psalm (151A and 151B, of which most of the second is lost). It tells of David's defeat of Goliath. Psalm 152 is extant only in Syriac, but may have been composed originally in Hebrew by a Palestinian Jew sometime in the first two or three centuries B.C.E. It describes David's cry for help in fighting the lion and wolf. Psalm 153 is also extant only in Syriac, but probably was originally composed in Hebrew by a Palestinian Jew sometime in the last two or three centuries B.C.E. It describes David's thanks for being delivered from the lion and wolf. Psalm 154 was written originally in Hebrew, a version of which is preserved at Qumran (11QPs^a = 11Q5). It is also extant in Syriac. It is probably second century B.C.E. It is a call to praise God. Psalm 155 was composed in Hebrew and is also extant in 11QPs^a and in Syriac. (NB: Syriac Psalms I–III = Psalms 151, 154, and 155.) It purports to be Hezekiah's cry for help when the Assyrians had surrounded Jerusalem. For these and other apocryphal psalms attested at Qumran, see chapter 3 below.

Text: W. BAARS, "Apocryphal Psalms," in *The Old Testament in Syriac according to the Peshitta Version*, part 4, fasc. 6 (Syriac); J. H. CHARLESWORTH ed., *DSSP* 4A:162–69 (Ps 151), 170–77 (Ps 154), 178–85 (Ps 155); F. GARCÍA MARTÍNEZ and E. J. C. TIGCHELAAR, *4Q274–11Q31* (vol. 2 of *The Dead Sea Scrolls Study Edition;* Leiden: Brill, 1998), 1172–74 (Ps 154), 1176 (Ps 155), 1178 (Ps 151); J. A. SANDERS, *The Psalms Scroll of Qumran Cave 11 (11QPs^a)*, 54–64 (Ps 151), 64–70 (Ps 154), 70–76 (Ps 155). *Survey:* J. H. CHARLESWORTH, *PMR* 202–9, 304; L. DiTOMMASO, *BPR* 901–18; S. C. PIGUÉ, "Psalms, Syriac (Apocryphal)," *ABD* 5:536–37. *Commentary and Critical Study:* J. H. CHARLESWORTH and J. A. SANDERS, "More Psalms of David," *OTP* 2:609–24; P. W. FLINT, *The Dead Sea Psalms Scrolls and the Book of Psalms* (STDJ 17; Leiden: Brill, 1997), 243–51; D. J. HARRINGTON, "Psalm 151," *HBC* 935–36; J. MAGNE, "Recherches sur les Psaumes 151, 154, et 155," *RevQ* 8 (1972–1975): 503–8; B. M. METZGER, "Psalm 151," *OAA* 330–31; A. SALVESEN, "Psalm 151," *ECB* 862–64; J. A. SANDERS, *The Dead Sea Psalms Scroll* (Ithaca, N.Y.: Cornell University Press, 1967); IDEM, *The Psalms Scroll of Qumran Cave 11 (11QPs^a);* IDEM, "Two Non-canonical Psalms in 11QPs^a," *ZAW* 76 (1964): 57–75; J. STRUGNELL, "Notes on the Text and Transmission of the Apocryphal Psalms 151, 154 (= Syr. II), and 155 (= Syr. III)," *HTR* 59 (1966): 257–81.

Prayer of Manasseh. Although part of the Apocrypha—that part that did not gain entry into the Catholic Bible at Trent in 1546—*OTP* places the Prayer of Manasseh in the Pseudepigrapha because of its pseudonymity. Inspired by 2 Chr 33:11–13, this document purports to be the prayer of repentance uttered by King Manasseh after his exile. It was probably composed originally in Greek (though several scholars are convinced that the original was Semitic) sometime in the first or second century B.C.E. See comments and bibliography in chapter 1 above.

Psalms of Solomon. The *Psalms of Solomon* is a collection of eighteen Hebrew psalms written around 50 B.C.E., probably in response to the Roman takeover a few years earlier. They are now extant in several Greek and Syriac manuscripts. The *Psalms* have had little influence on the NT. Major themes would include: (1) anticipation of fulfillment of promises (12:7), the coming of Messiah/King (17:21–18:9), who would rule by the power of God (17:37); (2) the "Conqueror" who is probably Pompey (63 B.C.E.; 17:14; 8:18–21); (3) sexual sin, which is viewed as particularly offensive; and (4) the "righteous" who are the Pharisees, while the "sinners" are the Sadducees. Traditionally it has been believed that the *Psalms* were composed by a Pharisee or Pharisaic group. Wright (1972), however, has called this conclusion into question.

Text: W. BAARS, "Psalms of Solomon," in *The Old Testament in Syriac according to the Peshitta Version,* part 4, fasc. 6, pp. 1–27 (Syriac); A.-M. DENIS, *CGPAT* 859–62 (Greek); O. VON GEBHARDT, Ψαλμοὶ Σολομῶντος: *Die Psalmen Salomo's, zum ersten Male mit Benutzung der Athoshandschriften und des Codex Casanatensis herausgegeben* (TU 13/2; Leipzig: Hinrichs, 1895) (Greek); H. E. RYLE and M. R. JAMES, Ψαλμοὶ Σολομῶντος— *Psalms of the Pharisees, Commonly Called the Psalms of Solomon,* 2–153 (Greek); H. B. SWETE, *The Psalms of Solomon with the Greek Fragments of the Book of Enoch* (Old Testament in Greek 3; Cambridge: Cambridge University Press, 1899), 1–23 (Greek). **Survey:** J. H. CHARLESWORTH, "Jewish Hymns, Odes, and Prayers," *EJMI* 415–16; IDEM, *PMR* 195–97, 303–4; L. DITOMMASO, *BPR* 873–93; D. FLUSSER, "Psalms, Hymns, and Prayers," *SJWSTP* 573–74; M. LATTKE, "Psalms of Solomon," *DNTB* 853–57; G. W. E. NICKELSBURG, *JLBM* 203–12; J. L. TRAFTON, "Solomon, Psalms of," *ABD* 6:115–17; J. C. VANDERKAM, *An Introduction to Early Judaism,* 128–32. **Commentary and Critical Study:** K. R. ATKINSON, "On the Use of Scripture in the Development of Militant Davidic Messianism at Qumran: New Light from *Psalm of Solomon 17,*" in *The Interpretation of Scripture in Early Judaism and Christianity* (ed. Evans), 106–23; S. P. BROCK, "The Psalms of Solomon," *AOT* 649–82; G. B. GRAY, "The Psalms of Solomon," *APOT* 2:625–52; J. R. HARRIS, *The Odes and Psalms of Solmon;* J. R. HARRIS and A. MINGANA, *The Odes and Psalms of Solomon,* vol. 2; S. HOLM-NIELSEN, "Die Psalmen Salomos," *JSHRZ* 4/2 (1977) 49–112; M. DE JONGE, "The Psalms of Solomon," *OOT* 159–77; H. E. RYLE and M. R. JAMES, Ψαλμοὶ Σολομῶντος— *Psalms of the Pharisees, Commonly Called the Psalms of Solomon;* J. L. TRAFTON, *The Syriac Version of the Psalms of Solomon: A Critical Evaluation* (SBLSCS 11; Atlanta: Scholars Press, 1985); R. B. WRIGHT, "Psalms of Solomon," *OTP* 2:639–70; IDEM, "The Psalms of Solomon, the Pharisees, and the Essenes," in *1972 Proceedings: International Organization for Septuagint and Cognate Studies and the Society of Biblical Literature Pseudepigrapha Seminar* (ed. R. A. Kraft; SCS 2; Missoula, Mont.: Society of Biblical Literature, 1972), 136–47.

Hellenistic Synagogal Prayers. Sixteen *Hellenistic Synagogal Prayers* are found "scattered among the Christian liturgy Books Seven and Eight of the *Apostolic Constitutions*" (D. A. Fiensy, *OTP* 2:671). There is no evidence that would suggest that these prayers were written in any language other than Greek, the language of the *Constitutions*. Because many of these prayers contain nothing distinctively Christian, or when they do, it usually has the appearance of an interpolation, it seems likely that these prayers are indeed Jewish and were composed sometime in the second or third century C.E. The prayers reflect the "orthodoxy" of emerging Judaism. The Christian interpolations are christological (e.g., Christ born of virgin, of line of David [6:2]; the divine Word [1:8; 5:20]; mediator [4:22; 6:13]).

Text: F. X. FUNK, *Didascalia et Constitutiones apostolorum* (Paderborn, Ger.: F. Schöningh, 1905). *Survey:* J. H. CHARLESWORTH, "Jewish Hymns, Odes, and Prayers," *EJMI* 411–36, esp. 416–17 (for a convenient list of ancient prayers, see p. 424); IDEM, *PMR* 288–89; L. DITOMMASO, *BPR* 525–28; D. A. FIENSY, "The Hellenistic Synagogal Prayers: One Hundred Years of Discussion," *JSP* 5 (1989): 17–27; IDEM, "Prayers, Hellenistic Synagogal," *ABD* 5:450–51. *Commentary and Critical Study:* J. H. CHARLESWORTH, "Christian and Jewish Self-Definition in Light of the Christian Additions to the Apocryphal Writings," in *Aspects of Judaism in the Graeco-Roman Period* (vol. 2 of *Jewish and Christian Self-Definition;* ed. E. P. Sanders et al.; Philadelphia: Fortress, 1981), 25–55, esp. 31–35; D. A. FIENSY, *Prayers Alleged to Be Jewish: An Examination of the Constitutiones apostolorum* (BJS 65; Chico, Calif.: Scholars Press, 1985); D. A. FIENSY and D. R. DARNELL, "Hellenistic Synagogal Prayers," *OTP* 2:671–97.

Prayer of Joseph. The *Prayer of Joseph* was composed either in Aramaic (if Jewish) or in Greek (if Christian) in the first century C.E. It is quoted by Origen, in his commentary on John (*Comm. Jo.* 2.31 [on John 1:6]). The book teaches that Jacob was the incarnation of the angel "Israel" who competed with the angel Uriel over their respective rank in heaven. Jonathan Smith (*OTP* 2:699) believes that "the text was most likely an extended testament developed out of Jacob's blessing of Joseph's sons in Genesis 48." "Israel" is understood to mean "one who sees God" (v. 3), rather than "prince of God." Only fragments are extant, amounting to no more than nine verses.

Text: A.-M. DENIS, *CGPAT* 901; IDEM, *FPSG* 61–62. *Survey:* J. H. CHARLESWORTH, *PMR* 140–42, 293; L. DITOMMASO, *BPR* 611–15; J. Z. SMITH, "Joseph, Prayer of," *ABD* 3:976. *Commentary and Critical Study:* J. Z. SMITH, "Prayer of Joseph," *OTP* 2:699–714; IDEM, "The Prayer of Joseph," in *Religions in Antiquity: Essays in Memory of Erwin Ramsdell Goodenough* (ed. J. Neusner; SHR 14; Leiden: Brill, 1968), 253–94, repr. in SMITH, *Map Is Not Territory: Studies in the History of Religions* (SJLA 23; Leiden: Brill, 1978), 24–66; E. STEIN, "Zur apokryphen Schrift 'Gebet Josephs,'" *MGWJ* 81 (1937): 280–86.

Prayer of Jacob. The *Prayer of Jacob* was probably originally composed in Greek sometime between the first and fourth centuries C.E. by a Jew apparently interested in magic. The author requests wisdom from God, perhaps even immortality.

Text: A.-M. DENIS, *FPSG* 235–36; *PGM* XXIIb.1–26 (= Preisendanz, 2:148–49). *Survey:* J. H. CHARLESWORTH, "Jacob, Prayer of," *ABD* 3:609; IDEM, *PMR* 139, 290; L. DITOM-MASO, *BPR* 557–58. *Commentary and Critical Study:* H. D. BETZ, ed., *The Greek Magical Papyri in Translation, Including the Demotic Spells* (2d ed.; Chicago: University of Chicago Press, 1996–), 1:261; J. H. CHARLESWORTH, "Prayer of Jacob," *OTP* 2:715–23.

Odes of Solomon. The *Odes of Solomon* were originally written in either Syriac or Aramaic in the late first or early second century C.E. "Forty of the forty-two *Odes of Solomon* are extant in Syriac, five are preserved in Coptic, and one in Greek" (Charlesworth, *PMR* 189). Contrary to older opinion the *Odes* are no longer viewed as gnostic or as Jewish, but as early Christian. It is therefore highly un-likely that the *Odes* themselves or the traditions they presuppose were drawn upon by the Fourth Evangelist. The theme of the *Odes* is one of thanksgiving for the advent of the promised Messiah. Dualism, the hypostatic and mediatorial role of the Word, and the concept of salvation are similar to the ideas in the Fourth Gospel. James Brownson has recently argued that the *Odes* may very well have been composed by a community that broke from the Johannine community. For evidence of this he cites several parallels between *Odes* and the Johannine Epistles. "The original language, Syriac, and the affinities with the Dead Sea Scrolls, the Johannine Literature, and Ignatius of Antioch indicate that the *Odes* may have been composed in or near Syrian Antioch" (Charlesworth, *PMR* 190).

Text: J. H. CHARLESWORTH, *The Odes of Solomon: The Syriac Texts* (Oxford: Clarendon, 1973; repr. with corrections, SBLTT 13; Pseudepigrapha Series 7; Missoula, Mont.: Schol-ars Press, 1977), 17–148 (Syriac text with notes); M. TESTUZ, ed., *Papyrus Bodmer X–XII* (Geneva: Bibliotheca Bodmeriana, 1959), 60–69 (Greek text of *Odes Sol.* 11). *Survey:* J. H. CHARLESWORTH, "Jewish Hymns, Odes, and Prayers," *EJMI* 417–18; IDEM, "Odes of Solo-mon," *DNTB* 749–52; IDEM, *PMR* 189–94, 301–3; IDEM, "Solomon, Odes of," *ABD* 6:114–15; L. DITOMMASO, *BPR* 851–72; M. LATTKE, *Forschungsgeschichtliche Bibliogra-phie, 1799–1984, mit kritischen Anmerkungen* (vol. 3 of *Die Oden Salomos in ihrer Bedeu-tung für Neues Testament und Gnosis;* OBO 25/3; Göttingen: Vandenhoeck & Ruprecht, 1986). *Commentary and Critical Study:* D. E. AUNE, "The Odes of Solomon and Early Christian Prophecy," *NTS* 28 (1981–1982): 435–60; G. R. BLASZCZAK, *A Formcritical Study of Selected Odes of Solomon* (HSM 36; Atlanta: Scholars Press, 1985); J. BROWNSON, "The Odes of Solomon and the Gospel of John," *JSP* 2 (1988): 46–69; J. H. CHARLESWORTH, *Critical Reflections on the Odes of Solomon* (JSPSup 22; Sheffield: Sheffield, 1998); IDEM, "Odes of Solomon," *OTP* 2:725–71; IDEM, *The Odes of Solomon: The Syriac Texts* (SBLTT 13; Pseudepigrapha Series 7; Missoula, Mont.: Scholars Press, 1978); IDEM, "The Odes of Solomon and the Jewish Wisdom Texts," in *The Wisdom Texts from Qumran and the Development of Sapiential Thought* (ed. C. Hempel et al.; BETL 159; Leuven: Leuven University Press, 2002), 323–49; IDEM, "The Odes of Solomon—Not Gnostic," *CBQ* 31 (1969): 357–69; IDEM, "Qumran, John, and the Odes of Solomon," in *John and Qumran* (ed. J. H. Charlesworth; London: Geoffrey Chapman, 1972; repr., *John and the Dead Sea Scrolls;* New York: Crossroad, 1990), 107–36; J. H. CHARLESWORTH and R. A. CULPEPPER, "The Odes of Solomon and the Gospel of John," *CBQ* 35 (1973): 298–322; J. A. EMERTON, "The Odes of Solomon," *AOT* 683–31; J. R. HARRIS, *The Odes and Psalms of Solomon;* J. R. HARRIS and A. MINGANA, *The Odes and Psalms of Solomon,* vol. 2; M. LATTKE, *Die Oden Salamos in ihrer Bedeutung für Neues Testament und Gnosis* (OBO 25/1–4; Göttingen:

Vandenhoeck & Ruprecht, 1979–1998); J. T. SANDERS, "Nag Hammadi, Odes of Solomon, and NT Christological Hymns," in *Gnosticism and the Early Christian World* (ed. J. E. Goehring et al.; J. M. Robinson FS; Sonoma, Calif.: Polebridge, 1990), 51–66; W. R. SCHOEDEL, "Some Readings in the Greek Ode of Solomon (Ode XI)," *JTS* 33 (1982): 175–82; E. YAMAUCHI, *Pre-Christian Gnosticism: A Survey of the Proposed Evidences* (Grand Rapids: Eerdmans, 1973), 91–94.

Part Six: Fragments

Philo the Epic Poet. Philo the Epic Poet was a Jew who may have lived in Alexandria and who composed in Greek in the third or second century B.C.E. All that has survived are fragments of his *On Jerusalem* quoted in Eusebius, *Praep. ev.* 9.20.1–2; 9.24.1; and 9.37.1–3. Imitating the classic style of Greek poets, the author lauds the patriarchs and the city of Jerusalem.

Text: A.-M. DENIS, *CGPAT* 920; IDEM, *FPSG* 203–4; C. R. HOLLADAY, *Poets* (vol. 2 of *Fragments from Hellenistic Jewish Authors*), 234–44; W. N. STEARNS, *Fragments from Graeco-Roman Writers*, 95–99. *Survey:* J. H. CHARLESWORTH, *PMR* 168–69; L. DiTOMMASO, *BPR* 1057–59; P. W. VAN DER HORST, "The Interpretation of the Bible by the Minor Hellenistic Jewish Authors," *Mikra* 525–26; G. W. E. NICKELSBURG, "The Bible Rewritten and Expanded," *SJWSTP* 118–20. *Commentary and Critical Study:* H. W. ATTRIDGE, "Philo the Epic Poet," *OTP* 2:781–84; Y. GUTMAN, "Philo the Epic Poet," in *Studies in Classics and Jewish Hellenism* (ed. R. Koebner; ScrHier 1; Jerusalem: Hebrew University and Magnes Press, 1954), 36–63; C. R. HOLLADAY, *Poets* (vol. 2 of *Fragments from Hellenistic Jewish Authors*), 205–99; N. WALTER, "Fragmente jüdisch-hellenistischer Epik," 139–53.

Theodotus. Theodotus, who was either Jewish or Samaritan, composed a piece of epic poetry probably entitled *On the Jews* in either the first or second century B.C.E. Written in Greek (and preserved in Eusebius, *Praep. ev.* 9.22.1–11), it tells of the rape of Jacob's daughter Dinah (Gen 34) and the slaughter of the men of Shechem.

Text: A.-M. DENIS, *CGPAT* 920; IDEM, *FPSG* 204–7; C. R. HOLLADAY, *Poets* (vol. 2 of *Fragments from Hellenistic Jewish Authors*), 51–204; W. N. STEARNS, *Fragments from Graeco-Roman Writers*, 100–105. *Survey:* J. H. CHARLESWORTH, *PMR* 210–11, 305; L. DiTOMMASO, *BPR* 1062–65; P. W. VAN DER HORST, "The Interpretation of the Bible by the Minor Hellenistic Jewish Authors," *Mikra* 526–28; G. W. E. NICKELSBURG, "The Bible Rewritten and Expanded," *SJWSTP* 121–25. *Commentary and Critical Study:* J. J. COLLINS, "The Epic of Theodotus and the Hellenism of the Hasmoneans," *HTR* 73 (1980): 91–104; M. DAISE, "Samaritans, Seleucids, and the Epic of Theodotus," *JSP* 17 (1998): 25–51; F. FALLON, "Theodotus," *OTP* 2:785–89; R. PLUMMER and M. ROUSSEL, "A Note on Theodotus and Homer," *JSJ* 13 (1982): 177–82; N. WALTER, "Fragmente jüdisch-hellenistischer Epik," 164–71.

Orphica. Orphica purports to be an oracle by one Orphaeus to his son and pupil Musaeus. Written by a Jew in archaizing Greek, probably in the first century B.C.E. or C.E., it describes the attributes of God. The fragments survive in the writings of

Ps.-Justin (*Cohortio ad Graecos* and *De monarchia*), Clement of Alexandria, Eusebius, Cyril of Alexandria, and Theodoret.

Text: A.-M. DENIS, *CGPAT* 911; IDEM, *FPSG* 163–67; C. R. HOLLADAY, *Orphica* (vol. 4 of *Fragments from Hellenistic Jewish Authors*), 104–53 (recension A), 174 (recension B), 194 (recension C). **Survey:** J. H. CHARLESWORTH, *PMR* 167–68, 297; L. DITOMMASO, *BPR* 1052–56. **Commentary and Critical Study:** C. R. HOLLADAY, *Orphica* (vol. 4 of *Fragments from Hellenistic Jewish Authors*); IDEM, "Pseudo-Orpheus: Tracking a Tradition," in *The Early Church in Its Context: Essays in Honor of Everett Ferguson* (ed. A. J. Malherbe et al.; NovTSup 90; Leiden: Brill, 1998), 192–220; M. LAFARGUE, "Orphica," *OTP* 2:795–801; N. WALTER, "Pseudepigraphische jüdisch-hellenistische Dichtung," 217–43.

Ezekiel the Tragedian. Ezekiel the Tragedian (as he is called by Eusebius, *Praep. ev.* 9.28.1) composed a drama in Greek entitled the *Exagoge* (*Leading Out*) in the second century B.C.E. Centering around the character of Moses, the drama is based on Exodus 1–15. The fragments of this writer's work are found in Clement of Alexandria (*Strom.* 1.23.155.1–7; 1.23.156.1–2), Epiphanius (*Pan.* 64.29.6–64.30.1), and Eusebius (*Praep. ev.* 9.28.4–5; 9.29.4–16).

Text: A.-M. DENIS, *CGPAT* 921–22; IDEM, *FPSG* 207–16; C. R. HOLLADAY, *Poets* (vol. 2 of *Fragments from Hellenistic Jewish Authors*), 301–529. **Survey:** J. H. CHARLESWORTH, *PMR* 110–11, 284; L. DITOMMASO, *BPR* 1035–41; P. W. VAN DER HORST, "Ezekiel the Tragedian," *ABD* 2:709; G. W. E. NICKELSBURG, "The Bible Rewritten and Expanded," *SJWSTP* 125–30. **Commentary and Critical Study:** N. L. COLLINS, "Ezekiel, the Author of the *Exagoge:* His Calendar and Home," *JSJ* 22 (1991): 201–11; C. R. HOLLADAY, *Poets* (vol. 2 of *Fragments from Hellenistic Jewish Authors*), 301–529; P. W. VAN DER HORST, "Moses' Throne Vision in Ezekiel the Dramatist," *JTS* 34 (1983): 21–29; R. G. ROBERTSON, "Ezekiel the Tragedian," *OTP* 2:803–19; E. VOGT, "Tragiker Ezechiel," *JSHRZ* 4/3 (1983) 113–33.

Fragments of Pseudo-Greek Poets. The *Fragments of Pseudo-Greek Poets* is a collection of poetic compositions by Jews in deliberate imitation of classical Greek poetry. These imitations were often combined with authentic materials. The purpose of these poems was to support Jewish thought by showing that it was paralleled by the best in the Greek tradition. Hesiod, Pythagoras, Aeschylus, Sophocles, Euripides, Philemon, Diphilus, and Menander are imitated. God, judgment, and the folly of the Greek myths are the main items of interest. Most of these second- or third-century B.C.E. fragments are preserved by Clement of Alexandria, a second-century Greek church father.

Text: A.-M. DENIS, *CGPAT* 922–23; IDEM, *FPSG* 161–74. **Survey:** J. H. CHARLESWORTH, *PMR* 168; L. DITOMMASO, *BPR* 1047–48. **Commentary and Critical Study:** H. W. ATTRIDGE, "Fragments of Pseudo-Greek Poets," *OTP* 2:821–30; N. WALTER, "Pseudepigraphische jüdisch-hellenistische Dichtung," 244–76.

Aristobulus. Aristobulus was originally composed in Greek, probably some time in the second century B.C.E., perhaps during the reign of Ptolemy VI Philometor (155–145 B.C.E.). Five fragments have survived: (1) Fragment 1 is concerned with the astronomical features of the Passover. (2) Fragment 2 is concerned with the nature of God, in which *Aristobulus* attempts to explain OT anthropomorphisms. (3) Fragment 3 claims that Plato and Pythagoras had borrowed from Jewish law in articulating their ethical theories. (4) Fragment 4, like frg. 2, discusses God's nature and, like frg. 3, suggests that various Greek poets had ideas similar to those of Moses. (5) Fragment 5 argues cosmologically for the holiness of the Sabbath and cites Homer, Hesiod, and (the mythical) Linus for evidence that even the Greeks regarded the Sabbath as holy. The fragments are found in Eusebius (*Hist. eccl.* 7.32.16–18; *Praep. ev.* 8.9.38–8.10.18; 13.11.3–13.12.16).

Text: A.-M. DENIS, *FPSG* 217–28; C. R. HOLLADAY, *Aristobulus* (vol. 3 of *Fragments from Hellenistic Jewish Authors*), 128–96. *Survey:* J. H. CHARLESWORTH, *PMR* 81–82, 274; L. DiTOMMASO, *BPR* 1001–8; C. R. HOLLADAY, "Aristobulus," *ABD* 1:383–84; B. L. MACK and R. E. MURPHY, "Wisdom Literature," *EJMI* 379–80. *Commentary and Critical Study:* A. Y. COLLINS, "Aristobulus," *OTP* 2:831–42; C. R. HOLLADAY, *Aristobulus* (vol. 3 of *Fragments from Hellenistic Jewish Authors*); F. SIEGERT, "Early Jewish Interpretation in a Hellenistic Style," in *Hebrew Bible/Old Testament: The History of Its Interpretation* (ed. M. Saebø; Göttingen: Vandenhoeck & Ruprecht, 1996), 1:130–98, esp. 154–62; N. WALTER, "Fragmente jüdisch-hellenistischer Exegeten," *JSHRZ* 3/2 (1975) 261–79.

Demetrius the Chronographer. Six fragments from Demetrius the Chronographer are all that survive this third-century B.C.E. work. The fragments deal with various periods in Israel's history. (1) Fragment 1 retells the story of the sacrifice of Isaac (Gen 22). (2) Fragment 2 retells the story of Jacob, his sons, and Joseph. It also provides part of Moses' genealogy. (3) Fragment 3 supplies the genealogies of Moses and his wife Zipporah. (4) Fragment 4 retells the story of making the bitter waters sweet (Exod 15:22–27). (5) Fragment 5 tells how the wandering Israelites obtained their weapons (from the drowned Egyptians). (6) Fragment 6 is supposedly from a work entitled *On the Kings in Judaea* in which a chronology from the deportations of Israel and Judah to the time of Demetrius is given. The fragments are found in Eusebius (*Praep. ev.* 9.19.4; 9.21.1–19; 9.29.1–3, 15–16).

Text: A.-M. DENIS, *CGPAT* 912–13; IDEM, *FPSG* 175–79; C. R. HOLLADAY, *Historians* (vol. 1 of *Fragments from Hellenistic Jewish Authors*), 62–78; W. N. STEARNS, *Fragments from Graeco-Jewish Writers*, 17–28. *Survey:* J. H. CHARLESWORTH, *PMR* 93–94, 277; L. DiTOMMASO, *BPR* 1018–23; C. R. HOLLADAY, "Demetrius the Chronographer," *ABD* 2:137–38; P. W. VAN DER HORST, "The Interpretation of the Bible by the Minor Hellenistic Jewish Authors," *Mikra* 528–32. *Commentary and Critical Study:* H. W. ATTRIDGE, "Historiography," *SJWSTP* 161–62; E. J. BICKERMAN, "The Jewish Historian Demetrios," in *Christianity, Judaism, and Other Greco-Roman Cults* (ed. J. Neusner; 4 vols.; SJLA 12; Leiden: Brill, 1974), 3:72–84; J. HANSON, "Demetrius the Chronographer," *OTP* 2:843–54; C. R. HOLLADAY, *Historians* (vol. 1 of *Fragments from Hellenistic Jewish Authors*), 51–91; N. WALTER, "Fragmente jüdisch-hellenistischer Exegeten," *JSHRZ* 3/2 (1975) 280–92.

Aristeas the Exegete. Aristeas the Exegete is a late second-or early first-century B.C.E. retelling of the book of Job. Since the account depends upon the LXX throughout, it is likely that Greek was the language of its original composition. In this account Job is a descendant of Esau. Because of a reference in the *Letter of*

Aristeas (§6) to a previous work concerning the Jews, it has been suggested that both works bearing the name Aristeas were authored by the same person. However, the scholarly consensus now is that the works derive from two persons. All that survives of the text are four verses quoted in Eusebius, *Praep. ev.* 9.25.1–4.

Text: A.-M. DENIS, *CGPAT* 917; IDEM, *FPSG* 195–96; C. R. HOLLADAY, *Historians* (vol. 1 of *Fragments from Hellenistic Jewish Authors*), 268–70; W. N. STEARNS, *Fragments from Graeco-Jewish Writers*, 57–59. *Survey:* J. H. CHARLESWORTH, *PMR* 80–81, 274; L. DiTOMMASO, *BPR* 998–1000; C. R. HOLLADAY, "Aristeas the Exegete," *ABD* 1:380. *Commentary and Critical Study:* R. DORAN, "Aristeas the Exegete," *OTP* 2:855–59; C. R. HOLLADAY, *Historians* (vol. 1 of *Fragments from Hellenistic Jewish Authors*), 261–75; N. WALTER, "Fragmente jüdisch-hellenistischer Exegeten," *JSHRZ* 3/2 (1975) 293–96.

Eupolemus. Eupolemus is a late second- or early first-century B.C.E. Jewish author whose work, perhaps originally entitled *On the Kings of Judea,* survives as only five fragments. The first four fragments are preserved in Eusebius, *Praep. ev.* 9.26.1; 9.30.1–9.34.18; 9.34.20; and 9.39.2–5. The fifth fragment is preserved in Clement of Alexandria, *Strom.* 1.141.4. The fragments deal with various persons and events in Israel's history. (1) Fragment 1 identifies Moses as the world's first sage, who invented the alphabet and wrote laws. (2) Fragment 2, the longest of all, traces the history of Israel from Moses to Solomon and the building of the temple. (3) Fragment 4 concerns King Jonachim (by which is probably meant King Joachim [=Jehoiakim]) and the destruction by Nebuchadnezzar.

Text: A.-M. DENIS, *CGPAT* 914–15; IDEM, *FPSG* 179–86; C. R. HOLLADAY, *Historians* (vol. 1 of *Fragments from Hellenistic Jewish Authors*), 112–34; W. N. STEARNS, *Fragments from Graeco-Jewish Writers*, 29–41. *Survey:* H. W. ATTRIDGE, "Historiography," *SJWSTP* 162–65; IDEM, "Jewish Historiography," *EJMI* 313–15; J. H. CHARLESWORTH, *PMR* 107–8, 283; L. DiTOMMASO, *BPR* 1024–29; C. R. HOLLADAY, "Eupolemus," *ABD* 2:671–72. *Commentary and Critical Study:* F. FALLON, "Eupolemus," *OTP* 2:861–72; C. R. HOLLADAY, *Historians* (vol. 1 of *Fragments from Hellenistic Jewish Authors*), 93–156; B. Z. WACHOLDER, *Eupolemus;* N. WALTER, "Fragmente jüdisch-hellenistischer Historiker," 93–108.

Pseudo-Eupolemus. In Eusebius's *Preparatio evangelica* there are two quotations, one supposedly from Eupolemus and another given as anonymous. Scholars assign both quotations to first-century B.C.E. Ps.-Eupolemus. The first fragment (9.17.2–9) describes Abraham as a master astrologer. The second fragment (9.18.2) traces Abraham's ancestry to the giants and claims that the patriarch taught astrology to the Phoenicians and later to the Egyptians. The language of the original fragments was very likely Greek.

Text: A.-M. DENIS, *CGPAT* 917; IDEM, *FPSG* 197–98; C. R. HOLLADAY, *Historians* (vol. 1 of *Fragments from Hellenistic Jewish Authors*), 170–76; W. N. STEARNS, *Fragments from Graeco-Jewish Writers*, 67–70. *Survey:* H. W. ATTRIDGE, "Historiography," *SJWSTP* 165–66; J. H. CHARLESWORTH, *PMR* 77–78, 108, 283; L. DiTOMMASO, *BPR* 1030–34; C. R. HOLLADAY, "Eupolemus, Pseudo-," *ABD* 2:672–73. *Commentary and Critical Study:* J. E. BOWLEY, "Ur of the Chaldees in Pseudo-Eupolemus," *JSP* 14 (1996): 55–63; R. DORAN, "Pseudo-Eupolemus," *OTP* 2:873–82; C. R. HOLLADAY, *Historians* (vol. 1 of *Fragments from Hellenistic Jewish Authors*), 157–87; B. Z. WACHOLDER, *Eupolemus,* 313–14; IDEM, "Pseudo-Eupolemus' Two Greek Fragments on the Life of Abraham," *HUCA* 34 (1963): 83–113; N. WALTER, "Fragmente jüdisch-hellenistischer Historiker," 141–43.

Cleodemus Malchus. Cleodemus Malchus's work survives only as a single Greek fragment quoted by Josephus (*Ant.* 1.15.1 §§239–241) and then later by Eusebius (*Praep. ev.* 9.20.2–4). In all likelihood the original text was Greek. In the fragment we are told that one "Keturah bore Abraham mighty sons" (*Ant.* 1.15.1 §240) named Surim, after whom Assyria was named, and Afera and Iafra, after whom Africa was named.

Text: A.-M. DENIS, *CGPAT* 917; IDEM, *FPSG* 196–97; C. R. HOLLADAY, *Historians* (vol. 1 of *Fragments from Hellenistic Jewish Authors*), 252–54; W. N. STEARNS, *Fragments from Graeco-Jewish Writers,* 60–61. *Survey:* J. H. CHARLESWORTH, *PMR* 92–93, 276; L. DiTOMMASO, *BPR* 1015–17; C. R. HOLLADAY, "Cleodemus Malchus," *ABD* 1:1062–63; P. W. VAN DER HORST, "The Interpretation of the Bible by the Minor Hellenistic Jewish Authors," *Mikra* 542–43. *Commentary and Critical Study:* R. DORAN, "Cleodemus Malchus," *OTP* 2:883–86; C. R. HOLLADAY, *Historians* (vol. 1 of *Fragments from Hellenistic Jewish Authors*), 245–59; N. WALTER, "Fragmente jüdisch-hellenistischer Historiker," 115–19.

Artapanus. Only three fragments of the second- or third-century B.C.E. work of Artapanus survive. These fragments tell of the cultural contributions of Abraham, Joseph, and Moses while they were in Egypt. Abraham taught astrology (frg. 1: Eusebius, *Praep. ev.* 9.18.1). Joseph excelled as manager and surveyor (frg. 2: *Praep. ev.* 9.23.1–4). Moses was mighty in magic and military strategy (frg. 3: *Praep. ev.* 9.27.1–37). An interesting feature in the story about Moses is that Chenephres, one of the several "kings" over Egypt, out of envy sought to do away with Moses by sending him out on a very dangerous military campaign. Much to everyone's surprise, Moses is victorious. When he returns to Egypt he demands the release of the Hebrews.

Text: A.-M. DENIS, *CGPAT* 915–16; IDEM, *FPSG* 186–95; C. R. HOLLADAY, *Historians* (vol. 1 of *Fragments from Hellenistic Jewish Authors*), 204–24; W. N. STEARNS, *Fragments from Graeco-Jewish Writers,* 42–56. *Survey:* H. W. ATTRIDGE, "Historiography," *SJWSTP* 166–68; J. H. CHARLESWORTH, *PMR* 82–83, 275; L. DiTOMMASO, *BPR* 1009–14; C. R. HOLLADAY, "Artapanus," *ABD* 1:461–63; P. W. VAN DER HORST, "The Interpretation of the Bible by the Minor Hellenistic Jewish Authors," *Mikra* 532–37. *Commentary and Critical Study:* J. J. COLLINS, "Artapanus," *OTP* 2:889–903; C. R. HOLLADAY, *Historians* (vol. 1 of *Fragments from Hellenistic Jewish Authors*), 189–243; D. L. TIEDE, *The Charismatic Figure as Miracle Worker* (SBLDS 1; Missoula, Mont.: Scholars Press, 1972), 146–77; N. WALTER, "Fragmente jüdisch-hellenistischer Historiker," 121–36.

Pseudo-Hecataeus. There are four fragments attributed to Hecataeus of Abdera, a historian who wrote about 300 B.C.E. Of these only one is likely the work of Ps.-Hecataeus (according to Doran, *OTP* 2:905–16; the ordering of fragments is different in Holladay). (1) Fragment 1 (*Let. Aris.* §31), probably authentic, refers to Hecataeus's description of the Jewish Scriptures as "holy and reverent." Holladay does not include this fragment. (2) Fragment 2 (Clement of Alexandria, *Strom.* 5.14.113.1–2; cf. Eusebius, *Praep. ev.* 13.13.40) claims that Hecataeus quoted Sophocles in his book, *On Abraham and the Egyptians.* This fragment probably derives from Ps.-Hecataeus (second century B.C.E.). Holladay identifies this passage as frg. 3. (3) Fragment 3 (Josephus, *Ag. Ap.* 2.4 §§42–43) reports Alexander the Great's tribute-free gift of Samaria to the Jews. Since the reference may very well be to the Samaritan revolt in 331 B.C.E., Doran judges this fragment to be genuine. Holladay identifies this passage as frg. 2. (4) Fragment 4 (Josephus, *Ag. Ap.* 1.22 §§183–205; cf. Eusebius, *Praep. ev.* 9.4.2–9), by far the longest, reports some of the events in the years following the death of Alexander the Great, especially those concerning the Jews. Holladay identifies this passage as frg. 1.

Text: A.-M. DENIS, *CGPAT* 918; IDEM, *FPSG* 199–202; C. R. HOLLADAY, *Historians* (vol. 1 of *Fragments from Hellenistic Jewish Authors*), 304–22; M. STERN, *Greek and Latin Authors on Jews and Judaism* (3 vols.; Jerusalem: Israel Academy of Sciences and Humanities, 1974), 1:35–37. *Survey:* H. W. ATTRIDGE, "Historiography," *SJWSTP* 169–71; J. H. CHARLES-WORTH, *PMR* 119–22, 287; L. DITOMMASO, *BPR* 1042–48; C. R. HOLLADAY, "Hecataeus, Pseudo-," *ABD* 3:108–9. *Commentary and Critical Study:* B. BAR-KOCHVA, *Pseudo-Hecataeus, On the Jews: Legitimizing the Jewish Diaspora* (HCS 21; Berkeley: University of California Press, 1996); R. DORAN, "Pseudo-Hecataeus," *OTP* 2:905–19; J. G. GAGER, "Hecataeus of Abdera," in *Moses in Greco-Roman Paganism* (SBLMS 16; Nashville: Abingdon, 1972), 26–37; C. R. HOLLADAY, *Historians* (vol. 1 of *Fragments from Hellenistic Jewish Authors*), 277–335; A. KASHER, "Hecataeus of Abdera on Mosollamus the Jewish Mounted Archer (*Contra Apionem* I,200–204)," in *Geschichte–Tradition–Reflexion* (ed. P. Schäfer; M. Hengel FS; 3 vols.; Tübingen: Mohr [Siebeck], 1996), 1:147–58; D. MENDELS, "Hecataeus of Abdera and a Jewish 'patrios politeia' of the Persian Period (Diodorus Siculus XL, 3)," *ZAW* 95 (1983): 96–110; N. WALTER, "Fragmente jüdisch-hellenistischer Historiker," 144–60.

Appendix (not treated in OTP)

5 Maccabees. Fifth Maccabees is extant in Arabic (cf. Paris Polyglot of 1645), though it is thought that it may have been written originally in Hebrew. (It is not to be confused with the "5 Maccabees" of the Syriac Codex Ambrosianus, which is no more than an excerpt from Josephus, *J.W.* 6.) It covers the period 184–6 B.C.E. (from the attempt on the treasury by Heliodorus to Herod's final brutal murders), and it is the longest of the books of Maccabees (59 chapters). It was written after 70 C.E., for there are allusions to a "third captivity" (9:5) and to the "destruction of the second house" (21:30). Because the writing does not appear in earlier collections of Scripture (such as the major codices of the LXX), scholars have assumed that *5 Maccabees* is nothing more than a late (possibly medieval) conflation of parts of the other books of Maccabees, Josephus's *Jewish Antiquities*, and the Hebrew chronicle of Jewish history called *Yosippon.* Some scholars have in fact suggested that *5 Maccabees* is an epitome of *Yosippon.* J. H. Charlesworth, however, does not think so. He believes that the book, utilizing some sources common to the books of Maccabees and *Yosippon*, may actually derive from the late first century. On *Yosippon,* see chapter 5 (and Charlesworth, *PMR* 154–55). A Latin translation is provided by Gabriel Sionita in G. M. Le Jay et al., eds., *Biblia hebraica, samaritana, chaldaica, graeca, syriaca, latina, arabica, quibus textus originales totius Scripturae Sacrae* (9 vols.; Paris: A Vitré, 1629–1645), 9:1–76. The Latin has been translated into English by Henry Cotton, *The Five Books of Maccabees in English: With Notes and Illustrations* (Oxford: Oxford University Press, 1832), 277–446. Cotton (p. xxx) believes that *5 Maccabees* was written in Hebrew and translated into the Greek, of which nothing now survives.

Text: B. WALTON, ed., *Biblia sacra polyglotta* (6 vols.; London: Roycroft, 1657; repr., Graz: Akademische Druck-und Verlagsanstalt, 1963–1965), 4:112–59 (Arabic text, where it is called "Arabic 2 Maccabees"). *Survey:* J. H. CHARLESWORTH, *PMR* 153–56, 296; L. DITOMMASO, *BPR* 706–7; W. GRUDEM, "Alphabetical List for Old Testament Apocrypha and Pseudepigrapha," *JETS* 19 (1976): 297–313, esp. 308. *Commentary and Critical Study:* E. C. BISSELL, "The Fifth Book of the Maccabees," in J. P. Lange, P. Schaff, and E. C. Bissell, *The Apocrypha of the Old Testament: With Historical Introductions, a Revised Translation, and Notes Critical and Introductory* (New York: Charles Scribner's Sons, 1880), 638–40; H. WILLRICH, "Jasons Verhältnis zum III and IV Makkabäerbuch, zur Arabischen Makkabäergeschichte und Josippon," in *Judaica: Forschungen zur hellenistisch-jüdischen Geschichte und Litteratur* (Göttingen: Vandenhoeck & Ruprecht, 1900), 163–76.

Themes

Because of the quantity and diversity of the materials that make up the OT Pseudepigrapha, it is difficult to speak of themes that are common to very many of them. For a convenient survey, see Charlesworth, *OTP* 1:xxi–xxxiv. There are four aspects of the Pseudepigrapha that have relevance for NT study.

1. *Pseudepigraphy.* Considering the literary convention of pseudepigraphy in the case of so many of the writings that make up the OT Pseudepigrapha might help us understand the presence and meaning of pseudonymity in the NT itself. For years scholars have suspected that the Pastorals, James, the Petrines, Jude, and sometimes other books are pseudepigraphal. How do the alleged Pseudepigrapha of the NT compare to the numerous pseudepigraphal writings of the period? What were the purposes of pseudepigraphy? Was the early church aware of pseudepigraphy and, if so, what was its attitude toward it? The church of the second and third centuries certainly was aware of pseudepigraphy and apparently took a dim view of it. According to the *Apostolic Constitutions and Canons:* "Among the ancients also some have written apocryphal books of Moses, and Enoch, and Adam, and Isaiah, and David, and Elijah, and of the three patriarchs, pernicious and repugnant to the truth" (6.16). Tertullian (*Bapt.* 17) defrocked an elder for authoring the *Acts of Paul* (see ch. 7). But does this mean that the early church believed that pseudepigraphy was in itself wrong? Recently David Meade has concluded that the early church condemned pseudepigraphy when it was used to promote heretical ideas. He notes, for example, that initially no one objected to the use of the *Gospel of Peter,* until it was discovered to contain heresy

(Eusebius, *Hist. eccl.* 6.12.15). Even the Muratorian Canon's rejection of forged Pauline epistles to the Laodiceans and to the Alexandrians seems motivated by concerns over Marcionite heresy (cf. Meade, 203–7).

Some scholars think that pseudepigraphy was motivated by the search for authority (cf. Collins 1977). Others suspect that it had something to do with the effort to establish claims over against rivals (cf. Beckwith). I think that both views are correct and that in many cases they complement one another. Just as the demise of the spirit of prophecy occasioned intertestamental pseudepigraphy, so the passing of the apostolic age occasioned the emergence of Christian pseudepigraphy (see ch. 8). The gnostic codices of Nag Hammadi also illustrate this phenomenon (see ch. 10). Writing in the names of various apostolic figures, diverse gnostic sects vie with one another for doctrinal legitimacy. In any case, understanding pseudepigraphy should significantly be aided by study of the OT Pseudepigrapha.

Bibliography: R. BECKWITH, "The Earliest Enoch Literature and Its Calendar: Marks of their Origin, Date and Motivation," *RevQ* 10 (1981): 365–403; D. A. CARSON, "Pseudonymity and Pseudepigraphy," *DNTB* 857–64; J. H. CHARLESWORTH, "Pseudepigraphy," in *Encyclopedia of Early Christianity* (ed. E. Ferguson; New York: Garland, 1990), 775–78; IDEM, "Pseudonymity and Pseudepigraphy," *ABD* 5:540–41; J. J. COLLINS, "Pseudonymity, Historical Reviews, and the Genre of the Revelation of John," *CBQ* 39 (1977): 329–43, esp. 331–32; J. D. G. DUNN, "The Problem of Pseudonymity," in *The Living Word* (London: SCM Press, 1987), 65–88; E. E. ELLIS, "Pseudonymity and Canonicity of New Testament Documents," in *Worship, Theology, and Ministry in the Early Church: Essays in Honour of Ralph P. Martin* (ed. M. J. Wilkins and T. Paige; JSNTSup 87; Sheffield: JSOT Press, 1992), 212–24; A. B. KOLENKOW, "The Literary Genre 'Testament,' " *EJMI* 264–66; D. G. MEADE, *Pseudonymity and Canon: An Investigation into the Relationship of Authorship and Authority in Jewish and Earliest Christian Tradition* (Grand Rapids: Eerdmans, 1987); B. M. METZGER, "Literary Forgeries and Canonical Pseudepigrapha," *JBL* 91 (1972): 3–24; D. S. RUSSELL, *The Method and Message of Jewish Apocalyptic* (Philadelphia: Westminster, 1964), 127–39, for a summary of approaches; M. E. STONE, "Apocalyptic Literature," *SJWSTP* 427–33.

2. *Idealization of the Past.* Related to the first point, there is a tendency in the Pseudepigrapha to glorify the biblical characters of long ago. Biblical heroes of the past become models of piety and faithfulness for later generations. Past events too are special, for future events will parallel them. Lying behind this concern is typological thinking where it is assumed that what has taken place in the past foreshadows what is happening in the present or what will happen in the future. For example, several writings allegedly speak of the first destruction of Jerusalem and the temple, while in reality they are speaking of the second destruction in 70 C.E. It is assumed that the horrible events of 70 are explained by the sad events of 586 B.C.E.

Bibliography: G. W. E. NICKELSBURG, *Faith and Piety in Early Judaism: Texts and Documents* (Philadelphia: Fortress, 1983); D. PATTE, *Early Jewish Hermeneutic in Palestine* (SBLDS 22; Missoula, Mont.: Scholars Press, 1975), 159–67.

3. *Apocalyptic.* The Apocalypses and the Testaments chiefly contain apocalyptic material. Even in the writings placed in "OT expansions," such as *Jubilees* or *Biblical Antiquities,* apocalyptic material is present. These writings describe visions of the future (most of which is biblical history usually presented in symbolic language). There is great interest in eschatology, that is, the events that culminate in the end of human history and of earth as we know it. There is great interest in resurrection, judgment, hell, and paradise. Messianic interest in those writings that are clearly Jewish (as opposed to Christian) is limited to five pseudepigrapha (*Psalms of Solomon, 2 Baruch,* 4 Ezra [=2 Esdras 3–14], *1 En.* 37–71, *3 Enoch*).

Bibliography: J. J. COLLINS, *The Apocalyptic Imagination;* IDEM, "Apocalyptic Literature," *EJMI* 345–70; D. S. RUSSELL, *The Method and Message of Jewish Apocalyptic* (Philadelphia: Westminster, 1964); M. E. STONE, "Apocalyptic Literature," *SJWSTP* 383–427, 433–41; J. C. VANDERKAM and W. ADLER, eds., *The Jewish Apocalyptic Heritage in Early Christianity* (CRINT 3.4; Minneapolis: Fortress, 1996).

4. *Rewritten Bible.* A phenomenon that is common in the OT Pseudepigrapha, but one that is not limited to it, is something that scholars call "rewritten Bible." Rewritten Bible refers to the retelling, usually with omissions, supplements, and loose paraphrases, of biblical narratives. What is left unclear, or unsaid, in the biblical narratives is explained either in narrative form, or with the insertion of a speech, prophecy, or hymn. Rewritten Bible is found in the Targumim (see ch. 6), in some of the writings of Qumran (see ch. 3), and even in the NT itself (as seen in the relationship of Matthew and Luke to Mark). There are two principal features involved. First, there is the question of what relationship the rewritten narratives have to the biblical writings. J. H. Charlesworth has addressed this question. He rightly claims that most of the OT Pseudepigrapha, even those writings which are not obvious examples of rewritten Bible, have drawn upon and interpreted the OT in important ways. He finds four categories: (1) *inspiration,* where the OT inspires in the pseudepigraphal writer a given theme or style (e.g., *Prayer of Manasseh* and Pss 151–155); (2) *framework,* where the OT provides the basis, or framework, for a new story (e.g., 4 Ezra, *2 Baruch, Testaments of the Twelve Patriarchs, Testament of Job*); (3) *launching,* where the OT narrative provides the point of departure for a continuation of the story (e.g., *1 Enoch,* which is in part launched by Gen 5:23–24); and (4) *inconsequential,* where pseudepigraphal writings are influenced by the OT in only the slightest way, often doing nothing more than borrowing the name and reputation of an ancient worthy (e.g., *Apocalypse of Adam* and *Treatise of Shem*). Other writings are obvious examples of rewritten Bible (e.g., *Jubilees* and Ps.-Philo [within the Pseudepigrapha], Josephus's *Jewish Antiquities* and 1QapGenesis [outside the Pseudepigrapha]). Charlesworth believes that ultimately the motivation behind the Pseudepigrapha, especially those that can be classified as instances of rewritten Bible, is to interpret Scripture.

This leads to the second question: What methods do these writings employ in their attempts to interpret Scripture? Reviewing *Jubilees* and Ps.-Philo we find condensation, omission, supplementation, and reshaping. Names and genealogies are added, problems are explained, discrepancies are resolved, new connections or associations are offered, speeches and prayers are rewritten, speeches, prayers, and hymns are added, biblical language is modernized, and biblical narratives are often enriched with details from similar biblical accounts. This last feature is one of the most striking aspects of the rewritten Bible: the tendency to utilize Scripture from elsewhere in the Bible to elaborate on the biblical story at hand. Not only is this genre valuable as a source of exegetical tradition for comparative purposes, but it sheds valuable light on the editorial techniques of the hagiographers (i.e., the authors of "sacred writings") of the intertestamental and NT periods. These editorial techniques could, for example, teach us much about the evangelists' use of their sources (cf. Bauckham; Evans).

Bibliography: P. S. ALEXANDER, "Retelling the Old Testament," in *It Is Written: Scripture Citing Scripture* (ed. D. A. Carson and H. G. M. Williamson; B. Lindars FS; New York: Cambridge University Press, 1988), 99–121; R. BAUCKHAM, "The Liber antiquitatum biblicarum of Pseudo-Philo and the Gospels as 'Midrash,'" in *Studies in Midrash and Historiography* (ed. R. T. France and D. Wenham; Gospel Perspectives 3; Sheffield: JSOT Press, 1983), 33–76; J. H. CHARLESWORTH, "The Interpretation of the Tanak in the Jewish Apocrypha and Pseudepigrapha," in *The Ancient Period* (vol. 1 of *A History of Biblical Interpretation;* ed. A. J. Hauser and D. F. Watson; Grand Rapids: Eerdmans, 2003), 253–82 (very helpful bibliography); IDEM, "The Pseudepigrapha as Biblical Exegesis," in *Early Jewish and Christian Exegesis* (ed. C. A. Evans and W. F. Stinespring; W. H. Brownlee FS; Homage 10; Atlanta: Scholars Press, 1987), 139–52; D. DIMANT, "Use and Interpretation of Mikra in the Apocrypha and Pseudepigrapha," *Mikra* 379–419; C. A. EVANS, "The Genesis Apocryphon and the Rewritten Bible," *RevQ* 13 (1988): 153–65; IDEM, "Luke and the Rewritten Bible: Aspects of Lucan Hagiography," in *The Pseudepigrapha and Early Biblical Interpretation* (ed. Charlesworth and Evans), 170–201; F. J. MURPHY, *Pseudo-Philo: Rewriting the Bible* (Oxford: Oxford University Press, 1993); G. W. E. NICKELSBURG, "The Bible Rewritten and Expanded," *SJWSTP* 89–156.

5. The Pseudepigrapha and the New Testament. In recent years, especially since the publication twenty years ago of the two-volume *Old Testament Pseudepigrapha,* edited by James H. Charlesworth, NT scholars have become much more aware of the significance of the pseudepigraphal writings for NT interpretation (see Charlesworth, *The Old Testament Pseudepigrapha and the New Testament*). These writings, which emanate from the OT, intertestamental, and NT periods, clarify important aspects of Jesus' ministry and virtually every writing found in the NT. A few examples may be surveyed here.

Pseudepigraphal traditions at many points cohere in meaningful ways with aspects of Jesus' teaching and ministry. After the death of the righteous Taxo and his sons, it is foretold that God's "kingdom will appear throughout his whole creation. Then the devil will have an end [*finem habebit*]" (*T. Mos.* 10:1). The association of the appearance of the kingdom of God and the demise of the devil is consistent with Jesus' proclamation of the kingdom and demonstration of its power through exorcism (e.g., Mark 3:14–15; 6:7; Luke 11:20). Indeed, Jesus' comment "If Satan . . . is divided, . . . his end has come [*telos echei*, lit. "he has an end"]" (Mark 3:26) verbally matches the language of the *Testament of Moses*. Moreover, the expectation that it will be through the death, the blood of Taxo and his sons, that the kingdom of God will appear and the devil will be destroyed coheres with Jesus' teaching that the kingdom of God will come in its fullness only after his suffering (cf. Mark 14:24–25).

Several pseudepigraphal traditions clarify Jesus as exorcist. Appeal to him as "Son of David" (Mark 10:47–48) recalls appeals to Solomon, the son of David, in *T. Sol.* 1:7; 5:10. Accusing Jesus of being in league with Beelzebul, the prince of demons (Mark 3:22), recalls Solomon's encounter with this being (*T. Mos.* 2:9; 3:5–6). Even the tradition of the ring/seal in the *Testament of Solomon*, by which Solomon can control the demons (*T. Sol.* 1:5–12), is attested in Josephus (*Ant.* 8.2.5 §§46–49). We should imagine that the exorcist outside Jesus' following, who invoked Jesus' name (Mark 9:38–39), may well have made use of such paraphernalia.

Jesus assures his disciples that he has given them the "authority to tread on snakes and scorpions, and over all the power of the enemy" (Luke 10:19). Jesus is alluding to Ps 91:13 ("You will tread on the lion and the adder"), but as this passage was interpreted in pseudepigraphal (*T. Levi* 18:10–12; *T. Sim.* 6:6; *T. Zeb.* 9:8) and targumic tradition (*Tg. Pss.* 91:5–6, 10, 13). The demonic interpretation of Psalm 91, attested at Qumran (cf. 11Q11), also clarifies the function of Ps 91:11–12 in the temptation narratives (Matt 4:5–7; Luke 4:9–12). Moreover, Jesus' declaration that he "watched Satan fall from heaven like a flash of lightning" (Luke 10:18) also coheres with pseudepigraphal (*T. Sol.* 20:16–17; *2 En.* 29:5) and targumic (*Tg. Isa.* 14:12) tradition.

Jesus' self-reference as "the Son of Man" unmistakably alludes to the mysterious figure of Dan 7:9–14, but with ideas probably clarified by the Similitudes of Enoch (i.e., *1 En.* 37–71), whose traditions were beginning to take shape, in all probability, in the early first century C.E. Jesus' daring allusion to Ps 110:1 and Dan 7:13 in his reply to Caiaphas may have been colored by ideas eventually reflected in *1 En.* 62:5: "and pain shall seize them when they see the Son of Man sitting on the throne of his glory."

Echoes of Enochic literature are found throughout the dominical tradition (see appendix 2). One of note is found in Matt 22:13, where, in the parable of the Marriage Feast (Matt 22:1–14), the intruder is to be bound "hand and foot" and cast "into the outer darkness" (Matt 22:13). This is a clear allusion to *1 En.* 10:4, where the angel Raphael is commanded, "Bind Azaz'el hand and foot (and) cast him into the darkness!"

There are points of coherence between the writings of Paul and the writings of the Pseudepigrapha. Indeed, in some cases the apostle has probably quoted pseudepigraphal texts. According to Paul, the heathen "did not honor [the Lord] as God or give thanks to him, but they became futile in their thinking and their senseless minds were darkened" (Rom 1:21). We are reminded of *1 En.* 99:6–9, where we are told that sinners "shall become wicked on account of the folly of their hearts . . . and shall worship stone" (cf. *T. Reu.* 3:7–8).

Paul's curious quotation "What no eye has seen, nor ear heard, nor the human heart conceived, what God has prepared for those who love him" (1 Cor 2:9) alludes to passages from Isaiah, to be sure (cf. Isa 52:15; 64:4; 65:17), but it also alludes to pseudepigraphal traditions (e.g., *L.A.B.* 26:13; cf. the Coptic version of the *Testament of Jacob*).

In late Pauline tradition, the tradition of the Egyptian false prophets Jannes and Jambres is invoked (cf. 2 Tim 3:8). A rich tradition in the writings of the Pseudepigrapha (*L.A.B.* 47:1; *Jannes and Jambres*), in the Scrolls (CD 5:17–19), in Aramaic tradition (*Tg. Ps.-J.* Exod 7:11; Num 22:22), and even in Greco-Roman literature (Pliny the Elder, *Nat.* 30.2.11) grew up around these two characters.

The Gospel of John invites comparison with pseudepigraphal traditions. One point of contact that calls for further investigation is *Jos. Asen.* 8:5, where Josephus tells Aseneth that the true believer is one who will "eat blessed bread of life and drink a blessed cup of immortality." This remarkable statement immediately recalls the Johannine "bread of life" (John 6:35, 48) and the promise that the one who eats it will live forever (John 6:51, 58). Moreover, drinking a cup of immortality recalls not only John 7:37 ("Let anyone who is thirsty come to me, and . . . drink"); the juxtaposition in *Joseph and Aseneth* of eating bread of life and drinking a cup of immortality, which coheres with John 6:53, 55, is remarkable.

In many places in the NT antilegomena, we have points of coherence with the Pseudepigrapha. One thinks of Heb 11:37 ("they were sawn in two") and *Mart. Ascen. Isa.* 5:1 ("and he sawed Isaiah in half with a wood saw"), of Christ's descent into hell in 1 Pet 3:19 and *1 En.* 10:11–15 and Ps.-Jeremiah (*apud* Justin Martyr, *Dial.* 72.4, et al.), and of Jude 1:9, where Michael argues with the devil over the body of Moses (probably an allusion to the *Testament of Moses*), or Jude 14–15, where part of *1 En.* 1:9 is quoted: "Behold, the Lord came with his holy myriads, to execute judgment on all, and to convict all the ungodly of all their deeds of ungodliness which they have committed in such an ungodly way, and of all the harsh things which ungodly sinners have spoken against him." The book of Revelation offers a treasure trove of parallels with pseudepigraphal literature.

Bibliography: S. AALEN, "St. Luke's Gospel and the Last Chapters of I Enoch," *NTS* 13 (1967): 1–13; R. J. BAUCKHAM, "Resurrection as Giving Back the Dead: A Traditional Image of Resurrection in the Pseudepigrapha and the Apocalypse of John," in *The Pseudepigrapha and Early Biblical Interpretation* (ed. Charlesworth and Evans), 269–91; M. BLACK, "The Maranatha Invocation and Jude 14, 15 (1 Enoch 1:9)," in *Christ and Spirit in the New Testament* (ed. B. Lindars and S. S. Smalley; C. F. D. Moule FS; Cambridge: Cambridge University Press, 1973), 189–96; F. H. BORSCH, "Mark XIV.62 and 1 Enoch LXII.5," *NTS* 14 (1968): 565–67; J. H. CHARLESWORTH, "The Historical Jesus in Light of Writings Contemporary with Him," *ANRW* 25.1:451–76; IDEM, *The Old Testament Pseudepigrapha and the New Testament;* P. H. DAVIDS, "The Use of the Pseudepigrapha in the Catholic Epistles," in *The Pseudepigrapha and Early Biblical Interpretation* (ed. Charlesworth and Evans), 228–45; C. W. FISHBURNE, "I Corinthians III. 10–15 and the Testament of Abraham," *NTS* 17 (1970): 109–15; O. HOFIUS, "Das Zitat 1 Kor 2:9 und das koptische Testament des Jakob," *ZNW* 66 (1975): 140–42; H. C. KEE, "Appropriating the History of God's People: A Survey of Interpretations of the History of Israel in the Pseudepigrapha, Apocrypha, and the New Testament," in *The Pseudepigrapha and Early Biblical Interpretation* (ed. Charlesworth and Evans), 44–64; R. A. KRAFT, "The Pseudepigrapha in Christianity," in *Tracing the Threads: Studies in the Vitality of Jewish Pseudepigrapha* (ed. J. C. Reeves; SBLEJL 6; Atlanta: Scholars Press, 1994), 55–86; M. MCNAMARA, "Traditions Relating to Moses, Jannes, and Jambres in the Palestinian Targum and in St. Paul," in *The New Testament and the Palestinian Targum to the Pentateuch*, 70–96; D. J. ROWSTON, "The Most Neglected Book in the New Testament," *NTS* 21 (1975): 554–63 G. STEINDORFF, *Die Apokalypse des Elias, eine unbekannte Apokalypse, und Bruchstücke der Sophonias-Apokalypse* (TU 17/3a; Leipzig: Hinrichs, 1899).

General Bibliography

Text: W. BAARS, *The Old Testament in Syriac according to the Peshitta Version* (Leiden: Brill, 1972–); K. BERGER, *Die griechische Daniel-Diegesis: Eine altkirchliche Apokalypse. Text, Übersetzung, und Kommentar* (SPB 27; Leiden: Brill, 1976); R. H. CHARLES, *The Assumption of Moses* (London: Adam and Charles Black, 1897); IDEM, *The Greek Versions of the Testaments of the Twelve Patriarchs* (London: Oxford University Press, 1908; repr., Hildesheim: Olms, 1960); J. H. CHARLESWORTH, *The Greek Recension* (vol. 1 of *The History of the Rechabites;* SBLTT 17; Pseudepigrapha Series 10; Chico, Calif.: Scholars Press, 1982); M. HENZE, *The Syriac Apocalypse of Daniel: Introduction, Text, and Commentary* (STAC 11; Tübingen: Mohr Siebeck, 2001); C. R. HOLLADAY, *Fragments from Hellenistic Jewish Authors* (SBLTT 20, 30, 39, 40; Pseudepigrapha 10, 12–14; Chico, Calif.: Scholars Press, 1983–1996); M. R. JAMES, *Apocrypha anecdota: A Collection of Thirteen Apocryphal Books and Fragments* (Texts and Studies 2/3; Cambridge: Cambridge University Press, 1893); IDEM, *Apocrypha anecdota: Second Series* (Texts and Studies 5/1; Cambridge: Cambridge University Press, 1897); IDEM, *The Testament of Abraham* (Texts and Studies 2/2; Cambridge: Cambridge University Press, 1892); A. JELLINEK, *Bet ha-Midrasch: Sammlung kleiner Midraschim und vermischter Abhandlungen aus der ältern jüdischen Literatur* (6 vols.; Leipzig: Friedrich Nies [vols. 1–2], C. W. Vollrath [vols. 3–4], Brüder Winter [vols. 5–6], 1853–1877; repr., 6 vols. in 2; Jerusalem: Wahrman Books, 1967); R. A. KRAFT and A.-E. PURINTUN, *Paraleipomena Jeremiou* (SBLTT 1; Pseudepigrapha Series 1; Missoula, Mont.: Society of Biblical Literature, 1972); C. C. MCCOWN, *The Testament of Solomon* (UNT 9; Leipzig: Hinrichs, 1922); G. MERCATI, *Note di letteratura biblica e christiana antica* (Studi e testi 5; Rome: Vaticana, 1901); H. ODEBERG, *3 Enoch, or the Hebrew Book of Enoch* (Cambridge: Cambridge University Press, 1928; repr., with prolegomenon by J. C. Greenfield; New York: Ktav, 1973); D. M. PARROTT, ed., *Nag Hammadi Codices V, 2–5 and VI with Papyrus Berolinensis 8502,1 and 4* (NHS 11; Leiden: Brill, 1979); H. E. RYLE and M. R. JAMES, Ψαλμοὶ Σολομῶντος— *Psalms of the Pharisees, Commonly Called the Psalms of Solomon: The Text Newly Revised from all the MSS* (Cambridge: Cambridge University Press, 1891); J. A. SANDERS, *The Psalms Scroll of Qumran Cave 11 (11QPsᵃ)* (DJDJ 4; Oxford: Clarendon, 1965); W. N. STEARNS, *Fragments from Graeco-Roman Writers* (Chicago:

University of Chicago Press, 1908); M. E. STONE, ed., *The Testament of Abraham: The Greek Recensions* (SBLTT 2; Pseudepigrapha Series 2; Missoula, Mont.: Scholars Press, 1972); N. S. TIKHONRAVOV, *Pamjatniki otrecennoj russkoj literatury* (2 vols.; St. Petersburg: Obshchestvenaia Polza, 1863); C. C. TORREY, *The Lives of the Prophets: Greek Text and Translation* (JBLMS 1; Philadelphia: Society of Biblical Literature, 1946); J. TROMP, *The Assumption of Moses: A Critical Edition with Commentary* (SVTP 10; Leiden: Brill, 1993); J. C. VANDERKAM, *The Book of Jubilees: A Critical Text* (2 vols.; CSCO 510; ScrAeth 87; Leuven: Peeters, 1989); O. WAHL, *Apocalypsis Esdrae, Apocalypsis Sedrach, Visio beati Esdrae* (PVTG 4; Leiden: Brill, 1977); N. WALTER, "Fragmente jüdisch-hellenistischer Epik: Philo, Theodotus," *JSHRZ* 4/3 (1983) 135–72; IDEM, "Fragmente jüdisch-hellenistischer Historiker: Eupolemus," *JSHRZ* 1/2 (1976) 91–160; IDEM, "Pseudepigraphische jüdisch-hellenistische Dichtung: Pseudo-Phokylides, Pseudo-Orpheus, gefälschte Verse auf Namen griechischer Dichter," *JSHRZ* 4/3 (1983) 173–276. **Principal Studies:** R. H. CHARLES, *APOT*; J. H. CHARLESWORTH, "The Concept of the Messiah in the Pseudepigrapha," *ANRW* 19.1:188–218; IDEM, *OTP*; IDEM, *The Pseudepigrapha and Modern Research, with a Supplement* (2d ed.; SCS 7; Chico, Calif.: Scholars Press, 1981); J. H. CHARLESWORTH and C. A. EVANS, eds., *The Pseudepigrapha and Early Biblical Interpretation* (JSPSup 14; Sheffield: Sheffield, 1993); E. G. CHAZO, "Moses' Struggle for His Soul: A Prototype for the *Testament of Abraham,* the *Greek Apocalypse of Ezra,* and the *Apocalypse of Sedrach,*" *SecCent* 5 (1985–1986): 151–64; A.-M. DENIS, *CGPAT*; IDEM, *FPSG*; IDEM, *Introduction aux pseudépigraphes grecs d'Ancien Testament* (SVTP; Leiden: Brill, 1970); L. DiTOMMASO, *BPR*; J. R. HARRIS, *The Odes and Psalms of Solmon* (Cambridge: Cambridge University Press, 1909); J. R. HARRIS and A. MINGANA, *The Odes and Psalms of Solomon* (2 vols.; Manchester, Eng.: Manchester University Press, 1916–1920); M. DE JONGE, *OOT*; M. A. KNIBB and P. W. VAN DER HORST, eds., *Studies on the Testament of Job* (SNTSMS 66; Cambridge: Cambridge University Press, 1989); R. A. KRAFT and G. W. E. NICKELSBURG, *EJMI*; M. E. STONE, *JWSTP*; B. Z. WACHOLDER, *Eupolemus: A Study of Judaeo-Greek Literature* (MHUC 3; Cincinnati: Hebrew Union College Press, 1974); T. W. WILLET, *Eschatology in the Theodicies of 2 Baruch and 4 Ezra* (JSPSup 4; Sheffield: JSOT Press, 1989). **Related Studies:** J. H. CHARLESWORTH, *The Old Testament Pseudepigrapha and the New Testament* (SNTSMS 54; Cambridge: Cambridge University Press, 1985); rev., *The Old Testament Pseudepigrapha and the New Testament: Prolegomena for the Study of Christian Origins* (Harrisburg, Pa.: Trinity Press International, 1998); IDEM, "Pseudepigrapha," *HBD* 836–40; J. H. CHARLESWORTH and C. A. EVANS, eds., *The Pseudepigrapha and Early Biblical Interpretation* (JSPSup 14; Sheffield: Sheffield, 1993); J. J. COLLINS, *The Apocalyptic Imagination: An Introduction to Jewish Apocalyptic Literature* (2d ed.; Biblical Resource Series; Grand Rapids: Eerdmans, 1998); C. A. EVANS, ed., *The Interpretation of Scripture in Early Judaism and Christianity: Studies in Language and Tradition* (JSPSup 33; SSEJC 7; Sheffield: Sheffield, 2000); G. E. LADD, "Pseudepigrapha," *ISBE* 4:1040–43; M. MCNAMARA, *The New Testament and the Palestinian Targum to the Pentateuch* (2d ed.; AnBib 27A; Rome: Pontifical Biblical Institute, 1978); C. C. NEWMAN et al., eds., *The Jewish*

Roots of Christological Monotheism: Papers from the St. Andrews Conference on the Historical Origins of the Worship of Jesus (JSPSup 63; Leiden: Brill, 1999); G. W. E. NICKELSBURG, *Faith and Piety in Early Judaism: Texts and Documents* (Philadelphia: Fortress, 1983); IDEM, *JLBM;* L. ROST, *Judaism outside the Hebrew Canon: An Introduction to the Documents* (Nashville: Abingdon, 1976), 100–154, 191–97; H. D. F. SPARKS, *AOT;* M. E. STONE and T. A. BERGREN, eds., *Biblical Figures outside the Bible* (Harrisburg, Pa.: Trinity Press International, 1998); J. C. VANDERKAM, *An Introduction to Early Judaism* (Grand Rapids: Eerdmans, 2001).

CHAPTER THREE

The Dead Sea Scrolls

Dead Sea Scrolls Selected List

QUMRAN

1QIsa[a,b] (Isaiah, copies a and b)

1QpHab (*Commentary on Habakkuk*)

1QpMic = 1Q14 (*Commentary on Micah*)

1QpZeph = 1Q15 (*Commentary on Zephaniah*)

1QpPs = 1Q16 (*Commentary on Psalms*)

1QJub[a,b] = 1Q17–18 (*Jubilees*, copies a and b)

1QNoah = 1Q19 (*Book of Noah*)

1QapGen = 1Q20 (*Genesis Apocryphon*)

1QTLevi ar = 1Q21 (Aramaic *Testament of Levi*)

1QDM = 1Q22 (*Words of Moses*)

1QEnGiants[a,b] = 1Q23–24 (*Book of Giants*)

1QMyst = 1Q27 (*Book of Mysteries*)

1QS (*Serek Hayahad* or *Rule of the Community*)

1QSa = 1Q28a (*Rule of the Congregation*)

1QSb = 1Q28b (*Rule of the Blessings*)

1Q29 (*Liturgy of the Three Tongues of Fire*)

1Q30–31 (*Liturgical Texts* A and B)

1QJN ar = 1Q32 (*New Jerusalem*)

1QM + 1Q33 (*Milḥamah* or *War Scroll*)

1QLitPr[a,b] = 1Q34 + 1Q34bis (*Festival Prayers*)

1QH[a] + 1QH[b] = 1Q35 (*Thanksgiving Hymns[a,b]*)

2QapMoses = 2Q21 (*Apocryphon of Moses*)

2QapDavid = 2Q22 (*Apocryphon of David*)

2QapProph = 2Q23 (apocryphal prophetic text)

2QJN ar = 2Q24 (*New Jerusalem*)

2Q25 (juridical text)

2QEnGiants ar = 2Q26 (Enochic *Book of Giants*)

3QpIsa = 3Q4 (*Commentary on Isaiah*)

3QJub = 3Q5 (*Jubilees*)

3QHymn = 3Q6 (*Hymn of Praise*)

3QTJud? = 3Q7 (*Testament of Judah*)

3QTreasure = 3Q15 (*Copper Scroll*)

4QSam[a] = 4Q51 (Samuel[a])

4Q88 = 4QPsAp[f] and 11Q11 = 11QApPs[a])

4QtgLev = 4Q156 (*Targum of Leviticus*)

4QtgJob = 4Q157 (*Targum of Job*)

(continued on next page)

Dead Sea Scrolls Selected List, cont'd

4QReworked Pentateuch = 4Q158

4QOrd^a = 4Q159 (*Ordinances* ^{a})

4QVisSam = 4Q160 (*Vision of Samuel*)

4QpIsa^a = 4Q161 (*Commentary on Isaiah^a*)

4QpIsa^b = 4Q162 (*Commentary on Isaiah^b*)

4QpIsa^c = 4Q163 (*Commentary on Isaiah^c*)

4QpIsa^d = 4Q164 (*Commentary on Isaiah^d*)

4QpIsa^e = 4Q165 (*Commentary on Isaiah^e*)

4QpHos^a = 4Q166 (*Commentary on Hosea^a*)

4QpHos^b = 4Q167 (*Commentary on Hosea^b*)

4QpMic(?) = 4Q168 (*Commentary on Micah[?]*)

4QpNah = 4Q169 (*Commentary on Nahum*)

4QpZeph = 4Q170 (*Commentary on Zephaniah*)

4QpPs^a = 4Q171 (*Commentary on Psalms^a*)

4QpUnid = 4Q172 (*Unidentified Commentary*)

4QpPs^b = 4Q173 (*Commentary on Psalms^b*)

4QFlor = 4Q174 (*Florilegium*) or 4QEschMidr (*Midrash on Eschatology*)

4QTest = 4Q175 (*Testimonia*)

4QTanh = 4Q176 (*Tanhumim*)

4QCatena^{a,b} = 4Q177 + 4Q182 (*Catena^{a,b}*)

4Q178 (unclassified fragments)

4QapocrLam A = 4Q179 (*Apocryphal Lamentations A*)

4QAgesCreat = 4Q180–181 (*Ages of Creation*)

4Q183 (*Historical Work*)

4QWiles = 4Q184 (*Wiles of the Harlot* or *of Lilith*)

4Q185 (*Sapiential Work*)

4Q186 (*Horoscope*)

4QTob^{a-d} ar = 4Q196–199 + 4QTob^e hebr = 4Q200 (Tobit)

4QEn$^{a,b,d-g}$ ar = 4Q201–202, 205–207, 212 (*1 Enoch*) + 4QEnGiants^{a,c} ar = 4Q203–204 (*Book of Giants*) + 4QEnastr^{a-d} ar = 4Q208–211 (*Astronomical Enoch*)

4QTLevi^{a-f} ar = 4Q213–214b, 214a + 4Q540–541 (Aramaic *Testament of Levi^{a-d}*)

4QTNaph = 4Q215 (*Testament of Naphtali*)

4Q215a (*Time of Righteousness*)

4QJub^{a-h} = 4Q216–224 (*Jubilees*) + 4QJub^{a-c} = 4Q225–227 (pseudo-*Jubilees*) + 4Q228 (a work citing *Jubilees*)

4QPrNab = 4Q242 (*Prayer of Nabonidus*)

4QpsDan^{a-c} ar = 4Q243–245 (pseudo-Daniel)

4Q246 (*Apocryphon of Daniel*)

4QApocWeeks? = 4Q247 (*Apocalypse of Weeks?*)

4Q248 (*Acts of a Greek King*)

4QMSM = 4Q249 + 4Q250 (*Midrash Sepher Moshe*)

4Q251 (*Halakah A*)

4QpGen^{a-d} = 4Q252–254a (*Commentaries on Genesis^{a-c}*)

4QS^{a-j} = 4Q255–264 + 4Q319 (*Rule of the Community*)

4Q264^a (*Halakah B*)

4QSD = 4Q265 (*Serek Damascus*)

4QD^{a-h} = 4Q266–273 (*Damascus Covenant*)

4Q274 + 4Q276–278 (*Tohorot*, or *Purification Rules*)

4Q275 (*Communal Ceremony*)

4Q279 (*Four Lots*)

4QBer = 4Q280 + 4Q286–290 (*Blessings*)

4Q281–282 (unidentified fragments)

(continued on next page)

Dead Sea Scrolls Selected List, cont'd

4Q284 (*Purification Liturgy*)

4Q284a (*Harvesting*)

4Q285 (*Sefer Hamilḥamah* or *Rule of War*)

4QBer^{a-e} = 4Q286–290 (*Berakot* or *Blessings*)

4Q291–293 (*Work Containing Prayers A, B, C*)

4Q294 (*Sapiential-Didactic Work*)

4QcryptA = 4Q298 (*Words of the Maskil to All Sons of Dawn*)

4Q299–301 (*Mysteries*)

4Q302/302a (*Admonitory Parable*)

4Q303–305 (*Meditation on Creation A, B, C*)

4Q306 (*People Who Err*)

4Q307 (*Proselyte/Temple*)

4QcryptMMT^g? = 4Q313 (*Cryptic A Miqsat Ma'ase ha-Torah^g?*)

4QAstrCrypt = 4Q317 (*Phases of the Moon*)

4QBr ar = 4Q318 (*Aramaic Brontologion*)

4Q319–330 (calendrical documents)

4QpapHistWork = 4Q331–333 (*Historical Work*)

4QOrdo = 4Q334 (*Order of Divine Office*)

4Q337 (fragment of a calendar)

4Q338 (a genealogical list)

4Q339 (*List of False Prophets ar*)

4Q340 (*List of Netinim*)

4Q341 (*List of Proper Names*, formerly 4QTherapeia)

4Q342–361 (miscellaneous papers)

4Q362–363a (cryptic texts)

4Q364–367 (*Reworked Pentateuch^{b-e}*)

4QapocrPent = 4Q368 (*Pentateuch Apocryphon*)

4QPEnosh = 4Q369 (*Prayer of Enosh*)

4Q370 (*Exhortation Based on Flood*)

4Q371–373 (*Apocryphon of Joseph^{a-c}*)

4QapocrMos A, B, C = 4Q374–375 + 4Q377 (*Apocryphon of Moses A, B, C*)

4Q376 (*Liturgy of the Three Tongues of Fire* or *Apocryphon of Moses$^{b?}$*)

4QPssJosh^{a,b} = 4Q378–379 (*Psalms of Joshua^{a,b}*)

4Q380–381 (*Noncanonical Psalms*)

4Qpap paraKings = 4Q382 (*Paraphrase of Kings*)

4Q383–384 + 4Q385b + 4Q387b (*Apocryphon of Jeremiah A, C^{a-f}*)

4QpsEzek = 4Q385 + 4Q386–388 (*pseudo-Ezekiel^{a-d}*)

4QpsMoses = 4Q385a + 4Q387a + 4Q388a–390 (*pseudo-Moses^{a-e}*)

4QpsEzek^c = 4Q391 (*pseudo-Ezekiel^c*)

4Q392–393 (*Liturgical Work*)

4QMMT = 4Q394–399 (*Miqsat Ma^{c}aśê ha-Torah*)

4QSirSabb^{a-h} = 4Q400–407 (*Song of the Sabbath*)

4Q408 + 4Q410–413 + 4Q415–419 + 4Q423–426 (various sapiential works)

4Q409 (*Liturgy*)

4Q414 (*Ritual Purity A*, formerly *Baptismal Liturgy*)

4Q421 (*Ways of Righteousness^a*)

4Q422 (*Paraphrase of Genesis and Exodus*)

4Q427–432 + 4Q433a +4Q440–440a (*Hymns^{a-f} + Hodayot*-like texts A–D)

4Q434–439 (*Barkhi Nafshi*)

4Q434a (*Grace after Meals*)

4Q441–442 + 4Q443 (*Individual Thanksgiving A, B + Personal Prayer*)

4Q444 (*Incantation*)

4Q445 (*Lament A*)

4Q446–447 (*Poetic Text A, B*)

4Q448 (*Apocryphal Psalm and Prayer*)

4Q449–457 (*Prayers*)

4Q458–463 + 4Q464a + 4Q467–468 (historical/pseudepigraphal narratives)

(continued on next page)

DEAD SEA SCROLLS SELECTED LIST, CONT'D

4Q464 (*Exposition on the Patriarchs*)

4Q469–470 (apocryphal texts)

4Q471 (*War Scroll^h*)

4Q472–476 (eschatological and sapiential works)

4Q477 (*Rebukes*)

4Q478 (fragment mentioning festivals)

4Q479 (text mentioning the seed of David)

4Q480 + 4Q481b + 4Q481e (narrative fragments)

4Q481 (small fragments)

4Q481a (*Apocryphon of Elisha*)

4Q481c (*Prayer for Mercy*)

4Q481d (fragments with red ink)

4Q482–483 (*Jubilees?*)

4QTJudah (?) = 4Q484 (*Testament of Judah*[?])

4Q485 (*Prophecy*)

4Q486–487 (*Sapiential Work? A, B*)

4Q488–490 (fragments of an apocalypse?)

4Q491–497 (*War Scroll^a-g*)

4Q498–499 (fragments of hymns)

4Q500 (*Vineyard Benediction*)

4Q501 (*Apocryphal Lamentations B*)

pap4QRitMar = 4Q502 (*Ritual of Marriage* papyrus)

4QpapPrQuot = 4Q503 (*Prières quotidiennes* or *Daily Prayers^a*)

4QDibHam^a-c = 4Q504–506 (*Words of the Luminaries^a-c*)

4QPrFêtes^a-c = 4Q507–509 (*Festival Prayers^a-c*)

4QShir^a,b = 4Q510–511 (*Songs of the Sage^a,b*)

4QpapRitPur B = 4Q512 (*Ritual Purity B*)

4Q513–514 (*Ordinances^b,c*)

4Q515–520 (unclassified fragments)

4Q521 (*Messianic Apocalypse*)

4Q522 (*Prophecy of Joshua*)

4Q523 (*Jonathan*)

4QTemple = 4Q524 (*Temple Scroll*)

4Q525 (*Beatitudes*)

4Q526 (*Testament?*)

4Q527 (*Liturgical Work D?*)

4Q528 (*Hymnic or Sapiential Work B*)

4Q529 (Aramaic *Words of Michael*)

4QEnGiants^b-e = 4Q530–533 (*Book of Giants*)

4QMess ar = 4Q534 (*Elect of God*)

4Q535–536 (formerly Birth of Noah^c,d ar)

4QTJacob (?) ar = 4QAJa ar = 4Q537 (Aramaic *Testament,* or *Vision,* or *Apocryphon of Jacob*)

4QTJudah = 4QAJu ar = 4Q538 (Aramaic *Testament* or *Apocryphon of Judah*)

4QapocrJoseph = 4QAJo ar = 4Q539 (Aramaic *Apocryphon of Joseph*)

4QapocrLevi^a,b(formerly c,d) ar = 4Q540–541 (*Apocryphon of Levi^a,b*)

4QTQahat ar = 4Q542 (Aramaic *Testament of Qahat*)

4QAmram^a-f = 4Q543–548 (*Visions of Amram^a-f*)

4Q549 (a work mentioning Hur and Miriam)

4QPrEsther^a-e = 4Q550–550^d (*Proto-Esther^a-e*)

4QDanSuz? ar = 4Q551 (*Susanna?*)

4QFour Kingdoms^a,b ar = 4Q552–553 (*Four Kingdoms^a,b*)

4QNJ^a,b ar = 4Q554–555 (*New Jerusalem*)

4QVision^a-c ar = 4Q556–558 (*Vision*)

4QpapBibChronology ar = 4Q559 (Aramaic *Biblical Chronology*)

4Q560 (Aramaic exorcistic text)

4QHor ar = 4Q561 (Aramaic *Horoscope*)

4Q562–575 (miscellaneous Aramaic fragments)

4QGen^n = 4Q576 (*Genesis^n*)

4Q577 (text mentioning the flood)

4Q578 (*Historical Text B*)

(continued on next page)

DEAD SEA SCROLLS SELECTED LIST, CONT'D

4QHymnic Work? = 4Q579 (*Hymnic Work?*)

5QapocrJosh = 5Q9 (*Apocryphon of Joshua*)

5QpMal or 5QapMal = 5Q10 (*Commentary on*, or *Apocryphon of, Malachi*)

5QS = 5Q11 (*Rule of the Community*)

5QD = 5Q12 (*Damascus Covenant*)

5QRègle = 5Q13 (*Rule*)

5QCurses = 5Q14 (*Curses*)

5QNJ ar = 5Q15 (*New Jerusalem*)

5Q16–25 (unclassified fragments)

6QpapEnGiants = 6Q8 (*Book of Giants*)

6Qpap apocrSam-Kgs = 6Q9 (*Samuel-Kings Apocryphon*)

6Q10 + 6Q12 (prophetic materials)

6QAllegory = 6Q11 (*Allegory of the Vine*)

6QPriestProph = 6Q13 (*Priestly Prophecy*)

6QApoc ar = 6Q14 (Aramaic apocalypse)

6QD = 6Q15 (*Damascus Document*)

6QpapBen = 6Q16 (*Benediction*)

6QpapCalenDoc = 6Q17 (calendrical document)

6QpapHymn = 6Q18 (*Hymn*)

6QGen? ar = 6Q19 (*Targum of Genesis?*)

6QDeut? = 6Q20 (Deuteronomy?)

6Q21 (prophetic text?)

6Q22–31 (mostly unclassified fragments)

7QLXXEpJer = 7Q2 (*Epistle of Jeremiah*)

7Q3, 5–7, 9–10, 15–18 (unclassified fragments)

7QpapEn gr = 7Q4, 8, 11–14 (*Enoch*)

7Q19 (papyrus imprint)

11QPs$^{a–e}$ = 11Q5–9 (*Psalms Scroll*)

11QtgJob = 11Q10 (*Targum of Job*)

11QApPs^a = 11Q11 (*Apocryphal Psalms^a*)

11QJub = 11Q12 (*Jubilees*)

11QMelch = 11Q13 (*Melchizedek Text*)

11QBer or 11QSepher ha-Milhamah = 11Q14 (*Blessings*)

11QHymns^{a,b} = 11Q15–16 (*Hymns^{a,b}*)

11QShirShabb = 11Q17 (*Songs of the Sabbath Sacrifice*)

11QJN ar = 11Q18 (*New Jerusalem*)

11QTemple^{a,b} = 11Q19–20 (*Temple Scroll*)

11QTemple? = 11Q21 (*Temple? Scroll*)

11Q22–31 (unidentified fragments)

MASADA

MURABBAᶜAT

NAHAL ḤEVER

NAHAL ṢEʾELIM (WADI SEIYÂL)

WADI SDEIR

NAHAL MISHMAR

KHIRBET MIRD

WADI ED-DALIYEH

CAIRO GENIZAH

CD

The Dead Sea Scrolls probably constitute the single most important biblically related literary discovery of the twentieth century. The Scrolls have contributed significantly to biblical scholarship in several fields: (1) the study of ancient writing and making of books/scrolls; (2) textual criticism of the OT; (3) linguistic studies in Hebrew and Aramaic; (4) apocryphal and pseudepigraphal studies; (5)

the study of sects and groups, particularly the Essenes, within Palestinian Jewry; (6) ancient methods of biblical interpretation; (7) intertestamental history; (8) first-century doctrines and religious ideas; and (9) NT background studies.

Contents

The exact number of scrolls now extant is not known. This is primarily because of the fragmentary condition of many scrolls, with the result that sometimes we do not know which fragments belong to which document. It is also because one or two (or more) scrolls neither photographed nor transcribed may well be in private hands. The best estimate is that there are 870–880 scrolls, of which about 220 are Bible scrolls. See S. A. Reed, *The Dead Sea Scrolls Catalogue: Documents, Photographs, and Museum Inventory Numbers* (ed. M. J. Lundberg; SBLRBS 32; Atlanta: Scholars Press, 1994). They are also listed in Alexander et al., *SBLHS* 183–233, and in E. Tov, "A List of the Texts from the Judaean Desert," in *The Dead Sea Scrolls after Fifty Years* (ed. Flint and VanderKam), 2:669–717.

The Discoveries in the Judaean Desert series (Oxford), nearly complete, constitutes the official *editio princeps* of this corpus. Most of these volumes are listed in *SBLHS* 178–79; a more up-to-date listing is provided below. Perhaps the most convenient presentation is that by F. García Martínez and E. J. C. Tigchelaar, whose two volumes present the non-Bible scrolls on facing pages, with Hebrew or Aramaic on the left and an English translation on the right. These volumes include not only the scrolls from the eleven Qumran caves; they include related materials from the Cairo Genizah. James Charlesworth and colleagues are preparing a similar presentation, but with critical apparatus and notes, as part of the Princeton Dead Sea Scrolls project. One should note the pointed version by Eduard Lohse (which contains almost none of the fragmentary texts and other more recently published texts) and the multivolume works by Ben Zion Wacholder and Martin Abegg (cited in the next paragraph). Finally, mention should be made of the photographs published by J. M. Robinson and R. H. Eisenman, *A Facsimile Edition of the Dead Sea Scrolls* (Washington: Biblical Archaeology Society, 1991), as well as the Brill edition on microfiche: E. Tov, with S. J. Pfann, *The Dead Sea Scrolls on Microfiche: A Comprehensive Facsimile Edition of the Texts from the Judean Desert* (Leiden: Brill, 1993).

Bibliography: Hebrew and Aramaic Text: K. BEYER, *Die aramäischen Texte vom Toten Meer: Ergänzungsband* (Göttingen: Vandenhoeck & Ruprecht, 1994); IDEM, *Die aramäischen Texte vom Toten Meer samt den Inschriften aus Palästina, dem Testament Levis aus der Kairoer Genisa, der Fastenrolle, und den alten talmudischen Zitaten* (Göttingen: Vandenhoeck & Ruprecht, 1984); DJD volumes (see list below); E. L. SUKENIK, *The Dead Sea Scrolls of the Hebrew University* (ed. N. Avigad and Y. Yadin; Jerusalem: Hebrew University and Magnes Press, 1955); E. TOV, *The Dead Sea Scrolls on Microfiche* (Leiden: Brill, 1993); B. Z. WACHOLDER and M. G. ABEGG Jr., *A Preliminary Edition of the Unpublished Dead Sea Scrolls: The Hebrew and Aramaic Texts from Cave Four* (4 fasc.; Washington, D.C.: Biblical Archaeology Society, 1991–1996). *Hebrew and Aramaic Text with English Translation:*

J. H. CHARLESWORTH et al., eds., *The Dead Sea Scrolls: Hebrew, Aramaic, and Greek Texts with English Translations* (Princeton Theological Seminary Dead Sea Scrolls Project; Louisville: Westminster John Knox, 1994–): vol. 1, *Rule of the Community and Related Documents* (1994); vol. 2, *Damascus Document, War Scroll, and Related Documents* (1995); vol. 4A, *Pseudepigraphic and Non-Masoretic Psalms and Prayers* (1997); vol. 4B, *Angelic Liturgy: Songs of the Sabbath Sacrifice* (1999); and vol. 6B, *Pesharim, Other Commentaries, and Related Documents* (2002); J. A. FITZMYER and D. J. HARRINGTON, *A Manual of Palestinian Aramaic Texts (Second Century B.C.–Second Century A.D.)* (BibOr 34; Rome: Pontifical Biblical Institute, 1978); F. GARCÍA MARTÍNEZ and E. J. C. TIGCHELAAR, *The Dead Sea Scrolls Study Edition* (Leiden: Brill, 1997–1978): vol. 1, *1Q1–4Q273* (1997); vol. 2, *4Q274–11Q31* (1998). **Pointed Hebrew Text with German Translation:** E. LOHSE, *Die Texte aus Qumran: Hebräisch und Deutsch* (3d ed.; Munich: Kösel, 1981). **English Translations:** A. DUPONT-SOMMER, *The Essene Writings from Qumran* (Gloucester, Mass.: Peter Smith, 1973) (based on French translation); F. GARCÍA MARTÍNEZ, *The Dead Sea Scrolls Translated: The Qumran Texts in English* (Leiden: Brill, 1994) (based on Spanish translation); G. VERMES, *The Dead Sea Scrolls in English* (4th ed., New York: Penguin, 1995); M. O. WISE, M. G. ABEGG Jr., and E. M. COOK, *The Dead Sea Scrolls: A New Translation* (San Francisco: HarperCollins, 1996). **English Translation of Bible Scrolls:** M. G. ABEGG, P. W. FLINT, and E. ULRICH, *The Dead Sea Scrolls Bible: The Oldest Known Bible Translated for the First Time into English* (San Francisco: HarperCollins, 1999). **Concordances:** M. G. ABEGG Jr. with J. E. BOWLEY and E. M. COOK, in consultation with E. TOV, *The Dead Sea Scrolls Concordance* (Boston: Brill, 2003–) (also available as a module for the Accordance software program); J. H. CHARLESWORTH, ed., *Graphic Concordance to the Dead Sea Scrolls* (Louisville: Westminster/John Knox, 1991); U. DAHMEN, "Nachträge zur Qumran-Konkordanz," *ZAH* 4 (1991): 213–35; K. G. KUHN et al., *Konkordanz zu den Qumrantexten* (Göttingen: Vandenhoeck & Ruprecht, 1960) (augmented, *RevQ* 4 [1963–1964]: 163–234). **Analysis of Qumran Hebrew and Aramaic:** M. G. ABEGG, "The Hebrew of the Dead Sea Scrolls," in *The Dead Sea Scrolls after Fifty Years* (ed. Flint and VanderKam), 1:325–58; E. M. COOK, "The Aramaic of the Dead Sea Scrolls," in *The Dead Sea Scrolls after Fifty Years* (ed. Flint and VanderKam), 1:359–78; E. QIMRON, *The Hebrew of the Dead Sea Scrolls* (HSS 29; Atlanta: Scholars Press, 1986). **Archaeology of Qumran:** Y. HIRSCHFELD, *Qumran in Context: Reassessing the Archaeological Evidence* (Peabody, Mass.: Hendrickson, 2004); J. MAGNESS, *The Archaeology of Qumran and the Dead Sea Scrolls* (Studies in the Dead Sea Scrolls and Related Literature; Grand Rapids: Eerdmans, 2002); C. MARTONE, "A Concordance to the Newly Published Qumran Texts," *Hen* 15 (1993): 155–206. **Qumran and Christian Origins:** C. M. PATE, *Communities of the Last Days: The Dead Sea Scrolls, the New Testament, and the Story of Israel* (Downers Grove, Ill.: InterVarsity, 2000); J. C. VANDERKAM and P. W. FLINT, *The Meaning of the Dead Sea Scrolls: Their Significance for Understanding the Bible, Judaism, Jesus, and Christianity* (San Francisco: HarperCollins, 2002).

Select Bibliography of Major Conference Volumes: G. J. BROOKE, *New Qumran Texts and Studies;* E. G. CHAZON and M. E. STONE, eds., *Pseudepigraphical Perspectives—the Apocrypha and Pseudepigrapha in Light of the Dead Sea Scrolls: Proceedings of the International Symposium of the Orion Centre, 12–14 January 1997* (STDJ 31; Leiden: Brill, 1999); F. H. CRYER and T. L. THOMPSON, eds., *Qumran between the Old and New Testament* (JSOTSup 290; Copenhagen International Seminar 6; Sheffield: Sheffield, 1998); D. DIMANT and U. RAPPAPORT, *The Dead Sea Scrolls;* D. DIMANT and L. H. SCHIFFMAN, *Time to Prepare the Way in the Wilderness;* P. W. FLINT and J. C. VANDERKAM, *The Dead Sea Scrolls after Fifty Years;* R. A. KUGLER and E. M. SCHULLER, eds., *The Dead Sea Scrolls at*

Fifty: Proceedings of the 1997 Society of Biblical Literature Qumran Section Meetings (SBLEJL 15; Atlanta: Scholars Press, 1999); T. H. LIM with L. W. HURTADO, A. G. AULD, and A. JACK, eds., *The Dead Sea Scrolls in Their Historical Context* (Edinburgh: T&T Clark, 2000); D. W. PARRY and E. ULRICH, *The Provo International Conference on the Dead Sea Scrolls;* S. E. PORTER and C. A. EVANS, *The Scrolls and the Scriptures;* L. H. SCHIFFMAN, E. TOV, and J. C. VANDERKAM, eds., *The Dead Sea Scrolls Fifty Years after Their Discovery: Proceedings of the Jerusalem Congress, July 20–25, 1997* (Jerusalem: Israel Exploration Society and Israel Antiquities Authority, 2000); M. E. STONE and E. G. CHAZON, *Biblical Perspectives—Early Use and Interpretation of the Bible in Light of the Dead Sea Scrolls;* J. TREBOLLE BARRERA and L. VEGAS MONTANER, *The Madrid Qumran Congress;* E. ULRICH and J. C. VANDERKAM, eds., *The Community of the Renewed Covenant: The Notre Dame Symposium on the Dead Sea Scrolls* (CJAS 10; Notre Dame, Ind.: University of Notre Dame Press, 1994); M. O. WISE et al., *Methods of Investigation of the Dead Sea Scrolls and the Khirbet Qumran Site.*

Discoveries in the Judaean Desert (DJDJ/DJD):

The Discoveries in the Judaean Desert series (= DJD; formerly, Discoveries in the Judaean Desert of Jordan = DJDJ), published by Oxford's Clarendon Press, is the official publication of the Dead Sea Scrolls. To date, this series is nearly complete, with thirty-six of the projected forty volumes published. Yet to appear are volumes 5a (a revision of the original 5), 17, 32, and 37. The volumes are listed below in serial sequence, with a listing of contents. In this chapter, references to these works follow the format "author (DJD/DJDJ + volume no.) page nos."

D. Barthélemy and J. T. Milik, *Qumran Cave I* (DJD 1; Oxford: Clarendon, 1955), xi + 163 pp. + 37 pls. (1Q1–72)

P. Benoit, J. T. Milik, and R. de Vaux, *Les grottes de Murabba^cat* (DJD 2; Oxford: Clarendon, 1961), xv + 314 pp. + 107 pls. (Mur 1–173)

M. Baillet, J. T. Milik, et R. de Vaux, *Les "petites grottes" de Qumrân* (DJDJ 3; Oxford: Clarendon, 1962), xiii + 315 pp. + 71 pls. (2Q1–33, 3Q1–15, 5Q1–25, 6Q1–31, 7Q1–19, 8Q1–5, 9Q1, 10Q1)

J. A. Sanders, *The Psalms Scroll of Qumran Cave 11 (11QPs^a)* (DJDJ 4; Oxford: Clarendon, 1965), xi + 97 pp. + 17 pls. (11Q5)

J. M. Allegro, with A. A. Anderson, *Qumran Cave 4.I (4Q158–4Q186)* (DJDJ 5; Oxford: Clarendon, 1968), 111 pp. + 31 pls. (4Q158–186)

M. J. Bernstein and G. J. Brooke, in consultation with J. C. VanderKam and M. Brady, *Qumran Cave 4.I (4Q158–186)* (rev. ed.; DJD 5a; Oxford: Clarendon, forthcoming) (a complete revision of the Pesher volume, containing 4Q158–186)

M. Baillet, R. de Vaux, and J. T. Milik, *Qumran grotte 4.II: I. Archéologie. II. Tefillin, mezuzot, et targums (4Q128–4Q157)* (DJD 6; Oxford: Clarendon, 1977), xi + 91 pp. + 28 pls. (4Q128–157)

M. Baillet, *Qumrân grotte 4.III (4Q482–4Q520)* (DJD 7; Oxford: Clarendon, 1982), xiv + 339 pp. + 80 pls. (4Q482–520)

E. Tov, *The Greek Minor Prophets Scroll from Nahal Hever (8HevXIIgr)* (DJD 8; Oxford: Clarendon, 1990), x + 169 pp. + 20 pls. (8Ḥev1)

P. W. Skehan, E. Ulrich, and J. E. Sanderson, with P. J. Parsons, *Qumran Cave 4.IV: Palaeo-Hebrew and Greek Biblical Manuscripts* (DJD 9; Oxford: Clarendon, 1992), xiii + 250 pp. + 47 pls. (4Q11–12, 22, 45–46, 101, 119–127)

E. Qimron and J. Strugnell, *Qumran Cave 4.V: Miqsat Ma'ase ha-Torah* (DJD 10; Oxford: Clarendon, 1994), xiv + 235 pp. + 8 pls. (4Q394–399)

E. Eshel, H. Eshel, C. Newsom, B. Nitzan, E. Schuller, and A. Yardeni, in consultation with J. C. VanderKam and M. Brady, *Qumran Cave 4.VI: Poetical and Liturgical Texts, Part 1* (DJD 11; Oxford: Clarendon, 1997), xi + 425 pp. + concordances + 32 pls. (4Q286–290, 380–381, 400–407, 448, Mas1k)

E. Ulrich and F. M. Cross, *Qumran Cave 4.VII: Genesis to Numbers* (DJD 12; Oxford: Clarendon, 1994), xv + 272 pp. + 49 pls. (4Q1–10, 13–21, 23–27)

H. W. Attridge, T. Elgvin, J. Milik, S. Olyan, J. Strugnell, E. Tov, J. VanderKam, and S. White, in consultation with J. C. VanderKam, *Qumran Cave 4.VIII: Parabiblical Texts, Part 1* (DJD 13; Oxford: Clarendon, 1994), x + 470 pp. + 43 pls. (4Q216–228, 364–367, 369, 382, 422)

E. Ulrich, F. M. Cross, S. W. Crawford, J. A. Duncan, P. W. Skehan, E. Tov, and J. Trebolle Barrera, *Qumran Cave 4.IX: Deuteronomy to Kings* (DJD 14; Oxford: Clarendon, 1995), xiii + 188 pp. + 37 pls. (4Q28–44, 47–50, 54)

E. Ulrich, F. M. Cross, R. E. Fuller, J. E. Sanderson, P. W. Skehan, and E. Tov, *Qumran Cave 4.X: The Prophets* (DJD 15; Oxford: Clarendon, 1997), xv + 325 pp. + 64 pls. (4Q55–82)

E. Ulrich et al., *Qumran Cave 4.XI: Psalms to Chronicles* (DJD 16; Oxford: Clarendon, 2000), xv + 302 pp. + 38 pls. (4Q83–100, 102–118, 522, 11Q8 frg. 3)

E. Ulrich, F. M. Cross, D. Parry, and R. Saley, *Qumran Cave 4.XII: 1–2 Samuel* (DJD 17; Oxford: Clarendon, forthcoming) (4Q51–53)

J. M. Baumgarten, *Qumran Cave 4.XIII: The Damascus Document (4Q266–273)* (DJD 18; Oxford: Clarendon, 1996), xix + 236 pp. + 42 pls. (4Q266–273)

M. Broshi, E. Eshel, J. Fitzmyer, E. Larson, C. Newsom, L. Schiffman, M. Smith, M. Stone, J. Strugnell, and A. Yardeni, in consultation with J. C. Vander-Kam, *Qumran Cave 4.XIV: Parabiblical Texts, Part 2* (DJD 19; Oxford: Clarendon, 1995), xi + 267 pp. + 29 pls. (4Q196–200, 339–340, 370, 374–376, 384, 391, 462–464b, 470)

T. Elgvin et al. in consultation with J. A. Fitzmyer, *Qumran Cave 4.XV: Sapiential Texts, Part 1* (DJD 20; Oxford: Clarendon, 1997), xi + 246 pp. + 18 pls. (4Q298–305, 411–413, 420–421, 425–426)

S. Talmon, J. Ben-Dov, and U. Glessmer, *Qumran Cave 4.XVI: Calendrical Texts* (DJD 21; Oxford: Clarendon, 2001), xi + 245 pp. + 13 pls. (4Q319–322, 323–324c, 324e–330, 334, 337, 394 frgs. 1–2)

G. J. Brooke, J. J. Collins, P. Flint, J. Greenfield, E. Larson, C. Newsom, É. Puech, L. H. Schiffman, M. Stone, and J. Trebolle Barrera, in consultation with J. VanderKam, partially based on earlier transcriptions by J. T. Milik and

J. Strugnell, *Qumran Cave 4.XVII: Parabiblical Texts, Part 3* (DJD 22; Oxford: Clarendon, 1996), xi + 352 pp. + 29 pls. (4Q213–215, 242–246, 252–254a, 275, 378–379, 473, 478–481e)

F. García Martínez, E. J. C. Tigchelaar, and A. S. van der Woude, *Manuscripts from Qumran Cave 11 (11Q2–18, 11Q20–30)* (DJD 23; Oxford: Clarendon, 1997), xiii + 457 pp. + concordances + 52 pls. (11Q2–4, 11Q5 frgs. E–F, 11Q6–18, 11Q20–31)

M. J. W. Leith, *Wadi Daliyeh Seal Impressions* (DJD 24; Oxford: Clarendon, 1997), xxv + 249 pp. + 24 pls.

É. Puech, *Qumran Cave 4.XVIII: Textes hébreux (4Q521–4Q528, 4Q576–4Q579)* (DJD 25; Oxford: Clarendon, 1997), xviii + 229 pp. + concordances + 15 pls. (4Q521–522, 523–528, 576–579)

P. S. Alexander and G. Vermes, *Qumran Cave 4.XIX: 4QSerekh Ha-Yahad and Two Related Texts* (DJD 26; Oxford: Clarendon, 1998), xvii + 253 pp. + 24 pls. (4Q255–264, 279)

H. M. Cotton and A. Yardeni, *Aramaic, Hebrew, and Greek Documentary Texts from Nahal Hever and Other Sites, with an Appendix Containing Alleged Qumran Texts* (DJD 27; Oxford: Clarendon, 1997), xxvii + 381 pp. + 33 figures and 61 pls. (4Q235, 342–348, 351–354, 356–359, 360a–361, Hev/Se7–50, XHev/Se60–169, Hev/Se?1–57)

D. Gropp, M. J. Bernstein, M. Brady, J. H. Charlesworth, P. W. Flint, H. Misgav, S. Pfann, E. Schuller, E. Tigchelaar, and J. VanderKam, *Wadi Daliyeh II and Qumran Cave 4.XXVIII: Miscellanea, Part 2* (DJD 28; Oxford: Clarendon, 2001), xv + 254 pp. + 63 pls. (4Q238, 313c, 317, 322a, 324d, 362–363b, 368, 371–373, 377, 468cc–dd, 11Q2, WDSP1–38)

E. Chazon et al. in consultation with J. C. VanderKam and M. Brady, *Qumran Cave 4.XX: Poetical and Liturgical Texts, Part 2* (DJD 29; Oxford: Clarendon, 1999), xiii + 478 pp. + 28 pls. (4Q280, 291–293, 392–393, 409, 427–440, 441–447, 449–454, 456–457b, 471b–471c, 476–476a)

D. Dimant, partially based on earlier texts by J. Strugnell, *Qumran Cave 4.XXVI: Parabiblical Texts, Part 4: Pseudo-Prophetic Texts* (DJD 30; Oxford: Clarendon, 2001), xiv + 278 pp. + 12 pls. (4Q383, 385–390)

É. Puech, *Qumran Grotte 4.XXII: Textes Arameens Premiere Partie (4Q529–549)* (DJD 31; Oxford: Clarendon, 2001), xviii + 439 pp. + 22 pls. (4Q203, 529–549)

P. W. Flint and E. Ulrich, *Qumran Cave 1.II: The Isaiah Scrolls* (DJD 32; Oxford: Clarendon, forthcoming) (1QIsa[a,b])

D. M. Pike and A. Skinner, with a contribution by T. L. Szink, in consultation with J. C. VanderKam and M. Brady, *Qumran Cave 4.XXIII: Unidentified Fragments* (DJD 33; Oxford: Clarendon, 2001), xv + 376 pp. + 41 pls.

J. Strugnell, D. J. Harrington, and T. Elgvin, in consultation with J. A. Fitzmyer, *Qumran Cave 4.XXIV: 4QInstruction (Musar leMevin): 4Q415* (DJD 34; Oxford: Clarendon, 1999), xvi + 584 pp. + 31 pls. (1Q26, 4Q274, 415)

J. M. Baumgarten, T. Elgvin, E. Eshel, E. Larson, M. R. Lehmann, S. Pfann, and L. H. Schiffman, based in part on earlier transcriptions by J. T. Milik,

Qumran Cave 4.XXV: Halakhic Texts (DJD 35; Oxford: Clarendon, 1999), xi
   + 173 pp. + xii pls. (4Q249, 251, 264a–265, 276–278, 284–284a, 414, 472a)
S. Pfann, P. S. Alexander, et al., *Qumran Cave 4.XXVI: Cryptic Texts and Miscellanea, Part 1* (DJD 36; Oxford: Clarendon, 2000), xvi + 739 pp. + Hebrew and
   Aramaic concordances + 49 pls. (4Q201, 203, 206, 208–209, 215a, 234,
   247–248, 249a–250j, 281a-f–282a-t, 285, 294, 306–313b, 318, 331–333,
   338, 341, 350, 355, 360, 408, 410–419, 423–424, 440a-b, 455, 458–461,
   466–468m-bb, 469, 471–471a, 472, 474–475, 477, KhQOstraca 1–3)
É. Puech in consultation with J. C. VanderKam and M. Brady, *Qumran Cave
   4.XXVII: Textes araméens, deuxième partie (4Q550–575, 580–582)* (DJD 37;
   Oxford: Clarendon, forthcoming) (4Q550–575, 580–582)
J. H. Charlesworth et al. in consultation with J. C. VanderKam and M. Brady,
   Miscellaneous Texts from the Judaean Desert (DJD 38; Oxford: Clarendon,
   2000), xvii + 250 pp. + 36 pls. (Jer 19c-h, Sdeir 1–4, 5/6Ḥev1, 8Ḥev 2, 4,
   XḤev/Se2–6, 1Mish 2, 34Se2–5)
E. Tov, with contributions by M. G. Abegg Jr., A. Lange, U. Mittmann-Richert,
   S. Pfann, E. J. C. Tigchelaar, E. Ulrich, and B. Webster, *The Texts from the
   Judaean Desert: Indices and an Introduction to the Discoveries in the Judaean
   Desert Series* (DJD 39; Oxford: Clarendon, 2002), x + 452 pp.

Identity of the Scrolls Community

There is debate over the origin of the Qumran community and its relationship to the group that Philo, Josephus, and others called the "Essenes." Philo
mentions the group in two places. In *Good Person* 75–91 he describes the
"Essaioi" as persons of high moral standards, who are "especially devout in the
service of God, not by offering sacrifices of animals, but by resolving to sanctify
their minds." They live communally in villages, they avoid cities, they are frugal,
modest, peaceful, egalitarian, and respectful of elders. They are called Essaioi,
Philo thinks, because the word is related to *hosiotēs* ("holiness"). In *Apologia pro
Judaeis,* a work that is lost but quoted by Eusebius (*Praep. ev.* 8.11.1–18), Philo repeats many of the things related in *That Every Good Person Is Free* and adds that
the Essaioi are made up mostly of older men ("there are no children of younger
years among the Essaioi, nor even adolescents or young men"), who are farmers,
shepherds, keepers of bees, and craftsmen of every sort. They constitute a self-
sufficient community. They hold all things common. They care for the sick.

Josephus mentions the Essenes many times; twice he dwells upon them
at length. In the *Jewish War* (2.8.2–11 §§119–158) Josephus calls the group
"Essenoi." He tells us that they renounce pleasure, disdain marriage, and adopt
young children in order to instruct them in their ways. They wear white garments. They live communally. They are sober and taciturn. Josephus also describes their requirements for membership and their strict regulations for daily
life. The Essenes believe in the eternal soul, which after death will either join the

abode of the righteous or the pit of Hades. Josephus then describes another order of Essenes which believes that marriage is proper and necessary, not for pleasure, but for the propagation of the human race. This passage is closely paralleled by Hippolytus, *Haer.* 9.18–28, and the latter may even be dependent upon the *Jewish War.* Josephus discusses the Essenes in a briefer account in *Ant.* 18.1.5 §§18–22. One important comment should be noted. He says that "they send offerings to the Temple, but offer no sacrifices there since the purifications to which they are accustomed are different. For this reason, they refrain from entering into the common enclosure, but offer sacrifices among themselves" (*Ant.* 18.1.5 §19). This is in essential agreement with what Philo had said (*Good Person* 12 §75). What Josephus meant when he said "offer sacrifices among themselves" is a matter of scholarly debate.

Pliny the Elder (ca. 75 C.E.) provides some useful information regarding the location of the Essenes (*Nat.* 5.17.4). According to him, the Essenes were situated west of the Dead Sea and north of Engedi and Masada. This is the same location where the Dead Sea Scrolls have been found. He goes on to say that although the Essenes did not practice marriage, their numbers grew because throngs of people sought to join them, having "repented" for their past lives. Probably drawing on the same source, Dio Chrysostom (ca. 100 C.E.), according to his biographer, Synesius, "praises the Essenes, who form an entire and prosperous city near the Dead Sea, in the center of Palestine, not far from Sodom" (Dio Chrysostom, *Disc. 3.2*).

Because of the similarities of doctrine and practice between the Essenes and the writers of the Dead Sea Scrolls and because of the location of this group near the Dead Sea, most scholars today have concluded that the scrolls were once part of the library of the Essenes. But what of the origin of this community? Here there is less agreement among scholars. Among the most plausible reconstructions is the hypothesis that the community was founded by the "Teacher of Righteousness," who criticized and was opposed by Jewish high priest and King Jannaeus (ca. 104–103 B.C.E.) and perhaps was put to death by Jannaeus's son Hyrcanus II (ca. 64 B.C.E.), the "Wicked Priest" (cf. 1QpHab 8:8–13; 9:9–12). Moreover, it has been suggested by R. Goossens that the Teacher of Righteousness was Onias the Righteous, a pious man remembered for his answered prayer (*m. Ta˓an.* 3:8; Josephus, *Ant.* 14.2.1 §22; see appendix 5). But this identification is not without difficulties and so has not won many followers. J. H. Charlesworth has suggested that the Wicked Priest was Jonathan, the younger brother of Judas Maccabeus and Simon. But it may be, as W. H. Brownlee argued, that the Wicked Priest was a technical term that referred to more than one Hasmonean high priest. I am inclined to agree. Like the Teacher of Righteousness, which probably came to be viewed as a title of office, so the Wicked Priest came to be understood as the title of the opposing office. Most scholars do agree, however, that the frequently appearing word "Kittim" refers to the Romans, which supports seeing the community as originating in the late second century B.C.E. and thriving on through the first century B.C.E. and into the first century C.E.

Bibliography: W. H. BROWNLEE, "A Comparison of the Covenanters of the Dead Sea Scrolls with pre-Christian Jewish Sects," *BA* 13 (1950): 50–72; IDEM, "The Historical Allusions of the Dead Sea Habakkuk Midrash," *BASOR* 126 (1952): 10–20; IDEM, "The Wicked Priest, the Man of Lies, and the Righteous Teacher—the Problem of Identity," *JQR* 73 (1982): 1–37; P. R. CALLAWAY, *The History of the Qumran Community: An Investigation* (JSPSup 3; Sheffield: JSOT Press, 1988); J. H. CHARLESWORTH, "The Origin and Subsequent History of the Authors of the Dead Sea Scrolls: Four Transitional Phases among the Qumran Essenes," *RevQ* 10 (1980): 213–33; D. DIMANT, "Qumran Sectarian Literature," *SJWSTP* 542–47; A. DUPONT-SOMMER, *The Jewish Sect of Qumran and the Essenes* (London: Vallentine, Mitchell, 1954); C. T. FRITSCH, "Herod the Great and the Qumran Community," *JBL* 74 (1955): 175–81; F. GARCÍA MARTÍNEZ and J. TREBOLLE BARRERA, *The People of the Dead Sea Scrolls: Their Writings, Beliefs, and Practices* (Leiden: Brill, 1995); R. GOOSSENS, "Les Kittim du Commentaire d'Habacuc," *La nouvelle Clio* 9 (1952): 138–70; IDEM, "Onias le juste, le messie de a nouvelle alliance, lapidé à Jérusalem en 65 av. J.-C.," *La nouvelle Clio* 7 (1950): 336–53; S. GORANSON, "Others and Intra-Jewish Polemic as Reflected in Qumran Texts," in *The Dead Sea Scrolls after Fifty Years* (ed. Flint and VanderKam), 2:534–51; G. JEREMIAS, *Der Lehrer der Gerechtigkeit* (SUNT 2; Göttingen: Vandenhoeck & Ruprecht, 1963); J. MURPHY-O'CONNOR, "Demetrius I and the Teacher of Righteousness (I Macc. x, 25–45)," *RB* 83 (1976): 400–420; IDEM, "Judean Desert," *EJMI* 139–43; L. H. SCHIFFMAN, *Archaeology and History in the Dead Sea Scrolls*; J. C. VANDER-KAM, "Identity and History of the Community," in *The Dead Sea Scrolls after Fifty Years* (ed. Flint and VanderKam), 2:487–533; A. S. VAN DER WOUDE, "Fifty Years of Qumran Research," in *The Dead Sea Scrolls after Fifty Years* (ed. Flint and VanderKam), 1:1–45; IDEM, "Wicked Priest or Wicked Priests? Reflections on the Identification of the Wicked Priest in the Habakkuk Commentary," *JJS* 33 (1982): 349–59; G. VERMES, "The Essenes and History," *JJS* 32 (1981): 18–31.

Normally, Qumran texts are cited, using arabic numerals, by column and line number, e.g., 1QS 9:3–6 means *Serek* ("Rule") from Qumran, Cave 1, column 9, lines 3 to 6. But in the case of most scrolls, because of their fragmentary condition, they are cited as follows: 4QpNah 3–4 i 6, which means fragments 3 and 4 (arabic numerals), column i (lowercase roman numerals), line 6 (arabic numerals).

The Dead Sea Scrolls constitute a vast and diverse body of written materials. These materials have been categorized according to the geographical regions in which they have been found. Of all the regions "Qumran" (from the gulch called Wadi Qumran) is best known. Recovered from eleven caves, the writings of Qumran number more than 800 documents. Many of these are in fragments (more than 20,000 fragments in all). J. H. Charlesworth (*JJ*, 184–86) subdivides the principal writings as "Qumran Rules" (ten documents), "Qumran Hymns and Prayers" (23 documents), "Qumran Commentaries" (21 documents), "Qumran Apocryphal and Other Works" (33 documents), and "Other" (nine documents). In many cases there are two or more fragmentary copies of these documents scattered among the caves. Counting the biblical books and the duplicates, the eleven caves of Qumran have yielded hundreds of documents (more than 600 from Cave 4 alone). The several regions are as follows:

Qumran
Masada
Murabbaʿat
Naḥal Ḥever (Wadi Khabra)
Naḥal Ṣeʾelim (Wadi Seiyâl)
Naḥal Mishmar (Wadi Mahras)
Khirbet Mird
Cairo Genizah

The chief finds of these regions will be summarized below, with most of the attention given to Qumran. Emphasis has been placed on the sectarian and apocryphal documents.

Summaries of Qumran Documents

Qumran, Cave 1

The Qumran caves are numbered according to the order of their discovery. Cave 1 was discovered, to the best of our knowledge, sometime late in 1947. Seventy-seven or seventy-eight scrolls were found in this cave, that is, 1Q1–72, 1QIsaiaha, 1QpHabakkuk, 1QapGenar (two scrolls that were never numbered), 1Q28a, 1Q28b (appendixes to 1Q28 [title] + 1QS, another otherwise unnumbered scroll), 1QM, and 1QH. 1Q1–12 + 1QIsaiaha are Bible scrolls (1QIsaiahb = 1Q8). 1Q13 is a phylactery, which comprises several quotations of Scripture. 1Q14–16 + 1QpHab are pesharim (on Micah, Habakkuk, Zephaniah, and Psalms). 1Q17–18 are copies of the pseudepigraphon *Jubilees*, known from other MSS. 1Q19–27 comprise various pseudepigraphal texts, some of them previously known (such as 1Q21 = Aramaic *Testament of Levi*, and 1Q23–24 = Enochic *Book of Giants*). 1Q28 + 1QS + 1Q28a–b comprise Cave 1's *Rule of the Community* and appendixes. 1Q29–31 comprise various liturgical texts, while 1Q32 describes the *New Jerusalem*, a text found in other caves. 1Q33 + M comprise the famous *War Scroll* or *Milḥamah*. 1Q34 + 1Q34bis comprise *Festival Prayers*, and 1Q35–40 are hymnic compositions. 1Q41–62 comprise unclassified Hebrew fragments, 1Q63–68 comprise unclassified Aramaic fragments, and 1Q69–70bis comprise unclassified papyrus fragments. And finally, 1Q71–72 have turned out to be small fragments of Daniel. All the identified and classified texts are briefly reviewed below.

1QIsaa,b (Isaiah, first and second copies). Two copies of Isaiah were discovered among the contents of Cave 1. Copy "a," also known as the *Great Isaiah Scroll*, is complete, while copy "b" (= 1Q8) is fragmentary (fragments of chs. 7–66). Whereas copy "a" follows the Hebrew preserved in the Masoretic tradition closely, copy "b" takes liberties with the text, almost to the point that it could be regarded as a sort of Hebrew Targum to Isaiah. For discussion of the possible exegetical significance in some of the variants in 1QIsaa, see Brownlee;

Rosenbloom; Steck (vol. 1). For discussion of other biblical scrolls from Qumran, see below.

Bibliography: W. H. BROWNLEE, *The Meaning of the Qumran Scrolls for the Bible* (New York: Oxford University Press, 1964), 155–259; M. BURROWS, *The Isaiah Manuscript and the Habakkuk Commentary* (vol. 1 of *The Dead Sea Scrolls of St. Mark's Monastery*), pls. I–LIV (photographs of 1QIsa^a); C. A. EVANS, "1QIsaiah^a and the Absence of Prophetic Critique at Qumran," *RevQ* 11 (1984): 560–70; G. GARBINI, "1QIsa^b et le texte d'Esaïe," *Hen* 6 (1984): 17–21; E. Y. KUTSCHER, *The Language and Linguistic Background of the Isaiah Scroll (1 QIsa^a)* (indexed and corrected by E. Qimron; STDJ 6A; Leiden: Brill, 1979); D. W. PARRY and E. QIMRON, eds., *The Great Isaiah Scroll (1QIsa^a): A New Edition* (STDJ 32; Leiden: Brill, 1998); J. R. ROSENBLOOM, *The Dead Sea Isaiah Scroll—a Literary Analysis: A Comparison with the Masoretic Text and the Biblia hebraica* (Grand Rapids: Eerdmans, 1970); O. H. STECK, *Die erste Jesajarolle von Qumran (1QIsa)* (2 vols.; SBS 173/1–2; Stuttgart: Katholisches Bibelwerk, 1998); E. L. SUKENIK, *The Dead Sea Scrolls of the Hebrew University* (Jerusalem: Magnes Press, 1955) (transcription of 1QIsa^b); S. TALMON, "1QIsa^a as a Witness to Ancient Exegesis of the Book of Isaiah," *ASTI* 1 (1962): 62–72, repr. in Talmon, *The World of Qumran from Within: Collected Studies* (Jerusalem: Magnes Press; Leiden: Brill, 1989), 131–41; J. C. TREVER, *Scrolls from Qumran Cave I*, 13–123 (black-and-white photographs on the left-hand side, color photographs on the right). P. W. Flint and E. Ulrich are preparing a new edition for DJD.

1QpHab (*Pesher* or *Commentary on Habakkuk*). The pesharim of Cave 1 include 1QpHab, 1QpMic (= 1Q14), 1QpZeph (= 1Q15), and 1QpPs (= 1Q16). They are discussed below under the heading "Pesharim: Qumran's Commentaries on Scripture."

Bibliography: M. J. BERNSTEIN, " 'Walking in the Festivals of the Gentiles': 4QpHosea^a 2.15–17 and *Jubilees* 6.34–38," *JSP* 9 (1991): 21–34; G. J. BROOKE, "Qumran Pesher: Towards the Redefinition of a Genre," *RevQ* 10 (1979–1981): 483–503; W. H. BROWNLEE, *The Midrash Pesher of Habakkuk* (SBLMS 24; Missoula, Mont.: Scholars Press, 1979); M. BURROWS, *The Isaiah Manuscript and the Habakkuk Commentary* (vol. 1 of *The Dead Sea Scrolls of St. Mark's Monastery*), pls. LV–LXI (photographs of 1QpHab); J. CARMIGNAC, "Interprétations de prophètes et de psaumes," *TQum* 2:45–128; J. H. CHARLESWORTH, *The Pesharim and Qumran History: Chaos or Consensus?* (Grand Rapids: Eerdmans, 2002); D. DIMANT, "Qumran Sectarian Literature," *SJWSTP* 505–14; M. P. HORGAN, "The Bible Explained (Prophecies)," *EJMI* 250–53; IDEM, *Pesharim*; J. MURPHY-O'CONNOR, "The Judean Desert," *EJMI* 134–35; A. E. PALUMBO Jr. "1QpHab 11:2–8 and the Death of James the Just," *QC* 3 (1993): 139–53; IDEM, "A New Interpretation of the Nahum Commentary," *FO* 29 (1992–1993): 153–62; L. H. SCHIFFMAN, "Pharisees and Sadducees in Pesher Nahum," in *Minhah le-Nahum* (ed. M. Brettler and M. Fishbane; JSOTSup 154; Sheffield: JSOT Press, 1993), 272–90; H. STEGEMANN, "Weitere Stücke von 4 Q p Psalm 37, von 4 Q Patriarchal Blessings und Hinweis auf eine unedierte Handschrift aus Höhle 4 Q mit Exzerpten aus dem Deuteronomium," *RevQ* 6 (1967): 193–227; J. C. TREVER, *Scrolls from Qumran Cave I*, 149–63 (black-and-white photographs on the left-hand side, color photographs on the right); A. S. VAN DER WOUDE, "Once Again: The Wicked Priests in the Habakkuk Pesher from Cave 1 of Qumran," *RevQ* 17 (1996): 375–84; IDEM, "Wicked Priest or Wicked Priests? Reflections on the Identification of the

Wicked Priest in the Habakkuk Commentary," in *Essays in Honour of Yigael Yadin* (ed. Vermes and Neusner), 349–59.

1QJub[a,b] = 1Q17–18. This text, along with other copies and related works, is discussed below under the heading "Apocrypha and Pseudepigrapha."

Bibliography: J. C. VANDERKAM, *Textual and Historical Studies in the Book of Jubilees* (HSM 14; Missoula, Mont.: Scholars Press, 1977); J. C. VANDERKAM and J. T. MILIK, "The First *Jubilees* Manuscript from Qumran Cave 4: A Preliminary Publication," *JBL* 110 (1991): 243–70.

1QNoah = 1Q19 (*Book of Noah*). This text, along with the other *Enoch* and related texts, is discussed below. The *Book of Noah* is related to *1 En.* 8:4–9:4; 106:9–10, in which the sins of the earth and the birth of Noah are described. See the discussion below under the heading "Apocrypha and Pseudepigrapha."

Bibliography: F. GARCÍA MARTÍNEZ, "4QMess ar and the Book of Noah," in *Qumran and Apocalyptic*, 1–44; J. T. MILIK, *BE* 55–60; L. T. STUCKENBRUCK, *The Book of Giants from Qumran* (TSAJ 62; Tübingen: Mohr [Siebeck], 1997).

1QapGen = 1Q20 (*Genesis Apocryphon*). The *Genesis Apocryphon* of Cave 1 is written in Aramaic and is a first-person retelling of some of the narratives of Genesis concerning the patriarchs. Lamech suspects that the birth of his son Noah was in some ways supernatural, so he goes to his father Methuselah. Methuselah, however, takes the matter to his father Enoch for an explanation. Enoch explains that sin had taken place in the days of his father Jared involving the sons of God (Gen 6:1–3). Therefore, God was about to bring upon the earth a fearful judgment. The Noah story is then retold with embellishments. The next hero is Abraham who is warned in a dream that men will try to kill him in order to take his wife. When Pharaoh learns of Sarah's beauty he takes her and tries to kill Abraham. Sarah saves his life by claiming that he was only her kinsman. (This is perhaps an attempt to justify the biblical account of Abraham's deceit.) The story continues with the adventures of Lot and the promise of a son to Abraham. The *Genesis Apocryphon* is quite similar in style to *Jubilees.*

Bibliography: J. CARMIGNAC, "L'Apocryphe de la Genèse," *TQum* 2:207–42; C. A. EVANS, "The Genesis Apocryphon and the Rewritten Bible," *RevQ* 13 (1988): 153–65; J. A. FITZMYER, *DSS* 137–40; IDEM, *The Genesis Apocryphon of Qumran Cave I: A Commentary* (2d ed.; BibOr 18A; Rome: Pontifical Biblical Institute, 1971) (Aramaic text, English translation, commentary, bibliography, and response to reviews of the 1966 edition); J. T. MILIK (DJD 1) 86–87; T. MURAOKA, "Notes on the Aramaic of the Genesis Apocryphon," *RevQ* 8 (1972): 7–51; J. C. REEVES, "What Does Noah Offer in 1QapGen X, 15?" *RevQ* 12 (1986): 415–19; R. C. STEINER, "The Heading of the *Book of the Words of Noah* on a Fragment of the Genesis Apocryphon: New Light on a 'Lost' Work," *DSD* 2 (1995): 66–71; J. C. VANDERKAM, "The Textual Affinities of the Biblical Citations in the Genesis Apocryphon," *JBL* 97

(1978): 45–55; M. WEINFELD, "Sarah and Abimelech (Genesis 20) against the Background of an Assyrian Law and the Genesis Apocryphon," in *Mélanges bibliques et orientaux en l'honneur de M. Mathias Delcor* (ed. A. Caquot, S. Légasse, and M. Tardieu; Neukirchen: Neukirchener Verlag, 1985), 431–36; R. T. WHITE, "Genesis Apocryphon," *ABD* 2:932–33.

1QTLevi ar = 1Q21 (*Testament of Levi*). This fragment seems to be related to the Greek *Testament of Levi* (cf. *T. Levi* 8:11). It also overlaps with CTLevi ar ("C" refers to Cairo Genizah), which also parallels 4Q213–214. This *Testament* and others are discussed below under the heading "Apocrypha and Pseudepigrapha."

Bibliography: J. T. MILIK (DJD 1) 87–91.

1QDM = 1Q22 (*Dibre Moshe*). The *Dibre Moshe*, or *Sayings of Moses*, purports to be Moses' farewell address to Israel. Moses exhorts the people to remain loyal to Yahweh and to abhor the idolatry of the pagans that they will encounter in the promised land. He reminds them to observe the Year of Release (every seventh year). The fragment ends with instructions regarding the day of Atonement.

Bibliography: J. CARMIGNAC, "Dires de Moïse," *TQum* 2:247–53; J. T. MILIK (DJD 1) 91–97; J. STRUGNELL, "Moses-Pseudepigrapha at Qumran: 4Q375, 4Q376, and Similar Works," in *Archaeology and History in the Dead Sea Scrolls* (ed. Schiffman), 221–56.

1QEnGiants[a,b] = 1Q23–24 (*Book of Giants*). 1Q23; 2Q26; 4Q203; 4Q530–532; 6Q8; and possibly 1Q24, 4Q206 frgs. 2–3, and 4Q556 are manuscripts of the *Book of Giants*, a work eventually incorporated into *Enoch*. See the discussion below under the heading "Apocrypha and Pseudepigrapha."

Bibliography: J. T. MILIK (DJD 1) 97–99; L. T. STUCKENBRUCK (DJD 36) 49–72; IDEM, "The Throne-Theophany of the Book of Giants: Some New Light on the Background of Daniel 7," in *The Scrolls and the Scriptures* (ed. Porter and Evans), 211–20.

1QMyst = 1Q27 (*Book of Mysteries*). The *Book of Mysteries* is a short fragment that warns of the certainty of the day of judgment when evil will at last be purged from the earth. It begins by noting that most people do not know what is coming, and it concludes by noting that most people recognize that sin is wrong. 4Q299–301 are related.

Bibliography: D. BARTHÉLEMY and J. T. MILIK, "Appendix I—1Q27: Book of Mysteries," *SBLSP* 19 (1980): 247–50; J. CARMIGNAC, "Livre des mystères," *TQum* 2:255–61; J. T. MILIK (DJD 1) 102–7.

1QS (*Serek Hayaḥad* [*Rule of the Community* or *Manual of Discipline*]). The *Rule of the Community* is among the most significant finds at Qumran. This scroll lays down the requirements for admission into the community. The would-be adherent is repeatedly told that he must no longer "walk in the stubbornness of his heart." Topics that are touched on include the two natures of human beings, social relations in the community, rules of holiness, duties, regulations concerning malicious speech and other sins, and rules concerning community leaders. There are two appendices to 1QS (1QSa, 1QSb). There are also several fragments of the text in Caves 4, 5, and (possibly) 11: 4Q255–264, 5Q11, 11Q29?. 6QpapBen (= 6Q16) may also be related.

Bibliography: D. C. ALLISON Jr., "The Authorship of 1QS III, 13–IV, 14," *RevQ* 10 (1979–1981): 257–68; W. H. BROWNLEE, *The Dead Sea Manual of Discipline: Translation and Notes* (BASORSup 10–12; New Haven: American Schools of Oriental Research, 1951); M. BURROWS, *Plates and Transcription of the Manual of Discipline* (vol. 2, fasc. 2 of *The Dead Sea Scrolls of St. Mark's Monastery*), pls. I–X (photographs of 1QS); J. H. CHARLESWORTH, "A Critical Comparison of the Dualism in 1QS 3:13–4:26 and the 'Dualism' Contained in the Gospel of John," in *John and the Dead Sea Scrolls* (ed. J. H. Charlesworth; New York: Crossroad, 1990), 76–106; D. DIMANT, "Qumran Sectarian Literature," *SJWSTP* 497–503, 517–18, 524; J. A. FITZMYER, *DSS* 130–31; P. GUILBERT, "La Règle de la communauté," *TQum* 1:9–80; A. R. C. LEANEY, *The Rule of Qumran and Its Meaning: Introduction, Translation, and Commentary* (NTL; London: SCM Press, 1966); J. A. LOADER, "The Model of the Priestly Blessing in 1QS," *JSJ* 14 (1983): 11–17; S. METSO, *The Textual Development of the Qumran Community Rule* (STDJ 21; Leiden: Brill, 1997); J. MURPHY-O'CONNOR, "Community, Rule of the (1QS)," *ABD* 1:1110–12; IDEM, "The Judean Desert," *EJMI* 128–29; E. QIMRON and J. H. CHARLESWORTH, "Rule of the Community (1QS)," *DSSP* 1:1–51; H. STEGEMANN, "Zu Textbestand und Grundgedanken von 1QS III, 13–IV, 26," *RevQ* 13 (1988): 95–131; J. C. TREVER, *Scrolls from Qumran Cave I*, 125–47 (black-and-white photographs on the left-hand side, color photographs on the right); P. WERNBERG-MØLLER, *The Manual of Discipline* (STDJ 1; Leiden: Brill, 1957).

1QSa = 1Q28a (*Rule of the Congregation*). 1QSa is a two-column appendix to the much larger 1QS (*Rule of the Community*). It is eschatological in orientation, in anticipation of all Israel joining the Community of the Renewed Covenant on the eve of the final victory. The *Rule of the Congregation* recapitulates order and rank for the community. Of great interest is 2:11–12, which provides instruction for seating at the great eschatological banquet, "when God has begotten the Messiah among them." Although some dispute the reading "begotten," the passage seems to be a clear allusion to Ps 2:2, 7, which speaks of the Messiah, whom the nations oppose and who is said to be God's "Son" and "begotten." On the various emendations that have been suggested, see Charlesworth and Stuckenbruck, *DSSP* 1:117 n. 64. The emendations are unnecessary.

Bibliography: J. M. BAUMGARTEN, "On the Testimony of Women in *1QSa*," in *Studies in Qumran Law* (SJLA 24; Leiden: Brill, 1977), 183–86; P. BORGEN, " 'At the Age of Twenty' in 1QSa," in *Paul Preaches Circumcision and Pleases Men* (Trondheim, Nor.: Trondheim University Press, 1983), 167–77; J. CARMIGNAC, "La Règle de la congrégation," *TQum* 2:9–27; J. H. CHARLESWORTH and L. T. STUCKENBRUCK, "Rule of the Congregation (1QSa)," *DSSP* 1:108–17; C. HEMPEL, "The Earthly Essene Nucleus of 1QSa," *DSD* 3 (1996): 253–69; É. PUECH, "Préséance sacerdotale et messie-roi dans la Règle de la congrégation

(1QSa ii 11–22)," *RevQ* 16 (1994): 351–65; L. H. SCHIFFMAN, *The Eschatological Community of the Dead Sea Scrolls: A Study of the Rule of the Congregation* (SBLMS 38; Atlanta: Scholars Press, 1989); H. STEGEMANN, "Some Remarks to 1QSa, to 1QSb, and to Qumran Messianism," *RevQ* 21 (1997): 479–505; Y. YADIN, "A Crucial Passage in the Dead Sea Scrolls," *JBL* 78 (1959): 238–41.

1QSb = 1Q28b (*Rule of the Blessings*). The fragment from the Schøyen Collection (MS 1909) helps fill out portions of col. 5. The *Rule of the Blessings* describes the rank and role of various key personages in renewed Israel. Of interest is what is said about the Messiah in col. 5, to whom various Scriptures are applied (e.g., Isa 11:2–5; Mic 4:13; Num 24:17).

Bibliography: M. G. ABEGG, "1QSb and the Elusive High Priest," in *Emanuel* (ed. Paul et al.), 3–16; G. J. BROOKE and J. M. ROBINSON, *A Further Fragment of 1QSb: The Schøyen Collection MS 1909* (Occasional Papers of the Institute for Antiquity and Christianity 30; Claremont: Institute for Antiquity and Christianity, 1994); J. CARMIGNAC, "Le recueil des Bénédictions," *TQum* 2:29–42; J. H. CHARLESWORTH and L. T. STUCKENBRUCK, "Blessings (1QSb)," *DSSP* 1:119–31; R. LEIVESTAD, "Enthalten die Segenssprüche 1QSb eine Segnung des Hohenpriesters der messianischen Zeit?" *ST* 31 (1977): 137–45; H. STEGEMANN, "Some Remarks to 1QSa, to 1QSb, and to Qumran Messianism," *RevQ* 21 (1997): 479–505; S. TALMON, "The 'Manual of Benedictions' of the Sect of the Judaean Desert," *RevQ* 2 (1960): 475–500.

1Q29 (*Liturgy of the Three Tongues of Fire*). See also 4Q376. This work concerns the tradition of the high priest discerning God's will from the Urim and Thummim (cf. Num 27:21; 1 Sam 28:6).

Bibliography: J. T. MILIK (DJD 1) 130–32; J. STRUGNELL, "Moses-Peudepigrapha at Qumran: 4Q375, 4Q376, and Similar Works," in *Archaeology and History in the Dead Sea Scrolls* (ed. Schiffman), 221–56.

1Q30–31 (*Liturgical Texts* A and B). J. T. Milik assigned 12 fragments to 1Q30. He restored line 2 of the first fragment to read, "Holy [Mes]iah." But most scholars now read "Holy Spirit." Two fragments are assigned to 1Q31. References to the "men of the Community [i.e., *Yahad*]," being ordered to take "plunder" (frg. 1), and "in the camps" and "to the war" (frg. 2) suggest that 1Q31 is not liturgical but related in some way to the *War Scroll*.

Bibliography: J. T. MILIK (DJD 1) 132–33; A. S. VAN DER WOUDE, *Die messianischen Vorstellungen der Gemeinde von Qumrân* (SSN 3; Assen, Neth.: Van Gorcum, 1957), 165.

1QJN ar = 1Q32 (*New Jerusalem*). Qumran's *New Jerusalem* is extant in Hebrew and Aramaic fragments discovered in several of the caves (cf. 2QJN ar = 2Q24; 4QJN[a,b] ar = 4Q554–555; 5QJN ar = 5Q15; and 11QJN ar = 11Q18). The document describes the future temple of the New Jerusalem of restored Israel. Modeled after Ezekiel 40–47 and Isa 54:11–12, it is presented as a vision in which precise measurements and liturgical practices for the new temple are clarified. The new Jerusalem is said to be 100 stades north to south and 140 stades east to west (or 13.3 x 18.6 miles). This text is relevant for the study of Revelation (cf. Rev 21:9–27).

Bibliography: M. BAILLET (DJDJ 3) 84–89; IDEM, "Fragments araméens de Qumrân 2: Description de la Jérusalem nouvelle," *RB* 62 (1955): 225–45; M. CHYUTIN, *The New Jerusalem Scroll from Qumran: A Comprehensive Reconstruction* (JSPSup 25; Sheffield: Sheffield, 1997); D. DIMANT, "Qumran Sectarian Literature," *SJWSTP* 531–32; F. GARCÍA MARTÍNEZ, *Qumran and Apocalyptic,* 180–213; J. T. MILIK (DJD 1) 134–35, 184–93; É. PUECH, "À propos de la Jérusalem nouvelle d'après les manuscrits de la mer Morte," *Semitica* 43–44 (1995): 87–102.

1QM + 1Q33 (*Milḥamah* or *War Scroll,* or *Rule of the War between the Sons of Darkness and the Sons of Light*). The *War Scroll* describes the great and final eschatological battle between the sons of light and the sons of darkness. In this battle the evil Prince of Darkness, also known as Belial (or Beliar), and his corrupt minions will be annihilated. The scroll provides detailed instructions for proper battle formations, formations which appear to reflect Roman military tactics. The righteous priests of the Qumran community play prominent rolls in the anticipated eschatological battle. Only those who are ritually pure may participate. The scroll also contains the thanksgiving hymn that is to be sung when the battle is won. There are several fragments of this text in Cave 4 (cf. 4QM[a-f] = 4Q491–496). 4Q285, 4Q497, and 11Q14 may also be related to the *War Scroll.*

Bibliography: M. BAILLET (DJD 7) 12–68; J. CARMIGNAC, "La Règle de la guerre," *TQum* 1:81–125; IDEM, *La Règle de la guerre des fils de lumière contre les fils de ténèbres* (Paris: Letouzey & Ané, 1958); P. R. DAVIES, *1QM, the War Scroll from Qumran: Its Structure and History* (BibOr 32; Rome: Pontifical Biblical Institute, 1977); D. DIMANT, "Qumran Sectarian Literature," *SJWSTP* 515–17; J. DUHAIME, "Étude comparative de 4QM[a] fgg. 1–3 et 1QM," *RevQ* 14 (1990): 459–72; IDEM, "War Scroll," *DSSP* 2:80–203; J. A. FITZMYER, *DSS* 141–43; J. T. MILIK (DJD 1) 135–36 (1Q33); J. MURPHY-O'CONNOR, "The Judean Desert," *EJMI* 132–33; J. P. M. VAN DER PLOEG, *Le rouleau de la guerre* (STDJ 2; Leiden: Brill, 1959); A. STEUDEL, "The Eternal Reign of the People of God—Collective Expectations in Qumran Texts (*4Q246* and *1QM*)," *RevQ* 17 (1996): 507–25; Y. YADIN, *The Scroll of the War of the Sons of Light against the Sons of Darkness* (Oxford: Oxford University Press, 1962).

1QLitPr[a,b] = 1Q34 + 1Q34bis (*Festival Prayers*). See also 4QPrFêtes[a-c] = 4Q507–509. These liturgical (or festival) prayers originally covered the entire year. They are petitions that the righteous enjoy God's blessing, while the wicked suffer "pains in their bones." There is also a petition that God renew his covenant with his people (cf. 1Q34bis frg. 3 ii 6).

Bibliography: M. BAILLET (DJD 7) 175–215; J. CARMIGNAC, "Recueil de Prières liturgiques," *TQum* 2:263–67; J. H. CHARLESWORTH and D. OLSON, "Prayers for Festivals,"

DSSP 4A:46–105; J. R. DAVILA, *Liturgical Works,* 15–40; J. T. MILIK (DJD 1) 136, 152–55; J. C. TREVER, "Completion of the Publication of Some Fragments from Qumran Cave I," *RevQ* 5 (1965): 323–36, esp. 328–33.

1QH^a + 1QH^b = 1Q35 (*Hodayot* or *Thanksgiving Hymns*). The *Thanksgiving Hymns* of Cave 1 powerfully describe the frame of mind of the covenanters of Qumran. Their separation from the corrupt world, their spiritual ascents into the heavens, and their pain at being opposed and rebuffed by nonbelievers constitute the main themes of these hymns. Some have suggested that hymn 8 was written by the Teacher of Righteousness himself, since the hymn concerns one whose insights have been rejected by "garblers of the truth." There are nineteen complete hymns and fragments of several others. NB: The Materials that make up *Hodayot* have been reorganized, with the result that the column numbers have changed.

Bibliography: J. CARMIGNAC, "Les Hymnes," *TQum* 1:127–282; D. DIMANT, "Qumran Sectarian Literature," *SJWSTP* 522–24; D. D. HOPKINS, "The Qumran Community and 1QHodayot: A Reassessment," *RevQ* 10 (1979–1981): 323–64; M. P. HORGAN and P. J. KOBELSKI, "The Hodayot (1QH) and New Testament Poetry," in *To Touch the Text: Biblical and Related Studies in Honor of Joseph A. Fitzmyer, S.J.* (ed. M. P. Horgan and P. J. Kobelski; New York: Crossroad, 1989), 179–93; B. KITTEL, *The Hymns of Qumran: Translation and Commentary* (SBLDS 50; Chico, Calif.: Scholars Press, 1981); M. MANSOOR, *The Thanksgiving Hymns* (STDJ 3; Grand Rapids: Eerdmans, 1961); E. H. MERRILL, *Qumran and Predestination: A Theological Study of the Thanksgiving Hymns* (STDJ 8; Leiden: Brill, 1975); J. MURPHY-O'CONNOR, "The Judean Desert," *EJMI* 130–32; É. PUECH, "Quelques aspects de la restauration du rouleau des Hymnes (1QH)," *JJS* 39 (1988): 38–55; IDEM, "Restauration d'un hymnique à partir de trois manuscrits fragmentaires: 1QH^a xv 37–xvi 4 (vii 34–viii 3), 1Q35 (H^b) 1,9–14, 4Q428 (H^b) 7," *RevQ* 16 (1995): 543–58; E. M. SCHULLER, "The Cave 4 Hodayot Manuscripts: A Preliminary Description," *JQR* 85 (1994): 137–50; E. M. SCHULLER and L. DiTOMMASO, "A Bibliography of the Hodayot, 1948–1996," *DSD* 4 (1997): 55–101.

Qumran, Cave 2

Qumran's Cave 2 contained approximately thirty-three scrolls: 2Q1–33 plus "debris in a box," which may or may not represent miniscule remains of additional scrolls. 2Q1–17 represent portions of the five books of Moses, one prophet (Jeremiah), and three Writings (Psalms, Job, and two Ruth scrolls). We also have fragments of Sirach (2Q18), *Jubilees* (2Q19–20), the Enochic *Book of Giants* (2Q26), some other apocryphal texts (2Q21–23), a juridical text (2Q25), and another copy of the Aramaic *New Jerusalem* (2Q24). 2Q27–33 are unclassified fragments.

2QapMoses = 2Q21 (*Apocryphon of Moses*). An apocryphal writing about Moses in the wilderness setting.

Bibliography: M. BAILLET (DJDJ 3) 79–81.

2QapDavid = 2Q22 (*Apocryphon of David*). The *Apocryphon of David* is an apocryphal story about David, and is perhaps part of a collection of apocryphal psalms (see 4QapPs). This apocryphon may be related to 4Q371–372.

Bibliography: M. BAILLET (DJDJ 3) 81–82; E. SCHULLER, "A Preliminary Study of 4Q373 and Some Related (?) Fragments," in *The Madrid Qumran Congress* (ed. Trebolle Barrera and Vegas Montaner), 2:515–25.

2QapProph = 2Q23 (an apocryphal prophetic text). In frg. 1, lines 6–7, we read, "you will be pushed away from the cornerstone of . . . which is full of demons . . ."

Bibliography: M. BAILLET (DJDJ 3) 82–84.

2QJN ar = 2Q24 (*New Jerusalem*). See the discussion of 1QJN ar = 1Q32 above (no. 15).

2Q25 Juridical text. Reference to "obligations" and "thus it is written in the book of Moses" create the impression that the three small fragments that make up 2Q25 were part of a juridical work. The fragments are dated to the first century B.C.E.

Bibliography: M. BAILLET (DJDJ 3) 90; J. H. CHARLESWORTH, "Juridical Fragment (2Q25)," *DSSP* 2:218–19.

2QEnGiants ar = 2Q26 (Enochic *Book of Giants*). This text is part of the *Book of Giants,* a document that is extant as part of *1 Enoch* (see chs. 6–11, 106–107). See also 6QEnGiants; 4QEnGiants^{a-f}. Other parts of *1 Enoch* are found in various caves (cf. 4QEn^{a-g}). See the discussion of *Enoch* below under the heading "Apocrypha and Pseudepigrapha."

Bibliography: M. BAILLET (DJDJ 3) 90–91; J. T. MILIK, *BE* 334; L. T. STUCKENBRUCK, *The Book of Giants from Qumran,* 63–66; IDEM (DJD 36) 73–75.

Qumran, Cave 3

Cave 3 has yielded fifteen documents: 3Q1–15, plus uninscribed fragments (3QX1–4), a leather knot (3QX4), debris in a box (3QX5), and a squeeze of Cave 3 clay (3QX6). There are three Bible scrolls (3Q1–3), representing Ezekiel, Psalms, and Lamentations. We have a pesher on Isaiah (3Q4), a fragment of *Jubilees* (3Q5), and what may be a fragment of a *Testament of Judah* (3Q7). By far the most interesting item is 3Q15, the *Copper Scroll.*

3QpIsa = 3Q4 (*Commentary on Isaiah*). For discussion, see below under the heading "Pesharim."

Bibliography: M. BAILLET (DJDJ 3) 95–96; M. P. HORGAN, "Isaiah Pesher 1 (3Q4 = 3QpIsa)," *DSSP* 6B:35–37; IDEM, *Pesharim,* 260–61.

3QJub = 3Q5 (*Jubilees*). For discussion, see below under the heading "Apocrypha and Pseudepigrapha."

Bibliography: M. BAILLET (DJDJ 3) 96–98; A. ROFÉ, "Further Manuscript Fragments of the Jubilees in the Third Cave of Qumran," *Tarbiz* 34 (1965): 333–36.

3QHymn = 3Q6 (*Hymn of Praise*). Only small fragments are extant.

Bibliography: M. BAILLET (DJDJ 3) 98.

3QTJud? = 3Q7 (possibly a fragment of the *Testament of Judah*). See 4QTJos ar below. For further discussion, see below under the heading "Apocrypha and Pseudepigrapha."

Bibliography: M. BAILLET (DJDJ 3) 99; J. T. MILIK, "Écrits préesséniens de Qumrân: D'Hénoch à Amram," in *Qumrân* (ed. Delcor), 91–106, esp. 98–99.

3QTreasure = 3Q15 (*Copper Scroll*). The *Copper Scroll* provides the directions to several hidden treasures of gold and silver. It has been debated whether the scroll tells of real treasure. The story of how this copper scroll was cut into strips without destroying any text is itself of interest. Albert Wolters proposes that the scroll speaks of the "cavern of the Shekinah" (at 12:10), since, according to Essene belief, the Shekinah of God no longer resides in the "house of the Shekinah," that is, the temple in Jerusalem.

Bibliography: G. J. BROOKE and P. R. DAVIES, eds., *Copper Scroll Studies* (JSPSup 40; New York: Sheffield, 2002); D. DIMANT, "Qumran Sectarian Literature," *SJWSTP* 531; P. K. MCCARTER, "The Mystery of the Copper Scroll," in *The Dead Sea Scrolls after Forty Years* (ed. H. Shanks et al.; Washington, D.C.: Biblical Archaeology Society, 1991), 41–54; J. MURPHY-O'CONNOR, "The Judean Desert," *EJMI* 135; A. WOLTERS, *The Copper Scroll: Overview, Text, and Translation* (Sheffield: Sheffield Academic Press, 1996); IDEM, "History and the Copper Scroll," in *Methods of Investigation of the Dead Sea Scrolls and the Khirbet Qumran Site* (ed. Wise et al.), 285–98; IDEM, "The Shekinah in the Copper Scroll: A New Reading of 3Q15 12.10," in *The Scrolls and the Scriptures* (ed. Porter and Evans), 382–93.

Qumran, Cave 4

Cave 4 has been described as the "mother lode." Discovered in 1952, just opposite the ruins at Qumran, this cave yielded up the fragments of over 500 documents, including some 125 Bible scrolls, one dozen or more pesharim, dozens of scrolls of apocryphal and pseudepgraphal texts, and a host of sectarian texts, including the *Rule of the Community,* the *Damascus Covenant, Hymns,* calendars of one sort or another, rules touching purity, and many others. Perhaps the single most important sectarian document found in this cave is the so-called MMT (*Miqsat Ma'ase ha-Torah* = *Some of the Works of the Law*), extant in six fragmentary copies (i.e., 4Q394–399). Several other texts have come to light that have great significance for understanding Jesus (e.g., 4Q246, 4Q500, 4Q521, and 4Q525).

4QSamᵃ = 4Q51. 4QSamᵃ should be noted because, in the words of Frank Cross (1980), "4QSamᵃ preserves lost bits of the text of Samuel" (p. 26). The most dramatic instance concerns material that probably originally belonged at the beginning of 1 Samuel 11, which explains why Nahash acted against the Gadites so severely.

Bibliography: F. M. CROSS, "The Ammonite Oppression of the Tribes of Gad and Reuben: Missing verses from 1 Sam 11 Found in 4QSamuelᵃ," in *The Hebrew and Greek Texts of Samuel: 1980 Proceedings IOSCS, Vienna* (ed. E. Tov; Jerusalem: Academon, 1980), 105–16; IDEM, "New Directions in Dead Sea Scroll Research: Original Biblical Text Reconstructed from Newly Found Fragments," *BRev* 1 (1985): 26–35; IDEM, "A New Qumran Biblical Fragment Related to the Original Hebrew Underlying the Septuagint," *BASOR* 132 (1953): 15–26; E. ULRICH, *The Qumran Text of Samuel and Josephus* (HSM 19; Chico, Calif.: Scholars Press, 1978); IDEM, "4QSamᶜ: A Fragmentary Manuscript of 2 Samuel 14–15 from the Scribe of *Serek Hayyahad* (1QS)," *BASOR* 235 (1979): 1–25.

4QtgLev = 4Q156 (*Targum of Leviticus* 16:12–15, 18–21). This small fragment of a Targum on Leviticus, along with 4QtgJob and 11QtgJob, provide evidence of written Targumim far earlier than previously thought. Although the three Targumim of Qumran do not agree with the wording of the complete Targumim that date from a later period, they attest the existence of Targumim in the NT period and earlier.

Bibliography: A. ANGERSTORFER, "Überlegungen zu Sprache und Sitz im Leben des Toratargums 4QtgLev (4Q156), sein Verhältnis zu Targum Onkelos," *BN* 55 (1990): 18–35; J. A. FITZMYER, "The Targum of Leviticus from Qumran Cave 4," *Maarav* 1 (1978): 5–21; J. T. MILIK and M. M. KASHER (DJD 6) 86–89, 92–93; L. T. STUCKENBRUCK, "Bibliography on 4QTgLev (4Q156)," *JSP* 10 (1992): 53–55.

4QtgJob = 4Q157 (*Targum of Job* 3:5–9; 4:16–5:4). See the discussion of the preceding entry. See also the discussion of 11QtgJob below.

Bibliography: E. KUTSCH, "Die Textgliederung im hebräischen Ijobbuch sowie in 4QTgJob und in 11QTgJob," *BZ* 27 (1983): 221–28; J. T. MILIK (DJD 6) 90; R. I. VASHOLZ, "4QTargum Job versus 11QTargum Job," *RevQ* 11 (1982): 109.

4QReworked Pentateuch = 4Q158. This Scroll, of which survive approximately one dozen fragments, consists mostly of Exodus. Its insertion of material from Deuteronomy into Exodus 20 (cf. frgs. 6–8) coheres with Samaritan textual tendencies.

Bibliography: J. M. ALLEGRO (DJDJ 5) 1–6; J. STRUGNELL, "Notes en marge du volume V des 'Discoveries in the Judaean Desert of Jordan,'" 163–276, esp. 168–76; E. TOV, "4QReworked Pentateuch: A Synopsis of Its Contents," *RevQ* 16 (1995): 647–53.

4QOrd^{a,b,c} = 4Q159 + 4Q513–514 (*Ordinances*). Some halakic rules and regulations. Apparently 4QOrd^a is critical of the requirement to pay the half-shekel temple tax annually: "as for the half-[shekel, the offering to the Lord] which they gave, each man as a ransom for his soul: only one [time] shall he give it all his days" (2:6–8; cf. Exod 30:13–16; Matt 17:24–27).

Bibliography: J. M. ALLEGRO, "An Unpublished Fragment of Essene Halakah (4Q Ordinances)," *JSS* 6 (1961): 71–73; J. LIVER, "The Half-Shekel Offering in Biblical and Postbiblical Literature," *HTR* 56 (1963): 173–98; L. H. SCHIFFMAN, "Ordinances and Rules (4Q159 = 4QOrd^a, 4Q513 = 4QOrd^b)," *DSSP* 1:145–75; F. D. WEINERT, "4Q159: Legislation for an Essene Community outside of Qumran?" *JSJ* 5 (1974): 179–207.

4QVisSam = 4Q160 (*Vision of Samuel*). This brief, fragmentary text retells the story of Samuel's dream (1 Sam 3:14–17). The young Samuel tells the dream to Eli and goes on to describe what appears to be an apocalyptic vision.

Bibliography: J. M. ALLEGRO (DJDJ 5) 9–11; J. STRUGNELL, "Notes en marge du volume V des 'Discoveries in the Judaean Desert of Jordan,'" 163–276, esp. 179–83.

4QpIsa^{a-e} = 4Q161–165 (*Commentary on Isaiah^{a-e}*) + 4QpHos^{a,b} = 4Q166–167 (*Commentary on Hosea^{a,b}*) + 4QpMic(?) = 4Q168 (*Commentary on Micah[?]*) + 4QpNah = 4Q169 (*Commentary on Nahum*) + 4QpPs^a = 4Q171 (*Commentary on Psalms^a*) + 4QpUnid = 4Q172 (*Unidentified Commentary*) + 4QpPs^b = 4Q173 (*Commentary on Psalms^b*). See further discussion below under the heading "Pesharim."

Bibliography: J. M. ALLEGRO (DJDJ 5); J. H. CHARLESWORTH, *The Pesharim and Qumran History: Chaos or Consensus?* (Grand Rapids: Eerdmans, 2002); J. H. CHARLESWORTH et al., *DSSP*, vol. 6B; M. P. HORGAN, *Pesharim*. Additional biography is provided below under the heading "Pesharim."

4QFlor = 4Q174 (*Florilegium* or 4QEschMidr [*Midrash on Eschatology*]). This document consists of several brief commentaries on various biblical passages (2 Sam 7:10–14; Exod 15:17–18; Amos 9:11; Ps 1:1; Isa 8:11; Ps 2:1; Dan 12:10; 11:32; Deut 33:8–11, 19–21). The theme is eschatological. The eschatological interpretation of 2 Samuel 7 is significant for NT studies (cf. Luke 1:32–33; Rom 1:4).

Bibliography: J. M. BAUMGARTEN, "The Exclusion of 'Netinim' and Proselytes in 4QFlorilegium," *RevQ* 8 (1972–1975): 87–96; G. J. BROOKE, *Exegesis at Qumran: 4QFlorilegium in Its Jewish Context* (JSOTSup 29; Sheffield: JSOT Press, 1985); J. CARMIGNAC, "Florilège," *TQum* 2:279–84; D. DIMANT, "Qumran Sectarian Literature," *SJWSTP* 518–21; D. R.

SCHWARTZ, "The Three Temples of 4QFlorilegium," *RevQ* 10 (1979–1981): 83–91; A. STEU-
DEL, *Der Midrasch zur Eschatologie aus der Qumrangemeinde (4QMidrEschat^{a,b})*; M. O.
WISE, "4QFlorilegium and the Temple of Adam," *RevQ* 15 (1991): 103–32.

4QTest = 4Q175 (*Testimonia*). 4QTestimonies is made up of a series of quotations looking forward to the appearance of the prophet of Deut 18:18 and the
"star of Jacob" and "scepter of Israel" of Num 24:17. It is not certain if a
Davidic Messiah is in view, or some sort of prophetic, even priestly, deliverer is
in view. The conflation of Deut 5:28–29 and 18:18–19 parallels the Samaritan
Pentateuch. 4Q175 parallels 4Q379 (*Apocryphon of Joshua*, formerly *Psalms of
Joshua*) frg. 22 ii (see Lim).

Bibliography: J. M. ALLEGRO, "Further Messianic References," *JBL* 75 (1956): 182–87;
J. CARMIGNAC, "Témoignages," *TQum* 2:273–78; J. A. FITZMYER, "4QTestimonia and the
New Testament," in Fitzmyer, *Essays on the Semitic Background of the New Testament* (Lon-
don: Geoffrey Chapman, 1971; repr., SBLSBS 5; Missoula, Mont.: Scholars Press, 1974),
59–89; T. LIM, "The 'Psalms of Joshua' (4Q379 fr. 22 col. 2): A Reconsideration of Its
Text," *JJS* 44 (1993): 309–12.

4QTanh = 4Q176 (*Tanhumim*). 4QTanh consists of various biblical quotations
(Ps 79:2–3; Isa 40:1–5; 41:8–9; 49:7, 13–17; 43:1–2, 4–6; 51:22–23; 52:1–3;
54:4–10 [then pesher]; 52:1–2; Zech 13:9). Fragments 19–21 are from *Jubilees*
and are now classified as 4Q176a.

Bibliography: J. M. ALLEGRO (DJDJ 5) 60–67; M. KISTER, "New Identified Fragments of
the Book of Jubilees: Jub. 23:21–23, 30–31," *RevQ* 12 (1985–1987): 529–36; C. D. STANLEY,
"The Importance of 4QTanhumim (4Q176)," *RevQ* 15 (1992): 569–82; J. STRUGNELL,
"Notes en marge du volume V des 'Discoveries in the Judaean Desert of Jordan,'"
163–276, esp. 229–36.

4QCatena^{a,b} = 4Q177 + 4Q182. The work consists of a series of predictions based
upon the interpretation of various prophetic texts (e.g., Hos 5:8; Isa 37:30;
32:7; 22:13).

Bibliography: J. M. ALLEGRO (DJDJ 5) 67–74; A. STEUDEL, *Der Midrasch zur Eschatologie
aus der Qumrangemeinde (4QMidrEschat^{a,b})*; J. STRUGNELL, "Notes en marge du volume
V des 'Discoveries in the Judaean Desert of Jordan,'" 163–276, esp. 236–48.

NB: 4Q178 comprises unclassified fragments.

4QapocrLam A = 4Q179 (*Apocryphal Lamentations A*). This text is reminiscent of
Lamentations, expressing regret for sin and sorrow over the destruction of Jerusalem, the temple, and cities. "Alas! All her palaces are desolate . . . Our inheritance has been turned into a desert . . . " (lines 10, 12). See also 4Q501.

Bibliography: J. M. ALLEGRO (DJDJ 5) 75–77; M. P. HORGAN, "4Q179: A Lament over Jerusalem," *JSS* 18 (1973): 222–34; J. STRUGNELL, "Notes en marge du volume V des 'Discoveries in the Judaean Desert of Jordan,'" 163–276, esp. 250–52.

4QAgesCreat = 4Q180–181 (*Ages of Creation*). *Ages of Creation* attempts to categorize world history into specific epochs of time (and is sometimes called *Epochs of Times*). From Adam to Noah and from Noah to Abraham are reckoned as ten generations apiece (cf. Matt 1:17 where "fourteen" generations are noted). The work then goes on to discuss the significance of the sin of the fallen angels (Gen 6:1–4). The fragmentary text concludes with an account of various events in the life of Abraham.

Bibliography: J. M. ALLEGRO (DJDJ 5) 77–80; D. DIMANT, "The 'Pesher on the Periods' (4Q180) and 4Q181," *IOS* 9 (1979): 77–102; J. J. M. ROBERTS, "Wicked and Holy (4Q180–181)," *DSSP* 2:204–13; J. STRUGNELL, "Notes en marge du volume V des 'Discoveries in the Judaean Desert of Jordan,'" 163–276, esp. 252–55.

4Q183 (*Historical Work*). References such as "they defiled their temple," "wars," and "expiated their iniquities through [their] sufferings" suggest that the subject is the Maccabean struggle against Antiochus IV.

Bibliography: J. M. ALLEGRO (DJDJ 5) 81–82; J. STRUGNELL, "Notes en marge du volume V des 'Discoveries in the Judaean Desert of Jordan,'" 163–276, esp. 256–63.

4QWiles = 4Q184 (*Wiles of the Harlot* or *of Lilith*). Cave 4 has yielded a sapiential work that describes what scholars at first thought were the "wiles of a wicked woman" or "harlot." Some think that none other than Lilith, the queen of the demons, is in view. The main danger of Lilith (or the harlot), according to this writing, is that she will steer men away from Torah.

Bibliography: J. M. ALLEGRO (DJDJ 5) 82–85; IDEM, "The Wiles of the Wicked Woman: A Sapiential Work from Qumran's Fourth Cave," *PEQ* 96 (1964): 53–55; J. M. BAUMGARTEN, "On the Nature of the Seductress in 4Q184," *RevQ* 15 (1991): 133–43; J. STRUGNELL, "Notes en marge du volume V des 'Discoveries in the Judaean Desert of Jordan,'" 163–276, esp. 263–68.

4Q185 (*Sapiential Work*). This work warns the wicked and pronounces beatitudes on those who hold fast to wisdom (cf. 4Q525).

Bibliography: J. M. ALLEGRO (DJDJ 5) 82–85; J. STRUGNELL, "Notes en marge du volume V des 'Discoveries in the Judaean Desert of Jordan,'" 163–276, esp. 269–73; T. H. TOBIN, "4Q185 and Jewish Wisdom Literature," in *Of Scribes and Scrolls: Studies on the Hebrew Bible, Intertestamental Judaism, and Christian Origins* (ed. H. W. Attridge et al.; J. Strugnell FS; Resources in Religion 5; Lanham, Md.: University Press of America, 1990), 145–52.

4Q186 (*Horoscope*). "And this is the sign in which he was born: the period of Taurus. He will be poor. And his animal is the bull" (frg. 1 ii 8–9).

Bibliography: J. M. ALLEGRO, "An Astrological Cryptic Document from Qumran," *JSS* 9 (1964): 291–94; IDEM (DJDJ 5) 82–85; J. CARMIGNAC, "Les horoscopes de Qumrân,"

RevQ 5 (1965): 199–227; J. STRUGNELL, "Notes en marge du volume V des 'Discoveries in the Judaean Desert of Jordan,'" 163–276, esp. 274–76.

NB: 4Q187–95. No manuscripts have been assigned to these numbers.

4QTob[a-d] ar = 4Q196–199 + 4QTob[e] hebr = 4Q200. Four MSS of Tobit in Aramaic and one in Hebrew. For further discussion, see below under the heading "Apocrypha and Pseudepigrapha."

Bibliography: J. A. FITZMYER (DJD 19) 7–76; IDEM, "The Qumran Texts of Tobit."

4QEn[a,b,d-g] ar = 4Q201–202, 205–207, 212 (*1 Enoch*) + 4QEnGiants[a,c] ar = 4Q203–204 (*Book of Giants*) + 4QEnastr[a-d] ar = 4Q208–211 (*Astronomical Enoch*). For discussion, see below under the heading "Apocrypha and Pseudepigrapha."

Bibliography: E. LARSON, *The Translation of Enoch from Aramaic into Greek* (JSJSup 53; Leiden: Brill, 1998); J. T. MILIK, *BE* 178–288, 310–17, 340–62; É. PUECH (DJD 31) 17–18; L. T. STUCKENBRUCK (DJD 36) 3–47; IDEM, *The Book of Giants from Qumran* (TSAJ 62; Tübingen: Mohr [Siebeck], 1997), 66–100, 191–96; E. J. C. TIGCHELAAR and F. GARCÍA MARTÍNEZ (DJD 36) 95–171.

4QTLevi[a-f] ar = 4Q213–214b, 214a + 4Q540–541 (Aramaic *Testament of Levi[a-d]*). For discussion, see below under the heading "Apocrypha and Pseudepigrapha."

Bibliography: G. J. BROOKE, "4QTestament of Levid(?) and the Messianic Servant High Priest," in *From Jesus to John* (ed. De Boer), 83–100; J. C. GREENFIELD and M. E. STONE, "Remarks on the Aramaic Testament of Levi from the Geniza," *RB* 85 (1978): 214–30; M. DE JONGE, "The Testament of Levi and 'Aramaic Levi,'" *RevQ* 13 (1988): 367–85; J. T. MILIK, *BE* 23–72; IDEM, "Le Testament de Lévi en araméen: Fragment de la grotte 4 de Qumrân," *RB* 62 (1955): 398–99; É. PUECH (DJD 31) 217–56; M. E. STONE and J. C. GREENFIELD (DJD 22) 1–41.

4QTNaph = 4Q215 (*Testament of Naphtali*). For discussion, see below under the heading "Apocrypha and Pseudepigrapha."

Bibliography: M. E. STONE (DJD 22) 73–82; IDEM, "The Hebrew Testament of Naphtali," *JJS* 47 (1996): 311–21.

4Q215a (*Time of Righteousness*). A large portion of what is identified as col. 2 survives, declaring that "the age of peace has arrived, and the laws of truth, and the testimony of justice, to instruct all in God's paths and in the mighty acts of his deeds" (frg. 1 ii 5–6).

Bibliography: G. W. NEBE, "Qumranica I: Zu unveröffentlichen Handschriften aus Höhle 4 von Qumran," *ZAW* 106 (1994): 315–22; M. E. STONE and E. CHAZON (DJD 36) 172–84.

4QJub^{a-h} = 4Q216–224 (*Jubilees*) + 4QJub^{a-c} = 4Q225–227 (pseudo-*Jubilees*) + 4Q228 (a work citing *Jubilees*). For discussion, see below under the heading "Apocrypha and Pseudepigrapha."

Bibliography: J. C. VANDERKAM, "4QJubc (4Q218) and 4QJube (4Q220): A Preliminary Edition," *Text* 17 (1994): 43–56 + pls. I–II; J. C. VANDERKAM and J. T. MILIK (DJD 13) 1–185.

4QPrNab = 4Q242 (*Prayer of Nabonidus*). The *Prayer of Nabonidus* closely resembles the story of Nebuchadnezzar in Daniel 4. It tells of the king's pride, his fall, and his eventual restoration. Some scholars think that the account in Daniel is based upon an actual illness that Nabonidus, the last king of the neo-Babylonian empire (555–539 B.C.E.), had suffered and that the Danielic version has retold the story. This is possible, but some caution is required, for the name of the king in 4QPrNab is actually "Nabunai." For further discussion, see below under the heading "Apocrypha and Pseudepigrapha."

Bibliography: J. CARMIGNAC, "Prière de Nabonide," *TQum* 2:289–94; J. J. COLLINS (DJD 22) 83–93; IDEM, "Nabonidus, Prayer of," *ABD* 4:976–77; F. M. CROSS, "Fragments of the Prayer of Nabonidus," *IEJ* 34 (1984): 260–64; F. GARCÍA MARTÍNEZ, *Qumran and Apocalyptic,* 116–36; G. W. E. NICKELSBURG, "Stories of Biblical and Early Post-biblical Times," *SJWSTP* 35–37; É. PUECH, "La Prière de Nabonide (4Q242)," in *Targumic and Cognate Studies* (ed. K. J. Cathcart and M. Maher; M. J. McNamara FS; JSOTSup 230; Sheffield: Sheffield, 1996), 208–27; A. S. VAN DER WOUDE, "Bemerkungen zum Gebet des Nabonid," in *Qumrân* (ed. Delcor), 121–29.

4QpsDan^{a-c} ar = 4Q243–245 (pseudo-Daniel), related to *Prayer of Nabonidus.* The text's train of thought cannot be followed, given the fragmentary condition of these scrolls. Evidently, Daniel provides the Babylonian king with an interpretation of Israel's history and future. The conclusion of the vision appears to be related to Daniel 7. For further discussion, see below under the heading "Apocrypha and Pseudepigrapha."

Bibliography: J. J. COLLINS, "Pseudo-Daniel Revisited," *RevQ* 17 (1996): 111–36; J. J. COLLINS and P. W. FLINT (DJD 22) 97–131, 153–64; P. W. FLINT, "4Qpseudo-Daniel ar^c (4Q245) and the Restoration of the Priesthood," *RevQ* 17 (1996): 137–50; F. GARCÍA MARTÍNEZ, *Qumran and Apocalyptic,* 137–61.

4Q246 (*Apocryphon of Daniel*). 4Q246 contains some lines that are of significance for NT interpretation: "[But your son] shall be great upon the earth, [O King! All (men) shall] make peace, and all shall serve [him. He shall be called the son of] the [G]reat [God], and by his name shall he be named [1:6–9]. . . . He shall be hailed (as) the Son of God, and they shall call him Son of the Most High. As comets (flash) to the sight, so shall be their kingdom. (For some) year[s] they shall rule upon the earth and shall trample upon people, city upon ci[t]y [*vacat*] until there arise the people of God, and everyone rests from the sword [2:1–4]" (Fitzmyer 1974, 393). The parallels with Luke 1:32–35 are evident.

Bibliography: J. J. COLLINS, "The Background of the 'Son of God' Text," *BBR* 7 (1997): 51–62; IDEM, "The 'Son of God' Text from Qumran," in *From Jesus to John* (ed. De Boer), 65–82; E. M. COOK, "4Q246," *BBR* 5 (1995): 43–66; J. D. G. DUNN, " 'Son of God' as 'Son of Man' in the Dead Sea Scrolls? A Response to John Collins on 4Q246," in *The Scrolls and the Scriptures* (ed. Porter and Evans), 198–210; J. A. FITZMYER, "The Contribution of Qumran Aramaic to the Study of the New Testament," *NTS* 20 (1974): 382–407, esp. 391–94; IDEM, "The 'Son of God' Document from Qumran," *Bib* 74 (1993): 153–74; D. FLUSSER, "The Hubris of the Antichrist in a Fragment from Qumran," *Imm* 10 (1980): 31–37; F. GARCÍA MARTÍNEZ, *Qumran and Apocalyptic*, 172–79; É. PUECH (DJD 22) 165–84; IDEM, "Fragment d'une apocalypse en araméen (4Q246 = pseudoDan^d) et le 'royaume de Dieu,' " *RB* 99 (1992): 98–131; A. STEUDEL, "The Eternal Reign of the People of God—Collective Expectations in Qumran Texts (*4Q246* and *1QM*)," *RevQ* 17 (1996): 507–25; J. ZIMMERMANN, "Observations on 4Q246—the 'Son of God,' " in *Qumran-Messianism: Studies on the Messianic Expectations in the Dead Sea Scrolls* (ed. J. H. Charlesworth, H. Lichtenberger, and G. S. Oegema; Tübingen: Mohr [Siebeck], 1998), 175–90.

4QApocWeeks? = 4Q247 (*Apocalypse of Weeks?*). The symbolic meaning of week (cf. line 2, "after it shall come the fifth week") and the mention of the "king of the Kittim" suggest that this text is an apocalypse related to the Daniel cycle.

Bibliography: M. BROSHI (DJD 36) 187–91; J. T. MILIK, *BE* 256.

4Q248 (*Acts of a Greek King*). Egypt and Greece are mentioned. The "city of the sanctuary" (probably Jerusalem) will be conquered. Again, we probably have a reference to the Maccabean struggle against Antiochus IV (so Broshi and Eshel).

Bibliography: M. BROSHI (DJD 36) 192–200; M. BROSHI and E. ESHEL, "The Greek King Is Antiochus IV (4QHistorical Text = 4Q248)," *JJS* 48 (1997): 120–29.

4QMSM = 4Q249 + 4Q250 (*Midrash Sepher Moshe*). These are cryptic texts. The recto of the first papyrus (i.e., 4Q249) speaks of pulling down a house and putting to death, while the verso (i.e., 4Q250) titles the text as "Interpretation [or Midrash] of the Book of Moses." Both 4Q249 and 4Q250 have been subdivided into a number of texts (i.e., 4Q249^{a-z} and 4Q250^{a-j}). Many of these smaller units are unidentified.

Bibliography: S. PFANN, "4Q249 Midrash Sefer Moshe," in *Legal Texts and Legal Issues* (ed. Bernstein et al.), 11–18; IDEM (DJD 36) 515–696.

4Q251 (*Halakah A*). Discussion of Sabbath law, compensation (*lex talionis*), firstfruit offerings, and kashrut.

Bibliography: J. M. BAUMGARTEN, "4QHalakah^a, the Law of Hadash, and the Pentecontad Calendar," *JJS* 27 (1976): 36–46; J. T. MILIK (DJDJ 3) 300.

4QpGen^{a-d} 4Q252–254a (*Commentaries on Genesis*^{a-c} or *Patriarchal Tales*^{a-c}), formerly 4QPBless (*Patriarchal Blessings*). Because the text comments on Gen 49:10, it was at one time known as 4QpGen 49. This part of the text is clearly messianic: "Until the Messiah of righteousness comes, the Branch of David; for to him and to his seed has been given the covenant of the kingship of his people for everlasting" (1:3–4). Note the allusion to 2 Samuel 7.

Bibliography: J. M. ALLEGRO, "Further Messianic References in Qumran Literature," *JBL* 75 (1956): 174–76; G. J. BROOKE (DJD 22) 185–232; IDEM, "The Thematic Content of 4Q252," *JQR* 85 (1994): 33–59; IDEM, "4Q252 as Early Jewish Commentary," *RevQ* 17 (1996): 385–401; IDEM, "4Q252 et le Nouveau Testament," in *Le déchirement: Juifs et chrétiens au premier siècle* (ed. D. Marguerat; MdB 32; Paris: Labor et Fides, 1996), 221–42; IDEM, "4Q253: A Preliminary Edition," *JSS* 40 (1995): 227–32; IDEM, "4Q254, Fragments 1 and 4, and 4Q254a: Some Preliminary Comments," in *Proceedings of the Eleventh World Congress of Jewish Studies, Division A: The Bible and Its World* (ed. D. Assaf; Jerusalem: World Union of Jewish Studies, 1994), 185–88; J. CARMIGNAC, "Paraphrase des Bénédictions patriarcales," *TQum* 2:285–88; T. LIM, "The Chronology of the Flood Story in a Qumran Text (4Q252)," *JJS* 43 (1992): 288–98; H. STEGEMANN, "Weitere Stücke von 4 Q p Psalm 37, von 4 Q Patriarchal Blessings und Hinweis auf eine unedierte Handschrift aus Höhle 4 Q mit Exzerpten aus dem Deuteronomium," *RevQ* 6 (1967): 193–227.

4QS^{a-j} = 4Q255–264 + 4Q319 (*Rule of the Community*). See the discussion of 1QS above.

Bibliography: P. ALEXANDER and G. VERMES (DJD 26) 27–38.

4Q264a (*Halakah B*). See the discussion of 4Q251 above.

Bibliography: J. M. BAUMGARTEN (DJD 35) 53–56.

4QSD = 4Q265 (*Serek Damascus*). A combination of *Rule* and *Damascus* elements.

Bibliography: J. M. BAUMGARTEN (DJD 35) 57–78; IDEM, "Purification after Childbirth and the Sacred Garden in 4Q265 and Jubilees," in *New Qumran Texts and Studies* (ed. Brooke), 3–10.

4QD^{a-h} = 4Q266–273 (*Damascus Covenant*). See below (CD).

Bibliography: P. ALEXANDER and G. VERMES (DJD 26) 201–11; J. M. BAUMGARTEN (DJD 18) 23–198; J. M. BAUMGARTEN and M. T. DAVIS, "Cave IV, V, VI Fragments Related to the Damascus Document," *DSSP* 2:59–75.

4Q274 + 4Q276–278 (*Tohorot*, or *Purification Rules*). Explication of the laws of purification, with a citation of Lev 13:45–46.

Bibliography: J. M. BAUMGARTEN (DJD 35) 99–122; IDEM, "The Laws about Fluxes in 4QTohora^a," in *Time to Prepare the Way in the Wilderness* (ed. Dimant and Schiffman),

1–8; IDEM, "The Red Cow Purification Rites in Qumran Texts," *JJS* 46 (1995): 112–19; J. MILGROM, "4QTohoraᵃ: A Unpublished Qumran Text on Purities," in *Time to Prepare the Way in the Wilderness* (ed. Dimant and Schiffman), 59–68.

4Q275 (*Communal Ceremony*). The mention of "genealogical register," "overseer," cursing, and disinheritance recall membership assessments and warnings found in *Rule* texts.

Bibliography: P. ALEXANDER and G. VERMES (DJD 26) 209–16.

4Q279 (*Four Lots*). This text probably concerns the division of wealth: "for the priests, the sons of Aaron, the first lot shall appear . . . and the third lot for the sons of Israel . . . and the fourth lot for the proselyte" (frg. 1, lines 4–6). The missing second lot probably falls to the Levites (cf. CD 14:3–4).

Bibliography: P. ALEXANDER and G. VERMES (DJD 26) 217–23; D. HAMIDOVIC, "4Q279, 4QLots, une interprétation du Psaume 135 appartenant à 4Q421, 4QWays of Righteousness," *DSD* 9 (2002): 166–86.

4QBer = 4Q280 + 4Q286–290 (*Blessings*), formerly 4QDb,e (*Melchizedek and Melkiresha*). The material is related to *Rule of the Community*. "Blessings" is a euphemism, for the text really concerns curses.

Bibliography: J. R. DAVILA, *Liturgical Works*, 41–82; J. T. MILIK, "Milkî-sedeq et Milkî-resa' dans les anciens écrits juifs et chrétiens," *JJS* 23 (1972): 95–144, esp. 126–34.

4Q281–282. Unidentified fragments.

Bibliography: J. A. FITZMYER (DJD 36) 212–15.

NB: No manuscript has been assigned to 4Q283.

4Q284 (*Purification Liturgy*). Rules regarding, and evidently a liturgy celebrating, purification.

Bibliography: J. M. BAUMGARTEN (DJD 35) 123–30.

4Q284a (*Harvesting*). The extant fragments are mostly concerned with gleaning.

Bibliography: J. M. BAUMGARTEN (DJD 35) 131–34.

4Q285 (*Sefer Hamilḥamah* or *Rule of War*). When 4Q285 was first made public, some claimed (without due regard to Hebrew syntax or the implications of context) that the text envisioned the slaying of the Messiah, the Branch of David, or Prince of the Congregation. But the text envisions precisely the opposite: the slaying of the king of the Kittim (almost certainly the Roman emperor) by the Messiah. The latter part of frg. 5, moreover, is to be restored as "with tambourine and dancing" (so Abegg; cf. Exod 15:20; Judg 21:23) and not "with wounds" or the like (as in Vermes and others), thus adding contextual support for the Messiah-slays-the king of the Kittim interpretation. 11Q14 overlaps with 4Q285 frgs. 1 and 5.

Bibliography: M. G. ABEGG Jr., "Messianic Hope and 4Q285: A Reassessment," *JBL* 113 (1994): 81–91; P. S. ALEXANDER, "A Reconstruction and Reading of 4Q285 (4QSefer ha-Milhamah)," *RevQ* 19 (2000): 333–48; P. S. ALEXANDER and G. VERMES (DJD 36) 228–46; R. P. GORDON, "The Interpretation of 'Lebanon' and 4Q285," *JJS* 43 (1992): 92–94; W. J. LYONS, "Clarifications concerning 4Q285 and 11Q14 Arising from Discoveries in the Judean Desert 23," *DSD* 6 (1999): 37–43; B. NITZAN, "Benedictions and Instructions for the Eschatological Community (11QBer, 4Q285)," *RevQ* 16 (1993): 77–90; J. C. O'NEILL, "Who Killed Whom (4Q285) without the Camp (Heb 13:12–13)?" *Journal of Higher Criticism* 9 (2002): 125–39; E. J. C. TIGCHELAAR, "Working with a Few Data: Relation between 4Q285 and 11Q14," *DSD* 7 (2000): 49–56; G. VERMES, "The Oxford Forum for Qumran Research: Seminar on the Rule of War from Cave 4 (4Q285)," *JJS* 43 (1992): 85–94.

4QBer[a-e] = 4Q286–290 (*Berakot* or *Blessings*). A litany of praise of God, for his creation and blessings, to which members of the community (*Yahad*) respond by saying, "Amen. Amen."

Bibliography: B. NITZAN, "4QBerakhot[a–e] (4Q286–290): A Covenantal Ceremony in the Light of Related Texts," *RevQ* 16 (1995): 487–506; IDEM (DJD 11) 7–74.

4Q291–293 (*Work Containing Prayers A, B, C*). God "Most High" is blessed and praised. The concluding injunction "Amen. Amen" is found.

Bibliography: B. NITZAN (DJD 29) 9–22.

4Q294 (*Sapiential-Didactic Work*). Almost no legible text survives. It is thought to have something to do with wisdom, because of line 4: "he meditates day (and night?)."

Bibliography: E. J. C. TIGCHELAAR (DJD 36) 247–48.

NB: *4Q295–97. No manuscripts have been assigned to these numbers.*

4QcryptA = 4Q298 (*Words of the Maskil to All Sons of Dawn*). 4Q298 is written in cryptic script (i.e., script A). To read the text, one must possess the code (which Scrolls scholars have managed to decipher). In this way only the initiated are able to read the scroll. The text enjoins the faithful to pursue justice and to walk humbly (cf. Mic 6:8).

Bibliography: M. KISTER, "Commentary to 4Q298," *JQR* 85 (1994): 237–49; S. J. PFANN, "4Q298: The Maskil's Address to All Sons of Dawn," *JQR* 85 (1994): 203–35; S. J. PFANN and M. KISTER (DJD 20) 1–30.

4Q299–301 (*Mysteries*). For discussion, see 1QMyst = 1Q27 above.

Bibliography: L. H. SCHIFFMAN, "4QMysteries: A Preliminary Edition," *RevQ* 62 (1993): 203–24; IDEM, "4QMysteriesª: A Preliminary Edition and Translation," in *Solving Riddles and Untying Knots* (ed. Zevit et al.), 207–60; IDEM (DJD 20) 33–123.

4Q302/302a (*Admonitory Parable*). Part of this fragmentary document relates a parable of a tree "which grows high, all the way to heaven" and "produces suc-culent fruit" and so forth. The parable itself and its admonition to "under-stand this, wise ones" parallels the parables of Jesus, which sometimes are accompanied with the admonition that to him "who has ears, let him hear" (cf. Mark 4:9). On the theme of the fruitful tree (which usually symbolizes Is-rael), see Matt 3:10; 7:17; Luke 13:6–9.

Bibliography: B. NITZAN; "4Q302/302A (Sap. A): Pap. Praise of God and Parable of the Tree: A Preliminary Edition," *RevQ* 17 (1996): 151–73; IDEM (DJD 20) 125–49; IDEM, "Post-biblical *rib* Pattern Admonitions in 4Q302/302A and 4Q381 69, 76–77," in *Biblical Perspectives—Early Use and Interpretation of the Bible in Light of the Dead Sea Scrolls* (ed. Stone and Chazon), 159–74.

4Q303–305 (*Meditation on Creation A, B, C*). In 4Q303 we again encounter the admonition "You who have understanding, listen." The reference to "a king for all of them" (line 7) is interesting. Lines 8–11 allude to Adam, Eve, and what may be the "tree of the knowledge of good and evil." The small extant fragment of 4Q305 may have treated the same theme. The creation theme seems to be treated in the tiny fragment of 4Q304 as well, where we find "earth" and "darkness."

Bibliography: T. H. LIM (DJD 20) 151–58.

4Q306 (*People Who Err*). This fragmentary text describes the people "who err and do not do" the law. Either they, or others (it is not clear who), see the error of their ways and will "seek the law . . . with all their soul. And they will be like those who grope for a path . . ." (frg. 1, lines 11–12).

Bibliography: T. H. LIM (DJD 36) 249–54.

4Q307 (*Proselyte/Temple*). Fragment 1, line 6 refers to "every proselyte who . . . with Israel in the lot of . . . ," and frg. 2 refers to "my soul . . . in the temple . . . those who serve."

Bibliography: T. H. LIM (DJD 36) 255–58.

NB: Few details are known of 4Q308–12; they cannot be located.

4QcryptMMTᵍ? = 4Q313 (*Cryptic A Miqsat Ma'ase ha-Torah*ᵍ?). Written in Hebrew cryptic script A and dating to the first century B.C.E., this text appears to be another fragmentary copy of MMT (see 4Q394–399 below).

Bibliography: S. J. PFANN (DJD 36) 697–99.

NB: *Few details are known of 4Q314–16; canceled.*

4QAstrCrypt = 4Q317 (*Phases of the Moon*). The lunar phases are plotted according to the solar calendar.

Bibliography: J. T. MILIK, *BE* 68–69; M. O. WISE, "Second Thoughts on קוד and the Qumran Synchronistic Calendars," in *Pursuing the Text* (ed. J. C. Reeves and J. Kampen; B. Z. Wacholder FS; JSOTSup 184; Sheffield: Sheffield, 1994), 98–120, esp. 111–16.

4QBr ar = 4Q318 (Aramaic *Brontologion*). *Brontologion*, or *Thunder Discourse*, explicates the Zodiac and evidently makes forecasts on the basis of thunder: "If it thunders in Gemini, fear and distress from foreigners and . . ." (frg. 2 ii 9).

Bibliography: J. C. GREENFIELD and M. SOKOLOFF (DJD 36) 259–74; IDEM, "An Astrological Text from Qumran (4Q318) and Reflections on Some Zodiacal Names," *RevQ* 16 (1995): 507–25; M. O. WISE, "Thunder in Gemini: An Aramaic Brontologion (4Q318) from Qumran," in *Thunder in Gemini*, 13–50.

4Q319–330 (calendrical documents). These calendrical texts, which are often called *mishmarot* ("watches"), attempt to synchronize various aspects of the Jewish calendar, such as jubilees, Sabbaths, festivals, celestial signs, solar and lunar issues, and priestly courses.

Bibliography: M. G. ABEGG, "The Calendar at Qumran," in *Theory of Israel* (vol. 1 of *The Judaism of Qumran: A Systemic Reading of the Dead Sea Scrolls*, part 5 of *Judaism in Late Antiquity*; ed. A. Avery-Peck, J. Neusner, and B. Chilton; Handbook of Oriental Studies, 1: Ancient Near East 56; Leiden: E. J. Brill, 2001), 145–71; J. BEN-DOV (DJD 21) 195–244 (3Q319); S. TALMON (DJD 28) 125–28 (4Q322a); IDEM, "A Calendrical Document from Qumran Cave 4 (Mishmarot D, 4Q325)," in *Solving Riddles and Untying Knots* (ed. Zevit et al.), 327–44; S. TALMON with J. BEN-DOV (DJD 21) 1–154 (4Q320–330); S. TALMON and I. KNOHL, "A Calendrical Scroll from a Qumran Cave: Mishmarot Bᵃ, 4Q321," in *Pomegranates and Golden Bells: Studies in Biblical, Jewish, and Near Eastern Ritual, Law, and Literature in Honor of Jacob Milgrom* (ed. D. P. Wright et al.; Winona Lake, Ind.: Eisenbrauns, 1995), 267–301; M. O. WISE, "Primo annales fuere: An Annalistic Calendar from Qumran," in *Thunder in Gemini*, 186–221 (4Q322).

4QpapHistWork = 4Q331–333 (*Historical Work*). This fragmentary text may refer to members of the Hasmonean dynasty. In 4Q331 frg. 1 i 6–7 we find "priest . . . Yohanan" and in ii 7 the name "Shelamzion" appears. In 4Q332 frg.

2, lines 1–6 we find "give to him honor among the Nabateans," "Shelamzion entered," and "Hyrcanus rebelled." In 4Q333 frg. 1, line 4 we read that on this day (i.e., the Feast of Booths) one "Amelios killed" someone.

Bibliography: J. A. FITZMYER (DJD 36) 275–89.

4QOrdo = 4Q334 (*Order of Divine Office*). A liturgical calendar.

Bibliography: J. CARMIGNAC, "Ordonnances," *TQum* 2:295–97; U. GLESSMER (DJD 21) 167–94.

NB: Few details are known of 4Q335–336; texts cannot be located.

4Q337 (fragment of a calendar). This is a small fragment; "sabbath" occurs three times.

Bibliography: S. TALMON with J. BEN-DOV (DJD 21) 155–56.

4Q338 (a genealogical list). The ink has almost vanished. The word "begot" appears twice; hence the suggestion that the text was a genealogical list.

Bibliography: J. T. MILIK, *BE* 139; E. TOV (DJD 36) 290.

4Q339 (*List of False Prophets ar*). An Aramaic list of false prophets, including Balaam (cf. Num 22–24), the "old man from Bethel" (cf. 1 Kgs 13:11–34), and others.

Bibliography: M. BROSHI and A. YARDENI (DJD 19) 77–79; IDEM, "On Netinim and False Prophets," in *Solving Riddles and Untying Knots* (ed. Zevit et al.), 29–37, esp. 29–33.

4Q340 (*List of Netinim*). A list of temple servants.

Bibliography: M. BROSHI and A. YARDENI (DJD 19) 81–84; IDEM, "On Netinim and False Prophets," in *Solving Riddles and Untying Knots* (ed. Zevit et al.), 29–37, esp. 33–37.

4Q341 (*List of Proper Names,* formerly 4QTherapeia). This small fragment consists of a list of names, some familiar, such as "Mephibosheth," "Hyrcanus," and "Aquila," and some unknown, probably meaningless. A similar list of names is found on two ostraca from Masada (nos. 608–9). Initially some scholars thought this text concerned medicine (and so was designated 4QTherapeia). It is now regarded as a writing exercise.

Bibliography: J. NAVEH (DJD 36) 291–93; IDEM, "A Medical Document or a Writing Exercise? The So-Called 4QTherapeia," *IEJ* 36 (1986): 52–55.

4Q342–361 (miscellaneous papers). These twenty or so texts (some of which are not identified) are mostly letters and legal papers, such as accounts, deeds, or acknowledgment of debt. At least one of the texts (i.e., 4Q347) is from Naḥal Ḥever.

Bibliography: A. YARDENI (DJD 27) 106–7, 285–99, 304–17.

4Q362–363a (cryptic texts). Small fragments with little decipherable text.

Bibliography: S. PFANN (DJD 28) pls. XLI–XLIII.

4Q364–367 (*Reworked Pentateuch*[b-e]). A reworked, perhaps annotated, version of the Pentateuch.

Bibliography: E. TOV, "The Textual Status of 4Q364–367," in *The Madrid Qumran Congress* (ed. Trebolle Barrera and Vegas Montaner), 43–82; E. TOV and S. A. WHITE (DJD 13) 187–351; S. A. WHITE, "4Q364 and 365: A Preliminary Report," in *The Madrid Qumran Congress* (ed. Trebolle Barrera and Vegas Montaner), 217–28.

4QapocrPent = 4Q368 (*Pentateuch Apocryphon*). Deuteronomy has contributed to the vocabulary of this work. Moses appears to play the central role.

Bibliography: J. C. VANDERKAM and M. BRADY (DJD 28) 131–49.

4QPEnosh = 4Q369 (*Prayer of Enosh*). Attridge, Strugnell, and Evans have argued that this fragmentary text is visionary, eschatological, and probably messianic (with David, more than likely, the template). The eschatological interpretation is perhaps supported by the reference to Enoch from "the seventh generation" (cf. Jude 14–15). The principal figure is designated "first-born son" and "prince and ruler," who perhaps is said to wear "the crown of the heaven and the glory of the clouds" (partially restored). Kugel, however, disagrees, arguing that the text is speaking about historical Israel, not a messianic prince. 4Q369 represents another example of rewritten Bible. For what may be another copy of this text, see 4Q499 below.

Bibliography: H. ATTRIDGE and J. STRUGNELL (DJD 13) 353–62; C. A. EVANS, "A Note on the 'First-Born Son' of 4Q369," *DSD* 2 (1995): 185–201; J. L. KUGEL, "'Prayer of Enosh' and Ancient Biblical Interpretation," *DSD* 5 (1998): 119–48.

4Q370 (*Exhortation Based on Flood*). The text appears to be a sermon based on the flood: "Consider the might of the Lord; remember his wonders" (2:7).

Bibliography: C. NEWSOM (DJD 19) 85–97.

4Q371–373 (*Apocryphon of Joseph*[a-c]). A retelling of portions of the Pentateuch, emphasizing God's deliverance of his people.

Bibliography: E. SCHULLER, "A Preliminary Study of 4Q373 and Some Related (?) Fragments," in *The Madrid Qumran Congress* (ed. Trebolle Barrera and Vegas Montaner), 2:515–25; E. SCHULLER and M. J. BERNSTEIN (DJD 28) 151–204.

4QapocrMos A, B, C = 4Q374–375 + 4Q377 (*Apocryphon of Moses* A, B, C). 4Q374 recounts the exodus and conquest, 4Q375 develops the theme of discerning true and false prophecy (cf. Deut 18:18–22), and 4Q377 extols Moses, the Lord's "anointed" and "man of God."

Bibliography: C. NEWSOM (DJD 19) 99–110 (4Q374); J. STRUGNELL (DJD 19) 111–119 (4Q375); J. C. VANDERKAM and M. BRADY (DJD 28) 205–17 (4Q377).

4Q376 (*Liturgy of the Three Tongues of Fire* or *Apocryphon of Moses*[b?]). See the discussion of 1Q29 above.

Bibliography: J. STRUGNELL (DJD 19) 121–36.

4QPssJosh[a,b] = 4Q378–379 (*Psalms of Joshua*[a,b]). Judging from what little is extant, the psalms seem to revolve around the theme of military victory over the powers of evil. A portion of this apocryphal work is quoted in 4QTestim (= 4Q175).

Bibliography: D. DIMANT, "Qumran Sectarian Literature," *SJWSTP* 518; C. NEWSOM (DJD 22) 241–88; IDEM, "The 'Psalms of Joshua' from Qumran Cave 4," *JJS* 39 (1988): 56–73.

4Q380–381 (*Noncanonical Psalms*). The first psalm (4Q380) consists of seven fragments written on leather. The first fragment speaks of Jerusalem as God's chosen city. The seventh fragment speaks of God's wisdom in creation. The second psalm (4Q381) consists of some 104 fragments. The first fragment is in praise of God the Creator and Sustainer of the land. In fragment 15 there is a call for God's help, a call which closely parallels Ps 89:14, 7. Fragment 24 calls for victory over enemies. Fragment 31 refers to the "prayer of the king of Judah." According to line 8 of fragment 33, this is none other than the "Prayer of Manasseh, king of Judah, when the king of Assyria imprisoned him." The penitent king admits to his sins. Is this apocryphal psalm related to the apocryphal Prayer of Manasseh? Eileen Schuller does not think so. She suspects that only later was the psalm associated with Manasseh.

Bibliography: E. M. SCHULLER (DJD 11) 75–172; IDEM, *Non-canonical Psalms from Qumran* (HSS 28; Atlanta: Scholars Press, 1986); IDEM, "Qumran Pseudepigraphic Psalms," *DSSP* 4A:1–39.

4Qpap paraKings = 4Q382 (*Paraphrase of Kings*). This text consists of 154 papyrus fragments, some of which appear to be a retelling of the Elijah-Elisha narratives from 1–2 Kings. Some of these fragments probably do not belong to this text.

Bibliography: S. OLYAN (DJD 13) 363–416.

4Q383–384 + 4Q385b + 4Q387b (*Apocryphon of Jeremiah* A, C^{a-f}). Distinctive terminology distinguishes this grouping of texts from the grouping below that is linked to Ezekiel. The Jeremiah texts seem to comprise a speech addressed to the prophet.

Bibliography: G. J. BROOKE, "Ezekiel in Some Qumran and New Testament Texts," in *The Madrid Qumran Congress* (ed. Trebolle Barrera and Vegas Montaner), 1:318–37; D. DIMANT (DJD 30) 91–260 (4Q383, 385b, 387b); M. SMITH (DJD 19) 137–52 (4Q384).

4QpsEzek = 4Q385 + 4Q386–388 (*pseudo-Ezekiel*^{a-d}). There is reference to the divine chariot throne.

Bibliography: D. DIMANT (DJD 30) 7–88.

4QpsMoses = 4Q385a + 4Q387a + 4Q388a–390 (*pseudo-Moses*^{a-e}). This cluster of texts is closely linked to the Jeremiah texts above.

Bibliography: D. DIMANT (DJDJ 3) 129–71 (4Q385a), 201–53 (4Q388a–390), 255–60 (4Q387a); IDEM, "New Light from Qumran on the Jewish Pseudepigrapha—4Q390," in *The Madrid Qumran Congress* (ed. Trebolle Barrera and Vegas Montaner), 2:406–683.

4QpsEzek^c = 4Q391 (*pseudo-Ezekiel*^c). This text is quite fragmentary; reference to the "river Chebar" in frg. 65 links it to the Ezekiel tradition (e.g., Ezek 1:1).

Bibliography: M. SMITH (DJD 19) 153–93.

4Q392–393 (*Liturgical Work*).

Bibliography: J. A. EMERTON, "A Note on Two Words in 4Q393," *JJS* 47 (1996): 348–51; D. K. FALK, "4Q393: A Communal Confession," *JJS* 45 (1994): 184–207; IDEM, "Biblical Adaptation in 4Q392 *Works of God* and 4Q393 *Communal Confession*," in *The Provo International Conference on the Dead Sea Scrolls* (ed. Parry and Ulrich), 126–46; IDEM (DJD 29) 23–61.

4QMMT = 4Q394–399 (*Miqṣat Ma^caśê ha-Torah*). This document, at one time called 4QMishnah, appears to be an irenic letter, in six fragments (of four or five copies), from the Qumran community (the Teacher of Righteousness?), or at least those who would eventually form the community, to the high priest of Jerusalem. The letter may represent a period just prior to the final split between the Qumran community and the temple establishment. In one of the fragments there is a reference to the contents of Scripture: "We have [written] to you [sg.], so that you might understand the book of Moses, and [the words of the pr]ophets, and Davi[d]" (my translation; cf. Luke 24:44). The irenic tone is in evidence here as well. Regarding the NT, the most important feature of this text is the reference to being reckoned righteous for doing the law. This point is discussed in the examples below.

Bibliography: M. G. ABEGG, "4QMMT C 27,31 and 'Works Righteousness,'" *DSD* 6 (1999): 139–47; J. D. G. DUNN, "4QMMT and Galatians," *NTS* 43 (1997): 147–53; E. QIMRON and J. STRUGNELL (DJD 10) 7–63; L. H. SCHIFFMAN, "The New Halakhic Letter (4QMMT) and the Origins of the Dead Sea Sect," *BA* 53, no. 2 (1990): 64–73.

4QSirSabb[a–h] = 4Q400–407 (*Song of the Sabbath*). This text describes the heavenly throne room and an angelic liturgy. See also 11QShirShabb and MasShirShabb. Of interest for NT study are the numerous references to the kingdom of God.

Bibliography: J. H. CHARLESWORTH et al., *DSSP*, vol. 4B; J. R. DAVILA, *Liturgical Works*, 83–167; D. DIMANT, "Qumran Sectarian Literature," *SJWSTP* 524–25; C. NEWSOM (DJD 11) 173–401; IDEM, *Songs of the Sabbath Sacrifice.*

4Q408 + 4Q410–413 + 4Q415–419 + 4Q423–426 (various sapiential works).

Bibliography: J. M. BAUMGARTEN, "Some Notes on *4Q408*," *RevQ* 18 (1997): 143–44; T. ELGVIN (DJD 34) 505–534 (4Q423); E. QIMRON (DJD 20) 169–71 (4Q413); IDEM, "A Work concerning Divine Providence: 4Q413," in *Solving Riddles and Untying Knots* (ed. Zevit et al.), 191–202; A. STEUDEL (DJD 36) 298–319 (4Q408 + 410); IDEM (DJD 20) 159–67 (4Q411–412), 203–224 (4Q425–426); J. STRUGNELL and D. J. HARRINGTON (DJD 34) 41–504 (4Q415–418c); S. TANZER (DJD 36) 320–46 (4Q419 + 424).

4Q409 (*Liturgy*). A blessing for various festivals (esp. Firstfruits).

Bibliography: J. R. DAVILA, *Liturgical Works*, 168–71; E. QIMRON (DJD 29) 63–67; IDEM, "Times for Praising God: A Fragment of a Scroll from Qumran (4Q409)," *JQR* 80 (1990): 341–47.

4Q414 (*Ritual Purity A*, formerly *Baptismal Liturgy*). A liturgy for ritual bathing.

Bibliography: J. R. DAVILA, *Liturgical Works*, 267–93; E. ESHEL (DJD 35) 135–54.

4Q421 (*Ways of Righteousness*[a]). Instruction in how to be a good disciple.

Bibliography: T. ELGVIN (DJD 20) 183–202; IDEM, "Wisdom in the Yahad: 4QWays of Righteousness," *RevQ* 17 (1996): 205–32.

4Q422 (*Paraphrase of Genesis and Exodus*). Written in Hasmonean script, this text consists of a paraphrase of the opening chapters of Genesis (esp. chs. 1–9) and Exodus (esp. chs. 1–7).

Bibliography: T. ELGVIN and E. TOV (DJD 13) 417–41.

4Q427–432 + 4Q433a + 4Q440–440a (*Hymns^{a-f}* + *Hodayot*-like texts A–D). See the discussion of 1QH above.

Bibliography: A. LANGE (DJD 36) 347–48 (4Q440a); E. M. SCHULLER (DJD 29) 69–232 (4Q427–432), 247–54 (4Q440).

4Q434–439 (*Barki Nafshi*). A series of texts devoted to blessing God; they receive their name from the refrain, "Bless, O my soul, the Lord." Several Scriptures are woven into these texts.

Bibliography: E. M. COOK, "A Thanksgiving for God's Help (4Q434 II–III)," in *Prayer from Alexander to Constantine: A Critical Anthology* (ed. M. Kiley et al.; New York: Routledge, 1997), 14–17; D. R. SEELY, "The Barki Nafshi Texts (4Q434–439)," in *Current Research and Technological Developments: Conference on the Texts from the Judean Desert, Jerusalem, 30 April 1995* (ed. D. W. Parry and S. D. Ricks; STDJ 20; Leiden: Brill, 1996), 194–214; IDEM, "The 'Circumcised Heart' in 4Q434 *Barki Naphshi*," *RevQ* 17 (1996): 527–35; M. WEINFELD and D. R. SEELY (DJD 29) 255–341.

4Q434a (*Grace after Meals*). A prayer of consolation, hope, and thanks: "As someone whose mother consoles him, so will he console them in Jerusalem" (frgs. 1–2, line 6).

Bibliography: J. R. DAVILA, *Liturgical Works,* 172–76; M. WEINFELD, "Grace after Meals in Qumran," *JBL* 111 (1992): 427–40; M. WEINFELD and D. R. SEELY (DJD 29) 279–81.

4Q441–442 + 4Q443 (*Individual Thanksgiving A, B + Personal Prayer*). These texts are quite fragmentary. 4Q443 uses juridical language: "(as) a witness in court you have appointed men . . . will argue for me, and his witnesses will testify for me" (frg. 2, lines 6–7).

Bibliography: E. CHAZON (DJD 29) 343–66.

4Q444 (*Incantation*). See also 4Q511 frg. 121. Reference to "all the spirits of the bastards and the spirit of uncleanness" suggests that 4Q444 may be an incantation. Note the frequent references of "unclean spirit(s)" in the NT (e.g., Mark 1:23, 26, 27; 3:11, 30; 5:2, 8, 13; 6:7; 7:25; 9:25).

Bibliography: E. CHAZON (DJD 29) 367–78.

4Q445 (*Lament A*). Although quite fragmentary, words such as "afflicted," "bereavement," and "I am forsaken and disgraced" suggest the text is a lament.

Bibliography: E. J. C. TIGCHELAAR (DJD 29) 379–84.

4Q446–447 (*Poetic Text A, B*). Only small fragments survive.

Bibliography: E. J. C. TIGCHELAAR (DJD 29) 385–90.

4Q448 (*Apocryphal Psalm and Prayer*). Column A, which overlaps with 11Q5 col. xvii, is clearly a psalm, for it begins, "Hallelujah. A psalm" (line 1). Column B is evidently a prayer; it begins, "Arise, Holy One, on behalf of King Jonathan, and the whole assembly of your people, Israel" (lines 1–4). Who is this Jonathan? Could he be the Hasmonean Alexander Jannaeus (ruled 103–76 B.C.E.) or Jonathan, son of Mattathias (ruled 160–142 B.C.E.)? Because the former, not the latter, was called "king," it seems better to conclude that the reference is to Jannaeus (who in 4QpNah frgs. 3–4 i 5 is called the "Lion of Wrath").

Bibliography: E. ESHEL, H. ESHEL, and A. YARDENI (DJD 11) 403–25; A. LEMAIRE, "Le roi Jonathan à Qoumrân (4Q448 B–C)," in *Qoumrân et les manuscrits de la mer Morte* (ed. E.-M. Laperrousaz; Paris: Cerf, 1997), 57–70; G. VERMES, "The So-Called King Jonathan Fragment (4Q448)," *JJS* 44 (1993): 294–300.

4Q449–457 (*Prayers*). An assortment of prayers, laments, and didactic works.

Bibliography: E. CHAZON (DJD 29) 391–419; IDEM (DJD 36) 351–52 (4Q455).

4Q458–463 + 4Q464a + 4Q467–468 (historical/pseudepigraphal narratives).

Bibliography: M. BROSHI (DJD 36) 401–11 (4Q468^{a-e}); D. ERNST and A. LANGE (DJD 36) 420–32 (4Q468^{k-bb}); E. ESHEL and M. E. STONE (DJD 19) 231–232 (4Q464a); A. LANGE (DJD 36) 412–19 (4Q468^{f-j}); E. LARSON (DJD 36) 353–93 (4Q458–461); D. PIKE (DJD 36) 398–400 (4Q467); M. SMITH (DJD 19) 195–214 (4Q462–463).

4Q464 (*Exposition on the Patriarchs*). A narrative of various events in the lives of the patriarchs.

Bibliography: E. ESHEL and M. STONE (DJD 19) 215–30; M. E. STONE and E. ESHEL, "An Exposition on the Patriarchs (4Q464) and Two Other Documents (4Q464^a and 4Q464^b)," *Mus* 105 (1992): 243–64.

4Q469–470 (apocryphal texts). 4Q469 seems to be related to 4Q439. There is mention of failing to receive discipline and being men of treachery. In 4Q470, better preserved, Michael and Zedekiah are mentioned. Michael says to Zediah, "I will make with you a covenant before the congregation . . ." (frg. 1, line 6). Fragment 3 recalls the wilderness wanderings, perhaps as part of the promise of making a (new?) covenant with Israel.

Bibliography: E. LARSON (DJD 36) 433–38 (4Q469); E. LARSON, L. SCHIFFMAN, and J. STRUGNELL (DJD 19) 235–44 (4Q470).

4Q471 (*War Scroll^h*) + 4Q471a (polemic work). See the discussion of 1QM above.

Bibliography: E. ESHEL and H. ESHEL (DJD 36) 439–45 (4Q471); E. ESHEL and M. KISTER (DJD 36) 446–50 (4Q471a).

4Q472–476 (eschatological and sapiential works). 4Q472 may describe the heavenly court (and frg. 2 mentions the *Yahad,* the community). 4Q473 elaborates on the Deuteronomistic "two ways." 4Q474 extols Rachel. 4Q475 speaks of a renewed earth. 4Q476 seems to be a Sabbath liturgy, and the two small fragments that make up 4Q476a seem to be concerned with heavenly liturgy.

Bibliography: T. ELGVIN (DJD 36) 450–55 (4Q472), 456–63 (4Q474), 464–73 (4Q475); IDEM (DJD 22) 289–94 (4Q473); IDEM (DJD 29) 437–46 (4Q476 + 476a).

4Q477 (*Rebukes*). This text appears to offer guidelines in how to rebuke members of the community. It contains words such as "Community" and "the Many," as well as personal names (Yohanan, Hananiah Notos, and Simon), which evidently are cited as examples.

Bibliography: E. ESHEL (DJD 36) 474–83; C. HEMPEL, "Who Rebukes in 4Q477?" *RevQ* 16 (1995): 127–28; S. A. REED, "Genre, Setting, and Title of 4Q477," *JJS* 47 (1996): 147–48.

4Q478 (fragment mentioning festivals). Very little text survives.

Bibliography: E. LARSON and L. H. SCHIFFMAN (DJD 22) 295–96.

4Q479 (text mentioning the seed of David). In frg. 1 we have "seed of David" and "David went out."

Bibliography: E. LARSON and L. H. SCHIFFMAN (DJD 22) 297–99.

4Q480 + 4Q481b + 4Q481e (narrative fragments). Little text survives; in 4Q481b we have "will bring back his scattered ones," "their camps," and "like the wilderness." 4Q481e criticizes those who did not listen to God's words. These narratives appear to be assessing Israel's history in a way that is consistent with Qumran's perspective.

Bibliography: E. LARSON and L. H. SCHIFFMAN (DJD 22) 301–2, 311–12, 321–22.

4Q481 (small fragments). Little text survives.

Bibliography: E. LARSON and L. H. SCHIFFMAN (DJD 22) 303–4.

4Q481a (*Apocryphon of Elisha*). An elaboration of 2 Kings 2.

Bibliography: J. TREBOLLE BARRERA (DJD 22) 305–9.

4Q481c (*Prayer for Mercy*). A very fragmentary text, part of which reads, "they will praise with all their mouth . . . for manifold are your mercies . . . and gather us" (lines 5–6, 8).

Bibliography: E. LARSON and L. H. SCHIFFMAN (DJD 22) 313–14.

4Q481d (fragments with red ink). These fragments appear to be a narrative. The words "strength of heart" (*tsur leb*) are written in red ink.

Bibliography: E. LARSON and L. H. SCHIFFMAN (DJD 22) 315–19.

4Q482–483 (*Jubilees?*). 4Q482 has been designated 4QpapJub? and 4Q483 has been designated 4QpapGen or papJub?. Both fragmentary texts may well belong to *Jubilees*, with 4Q482 matching *Jub.* 13:29 (cf. Gen 14:22–23) and 4Q483 matching *Jub.* 2:14 (cf. Gen 1:28). For more on *Jubilees*, see below under the heading "Apocrypha and Pseudepigrapha."

Bibliography: M. BAILLET (DJD 7) 1–2.

4QTJudah(?) = 4Q484 (*Testament of Judah*[?]). Only tiny fragments survive; it has been suggested that frg. 1 may match *T. Jud.* 25:1–2 and frg. 7 may match *T. Jud.* 25:2. For more on the *Testaments*, see below under the heading "Apocrypha and Pseudepigrapha."

Bibliography: M. BAILLET (DJD 7) 3.

4Q485 (*Prophecy*). There is a prophetic promise to restore someone's fortune.

Bibliography: M. BAILLET (DJD 7) 4.

4Q486–487 (*Sapiential Work?* A, B). Although quite fragmentary, sufficient text survives to suggest that these are sapiential works.

Bibliography: M. BAILLET (DJD 7) 4–10.

4Q488–490 (fragments of an apocalypse?). Only tiny fragments survive.

Bibliography: M. BAILLET (DJD 7) 10–11.

4Q491–497 (*War Scroll*[a-g]). Substantial text survives, with significant overlap with 1QM. See the discussion of this text above. 4Q491c has been identified as a hymn of self-glorification, in which the speaker appears to view himself as exalted in heaven and endowed with wisdom and knowledge far beyond any mortal (see Abegg; Smith). 4Q491c, which is probably not part of the *War Scroll*, may be related to 4Q427 and 4Q471b and may represent what all members of the community were to recite in this life and in heaven (see Wise 2000).

Bibliography: M. G. ABEGG, "Who Ascended to Heaven? 4Q491, 4Q427, and the Teacher of Righteousness," in *Eschatology, Messianism, and the Dead Sea Scrolls* (ed. Evans and Flint), 61–73 (4Q491c); M. BAILLET (DJD 7) 12–72 (4Q491–497); J. DUHAIME, "War Scroll: Cave IV Fragments," *DSSP* 2:142–203 (4Q491–497); M. SMITH, "Ascent to the Heavens and Deification in 4QM," in *Archaeology and History in the Dead Sea Scrolls* (ed. Schiffman), 181–88 (4Q491c); M. O. WISE, "מי כמוני באלים: A Study of 4Q491c, 4Q471b, 4Q427 7, and 1QH^A 25:35–26:10," *DSD* 7 (2000): 173–219.

4Q498–499 (fragments of hymns). 4Q498 consists of small fragments. 4Q499 seems to be another copy of the *Prayer of Enosh* (= 4Q369); at least frgs. 48 and 47 (in that order) appear to match fragmentary portions of this text (see Tigchelaar).

Bibliography: M. BAILLET (DJD 7) 73–77; E. J. C. TIGCHELAAR, "4Q499 48 + 47 (par 4Q369 1 ii): A Forgotten Identification," *RevQ* 18 (1997): 303–6.

4Q500 (*Vineyard Benediction*). Phrases "your winepress, built among stones" (line 3), "gate of the holy height" (line 4), and "your planting and your glorious channels" (line 5) suggest the restoration "your vineyard" (line 7) and almost certainly link this text to Isaiah's Song of the Vineyard (Isa 5:1–7) and interpretive tradition that had developed (as in *Targum Isaiah*). This text and its possible relevance for Jesus' parable of the Vineyard are treated below.

Bibliography: M. BAILLET (DJD 7) 78–79; J. M. BAUMGARTEN, "4Q500 and the Ancient Conception of the Lord's Vineyard," *JJS* 40 (1989): 1–6; G. J. BROOKE, "4Q500 1 and the Use of Scripture in the Parable of the Vineyard," *DSD* 2 (1995): 268–94.

4Q501 (*Apocryphal Lamentations B*). This lament begs God not to give Israel's inheritance to others but to "remember the sons of your covenant" (lines 1–2). See 4Q179 above.

Bibliography: M. BAILLET (DJD 7) 79–80; J. R. DAVILA, *Liturgical Works*, 177–80.

pap4QRitMar = 4Q502 (*Ritual of Marriage* papyrus). It has been assumed that the papyrus is some sort of marriage ritual, but J. M. Baumgarten has recently called this interpretation into question.

Bibliography: M. BAILLET (DJD 7) 81–105; J. M. BAUMGARTEN, "4Q502, Marriage or Golden Age Ritual?" *JJS* 34 (1983): 125–35; J. R. DAVILA, *Liturgical Works*, 181–207.

4QpapPrQuot = 4Q503 (*Prières quotidiennes* or *Daily Prayers^a*). This text appears to provide guidelines for what prayers are to be said on what days of the month.

Bibliography: M. BAILLET (DJD 7) 105–36; J. R. DAVILA, *Liturgical Works,* 208–38; D. T. OLSON, "Daily Prayers," *DSSP* 4A:235–85.

4QDibHam[a-c] = 4Q504–506 (*Words of the Luminaries*[a-c]). Of special interest is 4Q504 frgs. 1–2 col. iv: "And you chose the tribe of Judah, and established your covenant with David so that he would be like a shepherd, a prince over your people, and would sit in front of you on the throne of Israel for ever. And all the gentiles have seen your glory, for you have made yourself holy in the midst of your people, Israel" (lines 5–9).

Bibliography: M. BAILLET (DJD 7) 137–75; J. CARMIGNAC, "Paroles lumineuses," *TQum* 2:299–310; J. R. DAVILA, *Liturgical Works,* 15–40, 239–66; D. FALK, *Daily, Sabbath, and Festival Prayers in the Dead Sea Scrolls* (STDJ 27; Leiden: Brill, 1998), 60–94; D. T. OLSON, "Words of the Lights," *DSSP* 4 A:107–53.

4Q507–509 (*Festival Prayers*[a-c]). 4Q507 consists of a few small fragments; frg. 1 speaks of "sin from the womb" (cf. Ps 51:5). 4Q508 consists of larger fragments and seems to be penitential. 4Q509 consists of several large fragments, exhibits a penitential tone, appeals for divine help, recalls the covenant, and mentions the Feast of Booths.

Bibliography: M. BAILLET (DJD 7) 175–215; J. R. DAVILA, *Liturgical Works,* 15–40; D. K. FALK, *Daily, Sabbath, and Festival Prayers in the Dead Sea Scrolls* (STDJ 27; Leiden: Brill, 1998), 154–215 (4Q507); D. T. OLSON, "Prayers for Festivals," *DSSP* 4A: 54–105.

4QShir[a,b] = 4Q510–511 (*Songs of the Sage*[a,b]). 4Q510 and 4Q511 overlap at points. The texts are identified as *Songs of the Sage* because of the self-reference in 4Q510 frg. 1: "And I, a sage, declare the splendor of his radiance in order to frighten and terrify all the spirits of the ravaging angels and the bastard spirits, demons, Lilith, awls, and jackals . . ." (lines 4–5; cf. 4Q511 frg. 10). The idea of a wise man (*maskil*) who frightens away demons by calling upon God makes an important contribution to traditions of exorcism, which played a role in the preaching and ministry of Jesus and some of his earliest followers.

Bibliography: M. BAILLET (DJD 7) 215–62; J. CARMIGNAC, "Règle des chants pour l'holocauste du sabbat," *TQum* 2:311–20; B. NITZAN, "Hymns from Qumran—4Q510–4Q511," in *The Dead Sea Scrolls* (ed. Dimant and Rappaport), 53–63.

4QpapRitPur B = 4Q512 (*Ritual Purity B*). References to immersion, purification, clothes, and impurity of flesh indicate that this text is some sort of a purification ritual.

Bibliography: M. BAILLET (DJD 7) 262–86; J. M. BAUMGARTEN, "The Purification Rituals in DJD 7," in *The Dead Sea Scrolls* (ed. Dimant and Rappaport), 199–209; J. R. DAVILA, *Liturgical Works,* 267–95.

4Q513–514 (*Ordinances*[b,c]). 4Q513 concerns the sheqel tax and related ordinances. See 4Q159 above. 4Q514 concerns issues of impurity and purification, including ritual bathing.

Bibliography: M. BAILLET (DJD 7) 287–98; J. M. BAUMGARTEN, "Halakhic Polemics in New Fragments from Qumran Cave 4," in *Biblical Archaeology Today* (ed. A. Biran et al.; Jerusalem: Israel Exploration Society, 1993), 390–99; J. MILGROM, "Purification Rule," *DSSP* 1:177–79; L. H. SCHIFFMAN, "Rules," *DSSP* 1:159–75.

4Q515–520 (unclassified fragments).

Bibliography: M. BAILLET (DJD 7) 299–312.

4Q521 (*Messianic Apocalypse*). This much-discussed text is apparently a messianic apocalypse. The best-preserved portion is col. ii, which is mostly found in frg. 2 (with a small amount of the lower right-hand portion preserved in frg. 4). The apocalypse foretells the appearance of an anointed one (or Messiah), to whom heaven and earth will listen. The column goes on to say that marvelous things will take place, including the freeing of prisoners, the restoration of sight to the blind, the healing of the wounded, the reviving of the dead, and the proclamation of good news to the poor. Linkage of the Messiah with words and phrases from Isa 26:19, 35:5–6, and 61:1–2 makes this text relevant for understanding Jesus' reply to the imprisoned John the Baptist (cf. Matt 11:5 = Luke 7:22). This text is discussed below.

Bibliography: M. BECKER, "4Q521 und die Gesalbten," *RevQ* 18 (1997): 73–96; J. J. COLLINS, "The Works of the Messiah," *DSD* 1 (1994): 98–112; H. KVALBEIN, "The Wonders of the End-Time: Metaphoric Language in 4Q521 and the Interpretation of Matthew 11.5 par.," *JSP* 18 (1998): 87–110; M. PHILONENKO, "Adonaï, le messie, et le saoshyant: Observations nouvelles sur 4Q521," *RHPR* 82 (2002): 259–66; IDEM, "Le vivificateur: Étude d'eschatologie comparée (de 4Q521 aux Actes de Thomas)," *RHPR* 83 (2003): 61–69; É. PUECH (DJD 25) 1–38; IDEM, "Une apocalypse messianique (4Q521)," *RevQ* 15 (1992): 475–522; J. D. TABOR and M. O. WISE, " 'On Resurrection' and the Synoptic Gospel Tradition: A Preliminary Study," *JSP* 10 (1992): 150–61.

4Q522 (*Prophecy of Joshua*). References to boundaries, peoples, conquest, and Joshua himself suggest that 4Q522 is a prophecy or apocryphon of Joshua. It contains references to the "Rock of Zion" and to building the "house of YHWH" in frg. 9 ii, lines 4 and 5.

Bibliography: D. DIMANT, "The Apocryphon of Joshua—4Q522 9 ii: A Reappraisal," in *Emanuel* (ed. Paul et al.), 179–204; É. PUECH (DJD 25) 39–74; IDEM, "La pierre de Sion et l'autel des holocaustes d'après un manuscrit hébreu de la grotte 4 (4Q522)," *RB* 99 (1992): 676–96.

4Q523 (*Jonathan*). The fragmentary sentence "they have removed Jonathan" gives this text its name. Reference to God and Magog in frgs. 1–2, line 5 may presuppose an eschatological dimension in this text.

Bibliography: É. PUECH (DJD 25) 75–83; IDEM, "Jonathan le prête impie et les débuts de la communauté de Qumrân, *4QJonathan (4Q523)* et *4QPsAp (4Q448),*" *RevQ* 17 (1996): 241–60.

4QTemple = 4Q524 (*Temple Scroll*). There is considerable overlap between 4Q524 and 11Q19 (*Temple Scroll*[a]); for example, frgs. 6–10 match 11Q19 cols. lix–lx, frg. 14 matches 11Q19 lxiv, and frgs. 15–20 match 11Q19 lxvi. See the discussion of 11Q19 below.

Bibliography: G. BRIN, "Reading in 4Q524 frs. 15–22—DJD XXV," *RevQ* 19 (1999): 265–71; É PUECH (DJD 25) 85–114; IDEM, "Fragments du plus ancien exemplaire du Rouleau du temple (4Q524)," in *Legal Texts and Legal Issues* (ed. Bernstein et al.), 19–64; IDEM, "Notes sur *11Q19 LXIV 6–13* et *4Q524 14, 2–4:* À propos de la crucifixion dans le Rouleau du temple et dans le judaïsme ancien," *RevQ* 18 (1997): 109–24.

4Q525 (*Beatitudes*). 4Q525 is a wisdom text that, among other things, contains a string of beatitudes (frgs. 2 + 3 col. ii) and thus offers the closest literary parallel to the Beatitudes of Jesus (in Matthew 5 and Luke 6). Fragment 15 is also of interest. Its warnings of burning serpents, vipers' venom, flames of death, and the "pit" may contribute to our understanding of Jewish demonology in late antiquity and perhaps shed light on this aspect of Jesus' ministry (e.g., Luke 10:19, "See, I have given you authority to tread on snakes and scorpions, and over all the power of the enemy; and nothing will hurt you").

Bibliography: J. H. CHARLESWORTH, "The Qumran Beatitudes (4Q525) and the New Testament (Mt 5:3–11, Lk 6:20–26)," *RHPR* 80 (2000): 13–35; É. PUECH "4Q525 et les péricopes des béatitudes en Ben Sira et Matthieu," *RB* 98 (1991): 80–106; IDEM, "The Collection of Beatitudes in Hebrew and in Greek (4Q525 1–4 and Mt 5,3–12)," in *Early Christianity in Context: Monuments and Documents* (ed. F. Manns and E. Alliata; SBF: Collectio minor 38; Jerusalem: Franciscan Printing Press, 1993), 353–68; IDEM (DJD 25) 115–78; J. C. R. DE ROO, "Is 4Q525 a Qumran Sectarian Document?" in *The Scrolls and the Scriptures* (ed. Porter and Evans), 338–67; B. T. VIVIANO, "Beatitudes Found among the Dead Sea Scrolls," *BAR* 18, no. 6 (1992): 53–55, 66.

4Q526 (*Testament?*). One small fragment; the words "the Lord said to my father" suggest that this text may have been a testament.

Bibliography: É. PUECH (DJD 25) 179–81.

4Q527 (*Liturgical Work D?*). One small fragment; the words "stored for the feast of the Lord," "peace-offerings," and "the priest" suggest that the text may have been a liturgical work.

Bibliography: É. PUECH (DJD 25) 183–85.

4Q528 (*Hymnic or Sapiential Work B*). One small fragment; the statements "gather those who fear you, the sons of Israel," "you will redeem the perfect ones," and "Blessed are you, all who fear YHWH" suggest that this text might be sapiential.

Bibliography: É. PUECH (DJD 25) 187–90.

4Q529 (Aramaic *Words of Michael*). This text, which consists of two fragments, one large and one tiny, receives its name from its opening line: "Words of the book, which Michael spoke to the angels." Several times the deity is referred to as the "Great One, the Lord Eternal."

Bibliography: J. T. MILIK, *BE* 91; É. PUECH (DJD 31) 1–8.

4QEnGiants[b-e] = 4Q530–533 (*Book of Giants*). See below under the heading "Apocrypha and Pseudepigrapha."

Bibliography: J. T. MILIK, *BE* 304–13; É. PUECH (DJD 31) 9–115; L. T. STUCKENBRUCK, *The Book of Giants from Qumran*, 100–185.

4QMess ar = 4Q534 (Aramaic *Elect of God*, formerly *Messianic Text*). Fitzmyer notes that this text was originally misnamed, for it is not messianic. Rather, it speaks of the birth of God's elect (Noah?). It is probably related to 4Q536–537. See *Enoch* and related works below under the heading "Apocrypha and Pseudepigrapha."

Bibliography: J. A. FITZMYER, *ESBNT* 127–60; F. GARCÍA MARTÍNEZ, "4QMess Ar and the Book of Noah," in *Qumran and Apocalyptic*, 1–44; J. T. MILIK, *BE* 56; É. PUECH (DJD 31) 117–52; L. T. STUCKENBRUCK, *The Book of Giants from Qumran*, 214–17.

4Q535–536 (formerly Birth of Noah[c,d] ar). Related to the Enochic *Book of Giants* tradition; probably related to 4Q534. See below under the heading "Apocrypha and Pseudepigrapha."

Bibliography: É. PUECH (DJD 31) 153–70; L. T. STUCKENBRUCK, *The Book of Giants from Qumran*, 217–18.

4QTJacob (?) ar = 4QAJa ar = 4Q537 (Aramaic *Testament*, or *Vision*, or *Apocryphon of Jacob*). What survives of this text alternates between events in the life of Jacob and predictions of what lies ahead for Israel. Qumran's *Testaments* are discussed below under the heading "Apocrypha and Pseudepigrapha."

Bibliography: J. T. MILIK, "Écrits préesséniens de Qumrân: D'Hénoch à Amram," in *Qumrân* (ed. Delcor, 91–106, esp. 103–4; É. PUECH (DJD 31) 171–90; IDEM, "Fragments d'un apocryphe de Lévi et le personnage eschatologique, 4QTestLévi[c-d] (?) et 4QAJa," in *The Madrid Qumran Congress* (ed. Trebolle Barrera and Vegas Montaner), 2:449–501.

4QTJudah = 4QAJu ar = 4Q538 (Aramaic *Testament* or *Apocryphon of Judah*). See below under the heading "Apocrypha and Pseudepigrapha."

Bibliography: J. T. MILIK, "Écrits préesséniens de Qumrân: D'Hénoch à Amram," in *Qumrân* (ed. Delcor), 97–98; É. PUECH (DJD 31) 191–99.

4QAJo ar = 4Q539 (Aramaic *Apocryphon of Joseph*). Although clearly related to the genre of the *Testaments of the Twelve Patriarchs,* it is not clear that these Hebrew and Aramaic fragments lie behind the Greek Testaments. See the discussion of the *Testaments* below under the heading "Apocrypha and Pseudepigrapha."

Bibliography: J. T. MILIK, "Écrits préesséniens de Qumrân: D'Hénoch à Amram," in *Qumrân* (ed. Delcor), 97–102; É. PUECH (DJD 31) 201–11.

4QapocrLevi[a,b(formerly c,d)] ar = 4Q540–541 (*Apocryphon of Levi[a,b]*). See the discussion of *Testaments* below under the heading "Apocrypha and Pseudepigrapha."

Bibliography: J. J. COLLINS, "Asking for the Meaning of a Fragmentary Qumran Text: The Referential Background of 4QAaron A," in *Texts and Contexts: Biblical Texts in Their Textual and Situational Contexts* (ed. T. Fornberg and D. Hellholm; Oslo: Scandinavian University Press, 1995), 579–90; É. PUECH (DJD 31) 213–56; IDEM, "Fragments d'un apocryphe de Lévi et le personnage eschatologique, 4QTestLévi[c-d] (?) et 4QAJa," in *The Madrid Qumran Congress* (ed. Trebolle Barrera and Vegas Montaner), 2:449–501; M. PHILONENKO, "Son soleil éternel brillera (4QTestLevi[c-d (?)] ii 9)," *RHPR* 73 (1993–1994): 405–8.

4QTQahat ar = 4Q542 (Aramaic *Testament of Qahat*). The *Testament of Qahat (Kohat)* is related to, or perhaps part of, the *Visions of Amram* (see 4QAmram below), for Kohat is the son of Levi, father of Amram. See the discussion of *Testaments* below under the heading "Apocrypha and Pseudepigrapha."

Bibliography: A. CAQUOT, "Grandeur et pureté du sacerdoce: Remarques sur le Testament de Qahat (4Q542)," in *Solving Riddles and Untying Knots* (ed. Zevit et al.), 39–44; M. COOK, "Remarks on the Testament of Kohat from Qumran Cave 4," *JJS* 44 (1993): 205–19; J. T. MILIK, "4Q Visions de 'Amram et une citation d'Origène," *RB* 79 (1972): 77–97, esp. 97; É. PUECH (DJD 31) 257–82; IDEM, "Le Testament de Qahat en araméen de la grotte 4 (4QTQah)," *RevQ* 15 (1991): 23–54.

4QAmram[a-f] = 4Q543–548 (*Visions of Amram [a-f]*). In these visions, Amram, grandson of Levi, warns his family on the day of his death (cf. 4Q543 frg. 1 = 4Q545 frg. 1 i = 4Q546 frg. 1) of coming trials: "Amram, my son, I command . . . and to your sons and to their sons I command . . ." (4Q542 frg. 1 ii 9–10). The vision of the two beings (one evil, one righteous) quarreling over the patriarch (4Q544 frg. 1, lines 10–14) is reminiscent of Jude 9 (cf. Berger). Evidently, the evil one is Melkiresha (4Q544 frg. 2, line 3), whose name means "My King is Evil." It is not certain that 4Q548 is part of the *Visions of Amram.*

Bibliography: K. BERGER, "Der Streit des guten und des bösen Engels um die Seele: Beobachtungen zu 4Q'Amr^b und Judas 9," *JSJ* 4 (1973): 1–18; A. CAQUOT, "Les testaments qoumrâniens des pères du sacerdoce," *RHPR* 78 (1998): 3–26; J. A. FITZMYER, *ESBNT* 101–4; J. T. MILIK, "4Q Visions de 'Amram et une citation d'Origène," *RB* 79 (1972): 77–97, esp. 78–92; É. PUECH (DJD 31) 283–398.

4Q549 (a work mentioning Hur and Miriam). Apparently a narrative about the exodus and wilderness wandering. Note the phrase "to leave for the eternal dwelling" (frg. 2, line 6). Puech classifies this text with 4Q543–548.

Bibliography: A. CAQUOT, "Les testaments qoumrâniens des pères du sacerdoce," *RHPR* 78 (1998): 3–26; É. PUECH (DJD 31) 399–405.

4QPrEsther^{a-e} = 4Q550–550^d (*Proto-Esther^{a-e}*). This cycle of tales centers on a villain called Bagasraw (or Bagasro), who is mentioned by name in 4Q550^c col. ii, lines 5, 6, 7, 8; col. iii, lines 2, 5; 4Q550^d frg. 1, line 4 (restored). The story is reminiscent of the story of Esther (hence the name *Proto-Esther* for these texts). Bagasraw seems to play the role of Haman. Mordecai and Esther are not mentioned, but the story vaguely resembles the story of Esther (though the parallels have been exaggerated by Milik—see Collins and Green). We read about the Persian king Darius, his attendants, Jews, royal letters, an evil plot, complete with exaltation of the villain, and finally the demise of the villain. What implications this may have for the assumption that Esther was absent at Qumran is hard to say. There appears to be nothing about the calendar in these fragments (which was an important issue at Qumran), and these fragments—unlike Hebrew Esther—mention God (e.g., "the Most High" in 4Q550^c col. iii, line 1). 4Q550^e might be part of this cycle. It may also be related to the Ezra cycle (see Wechsler). The small fragment mentions "build Zion" and "Media and Persia, Assyria and the Sea." (lines 2 and 4). It is not clear that 4Q550^f is part of this collection of texts.

Bibliography: J. J. COLLINS and D. A. GREEN, "The Tales from the Persian Court (4Q550^{a-e})," in *Antikes Judentum und frühes Christentum* (ed. B. Kollmann, W. Reinbold, and A. Steudel; H. Stegemann FS; New York: de Gruyter, 1999), 39–50 and plates; J. T. MILIK, "Les modèles araméens du livre d'Esther dans la grotte 4 de Qumrân," *RevQ* 15 (1992): 321–406; É. PUECH (DJD 37) (forthcoming); M. G. WECHSLER, "Two Para-biblical Novellae from Qumran Cave 4: A Reevaluation of 4Q550," *DSD* 7 (2000): 130–72; S. WHITE-CRAWFORD, "Has Esther Been Found at Qumran? 4QProto-Esther and the Esther Corpus," *RevQ* 17 (1995): 306–25.

4QDanSuz? ar = 4Q551 (*Susanna?*). The small amount of surviving material seems to recount a tale similar to the story of Susanna, an addition to Daniel, in which someone is accused and someone responds with the warning "My brothers, do not act wickedly . . ." (line 5). Compare Sus 45–48. It is probably not the story of Susanna but a parallel story, as in the case of proto-Esther above.

Bibliography: J. T. MILIK, "Daniel et Susanne à Qumrân?" in *De la Tôrah au messie: Études d'exégèse et d'herméneutique bibliques offertes à Henri Cazelles* (ed. M. Carrez et al.; Paris: Desclée, 1981), 337–59; É. PUECH (DJD 37) (forthcoming).

4QFour Kingdoms[a,b] ar = 4Q552–553 (*Four Kingdoms[a,b]*). The text contains a vision of four trees that represent four kingdoms, analogous to the visions in Daniel.

Bibliography: É. PUECH (DJD 37) (forthcoming).

4QNJ[a,b] ar = 4Q554–555 (*New Jerusalem*). See the discussion of 1QJN ar above.

Bibliography: É. PUECH (DJD 37) (forthcoming).

4QVision[a-c] ar = 4Q556–558 (*Vision*). Evidently, it is the angel Gabriel who conveys the vision; at least his name is mentioned in 4Q557 frg. 1, line 2. Elijah appears in 4Q558 frg. 1 ii 4 ("to you I will send Elijah, before"); in frg. 2, line 4 there is mention of "the reign of Uzziah."

Bibliography: É. PUECH (DJD 37) (forthcoming).

4QpapBibChronology ar = 4Q559 (Aramaic *Biblical Chronology*). The fragments mention Levi, Qahat, Amram, Aaron (in frg. 3) and a few Gentile kings (in frg. 4).

Bibliography: É. PUECH (DJD 37) (forthcoming); M. O. WISE, "To Know the Times and the Season: A Study of the Aramaic Chronograph 4Q559," *JSP* 15 (1997): 3–51.

4Q560 (Aramaic exorcistic text). Fragment 1 i consists of a description of the ill effects of the demonic beings, and frg. 1 ii contains the exorcistic formula "O spirit, adjure . . . I enchant you, O spirit . . . on the earth, in clouds" (lines 5–7).

Bibliography: D. L. PENNEY and M. O. WISE, "By the Power of Beelzebub: An Aramaic Incantation Formula from Qumran (4Q560)," *JBL* 113 (1994): 627–50; É. PUECH (DJD 37) (forthcoming).

4QHor ar = 4Q561 (Aramaic *Horoscope*). The horoscope engages in physiognomy, e.g., "His nose long and handsome. And his teeth well aligned. And his beard will be thin . . ." (frg. 1 col. i, lines 2–4).

Bibliography: É. PUECH (DJD 37) (forthcoming).

4Q562–575 (miscellaneous Aramaic fragments). We find phrases such as "shall not take upon themselves the priesthood" (4Q562 frg. 1), "spoke the prophet" and "the place of the cemetery" (frg. 2), "judgments in their times" (4Q568), and "remember the poor" (4Q569).

Bibliography: É. PUECH (DJD 37) (forthcoming).

4QGen[n] = 4Q576 (Genesis[n]). A misplaced biblical text. Two small fragments of Genesis: frg. 1 = Gen 34:7–10; frg. 2 = Gen 50:3.

Bibliography: É. PUECH (DJD 25) 191–93.

4Q577 (text mentioning the flood). In frg. 4 we read, "flood . . . the Lord who saved them . . . everything that was decreed," and in frg. 7, "to destroy it . . . and all . . . the sons of men . . . destroy all . . ."

Bibliography: É. PUECH (DJD 25) 195–203.

4Q578 (*Historical Text B*). The name "Ptolemy" (פתלמיס) appears in lines 2 and 3.

Bibliography: É. PUECH (DJD 25) 205–8.

4QHymnic Work? = 4Q579 (*Hymnic Work?*). A few words and phrases can be deciphered from frg. 1: "with all works . . . all angels . . . abyss, causing to tremble . . ."

Bibliography: É. PUECH (DJD 25) 209–11.

Qumran, Cave 5

Cave 5 has yielded seven biblical scrolls (5Q1–7): Deuteronomy, Kings, Isaiah, Amos, Psalms, and two copies of Lamentations. There also is one phylactery (5Q8). See J. T. Milik (DJDJ 3) 169–78. The cave has also yielded seven identified nonbiblical texts (5Q9–15), all of which have their counterparts in other caves, and an estimated ten unidentified texts (5Q16–25).

5QapocrJosh = 5Q9 (*Apocryphon of Joshua*). Very little text survives. We find the names "Joshua" and "Qidah" in frg. 1 and "Kokhbah" in frg. 5.

Bibliography: J. T. MILIK (DJDJ 3) 179–80; E. TOV, "The Rewritten Book of Joshua as Found at Qumran and Masada," in *Biblical Perspectives—Early Use and Interpretation of the Bible in Light of the Dead Sea Scrolls* (ed. Stone and Chazon), 233–56, esp. 250–51.

5QpMal or 5QapMal = 5Q10 (*Commentary on,* or *Apocryphon of, Malachi*). The *Apocryphon of Malachi* is apparently based on Mal 1:13–14 in which those who offer blemished sacrifices are cursed.

Bibliography: J. CARMIGNAC, "Vestiges d'un pesher de Malachie," *RevQ* 4 (1963–1964): 97–100; J. T. MILIK (DJDJ 3) 180.

5QS = 5Q11 (*Rule of the Community*). A fragmentary text; it seems to parallel 1QS col. ii. See the discussion of 1QS above.

Bibliography: J. H. CHARLESWORTH, "Possible Fragment of the Rule of the Community," *DSSP* 1:105–7; S. METSO, *The Textual Development of the Qumran Community Rule* (STDJ 21; Leiden: Brill, 1997): 65–66; J. T. MILIK (DJDJ 3) 180–81.

5QD = 5Q12 (*Damascus Covenant*). 5Q12 matches CD 9:7–10. See the discussion of CD below.

Bibliography: J. M. BAUMGARTEN, "5Q12," *DSSP* 2:76–77; J. T. MILIK (DJDJ 3) 181.

5QRègle = 5Q13 (*Rule*). 5QRègle is similar to 1QS and CD.

Bibliography: J. T. MILIK (DJDJ 3) 181–83; L. H. SCHIFFMAN, "Sectarian Rule," *DSSP* 1:132–43.

5QCurses = 5Q14 (*Curses*). A liturgical text containing curses, e.g., "May your eyes fall out from you . . . may they destroy you from among all the . . ."

Bibliography: J. T. MILIK (DJDJ 3) 183–84.

5QNJ ar = 5Q15 (*New Jerusalem*). This scroll fragment preserves a substantial portion of this important work. See the discussion of 1QJN ar above.

Bibliography: J. T. MILIK (DJDJ 3) 184–93.

5Q16–25 (unclassified fragments). 5Q16 seems related to the *Rule* scrolls in that frg. 1 mentions "everlasting curses." This may be true also regarding 5Q17, which mentions "the whole congregation." 4Q19 frg. 2 enjoins "for you shall clean yourself," and 4Q20 frg. 1 mentions "the sons of Aaron."

Bibliography: J. T. MILIK (DJDJ 3) 193–97.

Qumran, Cave 6

Cave 6 has yielded seven biblical scrolls (6Q1–7): Genesis, Leviticus, Deuteronomy(?), Kings, Song of Songs, and Daniel. See M. Baillet (DJDJ 3) 105–16. Two other texts are related to biblical books and may even be recensions of them: Genesis (6Q19), which is Aramaic, and Deuteronomy (6Q20). See M. Baillet (DJDJ 3) 136–37. There are also twenty or more nonbiblical texts.

6QpapEnGiants = 6Q8 (*Book of Giants*). Part of the Enochic *Book of Giants*. See below under the heading "Apocrypha and Pseudepigrapha."

Bibliography: M. BAILLET (DJDJ 3) 116–19; J. T. MILIK, *BE* 300–301; L. T. STUCKENBRUCK (DJD 36) 76–94; IDEM, *The Book of Giants from Qumran*, 196–213.

6Qpap apocrSam-Kgs = 6Q9 (*Samuel-Kings Apocryphon*). Cave 6 has yielded a fragment of a Samuel-Kings Apocryphon in which the history of these OT books is retold. Very little text survives.

Bibliography: M. BAILLET (DJDJ 3) 119–23.

6Q10 + 6Q12 (prophetic materials) Cave 6 has yielded Hebrew prophetic texts that may be examples of pseudepigrapha.

Bibliography: M. BAILLET (DJDJ 3) 123–26.

6QAllegory = 6Q11 (*Allegory of the Vine*). This Hebrew text may contain an allegory of the vine, a metaphor in the OT that is often used of Israel (cf. Ps 80:8; Jer 2:21; Ezek 17:7–8; Isa 5:1–7 ["vineyard"]; Jer 12:10). We read, "and you shall say: 'I shall guard the planted vine . . .'" (line 6).

Bibliography: M. BAILLET (DJDJ 3) 125–26.

6QPriestProph = 6Q13 (*Priestly Prophecy*). The priestly character of this text is deduced from mention of "the sons of Phineas," and its prophetic character from the forecast that "it will happen in those days."

Bibliography: M. BAILLET (DJDJ 3) 126–27.

6QApoc ar = 6Q14 (Aramaic apocalypse). Very little text survives; there appear to be anticipations of destruction and weeping.

Bibliography: M. BAILLET (DJDJ 3) 127–28; L. T. STUCKENBRUCK, *The Book of Giants from Qumran*, 218–19.

6QD = 6Q15 (*Damascus Document*). See CD under "Cairo Genizah" below.

Bibliography: M. BAILLET (DJDJ 3) 123–31; J. M. BAUMGARTEN, "6Q15," *DSSP* 2:78–79.

6QpapBen = 6Q16 (*Benediction*). Small fragments survive; vocabulary such as "pleasant smell," "rewards," "covenant," and "blessings" suggests that the text is a form of benediction.

Bibliography: M. BAILLET (DJDJ 3) 131–32.

6QpapCalenDoc = 6Q17 (calendrical document). " . . . second month . . . thirty days . . ."

Bibliography: M. BAILLET (DJDJ 3) 132–33.

6QpapHymn = 6Q18 (*Hymn*). In frg. 2 we read, "eternal life and glory," "darkness and gloom," "son of Isaac," "in eternity they will not be destroyed," and a few other words and phrases. In frg. 5 we read, "angels of righteousness," "steadfast through the spirit of knowledge," and "in eternity they will not be destroyed."

Bibliography: M. BAILLET (DJDJ 3) 133–36.

6QGen? ar = 6Q19 (*Targum of Genesis?*). The tiny Aramaic fragment ("of the sons of Ham . . . the peoples . . .") coheres with Gen 10:20 ("These are the descendants of Ham, by their families, their languages, their lands, and their nations") and could be part of a Targum. For more discussion, see below under the heading "Targumim."

Bibliography: M. BAILLET (DJDJ 3) 136.

6QDeut? = 6Q20 (Deuteronomy?). The fragment is reminiscent of Deut 8:7; 11:10–12; 31:7.

Bibliography: M. BAILLET (DJDJ 3) 136–37.

6Q21 (prophetic text?). Only a handful of words can be made out: "[their] souls . . . my people . . . to harvest, to . . ."

Bibliography: M. BAILLET (DJDJ 3) 137.

6Q22–31 (mostly unclassified fragments). 6Q26 appears to have been accounts or contracts.

Bibliography: M. BAILLET (DJDJ 3) 137–41.

Qumran, Cave 7

Cave 7 yielded several Greek MSS, including 7QLXXExod = 7Q1 and 7QLXXEpJer = 7Q2 (Epistle of Jeremiah). Several unidentified fragments, which for about thirty years a few scholars have tried to identify as writings of the NT (esp. 7Q5 and Mark 6:52), have been recently identified as belonging to *Enoch*. Most of the fragments remain unidentified. The NT identifications have won very few followers.

7QLXXEpJer = 7Q2 (*Epistle of Jeremiah*). We have the last part of verse 43 and most of verse 44 (with restorations): "because she was not as attractive as herself and her cord was not broken. [44]Whatever is done for them is false. Why then must any one think that they are gods, or call them gods?" See the discussion below under the heading "Apocrypha and Pseudepigrapha."

Bibliography: M. BAILLET (DJDJ 3) 143.

7Q3, 5–7, 9–10, 15–18 (unclassified fragments). 7Q5 has had a few champions of identification with Mark 6:52–53.

Bibliography: M. BAILLET (DJDJ 3) 143–45. For bibliography concerned with possible identification of some of these fragments (and those in the next entry) with NT writings, see J. A. FITZMYER, *DSS* 168–72. For a conclusive challenge to the identification of 7Q5 with Mark 6, see R. H. GUNDRY, "No *Nu* in Line 2 of 7Q5: A Final Disidentification of 7Q5 with Mark 6:52–53." *JBL* 118 (1999): 698–707.

7QpapEn gr = 7Q4, 8, 11–14 (*Enoch*). Recently E. A. Muro has demonstrated that several of the fragments from Cave 7 are in fact the remains of a Greek version of Enoch. His identifications are as follows:

7Q11	*1 En.* 100:12
7Q4 frg. 1 + 7Q12 + 7Q14	*1 En.* 103:3–4
7Q8	*1 En.* 103:7–8
7Q13	*1 En.* 103:15
7Q4 frg. 2	*1 En.* 105:1

Bibliography: M. BAILLET (DJDJ 3) 144–45; E. A. MURO, "The Greek Fragments of Enoch from Qumran Cave 7 (*7Q4, 7Q8, & 7Q12 = 7QEn gr = Enoch 103:3–4, 7–8*)," *RevQ* 18 (1997): 307–12; É. PUECH, "Notes sur les fragments grecs du manuscrit 7Q4 = 1 Hénoch 103 et 105," *RB* 103–104 (1996): 592–600; IDEM, "Sept fragments grecs de la Lettre d'Hénoch (*1 Hén 100, 103, 105*) dans la grotte 7 de Qumrân (= *7QHén gr*)," *RevQ* 18 (1997): 313–23.

7Q19 (papyrus imprint). Baillet reads, "of creation . . . in the scriptures . . ."

Bibliography: M. BAILLET (DJDJ 3) 145–46.

Qumran, Caves 8–10

Eight texts have been recovered from Cave 8: A few fragments of Genesis (8Q1 = Gen 17:12–19 + 18:20–25), several fragments of the Psalms (8Q2 = Pss 17:5–9, 14; 18:6–9, 10–13), a phylactery with clusters of quotations from Exodus and Deuteronomy (8Q3), a mezuzah with Deut 10:12–11:21 (8Q4), and a hymn (8Q5) that appears to extol God: "In your name, O Mighty One, I spread fear . . ." See M. Baillet (DJDJ 3) 147–62.

Cave 9 yielded one unclassified papyrus fragment (9Qpap), and Cave 10 yielded one ostracon (10QOstracon) with only two letters (*yod, shin*) at the beginning of a word or name. See M. Baillet (DJDJ 3) 163–64.

Qumran, Cave 11

Discovered in 1956 and the last of the Qumran caves to give up written materials, Cave 11 offers several important finds. There are nine biblical scrolls: two of Leviticus (11Q1–2), one of Deuteronomy (11Q3), one of Ezekiel (11Q4), and five Psalms scrolls (11Q5–9). There are eleven identified nonbiblical scrolls (11Q10–20), including the important Temple texts (11Q19–20), and five unidentified or unclassified texts (11Q21–25).

11QPs[a-e] = 11Q5–9 (*Psalms Scroll*). The *Psalms Scroll* contains portions of some thirty canonical psalms, Psalms 151A, 151B, 154, 155, Sir 51:13–20, 30, and 2 Sam 23:7. For further discussion, see below under the heading "Apocrypha and Pseudepigrapha."

Bibliography: P. W. FLINT, *The Dead Sea Psalms Scrolls and the Book of Psalms* (STDJ 17; Leiden: Brill, 1997); F. GARCÍA MARTÍNEZ, E. J. C. TIGCHELAAR, and A. S. VAN DER WOUDE (DJD 23) 29–78; M. H. GOSHEN-GOTTSTEIN, "The Psalms Scroll (11QPsa)," *Text* 5 (1966): 22–33; J. A. SANDERS, *The Psalms Scroll of Qumran Cave 11 (11QPsª)* (DJDJ 4; Oxford: Clarendon, 1965); IDEM, "The Qumran Psalms Scroll [11QPsª] Reviewed," in *On Language, Culture, and Religion* (ed. M. Black and W. A. Smalley; E. A. Nida FS; The Hague: Mouton, 1974), 79–99; G. H. WILSON, *The Editing of the Hebrew Psalter* (SBLDS 76; Chico, Calif.: Scholars Press, 1985).

11QtgJob = 11Q10 (*Targum of Job*). The *Targum of Job* (fragments of Job 17:14–42:11), along with 4QtgLev, 4QtgJob, and possibly 6Q19 (*Targum of Genesis?*), proves the existence of written Targumim at the time of the emergence of Christianity. Certain features found in the major Targumim, such as the use of the periphrastic *memra* ("word"), do not occur in the Qumran Targumim.

Bibliography: B. JONGELING, C. J. LABUSCHAGNE, and A. S. VAN DER WOUDE, *Aramaic Texts from Qumran with Translations and Annotations* (SSS NS 4; Leiden: Brill, 1976), 1–73; S. A. KAUFMAN, "The Job Targum from Qumran," *JAOS* 93 (1973): 317–27; M. SOKOLOFF, *The Targum to Job from Qumran Cave XI* (Ramat-Gan: Bar-Ilan University Press, 1974); J. P. M. VAN DER PLOEG and A. S. VAN DER WOUDE, *Le Targum de Job de la grotte XI de Qumrân* (Leiden: Brill, 1971).

11QApPs[a] = 11Q11 (*Apocryphal Psalms[a]*). 11Q11 comprises fragments of four psalms, one of which appears to be a version of Psalm 91. Apparently these are psalms that were to be recited over the "stricken," that is, those thought to be demon-possessed. These may well be the "Davidic" psalms mentioned in 11Q5 27:9–10: "And songs to perform over the possessed: four." The embellishment of the Davidic/Solomonic legend with exorcistic tradition, including Psalm 91, is significant for Jesus research, especially for the story of the temptation, in which Satan appeals to Psalm 91 (Matt 4:1–11 = Luke 4:1–13).

Bibliography: F. García Martínez, E. J. C. Tigchelaar, and A. S. van der Woude (DJD 23) 181–205; J. P. M. van der Ploeg, "Un petit rouleau de psaumes apocryphes (11QPsAp^a)," in *Tradition und Glaube* (ed. Jeremias et al.), 128–39; É. Puech, "11QPsAp^a, un rituel d'exorcismes: Essai de reconstruction," *RevQ* 14 (1990): 377–408; idem, "Les deux derniers psaumes davidiques du rituel d'exorcisme 11QPsAp^a iv, 4–v, 14," in *The Dead Sea Scrolls* (ed. Dimant and Rappaport), 64–89; J. A. Sanders, "A Liturgy for Healing the Stricken," *DSSP* 4A: 216–33.

11QJub = 11Q12 (*Jubilees*). See below under the heading "Apocrypha and Pseudepigrapha."

Bibliography: F. García Martínez, E. J. C. Tigchelaar, and A. S. van der Woude (DJD 23) 207–20; J. T. Milik, "À propos de 11QJub," *Bib* 54 (1973): 77–78; J. C. VanderKam, *Textual and Historical Studies in the Book of Jubilees* (HSM 14; Missoula, Mont.: Scholars Press, 1977), 18–51, 97–99; A. S. van der Woude, "Fragmente des Buches Jubiläen aus Qumran Höhle XI (11QJub)," in *Tradition und Glaube* (ed. Jeremias et al.), 140–46.

11QMelch = 11Q13 (*Melchizedek Text*). This is a text treating the heavenly prince Melchizedek, a figure of great importance to the men of Qumran. The text is based on the Jubilee passage of Lev 25:13 and so describes the "Last Jubilee." Parts of Isa 61:1–3 and 52:7 are cited several times. We are told that "Melchizedek will carry out the vengeance of God's judgments, and on that day he will free them from the hand of Belial and from the hand of all the spirits of his lot" (col. ii, line 13). Jesus' appeal to his exorcisms as proof that the kingdom of God has come upon his contemporaries (cf. Luke 11:20) coheres with this eschatological expectation and may explain, at least in part, why the author of Hebrews chose to compare Jesus with Melchizedek, the mysterious priest of God Most High (cf. Hebrews 5–7).

Bibliography: F. García Martínez, E. J. C. Tigchelaar, and A. S. van der Woude (DJD 23) 221–41; M. de Jonge and A. S. van der Woude, "11QMelchizedek and the New Testament," *NTS* 12 (1966): 301–26; P. J. Kobelski, *Melchizedek and Melchiresa'* (CBQMS 10; Washington, D.C.: Catholic Biblical Association, 1981); M. P. Miller, "The Function of Isa. 61,1–2 in Melchizedek," *JBL* 88 (1969): 467–69; D. F. Miner, "A Suggested Reading for 11Q Melchizedek 17," *JSJ* 2 (1971): 144–48; É. Puech, "Notes sur le manuscrit de XIQMelkisédeq," *RevQ* 12 (1985–1987): 483–513; A. S. van der Woude, "Melchisedek als himmlische Erlösergestalt in den neugefundenen eschatologische Midraschim aus Qumran Höhle XI," *OtSt* 14 (1965): 354–73.

11QBer or 11QSepher ha-Milhamah = 11Q14 (*Blessings*). A benediction, part of which overlaps with 4Q285 (see above).

Bibliography: F. García Martínez, E. J. C. Tigchelaar, and A. S. van der Woude (DJD 23) 243–51; B. Nitzan, "Benedictions and Instructions from Qumran for the Eschatological Community (11QBer, 4Q285)," *RevQ* 16 (1993): 77–90; A. S. van der Woude, "Ein neuer Segensspruch aus Qumran (11QBer)," in *Bibel und Qumran: Beiträge zur Erforschung der Beziehung zwischen Bibel-und Qumranwissenschaft (ed. S. Wagner; Berlin: Evangelische Haupt-Bibelgesellschaft, 1968): 253–58.

11QHymns[a,b] = 11Q15–16 (*Hymns[a,b]*). Fragments of two hymns.

Bibliography: F. GARCÍA MARTÍNEZ, E. J. C. TIGCHELAAR, and A. S. VAN DER WOUDE (DJD 23) 253–58; J. P. M. VAN DER PLOEG, "Les manuscrits de la grotte 11 de Qumrân," *RevQ* 12 (1985): 3–15.

11QShirShabb = 11Q17 (*Songs of the Sabbath Sacrifice*). See the discussion of 4Q400–407 above.

Bibliography: F. GARCÍA MARTÍNEZ, E. J. C. TIGCHELAAR, and A. S. VAN DER WOUDE (DJD 23) 259–304.

11QJN ar = 11Q18 (*New Jerusalem*). See the discussion of 1QJN ar above.

Bibliography: F. GARCÍA MARTÍNEZ, E. J. C. TIGCHELAAR, and A. S. VAN DER WOUDE (DJD 23) 305–55.

11QTemple[a,b] = 11Q19–20 (*Temple Scroll*). The *Temple Scroll* is the largest single scroll from Qumran, measuring some 28 feet in length (67 cols. of text) in "Herodian" script. This script dates the scroll to sometime between 30 B.C.E. and 70 C.E. It is believed that the original work was composed in the time of John Hyrcanus (134–105 B.C.E.). The scroll contains various laws, with the first section concerned with the temple, and the second section based on Deuteronomy 12–26. Unlike Deuteronomy, the *Temple Scroll* gives the laws in the first person, directly by God. Of interest is to note that some of the laws are given slightly different readings or emphases in order to underscore the distinctive beliefs of the men of Qumran. 11QTemple[b] is a second, fragmentary copy of the *Temple Scroll.* There are at least three dozen fragments. Portions of the *Temple Scroll* are also found in Cave 4 (i.e., 4Q524).

Bibliography: G. J. BROOKE, *Temple Scroll Studies* (JSPSup 7; Sheffield: JSOT Press, 1989); P. R. CALLAWAY, "The Temple Scroll and the Canonization of the Jewish Law," *RevQ* 13 (Mémorial Jean Carmignac, 1988): 239–50; D. DIMANT, "Qumran Sectarian Literature," *SJWSTP* 526–30; J. A. FITZMYER, *DSS* 144–48; F. GARCÍA MARTÍNEZ, E. J. C. TIGCHELAAR, and A. S. VAN DER WOUDE (DJD 23) 357–409 (11Q20); M. HENGEL and J. H. CHARLESWORTH, "The Polemical Character of 'On Kingship' in the Temple Scroll: An Attempt at Dating 11QTemple," *JJS* 37 (1986): 28–38; J. MAIER, *The Temple Scroll: An Introduction, Translation, and Commentary* (JSOTSup 34; Sheffield: JSOT Press, 1985); IDEM, *Die Tempelrolle vom Toten Meer und das "Neue Jerusalem": 11Q19 und 11Q20; 1Q32, 2Q24, 4Q554–555, 5Q15 und 11Q18* (3d ed.; Uni-Taschenbücher 829; Munich: Reinhardt, 1997); J. MURPHY-O'CONNOR, "The Judean Desert," *EJMI* 136–37; L. H. SCHIFFMAN, "Laws concerning Idolatry in the Temple Scroll," in *Uncovering Ancient Stones: Essays in Memory of H. Neil Richardson* (ed. L. M. Hopfe; Winona Lake, Ind.: Eisenbrauns, 1994), 159–75;

H. STEGEMANN, "The Origins of the Temple Scroll," in *Congress Volume: Jerusalem, 1986* (ed. J. A. Emerton; VTSup 40; Leiden: Brill, 1988), 235–56; Y. YADIN, *The Temple Scroll* (3 vols.; Jerusalem: Israel Exploration Society, 1983).

11QTemple? = 11Q21 (*Temple? Scroll*). This text appears to be related to the *Temple Scroll* and may even be part of a third copy, for frg. 1 parallels 11Q19 col. iii.

Bibliography: F. GARCÍA MARTÍNEZ, E. J. C. TIGCHELAAR, and A. S. VAN DER WOUDE (DJD 23) 411–14.

11Q22–31 (mostly unidentified fragments). 11Q22 is written in paleo-Hebrew. 11Q23 is cryptic. 11Q24 is in Aramaic. 11Q29 appears to be related to the *Rule* scrolls, for lines 2–3 (the only legible lines) overlap with 1QS col. vii.

Bibliography: F. GARCÍA MARTÍNEZ, E. J. C. TIGCHELAAR, and A. S. VAN DER WOUDE (DJD 23) 415–46.

Summaries of Masada Documents

The Masada materials consist of a great number of ostraca and a few texts written upon leather. For a catalogue, see S. A. Reed, *The Dead Sea Scrolls Catalogue: Documents, Photographs, and Museum Inventory Numbers* (ed. M. J. Lundberg; SBLRBS 32; Atlanta: Scholars Press, 1994), 185–216.

1. *Scripture.* Fragments of Genesis (MasGen = Gen 46:7–11), Leviticus (two scrolls; MasLev[a,b] = Lev 4:3–9 + 8:31–11:40), Deuteronomy (MasDeut = Deut 33:17–34:6), Ezekiel (MasEzek = Ezek 35:11–38:14), Psalms (two scrolls; MasPs[a,b] = Pss 81:2–85:6 + 150:1–6), and Sirach (MasSir = Sir 37:27–43:30) have been found at Masada.

2. *Apocryphal texts.* Fragments of *Jubilees* or pseudo-*Jubilees* (MasJub or MaspsJub), an apocryphal book of Joshua (MasapocrJosh), an apocryphal book based on Genesis (MasapocrGen), an apocryphal work possibly related to Esther, and several fragments of the *Songs of the Sabbath Sacrifice* (MasShirShabb) have been found. See 4Q400–407 and 11Q17 above. The Joshua apocryphon may be related to 4Q378–379. There was also found a small papyrus text of Samaritan origin that mentions "Mount Gerizim."

3. *Greek and Latin papyri.* Nine Greek papyri (Mas 739–47), twenty-two Latin papyri (Mas 721–38), and two bilingual papyri (Mas 748–49) were recovered at Masada. Among the Latin papyri we have a fragment of Virgil's *Aeneid* (4.9; cf. Mas 721) as well as private letters and official correspondence, some of it military. One Latin papyrus (no. 722) mentions emperor Vespasian (ruled 69–79 C.E.).

4. *Ostraca.* About seven hundred Aramaic and Hebrew ostraca (Mas 1–701), twenty-three Greek ostraca (Mas 772–94), and twenty-two Latin ostraca (Mas 750–71), as well as a number of Latin (Mas 795–853) and Greek (Mas 854–927) *tituli*, were recovered at Masada. Several of these ostraca are of interest:

Mas 405 reads, "the daughter of Qatra." Some scholars seeing a relation to the high-priestly family of Qatros recall the stone weight, found near the Burnt House, that reads, "belonging to the son of Qatros." Mas 437 may read, "sons of light." Mas 441 reads, "tithe of the priest," and Mas 461 reads, "A[nani]as the high priest, 'Aqavia his son." Mas 474 reads, "Joseph the zealous." Mas 554 is a letter, petitioning overdue payment: " . . . son of Ma'uzi, peace. Have pity on me [and please] pay the silver, five denarii, account . . . bread . . . that you owe me. [Have p]ity, because I am (poor?) . . . and I do not possess . . ." Of great interest is the appearance of Herod's name on several wine amphorae (Mas 804–10, 812–13, 815–16): "for Herod, king of the Jews" (*Regi Herodi iudaico*).

5. *Coins.* Masada yielded up about 18 Ptolemaic and Seleucid coins, about 90 Hasmonean coins, nearly 400 coins minted by Herod (all but one from Jerusalem); 176 coins minted by Archelaus, about 500 coins minted by the Roman prefects and procurators, most by the prefect Pilate and the procurator Festus, about 113 coins minted by Agrippa I, and 2 coins minted by Agrippa II (whose coins are rarely found in Judea). Nabatean and Roman coins were also found at Masada, including the notorious *Iudaea capta* coin. In reference to Alexander Jannaeus, coin 19 reads in Hebrew, "The King Yehonathan." Coin 25 reads in Greek, "of King Alexander." Coins 96 and 103 read in Hebrew, "Yehonathan the high priest and colleague [*hever*] of the Jews." Several coins refer to Herod the Great: "of King Herod" (coins 110–18). The Jewish rebels also minted coins, most of which are overstrikes. About 3,000 have been found at Masada. Many of these coins date themselves "Year I of the freedom of Zion." Many also state "Sheqel of Israel."

Bibliography: L. H. FELDMAN, "Masada: A Critique of Recent Scholarship," in *Christianity, Judaism, and Other Greco-Roman Cults* (ed. J. Neusner; 4 vols.; Leiden: Brill, 1975) 3:218–48; Y. MESHORER, *Herod the Great through Bar Cochba* (vol. 2 of *Ancient Jewish Coinage;* New York: Amphora Books, 1982); C. NEWSOM, *Songs of the Sabbath Sacrifice* (HSS 27; Atlanta: Scholars Press, 1985), 167–84; C. NEWSOM and Y. YADIN, "The Masada Fragment of the Qumran Songs of the Sabbath Sacrifice," *IEJ* 34 (1984): 77–84; J. STRUGNELL, "Notes and Queries on 'The Ben Sira Scroll from Masada,'" in *W. F. Albright Volume* (Eretz-Israel 9; Jerusalem: Israel Exploration Society, 1969), 109–19; S. TALMON, "Hebrew Written Fragments from Masada," *DSD* 3 (1996): 168–77; IDEM, "Masada: Written Material," *EDSS* 1:521–25; Y. YADIN, *The Ben Sira Scroll from Masada, with Introduction, Emendations, and Commentary* (Jerusalem: Israel Exploration Society, 1965); IDEM, "The Excavation of Masada, 1963–1964: Preliminary Report," *IEJ* 15 (1965): 1–120; IDEM, *Masada: Herod's Fortress and the Zealots' Last Stand* (New York: Random House, 1966).

The publications of the 1963–1965 Yigael Yadin Masada Excavations are as follows:

Y. Yadin, J. Naveh, and Y. Meshorer, *Masada I: The Yigael Yadin Excavations, 1963–1965, Final Reports: The Aramaic and Hebrew Ostraca and Jar Inscriptions, the Coins of Masada* (Jerusalem: Israel Exploration Society, 1989).

H. M. Cotton and J. Geiger, *Masada II: The Yigael Yadin Excavations, 1963–1965, Final Reports: The Latin and Greek Documents* (Jerusalem: Israel Exploration Society, 1989).

E. Netzer, *Masada III: The Yigael Yadin Excavations, 1963–1965, Final Reports:* (Jerusalem: Israel Exploration Society, 1991).

D. Barag et al., *Masada IV: The Yigael Yadin Excavations, 1963–1965, Final Reports: Lamps, Textiles, Basketry, Cordage, and Related Artifacts, Wood Remains, Ballista Balls, Human Skeletal Remains* (Jerusalem: Israel Exploration Society, 1995).

G. Foerster, *Masada V: Art and Architecture* (Jerusalem: Israel Exploration Society, 1996).

S. Talmon and Y. Yadin, *Masada VI: The Yigael Yadin Excavations, 1963–1965, Final Reports: Hebrew Fragments from Masada, the Ben Sira Scroll from Masada* (Jerusalem: Israel Exploration Society, 1999).

Masada VII: Pottery, Weapons, Stone, and Other Artifacts (in preparation).

Summaries of Murabbaᶜat Documents

In Wadi Murabbaᶜat were found about 175 texts and ostraca. Most of these were edited by J. T. Milik, P. Benoit, and A. Grohman and published in DJD 2.

1. *Scripture.* Several fragments of Scripture have been found: Genesis (Mur 1:1–3), Exodus (Mur 1:4–5), Numbers (Mur 1:6–7), Deuteronomy (Mur 2), Isaiah (Mur 3), a Minor Prophets scroll (MurXII = Mur 88), a phylactery (Mur 4) with verses from Exodus and Deuteronomy, possibly a mezuzah (Mur 5), and a variety of other texts, mostly business or private.

2. *Nonliterary Documents and Letters.* Several contracts, writs of divorce, marriage contracts, deeds, letters (materials are in Aramaic, Hebrew, and Greek). Of special interest are letters from Simon Bar Kokhba (or ben Kosiba), (apparent messianic) leader of Israel's second revolt against Rome (132–135 C.E.): Mur 42 (Letter to Yeshua' ben Galgula'), Mur 43 (Letter of Shim'on ben Kosibah to Yeshua' ben Galgula') and Mur 44 (Letter of Shim'on ben Kosibah to Yeshua' ben Galgula'). Mur 17 is a palimpsest; the older, underlying text dates to the seventh century B.C.E. Mur 72 records a court decision and dates to 125–100 B.C.E.

Bibliography: P. BENOIT, J. T. MILIK, and R. DE VAUX (DJD 2); H. ESHEL, "Murabbaᶜat: Written Material," *EDSS* 1:583–86; Y. YADIN, "Expedition D," *IEJ* 11 (1961): 36–52, esp. 51–52.

Summaries of Naḥal Ḥever Documents

Scholars classify the materials found in the caves at Naḥal Ḥever in three groupings: (1) materials from Cave 5/6 (the Cave of Letters) and Cave 8 (the Cave of Horror), (2) materials known to have come from Naḥal Ḥever but that were not excavated by archaeologists, and (3) materials thought to have come from Naḥal Ḥever though some uncertainty remains. The Cave of Letters yielded up an assortment of documents ranging from the 90s C.E. to 135 C.E. Fragments of two Bible scrolls were found: Numbers (5/6Ḥev 1a) and Psalms (5/6Ḥev 1b). Of interest is the Babatha archive, mostly comprising various legal documents (5/6Ḥev

13–17, 21–27, 34–35). Of great interest also are the letters of Simon Bar Kokhba (5/6Ḥev 49–63), leader of the great revolt of 132–135 C.E. The Cave of Horror yielded up the fragmentary *Greek Minor Prophets Scroll* (8ḤevXII gr = 8Ḥev 1), with portions of Jonah, Micah, Nahum, Habakkuk, Zephaniah, and Zechariah.

Bibliography: H. M. COTTON, "Hever, Nahal: Written Material," *EDSS* 1:359–61; H. M. COTTON and A. YARDENI (DJD 27); J. C. GREENFIELD, "The Texts from Nahal Se'elim (Wadi Seiyâl)," in *The Madrid Qumran Congress* (ed. Trebolle Barrera and Vegas Montaner), 2:661–65; N. LEWIS, ed., *The Documents from the Bar Kokhba Period in the Cave of Letters: Greek Papyri* (JDS 2; Jerusalem: Israel Exploration Society, 1989); E. TOV, *The Greek Minor Prophets Scroll from Nahal Hever (8HevXIIgr)* (DJD 8; Oxford: Clarendon, 1990); Y. YADIN, *Bar-Kokhba: The Rediscovery of the Legendary Hero of the Second Jewish Revolt against Rome* (London: Weidenfeld & Nicolson, 1971), 124–253; IDEM, "Expedition D—the Cave of Letters," *IEJ* 12 (1962): 227–57; IDEM, *The Finds from the Bar Kokhba Period in the Cave of the Letters* (JDS 1; Jerusalem: Israel Exploration Society, 1963); IDEM, "The Nabataean Kingdom, Provincia Arabia, Petra, and En-Gedi in the Documents from Nahal hever," *Phoenix: Ex oriente lux* 17 (1963): 227–41; Y. YADIN, J. C. GREENFIELD, A. YARDENI, and B. A. LEVINE, *The Documents from the Bar Kokhba Period in the Cave of Letters: Hebrew, Aramaic, and Nabatean-Aramaic Papyri* (JDS 3; Jerusalem: Israel Exploration Society, 2002).

Summaries of Naḥal Ṣe'elim (Wadi Seiyâl) Documents

Most of what originally was labeled as found at Naḥal Ṣe'elim (or Wadi Seiyâl) is now thought to have been found at Naḥal Ḥever. Consequently, most of the recent publications bring these two collections together. None of the Seiyâl material published in DJD 8 and 27 has been traced to Naḥal Ṣe'elim. The written material that we know comes from Naḥal Ṣe'elim was discovered in 1960, in Cave 34, by Yohanan Aharoni and associates. This material includes fragments of a phylactery (34Ṣe 1), a fragment with Hebrew letters (34Ṣe 2), and fragments of Greek papyri (34Ṣe 4–8).

Bibliography: Y. AHARONI, "Expedition B," *IEJ* 11 (1961): 11–24; H. M. COTTON, "Se'elim, Nahal: Written Material," *EDSS* 2:860–61; H. M. COTTON and A. YARDENI (DJD 27) 1–6; J. C. GREENFIELD, "The Texts from Nahal Se'elim (Wadi Seiyâl)," in *The Madrid Qumran Congress* (ed. Trebolle Barrera and Vegas Montaner), 2:661–65; B. LIFSHITZ, "The Greek Documents from Nahal Seelim and Nahal Mishmar," *IEJ* 11 (1961): 53–62 (see corrections by P. BENOIT, "Bulletin," *RB* 68 [1961]: 466–67, and by J. SCHWARTZ, "Remarques sur des fragments grecs du Désert de Juda," *RB* 69 [1962]: 61–63).

Summaries of Wadi Sdeir Documents

In 1952 some bedouin found written materials in caves in Naḥal David. Scholars think that the site was the Cave of the Pool, in Wadi Sdeir, where in 1905 G. D. Sandel was taken by bedouin and where he observed clay jars. In 1958

Yohanan Aharoni surveyed this cave, and Nahman Avigad excavated it in 1960 and 1961. Four texts were found in Wadi Sdeir: Genesis (Sdeir 1 = Gen 35:6–8; 35:26–36:2; 36:5–17), pap ar (Sdier 2 = Aramaic papyrus contract concerning debt), Greek document on leather (Sdier 3), and a Greek document on paper (Sdeir 4). In the caves of Naḥal David, burial remains have been discovered, dating to the Herodian period and perhaps even to the Hasmonean period.

Bibliography: Y. AHARONI, "Expedition A," *IEJ* 11 (1961): 6–10; IDEM, "Expedition A— Nahal David," *IEJ* 12 (1962): 169–83; H. ESHEL, "Sdeir, Wadi," *EDSS* 2:851–62.

Summaries of Naḥal Mishmar Documents

Pessah Bar-Adon excavated Naḥal Mishmar in 1960 and 1961. In 1961 Bar-Adon found hundreds of items from the Chalcolithic period. The cave where they were found became known as the Cave of the Treasure. In this cave and in another (Cave 2), pottery, including glass, was found that dated to the Bar Kokhba period. Three papyri were also found: a small fragment with Hebrew (1Mish 1), a papyrus with a list of Greek names (1Mish 2), and a third papyrus on which are visible a few signatures in Aramaic and Greek (1Mish 3).

Bibliography: P. BAR-ADON, *The Cave of the Treasure: The Finds from the Caves in Nahal Mishmar* (Jerusalem: Israel Exploration Society, 1980); IDEM, "Expedition C," *IEJ* 11 (1961): 25–35; H. ESHEL, "Mishmar, Nahal," *EDSS* 1:568–69; B. LIFSHITZ, "The Greek Documents from Nahal Seelim and Nahal Mishmar," *IEJ* 11 (1961): 53–62.

Summaries of Khirbet Mird Documents

Khirbet ("ruins of") Mird are located at the site of Hyrcania, a Hasmonean fortress situated in the Judean desert (cf. Josephus, *Ant.* 13.16.3 §417). Byzantine monks later settled at this site. Two sets of Greek papyri, two sets of Arabic papyri, and a few Greek and Syriac texts have been found. There are four Christian texts in all. These include two fragments of Acts (Acts 10:28–29, 32–41 = Mird Acts cpa), a letter (papMird A), and a magical amulet (MirdAmul cpa). The Arabic papyri are Muslim (papMird 1–100 arab) and include a fragment of the Qur'an. The Greek papyri have not been published, but Barbara and Kurt Aland have identified several as fragments of the NT: Mird 16gr = Matt 20:23–26, Mird 16Bgr = Matt 20:30–31?, Mird 26gr = Mark 2:3–4, 4–5; John 17:3, Mird 26Bgr = Mark 2:8–9; John 17:7–8, Mird 27gr = Mark 6:30–31, 33–34, Mird 27Bgr = Mark 6:36–37, 39–41, Mird 8gr = Acts 11:29–12:1, and Mird 8Bgr = Acts 12:2–5. The Matthean fragments are assigned the P83 siglum, the Mark/John fragments the P84 siglum, and the Acts fragments Uncial 0244. For these assignments, see B. Aland and K. Aland, *The Text of the New Testament: An Introduction to the Critical Editions and to the Theory and Practice of Modern Textual Criticism* (rev. ed.; Grand Rapids: Eerdmans, 1989), 101, 126.

Bibliography: J. VAN HAELST, "Cinq texts provenant de Khirbet Mird," *Ancient History* 22 (1991): 297–317; J. PATRICH, "Mird, Khirbet," *EDSS* 1:563–66; C. PERROT, "Un fragment christo-palestinien découvert à Khirbet Mird (Actes des apôtres, X, 28–29; 32–41)," *RB* 70 (1963): 506–55; G. R. H. WRIGHT, "The Archaeological Remains of el-Mird in the Wilderness of Judaea," *Bib* 42 (1961): 1–21.

Summaries of Wadi Ed-Daliyeh Documents

Honeycombed with caves, Wadi ed-Daliyeh is located about halfway between Jericho and Samaria. In 1962 bedouin discovered caves in the wadi that contained pottery, coins, beads, bullae, and some rolls and fragments of papyri. One of the papyri was dated to the fourth century B.C.E. The finds were eventually purchased from the bedouin, and proper excavations subsequently were undertaken. More artifacts were discovered, including about fifty skeletons, thought to be the remains of Samaritans who had fled from Alexander the Great. Evidently these fugitives hid in the cave and then were suffocated when the Greeks built a fire at its mouth. About forty Aramaic papyri have been recovered; apparently all are official documents, mostly dealing with the buying and selling of slaves. Best preserved is WDSP papDeed of Slave Sale A ar, which begins, "On the twentieth of 'Adar, the second year, the accession year of [D]arius, the king, in Samar[ia the citadel, which is in Samaria the province. Hananiah, son of Beyad'el sold] a certain Yehohanan, son of Se'ilah . . ." (lines 1–2).

Bibliography: F. M. CROSS, "A Report on the Samaria Papyri," in *Congress Volume, Jerusalem, 1986* (ed. J. A. Emerton; VTSup 40; Leiden: Brill, 1988), 17–26; D. M. GROPP (DJD 28) 3–116; IDEM, "Daliyeh, Wadi ed-: Written Material," *EDSS* 1:162–65; P. W. LAPP and N. L. LAPP, eds., *Discoveries in the Wadi ed-Daliyeh* (AASOR 41; Cambridge: Cambridge University Press, 1974).

Summaries of Cairo Genizah Documents

These documents were not found in the vicinity of the Dead Sea; they are medieval copies of some of these texts. In the genizah (a place where old sacred books were retired) of the old Ben-Ezra Synagogue in Cairo three relevant items were found in 1896 or 1897: portions of Sirach (CSir), an Aramaic portion of the *Testament of Levi* (CTLevi ar), and the *Damascus Document* (CD). The latter was published in 1910 under the title, "Fragments of a Zadokite Work" (see Charles, *APOT* 2:785–834). Also of relevance are the fragments of Targumim (*C. Tg.;* for discussion of these, see ch. 6 below, where more will be said about the contents of the genizah of the Ben-Ezra Synagogue).

CD = Cairo *Damascus Document* (or *Damascus Covenant*). Two copies of this text were discovered in the Cairo synagogue's genizah. The longest, document A, dates to the tenth century and has sixteen columns of text. Document B dates to the twelfth century and has two columns. Eight manuscripts were also found in Qumran's Cave 4 (4Q266–273), one in Cave 5 (5Q12), and one in Cave 6 (6Q15). The fragments from Caves 4–6 supplement, as well as overlap, the longer and better-preserved texts from the genizah. The work is a summons to the "Sons of Light" to separate themselves from the men of perversity, who are leading Israel astray. The *Damascus Document* places the time of the Sons of Light into the context of a history of salvation, which will come to fulfillment 390 years after the destruction of the first temple. The text contains warnings of the snares of Belial (or Satan) and a list of laws to be heeded, including rules of conduct within the community. This work and the *Rule of the Community* (1QS and parallel texts) provide the rationale and framework for the *Yahad,* or Community of the Renewed Covenant.

Bibliography: J. M. BAUMGARTEN (DJD 18); J. M. BAUMGARTEN and D. R. SCHWARTZ, "Damascus Document," *DSSP* 2:4–57; G. J. BROOKE, "The Messiah of Aaron in the *Damascus Document," RevQ* 15 (1991): 215–30; M. BROSHI, ed., *The Damascus Document Reconsidered* (Jerusalem: Israel Exploration Society, 1992); E. COTHENET, "Le Document de Damas," *TQum* 2:129–204; P. R. DAVIES, *The Damascus Covenant: An Interpretation of the "Damascus Document"* (JSOTSup 25; Sheffield: JSOT Press, 1983); IDEM, "The Ideology of the Temple in the Damascus Document," in *Essays in Honour of Yigael Yadin* (ed. Vermes and Neusner), 287–301; D. DIMANT, "Qumran Sectarian Literature," *SJWSTP* 490–97; C. A. EVANS, "Covenant in the Qumran Literature," in *The Concept of the Covenant in the Second Temple Period* (ed. S. E. Porter and J. C. R. de Roo; JSJSup 71; Leiden: Brill, 2003), 55–80; J. A. FITZMYER, *DSS* 132–36; J. C. GREENFIELD and M. E. STONE, "Remarks on the Aramaic Testament of Levi from the Genizah," *RB* 86 (1979): 214–30; S. IWRY, "Further Notes on the Damascus Document," in *Proceedings of the Tenth World Congress of Jewish Studies, Division A: The Period of the Bible* (ed. D. Assaf; Jerusalem: World Union of Jewish Studies, 1990), 205–11; M. L. KLEIN, *Genizah Manuscripts of the Palestinian Targum to the Pentateuch* (2 vols.; Cincinnati: Hebrew Union College Press, 1986); M. A. KNIBB, "The Interpretation of *Damascus Document* VII, 9b–VIII, 2a and XIX, 5b–14," *RevQ* 15 (1991): 243–51; I. LÉVI, *The Hebrew Text of the Book of Ecclesiasticus* (SSS 3; Leiden: Brill, 1904); C. M. MURPHY, "The Disposition of Wealth in the *Damascus Document* Tradition," *RevQ* 19 (1999): 83–129; J. MURPHY-O'CONNOR, "The Judean Desert," *EJMI* 126–28; C. RABIN, *The Zadokite Documents* (rev. ed.; Oxford: Clarendon, 1958); S. SCHECTER and C. TAYLOR, *The Wisdom of Ben Sira: Portions of the Book Ecclesiasticus from Hebrew Manuscripts in the Cairo Genizah Collection Presented to the University of Cambridge by the Editors* (Cambridge: Cambridge University Press, 1899); S. ZEITLIN, *The Zadokite Fragments: Facsimile of the Manuscripts in the Cairo Genizah Collection in the Possession of the University Library, Cambridge, England* (JQRMS 1; Philadelphia: Dropsie College Press, 1952).

Apocrypha and Pseudepigrapha

A great number of the Dead Sea Scrolls belong to categories of texts that eventually came to be called (rightly or wrongly) the Old Testament Apocrypha and Pseudepigrapha. There are also many other Qumran texts that are related—

some closely related—to these writings. Although most of the apocryphal Greek additions to Daniel are not attested at Qumran, there are texts that appear to be part of the Daniel cycle. We find the same in the case of the so-called Pseudepigrapha. Although we have not found the equivalent of the Greek *Testaments of the Twelve Patriarchs,* we have found *Testaments* that seem to be part of this literature. The apocryphal and pseudepigraphal writings of Qumran provide us with a fuller, richer literary context in which all of this literature may be better appreciated. It has become clear that the apocryphal and pseudepigraphal texts known to exist before the discovery of the Dead Sea Scrolls constitute a remnant of what had been an extensive body of material in Jewish late antiquity.

1. Old Testament Apocrypha (see ch. 1 above)

Four, possibly five of the books of the Apocrypha (or deuterocanonical books) have been found among the Dead Sea Scrolls: Sirach, Tobit, the Epistle of Jeremiah (= Baruch 6), Susanna (an addition to the book of Daniel), and Psalm 151. Some other texts closely related to Daniel and Esther may be remnants of expansive cycles, of which the better-known Greek additions are only a part.

Sirach. Sirach, or the Wisdom of Yeshu'a ben Sira, survives in its entirety in Greek, translated by the sage's grandson (as stated in the prologue), in Latin, and in other versions. Solomon Schechter found four Hebrew manuscripts (i.e., MSS A–D) of this book in the Cairo Genizah in 1896. A fifth was later found in the collection at the Jewish Theological Seminary of America in New York and a sixth in Cambridge, England (MSS E–F) These manuscripts preserve much, but not all, of the Hebrew text. Qumran (2Q18) preserves fragments of 6:14–15 (or 1:19–20) and 6:20–31. Cave 11's *Psalms Scroll,* which contains apocryphal psalms as well as psalms found in the Masoretic Psalter, preserves Sir 51:13–19, 30. Masada preserves Sir 39:27–43:30 and is nearly identical to the text preserved in the Cairo Genizah fragments. See P. C. Beentjes, *The Book of Ben Sira in Hebrew* (VTSup 68; Leiden: Brill, 1997).

Tobit. Tobit survives in its entirety in Greek, Latin, and other versions. It was long thought that Tobit was originally composed in either Aramaic or Hebrew. Discovery of four fragmentary Aramaic scrolls (4QTob^a-d ar = 4Q196–199) and one Hebrew scroll (4QTob^e hebr = 4Q200) has borne out this suspicion. The Hebrew appears to be a translation of the Aramaic. These scrolls preserve about one-fifth of the book. Indeed, Jerome admits that the Hebrew Tobit that he translated into Latin was itself a translation of an Aramaic text (*Epistula Ad Chromatium et Heliodorum;* cf. PL 29:23–26). See J. A. Fitzmyer (DJD 19) 1–76; idem, "The Aramaic and Hebrew Fragments of Tobit from Cave 4," *CBQ* 57 (1995): 655–75; idem, "The Qumran Texts of Tobit."

Epistle of Jeremiah. A small fragment of the Epistle of Jeremiah is among the Greek fragments of Cave 7 (7QLXXEpJer = 7Q2). Only the last part of verse 43 and most of verse 44 are extant. See M. Baillet (DJDJ 3) 143.

Daniel. The Daniel cycle is richly attested at Qumran. We may have an Aramaic exemplar for Susanna (4QDanSuz? ar = 4Q551). This fragmentary text seems to match Greek Sus 45–48. We also have several texts not paralleled by the Greek additions to Daniel: the *Prayer of Nabonidus* (4Q242) and three other texts dubbed *Pseudo-Daniel* (4QpsDan ar[a-c] = 4Q243–245). The *Aramaic Apocalypse* (4Q246), which foretells the coming of one who will be called "Son of God" and "Son of the Most High," may also be a part of the Daniel cycle, in which we have a Daniel figure who interprets the meaning of a vision (cf. Dan 2:1–45; 5:1–28). The *Apocalypse of Weeks* (4QApocWeeks? = 4Q247) may also be part of this cycle (cf. Dan 9:24–27), as well as the *Four Kingdoms* texts (4QFour Kingdoms[a,b] ar = 4Q552–553; cf. Dan 7:3, 6, 17; 8:8, 22). See J. J. Collins, "Pseudo-Daniel Revisited," *RevQ* 17 (1996): 111–36; J. J. Collins and P. W. Flint (DJD 22) 97–131, 153–64; P. W. Flint, "4Qpseudo-Daniel ar[c] (4Q245) and the Restoration of the Priesthood," *RevQ* 17 (1996): 137–50; F. García Martínez, *Qumran and Apocalyptic*, 137–61.

Esther. We have no obvious matches with the Greek Additions to Esther, but the tales that comprise 4Q550–550d (or 4QPrEsther[a-e]), which are also called *Proto-Esther[a-e]*, are reminiscent of the general plot of Esther, and—like the Additions—they refer to the divine name (which Hebrew Esther of the MT does not). 4Q550–550d may represent remnants of an Esther cycle somewhat analogous to what we see in the case of Daniel and related texts.

Psalm 151. The apocryphal Psalm 151 is represented at Qumran (in two recensions, Psalm 151A and 151B; cf. 11QPs[a] 28:3–12 + 28:13–14), along with a series of apocryphal psalms. For more examples and bibliography, see the next section.

2. Old Testament Pseudepigrapha (see ch. 2 above)

Two of the books of the Pseudepigrapha are well attested among the Dead Sea Scrolls: *Enoch* (or *1 Enoch*) and *Jubilees* (or the *Little Genesis*). There also is a host of *Testaments,* some of which are related to the Greek *Testaments of the Patriarchs* and to some of the other testamentary writings. There are also pseudepigraphal psalms, some of which correspond to the additional psalms found in the Syriac Psalter. It is interesting to observe, regarding *Enoch* and *Jubilees,* that only the biblical books Genesis, Exodus, Deuteronomy, Isaiah, and Psalms are better represented at Qumran.

1 Enoch. The Ethiopic version of *1 Enoch* comprises 108 chapters. Aramaic and Greek fragments of chapters 1–36 and 72–107 have been recovered from Qumran. It is significant that nothing of the Similitudes (or Parables) that comprise chapters 37–71 has been found. The Qumran texts, including the related *Giants* materials, comprise 1Q23–24 (1QEnGiants[a,b] ar), 2Q26 (2QEnGiants ar), 4Q201–202, 205–207, 212 (4QEn[a,b,d-g] ar), 4Q203–204 (4QEnGiants[a,c]), 4Q208–211 (4QEnastr[a-d] ar), 4Q530–532 (4QEnGiants[b-e]), 6Q8 (6QpapEnGiants), and 7Q4,

8, 11–14 (7QpapEn gr). Other texts that may be part of the wider Enochic cycle include 4Q534 (Aramaic *Elect of God,* formerly *Messianic Text*) and 4Q535–536 (formerly Birth of Noah[c,d] ar). Enochic tradition is mentioned in Qumran's sectarian texts (e.g., CD 1:7; 2:18). See J. T. Milik, *BE;* L. T. Stuckenbruck (DJD 36) 73–75; idem, *The Book of Giants from Qumran.*

Jubilees. Many fragmentary copies of *Jubilees* and closely related texts have been found at Qumran. These include 1Q17–18 (*Jub.* 27:19–21; 35:8–10; 36:12[?]), 2Q19–20 (*Jub.* 3:7–8; 46:1–3), 3Q5 (*Jub.* 23:6–7, 12–13, 23[?]), 4Q176a, 4Q216–224 (*Jub.* 21:22–24; 23:21–23, 30–31), 4Q225–227 (= pseudo-*Jubilees*), 4Q228 (a work citing *Jubilees*), 4Q482–483 (*Jubilees?*), and 11Q12 (*Jub.* 3:25–27; 4:7–11, 13–14, 16–17, 29–30; 5:1–2; 6:12(?); 12:15–17, 28–29). See J. C. VanderKam and J. T. Milik (DJD 13) 1–185.

Related to *Jubilees* and Ps.-Philo's *Biblical Antiquities* are several examples of rewritten Bible at Qumran. Some of these texts include 4Q158 + 4Q364–367 (*Reworked Pentateuch*), 4Q368 (*Pentateuch Apocryphon*), 4Q382 (*Paraphrase of Kings*), 4Q422 (*Paraphrase of Genesis and Exodus*), 4Q458–463 + 4Q464a + 4Q467–468 (historical/pseudepigraphal narratives), 4Q464 (*Exposition on the Patriarchs*), 4Q480 + 4Q481b + 4Q481e (narrative fragments), and 6Q9 (*Samuel-Kings Apocryphon*). Other works appear to retell and embellish the stories and prophecies of famous prophets, such as Jeremiah (4Q383–384 + 4Q385b + 4Q387b) and Ezekiel (4Q385 + 4Q386–388 + 4Q391). See G. J. Brooke, "Parabiblical Prophetic Narratives," in *The Dead Sea Scrolls after Fifty Years* (ed. Flint and VanderKam), 1:271–301; E. Tov, "Excerpted and Abbreviated Biblical Texts from Qumran," *RevQ* 16 (1993–1995): 581–600; E. Tov and S. A. White (DJD 13) 187–351.

Testaments. Among the Dead Sea Scrolls are numerous *Testaments,* some of which seem to be related to the Greek *Testaments of the Twelve Patriarchs.* We have 1Q21 (TLevi ar), 3Q7 (TJudah?), 4Q213–214b, 214a + 4Q540–541 + 4Q548 (TLevi ar), 4Q215 (TNaphtali), 4Q484 (TJudah?), 4Q537 (TJacob? ar), 4Q538 (TJudah or apocrJudah), 4Q539 (TJoseph or apocrJoseph). One should also compare 4Q542 (TQahat ar). The most important are the Levi texts (1Q21, 4Q213–214, 4Q540–541 + 4Q548), which overlap with the Greek *Testament of Levi.* See R. A. Kugler, *From Patriarch to Priest: The Levi-Priestly Tradition from Aramaic Levi to Testament of Levi* (SBLEJL 9; Atlanta: Scholars Press, 1996); M. E. Stone (DJD 22) 1–82.

Psalms. Besides two recensions of Psalm 151 (see above), the Dead Sea Scrolls preserve Psalms 154–155 (= Syriac Psalms II–III; cf. 11Q5 = 11QPs[a] 18:1–16 + 24:3–17) and several other previously unknown psalms (e.g., 4Q380–381, 4Q448; see esp. 4Q88 = 4QPsAp[f] and 11Q11 = 11QApPs[a]). These include *Plea for Deliverance* (11Q5 19:1–18 + 11Q6 frgs. a and b), *Hymn to the Creator* (11Q5 26:9–15), *Apostrophe to Zion* (11Q5 22:1–15 + 4Q88 7:14–8:15), *Eschatological Hymn* (4Q88 9:1–15), *Apostrophe to Judah* (4Q88 10:4–15), and *David's Compositions*

(11Q5 27:2–11). The Hebrew text of these psalms are conveniently presented, with English facing pages, in J. H. Charlesworth et al., *DSSP* 4A:192–215; P. W. Flint, *The Dead Sea Psalms Scrolls and the Book of Psalms* (STDJ 17; Leiden: Brill, 1997), 243–51; J. A. Sanders (DJDJ 4).

The Biblical Text at Qumran. The Biblical manuscripts recovered from Qumran and neighboring sites reveal affiliations with what would later become the MT, the Hebrew underlying the LXX (or Old Greek), the Samaritan, and an unknown Hebrew version. All of these texts have become available only recently, so it will be some time before a complete analysis is achieved. The diversity of the Hebrew textual tradition must be acknowledged. What must be avoided is a commitment to explain every difference with the MT as an error or corruption (as in Rosenbloom's analysis of the *Great Isaiah Scroll*). Much more difficult to assess are variants found in the pesharim, which in some cases were probably exegetically motivated (on this problem, see Brooke 1987).

Bibliography: M. G. ABEGG, P. W. FLINT, and E. ULRICH, *The Dead Sea Scrolls Bible: The Oldest Known Bible Translated for the First Time into English* (San Francisco: HarperCollins, 1999) (English translation, with MSS and variants indicated in footnotes); G. J. BROOKE, "The Biblical Texts in the Qumran Commentaries: Scribal Errors or Exegetical Variants?" in *Early Jewish and Christian Exegesis* (ed. C. A. Evans and W. F. Stinespring; W. H. Brownlee FS; Homage 10; Atlanta: Scholars Press, 1987), 85–100; F. M. CROSS and S. TALMON, eds., *Qumran and the History of the Biblical Text* (Cambridge: Harvard University Press, 1975); J. R. ROSENBLOOM, *The Dead Sea Isaiah Scroll—a Literary Analysis: A Comparison with the Masoretic Text and the Biblia hebraica* (Grand Rapids: Eerdmans, 1970); J. E. SANDERSON, *An Exodus Scroll from Qumran: 4QpaleoExod^m and the Samaritan Tradition* (HSS 30; Atlanta: Scholars Press, 1986); L. A. SINCLAIR, "A Qumran Biblical Fragment: Hosea 4QXII^d (Hosea 1:7–2:5)," *BASOR* 239 (1980): 61–65; P. W. SKEHAN, "Exodus in the Samaritan Recension from Qumran," *JBL* 74 (1955): 182–87 (on 4QpaleoExod^m); IDEM, "A Fragment of the 'Song of Moses' (Deut 32) from Qumran," *BASOR* 136 (1954): 12–15 (on 4QDeut^q); IDEM, "A Psalm Manuscript from Qumran (4QPs^b)," *CBQ* 26 (1964): 313–22; E. TOV, "Hebrew Biblical Manuscripts from the Judaean Desert: Their Contribution to Textual Criticism," *JJS* 39 (1988): 5–37; E. ULRICH, "The Dead Sea Scrolls and the Biblical Text," in *The Dead Sea Scrolls after Fifty Years* (ed. Flint and VanderKam), 1:79–100 (very important assessment of the state of the question); IDEM, "Pluriformity in the Biblical Text, Text Groups, and Questions of Canon," in *The Madrid Qumran Congress* (ed. Trebolle Barrera and Vegas Montaner), 23–41; J. DE WAARD, *A Comparative Study of the Old Testament Text in the Dead Sea Scrolls and in the New Testament* (Leiden: Brill, 1965).

Pesharim: Qumran's Commentaries on Scripture

Perhaps the most distinctive genre among the Dead Sea Scrolls is the *pesher* ("interpretation," pl. *pesharim*). Although the formal pesharim are limited to the Prophets and Psalms, there are similar interpretive texts focusing on narrative biblical books, particularly Genesis (e.g., 4Q252–254). See the bibliography supplied above in the individual entries.

Isaiah. There are fragments of at least five pesharim on the prophecy of Isaiah: 4Q161–165 (= 4QpIsa^a-e). 4Q161 comments on Isa 10:22–11:3, 4Q162 comments on Isa 5:5–30 (and possibly also Isa 6:9), 4Q163 comments on Isa 8:7–31:1 (with many gaps), 4Q164 comments on Isa 54:11–12, and 4Q165 comments on Isa 40:11–12; 14:19; 15:4–5; 21:10–15; 32:5–7; 11:11–12. Much of this commentary is quite fragmentary; sometimes all that can be restored is the text of Isaiah itself. 3Q4 (or 3QpIsa) is a small fragment of what may be another pesher on Isaiah (i.e., on Isa 1:1–2). 4Q500 (*Vineyard Benediction*) may be a commentary on Isa 5:1–7, but there is nothing about this small fragment suggesting that it is a pesher. The interpretation of Isa 10:34–11:5 in 4Q161 frgs. 7–10 iii coheres with the prophecy of 4Q285, in which the Messiah is expected to defeat Rome. One should also see 11Q13 (= 11QMelchizedek), which comments on Isa 52:7 and 61:1–3, in relation to the jubilee legislation of Lev 25:13.

Hosea. There are fragments of two pesharim on the prophecy of Hosea: 4Q166–167. 4Q166 (= 4QpHos^a) comments on Hos 2:8–14, and 4Q167 + 4Q168 frg. 2 i–ii (= 4QpHos^b) comments on Hos 5:13–8:14.

Micah. There is at least one pesher (1Q14) on the prophecy of Micah; there may also be a second (4Q168). 1Q14 (= 1QpMic) comments on Mic 1:2–9 and 6:15–16. 4Q168 (= 4QpMic?), if it is a pesher, comprises only the text of Mic 4:8–12. The commentary, if any, is lost.

Nahum. The better part of four columns of text of 4Q169 (= 4QpNah) survives. These columns comment on Nah 1:3–3:14, but there are gaps. This pesher is second in importance only to the fully preserved pesher on Habakkuk. The Nahum commentary refers to Demetrius, king of Greece (probably Demetrius III, who ruled 95–88 B.C.E.), the "Lion of Wrath" (possibly Alexander Jannaeus, who ruled Israel 103–76 B.C.E.), Antiochus (probably Antiochus IV Epiphanes, who ruled Syria and Israel 175–164 B.C.E.), the "seekers after smooth things" (probably the Pharisees, who opposed Alexander Jannaeus), and "his nobles" (perhaps Sadducees, who were allies of Jannaeus). Accordingly, the pesher on Nahum is of strategic importance in placing the Qumran community in historical context. On this question, see J. C. VanderKam, "Pesher Nahum and Josephus," in *When Judaism and Christianity Began: Essays in Memory of Anthony J. Saldarini* (ed. A. J. Avery-Peck, D. J. Harrington, and J. Neusner; 2 vols.; JSJSup 85; Leiden: Brill, 2004), 1:299–311.

Habakkuk. The pesher on Habakkuk is the best preserved of the pesharim; in fact, we may well have the commentary in its entirety (with the exception of a few lost words here and there at the bottom of the scroll). 1QpHab (to which no number was assigned) comprises thirteen columns, with commentary on Hab 1:1–2:20. This pesher is well known for explaining the role of the Teacher of Righteousness: " 'The wicked surround the righteous' [Hab 1:4]: Its interpretation—the wicked one is the Wicked Priest, and the righteous one is the Teacher of Righteousness"

(1:12–13); " . . . and God told Habakkuk to write down the things that are going to come upon the last generation, but the fulfillment of the end-time he did not make known to him. And when it says, 'so that he can run who reads it' [Hab 2:2], its interpretation concerns the Teacher of Righteousness, to whom God made known all the mysteries of the words of his servants the prophets" (7:1–5).

Zephaniah. There are two fragments of pesharim on the prophecy of Zephaniah: 1Q15 and 4Q170. 1Q15 (= 1QpZeph) comments on Zeph 1:18–2:2, with very little surviving commentary: "The interpretation . . . the land of Judah . . ." 4Q170 (= 4QpZeph) comprises two fragments, commenting on Zeph 1:12–13. Almost nothing of the commentary survives.

Malachi. Among the fragments originally assigned to 4Q253, a commentary on Genesis, a fragment has been identified as belonging rather to a pesher on Malachi. This fragment is numbered 4Q253a. It comprises portions of two columns that quote and comment on Mal 3:16–18. Very little commentary survives. 5Q10 (= 5QpMal?) may represent a second pesher on Malachi, commenting on Mal 1:14. Because the distinctive word *pesher* has to be restored, it is not certain that this text actually is a pesher.

Psalms. Three pesharim on the Psalms were found at Qumran: 1Q16, 4Q171, and 4Q173. 1Q16 (= 1QpPs) comments on Ps 68:13–31. Only frgs. 3, 8, and 9 preserve significant text. 4Q171 (= 4QPs^a) comments on Pss 37:2–39; 45:1–2; 69:8–9, and 4Q173 (= 4QPs^b) comments on Ps 129:7–8. Little commentary survives.

Canticles? 4Q240 may be a pesher on Canticles, but text and details are unknown. This text, originally assigned to J. T. Milik, is evidently lost.

Clusters and Commentaries on Collected Passages of Scripture. Among the Dead Sea Scrolls are several texts related to the pesharim but composed principally of clusters of scriptural passages, sometimes with commentary. These include 4Q174 (*Florilegium*), which may be a part of 4Q177 (*Catena^a*). The former quotes several passages (e.g., Ps 89:23; 2 Sam 7:10–14; Exod 15:17–18; Amos 9:11; Isa 8:11; Ezek 44:10; Ps 2:1; Dan 12:10; 11:32) and provides commentary and context for most. The text is eschatological, rooted in the Davidic covenant of 2 Samuel 7, and anticipates the appearance of the Messiah, who will support Qumran's priestly leadership. 4Q177 quotes and comments on several passages (e.g., Isa 37:30; 32:7; Ps 11:1; Mic 2:10–11; et passim). 4Q175 (*Testimonia*) quotes several important texts (e.g., Deut 5:28–29; 18:18–19; Num 24:15–17; Deut 33:8–11; Josh 6:26) with little commentary. 4Q176 (*Tanhumim*) cites a series of consoling passages (such as Isa 40:1–5, "Comfort, comfort my people . . ."). 4Q182 (*Catena^b*) is a fragment of a quotation from, and commentary on, Jer 5:7. Finally, there are some unidentified fragments that may have been parts of pesharim (cf. 4Q172, 4Q178, 4Q239).

Targumim

One of the big surprises at Qumran was the discovery of written Targumim among the scrolls. The extant Targumim known from rabbinic and synagogue sources date to the Middle Ages, although they contain traditions that reach back to the NT period. Until this discovery, not all scholars believed that they reached back that far. But the discovery of Targumim at Qumran, which date to the first century B.C.E., prove that written Targumim were indeed in circulation in the NT period and even a bit before. Still, it must be made clear that the Qumran Targumim are not identical to, or recensions of, the later rabbinic Targumim. The Qumran Targumim are surveyed here briefly; the complicated issue of the date of the Targumim and their relevance for NT interpretation will be taken up in chapter 6 below. See the bibliography supplied above in the individual entries.

Genesis. 6Q19 (*Targum of Genesis?*) may preserve a tiny fragment of a Targum of Genesis. What little text can be deciphered seems to cohere with Gen 10:20. See the discussion of this entry above.

Leviticus. Among the Qumran scrolls appears to be a Targum of Leviticus: 4Q156 (= 4QtgLev). The two surviving fragments contain a very literal Aramaic translation of Lev 16:12–15 and 16:18–21. It has been suggested that this may only be an Aramaic text and not a Targum, of which only a quotation of Leviticus 16 survives. This is possible, but the length of the quotation and the survival of no nonbiblical portion of text support the traditional identification of 4Q156 as a Targum. Moreover, the existence of two Targumim of Job proves that written Targumim did in fact circulate in the time of Jesus.

Job. Qumran provides us with two Targumim of Job: 4Q157 (= 4QtgJob) and 11Q10 (= 11QtgJob). The Cave 4 text provides only small fragments (3:5–9 [?]; 4:16–5:4), but Cave 11 preserves a significant portion of the text (17:14–42:11). These Targumim show no affinities with the complete rabbinic Targum, which dates from a much later period.

Themes

In the introductory paragraphs above the point was made that the Dead Sea Scrolls provide valuable background information for NT study. In the paragraphs below a few of the major parallels between the Scrolls and John the Baptist and Jesus will be considered.

John the Baptist and Qumran. The discovery of the Qumran scrolls has raised again the question of John's possible relationship with the Essenes. There are at least six important parallels between the Baptist and Qumran: (1) Both John and

Qumran appealed to Isaiah 40:3 ("The voice of one crying the wilderness, 'Prepare the way of the Lord'") for their rationale for retreating to the wilderness (cf. 1QS 8:12–16; 9:19–20; Matt 3:1–3; Mark 1:2–4; Luke 3:2–6; John 1:23). John's upbringing in the wilderness (cf. Luke 1:80) allows for the possibility of his association with the wilderness community (cf. Josephus, *J.W.* 2.8.2 §120: "The Essenes . . . adopt the children of others at a tender age in order to instruct them"). Essenes and Christians may have called their respective faiths "the Way" (1QS 9:17–18; Luke 20:21; Acts 9:2; 16:17; 18:26; cf. John 14:6) because of Isa 40:3. (2) Both John and Qumran called for repentance and practiced baptism (cf. 1QS 5:7–15; Pliny the Elder, *Nat.* 5.17.4; Matt 3:5; Mark 1:4–5; Luke 3:7; John 1:25). (3) Both John and Qumran anticipated the imminent appearance of the kingdom of God (1QS 8:13–14; Matt 3:2; Mark 1:7). (4) John and Qumran employ similarly the words "water, spirit, and fire" (cf. 1QS 4:11–21; Matt 3:11–12; Mark 1:8; Luke 3:16; John 1:26; Isa 5:24). (5) John's strange diet may reflect the strict *kashruth* observed by the Essenes (cf. Josephus, *J.W.* 2.8.8 §143 ["he cannot share the food of others . . . he eats grass"]; 2.8.10 §152; CD 6:17; Matt 3:4 ["locusts and wild honey"]; 11:18 ["John came neither eating nor drinking"]; Mark 1:6; Luke 1:15). (6) John's harsh criticism of the religious leaders (Matt 3:7–9: "You brood of vipers . . .") coheres with harsh epithets frequently found in the writings of Qumran (1QpHab 2:1–2 ["Man of Lies"]; 8:8 ["Wicked Priest"]; 10:9 ["Preacher of Lies"]; 1QS 9:16 ["men of the Pit"]; 9:17 ["men of perversity"]; 1QM 1:1 ["sons of darkness"]; 15:2–3 ["host of Belial"]).

The possibility that John was at one time an Essene is important, since Jesus in all likelihood had himself been a disciple or an associate of John. The writings of Qumran, therefore, in all probability are vital for understanding the ministry of John and perhaps aspects of the ministry of Jesus.

Bibliography: O. BETZ, "Was John the Baptist an Essene?" *BRev* 6, no. 6 (1990): 18–25; W. H. BROWNLEE, "John the Baptist in the New Light of Ancient Scrolls," *Int* 9 (1955): 71–90, repr. in *The Scrolls and the New Testament* (ed. K. Stendahl; London: SCM Press, 1958), 33–53, 252–56; S. L. DAVIES, "John the Baptist and Essene Kashruth," *NTS* 29 (1983): 569–71; A. S. GEYSER, "The Youth of John the Baptist," *NovT* 1 (1956): 70–75; S. MASON, *Josephus and the New Testament;* J. A. T. ROBINSON, "The Baptism of John and the Qumran Community," *HTR* 50 (1957): 175–91, repr. in Robinson, *Twelve New Testament Studies* (SBT 34; London: SCM, 1962), 11–27.

Jesus and Qumran. There are many suggestive similarities between the teachings and ministry of Jesus and those of Qumran. (1) Jesus was critical of an avaricious and oppressive temple establishment (Mark 12:38–13:2). So were the members of Qumran (1QpHab 8:11–12; 9:4–5; 10:1). (2) Both Jesus and Qumran apparently opposed the annual half-sheqel temple tax (Matt 17:24–27; 4QOrd[a] 2:6–8), which, much to the consternation of some rabbis, the priests themselves did not pay (*m. Šeqal.* 1:4). Jesus may also have questioned the temple establishment's role in assisting Rome in the collection of imperial taxes (Mark 12:13–17; Luke 23:2). (3) Both Jesus and Qumran interpreted Gen 1:27 in such a way as to forbid divorce and remarriage (Matt 19:4; Mark 10:6; CD 4:20–5:2). (4) Both Jesus and

Qumran spoke in terms of spiritual offerings, as opposed to literal animal offerings (Matt 9:13; 12:7 [cf. Hos 6:6]; Mark 12:28–34; cf. Philo, *Good Person* 12 §75; Josephus, *Ant.* 18.1.5 §19; and possibly 4Q174 1 i 6–7). Compare also Paul's statement in Rom 12:1: "present your bodies as a living sacrifice, holy and acceptable to God, which is your spiritual worship." (5) 4Q525 presents a string of beatitudes that offers a striking parallel to the strings of beatitudes attributed to Jesus in Matthew 5 and Luke 6. (6) Psalm 91 at Qumran is contextualized as an exorcistic psalm, which coheres with the temptation narratives (Matthew 4 and Luke 4), in which this psalm is quoted by Satan. This contextualization also coheres with *Targum Psalms,* which exaggerates the demonic element. (7) 4Q500's cultic interpretation of Isa 5:1–7 coheres with Jesus' application of this passage to the ruling priests in his parable of the Wicked Vineyard Tenants (Mark 12:1–12). Again, this interpretive orientation coheres with the Targum. (8) The *Songs of the Sabbath Sacrifice* frequently refer to God's kingdom ("your kingdom," "his kingdom," and the like), thus attesting the currency of the concept, which Jesus' proclamation must have presupposed. (9) The recounting of exaltation in 4Q491c, in which the speaker depicts himself as installed in heaven among the angels, could shed light on Jesus' remarkable reply to the high priest that as "Son of Man" he would sit at the right hand of God (Mark 14:61–62; cf. Mark 2:10, where Jesus claims, as Son of Man, to have "authority on earth"). Finally (10), we have astounding coherence between 4Q521 and Jesus' reply to the imprisoned John the Baptist (Matt 11:2–5 = Luke 7:19–22). According to 4Q521, when the Messiah appears, whom heaven and earth will obey, the wounded will be healed, the eyes of the blind will be opened, the dead will be made alive, and the poor will have the good news proclaimed to them (frgs. 2 + 4 ii 1–12). We have here allusions to Isa 26:19, 35:5–6, and 61:1–2, the very passages to which Jesus alludes in his reply to John. The messianic orientation of 4Q521 confirms the messianic nature of Jesus' statement, which the Matthean evangelist rightly understood (cf. Matt 11:2 "When John heard in prison what the Messiah was doing").

Bibliography: J. H. CHARLESWORTH, ed., *Jesus and the Dead Sea Scrolls* (ABRL; New York: Doubleday, 1992); C. A. EVANS, "Jesus and the Dead Sea Scrolls," in *The Dead Sea Scrolls after Fifty Years* (ed. Flint and VanderKam), 2:573–98; IDEM, "The Recently Published Dead Sea Scrolls and the Historical Jesus," in *Studying the Historical Jesus: Evaluations of the State of Current Research* (ed. B. D. Chilton and C. A. Evans; NTTS 19; Leiden: Brill, 1994), 547–65; W. S. LASOR, *The Dead Sea Scrolls and the New Testament,* 206–46.

Paul and Qumran. Paul's vocabulary, often ecclesiastical, is illustrated and sometimes defined by the terminology of the Dead Sea Scrolls. For example, Paul's reference to "the many" (*pleion;* cf. 2 Cor 2:5–6), as referring to the membership of the community, is identical to Qumran's use of *harabbim* (cf. 1QS 6:11b-12). Paul's understanding of bishop (*episkopos;* cf. Phil 1:1) is probably the equivalent of Qumran's *mabeqqer* (cf. 1QS 6:12). The appearance of *harabbim* ("the many") and *mabeqqer* ("overseer") in the same line adds to the conviction that Qumran's terminology parallels Paul's. Several other phrases that are common in Paul are also found in the Scrolls: "righteousness of God" (Rom 1:17; 3:21; 1QS 1:21; 10:23, 25; 11:12), "grace of God" (Rom 5:15; 1 Cor 3:10; 1QS 11:12), "works of the law" (Rom 3:20, 28; Gal 2:16; 3:2, 5, 10; 1QS 6:18; 4Q398 14–17 ii 3 = 4Q399 1 i 11), "church of God" (1 Cor 1:2; 10:32; 11:16; 15:9; 2 Cor 1:1; Gal 1:13; 1 Thess 2:14; 2 Thess 1:4; 1QM 4:10), and "new covenant" (2 Cor 3:6; CD [B] 19:33; 20:12; 1QpHab 2:3).

Paul's understanding of the curse mentioned in Deut 21:22 and his application of this passage to the crucified Jesus (Gal 3:13) agrees with 4QpNah frgs. 3–4 i 4–9 and 11QTemple 64:6–13. The Nahum pesher alludes to Alexander Jannaeus, the "Lion of Wrath," who crucified eight hundred Pharisees (cf. Josephus, *Ant.* 13.14.2 §380; idem, *J.W.* 1.4.5–6 §§93–98). Qumran's usage shows that Deut 21:22, originally not concerned with crucifixion, had come to mean crucifixion by the time of Paul.

Probably the most significant topic clarified by the Dead Sea Scrolls in Pauline studies concerns the question of righteousness and "works of the law." Paul asserts that "we know that a person is justified not by the works of the law but through faith in Jesus Christ. And we have come to believe in Christ Jesus, so that we might be justified by faith in Christ, and not by doing the works of the law, because no one will be justified by the works of the law" (Gal 2:16). The scriptural basis for Paul's argument that justification is from faith, not from works, is the example of Abraham, the father of the Jewish race, who "believed God, and it was reckoned to him as righteousness' [Gen 15:6]" (Gal 3:6; cf. Romans 4). In 4QMMT ("Some of the Works of the Law") we find similar language but a very different argument: "Now, we have written to you some of the *works of the Law*, those which we determined would be beneficial for you and your people, because we have seen [that] you possess insight and knowledge of the Law. Understand all these things and beseech Him to set your counsel straight and so keep you away from evil thoughts and the counsel of Belial. Then you shall rejoice at the end time when you find the essence of our words to be true. And *it will be reckoned to you as righteousness*, in that you have done what is right and good before Him, to your own benefit and to that of Israel" (4QMMT C26–32; italics added). The author is probably not alluding to Gen 15:6 but to Ps 106:30–31: "Then Phinehas stood up and interceded, and the plague was stopped. And that has been reckoned to him as righteousness from generation to generation forever." Thus, it is Phinehas the priest whose zeal for the law resulted in his being reckoned righteous. For the priestly Qumran community, this is the ideal model, and it is the model—or at least one very much like it—that Paul opposes in his letters.

Bibliography: M. G. ABEGG, "Paul, 'Works of the Law,' and MMT," *BAR* 20, no. 6 (1994): 52–55, 82; J. D. G. DUNN, "4QMMT and Galatians," *NTS* 43 (1997): 147–53; J. A. FITZMYER, "Paul and the Dead Sea Scrolls," in *The Dead Sea Scrolls after Fifty Years* (ed. Flint and VanderKam), 2:599–621; H.-W. KUHN, "The Impact of the Qumran Scrolls on the Understanding of Paul," in *The Dead Sea Scrolls* (ed. Dimant and Rappaport), 327–39; W. S. LASOR, *The Dead Sea Scrolls and the New Testament*, 168–78; J. MURPHY-O'CONNOR, ed., *Paul and Qumran: Studies in New Testament Exegesis* (London: Chapman, 1968); repr. J. H. Charlesworth, ed., *Paul and the Dead Sea Scrolls* (New York: Crossroad, 1990); E. P. SANDERS, *Paul and Palestinian Judaism: A Comparison of Patterns of Religion* (Philadelphia: Fortress, 1977).

General Bibliography

M. BERNSTEIN et al., eds., *Legal Texts and Legal Issues: Proceedings of the Second Meeting of the International Organization for Qumran Studies, Cambridge, 1995, Published in Honour of Joseph M. Baumgarten* (STDJ 23; Leiden: Brill, 1997); M. BLACK, *The Scrolls and Christian Origins: Studies in the Jewish Background of the New Testament* (BJS 48; Chico, Calif.: Scholars Press, 1983); IDEM, ed., *The Scrolls and Christianity* (London: SPCK, 1969); G. J. BROOKE, ed., *New Qumran Texts and Studies: Proceedings of the First Meeting of the International Organization for Qumran Studies, Paris, 1992* (STDJ 15; Leiden: Brill, 1994); M. BURROWS, ed., *The Dead Sea Scrolls of St. Mark's Monastery* (2 vols.; New Haven: American Schools of Oriental Research, 1950); F. M. CROSS Jr., *The Ancient Library of Qumran and Modern Biblical Studies* (rev. ed.; Garden City, N.Y.: Doubleday, 1961; repr., Grand Rapids: Baker, 1980); P. R. DAVIES, "Biblical Interpretation in the Dead Sea Scrolls," in *The Ancient Period* (vol. 1 of *A History of Biblical Interpretation;* ed. A. J. Hauser and D. F. Watson; Grand Rapids: Eerdmans, 2003), 144–66 (bibliography); J. R. DAVILA, *Liturgical Works* (ECDSS; Grand Rapids: Eerdmans, 2000); M. C. DE BOER, ed., *From Jesus to John: Essays on Jesus and New Testament Christology in Honour of Marinus de Jonge* (JSNTSup 84; Sheffield: JSOT Press, 1993); M. DELCOR, ed., *Qumrân: Sa piété, sa théologie, et son milieu* (BETL 46; Paris: Duculot, 1978); D. DIMANT and L. H. SCHIFFMAN, eds., *Time to Prepare the Way in the Wilderness* (STDJ 16; Leiden: Brill, 1995); D. DIMANT and U. RAPPAPORT, eds., *The Dead Sea Scrolls: Forty Years of Research* (STDJ 10; Leiden: Brill, 1992); C. A. EVANS and P. W. FLINT, eds., *Eschatology, Messianism, and the Dead Sea Scrolls* (Studies in the Dead Sea Scrolls and Related Literature 1; Grand Rapids: Eerdmans, 1997); J. A. FITZMYER, "The Dead Sea Scrolls," *HBD* 915–17; IDEM, "The Qumran Texts of Tobit," in *The Dead Sea Scrolls and Christian Origins* (Studies in the Dead Sea Scrolls and Related Literature; Grand Rapids: Eerdmans, 2000), 159–235; P. W. FLINT and J. C. VANDERKAM, eds., *The Dead Sea Scrolls after Fifty Years: A Comprehensive Assessment* (2 vols.; Leiden: Brill, 1998–1999); D. FLUSSER, *Judaism and the Origins of Christianity* (Jerusalem: Magnes Press, 1988), 3–225; F. GARCÍA MARTÍNEZ, *Qumran and Apocalyptic: Studies on the Aramaic Texts from Qumran* (STDJ 9; Leiden: Brill, 1992); M. P. HORGAN, *Pesharim: Qumran Interpretations of Biblical Books* (CBQMS 8; Washington, D.C.: Catholic Biblical Association, 1979); G. JEREMIAS et al., eds., *Tradition und Glaube: Das frühe Christentum in seiner Umwelt* (K. G. Kuhn FS; Göttingen: Vandenhoeck & Ruprecht, 1971); W. S. LASOR, *The Dead Sea Scrolls and the New Testament* (Grand Rapids: Eerdmans, 1972); C. NEWSOM, *Songs of the Sabbath Sacrifice: A Critical Edition* (HSS 27; Atlanta: Scholars Press, 1985); D. W. PARRY and E. ULRICH, eds., *The Provo International Conference on the Dead Sea Scrolls: Technological Innovations, New Texts, and Reformulated Issues* (STDJ 30; Leiden:

Brill, 1998); S. PAUL et al., eds., *Emanuel: Studies in Hebrew Bible, Septuagint, and Dead Sea Scrolls in Honor of Emanuel Tov* (VTSup 94; Boston: Brill, 2003); S. E. PORTER and C. A. EVANS, eds., *The Scrolls and the Scriptures: Qumran Fifty Years After* (JSPSup 26; RILP 3; Sheffield: Sheffield, 1997); L. ROST, *Judaism outside the Hebrew Canon: An Introduction to the Documents* (Nashville: Abingdon, 1976), 155–90; L. H. SCHIFFMAN, ed., *Archaeology and History in the Dead Sea Scrolls* (Y. Yadin FS; JSPSup 8; JSOT/ASOR Monograph Series 2; Sheffield: JSOT Press, 1990); H. SHANKS, *The Mystery and Meaning of the Dead Sea Scrolls* (New York: Random House, 1998); IDEM, ed., *Understanding the Dead Sea Scrolls: A Reader from the Biblical Archaeological Review* (New York: Random House, 1992); K. STEN-DAHL, ed., *The Scrolls and the New Testament* (New York: Harper, 1957; repr., with introduction by J. H. Charlesworth; New York: Crossroad, 1992); A. STEUDEL, *Der Midrasch zur Eschatologie aus der Qumrangemeinde (4QMidrEschat*[a,b]*): Materielle Rekonstruktion, Textbestand, Gattung, und Traditionsgeschichtliche Einordnung des durch 4Q174 ("Florilegium") und 4Q177 ("Catena*[a]*") repräsentierten Werkes aus den Qumranfunden* (STDJ 13; Leiden: Brill, 1994); M. E. STONE and E. G. CHAZON, eds., *Biblical Perspectives—Early Use and Interpretation of the Bible in Light of the Dead Sea Scrolls: Proceedings of the First International Symposium of the Orion Center, 12–14 May 1996* (STDJ 28; Leiden: Brill, 1998); J. STRUGNELL, "Notes en marge du volume V des 'Discoveries in the Judaean Desert of Jordan,'" *RevQ* 7 (1969–1971): 163–276; L. T. STUCKENBRUCK, *The Book of Giants from Qumran: Texts, Translation, and Commentary* (TSAJ 63; Tübingen: Mohr [Siebeck], 1997); J. TREBOLLE BARRERA and L. VEGAS MONTANER, eds., *The Madrid Qumran Congress: Proceedings of the International Congress on the Dead Sea Scrolls, Madrid, 18–21 March 1991* (2 vols.; STDJ 11; Leiden: Brill, 1992); J. C. TREVER, *Scrolls from Qumran Cave I* (Jerusalem: Albright Institute of Archaeological Research; Shrine of the Book, 1972); J. C. VANDERKAM, *The Dead Sea Scrolls Today* (London: SPCK; Grand Rapids: Eerdmans, 1994); IDEM, *An Introduction to Early Judaism* (Grand Rapids: Eerdmans, 2001), 150–66; G. VERMES and J. NEUSNER, eds., *Essays in Honour of Yigael Yadin* (Journal of Jewish Studies 33; Oxford: Oxford Centre for Postgraduate Hebrew Studies, 1983); M. O. WISE, *Thunder in Gemini: And Other Essays on the History, Language, and Literature of Second Temple Palestine* (JSPSup 15; Sheffield: Sheffield, 1994); M. O. WISE et al., eds., *Methods of Investigation of the Dead Sea Scrolls and the Khirbet Qumran Site: Present Realities and Future Prospects* (Annals of the New York Academy of Sciences 722; New York: New York Academy of Sciences, 1994); Z. ZEVIT et al., eds., *Solving Riddles and Untying Knots: Biblical, Epigraphic, and Semitic Studies in Honor of Jonas C. Greenfield* (Winona Lake, Ind.: Eisenbrauns, 1995).

CHAPTER FOUR

Versions of the Old Testament

ANCIENT VERSIONS

HEBREW	GREEK
Masoretic Text	Septuagint
Samaritan Pentateuch	Recensions
Dead Sea Scrolls	
	SYRIAC
LATIN	Peshitta
Old Latin	
Vulgate	

Study of the versions of the OT is essential not only for determining the most primitive reading of the text, but also for determining the range of possible readings available to the NT authors. The versions themselves often yield valuable clues as to how a given passage of Scripture was understood.

Summaries

The versions treated in this chapter represent several languages: Hebrew, Greek, Latin, and Syriac. Most of these languages are represented by more than one recension. (Because of their special features the Aramaic versions, known as the Targumim, are treated in a separate chapter; see ch. 6.) This field of study is therefore very complex. The purpose of this chapter, in keeping with the overall purpose of the present book, is to provide the reader with a basic overview. Those interested in pursuing matters further are directed to the major scholarly works, mostly in English, which are cited in the respective bibliographies.

Hebrew

When scholars speak of versions of the OT, they usually have in mind the LXX or the Vulgate, but not the Hebrew. In view of the plethora of Hebrew manuscripts that have been uncovered this century (e.g., the Cairo Genizah fragments and the Dead Sea Scrolls) and the increasing evidence of the pluralism of the biblical text in the first century, it is probably better to regard all of the extant materials as versions. The Hebrew may have been the original language in which most of the OT was written, but it is extant today in at least three distinct Hebrew traditions: the Masoretic Text (MT), the Samaritan Pentateuch (SP), fragments from the Cairo Genizah, and more than two hundred scrolls from Qumran, some of which exhibit a form of Hebrew text that corresponds with the Old Greek (or LXX). It is clear that no one of these extant traditions represents the exact original form. Therefore, it is appropriate to speak of all of these traditions, including the MT, as versions of the OT.

Masoretic Text. The official version of the OT for Judaism and Christianity since the early Middle Ages is the MT. (Of course, only for Christians is the Hebrew Bible the "OT"; for Jews it is the Bible, Mikra, or Tanak.) This version is called the MT because the scribes who preserved, edited, and pointed (i.e., added vowel signs, accents, and punctuation of a sort) it were called the Masoretes. Their notes are called the Masora. (Masora/Masoretic can be spelled with one *s* or with two, depending on which of two etymologies one thinks relates to the word.) The Western Masoretes are from Palestine, the Eastern Masoretes from Babylon. The Masoretic tradition probably originated in the late first or early second century. The Masora provides an interesting and complex array of sigla, whereby the scribes (or sopherim) noted their alterations of or reservations about this passage or that. Best known is *ketib/qere* ("written"/"spoken"). In these cases, reluctant to change the written text, the scribes wrote in the margin what should be read aloud. The Masora *marginalis* is the material written in the four margins of the page. The Masora *finalis* represents an alphabetical compilation at the end of the OT. The Masora *parva* ("small Masora") is found in the side margins, while the Masora *magna* ("large Masora") is found at the top and bottom margins. The oldest MT manuscripts date from the late ninth century C.E. (e.g., Codex Cairensis [C] on the Prophets). No complete manuscript is earlier than the tenth century (e.g., the Aleppo Codex, which in fact is not complete). Fragments from the Cairo Genizah date from the sixth (possibly fifth) to the eighth centuries. Codex Leningrad, on which the modern critical Hebrew Bible is based, dates to 1008 C.E.

The principal text is that edited by R. Kittel, with P. Kahle, *Biblia hebraica* (Stuttgart: Württembergische Bibelanstalt, 1968); the more recent edition is K. Elliger and W. Rudolph, *Biblia hebraica stuttgartensia* (Stuttgart: Deutsche Bibelgesellschaft, 1983). A smaller and less expensive edition has been produced by N. H. Snaith, *Tora, Nebi'im, Ketubim* (London: British and Foreign Bible Society, 1958). The standard concordance is G. Lisowsky, *Konkordanz zum hebräischen*

Alten Testament (2d ed.; Stuttgart: Württembergische Bibelanstalt, 1958), though computer-accessed databases have made this work obsolete. A series of volumes devoted to the textual variants is being prepared by D. Barthélemy, ed., *Critique textuelle de l'Ancien Testament* (OBO 50; Fribourg, Switz.: Editions Universitaires, 1982–). Three volumes have appeared: vol. 1 (OBO 50/1; 1982), which covers Joshua, Judges, Ruth, Samuel, Kings, Chronicles, Ezra, Nehemiah, and Esther; vol. 2 (OBO 50/2; 1986), which covers Isaiah, Jeremiah, and Lamentations; and vol. 3 (OBO 50/3; 1992), which covers Ezekiel, Daniel, and the Twelve. A fourth volume will appear soon (posthumously; Barthélemy passed away in 2002). This volume, edited by A. Schenker, covers the Psalter. Presumably, a fifth and final volume, covering the Pentateuch, is still planned. For a discussion of the materials and principles, see D. Barthélemy, ed., *Preliminary and Interim Report on the Hebrew Old Testament Project* (5 vols.; New York: United Bible Societies, 1973–1980). Barthélemy's introductions in the first three volumes of *Critique textuelle de l'Ancien Testament* will eventually be published in English. For discussion of the Hebrew Bible, see F. E. Deist, *Towards the Text of the Old Testament* (2d ed.; Pretoria: N.G. Kerkboeckhandel Transvaal, 1981); A. Dotan, "Masorah," *EncJud* 16:1401–82; M. Gertner, "The Masorah and the Levites," *VT* 10 (1960): 241–84; L. Goldschmidt, *The Earliest Editions of the Hebrew Bible* (New York: Aldus, 1950); M. J. Mulder, "The Transmission of the Biblical Text," *Mikra* 87–135; S. Talmon, "Old Testament Text," in *Cambridge History of the Bible* (ed. P. R. Ackroyd and C. F. Evans; 3 vols.; Cambridge: Cambridge University Press, 1963–1970), 1:159–99; E. Tov, *Textual Criticism of the Hebrew Bible* (Minneapolis: Fortress, 1992). Eugene Ulrich and others are preparing a Hebrew Bible based on the Dead Sea Scrolls. For an English translation of the Bible as preserved at Qumran and other locations in the Dead Sea region, see M. G. Abegg, P. W. Flint, and E. Ulrich, *The Dead Sea Scrolls Bible: The Oldest Known Bible Translated for the First Time into English* (San Francisco: HarperCollins, 1999). The best English translations are the RSV, NRSV, NASB, and the recently published NET Bible, available on the Internet at http://www.bible.org/netbible/.

Samaritan Pentateuch. As a distinct recension the Samaritan Pentateuch (SP) probably owes its origin to the schism in the second century B.C.E. There are 150 manuscripts of the SP, many nothing more than fragments, and most in Hebrew, though some Aramaic and Arabic are found. What makes the SP interesting is that in approximately 1,900 places it agrees with the LXX over against the MT. In some places it agrees with the NT over against both the LXX and the MT (e.g., Acts 7:4, 32). There are some fragments of the Pentateuch at Qumran reflecting a form of the text on which the SP was apparently based (cf. 4QpaleoExod[m14]; 4Q158[15]; 4Q364; 4QNum[b]; 4QDeut[n19]; 4Q175). The rabbis may have known of the SP: "Said Rabbi Eleazar ben R. Simeon, 'I stated to Samaritan scribes, "You have forged your own Torah, and it has done you no good" ' " (*y. Soṭah* 7.3).

S. Noja has argued that the SP was translated into Greek as the *Samareiticon*, a version that Origen often cited. Fragments of the *Samareiticon* survive in a fourth-century manuscript. Could this explain the agreements with the book of Acts, whose author likely did not know Hebrew? E. Tov disagrees, saying the evidence points only to a version of the LXX edited by the Samaritans. But others disagree with Tov.

The Samaritans awaited a Taheb, a sort of redeemer modeled after the prophet-like-Moses of Deut 18:15–19. It is perhaps because of this emphasis that Deut 18:18–22 has been inserted into Exod 20:22. The command to build an altar at Mount Gerizim is added to Exod 20:17, and the reading "Gerizim" in place of "Ebal" appears in Deut 27:4. Origen, Eusebius of Caesarea, Epiphanius, and Cyril of Jerusalem knew of the SP. Jerome used it in preparing his Latin translation of the Pentateuch.

The text of the SP has been edited by A. F. von Gall, *Der hebräische Pentateuch der Samaritaner* (5 vols.; Giessen: Töpelmann, 1914–1918; repr., Berlin: Töpelmann, 1963–1966). See also A. Sadaqa and R. Sadaqa, *The Samaritan Pentateuch: Jewish Version–Samaritan Version of the Pentateuch* (5 vols.; Tel Aviv: Rubin Mass, 1961–1965). There is no English translation. For studies of the Samaritan Pentateuch, see R. T. Anderson, "Samaritan Pentateuch: General Account," in *The Samaritans* (ed. Crown), 390–96; S. Noja, "The Samareitikon," in *The Samaritans* (ed. Crown), 408–12; J. D. Purvis, *The Samaritan Pentateuch and the Origin of the Samaritan Sect* (HSM 2; Cambridge: Harvard University Press, 1968); S. Talmon, "The Samaritan Pentateuch," *JJS* 2 (1951): 144–50; B. Waltke, "The Samaritan Pentateuch and the Text of the Old Testament," in *New Perspectives on the Old Testament* (ed. J. B. Payne; Dallas: Word, 1970), 212–39.

Dead Sea Scrolls. The discovery of the Dead Sea Scrolls, both those of Qumran and those of Murabbaʿat and Masada, witnesses to the Hebrew text dating from the turn of the era. Probably best known is the *Great Isaiah Scroll* (1QIsa^a). For a summary of the materials, see chapter 3 above. For an assessment of the implications of the Dead Sea Scrolls for the biblical text, see F. M. Cross and S. Talmon, eds., *Qumran and the History of the Biblical Text* (Cambridge: Harvard University Press, 1975); E. Tov, "Une inscription grecque d'origine samaritaine trouvée à Thessalonique," *RB* 81 (1974): 394–99; idem, "Proto-Samaritan Texts and the Samaritan Pentateuch," in *The Samaritans* (ed. Crown), 397–407; G. E. Weil, *Initiation à la Massorah* (Leiden: Brill, 1964).

Greek

Septuagint. The Septuagint (from the Latin *septuaginta,* "seventy") is the Greek translation of the OT (including the Apocrypha) and is abbreviated as LXX, the roman numeral for seventy. The name comes from the legend found in the pseudepigraphal *Letter of Aristeas* (see ch. 2), in which it is claimed that King Ptolemy II Philadelphus (285–247 B.C.E.) commissioned for the royal library seventy-two Palestinian scribes to translate the Hebrew Pentateuch into Greek. In isolation on the island of Pharos the scribes finished the task in seventy-two days. The story is recounted by Josephus (cf. *Ant.* 12.2.1 §11–12.2.15 §118). Philo himself accepted the story and regarded the translation as inspired, given, as it were, by divine dictation (cf. *Moses* 2.7 §37), a view that came to be held by many of the early Fathers of the Christian church.

For several reasons the legendary account of Aristeas cannot be accepted. Although the date of the LXX, at least as it concerns the Pentateuch, may be as ancient as *Aristeas* purports, the reason for the translation was to make the Bible more readily accessible to the Greek-speaking Jews of Alexandria. The remaining portions of the Bible were translated in succeeding generations, perhaps not being completed until the first century C.E. Evidently several translators were involved in this long process, for the style varies from one book to another.

The LXX is an important pre-MT witness. Some of its readings that differ from the MT agree with readings found in the Dead Sea Scrolls. Some of its differing readings appear in the NT, whose authors follow the LXX in more than one-half of their quotations of the OT. The diversity of the first-century Greek OT text has been documented by the discovery and publication of 8ḤevXIIgr, a fragmentary Greek scroll of the Minor Prophets (see Tov 1990). This text differs from the LXX at several points, and agrees with at least three of the recensions (Aquila, Symmachus, and Theodotion) at several points.

The principal text of the LXX is A. Rahlfs, *Septuaginta* (2 vols.; Stuttgart: Württembergische Bibelanstalt, 1935). A multivolume critical edition is A. Rahlfs et al., eds., *Septuaginta: Vetus Testamentum graecum* (Göttingen: Vandenhoeck & Ruprecht, 1931–). About two dozen volumes have appeared to date. The standard concordance is E. Hatch and H. A. Redpath, *A Concordance to the Septuagint and the Other Greek Versions of the OT* (2 vols.; Oxford: Clarendon, 1897; repr., Grand Rapids: Baker, 1983); again, computer-accessed databases have rendered this work obsolete. There are two English translations of the Septuagint: C. Thomson, *The Holy Bible, Containing the Old and the New Covenant, Commonly Called the Old and the New Testament* (4 vols.; Philadelphia: Jane Aitken, 1808); and L. C. L. Brenton, *The Septuagint Version of the Old Testament, according to the Vatican Text* (2 vols.; London: S. Bagster & Sons, 1844; repr., Peabody, Mass.: Hendrickson, 1986). The International Organization for Septuagint and Cognate Studies (IOSCS) has launched a New English translation of the LXX (NETS). The first fascicle to appear is A. Pietersma, *The Psalms: A New English Translation of the Septuagint* (Oxford: Oxford University Press, 2000). Members of the IOSCS are also preparing a commentary on the LXX. Their work will take into account the manner in which the Greek translators rendered the underlying Hebrew. Taking a different approach, a team of scholars assembled by S. E. Porter is preparing a commentary on the LXX that emphasizes the LXX as Greek literature, read by Greek speakers.

For more studies on the LXX, see S. Brock, *The Recensions of the Septuagint Version of I Samuel* (Turin: S. Zamorani, 1996); S. P. Brock, C. T. Fritsch, and S. Jellicoe, *A Classified Bibliography of the Septuagint* (ALGHJ 6; Leiden: Brill, 1973); G. J. Brooke and B. Lindars, eds., *Septuagint, Scrolls, and Cognate Writings* (SBLSCS 33; Atlanta: Scholars Press, 1992); P. Churgin, "The Targum and the Septuagint," *AJSL* 50 (1933): 41–65; F. C. Conybeare and St. G. Stock, *Grammar of Septuagint Greek* (Boston: Ginn, 1905; repr., Peabody, Mass.: Hendrickson, 1989);

L. Greenspoon, "Hebrew into Greek: Interpretation in, by, and of the Septuagint," in *The Ancient Period* (ed. Hauser and Watson), 80–113 (with helpful bibliography); R. J. V. Hiebert, C. E. Cox, and P. J. Gentry, eds., *The Old Greek Psalter*
(A. Pietersma FS; JSOTSup 332; Sheffield: Sheffield, 2001); D. Hill, *Greek Words
and Hebrew Meanings* (SNTSMS 5; Cambridge: Cambridge University Press,
1967); S. Jellicoe, *The Septuagint and Modern Study* (Oxford: Oxford University
Press, 1968); idem, *Studies in the Septuagint: Origins, Recensions, and Interpretations* (New York: Ktav, 1974); K. H. Jobes and M. Silva, *Invitation to the Septuagint*; R. W. Klein, *Textual Criticism of the Old Testament: The Septuagint after
Qumran* (Philadelphia: Fortress, 1974); R. T. McLay, *The Use of the Septuagint in
New Testament Research* (Grand Rapids: Eerdmans, 2003); S. Olofsson, *The LXX
Version: A Guide to the Translation Technique of the Septuagint* (ConBOT 30;
Stockholm: Almqvist, 1990); A. J. Saldarini, "Septuagint," *HBD* 925; I. L. Seelig-
man, *The Septuagint Version of Isaiah: A Discussion of Its Problems* (Leiden: Brill,
1948); A. Sperber, "NT and the Septuagint," *JBL* 59 (1940): 193–293; H. B. Swete,
An Introduction to the Old Testament in Greek (2d ed., rev. R. R. Ottley; Cambridge: Cambridge University Press, 1914; repr., Peabody, Mass.: Hendrickson,
1989); H. St. J. Thackeray, *A Grammar of the Old Testament in Greek according to
the Septuagint* (Cambridge: Cambridge University Press, 1909; repr., 1970);
E. Tov, *A Classified Bibliography of Lexical and Grammatical Studies on the Language of the Septuagint* (rev. ed.; Jerusalem: Academon, 1982); idem, *The Greek
Minor Prophets Scroll from Nahal Hever (8HevXIIgr)* (DJD 8; Oxford: Clarendon,
1990); idem, "Pap. Giessen 13, 19, 22, 26: A Revision of the LXX?" *RB* 78 (1971):
355–83; idem, "The Septuagint," *Mikra* 161–88; idem, *The Text-Critical Use of the
Septuagint in Biblical Research* (2d ed.; JBS 8; Jerusalem: Simor, 1997); E. Tov and
R. A. Kraft, "Septuagint," *IDBSup* 807–15; P. Walters, *The Text of the Septuagint:
Its Corruptions and Their Emendations* (ed. D. W. Gooding; Cambridge: Cam-
bridge University Press, 1973); J. W. Wevers, *Notes on the Greek Text of Genesis*
(SBLSCS 35; Atlanta: Scholars Press, 1993); idem, *Notes on the Greek Text of Exo-
dus* (SBLSCS 30; Atlanta: Scholars Press, 1990); idem, *Notes on the Greek Text of
Leviticus* (SBLSCS 44; Atlanta: Scholars Press, 1997); idem, *Notes on the Greek
Text of Numbers* (SBLSCS 46; Atlanta: Scholars Press, 1998); idem, *Notes on the
Greek Text of Deuteronomy* (SBLSCS 39; Atlanta: Scholars Press, 1995).

Greek Recensions. For various reasons, several recensions of the LXX were produced in the second and third centuries C.E. The oldest was by Aquila, who may
have been a disciple of Rabbi Aqiba and who may be the Onqelos associated with
the Pentateuch Targum of that name (cf. *b. Giṭ.* 56b; *b. Meg.* 3a). Aquila's Greek
recension, which is really a new, woodenly literal translation of the Hebrew text,
was published about 130 C.E. His recension survives in quotations, Hexaplaric
fragments, and on a few sixth-century palimpsests. Symmachus produced a
recension about 170 C.E. that represented a much more stylish Greek than that of
Aquila. According to Eusebius and Jerome, Symmachus was a Jewish Christian,
but according to Epiphanius he was a Samaritan who had converted to Judaism.
His work survives in a few Hexapla fragments. Following the Hebrew text

Theodotion revised the LXX (or at least a Greek text that was very similar) some-time toward the end of the second century. Only fragments of Theodotion's translation are extant (principally in quotations). Scholars are beginning to think that what had passed as Theodotion's version of Daniel, which had all but dis-placed the LXX version, may not be Theodotionic after all.

There are three other recensions, all later, that we know of. Best known is Origen's *Hexapla*. His six parallel columns contained: (1) the Hebrew text, (2) the Hebrew text transliterated with Greek letters, (3) Aquila, (4) Symmachus, (5) the LXX (with readings distinctly Origen's), and (6) Theodotion. Origen also pro-duced the *Tetrapla*, which contained only the Greek versions. For the most part all that remains of this great work are fragments. However, there are a few manu-scripts that preserve Origen's version of the LXX. There is also a Syriac translation of it known as the Syro-Hexapla. The best source for the fragments of these recensions is F. FIELD, *Origenis Hexapla* (2 vols.; Hildesheim: Georg Olms, 1964). There are plans to update this work. Finally, according to Jerome there were two other recensions, those by Lucian and Hesychius. Of the latter we know nothing. Of the former we know that he had been a presbyter from Antioch (d. 312). His recension survives in the quotations of Chrysostom and Theodoret of Cyrrhus and in several miniscules.

For more studies of the Greek recensions, see D. Barthélemy, *Les devanciers d'Aquila* (VTSup 10; Leiden: Brill, 1962); D. W. Gooding, *Recensions of the Septu-agint Pentateuch* (London: Tyndale, 1955); B. M. Metzger, "Lucian and the Lucianic Recension of the Greek Bible," *NTS* 8 (1962): 189–203; K. G. O'Connell, "Greek Versions," *IDBSup* 377–81; J. Reider and N. Turner, *An Index to Aquila* (VTSup 12; Leiden: Brill, 1966); E. Tov, "The Septuagint," *Mikra* 181–87.

Latin

Old Latin. The Old Latin (OL) survives in fragmentary manuscripts, liturgical books, and quotations of early Latin Fathers (e.g., Tertullian, Cyprian, Ambrose). A few books survive in complete form as part of the Vulgate (Baruch, Epistle of Jeremiah, Wisdom, Sirach, 1 and 2 Maccabees). Jerome did not edit these books because he regarded them as uninspired (principally because they were not ex-tant in Hebrew or Aramaic, and because they were not as ancient as the other books). The OL represents various translations of the LXX. The value of the OL is that it witnesses to the text of the LXX before the influences of the Greek re-censions. It also includes the NT.

A multivolume critical edition of the OL has been undertaken by B. Fischer et al., *Vetus latina: Die Reste der altlateinischen Bibel, nach Petrus Sabatier neu gesammelt und herausgegeben von der Erzabtei Beuron* (Freiburg in Breisgau: Herder, 1949–). The work is not yet complete. Each volume appears a fascicle at a time over a period of years. Some of the volumes released include Genesis by Fischer (vol. 2, 1951–1954), Ephesians by H. J. Frede (vol. 24/1, 1962–1964), Philippians and Colossians by Frede (vol. 24/2, 1966–1971), and the Catholic

Epistles by W. Thiele (vol. 26/1, 1956–1969). For an example, see W. Thiele, *Sapientia Salomonis* (vol. 11/1 of *Vetus latina*; 4 fasc.; Freiburg in Breisgau: Herder, 1977–1980).

Vulgate. In 382 Pope Damasus I commissioned Jerome to prepare a reliable Latin translation of the Bible. Despite Augustine's protests, Jerome based the OT translation on the Hebrew, having for years studied Hebrew in Bethlehem. (See Jerome's letter to Pope Damasus [*Epistulae* 18, ca. 381], where he defends the priority of the Hebrew over the Greek.) This work became the official Bible of the church, and eventually became known as the "Vulgate" (meaning "common"). It was not, however, until the ninth century that Jerome's version finally displaced the popular OL. The reluctance of many of the church's theologians to depart from the OL was because, unlike the Vulgate, it was dependent upon the LXX, regarded by many (e.g., Augustine) as divinely inspired. The major value of the Vulgate is that it represents an early witness to the Hebrew text.

The principal edition of the Vulgate is by R. Weber, ed., *Biblia Sacra iuxta vulgatam versionem* (2 vols.; 3d ed.; Stuttgart: Deutsche Bibelgesellschaft, 1985). There are various English translations available. An old classic is the Douay-Rheims, so called because it combines the Douay English translation of the OT (1609) with the Rheims English translation of the NT (1582): *The Holy Bible Translated from the Latin Vulgate* (New York: P. J. Kennedy & Sons, 1914). A multivolume critical edition has also been produced by the Benedictine Order, *Biblia Sacra iuxta latinam vulgatam versionem* (16 vols.; Rome: Typis Polyglottis Vaticanis, 1926–1981). For a concordance, see B. Fischer, ed., *Novae concordantiae Bibliorum Sacrorum iuxta vulgatam versionem critice editam* (5 vols.; Stuttgart: Frommann-Halzboog, 1977).

For more studies of the Vulgate and Latin versions, see J. Barr, "St. Jerome and the Sounds of Hebrew," *JSS* 12 (1967): 1–36; idem, "St. Jerome's Appreciation of Hebrew," *BJRL* 49 (1966–67): 281–302; D. Brown, "Jerome and the Vulgate," in *The Ancient Period* (ed. Hauser and Watson), 355–79 (very helpful bibliography); C. A. Evans, "Jerome's Translation of Isaiah 6:9–10," *VC* 38 (1984): 202–4; B. Kedar, "The Latin Translations," *Mikra* 299–338; W. Schwarz, *Principles and Problems of Biblical Translation* (Cambridge: Cambridge University Press, 1955), 25–37; H. F. D. Sparks, "Jerome as Biblical Scholar," in *Cambridge History of the Bible* 1 (ed. P. R. Ackroyd and C. F. Evans; 3 vols.; Cambridge: Cambridge University Press, 1963–1970), 1:510–41.

Syriac

The Peshitta. The Syriac version of the Bible came to be called the Peshitta (or Peshitto), which means "simple" (compare the Aramaic word *pešîṭā*, "plain [meaning]"). One of the oldest manuscripts is MS Add. 14,425 of the British Museum (containing the Pentateuch, minus Leviticus), which is dated 464 C.E. The origin of the Peshitta is obscure. Scholars are now aware of this version's close relationship to the Targumim. In one case the Targum (i.e., Proverbs Targum) may actually depend on the Peshitta. In all other cases, however, the relationship appears to be the reverse: the Peshitta relies on the Targum. My own work on Isaiah 6 suggests that the Peshitta is dependent on both *Targum Isaiah* and the LXX. Several Syriac words reflect distinctive targumic readings (esp. "forgive" in v. 10), on the one hand, and even syntax and words from the LXX (e.g., *gyr*, "for" in v. 10), on the other. Similar examples could be offered from other portions of Syriac Isaiah.

The principal edition of the Peshitta is A. M. Ceriani, *Translatio Syra Pescitto Veteris Testamenti ex Codice Ambrosiano II* (Milan: Impensis Bibliothecae Ambrosianae, 1876–1883). The Peshitta Institute of Leiden has sponsored a critical edition on behalf of the International Organization for the Study of the Old Testament. The text has been divided into four major parts, with two or more fascicles making up each part, in the Brill series Vetus Testamentum syriace: Genesis and Exodus (fasc. 1/1a; 1977); Leviticus–Joshua (1/2, 2/1b; 1990; repr., 2003); Judges and Samuel (2/2; 1978); Kings (2/4; 1976); Isaiah (3/1; 1987; repr., 1993); Jeremiah (3/2; forthcoming); Ezekiel (3/3; 1985; repr., 1993); the Minor Prophets, Daniel, and Bel and the Dragon (3/4; 1980); the Psalms (2/3; 1980); Job (2/1a; 1982; repr., 1993); Proverbs, Wisdom, Ecclesiastes, and Song of Songs (2/5; 1979); *Apocalypse of Baruch* and 4 Esdras (4/3; 1973); *Odes,* Prayer of Manasseh, apocryphal psalms, *Psalms of Solomon,* Tobit, and 3 Esdras (4/6; 1972). For an example, see S. P. Brock, *Isaiah* (VTS 3/1; Leiden: Brill, 1987). Several fascicles are still in preparation. An English translation of the Syriac Bible (based on Codex Ambrosianus) has been produced by G. Lamsa, *The Holy Bible from Ancient Manuscripts* (Nashville: Holman Bible Publishers, 1957). The standard lexicon is R. Payne Smith, *A Compendious Syriac Dictionary* (Oxford: Clarendon, 1903; repr., 1976). For a concordance, see P. G. Borbone and K. D. Jenner, eds., *Concordance to the Old Testament in Syriac* (Leiden: Brill, 1997–).

For more studies on the Peshitta and Syriac tradition, see W. Baars, *New Syro-Hexaplaric Texts: Edited, Commented upon, and Compared with the Septuagint* (Leiden: Brill, 1968); P. A. H. de Boer and W. Baars, *The Old Testament in Syriac according to the Peshitta Version* (Leiden: Brill, 1972); F. C. Burkitt, *Early Eastern Christianity* (New York: Dutton, 1904) (argues that the Peshitta derives from the first century C.E.); P. B. Dirksen, "The Old Testament Peshitta," *Mikra* 255–97; P. B. Dirksen and A. van der Kooij, eds., *The Peshitta as a Translation: Papers Read at the II Peshitta Symposium, Held at Leiden, 19–21 August 1993* (Monographs of the Peshitta Institute 8; Leiden: Brill, 1995); P. B. Dirksen and M. J. Mulder, eds., *The Peshitta, Its Early Text and History: Papers Read at the "Peshitta Symposium," Held at Leiden, 30–31 August 1985* (Monographs of the Peshitta Institute 4; Leiden: Brill, 1988); J. E. Erbes, *The Peshitta and the Versions: A Study of the Peshitta Variants in Joshua 1–5 in Relation to Their Equivalents in the Ancient Versions* (Uppsala: Uppsala University Press, 1999); C. A. Evans, *To See and Not Perceive: Isaiah 6.9–10 in Early Jewish and Christian Interpretation* (JSOTSup 64; Sheffield: JSOT Press, 1989), 77–80, 195; J. H. Hospers, "The Present-Day State of Research on the Pesitta (since 1948)," in *Verbum* (ed. T. P. van Baaren;

H. W. Obbink FS; STR-T 6; Utrecht: Kemink, 1964), 148–56; idem, "Some Remarks with Regard to the Text and Language of the Old Testament Peshitta," in *Von Kanaan bis Kerala* (ed. W. C. Delsman et al.; J. P. M. van der Ploeg FS; Neukirchen-Vluyn: Neukirchener Verlag, 1982), 443–55; S. Isenberg, "Jewish-Palestinian Origins of the Peshitta," *JBL* 90 (1971): 69–81; G. A. Kiraz, *Comparative Edition of the Syriac Gospels: Aligning the Siniaticus, Curetonianus, Peshîttâ, and Harklean Versions* (4 vols.; NTTS 21; Leiden: Brill, 1996); idem, *A Computer-Generated Concordance to the Syriac New Testament* (6 vols.; New York: Brill, 1993); idem, *Lexical Tools to the Syriac New Testament* (JSOT Manuals 7; Sheffield: JSOT Press, 1994); J. P. M. van der Ploeg, "The Peshitta of the Old Testament," in *The Malabar Church* (ed. J. Vellian; OrChrAn 186; Rome: Pontificium Institutum Orientalium Studiorum, 1970), 23–32.

Themes

Textual Criticism. Several of the above versions appear to be represented by the numerous quotations of the OT in the writings of the NT. In some cases one particular version serves the NT writer's purposes better than the others. The second example below will illustrate this point. Sometimes the versions are also helpful in determining the antiquity, if not original form, of a given reading. The first and third examples not only illustrate how the versions contribute to OT textual criticism, they also help clear up problems involving the NT itself.

Deuteronomy 32:43. In Rom 15:10 Paul quotes part of Deut 32:43 ("Rejoice, O Gentiles, with his people") according to the LXX and not the MT. Similarly, in Heb 1:6 the author cites another line from Deuteronomy's Song of Moses (cf. Deut 32:1–43) and applies it to Jesus: "Let all the angels of God worship him." The quotation is again taken from the LXX (perhaps from the parallel *Odes Sol.* 2:43 or LXX Ps 96:7 ["Worship him, all his angels"], rather than Deut 32:43). Again, however, the MT has no Hebrew equivalent, nor do the Pentateuch Targumim. Are the clauses in LXX Deut 32:43 later scribal glosses? Have the NT writers followed a Greek tradition that has no basis in the Hebrew original? Probably not. 4QDeuteronomy[a] provides a Hebrew reading that comes very close to what the LXX translator may have been looking at: "Rejoice, O heavens, with him; and worship him, sons of God. Let all the sons of God praise him. Rejoice, O Gentiles, with his people. . . ." The presence in the Hebrew of "sons of God," instead of "angels," presents no difficulty, since the LXX sometimes translates "gods" (*'ĕlōhîm*) as "angels" (cf. Pss 8:5; 96[97]:7) and "sons of the gods" (*bĕnê 'ĕlōhîm*) as "angels" (cf. Job 38:7). It is likely that 4QDeut[a] provides the original reading, which the MT in this instance has omitted through a scribal error.

Isaiah 6:9–10. According to Mark 4:11–12 Jesus tells parables "in order that" (*hina*) those who see will not perceive and those who hear will not understand, "lest they repent and be forgiven" (cf. Isa 6:9–10). Jesus has alluded to a version of Isaiah that approximates what we now find in *Targum Isaiah* (see esp. "forgive" in v. 10). Seemingly he stated that the purpose of his parables was to keep "outsiders" in the dark. This seems to be the basic idea of *Targum Isaiah* as well. There the prophet is to speak to those "people who hear but do not listen, and see but do not understand." The prophet is to "Make dull their heart and make heavy their ears." In other words, according to the Targum, the prophet is to harden only those who do not listen (i.e., the "outsiders"). This differs from the way it reads in the MT, in which the prophet is to harden the whole people. The Marcan passage has struck interpreters, ancient and modern, as very strange. Matthew, one of the first interpreters of this passage, paraphrased the text this way: "I speak parables to them, because [*hoti*] seeing they do not see and hearing they do not understand. And the prophecy of Isaiah is fulfilled which says, 'You will indeed hear but not understand . . . for the heart of this people has become fat . . .'" (Matt 13:13–15). Matthew has changed Mark's *hina* to *hoti,* from "in order that" to "because," and so has changed the idea of purpose to that of cause. He then reinforces his alteration by citing the LXX version of Isa 6:9–10 verbatim. For his part Luke abbreviates the Marcan passage (cf. Luke 8:10), omitting the offensive "lest they repent" clause. At the conclusion of Acts he will cite verbatim the full text of LXX Isa 6:9–10 (cf. Acts 28:26–27). John also quotes Isa 6:10, though in a completely different context: "He has blinded their eyes and hardened their heart . . . lest they should . . . turn for me to heal them" (John 12:40). Earlier John may have paraphrased Isa 6:9 in John 9:39: "I came into this world, in order that [*hina*] those who do not see should see, and those who see should become blind." Interpreters are undecided as to which OT version the Fourth Evangelist has followed. Some think that he has produced a free translation of the Hebrew. Thus, what we have in the four Gospels in this one instance are two (the Aramaic and the Greek) and possibly three (the Hebrew) OT versions represented in their respective quotations of a single OT passage.

Isaiah 6:13. Because the final clause of Isa 6:13 ("a holy seed is its stump") is missing in the LXX, some scholars have viewed its presence in the MT as a later scribal gloss. (Aquila and Symmachus retain it, while Origen and Theodotion mark it off with asterisks.) The fact that this clause is present in the Targum and Vulgate does not prove authenticity, only antiquity. But its presence in 1QIsa[a] argues strongly for its antiquity, if not its authenticity. It seems better to view the absence of the clause in the LXX as due to scribal homoioteleuton, that is, an error of jumping from one place in the text to another that follows the same word or a word with a similar ending. In this case, the Greek scribe apparently jumped (parablepsis) from the *autēs* of 6:13b to 7:1, thus omitting the line containing *autēs* at the end of 6:13c.

Amos 9:11–12. In his speech to the Jerusalem council, James quotes Amos 9:11–12: "After this I will return, and I will rebuild the dwelling of David, which has fallen; from its ruins I will rebuild it, and I will set it up, so that all other peoples may seek the Lord—even all the Gentiles over whom my name has been called. Thus says the Lord, who has been making these things known from long ago" (Acts 15:16–18). The quotation of Amos that is credited to James agrees exactly with neither the Hebrew nor the Old Greek. The most noticeable difference occurs in part of verse 12, which in the Hebrew reads, "that they may possess the remnant of Edom and all the nations who are called by my name." The Greek reads, "that the remnant of humanity [or man] may seek, even all the nations, upon whom my name has been invoked." This variation can be explained mainly in terms of different vocalization (i.e., *adam*, "man" or "humanity," instead of *edom*, "Edom") and the confusion between the look-alike letters *resh* (in *yarash*, "possess") and *dalet* (in *darash*, "seek"). The rendering in the Old Greek facilitates the further development that we see in Acts, thus making the prophecy of Amos speak more forcefully to the new context in the post-Easter setting.

Bibliography: W. F. ALBRIGHT, "New Light on Early Recensions of the Hebrew Bible," *BASOR* 140 (1955): 32–33 (on 4QDeutª); J. A. EMERTON, "The Translation and Interpretation of Isaiah vi. 13," in *Interpreting the Hebrew Bible* (ed. J. A. Emerton and S. C. Reif; E. I. J. Rosenthal FS; UCOP 32; Cambridge: Cambridge University Press, 1982), 85–118; C. A. EVANS, *To See and Not Perceive: Isaiah 6.9–10 in Early Jewish and Christian Interpretation* (JSOTSup 64; Sheffield: JSOT Press, 1989); K. H. JOBES and M. SILVA, *Invitation to the Septuagint*, 193–95; R. T. MCLAY, *The Use of the Septuagint in New Testament Research* (Grand Rapids: Eerdmans, 2003), 137–70; P. W. SKEHAN, "A Fragment of the 'Song of Moses' (Deut 32) from Qumran," *BASOR* 136 (1954): 12–15.

General Bibliography

K. ALAND and B. ALAND, *The Text of the New Testament: An Introduction to the Critical Editions and to the Theory and Practice of Modern Textual Criticism* (rev. ed.; Grand Rapids: Eerdmans, 1989); A. D. CROWN, ed., *The Samaritans* (Tübingen: Mohr [Siebeck], 1989); A. J. HAUSER and D. F. WATSON, eds., *The Ancient Period* (vol. 1 of *A History of Biblical Interpretation;* Grand Rapids: Eerdmans, 2003); K. H. JOBES and M. SILVA, *Invitation to the Septuagint* (Grand Rapids: Baker, 2000); F. G. KENYON, *The Text of the Greek Bible* (London: Gerald Duckworth, 1950); B. J. ROBERTS, *The Old Testament Text and Versions: The Hebrew Text in Transmission and the History of the Ancient Versions* (Cardiff: University of Wales, 1951); A. SUNDBERG, *The Old Testament of the Early Church* (HTS 20; Cambridge: Harvard University Press, 1964); J. WEINGREEN, *Introduction to the Critical Study of the Text of the Hebrew Bible* (Oxford: Clarendon, 1982); E. WÜRTHWEIN, *The Text of the Old Testament* (Grand Rapids: Eerdmans, 1979).

CHAPTER FIVE

Philo and Josephus

PHILO

1. *De Opificio Mundi (On the Creation of the World)*
   Legum Allegoriae (Allegories of the Law)
2. *De Cherubim (On the Cherubim)*
   De Sacrificiis Abelis et Caini (On the Sacrifices of Abel and Cain)
   Quod Deterius Potiori insidiari solet (The Worse Attacks the Better)
   De Posteritate Caini (On the Posterity of Cain)
   De Gigantibus (On the Giants)
3. *Quod Deus immutabilis sit (On the Unchangeableness of God)*
   De Agricultura (On Agriculture)
   De Plantatione (On Planting)
   De Ebrietate (On Drunkenness)
   De Sobrietate (On Sobriety)
4. *De Confusione Linguarum (On the Confusion of the Languages)*
   De Migratione Abrahami (On the Migration of Abraham)
   Quis Rerum Divinarum Heres (Who Is the Heir?)
   De Congressu quaerendae Eruditionis gratia (On the Preliminary Studies)
5. *De Fuga et Inventione (On Flight and Finding)*
   De Mutatione Nominum (On the Change of Names)
   De Somniis (On Dreams)
6. *De Abrahamo (On Abraham)*
   De Iosepho (On Joseph)
   De Vita Mosis (On the Life of Moses)
7. *De Decalogo (On the Decalogue)*
   De Specialibus Legibus I–III (On the Special Laws, Books I–III)
8. *De Specialibus Legibus IV (On the Special Laws, Book IV)*
   De Virtutibus (On the Virtues)
   De Praemiis et Poenis (On Rewards and Punishments)
9. *Quod Omnis Probus Liber sit (That Every Good Man Is Free)*
   De Vita Contemplativa (On the Contemplative Life)
   De Aeternitate Mundi (On the Eternity of the World)
   In Flaccum (To Flaccus)
   Apologia pro Iudaeis (Hypothetica)
   De Providentia (On Providence)
10. *De Legatione ad Gaium (On the Embassy to Gaius)*
11. *Quaestiones et Solutiones in Genesin (Questions and Answers on Genesis)*
12. *Quaestiones et Solutiones in Exodum (Questions and Answers on Exodus)*

JOSEPHUS	
Vita (Life) [vol. 1*]	*Antiquitates Judaicae (Jewish*
Contra Apionem (Against Apion) [vol.	*Antiquities)* [vols. 4–9]
1]	*Versions*
Bellum Judaicum (Jewish War) [vols.	Hegesippus (Latin)
2–3]	Slavonic Josephus (Old Russian)
	Yosippon (Hebrew)

*Indicates vol. number in LCL.

Philo

Philo (Judaeus) of Alexandria (ca. 20 B.C.E.–50 C.E.) was a prolific writer. Although he was Jewish, his language was Greek, the principal language of his city. What did he write? Most of his writings are extant, but scholars dispute whether they represent exegesis, philosophy, apologetics, or even psychology. Philo's writings probably reflect all of these interests, but his chief purpose, in my judgment, is to show that Judaism, particularly as seen in the Scriptures of Judaism, constitutes a superior worldview. His allegorical "exegesis" should be understood in this light. Philo was interested not in what actually happened, but in how the biblical story could speak to thinking persons of the Greco-Roman world. Philo carried out this purpose by interpreting the biblical stories (mostly those of the Pentateuch) in terms of neoplatonism (i.e., the view that what the physical senses perceive on earth below is but an imperfect reflection of the true and perfect reality of heaven above). Philo's approach resembles that of Stoic philosophers who allegorized Homer's epics. Similarly, Philo read allegorical meanings into the biblical narratives. For example, Cain is to be understood as "foolish opinion," which is to be replaced by Abel, to be understood as "good conviction" (*Sacrifices* 2 §5). Or again, when Abram was commanded to depart from his home country, the patriarch was actually commanded to escape the prison-house of his physical body and turn his thoughts God-ward (*Migration* 1–2 §1–12).

Of special interest to the present book is the question of the relationship of Philo's exegesis to the targumic traditions of the synagogue and to the midrashic traditions of the rabbinic academies. Some studies have attempted to relate Philo's legal interpretations (i.e., halakah) to those of the rabbis. Erwin R. Goodenough (*The Jurisprudence of the Jewish Courts of Egypt* [New Haven: Yale University Press, 1929; repr., Amsterdam: Philo, 1968]) and Isaak Heinemann (*Philons griechische und jüdische Bildung* [Breslau: M. & H. Marcus, 1932; repr., Hildesheim: Olms, 1962]) have concluded that Philo's halakic interpretation is distinctive to Alexandria. Edmund Stein (*Philo und Midrasch* [BZAW 57; Giessen: Töpelmann, 1931]) and Samuel Belkin (*Philo and the Oral Law* [Cambridge: Harvard University Press, 1940]) disagree, thinking that it is in basic continuity with Palestinian halakah. For a recent assessment, see the studies by Richard D. Hecht, "The Exegetical Contexts of Philo's Interpretation of Circumcision," in *Nourished with Peace: Studies in Hellenistic Judaism in Memory of Samuel Sandmel* (ed. F. E. Greenspahn et al.; Homage 9; Chico, Calif.: Scholars Press, 1984), 51–79; idem, "Preliminary Issues in the Analysis of Philo's *De specialibus legibus*," *SPhilo* 5 (1979): 1–56. Comparing haggadic traditions, Samuel Sandmel (*Philo's Place in Judaism: A Study of Conceptions of Abraham in Jewish Literature* [New York: Ktav, 1971]) concluded that Philo and early Palestinian rabbis have very different interpretive intentions. This may be so, but the similarities call for explanation (as seen in Borgen 1965; Meeks). One should also consult David T. Runia, *Philo in Early Christian Literature* (CRINT 3.3; Minneapolis: Fortress, 1993).

Philo's allegorical interpretation of Scripture has shed some light on the NT. Peder Borgen (*Bread from Heaven: An Exegetical Study of the Concept of Manna in the Gospel of John and the Writings of Philo* [NovTSup 10; Leiden: Brill, 1965; repr., 1981]) has shown that the use of the manna tradition in John 6 coheres at many points with Philonic and early rabbinic interpretation. Two years later Wayne Meeks (*The Prophet-King: Moses Traditions and the Johannine Christology* [NovTSup 14; Leiden: Brill, 1967]) found additional points of coherence between John and Philo (and other early Jewish materials) in their respective interpretations of Moses (for further comparisons between John and Philo see the general bibliography.). Hebrews has been another NT writing that has often been compared to Philonic principles of interpretation; see L. K. K. Dey, *The Intermediary World and Patterns of Perfection in Philo and Hebrews* (SBLDS 25; Missoula, Mont.: Scholars Press, 1975); S. G. Sowers, *The Hermeneutics of Philo and Hebrews: A Comparison of the Interpretation of the Old Testament in Philo Judaeus and the Epistle to the Hebrews* (BST 1; Richmond, Va.: John Knox, 1965); R. Williamson, *Philo and the Epistle to the Hebrews* (ALGHJ 4; Leiden: Brill, 1970). This NT writer's comparisons between the earthly priesthood and the heavenly, the earthly tabernacle and the heavenly, and the earthly sacrifice and the eternal are very much in step with the neoplatonic approach taken by Philo. Paul's Sarah/Hagar allegory in Galatians 4 probably represents another example of this kind of thinking.

The standard critical edition of Philo's works is L. Cohn et al., eds., *Philonis Alexandrini Opera quae supersunt* (7 vols.; Berlin: G. Reimer, 1896–1930; repr., 1962). Volume 7, parts 1 and 2 (published by de Gruyter, 1926–1930), constitutes an index compiled by H. Leisegang. The Loeb Classical Library offers an edition containing the Cohn-Wendland Greek text and an English translation: F. H. Colson and G. H. Whitaker, trans., *Philo* (10 vols.; Cambridge: Harvard University Press, 1927–1962) (with J. W. Earp for vol. 10, which contains a Scripture index; see abbreviations, 1:xxiii–xxiv); the series also offers R. Marcus, *Philo Supplement I: Questions and Answers on Genesis* (LCL; Cambridge: Harvard University Press, 1953); idem, *Philo Supplement II: Questions and Answers on Exodus* (LCL; Cambridge: Harvard University Press, 1953). See also C. D. Yonge, trans., *The Works of Philo* (London: H. G. Bohn, 1854; repr., Peabody, Mass.: Hendrickson, 1993). There are two concordances available: G. Mayer, *Index philoneus* (New

York: de Gruyter, 1974); and P. Borgen, K. Fuglseth, and R. Skarsten, *The Philo Index* (Grand Rapids: Eerdmans, 2000). The last volume of the series Biblia patristica indexes quotations of Scripture in Philo: A. Benoit et al., *Biblia patristica: Supplément, Philon d'Alexandrie* (vol. 5; Paris: Centre National de la Recherche Scientifique, 1982).

At one time it was thought that Philo was the author of *Liber antiquitatum biblicarum (Biblical Antiquities)*. This pseudepigraphal work often circulated along with the Latin translations of Philo's authentic writings. A century ago scholars abandoned the traditional view that Philo had written this work. They did so for two reasons: (1) The interpretive approach taken by the author of *Biblical Antiquities* is not allegorical. (2) *Biblical Antiquities* was probably written in Hebrew before later being translated into Greek and then eventually into Latin. Most scholars today believe that whereas Philo may have known a little Hebrew, he never would have been able to compose in that language. Greek was Philo's language. For further discussion of *Biblical Antiquities* see chapter 2.

Philo and the New Testament

The Logos. According to the well-known words of John 1, "in the beginning was the Word, and the Word was with God, and the Word was God . . . and through him (the Word) all things came into being" (vv. 1, 3). Interpreters have frequently appealed to Philo's use of Word (or Logos) for aid in understanding the background against which the Johannine Prologue should be understood. According to these opening verses the Word is from the beginning, in God's presence, is in some sense to be identified with God, and is the agent of creation. Philo assigns similar qualities to the Word: "[God] created the world through the Word" (*On Flight and Finding* 18 §95); "let him press to take his place under God's First-Born, the Word, who holds eldership among the angels, their ruler as it were. And many names are his, for he is called, 'the Beginning,' 'Name of God,' 'Word,' and 'Man after His Image'" (*Confusion* 28 §146); "Nothing mortal can be made in the likeness of the most High One and Father of the universe but (only) in that of the second God, who is his Word" (*QG* 2.62 [on Gen 9:6]); "[Scripture] gives the title of 'God' to His chief Word" (*On Dreams* 2.39 §230). These ideas are not only relevant to the Johannine Logos, but significantly contribute to the background of other christological confessions in the NT. One thinks of Col 1:15–16 ("He is the image of the invisible God, the first-born of all creation, because in him all things were created") and Heb 1:3 ("[The Son] reflects the glory of God and bears the very stamp of his nature, upholding the universe by his word of power").

Philo's Logos may also be related to the targumic Memra (Aramaic for "Word"). Philo had asserted that God's Logos, also called "the Beginning," was the agent through whom the world was created. Similarly, *Targum Neofiti* (see ch. 6) paraphrases Gen 1:1: "From the beginning with wisdom the Word of the Lord perfected the heavens and the earth" (cf. also *Tg. Neof.* Gen 1:26–27: "And the

Lord said: 'Let us create man . . .' and the Word of the Lord created man in his own image"). Recall that the Johannine Logos is introduced in a manner that clearly echoes Genesis 1: "In the beginning was the Word." It is possible, therefore, that the Logos was suggested to Philo by its usage in the synagogue (where the Targumim took shape) as much as by its usage in Stoic and neoplatonic circles.

Bibliography: A. W. ARGYLE, "Philo and the Fourth Gospel," *ExpTim* 63 (1951): 385–86; P. BORGEN, "Observations on the Targumic Character of the Prologue of John," *NTS* 16 (1970): 288–95; IDEM, "Philo of Alexandria," *SJWSTP* 273–74; D. A. HAGNER, "The Vision of God in Philo and John: A Comparative Study," *JETS* 14 (1971): 81–93; L. HURTADO, *One God, One Lord: Early Christian Devotion and Ancient Jewish Monotheism* (Philadelphia: Fortress, 1988); R. MIDDLETON, "Logos and Shekinah in the Fourth Gospel," *JQR* 29 (1933): 101–33; T. H. TOBIN, "The Prologue of John and Hellenistic Jewish Speculation," *CBQ* 52 (1990): 252–69; R. McL. WILSON, "Philo and the Fourth Gospel," *ExpTim* 65 (1953): 47–49.

The Perfect Man. Paul's Adam-Christ typology is similar to and may even reflect Philo's interesting interpretation of the two creation accounts. According to Philo, the Adams of the two creation accounts must be distinguished (*Confusion* 14 §§62–63; *QG* 1.4 [on Gen 2:7]). The Adam of the first creation account was "created in the image of God" (Gen 1:26–27). This Adam did not fall, but remained perfect. He is the "heavenly man." But the Adam of the second creation account was "formed from the dust of the earth" (Gen 2:7). Because he was sensual, his need for physical gratification clouded his reason and he fell when tempted: "Yet though he should have kept that image undefiled . . . when the opposites were set before him to choose or avoid, good and evil, honorable and base, true and false, he was quick to choose the false, the base, and the evil . . . with the natural consequence that he exchanged mortality [*thnēton*] for immortality [*athanatos*], forfeited his blessedness and happiness, and found an easy passage to a life of toil and misery" (*Virtues* 37 §205). Those who aspire "to be called a son of God" must follow the example of the man created in God's image (*eikōn*) (*Confusion* 28 §146).

This interpretation may have assisted Paul in working out his Adam-Christ typology. The first Adam was weak and fell prey to temptation, the second Adam, Christ, was perfect and did not succumb to temptation. In 1 Corinthians 15 the apostle quotes from Gen 2:7, "The first man, Adam became a living soul. The last Adam [i.e., Christ] became a life-giving spirit" (1 Cor 15:45). Two verses later he adds, "The first man [i.e., Adam] is from the earth, earthy [alluding to Gen 2:7]; the second man [i.e., Christ] is from heaven" (1 Cor 15:47). Two verses later Paul's typology draws still closer to Philo's allegory: "Just as we have borne the image of the earthy, we shall also bear the image [*eikōn*] of the heavenly" (1 Cor 15:49). Paul's typology may be assuming a distinction between the Adams of the two creation accounts that approximates Philo's exegesis. That is, the first Adam (i.e., the one formed of the dust of the earth) sinned, but Jesus Christ, the second Adam (i.e., the one modeled after the one created in the image of God, the one who is from heaven) was obedient and becomes himself a model for those who wish to aspire to heavenly virtue, or, as Philo puts it, to aspire to becoming a "son of God" (cf. Rom 8:14, 19, 29 ["predestined to be conformed to the image of his Son"]). Finally, Paul's reference to the resurrection hope may echo Philo's exegesis: "Flesh and blood cannot inherit the kingdom of God, nor does the perishable inherit the imperishability. . . . For this perishable nature must put on the imperishable, and this mortal nature [*thnēton*] must put on immortality [*athanasia*]" (1 Cor 15:50, 53). Philo's distinction between the two Adams is not precisely the same as Paul's, but his language does illuminate the context in which Paul's discussion may be better understood.

Shadow and Substance. In keeping with neoplatonic language (cf. Plato, *Resp.* 514A–518B) Philo speaks of the contrast between "shadow" and "substance": "Monstrous it is that shadow [*skia*] should be preferred to substance [*sōma*] or a copy to originals . . . and it behooves the man, whose aim it is to be rather to seem, to dissociate himself from the former [i.e., the shadow] and hold fast to the latter [i.e., the substance]" (*Migration* 2 §12). One is reminded of the polemic directed against Colossian errorists: "Let no one judge you in eating and in drinking or with regard to a festival or a new moon or a sabbath, which is a shadow [*skia*] of things to come, while the substance [*sōma*] is of Christ" (Col 2:16–17). Those who are concerned with eating and drinking are those who do not "hold fast" to Christ (Col. 2:19). The dichotomy between earthly shadow and heavenly substance may explain Luke's editing of the account of Jesus' baptism: "the Holy Spirit descended upon him in bodily form [*sōmatikōs*], like a dove" (Luke 3:22; cf. Mark 1:10). By inserting the word *sōmatikōs* the third evangelist may have wished to interpret the dove symbol in language that the educated readers of his time would have understood.

Bibliography: P. BORGEN, *Philo, John, and Paul: New Perspectives on Judaism and Early Christianity* (BJS 131; Atlanta: Scholars Press, 1987); H. CHADWICK, "St. Paul and Philo of Alexandria," *BJRL* 48 (1966): 286–307; H. CONZELMANN, *1 Corinthians* (Hermeneia; Philadelphia: Fortress, 1975), 286; J. D. G. DUNN, "I Corinthians 15:45—Last Adam, Life-Giving Spirit," in *Christ and the Spirit in the New Testament* (ed. B. Lindars and S. Smalley; C. F. D. Moule FS; Cambridge: Cambridge University Press, 1973), 127–41; E. KÄSEMANN, *Commentary on Romans* (Grand Rapids: Eerdmans, 1980), 144–47; J. MURPHY-O'CONNOR, "Philo and 2 Cor 6:14–7:1," *RB* 95 (1988): 55–69; P. T. O'BRIEN, *Colossians, Philemon* (WBC 44; Dallas: Word, 1982), 139–40; A. J. M. WEDDERBURN, "Philo's 'Heavenly Man,'" *NovT* 15 (1973): 301–26; R. WILLIAMSON, *Philo and the Epistle to the Hebrews* (ALGHJ 4; Leiden: Brill, 1970); IDEM, "Philo and New Testament Christology," in *Studia biblica, 1978* (ed. E. A. Livingstone; 3 vols.; Sheffield: JSOT Press, 1980), 3:439–45; N. T. WRIGHT, "Adam in Pauline Christology," *SBLSP* 22 (1983): 359–89.

General Bibliography for Philo

M. ALEXANDRE, "Rhetorical Argumentation as an Exegetical Technique in Philo of Alexandria," in *Hellenica et judaica* (ed. A. Caquot, M. Hadas-Lebel, and

J. Riaud; V. Nikiprowetzky FS; Leuven: Peeters, 1986), 13–27; Y. AMIR, "Authority and Interpretation of Scripture in the Writings of Philo," *Mikra* 421–53; H. W. ATTRIDGE, "Jewish Historiography," *EJMI* 322–24; P. BORGEN, "Philo of Alexandria," *SJWSTP* 233–82; IDEM, "Philo of Alexandria: A Critical and Synthetical Survey of Research since World War II," *ANRW* 21.1: 98–154; IDEM, "Philo of Alexandria as Exegete," in *The Ancient Period* (vol. 1 of *A History of Biblical Interpretation;* ed. A. J. Hauser and D. F. Watson; Grand Rapids: Eerdmans, 2003), 114–43 (very helpful bibliography); IDEM, "Quaestiones et solutiones: Some Observations on the Form of Philo's Exegesis," *SPhilo* 4 (1976–77): 1–15; H. BURKHARDT, *Die Inspiration heiliger Schriften bei Philo von Alexandrien* (Monographien und Studienbücher 340; Giessen, Ger.: Brunnen, 1988); F. M. COLSON, "Philo's Quotations from the Old Testament," *JTS* 41 (1940): 237–51; L. H. FELDMAN, *Scholarship on Philo and Josephus (1937–1962)* (Yeshiva Studies in Judaica 1; New York: Yeshiva University Press, 1963); E. R. GOODENOUGH, *An Introduction to Philo Judaeus* (2d ed.; Oxford: Blackwell, 1962); H. L. GOODHART and E. R. GOODENOUGH, "A General Bibliography of Philo Judaeus," in E. R. Goodenough, *The Politics of Philo Judeaus* (New Haven: Yale University Press, 1938), 130–321; L. L. GRABBE, *Etymology in Early Jewish Interpretation: The Hebrew Names in Philo* (BJS 115; Atlanta: Scholars Press, 1988); R. D. HECHT, "Philo and Messiah," in *Judaisms and Their Messiahs at the Turn of the Christian Era* (ed. J. Neusner, W. S. Green, and E. Frerichs; Cambridge: Cambridge University Press, 1987), 139–68; E. HILGERT, "Bibliographia philoniana, 1935–1981," *ANRW* 21.1:47–97; IDEM, "A Bibliography of Philo Studies, 1963–1970," *SPhilo* 1 (1972): 57–71, with updates in 2 (1973): 51–54; 3 (1974–75): 117–25; 4 (1976–1977): 79–85; 5 (1978): 113–20; 6 (1979–1980): 197–200; IDEM, "Philo Judaeus et Alexandrinus: The State of the Problem," in *The School of Moses: Studies in Philo and Hellenistic Religion in Memory of Horst R. Moehring* (ed. J. P. Kenney; BJS 304; Atlanta: Scholars Press, 1995), 1–15; W. L. KNOX, "A Note on Philo's Use of the Old Testament," *JTS* 41 (1940): 30–34; B. L. MACK, "Wisdom Literature," *EJMI* 387–95; D. T. RUNIA, *Philo in Early Christian Literature* (CRINT 3.3; Minneapolis: Fortress, 1993); S. SANDMEL, *Philo of Alexandria* (New York: Oxford University Press, 1979); IDEM, "Philo's Environment and Philo's Exegesis," *JBR* 22 (1954): 248–53; E. M. SMALLWOOD, *Philonis Alexandrini Legatio ad Gaium* (2d ed.; Leiden: Brill, 1970); T. H. TOBIN, *The Creation of Man: Philo and the History of Interpretation* (CBQMS 14; Washington, D.C.: Catholic Biblical Association, 1983); J. C. VANDERKAM, *An Introduction to Early Judaism,* 138–42; R. WILLIAMSON, *Jews in the Hellenistic World: Philo* (CCWJCW 1/2; Cambridge: Cambridge University Press, 1989).

Josephus

The writings of Josephus provide us with invaluable information touching history, politics, religious ideas, Jewish sects, and biblical interpretation. Born in the year of Gaius Caligula's accession (37/38 C.E.), young Joseph ben Matthias

studied Jewish law, contemplated which sect he would join (Pharisees, Sadducees, or Essenes), and visited the Roman capital. When the first war with Rome
broke out, Josephus (as he later calls himself) assumed command of part (or of
all) of Galilee. Besieged at Jotapata for forty-seven days, he surrendered to the
Romans and prophesied that Vespasian, the commander of the Roman forces in
Israel, would someday become the Roman emperor. When his prophecy came to
pass in 69 C.E., Josephus was released and was made part of Titus's advisory council. Shortly after the war ended in 70, Josephus went to Rome where he was
granted Roman citizenship. He took the name "Flavius" from the family name of
Vespasian and Titus. In the late 70s he wrote the *Jewish War* (seven books). (An
earlier version of this work, written in Aramaic, was sent to Jews of Mesopotamia
to discourage them from revolt.) In the mid-90s he completed the *Jewish Antiquities* (twenty books). Shortly after 100 C.E. he published his *Life* (an appendix to
Jewish Antiquities) and *Against Apion* (two books). (From *Ant.* 20.12.1 §267 one
may infer that much of the *Life* had been written by 93–94 C.E., although it would
not be published for another seven years or so.) Josephus died in the early years
of the second century. All of his writings, with the exception of the aforemen-
tioned earlier draft of *Jewish War*, were originally published in Greek. Greek was
not Josephus's mother-tongue, but he had studied it and could with some difficulty write and speak it. In composing his books he had assistance with the Greek
(*Ag. Ap.* 1.9 §50).

There are several topics treated in the writings of Josephus that are especially relevant to NT study. His description of the religious/political sects (i.e.,
Pharisees, Sadducees, Essenes, and the "Fourth Philosophy") is of great importance (cf. *Life* 2 §§10–12; *J.W.* 2.8.2–14 §§119–166; *Ant.* 18.1.2–6 §§11–23). His
description of the Samaritan-Jewish hostility (*J.W.* 2.12.3 §§232–244; *Ant.* 18.2.2
§30; 20.6.1–3 §§118–136) aids us in understanding what the NT presupposes
(Matt 10:5; Luke 9:52; 10:30–39; John 4:9; 8:48). His portrait of Pontius Pilate
as insensitive and brutal is illuminating (*Ant.* 18.3.1–2 §§55–62; *J.W.* 2.9.2–4
§§169–177; cf. Philo *Embassy* 38 §§299–305) and coheres with the NT (Luke
13:1–2; Acts 4:27). His portrait of the high priesthood indicates corruption, avarice, collaboration with Rome, and on occasion violence (*Ant.* 20.8.8 §181; 20.9.2
§§206–207), details which certainly cohere with the portrait in the Gospels and
Acts (Mark 14:1, 43, 53–65; 15:1–15, 31–32; Acts 4:1–3; 5:17–18; 7:1; 8:1; 9:1–2;
23:2; 24:1). Jesus' critical stance toward the ruling priests is thus clarified (Mark
11:15–17, 27–33; 12:1–12, 38–40, 41–44). His personal prophecies (*J.W.* 3.8.3
§§351–352; 6.2.1 §109; 6.4.5 §250; 6.5.4 §311) and the prophecies of others (*J.W.*
6.5.3 §§301–309) that he records regarding the destruction of Jerusalem and the
temple are instructive in making comparison with Jesus' similar prophecies
(Mark 13:1–2; Luke 19:41–44; 23:27–31). His description of would-be kings and
prophets, his retelling of the biblical narratives, and his references to John the
Baptist and Jesus will be considered in the section below.

There are two critical editions of the writings: S. A. Naber, *Flavii Josephi Opera
omnia* (6 vols.; Leipzig: Teubner, 1888–1896); and B. Niese, *Flavii Josephi Opera*
(7 vols.; Berlin: Weidmann, 1885–1895). The Greek text with English translation

appears in H. St. J. Thackeray et al., trans., *Josephus* (10 vols.; LCL; Cambridge: Harvard University Press, 1926–1965). The standard concordance is K. H. Rengstorf, ed., *A Complete Concordance to Flavius Josephus* (4 vols.; Leiden: Brill, 1973–1983). A helpful selected-subject concordance is Cleon L. Rogers Jr., *The Topical Josephus* (Grand Rapids: Zondervan, 1992). S. Mason, ed., *Flavius Josephus: Translation and Commentary* (Leiden: Brill), is a multivolume translation and commentary being published. To date, three volumes have appeared: vol. 3, L. H. Feldman, *Judean Antiquities 1–4* (2000); vol. 4, C. T. Begg, *Judean Antiquities 5–7* (2005); vol. 9, S. Mason, *Life of Josephus* (2001). This series promises to become the most important work available on Josephus.

Bibliography: T. S. BEALL, *Josephus' Description of the Essenes Illustrated by the Dead Sea Scrolls* (SNTSMS 58; Cambridge: Cambridge University Press, 1988); M. BLACK, "The Account of the Essenes in Hippolytus and Josephus," in *The Background of the New Testament and Its Eschatology* (ed. W. D. Davies and D. Daube; C. H. Dodd FS; Cambridge: Cambridge University Press, 1956), 172–75; J. BLENKINSOPP, "Prophecy and Priesthood in Josephus," *JJS* 25 (1974): 239–62; R. J. COGGINS, "The Samaritans in Josephus," in *Josephus, Judaism, and Christianity* (ed. Feldman and Hata), 257–73; I. HAHN, "Josephus und Die Eschatologie von Qumran," in *Qumran-Probleme* (ed. H. Bardtke; Berlin: Akademie, 1963), 167–91 (thinks that the prophecies of *Ant.* 6.13.9 §312 and *J.W.* 3.8.3 §352 are of Essene origin); J. NEUSNER, "Josephus's Pharisees," in *Ex orbe religionum* (ed. C. J. Bleeker et al., eds.; G. Widengren FS; 2 vols.; SHR 21; Leiden: Brill, 1972), 1:224–44; M. SMITH, "The Description of the Essenes in Josephus and the Philosophoumena," *HUCA* 29 (1958): 273–313; G. VERMES and M. GOODMAN, *The Essenes according to the Classical Sources* (Sheffield: Sheffield, 1989).

Josephus and the New Testament

Brigands and Prophets of Salvation. Josephus's descriptions of the ambitions and activities of those who hoped to lead Israel to freedom and renewal help us understand better how the authorities responded to Jesus and possibly how Jesus understood his mission. Several claimed kingship following the death of Herod: Judas of Gamala (*Ant.* 18.1.1 §4; *J.W.* 2.17.8 §§433–434; cf. Acts 5:37), Judas of Sepphoris (*Ant.* 17.10.5 §§271–272; *J.W.* 2.4.1 §56), Simon of Perea (*Ant.* 17.10.6 §§273–276; *J.W.* 2.4.2 §§57–59), Athronges the shepherd of Judea (*Ant.* 17.10.7 §§278–284; *J.W.* 2.4.3 §§60–65). Others had royal ambitions during the war with Rome: Menahem (*J.W.* 2.17.8–10 §§433–448), John of Gischala (*J.W.* 4.7.1 §§389–394), and Simon bar Gioras (*J.W.* 4.9.4 §510; 7.1.2 §29). There were also prophets who proclaimed deliverance: Theudas (*Ant.* 20.5.1 §§97–98; cf. Acts 5:36), who claimed that at his command the Jordan River would be parted, the Egyptian Jew (*Ant.* 20.8.6 §§169–170; cf. Acts 21:38), at whose command the walls of Jerusalem would collapse, Jonathan the refugee (*J.W.* 7.11.1 §§437–438; *Life* 76 §§424–425), who promised the people signs in the wilderness, and others (*Ant.* 20.8.10 §188). Although Josephus regularly calls the would-be kings "brigands" (*lēstai*) and the prophets "false prophets" (*pseudoprophētai*) and "impostors" (*goētēs*), it is probable that most of these people were sincere messianic claimants and visionaries who had hopes of delivering Israel. The Roman response in almost every case was swift and ruthless. The prophets' habit of promising signs in the wilderness, many of which are reminiscent of the events of the Exodus and Conquest under Moses and Joshua, are particularly illuminating for Jesus research. On NT warnings regarding the dangers of "false christs" and "false prophets" see Matt 24:11, 24; Mark 13:5, 22. For fuller details see appendix 6.

Bibliography: L. H. FELDMAN, "Prophets and Prophecy in Josephus," *JTS* 41 (1990): 386–422; D. HILL, "Jesus and Josephus' 'Messianic Prophets,'" in *Text and Interpretation* (ed. E. Best and R. McL. Wilson; M. Black FS; New York: Cambridge University Press, 1979), 143–54; R. A. HORSLEY and J. S. HANSON, *Bandits, Prophets, and Messiahs: Popular Movements at the Time of Jesus* (San Francisco: Harper & Row, 1985); S. MASON, *Flavius Josephus on the Pharisees: A Composition-Critical Study* (SPB 39; Leiden: Brill, 1991); IDEM, *Josephus and the New Testament;* J. REILING, "The Use of ψευδοπροφήτης in the Septuagint, Philo, and Josephus," *NovT* 13 (1971): 147–56.

Josephus and Miracles. In two studies Otto Betz has discussed Josephus's understanding of miracles and magic. He studies Josephus's descriptions of various persons who claimed to have miraculous powers (*J.W.* 2.13.4 §259; 2.13.5 §262; *Ant.* 20.5.1 §97; 20.8.6 §170), observing that the first-century historian does not distinguish between miracle and magic as sharply as do the rabbis (cf. *Ant.* 14.2.1 §§22–24 [on Onias the Righteous]). Betz concludes that Josephus's understanding of miracle (e.g., Exod 7:1–13) has been influenced by his knowledge of miracle-workers of his time. Josephus frequently calls miracle-workers, particularly those who promised Israel deliverance, "imposters" (*goētēs*). The word *goēs* occurs in 2 Tim 3:13: "evil men and impostors [*goētai*] will go from bad to worse, deceiving and being deceived." According to Philo: "If anyone cloaking himself under the name and guise of a prophet and claiming to be possessed by inspiration lead us on to the worship of the gods recognized in the different cities, we ought not to listen to him and be deceived by the name of a prophet. For such a one is no prophet, but an impostor [*goēs*], since his oracles and pronouncements are falsehoods invented by himself" (*Spec. Laws* 1.58 §315). For several examples of positive accounts of miracle-workers, see appendix 5.

Bibliography: O. BETZ, "Jesu heiliger Krieg," *NovT* 2 (1957): 116–37; IDEM, "Miracles in the Writings of Flavius Josephus," in *Josephus, Judaism, and Christianity* (ed. Feldman and Hata), 212–35; IDEM, "Das Problem des Wunders bei Flavius Josephus im Vergleich zum Wunderproblem bei den Rabbinen und im Johannesevangelium," in *Josephus-Studien* (ed. Betz, Haacker, and Hengel), 23–44; G. DELLING, "Josephus und das Wunderbare," *NovT* 2 (1958): 291–309; D. C. DULING, "The Eleazar Miracle and Solomon's Magical Wisdom in Flavius Josephus," *HTR* 78 (1985): 1–25; W. G. MACRAE, "Miracle in *The Antiquities* of Josephus," in *Miracles: Cambridge Studies in Their Philosophy and History* (ed. C. F. D. Moule; London: Mowbray, 1965), 127–47.

Josephus and the Rewritten Bible. Josephus's motives and techniques of retelling biblical history shed light on synoptic relationships. In his study of *Jewish Antiq-*

uities, Harold Attridge (1976, 181) has concluded that Josephus redefined Jewish history and tradition so that they would become "relevant, comprehensible and attractive in a new environment." Gospel interpreters have for years assumed that this is what the evangelists did when they edited their sources and composed their respective accounts. As a case in point, F. G. Downing has compared Josephus's rewriting of the Joshua-Judges narratives in *Jewish Antiquities* to Luke. He observes five basic ways in which Josephus rewrites the biblical narrative. (1) Josephus omits material to avoid discrepancies in multiple accounts, to avoid repetition, to avoid interruptions in the flow of the story, to avoid miraculous and magical details, to excise inappropriate theology, and to excise apologetically awkward material. (2) Josephus adds material to promote harmony and continuity in the narrative, to advance his view of divine providence and prophetic fulfillment, to emphasize the piety of major biblical characters, to promote Jewish apologetic, and to clarify and stimulate interest in the biblical story. (3) Josephus rearranges materials to promote harmony and continuity in the biblical narrative. (4) Josephus assembles and compiles his materials so as to unify the narrative around specific themes and verbal similarities. (5) Finally, Josephus conflates parallel accounts to promote harmony and continuity. When parallel accounts differ greatly, however, he often abandons conflation and opts, instead, to write a fresh account. Downing concludes that Luke's rewriting of Mark corresponds almost exactly to Josephus's rewriting.

Bibliography: H. W. ATTRIDGE, *The Interpretation of Biblical History in the Antiquitates judaicae of Flavius Josephus* (HDR 7; Missoula, Mont.: Scholars Press, 1976); IDEM, "Jewish Historiography," *EJMI* 324–28; H. W. BASSER, "Josephus as Exegete," *JAOS* 107 (1987): 39–54; J. E. BOWLEY, "Josephus's Use of Greek Sources for Biblical History," in *Pursuing the Text* (ed. Reeves and Kampen), 202–15; N. G. COHEN, "Josephus and Scripture: Is Josephus' Treatment of the Scriptural Narrative Similar throughout the Antiquities I–XI?" *JQR* 54 (1963–1964): 311–32; D. DAUBE, "Typology in Josephus," *JJS* 31 (1980): 18–36; F. G. DOWNING, "Redaction Criticism: Josephus' Antiquities and the Synoptic Gospels," *JSNT* 8 (1980): 46–65; 9 (1980): 29–48; L. H. FELDMAN, "Josephus's Biblical Paraphrase as a Commentary on Contemporary Issues," in *The Interpretation of Scripture in Early Judaism and Christianity: Studies in Language and Tradition* (ed. C. A. Evans; JSPSup 33; SSEJC 7; Sheffield: Sheffield, 2000), 124–201; IDEM, *Josephus's Interpretation of the Bible* (HCS 27; Berkeley: University of California Press, 1998) (a massive work); IDEM, *Studies in Josephus' Rewritten Bible* (JSJSup 58; Leiden: Brill, 1998); IDEM, "Use, Authority, and Exegesis of Mikra in the Writings of Josephus," *Mikra* 455–518; T. W. S. FRANXMAN, *Genesis and the "Jewish Antiquities" of Flavius Josephus* (BibOr 35; Rome: Pontifical Biblical Institute, 1979); K.-S. KRIEGER, *Geschichtsschreibung als Apologetik bei Flavius Josephus* (Tübingen: A. Francke, 1994); S. SOWERS, "On the Reinterpretation of Biblical History in Hellenistic Judaism," in *Oikonomia: Heilgeschichte als Thema der Theologie* (ed. F. Christ; O. Cullmann FS; Hamburg: Reich, 1967), 18–25.

References to John the Baptist and Jesus. In three passages Josephus refers to John the Baptist and Jesus. The authenticity of the passage concerned with John is not disputed:

But to some of the Jews the destruction of Herod's army seemed to be divine vengeance, and certainly a just vengeance, for his treatment of John, surnamed the Baptist. For Herod had put him to death, though he was a good man and had exhorted the Jews to lead righteous lives, to practise justice towards their fellows and piety towards God, and so doing to join in baptism. In his view this was a necessary preliminary if baptism was to be acceptable to God. They must not employ it to gain pardon for whatever sins they committed, but as a consecration of the body implying that the soul was already thoroughly cleansed by right behaviour. When others too joined the crowds about him, because they were aroused to the highest degree by his sermons, Herod became alarmed. Eloquence that had so great an effect on mankind might lead to some form of sedition, for it looked as if they would be guided by John in everything that they did. Herod decided therefore that it would be much better to strike first and be rid of him before his work led to an uprising, than to wait for an upheaval, get involved in a difficult situation and see his mistake. Though John, because of Herod's suspicions, was brought in chains to Machaerus, the stronghold that we have previously mentioned, and there put to death, yet the verdict of the Jews was that the destruction visited upon Herod's army was a vindication of John, since God saw fit to inflict such a blow on Herod. (*Ant.* 18.5.2 §§116–119 [LCL])

Some think that this account is at variance with the Synoptics' account (cf. Mark 6:17–29) where it is said that Herod imprisoned John for condemning the marriage to Herodias. While it is true that in the above passage Josephus underscores Herod's political motives and fears for eliminating John, later he does disapprove of the union: "Herodias, taking it into her head to flout the way of our fathers, married Herod, her husband's brother by the same father, who was tetrarch of Galilee; to do this she parted from a living husband" (*Ant.* 18.5.4 §136).

On James, brother of Jesus (not disputed). "And so he [Ananus the high priest] convened the judges of the Sanhedrin and brought before them a man called James, the brother of Jesus who was called the Christ, and certain others. He accused them of having transgressed the law and delivered them up to be stoned" (*Ant.* 20.9.1 §§200–203 [LCL]).

On Jesus (disputed).

> About this time there lived Jesus, a wise man, *if indeed one ought to call him a man.* For he was one who wrought surprising feats and was a teacher of such people as accept the truth gladly. He won over many Jews and many of the Greeks. *He was the Messiah.* When Pilate, upon hearing him accused by men of the highest standing amongst us, had condemned him to be crucified, those who had in the first place come to love him did not give up their affection for him. *On the third day he appeared to them restored to life, for the prophets of God had prophesied these and countless other marvellous things about him.* And the tribe of Christians, so called after him, has still to this day not disappeared (*Ant.* 18.3.3 §§63–64 [LCL]; italics indicate probable glosses).

This passage is repeated, with a couple of very slight differences, in Eusebius (*Hist. eccl.* 1.11.7–8; *Defense of the Gospel* 3.5.105).

Very few scholars have argued that this passage is wholly authentic; they include F. C. Burkitt, "Josephus and Christ," *ThT* 47 (1913): 135–44; F. Dornseiff, "Zum Testimonium flavianum," *ZNW* 46 (1955): 245–50; and J. Salvador, "E autêntico o 'Testimonium flavianum'?" *RCB* 2 (1978): 137–51. Ernst Bammel ("Zum Testimonium flavianum," in *Josephus-Studien* [ed. Betz, Haacker, and Hengel], 9–22) and Albert A. Bell Jr. ("Josephus the Satirist? A Clue to the Original form of the Testimonium flavianum," *JQR* 68 [1976]: 16–22) have argued that the passage is essentially authentic but was originally intended to be understood in terms of satire. Solomon Zeitlin ("The Christ Passage in Josephus," *JQR* 18 [1927–1928]: 231–55) argues that the passage as a whole is nothing more than an interpolation. Most argue, however, that Josephus did refer to Jesus but Christians have tampered with the text: Z. Baras, "Testimonium flavianum: The State of Recent Scholarship," in *Society and Religion in the Second Temple Period* (ed. M. Baras and Z. Baras; Jerusalem: Masada, 1977), 303–13, 378–85; S. G. F. Brandon, "The Testimonium Flavium," *History Today* 19 (1969): 438; A. M. Dubarle, "Le témoignage de Josèphe sur Jésus d'après des publications récentes," *RB* 94 (1977): 38–58; L. H. Feldman, "The *Testimonium flavianum:* The State of the Question," in *Christological Perspectives* (ed. R. F. Berkey and S. A. Edwards; H. K. McArthur FS; New York: Pilgrim, 1982), 179–99, 288–93; John P. Meier, "Jesus in Josephus: A Modest Proposal," *CBQ* 52 (1990): 72–103; P. Winter, "Josephus on Jesus," *Journal of Historical Studies* 1 (1967–1968): 289–302. This is likely the correct position. Although some Christian writers knew of the passage (such as Eusebius, ca. 324), none of the early Fathers thought that Josephus regarded Jesus as the Messiah (see Origen [ca. 280], *Cels.* 1.47; idem, *Comm. Matt.* 13.55). This could hardly have been the case if there had been no passage at all or that the pro-Christian version that is now extant was original. The best explanation is that Josephus did refer to Jesus, but not in such positive, almost confessional terms. Moreover, as Louis Feldman and others have shown, the passage for the most part betrays the writing style of Josephus. Only in one or two places do words or phrases occur that are uncharacteristic of his style. This leads Feldman to conclude that "our text represents what Josephus substantially wrote, but that some alterations have been made by a Christian interpolator" (LCL 9, p. 49, n. *b*).

How, then, did the passage originally read? Joseph Klausner (pp. 55–56) thought that the passage originally read something like this:

> Now, there was about this time Jesus, a wise man; for he was a doer of wonderful works, a teacher of such men as receive the truth with pleasure. He drew over to him both many of the Jews and many of the Gentiles. And when Pilate, at the suggestion of the principal men among us, had condemned him to the cross, those that loved him at the first ceased not so [to do]; and the race of Christians, so named from him, are not extinct even now.

Robert Eisler thought that the passage originally had a critical and cynical slant. He argued (pp. 61–62) that the original text read like this:

Now about this time arose (an occasion for new disturbances) a certain Jesus, a wizard of a man, if indeed he may be called a man (who was the most monstrous of all men, whom his disciples call a son of God, as having done wonders such as no man hath every yet done). . . . He was in fact a teacher of astonishing tricks to such men as accept the abnormal with delight.

And he seduced many Jews and many also of the Greek nation, and (was regarded by them as) the Messiah.

And when, on the indictment of the principal men among us, Pilate had sentenced him to the cross, still those who before had admired him did not cease (to rave). For it seemed to them that having been dead for three days, he had appeared to them alive again, as the divinely-inspired prophets had foretold—these and ten thousand other wonderful things—concerning him. And even now the race of those who are called "Messianists" after him is not extinct.

Klausner's more or less neutral reconstruction, however, enjoys the support of the Arabic version found in Agapius's *Book of the Title*, as translated by S. Pines p. 16):

Similarly Josephus the Hebrew. For he says in the treatises that he has written on the governance [?] of the Jews: "At this time there was a wise man who was called Jesus. And his conduct was good, and [he] was known to be virtuous. And many people from among the Jews and the other nations became his disciples. Pilate condemned him to be crucified and to die. And those who had become his disciples did not abandon his discipleship. They reported that he had appeared to them three days after his crucifixion and that he was alive; accordingly he was perhaps the Messiah concerning whom the prophets have recounted wonders."

Bibliography: J. N. BIRDSALL, "The Continuing Enigma of Josephus's Testimony about Jesus," *BJRL* 67 (1985): 609–22; R. EISLER, *The Messiah Jesus and John the Baptist*, 36–62; M. GOGUEL, *The Life of Jesus* (London: Allen and Unwin, 1932), 75–91; J. KLAUSNER, *Jesus of Nazareth* (New York: Macmillan, 1925), 55–60; S. PINES, *An Arabic Version of the Testimonium flavianum and Its Implications* (Jerusalem: Israel Academy of Sciences and Humanities, 1971).

Versions of Josephus's Writings

Some of Josephus's writings have been translated, edited, and abridged in a variety of languages and forms. The three principal versions will be briefly considered.

Hegesippus (Latin Josephus). By the sixth century the writings of Josephus had been translated into Latin. In the fourth century a loose Latin paraphrase of the *Jewish War* appeared under the name of a certain Hegesippus. The name is probably not genuine. The significance of the readings found only in Hegesippus is disputed. Some think that they may witness authentic Josephan traditions. Most suspect that they represent nothing more than later embellishments and legends. Solomon Zeitlin has argued that Hegesippus made use of the *Yosippon*. His argument, however, rests on the unlikely prior conclusion that the *Yosippon* is quite old (see discussion of the *Yosippon* below).

Bibliography: A. A. BELL Jr., "Classical and Christian Traditions in the Work of Pseudo-Hegesippus," *Indiana Social Studies Quarterly* 33 (1980): 60–64 (discusses the relationship of Hegesippus and *Yosippon*); IDEM, "Josephus and Pseudo-Hegesippus," in *Josephus, Judaism, and Christianity* (ed. Feldman and Hata), 349–61; F. BLATT, *Introduction and Text: The Antiquities, Books I–IV* (vol. 1 of *The Latin Josephus*; Acta jutlandica 30/1; Aarhus, Den.: Universitatsvorlaget, 1958); K. BOYSEN, *De Judaeorum vetustate sive Contra Apionem* (part 6 of *Flavii Josephi Opera ex versione latina antiqua* (CSEL 37; Vienna: F. Tempsky, 1898; repr., New York: Johnson, 1964); V. USSANI, *Hegesippi qui dicitur Historiae libri V* (CSEL 66; Vienna: Hölder-Pichler-Tempsky, 1932) (critical text of Hegesippus); S. ZEITLIN, "Josippon," *JQR* 53 (1962–1963): 277–97.

Slavonic Josephus (Old Russian). The Slavonic (or Old Russian) version of Josephus's *Jewish War* contains numerous passages not found in the Greek version. Many of these passages relate to John the Baptist or Jesus. It is thought that the Slavonic version may be a translation of a different, perhaps unedited, version of the Greek, or perhaps it may be a translation of the earlier Aramaic version of the Jewish War. Scholars are divided over every question pertaining to the origin, authenticity, and historical value of the Slavonic "additions." Here are a few of the most relevant texts:

> His [Jesus'] works, that is to say, were godly, and he wrought wonder-deeds amazing and full of power. Therefore it is not possible for me to call him a man. But again, looking at the existence he shared with all, I would not call him an angel. [follows 2.9.3, between §§174 and 175]

> Some said of him, that our first Lawgiver has risen from the dead and shows forth many cures and arts. [follows 2.9.3, between §§174 and 175]

> But when they saw his power, that he accomplished everything that he would by word, they urged him that he should enter the city and cut down the Roman soldiers and Pilate and rule over us. But that one scorned it. [follows 2.9.3, between §§174 and 175]

> [The temple curtain] had, you should know, been suddenly rent from top to the ground.... [follows 5.5.4 §214]

> And over these [gates] with inscriptions hung a fourth tablet with inscription in these [Greek, Roman, and Jewish] characters, to the effect: Jesus has not reigned as king; he has been crucified by the Jews because he proclaimed the destruction of the city and the laying waste of the Temple. [inserted in 5.5.2 §195]

> Some indeed by this understood Herod, but others the crucified wonder-doer Jesus, others say again Vespasian. [inserted at 6.5.4, replacing §313]

A. J. Berendts concluded that they are genuine. Robert Dunkerley agrees that they probably do go back to Josephus, but they are not necessarily historically accurate. J. Frey argued that they were early interpolations. J. M. Creed and J. W. Jack agree, arguing that the additions are late, spurious, and completely worthless. H. St. J. Thackeray translated into English the principal passages.

Bibliography: A. J. BERENDTS, *Die Zeugnisse vom Christentum im slavischen "De bello judaico" des Josephus* (TUGAL 29 [= NS 14]; Leipzig: Hinrichs, 1906); J. M. CREED, "The Slavonic Version of Josephus' History of the Jewish War," *HTR* 25 (1932): 277–319; R. DUNKERLEY, "The Riddles of Josephus," *HibJ* 53 (1954–1955): 127–34; R. EISLER, *The Messiah Jesus and John the Baptist*, 113–69; J. FREY, *Der slavische Josephusbericht über die urchristliche Geschichte nebst seinen Parallelen* (Dorpat: Mattiesen, 1908); J. W. JACK, *The Historic Christ* (London: Clarke, 1933); H. LEEMING and K. LEEMING, eds., *Josephus' Jewish War and Its Slavonic Version: A Synoptic Comparison of the English Translation by H. St. J. Thackeray with the Critical Edition by N. A. Mescerskij of the Slavonic Version in the Vilna Manuscript* (trans. H. Leeming and L. Osinkina; AGJU 46; Leiden: Brill, 2003); G. R. S. MEAD, *The Gnostic John the Baptizer* (London: Watkins, 1924), 97–119; É. NODET, "Jewish Features in the 'Slavonic' War of Josephus," in *Internationales Josephus-Kolloquium, Amsterdam, 2000* (ed. J. Kalms; Münsteraner judaistische Studien 10; Münster: LIT, 2001), 105–31; A. RUBINSTEIN, "Observations on the Old Russian Version of Josephus' Wars," *JJS* 2 (1957): 329–48; H. St. J. THACKERAY, "The Principal Additional Passages in the Slavonic Version," in Thackeray, *The Jewish War, Books IV–VII* (vol. 3 of *Josephus;* LCL 210; Cambridge: Harvard University Press, 1928), 635–58 (English translation); S. ZEITLIN, *Josephus on Jesus: With Particular Reference to Slavonic Josephus and the Hebrew Josippon* (Philadelphia: Dropsie College Press, 1931), 52–60; IDEM, "The Slavonic Josephus and Its Relation to Yosippon and Hegesippus," *JQR* 20 (1929–1930): 1–50.

Yosippon (Hebrew Josephus). In the Middle Ages a Hebrew translation based on the *Jewish War, Jewish Antiquities, Against Apion,* and even the Latin Hegesippus appeared under the name of *Yosippon* (or *Josippon*), which is the Hebraizing form of the Greek name Josephus. Many rabbis of the Middle Ages believed that the *Yosippon* was the work of Josephus. The Constantinople version of the *Yosippon* claims that Josephus was the author: "Behold, this book I, Joseph ben Gorion the Priest, wrote for Israel" (i.e., in Hebrew, as opposed to Greek, which was for the Romans). The name "ben Gorion" probably arose from confusing Josephus with a general named "Joseph ben Gorion." (Josephus, it should be remembered, had also been a general.) One of the manuscripts of the *Yosippon* claims that the work was written in 953 C.E. From this it is inferred that the *Yosippon* was composed in the tenth century. Solomon Zeitlin disagrees, claiming that the work is late third or early fourth century, though edited in later centuries. He claims that the author made use of the Babylonian Talmud, the Greek Apocrypha, and classical Greek authors. Few scholars follow Zeitlin, however. Since the *Yosippon* has made use of many sources, including the Talmud, the later date is more likely. Louis Feldman, moreover, has concluded (*Josephus and Modern Scholarship*, 68) that Hegesippus was the *Yosippon*'s main source. Therefore, in all probability the work is quite late (probably ninth or tenth century).

Did the original *Yosippon* mention Jesus? All of the early manuscripts give evidence of the work of the censors, both Jewish and Christian. Christian censors required offensive materials to be deleted, but often Jewish converts to Christianity would add confessional elements that later Jewish censors would delete. The net result is that *Yosippon*'s witness to Jesus, if there every was any, is mutilated. Robert Eisler thinks that the *Yosippon* did mention Jesus. Comparing three manuscripts, he has reconstructed what he thinks the original contained (p. 111):

> in those days there were wars and quarrels in Judaea between the Pharisees and the "robbers of our nation" who strayed after Jesus, son of Joseph. And there went out some of those robbers and wandered in the wilderness where this is no way, and made unto themselves signs and miracles through their sorceries. And there came some of the sons of the city of Edom, robbers (too), and they (all) went into the hiding-places of Edom and seduced many (saying): "in the days (of . . .) Jesus came to . . . (us). . . . Arrived has the angel (messenger) of God foretold by the prophets throughout the ages, and he has said . . . but they listened not to him, but sought how they might kill him.

In support of his reconstruction he notes that the *Toledot Yeshu* (see ch. 7) apparently depends upon the earlier anti-Christian versions of the *Yosippon*. The opening paragraphs of this curious book may support Eisler's reconstruction.

The *Yosippon* has been translated into Arabic, Ethiopic, Latin, and Old Slavonic. Various Hebrew editions are available (see Flusser, "Josippon," *EncJud*; "Jossipon, a Medieval Hebrew Version"). An old and unreliable English translation is Peter Morvvyng, *A Compendious and Most Marvelous History of the Latter Tymes of the Jewes Commune-Weale* (1558; republished about twelve times from 1561 to 1662). The title page of this work adds, "in Hebrew by Joseph ben Gorion, a nobleman of the same countrey, who saw the most things himselfe, and was the author and doer of a great part of the same" (Reiner 1969–1970, "Yosippon," 132 n. 12).

Bibliography: E. BAMMEL, "Jesus as a Political Agent in a Version of the Josippon," in *Jesus and the Politics of His Day* (ed. E. Bammel and C. F. D. Moule; Cambridge: Cambridge University Press, 1984), 197–209; S. BOWMAN, "Dates in *Sepher Yosippon*," in *Pursuing the Text* (ed. Reeves and Kampen), 349–59; R. EISLER, *The Messiah Jesus and John the Baptist*, 93–112; D. FLUSSER, "Josippon," *EncJud* 10:296–98; IDEM, "Josippon, a Medieval Hebrew Version of Josephus," in *Josephus, Judaism, and Christianity* (ed. Feldman and Hata), 386–97; A. A. NEUMAN, "Josippon and the Apocrypha," *JQR* 43 (1952–1953): 1–26; IDEM, "A Note on John the Baptist and Jesus in Josippon," *HUCA* 23 (1950–1951): 137–49; J. REINER, "The English Yosippon," *JQR* 58 (1967–1968): 126–42; IDEM, "The Original Hebrew Yosippon in the Chronicle of Jerahmeel," *JQR* 60 (1969–1970): 128–46; H. L. STRACK and G. STEMBERGER, *ITM* 358–59; S. ZEITLIN, "Josippon," *JQR* 53 (1962–1963): 277–97.

General Bibliography for Josephus

H. W. ATTRIDGE, "Josephus and His Works," *SJWSTP* 185–232; D. A. BARISH, "The Autobiography of Josephus and the Hypothesis of a Second Edition of his

Antiquities," *HTR* 71 (1978): 61–75; O. BETZ, K. HAACKER, and M. HENGEL, *Josephus-Studien: Untersuchungen zu Josephus, dem antiken Judentum, und dem Neuen Testament* (O. Michel FS; Göttingen: Vandenhoeck & Ruprecht, 1974); P. BILDE, *Flavius Josephus between Jerusalem and Rome: His Life, His Works, and Their Importance* (JSPSup 2; Sheffield, Eng.: JSOT Press, 1988); S. J. D. COHEN, *Josephus in Galilee and Rome: His Vita and Development as a Historian* (Studies in the Classical Tradition 8; Leiden: Brill, 1979); R. EISLER, *The Messiah Jesus and John the Baptist* (New York: Dial, 1931); L. H. FELDMAN, *The Importance of Jerusalem as Viewed by Josephus* (Ramat Gan: Bar-Ilan University Press, 1998); IDEM, *Josephus and Modern Scholarship (1937–1980)* (New York: de Gruyter, 1984) (bibliography on Slavonic Josephus, pp. 48–56; on *Yosippon*, pp. 57–74); L. H. FELDMAN and G. HATA, eds., *Josephus, the Bible, and History* (Detroit: Wayne State University Press, 1987); IDEM, *Josephus, Judaism, and Christianity* (Detroit: Wayne State University Press, 1987); G. HATA, "Is the Greek Version of Josephus' Jewish War a Translation or a Rewriting of the First Version?" *JQR* 66 (1975): 89–108; S. MASON, *Josephus and the New Testament* (2d ed.; Peabody, Mass.: Hendrickson, 2003); T. RAJAK, *Josephus: The Historian and His Society* (Philadelphia: Fortress, 1983); J. C. REEVES and J. KAMPEN, eds., *Pursuing the Text* (B. Z. Wacholder FS; JSOTSup 184; Sheffield, Eng.: Sheffield Academic Press, 1994); H. SCHRECKENBERG, *Bibliographie zu Flavius Josephus* (ALGHJ 1; Leiden: Brill, 1968); IDEM, *Bibliographie zu Flavius Josephus: Supplementband mit Gesamtregister* (ALGHJ 14; Leiden: Brill, 1979); R. J. H. SHUTT, *Studies in Josephus* (London: SPCK, 1961); H. St. J. THACKERAY, *Josephus, the Man and the Historian* (New York: Jewish Institute of Religion, 1929; repr., New York: Ktav, 1967) (regarded by Attridge as the best general introduction available); G. E. STERLING, *Historiography and Self-Definition: Josephos, Luke-Acts, and Apologetic Historiography* (New York: Brill, 1992); J. C. VANDERKAM, *An Introduction to Early Judaism* (Grand Rapids: Eerdmans, 2001), 142–46.

The Targums

Produced over generations in the homiletical and liturgical setting of the synagogue, the Targumim constitute an Aramaic translation/paraphrase/interpretation of the Hebrew Bible. The word "Targum," from the Aramaic word *trgm*, "to translate," basically means a paraphrase or interpretive translation. The Aramaic translator was called the meturgeman. Targumim to all of the books of the OT, with the exceptions of Ezra-Nehemiah and Daniel (large portions of which were already in Aramaic), are extant in manuscripts which date, for the most part, from the Middle Ages. Until recent years NT interpreters have made little use of them, primarily because it was assumed that they originated too late to be relevant. However, Paul Kahle's discovery and publication of the Cairo Genizah fragments and the discovery of Targum fragments among the Dead Sea

Scrolls (4QtgLev, 4QtgJob, 11QtgJob, and possibly 6Q19, which may be a Targum on Genesis) have led several scholars to reconsider this assumption.

Martin McNamara, in addition to others, has argued that there existed in NT times, and probably even earlier, a Palestinian Targum, which, he thinks, "is now found in its entirety in Codex Neofiti, and in part in the texts of Pseudo-Jonathan, the Fragment Targum and in fragments from the Cairo Geniza" (*Targum and Testament*, 12). Joseph Fitzmyer, in reviews of McNamara's *The New Testament and the Palestinian Targum* (*see TS* 29 [1968]: 321–26) and of Matthew Black's *An Aramaic Approach* on the Aramaic tradition underlying the Gospels (*see CBQ* 30 [1968]: 417–28) thinks that it is more appropriate to speak of Palestinian Targumim. Moreover, he is skeptical of the relevance of the Targumim for NT research, for he is not persuaded of their great antiquity by the arguments presented thus far. He thinks that appeals to parallels with the NT lead to circular reasoning: A parallel with the NT suggests antiquity of Targum, therefore Targum is relevant for NT comparison. McNamara has said by way of reply that parallels also occur in other datable traditions (such as early Fathers, early Jewish art, Qumran, early OT Pseudepigrapha, early translations of the OT, and early Jewish liturgy). From such comparative work he concludes, and I think rightly, that the Targumim do preserve some tradition that dates to, and possibly before, the time of the NT. Bruce Chilton's approach, by which he searches for "dictional" and "thematic coherence" between Jesus' sayings and readings distinctive of the Isaiah Targum, has sharpened comparative analysis, with positive results (see discussion of the *Targum Isaiah* below, as well as "Themes," in which NT examples are given).

The standard Aramaic edition is A. Sperber, *The Bible in Aramaic Based on Old Manuscripts and Printed Texts* (4 vols.; Leiden: Brill, 1959–1968). Other Aramaic editions will be noted below. A *Comprehensive Aramaic Lexicon* (Baltimore: Johns Hopkins University Press) is being prepared under the direction of Delbert R. Hillers, Stephen A. Kaufman, and Joseph A. Fitzmyer. The English translation of all extant Targumim in the series The Aramaic Bible, from Publisher Michael Glazier (and now Liturgical Press), is nearly complete. The project director is Martin McNamara. The volumes that have appeared to date are listed in the relevant sections below.

Although dated, B. Grossfeld, *A Bibliography of Targum Literature* (3 vols.; vols. 1–2; Bibliographica Judaica 3, 8; Cincinnati: Hebrew Union College; vol. 3, New York: Sepher-Hermon, 1972–1990), is still very useful, especially for accessing older material.

A new journal devoted to Aramaic research has been launched, initially under the title *Journal for the Aramaic Bible* (1999–2001) and continued under the title *Aramaic Studies* (2003–). The journal provides bibliography. Several Targum modules are being prepared for the Accordance computer search engine.

Bibliography: D. R. G. BEATTIE and M. J. MCNAMARA, eds., *The Aramaic Bible: Targums in their Historical Context* (JSOTSup 166; Sheffield: Sheffield, 1994); M. BLACK, *An Aramaic Approach to the Gospels and Acts,* 35–49; K. J. CATHCART and M. MAHER, *Targumic and Cognate Studies;* B. D. CHILTON, "Rabbinic Literature: Targumim," *DNTB* 902–9; P. V.

M. FLESHER, ed., *Textual and Contextual Studies in the Pentateuchal Targums* (vol. 1 of *Targum Studies*); D. W. GOODING, "On the Use of the LXX for Dating Midrashic Elements in the Targums," *JTS* 25 (1974): 1–11; M. H. GOSHEN-GOTTSTEIN, *Aramaic Bible Versions: Comparative Selections and Glossary, Including Unpublished Chapters from the Palestinian Targum* (Jerusalem: Hebrew University Students Printing and Publishing House, 1963); S. A. KAUFMAN, "Dating the Language of the Palestinian Targums and Their Use in the Study of First Century C.E. Texts," in *The Aramaic Bible* (ed. Beattie and McNamara), 118–41; IDEM, "On Methodology in the Study of the Targums and Their Chronology," *JSNT* 23 (1985): 117–24; R. LE DÉAUT, *The Message of the New Testament and the Aramaic Bible (Targum)* (SubBi 5; Rome: Pontifical Biblical Institute, 1982); M. MCNAMARA, *The New Testament and the Palestinian Targum to the Pentateuch;* IDEM, *Targum and Testament;* IDEM, "Targumic Studies," *CBQ* 28 (1966): 1–19; A. SALVESEN, "Symmachus and the Dating of Targumic Traditions," *JAB* 2 (2000): 233–45; P. WERNBERG-MØLLER, "An Inquiry into the Validity of the Text-Critical Argument for an Early Dating of the Recently Discovered Palestinian Targum," *VT* 12 (1962): 312–31; A. D. YORK, "The Dating of Targumic Literature," *JSJ* 5 (1974): 49–62; IDEM, "The Targum in the Synagogue and the School," *JSJ* 10 (1979): 74–86.

Summaries

Targumim to the Pentateuch. Most of the Targumim are to the Pentateuch. The extant manuscripts and the traditions underlying them range in date from NT times to well into the Middle Ages. Four of these Targumim are complete (*Onqelos, Pseudo-Jonathan, Neofiti,* and the *Samaritan Targum*), one represents a selection of texts *(Fragmentary Targum),* and others are extant only as fragments (Cairo Genizah fragments and 4QtgLeviticus).

Targum Onqelos. Targum Onqelos is regarded as the official Targum to the Pentateuch. It is the most literal of the Targumim to the Pentateuch, but it is not without some noteworthy interpretive elements, including mishnaic material (e.g., See Gen 6:1–6; 49:1–27; Num 24; Deut 32–33). Some scholars think that a "proto-Onqelos" may have originated in Palestine prior to the defeat of Simon Bar Kokhba, with the final redaction taking shape sometime in the third century and probably with Babylonian influence. This conclusion may receive a measure of support from rabbinic tradition. According to the Babylonian Talmud (cf. *b. Giṭ.* 56b; *b. Meg.* 3a) the author was Onqelos the Proselyte, a disciple of Rabbi Eliezer ben Hyrcanus (and possibly Aqiba). However, this Onqelos, who is referred to as Aqylos in the Palestinian Talmud (*y. Meg.* 1.9) may actually be the translator of the Greek recension of the LXX, which goes by the name of Aquila. In any case, the possibility of a Pentateuch Targum existing as early as the first century has to be taken seriously in view of the discovery among the Qumran writings of Targumim to Job and Leviticus.

The SBL abbreviation for *Targum Onqelos* is *Tg. Onq.* The biblical book, with chapter and verse, is cited in the conventional manner: *Tg. Onq.* Lev 3:2.

Text: A. BERLINER, *Text, nach editio Sabioneta* (vol. 1 of *Targum Onkelos;* Berlin: Gorze-lanczyk, 1884); A. SPERBER, *The Pentateuch according to Targum Onkelos* (vol. 1 of *The Bible in Aramaic Based on Old Manuscripts and Printed Texts;* Leiden: Brill, 1959). *Translation:* M. ABERBACH and B. GROSSFELD, *Targum Onkelos to Genesis* (Hoboken, N.J.: Ktav, 1982) (Aramaic with English translation); I. DRAZIN, *Targum Onkelos to Deuteronomy* (Hoboken, N.J.: Ktav, 1982) (Aramaic with English translation); IDEM, *Targum Onkelos to Exodus* (New York: Ktav, 19907) (Aramaic with English translation); IDEM, *Targum Onkelos to Leviticus* (Hoboken, N.J.: Ktav, 1994) (Aramaic with English translation); IDEM, *Targum Onkelos to Numbers* (Hoboken, N.J.: Ktav, 1998) (Aramaic with English translation); J. W. ETHERIDGE, *The Targum of Onkelos and Jonathan ben Uzziel on the Pentateuch with the Fragments of the Jerusalem Targum* (unreliable in places); B. GROSSFELD, *Targum Onqelos to Genesis; Targum Onqelos to Exodus; The Targum Onqelos to Leviticus and the Targum Onqelos to Numbers; The Targum Onqelos to Deuteronomy* (ArBib 6–9; Wilmington, Del.: Glazier, 1988). *Critical Study:* M. ABERBACH, "Patriotic Tendencies in Targum Onkelos," *JHebS* 1 (1969): 13–24; H. BARNSTEIN, *The Targum of Onkelos to Genesis: A Critical Inquiry into the Value of the Text Exhibited by Yemen MSS Compared with That of the European Recension, Together with Some Specimens of the Oriental Text* (London: David Nutt, 1896); A. BERLINER, *Einleitung in das Targum* (vol. 2 of *Targum Onkelos;* Berlin: Gorze-lanczyk, 1884); J. W. BOWKER, "Haggadah in the Targum Onqelos," *JSS* 12 (1967): 51–65; E. BREDEREK, *Konkordanz zum Targum Onkelos* (BZAW 9; Giessen: Töpelmann, 1906); P. V. M. FLESHER, ed., *Targum and Peshitta* (vol. 2 of *Targum Studies*); M. H. GOSHEN-GOTTSTEIN, "The Language of Targum Onqelos and the Model of Literary Diaglossia in Aramaic," *JNES* 37 (1978): 169–79; B. GROSSFELD, "Targum Onqelos, Halakha, and the Halakhic Midrashim," in *The Aramaic Bible* (ed. Beattie and McNamara), 228–46; M. L. KLEIN, "Manuscripts of Proto-Massorah to Onqelos," in *Estudios masoréticos (X Congreso de la IOMS)* (ed. E. Fernández Tejero; Textos y estudios Cardenal Cisneros 55; Madrid: Consejo Superior de Investigaciones Científicas, 1993), 73–88; G. J. KUIPER, "A Study of the Relationship between 'a Genesis Apocryphon' and the Pentateuchal Targumim in Genesis 14:1–12," in *In Memoriam Paul Kahle* (ed. M. Black and G. Fohrer), 149–61; C. MÜLLER-KESSLER, "The Earliest Evidence for Targum Onqelos from Babylonia and the Question of Its Dialect and Origin," *JAB* 3 (2001): 181–98; G. VERMES, "Haggadah in the Onkelos Targum," *JSS* 8 (1963): 159–69.

Targum Pseudo-Jonathan. Pseudo-Jonathan (also called *Targum Yerushalmi I*) was at one time called *Targum Jonathan,* perhaps because of the confusion caused by the abbreviation "T.Y." inscribed on one of the major manuscripts. "T.Y." was an abbreviation for *Targum Yerushalmi* (i.e., Jerusalem) but was probably taken as an abbreviation for *Targum Yehonathan* (i.e., Jonathan). It came to be called *Pseudo-Jonathan* so as not to be confused with *Targum Jonathan* to the Prophets. *Pseudo-Jonathan* contains a diversity of traditions. Some of it is early (e.g., Gen 37:36); some of it is late (Gen 21:21, where the names of Mohammed's wife and daughter appear). Some is Palestinian; some is European. Scholars are divided over the questions of this Targum's origin and relation to the other Targumim. Martin McNamara and others have pointed out that some of its distinctive readings offer remarkable parallels to the NT. Its paraphrase of Lev 22:28 reads: "My people, children of Israel, as our Father is merciful in heaven, so shall you be merciful on earth." This reading is quite close to a saying of Jesus found in Q (Matt 5:48; Luke 6:36: "Be merciful, even as your Father is merciful"). Its midrashic paraphrase of the story of Jannes and Jambres (Exod 7:11–12) parallels 2 Tim 3:8.

The SBL abbreviation is *Tg. Ps.-J.*, e.g., *Tg. Ps.-J.* Num 11:8.

Text: E. G. CLARK, *Targum Pseudo-Jonathan of the Pentateuch: Text and Concordance* (Hoboken, N.J.: Ktav, 1984) (British MS Add. 27031); M. GINSBURGER, *Pseudo-Jonathan: Thargum Jonathan ben Usiël zum Pentateuch* (Berlin: Calvary, 1903; repr., Jerusalem: Makor, 1969; Hildesheim: Olms, 1971); D. RIEDER, *Pseudo-Jonathan: Targum Jonathan ben Uzziel on the Pentateuch Copied from the London MS (British Museum Add. 27031)* (Jerusalem: Salomon's, 1974). *Translation:* J. BOWKER, *The Targums and Rabbinic Literature* (Cambridge: Cambridge University Press, 1969), 95–297 (most of Genesis, with comparative notes); E. G. CLARKE, *Targum Pseudo-Jonathan: Deuteronomy* (ArBib 5B; Collegeville, Minn.: Liturgical Press, 1998); J. W. ETHERIDGE, *The Targum of Onkelos and Jonathan ben Uzziel on the Pentateuch with the Fragments of the Jerusalem Targum* (unreliable in places); M. MAHER, *Targum Pseudo-Jonathan: Genesis* (ArBib 1b; Wilmington, Del.: Glazier, 1992); M. MCNAMARA and E. G. CLARKE, *Targum Neofiti 1 and Pseudo-Jonathan: Numbers* (ArBib 4; Collegeville, Minn.: Liturgical Press, 1995); M. MCNAMARA, R. HAYWARD, and M. MAHER, *Targum Neofiti 1 and Pseudo-Jonathan: Exodus* (ArBib 2; Collegeville, Minn.: Liturgical Press, 1994); IDEM, *Targum Neofiti 1 and Pseudo-Jonathan: Leviticus* (ArBib 3; Collegeville, Minn.: Liturgical Press, 1994). *Critical Study:* E. CASHDAN, "Names and the Interpretation of Names in the Pseudo-Jonathan Targum to the Book of Genesis," in *Essays Presented to Chief Rabbi Israel Brodie on the Occasion of His Seventieth Birthday* (ed. H. J. Zimmels et al.; London: Jew's College Press, 1967), 31–39; R. HAYWARD, "Red Heifer and Golden Calf: Dating Targum Pseudo-Jonathan," in *Textual and Contextual Studies in the Pentateuchal Targums* (vol. 1 of *Targum Studies;* ed. Flesher), 9–32; G. J. KUIPER, *The Pseudo-Jonathan Targum and Its Relationship to Targum Onkelos* (SEAug 9; Rome: Institutum Patristicum Augustinianum, 1972); M. MAHER, "Targum Pseudo-Jonathan of Deuteronomy 1.1–8," in *The Aramaic Bible* (ed. Beattie and McNamara), 264–90; IDEM, "Targum Pseudo-Jonathan of Exodus 2.21," in *Targumic and Cognate Studies* (ed. Cathcart and Maher), 81–99; R. SYRÉN, "Ishmael and Esau in the Book of *Jubilees* and Targum Pseudo-Jonathan," in *The Aramaic Bible* (ed. Beattie and McNamara), 310–15; H. SYSLING, "The Use of Dramatic and Erotic Elements as a Literary Technique in Targum Pseudo-Jonathan," *JAB* 1 (1999): 147–61.

Fragmentary Targum. The *Fragmentary Targum* (also called *Targum Yerushalmi II*) is aptly named, for it is made up of a selection of texts and targumic paraphrases (about 30 percent of the Pentateuch). There are five manuscripts extant. Since they cover approximately the same passages, it is assumed that they derive from a common ancestor. Again scholars are divided as to its origin, purpose, and relation to the other Targumim. It is valuable because it contains some unique readings, some of which appear to be quite early.

In the Michael Glazier Aramaic Bible, English translations of, and notes concerning, the *Fragmentary Targum* are interspersed in the volumes treating *Targum Neofiti* (ArBib 1a, 2, 3, 4, and 5a). Michael Klein presents the texts of the following MSS:

MS P = Paris–Bibliothèque nationale Hébr. 110
MS V = Vatican Ebr. 440
MS L = Leipzig–Universität B. H. fol. 1
MS N = Nürnberg
MS J = Jewish Theological Seminary 605
MS Br = British Museum Or. 10794List

The SBL abbreviation is *Frg. Tg.*, e.g., *Frg. Tg.* Num 11:26.

Text: M. GINSBURGER, *Das Fragmententhargum* (Berlin: Calvary, 1899; repr., Jerusalem: Makor, 1969) (MS Paris). *Text and Translation:* M. L. KLEIN, *The Fragment-Targums of the Pentateuch* (2 vols.; AnBib 76; Rome: Pontifical Biblical Institute, 1980) (MS Vatican). *Critical Study:* J. BASSFREUND, "Das Fragmenten-Targum zum Pentateuch: Sein Ursprung und Charakter und sein Verhältnis zu den anderen pentateuchischen Targumim," *MGWJ* 40 (1896): 1–14, 49–67, 97–109, 145–63, 241–52, 353–65, 396–405; M. C. DOUBLES, "Indications of Antiquity in the Orthography and Morphology of the Fragment Targum," in *In Memoriam Paul Kahle* (ed. M. Black and G. Fohrer), 79–89; M. GINSBURGER, "Die Fragmente des Thargum Jeruschalmi zum Pentateuch," *ZDMG* 57 (1903): 67–80; IDEM, "Zum Fragmententhargum," *MGWJ* 41 (1897): 289–96, 340–49; M. L. KLEIN, "The Extant Sources of the Fragmentary Targum to the Pentateuch," *HUCA* 46 (1975): 115–37; IDEM, "A Neglected MS of a Palestinian Fragment-Targum from the Cairo Genizah," *Text* 10 (1982): 26–36.

Targum Neofiti. Alejandro Díez Macho's discovery of *Targum Neofiti* (or *Neophyti*) was a sensation for Targum scholars. Some scholars think that it may have originated in the second century C.E. or even earlier. It is sometimes called *Neofiti 1* because it is manuscript 1 of the Neofiti collection of the Vatican Library. The SBL abbreviation is *Tg. Neof.*, e.g., *Tg. Neof.* Gen 1:1.

Text and Translation: A. DÍEZ MACHO, *Neophyti 1* (6 vols.; Madrid and Barcelona: Consejo Superior de Investigaciones Cientificas, 1968–1979); M. MCNAMARA, *Targum Neofiti 1: Deuteronomy* (ArBib 5A; Collegeville, Minn.: Liturgical Press, 1997); IDEM, *Targum Neofiti 1: Genesis* (ArBib 1a; Wilmington, Del.: Glazier, 1992); M. MCNAMARA and E. G. CLARKE, *Targum Neofiti 1 and Pseudo-Jonathan: Numbers* (ArBib 4; Collegeville, Minn.: Liturgical Press, 1995); M. MCNAMARA, R. HAYWARD, and M. MAHER, *Targum Neofiti 1 and Pseudo-Jonathan: Exodus* (ArBib 2; Collegeville, Minn.: Liturgical Press, 1994); IDEM, *Targum Neofiti 1 and Pseudo-Jonathan: Leviticus* (ArBib 3; Collegeville, Minn.: Liturgical Press, 1994). *Critical Study:* B. J. BAMBERGER, "Halakic Elements in the Neofiti Targum: A Preliminary Statement," *JQR* 66 (1975): 27–38; S. BROCK, "The Two Ways and the Palestinian Targum" in *A Tribute to Geza Vermes: Essays on Jewish and Christian Literature and History* (ed. P. R. Davies and R. T. White; JSOTSup 100; Sheffield: JSOT Press, 1990), 139–52; A. DÍEZ MACHO, "The Recently Discovered Palestinian Targum: Its Antiquity and Relationship with the Other Targums," in *Congress Volume, Oxford, 1957* (VTSup 7; Leiden: Brill, 1960), 222–45; M. C. DOUBLES, "Towards the Publication of the Extant Texts of the Palestinian Targum(s)," *VT* 15 (1965): 16–26; B. B. LEVY, *Targum Neophyti 1: A Textual Study* (2 vols.; New York: University Press of America, 1986–1987); S. LUND, "The Sources of the Variant Readings to Deuteronomy 1:1–29:17 of Codex Neofiti I," in *In Memoriam Paul Kahle* (ed. M. Black and G. Fohrer), 167–73; S. LUND and J. FOSTER, *Variant Versions of Targumic Traditions within Codex Neofiti 1* (SBLAS 2; Missoula, Mont.: Scholars Press, 1977); M. F. MARTIN, "The Palaeographical

Character of Codex Neofiti I," *Text* 3 (1963): 1–35; E. M. MENN, "Sanctification of the (Divine) Name: Targum Neofiti's 'Translation' of Genesis 38.25–26," in *The Function of Scripture in Early Jewish and Christian Tradition* (ed. C. A. Evans and J. A. Sanders; JSNTSup 154; SSEJC 6; Sheffield: Sheffield, 1998), 206–40.

Cairo Genizah Fragments. Sometime in the 1880s or 1890s, avaricious officials of the Ben-Ezra Synagogue began selling medieval documents from the synagogue's genizah. (A genizah [from Aramaic *genaz*, "to set aside" or "hide"] is a closet where sacred books that have been set aside or withdrawn from service are placed in storage.) Most of these documents were a thousand years old and for some reason had not been disposed of. These purchased documents began to appear in universities, libraries, and museums throughout Europe and North America. This led Solomon Schechter, reader in talmudic literature at the University of Cambridge, in the winter of 1896–1897 to journey to Cairo, where he was able to take possession—with the chief rabbi's permission—of some 140,000 documents (see Reif 1979). It is estimated that there may have been as many as 200,000 fragments from this genizah (though it is speculated that the genizot of other synagogues and burial places also contributed to his vast lot). Most of these fragments are of biblical manuscripts, the Mishna, the Tosefta, the Talmud, Targumim, and a variety of other writings, including poetry, medicine, and magic. Manuscripts are in Hebrew, Aramaic, Latin, Greek, and Arabic. It is estimated that the Cairo synagogue genizah yielded about 2,000 Targum MSS and fragments. What Qumran has been for biblical studies and the study of early Judaism and Christianity, the Cairo Genizah has been for Targum studies.

In 1930 Paul Kahle published the fragments of six manuscripts found in the genizah. Some believe that these fragments represent the Palestinian Targum. Alejandro Díez Macho eventually published four additional fragments of a seventh manuscript. Kahle dated the oldest fragments to 600–800 C.E. (for more on this question, see Hopkins). Michael Klein has published more materials. Other than the targumic materials found at Qumran, these fragments are several centuries older than the other extant Targum manuscripts. Their discovery cast Targum studies into a new light. What follows is a partial listing of the contents of the Palestinian Targum, not including the Tosefta Targumim (based on Kahle and Klein):

MS A:	Exod 4:7–11; 20:24–23:14
MS B:	Gen 2:17–3:6; 4:4–16
MS C:	Gen 31:38–54; 32:13–29; 34:9–25; 35:6–15; 41:32–41
MS D:	Gen 7:17; 8:8; 36:8–9, 24; 37:19–34; 38:16–26; 43:7–44:23; 46:26–47:5; 47:29–48:21; Exod 5:20–6:10; 7:10–22; 9:21–33; 39:23–37; 40:9–27; Deut 5:19–26; 26:18–27:11; 28:15–18, 26–29
MS E:	Gen 6:18–7:15; 9:5–23; 28:17–31:34; 37:15–44; 38:16–39:10; 40:5–18; 40:43–53; 41:6–26, 43–57; 42:34–43:10; 43:23–44:4
MS H:	Gen 15:1–4
MS Z:	Gen 44:16–20; 47:27–49:17

There is no SBL abbreviation for the Cairo Genizah fragments. I would recommend using "*C. Tg.*" for Cairo Genizah, followed by the letter designating the
appropriate MS, e.g., *C. Tg.* A Exod 21:1, *C. Tg.* B Gen 4:4, *C. Tg.* C Gen 31:38, and
so forth.

Text: P. KAHLE, "Das palästinische Pentateuch-Targum," in *Masoreten des Westens* (2 vols.;
Stuttgart: Kohlhammer, 1930; repr., Hildesheim: Olms, 1967), 2:1–13. *Text and Translation:* M. L. KLEIN, *Genizah Manuscripts of Palestinian Targum to the Pentateuch* (2 vols.;
Cincinnati: Hebrew Union College Press, 1986) (vol. 1 presents English and Aramaic on
facing pages; vol. 2 presents plates). *Critical Study:* A. DÍEZ MACHO, "Nuevos fragmentos
del Targum palestinense," *Sef* 15 (1955): 31–39; S. HOPKINS, "The Oldest Dated Document in the Genizah?" in *Studies in Judaism and Islam* (ed. S. Morag; S. D. Goitein FS; Jerusalem: Magnes Press, 1981), 83–98; P. KAHLE, *The Cairo Geniza* (2d ed.; Oxford:
Blackwell, 1959); M. L. KLEIN, "Cairo Genizah Targum Texts: Old and New," in *The Ara-
maic Bible* (ed. Beattie and McNamara), 18–29; IDEM, "New Fragments of Palestinian
Targum from the Cairo Genizah," *Sef* 49 (1989): 123–33; IDEM, *Targum Manuscripts in the
Cambridge Genizah Collections* (Cambridge: Cambridge University Press, 1992); S. C.
REIF, "The Cairo Genizah and Its Treasures with Special Reference to Biblical Studies," in
The Aramaic Bible (ed. Beattie and McNamara), 30–50; IDEM, *A Guide to the Taylor-
Schechter Genizah Collection* (2d ed.; Cambridge: Cambridge University Library, 1979).

6QGen? ar. 6QGen? ar (= 6Q19 *Targum of Genesis?*) is a small Aramaic fragment
that may constitute a fragment of a Genesis Targum. The surviving words, "of the
sons of Ham . . . the peoples . . . ," cohere with Gen 10:20 ("These are the descendants of Ham, by their families, their languages, their lands, and their nations")
but do not match exactly any of the extant Targumim. The text, however, is too
limited to decide the question.

Text: M. BAILLET, J. T. MILIK, and R. DE VAUX, *Les 'petites grottes' de Qumrân* (DJDJ 3; Oxford: Clarendon, 1962), 136. *Text and Translation:* F. GARCÍA MARTÍNEZ and E. J. C.
TIGCHELAAR, *4Q274–11Q31* (vol. 2 of *The Dead Sea Scrolls Study Edition*), 1156–57.

4QtgLev. 4QtgLev (= 4Q156) is a fragment of a Targum to Leviticus found in
Cave 4 of the caves near Qumran. All that is extant is Lev 16:12–15, 18–21. This
fragment proves that written Targumim to the Pentateuch existed as early as the
first century C.E.

Text: R. DE VAUX and J. T. MILIK, *Qumrân grotte 4,II*, 86–89, 92–93. *Text and Translation:*
F. GARCÍA MARTÍNEZ and E. J. C. TIGCHELAAR, *1Q1–4Q273* (vol. 1 of *The Dead Sea Scrolls
Study Edition*), 302–3. *Critical Study:* A. ANGERSTORFER, "Überlegungen zu Sprache und
Sitz im Leben des Toratargums 4QtgLev (4Q156), sein Verhältnis zu Targum Onkelos,"
BN 55 (1990): 18–35; J. A. FITZMYER, "The Targum of Leviticus from Qumran Cave 4,"
Maarav 1 (1978): 5–21; L. T. STUCKENBRUCK, "Bibliography on 4QTgLev (4Q156)," *JSP*
10 (1992): 53–55.

Samaritan Targum. The *Samaritan Targum* survives in eight extant manuscripts,
only one of which is complete. Of these manuscripts the oldest one dates to the
twelfth century. Unlike the Jewish Targumim, the *Samaritan Targum* represents

an attempt to translate word for word (though some paraphrase is present). Portions of the *Samaritan Targum* are quoted in other Samaritan writings, such as *Memar Marqah* (see ch. 11). The *Samaritan Targum*, of course, translates only the Pentateuch (see also discussion of the Samaritan Pentateuch in ch. 4). The SBL abbreviation is *Sam. Tg.*, e.g., *Sam. Tg.* Gen 2:7.

Text: A. BRÜLL, *Das samaritanische Targum zum Pentateuch* (5 vols.; Frankfurt am Main: Wilhelm Erras, 1873–1876; repr., 5 vols. in 1; New York: Olms, 1971); J. W. NUTT, *Fragments of a Samaritan Targum* (London: Trübner, 1874; repr., New York: Olms, 1980); A. TAL, *The Samaritan Targum of the Pentateuch: A Critical Edition* (3 vols.; Tel Aviv: Tel Aviv University Press, 1980–1983). *Critical Study:* M. FLORENTIN, "The Object Suffixes in Samaritan Aramaic and the Modes of Their Attachment to the Verb," *AbrN* 29 (1991): 67–82; A. TAL, "Divergent Traditions of the Samaritan Pentateuch as Reflected by Its Aramaic Targum," *JAB* 1 (1999): 297–314; IDEM, "Euphemisms in the Samaritan Targum of the Pentateuch," *AramSt* 1 (2003): 109–29; IDEM, "The Samaritan Targum in the Pentateuch—Its Distinctive Characteristic and its Metamorphosis," in *Proceedings of the Sixth World Congress of Jewish Studies, Division A: The Period of the Bible* (ed. A. Shinan; Internationaler Kongress für Studien zum Judentum 6; Jerusalem: World Union of Jewish Studies, 1977), 111–17; IDEM, "The Samaritan Targum of the Pentateuch," *Mikra* 189–216; IDEM, "The Samaritan Targumic Version of 'The Blessing of Moses' (Dtn 33) according to an Unpublished Ancient Fragment," *AbrN* 24 (1986): 178–95; IDEM, "The So-Called Cuthean Words in the Samaritan Aramaic Vocabulary," *AramSt* 2 (2004): 107–17.

Targum of the Prophets. It is conventional to refer to "Targum Jonathan to the Prophets," a convention that probably originated with the tradition that the *Targum of the Prophets* was composed by Jonathan ben Uzziel (*b. Meg.* 3a). Some scholars (e.g., Smolar and Aberbach) have argued that the Targum was produced by the school of Aqiba, but this hypothesis is problematic. Bruce Chilton has argued that the Targum reflects layers of tradition, so that it is better to speak of editions and meturgemanim, rather than sources and one principal meturgeman (or school). He also thinks that it is better to view the respective Targumim to the various prophets as more or less distinctive works. In other words, there really is not a unified "Jonathan Targum" with its own distinctive features, as in the case of *Onqelos* over against *Neofiti.* Samson Levey's survey of the appearance of "Messiah" seems to bear this out, for the appearance and function of the messianic idea varies, at times greatly, from one prophet to the next (compare Ezekiel with Isaiah, for example).

The *Targumim of the Prophets* are abbreviated thus: *Tg. Isa.* 5:1–7, *Tg. Jer.* 23:1, and so forth.

Text: P. DE LAGARDE, *Prophetae chaldaice* (Leipzig: Teubner, 1872; repr., Osnabrück: Zeller, 1967); A. SPERBER, *The Bible in Aramaic Based on Old Manuscripts and Printed Texts:* vol. 2, *The Former Prophets according to Targum Jonathan* (Leiden: Brill, 1959); vol. 3, *The Latter Prophets according to Targum Jonathan* (Leiden: Brill, 1962) (for fragments of the Palestinian *Targum of the Prophets* in vol. 3, see pp. 23–25 [Isa 10:32–33], 462–65 [Hab 3:1–5:11], 479–80 [Zech 2:14–15]). *Critical Study:* W. BACHER, "Kritische Untersuchungen zum Prophetentargum," *ZDMG* 28 (1874): 1–72; IDEM, "Notes on the Critique of the Text to the Targum of the Prophets," *JQR* 11 (1899): 651–55; P. CHURGIN, *Targum Jonathan to the Prophets* (YOSR 14; New Haven: Yale University Press, 1927; repr., New York: Ktav, 1983); C. H. CORNILL, "Das Targum zu den Propheten," *ZAW* 7 (1887): 177–202; R. P. GORDON, "Targum as Midrash: Contemporizing in the Targum to the Prophets," in *Proceedings of the Ninth World Congress of Jewish Studies, Division A* (ed. Assaf), 61–73; IDEM, "*Terra sancta* and the Territorial Doctrine of the Targum to the Prophets," in *Interpreting the Hebrew Bible* (ed. J. A. Emerton and S. C. Reif; E. I. J. Rosenthal FS; UCOP 32; Cambridge: Cambridge University Press, 1982), 119–31; R. HAYWARD, "Some Notes on Scribes and Priests in the Targum of the Prophets," *JJS* 36 (1985): 210–21; S. H. LEVEY, "The Date of Targum Jonathan to the Prophets," *VT* 21 (1971): 186–96; L. SMOLAR and M. ABERBACH, *Studies in Targum Jonathan to the Prophets* (New York: Ktav, 1983); A. SPERBER, "Zur Sprache des Prophetentargums," *ZAW* 45 (1927): 267–87.

The Former Prophets. The *Targum to the Former Prophets* (Joshua, Judges, 1–2 Samuel, and 1–2 Kings) contains traditions ranging from the second (and possibly earlier) to the seventh century. In many places the biblical narrative has been edited to reflect rabbinic law. One of the more interesting passages is 1 Sam 2:1–10, where Hannah's song of praise is transformed into an apocalypse. Israel's enemies will be routed, the wicked will be consigned to Gehenna, and the kingdom of the Messiah will be magnified (cf. 2:10). It is interesting to recall that Mary's Magnificat (Luke 1:46–55), which speaks of the overthrow of the mighty and the exaltation of the humble, was modeled after Hannah's song.

Bibliography: D. J. HARRINGTON and A. J. SALDARINI, *Targum Jonathan of the Former Prophets* (ArBib 10; Wilmington, Del.: Glazier, 1987); J. RIBERA FLORIT, "The Image of the Prophet in the Light of the Targum Jonathan and Jewish Literature in the Post-biblical Period," in *Proceedings of the Ninth World Congress of Jewish Studies, Division A* (ed. Assaf), 127–34; A. J. SALDARINI, "'Is Saul Also among the Scribes?': Scribes and Prophets in *Targum Jonathan*," in *"Open Thou Mine Eyes . . .": Essays on Aggadah and Judaica* (ed. H. J. Blumberg et al.; W. G. Braude FS; New York: Ktav, 1992), rev. and repr. in *The Interpretation of Scripture in Early Judaism and Christianity* (ed. Evans), 375–89; J.-W. WESSELIUS, "Completeness and Closure in Targumic Literature: The Emulation of Biblical Hebrew Poetry in Targum Jonathan to the Former Prophets," *JAB* 3 (2001): 237–47. *Joshua:* M. GASTER, "Das Buch Josua in hebräisch-samaritanischer Rezension," *ZDMG* 62 (1908): 494–549; F. PRAETORIUS, *Das Targum zu Josua in jemenischer Überlieferung* (Berlin: Reuther & Reichard, 1899). *Judges:* D. J. HARRINGTON, "The Prophecy of Deborah: Interpretive Homiletics in Targum Jonathan of Judges 5," *CBQ* 48 (1986): 432–42; F. PRAETORIUS, *Das Targum zum Buch der Richter in jemenischer Überlieferung* (Berlin: Reuther & Reichard, 1900); W. F. SMELIK, "Trouble in the Trees! Variant Selection and Tree Construction Illustrated by the Texts of Targum Judges," *AramSt* 1 (2003): 247–88. *1–2 Samuel:* R. P. GORDON, "Saul's Meningitis according to 1 Samuel XIX,4," *VT* 37 (1987): 39–49; D. J. HARRINGTON, "The Apocalypse of Hannah: Targum Jonathan of 1 Samuel 2:1–10," in *"Working with No Data": Semitic and Egyptian Studies* (ed. D. M. Golomb; T. O. Lambdin FS; Winona Lake, Ind.: Eisenbrauns, 1987), 147–52; E. VAN STAALDUINE-SULMAN, "Reward and Punishment in the Messianic Age (Targ. 2 Sam. 23.1–8)," *JAB* 1 (1999): 273–96; IDEM, "Translating with Subtlety: Some Unexpected Translations in the Targum of Samuel," *JAB* 3 (2001): 225–35; F. STUMMER, "Jüdische Traditionen in den Büchern Samuel und Könige," *Bib* 10 (1929): 3–30. *1–2 Kings:* F. STUMMER, "Jüdische Traditionen in den Büchern Samuel und Könige," *Bib* 10 (1929): 3–30.

The Latter Prophets. As briefly mentioned above, the Targumim to the Latter Prophets (Isaiah, Jeremiah, Ezekiel, and the Twelve Minor Prophets) bear individual characteristics. They will be considered briefly.

Targum Isaiah. Bruce Chilton has concluded that *Targum Isaiah* contains early traditions (i.e., first and second centuries C.E.), though the process of interpretation and redaction continued into the Islamic period. This Targum has proven to be valuable for NT study, particularly in Jesus research (see examples below). Chilton notes special interest in the Messiah (an idea largely shaped in the period between the two wars with Rome) and the regathering of the Jewish exiles. Isaiah 53 (or 52:13–53:12 to be precise) is interpreted messianically. But the Messiah is not a suffering Servant; he is a glorious and conquering hero. For example, whereas the Hebrew of 53:9 reads, "they made [the Servant's] grave with the wicked," *Targum Isaiah* reads, "[the Servant] will hand over the wicked to Gehenna." This Messiah will build the Sanctuary (53:5) and God will establish his kingdom (53:10).

Bibliography: B. D. CHILTON, *The Isaiah Targum* (ArBib 11; Wilmington, Del.: Glazier, 1987) (English translation, with bibliography); IDEM, *The Glory of Israel* (an important critical study of *Targum Isaiah*); S. R. DRIVER and A. NEUBAUER, *The Fifty-Third Chapter of Isaiah according to the Jewish Interpreters* (2 vols.; Oxford: J. Parker, 1876–1877; repr., New York: Ktav, 1969); A. HOUTMAN, "Targum Isaiah according to Felix Pratensis," *JAB* 1 (1999): 191–202; J. C. DE MOOR, "Multiple Renderings in the Targum of Isaiah," *JAB* 3 (2001): 161–80; D. MUÑOZ LÉON, "Memra in the Targum to Isaiah," in *Proceedings of the Ninth World Congress of Jewish Studies, Division A* (ed. Assaf), 135–42; J. F. STENNING, *The Targum of Isaiah* (Oxford: Clarendon, 1949) (Aramaic text with English translation); J. B. VAN ZIJL, *A Concordance to the Targum of Isaiah* (SBLAS 3; Missoula, Mont.: Scholars Press, 1979); IDEM, "Errata in Sperber's Edition of Targum Isaiah," *ASTI* 4 (1965): 189–91; 7 (1968–1969): 132–34.

Targum Jeremiah. Robert Hayward has concluded that the evidence suggests that *Targum Jeremiah* originated in the first century, perhaps even earlier (see 2:23–25, where the references to pagan idolatry might reflect the struggle with Antiochus IV and his successors). Of interest for Jesus research, Hayward concludes that *Targum Jeremiah*'s criticism of the high priesthood probably reflects first-century abuses. For example, see *Tg. Jer.* 8:10 ("robbers of money, both scribe and priest"). This emphasis could clarify and perhaps even corroborate the Synoptic portrait of Jesus' action in the temple (Mark 11:15–17).

Bibliography: R. HAYWARD, "Jewish Tradition in Jerome's Commentary on Jeremiah and the Targum of Jeremiah," *PIBA* 9 (1985): 100–120; IDEM, *The Targum of Jeremiah* (ArBib 12; Wilmington, Del.: Glazier, 1987) (English translation, with bibliography); W. MCKANE, "Jeremiah II 23–25: Observations on the Versions and History of Exegesis," *OtSt* 17 (1972): 73–88; H. P. SMITH, "The Targum to Jeremiah," *Hebraica* 4 (1888): 140–45.

Targum Ezekiel. Samson Levey thinks that much of the tradition of *Targum Ezekiel* derives from the late first century, perhaps reflecting the editorial hand of Yohanan ben Zakkai, who replaced messianic expectation and speculation with Merkabah mysticism. The fact that the word "messiah" never occurs in *Targum Ezekiel,* though messianic ideas are present, coheres with Levey's views. In other matters, especially those pertaining to halakah, *Targum Ezekiel* reflects the thinking of Rabbi Aqiba.

Bibliography: Y. KOMLOSH, "The Expository Traits of the Targum to Ezekiel," in *Essays on the Seventieth Anniversary of the Dropsie University (1909–1979)* (ed. A. I. Katsch and L. Nemoy; Philadelphia: Dropsie University Press, 1980), 289–96; S. H. LEVEY, *The Targum of Ezekiel* (ArBib 13; Wilmington, Del.: Glazier, 1987) (English translation, with bibliography); IDEM, "The Targum to Ezekiel," *HUCA* 46 (1975): 139–58; J. RIBERA FLORIT, "The Image of Israel according to the Targum of Ezekiel," in *Targumic and Cognate Studies* (ed. Cathcart and Maher), 111–21; IDEM, "The Use of the *Derash* Method in the *Targum of Ezekiel,*" in *The Interpretation of Scripture in Early Judaism and Christianity* (ed. Evans), 406–22.

Targum of the Minor Prophets. The *Targum of the Minor Prophets* originated in Palestine and was subsequently edited in Babylon. Although some traditions in all likelihood are pre-70 C.E., as coherence at points with 1QpHab would suggest (see Brownlee), most of the interpretive tradition took shape after the Roman destruction of Jerusalem. The *Targum of the Minor Prophets* offers several points of theological interest. In at least two places the Memra seems to take on the role of personality (cf. Amos 4:11; Hab 1:12). This could bear on the question of the relation of the Johannine Logos to the targumic Memra. There is also anticipation of resurrection in the Messianic Age (cf. Hos 6:2; 14:8; Zech 3:7) and hope for a new world (Mic 7:14; Hab 3:2).

Bibliography: K. J. CATHCART and R. P. GORDON, *The Targum of the Minor Prophets* (ArBib 14; Wilmington, Del.: Glazier, 1989) (English translation, with bibliography); G. FEIGON, *Yemenite Targum Manuscript to the Twelve Minor Prophets* (Enelow Memorial Collection at the Jewish Theological Seminary 27; San Diego, Calif.: Bureau of Jewish Education, 1971); R. P. GORDON, *Studies in the Targum to the Twelve Prophets;* IDEM, "The Targum to the Minor Prophets and the Dead Sea Texts: Textual and Exegetical Notes," *RevQ* 8 (1974): 425–29. **Hosea:** K. J. CATHCART, "Targum Jonathan to Hosea 1–3," *IBS* 10 (1988): 37–43. **Joel:** Y. KOMLOSH, "The Exegetical Method in Targum to Joel," in *Beer Sheba II: Studies by the Department of Bible and Ancient Near East* (ed. M. Cogan; S. Abramsky FS; Jerusalem: Magnes Press, 1985), 131–35. **Amos:** A. DÍEZ MACHO and A. G. LARRAYA, "El Ms. 4083f.9 de la Biblioteca Nacional y Universitaria de Estrasburgo (Fragmento de Amós 1:8–3:7, en hebreo y targum babilónnico)," *EstBib* 19 (1960): 91–95. **Obadiah:** E. LIPINSKI, "Obadiah 20," *VT* 23 (1973): 368–70; L. SMOLAR and M. ABERBACH, *Studies in Targum Jonathan to the Prophets* (New York: Ktav, 1983), 99–100, 122. **Jonah:** E. LEVINE, *The Aramaic Version of Jonah* (New York: Sepher-Hermon, 1975) (Aramaic with English translation). **Micah:** A. BAUMSTARK, "Neue orientalistische Probleme biblischer Textgeschichte," *ZDMG* 89 (1935): 89–118, here 115; IDEM, "Die Zitate des Mt.-Evangeliums aus dem Zwölfprophetenbuch," *Bib* 37 (1956): 296–313, here 299. **Nahum:** M. ADLER, "A Specimen of a Commentary and Collated Text of the Targum to the Prophets: Nahum," *JQR* 7 (1895): 630–57; R. P. GORDON, *Studies in the Targum to the Twelve*

Prophets, 41–45; J. RIBERA FLORIT, "La versión aramaica del profeta Nahum," *Anuario* 6 (1980): 291–322. **Habakkuk:** W. H. BROWNLEE, "The Habakkuk Midrash and the Targum of Jonathan," *JJS* 7 (1956): 169–86; R. P. GORDON, *Studies in the Targum to the Twelve Prophets,* 45–49, 83–95; N. WIEDER, "The Habakkuk Scroll and the Targum," *JJS* 4 (1953): 14–18. **Zephaniah:** R. P. GORDON, *Studies in the Targum to the Twelve Prophets,* 49–52; J. RIBERA FLORIT, "La versión aramaica del profeta Sofonías," *Estbib* 40 (1982): 127–58. **Haggai:** J. RIBERA FLORIT, "La versión aramaica del profeta Ageo," *Anuario* 4 (1978): 283–303. **Zechariah:** R. P. GORDON, "An Inner-Targum Corruption (Zech. I,8)," *VT* 25 (1975): 216–19; IDEM, *Studies in the Targum to the Twelve Prophets,* 52–56, 96–122; P. GRELOT, "Une Tosephta targoumique sur Zacharie, II, 14–15," *RB* 73 (1966): 197–211; T. JANSMA, "Inquiry into the Hebrew Text and the Ancient Versions of Zechariah IX–XIV: The Targum," *OtSt* 7 (1950): 9–23. **Malachi:** R. P. GORDON, *Studies in the Targum to the Twelve Prophets,* 56–61, 123–29; L. KRUSE-BLINKENBERG, "The Pesitta of the Book of Malachi," *ST* 20 (1966): 95–119; J. RIBERA FLORIT, "El Targum de Malaquias," *Estbib* 48 (1990): 171–97.

Targumim of the Writings. There is no official version of the *Targumim of the Writings* (Psalms, Proverbs, Job, Song of Songs, Ruth, Lamentations, Qohelet, Esther, and 1–2 Chronicles). There are no traditions of authors or relationship, as in the case of the Pentateuch or the Prophets, and so it is probably best to treat them as relatively independent works. Furthermore, these Targumim played no official role in the synagogue, though the Five Megilloth (Ruth, Qohelet, Song of Songs, Lamentations, Esther) functioned in holiday liturgy.

Bibliography: P. CHURGIN, *The Targum to Hagiographa* (New York: Horeb, 1945); B. GROSSFELD, ed., *The Targum to the Five Megilloth* (New York: Hermon, 1973); P. DE LAGARDE, *Hagiographa chaldaice* (Leipzig: Teubner, 1873; repr., Osnabrück: Zeller, 1967) (Aramaic text); E. LEVINE, *The Targum to the Five Megillot: Ruth, Ecclesiastes, Canticles, Lamentations, Esther* (Jerusalem: Makor, 1977) (Aramaic with English translation); A. SPERBER, *The Hagiographa* (vol. 4A of *The Bible in Aramaic;* Leiden: Brill, 1968) (Aramaic text of only Chronicles, Ruth, Song of Songs, Lamentations, Qohelet, and Esther).

Psalms. Targum Psalms, like most of the other Targumim to the Writings, contains traditions spanning centuries. Much appears to date from the Roman period. (The western Roman Empire is mentioned in 108:10.) Indeed, the earliest traditions likely derive from the first century C.E., and perhaps even earlier. One interesting reading may have something to do with the function of Ps 118:22 at the conclusion of the parable of the Wicked Vineyard Tenants (Mark 12:1–12). Whereas the Hebrew reads, "the stone which the builders rejected," the Aramaic reads, "the child [or son] which the builders rejected" thus linking the quotation more obviously to the rejected son of the parable proper. This passage will be discussed further in chapter 12 below. Some eight passages are interpreted overtly as messianic (see discussion below).

Bibliography: W. BACHER, "Das Targum zu den Psalmen," *MGWJ* 21 (1872): 408–16, 463–73; M. BERNSTEIN, "The 'Righteous' and the 'Wicked' in the Aramaic Version of Psalms," *JAB* 3 (2001): 5–26; IDEM, "Torah and Its Study in the Targum of Palms," in *Nazon Nahum: Studies in Jewish Law, Thought, and History* (ed. Y. Elman and J. S. Gurock;

N. Lamm FS; New York: Yeshiva University Press, 1997), 39–67; IDEM, "Translation Technique in the Targum to Psalms: Two Test Cases—Psalms 2 and 137," in *SBL Seminar Papers, 1994* (ed. E. H. Lovering; SBLSP 33; Atlanta: Scholars Press, 1994), 326–45; L. DÍEZ MERINO, "Haggadaic Elements in the Targum of Psalms," in *Proceedings of the Eighth World Congress of Jewish Studies, Division A: The Period of the Bible* (ed. D. Krone; Jerusalem: World Union of Jewish Studies, 1982), 131–37; IDEM, *Targum de Salmos: Edición príncipe del MS. Villa-Amil no. 5 de Alfonso de Zamora* (Bibliotheca hispana biblica 6; Madrid: Consejo de Investigaciones Cientificos, 1982); C. A. EVANS, "The Aramaic Psalter and the New Testament" (characteristics of the Aramaic Psalter are discussed on pp. 45–75); H. D. PREUSS, "Die Psalmenüberschriften in Targum und Midrash," *ZAW* 71 (1959): 44–54; J. SHUNARY, "Avoidance of Anthropomorphism in the Targum of Psalms," *Text* 5 (1966): 133–44; S. SPEIER, "Sieben Stellen des Psalmentargums in Handschriften und Druckausgaben: 3,7 44,17 45,6 49,11 68,15.20 125,1," *Bib* 48 (1967): 491–508; G. L. TECHEN, *Das Targum zu den Psalmen* (2 Vols.; Wismar: Grosse Stadtschule zu Wismar, 1896–1907); M. WILCOX, "The Aramaic Targum to Psalms," in *Proceedings of the Ninth World Congress of Jewish Studies, Division A* (ed. Assaf), 143–50.

Proverbs. Targum Proverbs presents scholars with a very curious feature: It appears that this Targum is based directly on the Syriac version of the OT (i.e., the Peshitta), rather than on the Hebrew Bible. Matthew Black (*Aramaic Approach,* 25) thinks that this is improbable, since it is hard to believe that in producing a Targum the Synagogue would depend on a Christian version of the Bible. But most scholars are persuaded that the evidence cannot be explained in any other way. If this is correct, the Targum cannot be older than the mid-second century, when the Peshitta first emerged. Another oddity about this Targum is the absence of midrashic expansions. There are modifications, but not to the degree one finds in the other Targumim.

Bibliography: V. APTOWITZER, "Mélanges: La traduction du Tétragramme dans le Targoum des Proverbes," *REJ* 54 (1907): 57–63; L. DÍEZ MERINO, *Targum de Proverbios: Edición principe del Ms. Villa–Amil no. 5 de Alfonso de Zamora* (Bibliotheca hispana biblica 11; Madrid: Consejo de Investigaciones Cientificos, 1984); J. F. HEALEY, "The Targum of Proverbs," in Mangan, Healey, and Knobel, *The Targums of Job, Proverbs, Qohelet* (English translation, with bibliography); A. KAMINKA, "Septuaginta und Targum zu Proverbia," *HUCA* 8–9 (1931–1932): 169–91.

Job. Céline Mangan has concluded that *Targum Job* probably represents an edited compilation of various Targumim of Job, extending from the first century into the eighth and ninth centuries. The likelihood that some traditions derived from the first century is supported by three facts: (1) Two copies of a Job Targum have been discovered at Qumran (11QtgJob = Job 17:14–42:11; 4QtgJob [4Q157] = Job 3:5–9; 4:16–5:4). (2) The Babylonian Talmud relates a story of a Job Targum found near the temple mount and shown to Hillel the Elder (ca. 50 C.E.; cf. *b. Šabb.* 115a). (3) There are several significant points of dictional coherence between *Targum Job* and first-century materials such as the NT and some of the Pseudepigrapha (some of these are discussed below).

Bibliography: L. DÍEZ MERINO, *Targum de Job: Edición principe del Ms. Villa–Amil no. 5 de Alfonso de Zamora* (Bibliotheca hispana biblica 8; Madrid: Consejo de Investigaciones Cientificos, 1984); J. A. FITZMYER, "Some Observations on the Targum of Job from Qumran Cave 11," *CBQ* 36 (1974): 503–24; F. GARCÍA MARTÍNEZ and E. J. C. TIGCHELAAR, *The Dead Sea Scrolls Study Edition. Volume One: 1Q1–4Q273* (Leiden, Brill, 1997), 303–4 (4QtgJob); IDEM, *The Dead Sea Scrolls Study Edition. Volume Two: 4Q274–11Q31.* (Leiden, Brill, 1998), 1184–1201 (11QtgJob); F. GARCÍA MARTÍNEZ, E. J. C. TIGCHELAAR, and A. S. VAN DER WOUDE, *Qumran Cave 11,II: 11Q2–18, 11Q20–30* (DJD 23; Oxford: Clarendon, 1998), 79–180 (11QtgJob); S. L. GOLD, "Targum or Translation: New Light on the Character of Qumran Job (11Q10) from a Synoptic Approach," *JAB* 3 (2001): 101–20; J. GRAY, "The Massoretic Text of the Book of Job, the Targum and the Septuagint Version in the Light of the Qumran Targum," *ZAW* 86 (1974): 331–50; S. A. KAUFMAN, "The Job Targum from Qumran," *JAOS* 93 (1973): 317–27; E. KUTSCH, "Die Textgliederung im hebräischen Hiobbuch sowie in 4QtgJob und in 11QtgJob," *BZ* 27 (1983): 221–28; C. MANGAN, "The Attitude to Women in the Prologue of Targum Job," in *Targumic and Cognate Studies* (ed. Cathcart and Maher), 100–110; IDEM, "Some Observations on the Dating of Targum Job," in *Back to the Sources: Biblical and Near Eastern Studies in Honour of Dermot Ryan* (ed. K. J. Cathcart and J. F. Healey; Dublin: Glendale, 1989), 67–78; IDEM, "Some Similarities between Targum Job and Targum Qohelet," in *The Aramaic Bible* (ed. Beattie and McNamara), 349–53; IDEM, "The Targum of Job," in Mangan, Healey, and Knobel, *The Targums of Job, Proverbs, Qohelet* (includes introduction and bibliography); T. MURAOKA, "The Aramaic of the Old Targum of Job from Qumran Cave XI," *JJS* 25 (1974): 425–43; M. SOKOLOFF, *The Targum to Job from Qumran Cave XI* (Ramat-Gan: Bar-Ilan University Press, 1974); R. I. VASHOLZ, "4QTargum Job versus 11QTargum Job," *RevQ* 11 (1982): 109; R. DE VAUX and J. T. MILIK, *Qumrân grotte 4,II*, 90 (4QtgJob); R. WEISS, *The Aramaic Targum of Job* (Tel Aviv: Tel Aviv University Press, 1979).

Song of Songs. Targum Song of Songs interprets the biblical book as an allegory of the relationship of God with Israel and with Israel's history. Although there is little in the Song of Songs that carries with it a messianic implication, the Targum introduces messianic ideas in half a dozen passages (see tabulation below). The traditional association of Song of Songs with King Solomon, son of David, probably accounts for this.

Bibliography: P. S. ALEXANDER, "From Poetry to Historiography: The Image of the Hasmoneans in Targum Canticles and the Question of the Targum's Provenance and Date," *JSP* 19 (1999): 103–28; IDEM, *The Targum of Canticles* (ArBib 17A; Collegeville, Minn.: Liturgical Press, 2003); IDEM, "Textual Criticism and Rabbinic Literature: The Case of the Targum of the Song of Songs," *BJRL* 75 (1993): 159–73; IDEM, "Tradition and Originality in the Targum of the Song of Songs," in *The Aramaic Bible* (ed. Beattie and McNamara), 318–39; L. DÍEZ MERINO, "El Targum al Cantar de los Cantares (Tradición Sefardi de Alfonso de Zamora)," *EstBib* 38 (1979–1980): 295–357; L. J. LIEBREICH, "The Benedictory Formula in the Targum to the Song of Songs," *HUCA* 18 (1944): 177–97; R. J. LOEWE, "Apologetic Motifs in the Targum to the Song of Songs," in *Biblical Motifs* (ed. A. Altmann; Lown Institute Studies and Texts 3; Cambridge: Harvard University Press, 1966), 159–96; IDEM, "The Sources of the Targum to the Song of Songs," in *Proceedings of the Twenty-Seventh International Congress of Orientalists, at Ann Arbor, Michigan, 1967* (ed. D. Sinor et al.; Wiesbaden: Harrassowitz, 1971), 104–5; R. H. MELAMED, "The

Targum to Canticles according to Six Yemen MSS.," *JQR* 10 (1919–1920): 377–410; 11 (1920–1921): 1–20; 12 (1921–1922): 57–117, repr., *The Targum to Canticles according to Six Yemen MSS.* (Philadelphia: Dropsie College Press, 1921); E. M. MENN, "Targum of the Song of Songs and the Dynamics of Historical Allegory," in *The Interpretation of Scripture in Early Judaism and Christianity* (ed. Evans), 423–45.

Ruth. Hebrew Ruth was used liturgically during the Feast of Weeks, but the Aramaic version was not. *Targum Ruth* has much in common with the other Megilloth Targumim. Palestinian in origin, the Targum contains some pre-70 C.E. halakic traditions. The haggadic elements are more diverse, but they too point to an early, Palestinian origin. *Targum Ruth* twice introduces the Messiah (after the ten famines in 1:1, and as one of the six blessings in 3:15).

Bibliography: D. R. G. BEATTIE, "Ancient Elements in the Targum to Ruth," in *Proceedings of the Ninth World Congress of Jewish Studies, Division A* (ed. Assaf), 159–65; IDEM, "The Targum of Ruth—a Sectarian Composition?" *JJS* 36 (1985): 222–29; IDEM, "The Textual Tradition of Targum Ruth," in *The Aramaic Bible* (ed. Beattie and McNamara), 340–48; IDEM, "The Yemenite Tradition of Targum Ruth," *JJS* 41 (1990): 49–56; D. R. G. BEATTIE and J. S. MCIVOR, *The Targum of Ruth, the Targum of Chronicles* (ArBib 19; Collegeville, Minn.: Liturgical Press, 1994); L. DÍEZ MERINO, "El Targum de Rut: Estado de la cuestión y traducción castellana," in *El misterio de la palabra* (ed. V. Collada and E. Zurro; L. Alonso Schökel FS; Madrid: Cristiandad, 1983), 245–65; E. LEVINE, *The Aramaic Version of Ruth* (AnBib 58; Rome: Pontifical Biblical Institute, 1973) (Aramaic with English translation).

Lamentations. Much of the tradition of *Targum Lamentations* probably derives from the period following the destruction of the second temple, though some of it could be earlier. There is later tradition in which a measure of polemic with Christianity may be in evidence (though I think Levine reads into some passages nuances that are not there). In its earliest form the Targum was Palestinian, though it has been influenced in later years by the eastern Aramaic of the Babylonian Talmud. The hope that God would send the Messiah becomes part of the prophet's plea in behalf of vanquished Judah (2:22). When Israel's sins are expiated, deliverance will come at the hands of the King Messiah and Elijah the high priest (4:22).

Bibliography: P. S. ALEXANDER, "The Textual Tradition of Targum Lamentations," *AbrN* 24 (1986): 1–26; C. M. M. BRADY, "The Date, Provenance, and Sitz im Leben of Targum Lamentations," *JAB* 1 (1999): 5–29; IDEM, "Vindicating God: The Intent of Targum Lamentations," *JAB* 3 (2001): 27–40; B. GROSSFELD, "Targum to Lamentations 2:10," *JJS* 28 (1977): 60–64; A. VAN DER HEIDE, *The Yemenite Tradition of the Targum of Lamentations: A Critical Text and Analysis of the Variant Readings* (SPB 32; Leiden: Brill, 1981); E. LEVINE, *The Aramaic Version of Lamentations* (New York: Sepher-Hermon, 1976) (Aramaic with English translation).

Qohelet. *Targum Qohelet* (or *Ecclesiastes*) probably emerged in the late Roman period (see 10:6, where "Edom" probably refers to Rome), though it may contain traditions from earlier periods. The Targum explicitly identifies King Solomon as the Preacher. Through the Holy Spirit the famous king predicts the division of the Israelite kingdom and the destruction of the temple. The entire book is cast as a prophecy: Whereas the Hebrew reads, "The words of the Preacher, the son of David," the Targum reads, "The words of the prophecy which the Preacher, that is, Solomon the son of David . . . prophesied" (1:1; cf. 1:4; 3:11; 4:15; 9:7). This interpretation coheres with the haggadic tradition that Solomon was a prophet (cf. *Sipre Deut.* §1 [on 1:1]; *Tg. 1 Kgs.* 5:13; *m.* ꜥ*Ed.* 5:3 ["it {Qohelet} defiles the hands {because it is inspired}"]; *t. Yad.* 2.14 ["it was said by the Holy Spirit"]). The Targum introduces the Messiah in two passages (1:11; 7:24). *Targum Qohelet* seems closer in language to *Pseudo-Jonathan* than to either *Onqelos* or *Neofiti.*

Bibliography: L. Díez Merino, *Targum de Qohelet: Edición principe del Ms. Villa–Amil no. 5 de Alfonso de Zamora* (Bibliotheca hispana biblica 13; Madrid: Consejo de Investigaciones Cientificos, 1987); P. S. Knobel, "The Targum of Qohelet," in Mangan, Healey, and Knobel, *The Targums of Job, Proverbs, Qohelet* (English translation, with bibliography); E. Levine, *The Aramaic Version of Qohelet* (New York: Sepher-Hermon, 1978) (Aramaic with English translation); A. Levy, *Das Targum zu Koheleth, nach südarabischen Handschriften herausgegeben* (Breslau: H. Fleischmann, 1905); C. Mangan, "Some Similarities between Targum Job and Targum Qohelet," in *The Aramaic Bible* (ed. Beattie and McNamara), 349–53.

Esther. There are two Targumim to Esther: *Targum Rishon* (or *First Targum of Esther*) and *Targum Sheni* (or *Second Targum of Esther*). *Targum Rishon* (ca. 500 C.E.) is written in western (i.e., Palestinian) Aramaic. (Grossfeld assigns it to lower Galilee.) Its translation is fairly literal. *Targum Sheni* (ca. 650 C.E.), also written in western Aramaic, extensively embellishes the story. The Targumim are so different that Grossfeld (1983, v) believes that "they are two independent compositions." The messianic idea is introduced by *Sheni* as part of a historical scheme made up of ten kingdoms (1:1). The ninth kingdom is that of the Messiah (and the tenth is that of God).

Although arguments have been made that the *Antwerp Polyglot Bible* preserves a third Esther Targum (e.g., P. Grelot 1975), others we have to do only with a pruned version of *Rishon* (so M. H. Goshen-Gottstein; B. Grossfeld 1983, 1984, 1992; and R. Le Déaut 1991).

Bibliography: M. David, *Das Targum Scheni, nach Handschriften herausgegeben und mit einer Einleitung versehen* (Berlin: M. Poppelauer, 1898); B. Ego, "All Kingdoms and Kings Trembled before Him: The Image of King Solomon in Targum Sheni on Megillat Esther," *JAB* 3 (2001): 57–73; idem, "God as Ruler of History: Main Thematic Motives of the Interpretation of Megilla Esther in Targum Sheni," *JAB* 2 (2000): 189–201; idem, *Targum Scheni zu Ester: Übersetzung, Kommentar, und theologische Deutung* (TSAJ 54; Tübingen: Mohr [Siebeck], 1996); idem, "Targumization as Theologization: Aggadic Additions in the Targum Sheni of Esther," in *The Aramaic Bible* (ed. Beattie and McNamara), 354–59; M. H. Goshen-Gottstein, "The 'Third Targum' on Esther and MS. Neofiti 1," *Bib* 56 (1975): 301–29; P. Grelot, "Observations sur les Targums I et III d'Esther," *Bib* 56 (1975): 53–73; B. Grossfeld, *Concordance of the First Targum to the Book of Esther* (SBLAS 5; Missoula, Mont.: Scholars Press, 1984); idem, *The First Targum to Esther* (New York: Sepher-Hermon, 1983)

(Aramaic with English translation); IDEM, *The Two Targums of Esther* (ArBib 18; Wilmington, Del.: Glazier, 1992) (English translation, with bibliography); B. GROSSFELD and R. LE DÉAUT, "The Origin and Nature of the Esther Targum in the Antwerp Polyglot: Exit Targum Esther III?" *Text* 17 (1991): 1–21; A. SULZBACH, *Targum Scheni zum Buch Esther* (Frankfurt am Main: Kaufmann, 1920).

Chronicles. Targum Chronicles offers a literal rendering, with occasional midrashic expansion (e.g., 1 Chr 1:20–21; 4:18; 7:21; 11:11–12; 12:32; 2 Chr 2:6; 3:1; 23:11). The meturgeman made use of the Palestinian Targumim to the Pentateuch (e.g., Gen 10:20 and 1 Chr 1:21; Gen 36:39 and 1 Chr 1:43) and was familiar with the Prophets Targumim. Vocabulary (including Greek and Latin loan words), place names, and style suggest a Palestinian provenance for *Targum Chronicles.* In only one place does the meturgeman show any interest in the Messiah theme. Seizing upon the name Anani (1 Chr 3:24), which approximates "clouds of," an association is made with Dan 7:13: "Behold, with the clouds of [*'anānê*] heaven came one like a son of man." This association leads the meturgeman to understand "Anani" as the actual name of the Messiah: " . . . and Anani, who is the King Messiah who is destined to be revealed."

Bibliography: D. R. G. BEATTIE and J. S. MCIVOR, *The Targum of Ruth, the Targum of Chronicles* (ArBib 19; Collegeville, Minn.: Liturgical Press, 1994); R. LE DÉAUT and J. ROBERT, *Targum des Chroniques* (2 vols.; AnBib 51; Rome: Pontifical Biblical Institute, 1971) (vol. 1: introduction and French translation; vol. 2: Aramaic text and glossary); E. NESTLE, "Das eherne Maultier der Manasse," *ZAW* 22 (1902): 309–12; M. ROSENBERG and K. KOHLER, "Das Targum zur Chronik," *JZWL* 8 (1870): 72–80, 135–63, 263–78.

Themes

Messianic emphases in the Targumim. "Messiah" occurs in the following targumic passages (as identified by Samson Levey; *Targum Neofiti* has also been taken into account):

Gen 3:15 *(Tg. Ps.-J.; Frg. Tg.; Tg. Neof.)*	Deut 25:19 *(Tg. Ps.-J.)*
Gen 35:21 *(Tg. Ps.-J.)*	Deut 30:4–9 *(Tg. Ps.-J.)*
Gen 49:1 *(Tg. Ps.-J.; Frg. Tg.)*	1 Sam 2:7–10
Gen 49:10–12 *(Tg. Onq.; Tg. Ps.-J.; Frg. Tg.; Tg. Neof.)*	1 Sam 2:35
	2 Sam 22:28–32
Exod 12:42 *(Frg. Tg.; Tg. Neof.)*	2 Sam 23:1–5
Exod 17:16 *(Tg. Ps.-J.)*	1 Kgs 5:13
Exod 40:9–11 *(Tg. Ps.-J.)*	Isa 4:1–6
Num 11:26 *(Frg. Tg.; Tg. Neof.)*	Isa 9:5–6
Num 23:21 *(Tg. Ps.-J.)*	Isa 10:24–27
Num 24:7 *(Frg. Tg.; Tg. Neof.)*	Isa 11:1–16
Num 24:17–24 *(Tg. Onq.; Tg. Ps.-J.; Frg. Tg.; Tg. Neof.)*	Isa 14:29–30
	Isa 16:1–5

Isa 28:5–6	Ps 21:1–8
Isa 42:1–9	Ps 45:7–18
Isa 43:10	Ps 61:7–9 [ET 6–8]
Isa 52:13–53:12	Ps 72:1–20
Jer 23:1–8	Ps 80:15–18 [ET 14–17]
Jer 30:8–11	Ps 89:51–52
Jer 30:21	Ps 132:10–18
Jer 33:12–26	Song 1:8
Ezek 17:22–24	Song 1:17
Ezek 34:20–31	Song 4:5
Ezek 37:21–28	Song 7:4
Hos 2:2	Song 7:12–14
Hos 3:3–5	Song 8:1–4
Hos 14:5–8	Ruth 1:1
Mic 4:8	Ruth 3:15
Mic 5:1–3	Lam 2:22
Hab 3:17–18	Lam 4:22
Zech 3:8	Qoh 1:11
Zech 4:7	Qoh 7:24
Zech 6:12–13	Esth (II) 1:1
Zech 10:4	1 Chr 3:24
Ps 18:28–32 [ET 27–31]	

Bibliography: K. H. BERNHARDT, "Zu Eigenart und Alter der messianisch-eschatologischen Zusätze im Targum Jeruschalmi I," in *Gott und die Götter* (ed. H. Bardtke; E. Fascher FS; Berlin: Evangelische Verlagsanstalt, 1958), 68–83; J.-J. BRIERRE-NARBONNE, *Exégèse targumique des prophéties messianiques* (Paris: P. Geuthner, 1936); C. A. EVANS, "Early Messianic Traditions in the Targums," in Evans, *Jesus and His Contemporaries: Comparative Studies* (AGJU 25; Leiden: Brill, 1995), 155–81; P. HUMBERT, "Le messie dans le Targum des Prophètes," *RTP* 43 (1910): 420–47; 44 (1911): 5–46; S. H. LEVEY, *The Messiah: An Aramaic Interpretation* (MHUC 2; Cincinnati: Hebrew Union College–Jewish Institute of Religion, 1974).

The Targumim and the Teaching of Jesus. Through analysis of dictional, thematic, and stylistic coherence, Bruce Chilton has shown how Jesus' statements and language at points reflect targumic tradition. Comparative study can lead to a better understanding of the saying in question and, in some cases, to firmer grounds for regarding a given saying as authentic. Chilton and others find dictional coherence in the following examples:

1. According to Mark 4:12, Jesus paraphrased Isa 6:9–10 to explain in part why some did not comprehend or respond supportively to his teaching: " . . . in order that seeing they should see and not perceive, and hearing they should hear and not understand, lest they should turn [i.e., repent] and it be forgiven them." Only *Targum Isaiah* reads "forgive"; the Hebrew (MT and 1QIsaᵃ) and the LXX read "heal." (The Peshitta also reads "forgive," either because it has followed the Targum or because it has been influenced by the version found in Mark.) I might

add that not only is there dictional coherence, there may be thematic coherence as well. According to the Targum, the prophet is to speak the word of obduracy to those *who* do not hear and do not see. In other words, the word of obduracy is directed only to the obdurate. In the Marcan context Jesus' word is directed to "outsiders." This application approximates the idea of the Targum. Jesus' quotation, therefore, appears to have been influenced by an Aramaic reading heard in the synagogue of his day (see Chilton 1984, 90–98; Evans 1982, 417).

2. According to Matt 26:52, Jesus rebuked Peter for his rash act of striking the high priest's servant: "All who take a sword on the sword will be destroyed" (only in Matthew). Chilton (1984, 98–101) suspects that Jesus has alluded to the Aramaic version of Isa 50:11: "Behold, all you kindling a fire, *grasping a sword,* go, fall in the fire you kindled and *on the sword* you grasped. This is yours from my word: you shall return to your *destruction*" (with the distinctive elements of the Targum emphasized). The Greek words of Jesus' saying ("take a sword," "on the sword," "destroyed") cohere with the distinctive elements of the Targum.

3. When Jesus warns his followers to beware of being cast into "Gehenna" (Mark 9:47), he quotes part of Isa 66:24: "where 'their worm does not die and the fire is not quenched'" (Mark 9:48). The Hebrew version of Isaiah says nothing about Gehenna, but the Targum does: "for their *breaths* will not die and their fire shall not be quenched, and *the wicked* shall be *judged in Gehenna*" (with the distinctive elements of the Targum emphasized). Again, Jesus' use of this verse from Isaiah may very well reveal a familiarity with the Aramaic tradition that is now preserved in *Targum Isaiah* (see Chilton 1984, 101–7). Moreover, Jesus' warning that the one who hates his brother is liable to be cast into the "Gehenna of fire" (Matt 5:22; 18:9) may also echo targumic diction: "a fire *of Gehenna* not fanned will consume him" (*Tg. Job* 20:26, with the distinctive element emphasized; cf. *Tg. Neof.* Gen 15:17).

4. In a tradition that enjoys multiple attestation Jesus avers: "With the measure you measure shall it be measured to you" (Q: Matt 7:2 = Luke 6:38; cf. Mark 4:24). Jesus' expression appears to echo the diction of the Aramaic tradition: "With *the* measure *with which you were measuring they will measure to you*" (*Tg. Isa.* 27:8, with the distinctive elements of the Targum emphasized). Jesus' saying follows neither the obscure Hebrew reading ("measure by measure") nor the LXX. Although similar sayings are found in the rabbinic writings (*b. Šabb.* 127b; *b. Meg.* 28a; *b. Roš Haš.* 16b), the language of the Targum provides the closest parallel (see Chilton 1984, 123–25).

5. Jesus' metaphorical saying about new wine bursting old wineskins (Mark 2:22 par.) coheres with Job 32:19: "My heart is like wine that has no vent; like new wineskins, it is ready to burst." The *Job Targum* parallels it even more closely: "My belly is like *new* wine" (*Tg. Job* 32:19, with the distinctive element of the Targum emphasized).

6. In Luke 16:9 Jesus tells his disciples to "make friends of the mammon of injustice [*or* dishonesty]." Although the Aramaic word *māmônā'* occurs in the Talmuds, especially the Palestinian version, the expression "mammon of injustice/ dishonesty" coheres with the targumic description of bribery as "mammon of

falsehood/deceit" (cf. *Tg. 1 Sam.* 12:3; *Tg. Hos.* 5:11; *Tg. Isa.* 5:23; 33:15; *Tg. Job* 27:8). The targumic expression, especially since it often has to do with political corruption or economic oppression, appears to offer a closer parallel than the Qumranic expressions "wealth of violence" (1QS 10:19) or "wealth of evil" (CD 6:15). Not only are the respective concerns different, Qumran used the word *hôn*, not *māmônā'*. The appearance of *māmônā'* in 11QtgJob 11:8 (at MT Job 27:17) proves, moreover, that the word was utilized in the targumic tradition in the first century (see Chilton 1984, 117–23).

7. In Matt 6:19–20, Jesus admonishes his disciples, "Do not store up for yourselves treasures on earth, where moth and rust consume and where thieves break in and steal, but store up for yourselves treasures in heaven, where neither moth nor rust consumes and where thieves do not break in and steal." The promises of future reward coheres with *Tg. Neof.* Gen 15:1: "the reward of your good works is prepared for you before Me in the world to come."

8. We find in Luke 11:27–28, "While he was saying this, a woman in the crowd raised her voice and said to him, 'Blessed is the womb that bore you and the breasts that nursed you!' But he said, 'Blessed rather are those who hear the word of God and obey it!'" We find in *Tg. Neof., Tg. Ps.-J.* Gen 49:25, "Blessed are the breasts that you sucked and the womb that bore you." A nearly identical form of this saying appears in *Gen. Rab.* 98.20 (on Gen 49:25), but this later midrash may in fact be dependent upon the Targumim. The woman's utterance may well reflect targumic tradition.

9. Jesus' confident expectation of being raised up "*on* the third day" or "*after* three days" appears to be based on Hos 6:2 in the Aramaic. According to Mark 8:31, "Then he began to teach them that the Son of Man must undergo great suffering, and be rejected by the elders, the chief priests, and the scribes, and be killed, and *after* three days rise again" (cf. Mark 9:31; 10:34). According to Luke 18:33, "After they have flogged him, they will kill him, and *on* the third day he will rise again" (cf. Luke 24:7). The *after* and *on* prepositional phrases in the NT tradition probably reflect the synonymous parallel prepositional phrases of Hos 6:2. The Hebrew reads, "*After* (*min*) two days he will revive [lit. "make alive"] us; *on* (*be*) the third day he will raise us up, that we may live before him"; the LXX reads, "*After* two days he will heal us; *on* the third day we shall be raised up and shall live before him"; but the Aramaic reads, "*on the day of resurrection from the dead* he will raise us up and we shall live before him." The explicit reference in the Aramaic version to resurrection strongly suggests that Jesus' allusive usage of this text reflects more the Aramaic than either the Hebrew or the Greek texts (cf. Evans 1999).

10. Luke 10:25–28 provides an instance of exegetical coherence. When an expert in the Mosaic law answered his own question, "What must I do to inherit eternal life?" (Luke 10:25), by reciting the "double commandment" (Luke 10:27; cf. Deut 6:5; Lev 19:18), Jesus is said to have replied, "do this, and you will live" (Luke 10:28). These words constitute a paraphrase of Lev 18:5 "by doing so one shall will live." Leviticus 18 concerns long life and prosperity in the promised land, as a reward for obeying the laws of the covenant. It has nothing to do with

eternal life, so why would appeal to it give reassurance to the man who asked the question about eternal life? Jesus' understanding of Lev 18:5 reflects targumic exegesis. According to *Onqelos:* "You shall therefore keep my statutes and my ordinances, by doing which a person shall live through them *in eternal life;* I am the LORD." According to *Pseudo-Jonathan:* "You shall therefore keep my statutes and my ordinances, by doing which a person shall live *in eternal life, and his portion shall be with the righteous;* I am the LORD" (cf. Evans 1997; Stegner 1985).

There are also instances of thematic coherence between targumic traditions and Jesus' teaching. Two examples may be considered:

1. Jesus bases his parable of the Wicked Vineyard Tenants (Mark 12:1–11) upon Isaiah's Song of the Vineyard (Isa 5:1–7). When the parable is finished, the chief priests perceive that he has told the parable against them (Mark 12:12). Although Jesus has clearly drawn upon Isaiah's song for the imagery of his parable, it is not clear that he has drawn upon its message. According to the Hebrew and Greek versions of Isaiah, the people of Judah as a whole are guilty of fruitlessness, and it is they who are in danger of judgment. But according to Jesus' parable it is the religious leaders, not the people, who are guilty and in danger of judgment. From *Targum Isaiah* we are able to explain this apparent discrepancy. According to it God did not build a *tower* (as in the MT and LXX), but his *sanctuary* in the midst of his people. He did not provide a *wine vat* (as in the MT and LXX), but his *altar to atone for their sins.* But despite these benefits the people did not produce *good deeds* (instead of the MT's "grapes"); they produced *evil deeds.* Therefore God will remove his *Shekinah* and will break down their *sanctuaries* (i.e., temple and synagogues). *Targum Isaiah* has narrowed the focus from the people of Judah to the temple establishment (as is also attested in 4Q500). It is therefore quite probable that Jesus' usage of Isa 5:1–7, which was directed against the temple establishment, presupposed the interpretation that is now reflected in *Targum Isaiah* (see Chilton 1984, 111–14). See chapter 12 for further discussion of this passage.

2. One of the most obvious characteristics of Jesus' public ministry is his proclamation of the in-breaking kingdom of God (cf. Mark 1:15; 9:1; 14:25; Luke 11:20). Chilton has observed an important point of coherence with *Targum Isaiah* that may clarify Jesus' proclamation. He finds that at many points the Targum inserts hopeful expressions of the revelation of the kingdom. Where the MT reads, "because the Lord of hosts reigns on Mount Zion" (Isa 24:23), the Targum reads: "because the kingdom of the Lord of hosts will be revealed on Mount Zion" (cf. the MT and Targum at 31:4; 40:9; 52:7). What the meturgeman hoped would soon be revealed, Jesus declared imminent and in some sense present in his ministry (see Chilton 1984, 58–63; idem, *Glory of Israel,* 77–81; idem, "Regnum Dei").

Finally, two examples of stylistic coherence between targumic traditions and Jesus' teaching may be considered:

1. One of the distinctive stylistic characteristics of Jesus' speech was his practice of prefacing certain solemn statements with the word "amen" (probably the Aramaic form; from *'āman,* "to be certain" or "sure"): "Amen, I say to you, all sins will be forgiven the sons of men" (Mark 3:28; cf. 8:12; 9:1 passim). Its rarity in Judaica led some scholars to suppose that Jesus' usage was unique. The closest

parallel that Gustaf Dalman could find was *hemānûtā'* (which is from the *'āman* stem) in two places in the Babylonian Talmud (*b. Ned.* 49b [of Judah ben Ilai, ca. 150 C.E.]; *b. Sanh.* 38b; see Dalman, 226–29). However, Chilton thinks that Jesus' practice may reflect a similar practice in the Targumim, where "amen" sometimes prefaced "a sentence as a solemn asseveration" (Chilton 1984, 202). Two helpful examples are found in *Targum Isaiah:* "They will . . . *give thanks, saying, 'Amen,* God is with you'" (*Tg. Isa.* 45:14); and, "*Amen,* you are God" (*Tg. Isa.* 45:15, with the distinctive elements of the Targum emphasized). (*Tg. Isa.* 37:18 is less helpful, since *'āman* is present in the Hebrew text as well.) Jesus' style of speaking evidently was not unique, but reflected a convention which his contemporaries would have heard in the synagogue.

2. Some twenty-one times Jesus speaks of "your/our Father in heaven" (Mark 11:25; Matt 5:45; 6:1, 9; 18:10 passim). This expression does not occur in the OT or the OT Apocrypha. But "Father in heaven" qualified by a personal pronoun does occur in the Targumim (*Tg. Ps.-J.* Exod 1:19; *Frg. Tg.* Gen 21:33; *Frg. Tg.* [MS M] Exod 17:11; *Frg. Tg.* Num 21:9; *Tg. Ps.-J.* Deut 28:32 passim). Since it occurs elsewhere in early Judaica (e.g., *m. 'Abot* 5:20; *Mek.* on Exod 20:6 [*Bahodesh* §6.143]), one cannot claim that its derivation is distinctly targumic. However, since its function seems often to be liturgical, the provenance of the synagogue, in which the targumic tradition grew, does suggest itself. Perhaps here again Jesus' style of speaking (and praying) may be clarified by comparison with the Targumim (see McNamara, *Targum and Testament,* 115–19).

Bibliography: B. D. CHILTON, *A Galilean Rabbi and His Bible: Jesus' Use of the Interpreted Scripture of His Time* (GNS 8; Wilmington, Del.: Glazier, 1984); IDEM, *The Glory of Israel;* IDEM, "Regnum Dei Deus est," *SJT* 31 (1978): 261–70; G. DALMAN, *The Words of Jesus* (Edinburgh: T&T Clark, 1902); C. A. EVANS, "Did Jesus Predict His Death and Resurrection?" in *Resurrection* (ed. S. E. Porter, M. A. Hayes, and D. Tombs; JSNTSup 186; RILP 5; Sheffield: Sheffield, 1999), 82–97; IDEM, "'Do This and You Will Live': Targumic Coherence in Luke 10:25–28," in B. Chilton and C. A. Evans, *Jesus in Context: Temple, Purity, and Restoration* (AGJU 39; Leiden: Brill, 1997), 377–93; IDEM, "The Text of Isaiah 6:9–10," *ZNW* 94 (1982): 415–18; K. KOCH, "Offenbaren wird sich das Reich Gottes: Die Malkuta Jahwäs im Profeten-Targum," *NTS* 25 (1978–1979): 158–65; M. MCNAMARA, *Targum and Testament;* S. SCHULZ, "Die Bedeutung der neuen Targumforschung für die synoptische Tradition," in *Abraham unser Vater* (ed. M. Hengel et al.; O. Michel FS; Leiden: Brill, 1973), 425–36; A. SHINAN, "Sermons, Targums, and the Reading from Scriptures in the Ancient Synagogue," in *The Synagogue in Late Antiquity* (ed. L. I. Levine; Philadelphia: American Schools of Oriental Research, 1987), 97–110; W. R. STEGNER, "The Parable of the Good Samaritan and Leviticus 18:5," in *The Living Text* (ed. D. E. Groh and R. Jewett; E. W. Saunders FS; Lanham, Md.: University Press of America, 1985), 27–38; IDEM, "The Rebuke Tradition in the Targums and the Narrative of the Temptation," in *Textual and Contextual Studies in the Pentateuchal Targums* (vol. 1 of *Targum Studies;* ed. Flesher), 33–59; M. WILCOX, "The Aramaic Background of the New Testament," in *The Aramaic Bible* (ed. Beattie and McNamara), 362–78.

The Targumim and the Gospel of Matthew. Interpreters have long believed that the Gospel of Matthew emerged from a Jewish context. Recent studies have identified points of contact with Jewish scribal and interpretative traditions (cf. Wills), some of which cohere with the Targumim (esp. *Targum Isaiah;* cf. Evans, "Targumizing Tendencies").

1. Like the Isaiah meturgeman, the Matthean evangelist holds to a very high view of the law (cf. Matt 5:17–18; 7:12; 12:5; 22:36, 40; 23:23). The latter passage, where Jesus contrasts the Pharisees' practice of tithing dill and cumin with their neglect of the weightier matters of the law, is very interesting. Scattering dill and sowing cumin in Hebrew Isa 28:25 becomes, in the Targum, doing the law.

2. A. J. Saldarini has remarked upon the interest in the scribe in both *Targum Isaiah* and in the Gospel of Matthew. *Scribe* sometimes replaces *prophet*, e.g., Isa 28:7 "The priest and the prophet reel with strong drink" becomes, in the Targum, "Priest and scribe are filled with old wine." Similarly, Matthew inserts references to scribes, as seen in Matt 23:34 ("Therefore I send you prophets, sages, and scribes"), compared with the parallel passage in Luke 11:49 ("I will send them prophets and apostles"). See also the programmatic Matt 13:52 ("Therefore every scribe who has been trained for the kingdom of heaven").

3. According to 2 Sam 5:8, David declared that "the blind and the lame shall not come into the house." He said this because of the Jebusites' earlier taunt that only the blind and lame would be needed to thwart David's attempt to take Jerusalem. But in the Targum, David says, "The sinners and the guilty shall not go up to the house." It is this passage, especially as rendered in the Aramaic, that lies behind Matthew's unique story that the blind and the lame came to Jesus "in the temple" to be healed, with the result that Jesus was hailed as "Son of David" (Matt 21:14–15). The equation of the *blind* and the *lame* with *sinners* and the *guilty* reflects assumptions about sin and health in late antiquity (e.g., John 9:2, "Rabbi, who sinned, this man or his parents, that he was born blind?"). By healing the blind and the lame in the temple precincts, Jesus the "Son of David" has reversed the policy of his illustrious ancestor, as a token of the healing and restorative rule of God. The Aramaic tradition provides the vital link between the Matthean story and the scriptural backdrop (cf. Evans 1997).

Bibliography: B. D. CHILTON, *The Glory of Israel;* C. A. EVANS, "A Note on Targum 2 Samuel 5.8 and Jesus' Ministry to the 'Maimed, Halt, and Blind,'" *JSP* 15 (1997): 79–82; IDEM, "Targumizing Tendencies in Matthean Redaction," in *When Judaism and Christianity Began: Essays in Memory of Anthony J. Saldarini* (ed. A. J. Avery-Peck, D. J. Harrington, and J. Neusner; 2 vols.; JSJSup 85; Leiden: Brill, 2004), 1:93–116; R. H. GUNDRY, *The Use of the Old Testament in St. Matthew's Gospel with Special Reference to the Messianic Hope* (NovTSup 18; Leiden: Brill, 1967); A. J. SALDARINI, "'Is Saul Also among the Scribes?' Scribes and Prophets in *Targum Jonathan*," in *The Interpretation of Scripture in Early Judaism and Christianity* (ed. Evans), 375–89; L. M. WILLS, "Scribal Methods in Matthew and Mishnah Abot," *CBQ* 63 (2001): 241–57.

The Targumim and Luke-Acts. That there are several examples of dictional and thematic coherence between the Targumim and Luke-Acts is especially interesting, given the probability that the author of Luke-Acts was non-Jewish. Targumic coherence may lend a measure of support to proposals that the author had been a

God-fearer and thus exposed to the reading and interpretation of Scripture in the synagogue setting.

1. The equivalence of *sin* and *debt* becomes evident in the exchange between Jesus and Simon the Pharisee: "Now when the Pharisee who had invited him saw it, he said to himself, 'If this man were a prophet, he would have known who and what kind of woman this is who is touching him—that she is a sinner.' . . . 'A certain creditor had two debtors. . . . Therefore, I tell you, her sins, which were many, have been forgiven; hence she has shown great love; but the one to whom little is forgiven, loves little'" (Luke 7:39, 41, 47). The interchangeable "sins" and "debts" in Jesus' teaching probably reflect Aramaic tradition: "This people have sinned great debts" (*Tg. Neof.* Exod 32:31). Here the expression "great debts" approximates Jesus' remark that the woman's sins/debts are "many." One should also compare Matt 6:12, "And forgive us our debts, as we also have forgiven our debtors," with Luke 11:4, "And forgive us our sins, for we ourselves forgive everyone indebted to us." The equivalence of "debts" and "sins" is plainly evident.

2. The curious beatitude of the woman in the crowd ("Blessed is the womb that bore you and the breasts that nursed you!" Luke 11:27) echoes targumic language: "Blessed are the breasts that you sucked and the womb that bore you" (*Tg. Neof., Tg. Ps.-J.* Gen 49:25). A nearly identical form of this saying appears in *Gen. Rab.* 98.20 (on Gen 49:25), but this later midrash is probably dependent upon the Targum.

3. A detail in the Pentecost story may reflect targumic tradition: "Divided tongues, as of fire, appeared among them, and a tongue rested on each of them" (Acts 2:3). The concept of the Spirit "resting" on someone and enabling him to prophesy may be clarified by *Frg. Tg.* Num 11:26, which says that "the Holy Spirit rested upon them," that is, upon Eldad and Modad, both of whom then "prophesied in the camp."

4. The evangelist commands: "Repent therefore from this wickedness of yours . . ." (Acts 8:22). To "repent from" something coheres with targumic diction, as in *Frg. Tg.* Gen 18:21 " . . . to repent from their evil deeds," *Frag. Tg.* Gen 19:24 ". . . that they might make repentance from their evil deeds," *Frag. Tg.* Exod 10:28 "Repent from these evil things," and *Frag. Tg.* Exod 14:29 " . . . the sea repented from its waves." See also Jer 8:6, which in the Hebrew says "there is no man who feels remorse over his evil." But in the Aramaic it reads: "There is no man who repents from his evil."

5. In Acts 11:15–18, Peter reports that the Holy Spirit fell upon Cornelius and his household. From this he infers, "If then God gave them the same gift that he gave us when we believed in the Lord Jesus Christ, who was I that I could hinder God?" The apostles concur and so recognize that "God has given even to the Gentiles the repentance that leads to life." The giving of the Spirit as proof of being God's people seems to be the point in *Tg. Ps.-J.* Exod 33:16 "For how will it be known that I have found *mercy before You,* I and your people," Moses asks God, "unless *Your Shekinah speaks* with us and *wonders are performed for us when you remove the spirit of prophecy from the nations and speak in the Holy Spirit to* me

and *to* your people, *so that we become different* from all the peoples that are on the face of the earth?"

6. Against the false prophet, Paul says, "And now listen—the hand of the Lord is against you, and you will be blind for a while, unable to see the sun" (Acts 13:11). The expression to be "blind . . . unable to see the sun" may allude to Ps 58:9: "Let them be like the snail that dissolves into slime, like the untimely birth that never sees the sun" (Eng. v. 8). This is a Semitic idiom, but it is only in the Targumim that blindness and not being able to see the sun are linked: "Like the crawling snail whose way is slimy, like the abortion and the mole who are *blind and do not see the sun.*" We may have here an example of dictional coherence.

7. Under arrest and soon to be sent to Rome, Paul defends the gospel before Agrippa and Festus. After Paul declares his belief in the resurrection and the fulfillment of prophecy, the Roman governor asserts, "You are out of your mind, Paul! Too much learning is driving you insane!" (Acts 26:24). The notion that great learning could lead to madness is attested in *Tg. Ps.-J.* Num 22:5, in a greatly expanded paraphrase of the story of Balak's summons to Balaam the prophet to pronounce a curse on the approaching tribes of Israel. Balak sends to "Balaam . . . the son of Beor, who *acted foolishly from the greatness of his wisdom.*" The governor's comment is not necessarily critical or dismissive (and Plato speaks of philosophical "madmen" in *Phaedr.* 245A, 249D). The targumic tradition is being critical of Balaam, but the association of "great wisdom" with madness or "foolish" behavior is evident.

Bibliography: M. BLACK, *An Aramaic Approach to the Gospels and Acts*; M. WILCOX, *The Semitisms of Acts* (Oxford: Clarendon, 1965).

The Targumim and the Fourth Gospel. There are numerous parallels between targumic diction and concepts in the Fourth Gospel:

1. When Jesus' brothers say to him, "show yourself to the world" (John 7:4), echoed here may be the targumic idea of the revelation of the Messiah: "the King Messiah is destined to reveal himself at the end of days" (*Tg. Ps.-J.* Gen 35:21; cf. *Tg. Zech.* 3:8; 4:7; 6:12; *Tg. Song* 8:1; *Tg. 1 Chr.* 3:24; McNamara, *Targum and Testament,* 140).

2. The idiom "taste death" (John 8:52; cf. Mark 9:1), which is not found in the Hebrew or Greek versions of the OT, is found in the Targumim (cf. *Frg. Tg.* and *Tg. Ps.-J.* Deut 32:1).

3. In response to Jesus' cry that the Father glorify his name, "a voice came from heaven, 'I have glorified it, and I will glorify it again'" (John 12:28). Traditions of the *bat qol* occur in rabbinic writings (cf. *ʾAbot* 6:2; *t. Soṭah* 13.2; *b. Ker.* 5b; *Lev. Rab.* 6.5 [on Lev 5:1]; other examples are considered below) and in the Targumim. But the form and context of this Johannine example coheres with what is found in the Targumim: on the day that Moses died, "a voice fell from heaven," enjoining the people to behold the great lawgiver, a man to whom the "glory of the Shekinah of the Lord was revealed" (*Tg. Ps.-J.* Deut 34:5; cf. John

12:28; McNamara, *Targum and Testament*, 113–14). Josephus witnesses to the antiquity of the *bat qol* tradition (cf. *Ant.* 13.10.3 §282).

4. Jesus' statement "In my Father's house there are many dwelling places" (John 14:2) probably reflects targumic language: "The glory of my Shekinah will accompany among you and will prepare a resting place for you" (*Tg. Neof.* Exod 33:14; cf. *Tg. Neof.* Gen 46:28; *Tg. Onq.* and *Tg. Neof.* Deut 1:33; McNamara, *Targum and Testament*, 142). The antiquity of the idea is attested by *1 En.* 39:4–8.

5. The expression "cup [of death]" (John 18:11) is found in the Targumim: "Joseph . . . put his trust in flesh . . . which will taste the cup of death" (*Frg. Tg.* and *Tg. Neof.* Gen 40:23; Le Déaut, "Targumic Literature," 246).

6. The Fourth Gospel's reference to "blood and water" issuing forth from the side of Jesus (19:34) may have been intended as an echo of the tradition that blood and water issued forth from the rock that Moses struck, a tradition preserved in the Targumim (cf. *Tg. Ps.-J.* Num 20:11; Le Déaut, "Targumic Literature," 277).

7. When Jesus says that his disciples will see "heaven opened and the angels of God ascending and descending upon the Son of Man" (John 1:51), we have coherence with the kind of interpretation preserved in *Frg. Tg.* and *Tg. Neof.* Gen 28:12 (cf. *Gen. Rab.* 68.12 [on Gen 28:12]), in which it is said that the angels ascended and descended upon Jacob rather than upon the stairway (Neyrey 1982; McNamara, *Targum and Testament*, 146–47; Rowland).

8. The exchange between Jesus and the woman at the well of Jacob offers another example of coherence with targumic tradition. Jesus' promise to provide living water that will spring up into eternal life (John 4:12–13) is probably a deliberate comparison to the haggadah that claimed that the well surged up during the twenty years that Jacob lived in Haran (*Frg. Tg.* and *Tg. Neof.* Gen 28:10; McNamara, *Targum and Testament*, 145–46; Neyrey 1979).

Bibliography: P. BORGEN, "Observations on the Targumic Character of the Prologue of John," *NTS* 16 (1970): 288–95; B. D. CHILTON, "Typologies of *memra* and the Fourth Gospel," in *Textual and Contextual Studies in the Pentateuchal Targums* (vol. 1 of *Targum Studies;* ed. Flesher), 89–100; C. A. EVANS, *Word and Glory: On the Exegetical and Theological Background of John's Prologue* (JSNTSup 89; Sheffield: JSOT Press, 1993), 114–45; R. LE DÉAUT, "Targumic Literature and New Testament Interpretation"; M. MCNAMARA, "The Targums and Johannine Literature," in McNamara, *Targum and Testament*, 142–59; J. H. NEYREY, "The Jacob Allusions in John 1:51," *CBQ* 44 (1982): 586–605; IDEM, "Jacob Traditions and the Interpretation of John 4:10–26," *CBQ* 41 (1979): 419–37; C. ROWLAND, "John 1.51, Jewish Apocalyptic, and Targumic Tradition," *NTS* 30 (1984): 498–507.

The Targumim and Paul. At many points, Paul's language and interpretation of Scripture cohere with the targumic tradition.

1. In Rom 2:4, Paul asks, "Or do you despise the riches of his kindness and forbearance and patience? Do you not realize that God's kindness is meant to lead you to repentance?" God's forbearance and patience are intended to give humanity time to repent. The concept is found in *Tg. Neof.* Gen 6:3 "*Behold, I have given the span of one hundred and twenty years that they might do repentance, but they*

have not done so" (so also the *Fragmentary Targum* and *Pseudo-Jonathan*); "*This wicked generation shall not endure before Me* forever, because they are flesh *and their deeds are evil; let an extension of* one hundred and twenty years *be granted to them that they might repent*" (*Tg. Onq.*) (targumic innovations in italic).

2. In reference to Abraham, Paul declares: "No distrust made him waver concerning the promise of God, but he grew strong in his faith as he gave glory to God" (Rom 4:20). But according to Gen 17:17, "Abraham fell on his face and laughed, and said to himself, 'Can a child be born to a man who is a hundred years old? Can Sarah, who is ninety years old, bear a child?'" The Targumim paraphrase the passage. According to *Onqelos*, Abraham did not laugh; he "rejoiced," and in *Pseudo-Jonathan*, Abraham "was amazed." Perhaps more germane is *Tg. Neof.* Gen 22:14, where Abraham prays, "*there was no division in my heart the first time you said to me to offer my son Isaac. . . . I immediately arose early in the morning and diligently put your words into practice with gladness and fulfilled your decree*" (targumic innovations in italic). Neofiti's "no division in my heart" approximates Paul's statement that Abraham did not waver in unbelief.

3. Paul declares that the "law is holy, and the commandment is holy and just and good" (Rom 7:12). This idea appears also in the Targumim: "*For the Law is a* tree of life *for everyone who toils in it and keeps the commandments. He lives and endures like* the tree of life *in the world to come. The Law is good for all who labor in it in this world like the fruit of the tree of life*" (*Tg. Neof.* Gen 3:24b) (targumic innovations in italic).

4. Paul admonishes the faithful, "Beloved, never avenge yourselves, but leave room for the wrath of God; for it is written, 'Vengeance is mine, I will repay, says the Lord'" (Rom 12:19). Paul is quoting Deut 32:35, though not according to the Hebrew or the Greek ("In the day of vengeance I shall repay"). Paul may be paraphrasing the text under the influence of Aramaic interpretation, as possibly attested in *Neofiti*: "Vengeance *is* mine, and *I am he who will repay*." Even more important, *Neofiti* goes on to speak of future judgment, which Paul probably has in mind as well: "for the day of the breaking of *the wicked* is near, and *the fire of Gehenna* is prepared for them, *and retribution hastens to come upon them in the world to come*" (targumic innovations in italic).

5. Paul enjoins the Corinthian Christians, "Do not become idolaters as some of them did; as it is written, 'The people sat down to eat and drink, and they rose up to play.' We must not indulge in sexual immorality as some of them did" (1 Cor 10:7). Paul is quoting part of Exod 32:6 and alluding to the sorry episode of the golden calf. But that story says nothing about sexual immorality. According to Exod 32:6 in the Hebrew: "They rose early the next day, and offered burnt offerings and brought sacrifices of well-being; and the people sat down to eat and drink, and rose up to revel [lit. 'and rose up to laugh']." The LXX reads, "and the people sat down to eat and drink and arose to dance." Paul has followed the LXX, but his warning not to indulge in sexual immorality may reflect the Aramaic paraphrase: "and the people sat down to eat and drink and rose up to *play obscenely* [*getak*] *in foreign worship*" (*Tg. Neof.*). In Aramaic, *getak* means either "to laugh" or "to jest," as does *tsahaq* in Hebrew, but it also means "to be obscene,"

particularly with reference to idolatry (see Jastrow, *Dictionary,* 233), e.g., *Tg. 2 Chr.* 15:16: "she had made *idols, so that she could indulge in obscene practices before the Asherahs*" (targumic innovations in italic). In antiquity, pagan worship often involved temple prostitutes. It is this aspect that the Targum may reflect and that Paul also presupposes; hence his warning to avoid sexual immorality.

Bibliography: B. D. CHILTON, "Aramaic and Targumic Antecedents of Pauline 'Justification,'" in *The Aramaic Bible* (ed. Beattie and McNamara), 379–97; M. MCNAMARA, *The New Testament and the Palestinian Targum to the Pentateuch,* 70–96.

The Aramaic Psalter and the New Testament. Targum Psalms is much neglected and, regarding NT research, remains an undiscovered country, mainly because there is no established text. Because there is no published English translation, NT interpreters rarely refer to it. The English edition in the Michael Glazier Aramaic Bible series is anticipated soon. Below are several examples where the Aramaic tradition may clarify passages in the NT.

1. When Jesus is baptized, the heavenly voice declares, "You are my Son, the Beloved [*agapētos*], with you I am well pleased" (Mark 1:11; cf. 9:7). Most commentators refer to Ps 2:7, which in the Hebrew and in the Greek reads, "You are my son; today I have begotten you." To explain the presence of "Beloved" in the Markan saying, some appeal to Isa 42:1 ("in whom my soul delights"), or perhaps Gen 22:2, in which "beloved" appears in the Greek version. "Beloved" is present, however, in the Aramaic version of Ps 2:7: "Beloved [*habib*] as a son to a father you are to me."

2. During the temptation, the Devil appeals to Ps 91:11–12 to assure Jesus of divine protection. That this psalm comes into play is interesting, for in the Aramaic it makes explicit reference to demons (cf. *Tg. Pss.* 91:5–6, 9–10). The antiquity of this orientation is attested not only by this remarkable coherence with first-century tradition but also by Psalm 91's association with a collection of apocryphal exorcistic psalms at Qumran (cf. 11Q11 = 11QApocryphal Psalms[a]).

3. The appeal of the crowd to Ps 118:25–26 during Jesus' entrance into the city of Jerusalem, on his way to the temple precincts (Mark 11:9–10), and Jesus' appeal to Ps 118:22–23 at the conclusion of his parable of the Wicked Vineyard Tenants (Mark 12:10–11) almost certainly reflect Ps 118:19–27 in the Aramaic. In the Targum this part of the psalm recounts the story of David's initial rejection and later acceptance by Samuel the priest and his colleagues (cf. vv. 22, 28: "the boy that the builders abandoned was among the sons of Jesse; and he was worthy to be appointed king and ruler. . . . 'I will praise you,' said David"). The Davidic orientation of this psalm not only explains why Ps 118:22–23 was chosen as the scriptural conclusion to a parable about a rejected son; it also clarifies the language of the crowd, which shouted, "Blessed is the coming kingdom of our ancestor David! Hosanna in the highest heaven!" (Mark 11:10). There is no reference to David in the Hebrew or in the Greek; it is only in the Aramaic.

4. In various sermons, the apostle Peter refers to David as a prophet and as speaking through "the Holy Spirit" (Acts 1:16–20, appealing to Ps 69:25; and Acts

2:25–31, appealing to Ps 16:8–11). The larger Christian community also refers to the Holy Spirit speaking through David in a prophetic sense (Acts 4:24–26, appealing to Pss 146:6; 2:2). These ideas are consistent with the Aramaic Psalter's view of David as possessing a spirit of prophecy (cf. *Tg. Pss.* 14:1; 18:1).

5. Quoting and expanding upon Gen 2:7, Paul calls Adam the "first" man (1 Cor 15:45–47). Four times the Aramaic Psalter innovatively refers to the "first Adam" (cf. *Tg. Pss.* 49:2; 69:32; 92:1; 94:10).

6. In Eph 4:8, the Pauline author quotes Ps 68:18 (Hebr. v. 19): "Therefore it is said, 'When he ascended on high he made captivity itself a captive, and he gave gifts to his people.'" The Hebrew reads, "You ascended the high mount, leading captives in your train and receiving gifts from people," but the LXX reads, "You ascended to the height; having taken captive captivity, you received gifts among people." Both the Hebrew and the Greek speak of God *receiving* gifts, but the quotation in Ephesians says "gave gifts to" people. The paraphrase in Ephesians agrees with the Aramaic, which reads, "You ascended to the height, *O prophet Moses;* you captured captives, *you taught the words of Torah,* you *gave them as* gifts *to* the sons of men, and even the stubborn *who are converted turn in repentance*" (italics indicate departures from the Hebrew).

Bibliography: C. A. EVANS, "The Aramaic Psalter and the New Testament: Praising the Lord in History and Prophecy," in *From Prophecy to Testament: The Function of the Old Testament in the New* (ed. C. A. Evans; Peabody, Mass.: Hendrickson, 2004), 44–91, here 90–91; M. MCNAMARA, *The New Testament and the Palestinian Targum to the Pentateuch* (2d ed.; AnBib 27A; Rome: Pontifical Biblical Institute, 1978), 78–81.

General Bibliography

P. S. ALEXANDER, "Jewish Aramaic Translations of Hebrew Scriptures," *Mikra* 217–53; IDEM, "Targum, Targumim," *ABD* 6:320–31; D. ASSAF, ed., *Proceedings of the Ninth World Congress of Jewish Studies, Division A: The Period of the Bible* (Jerusalem: World Union of Jewish Studies, 1986); D. R. G. BEATTIE and M. J. MCNAMARA, eds., *The Aramaic Bible: Targums in Their Historical Context* (JSOTSup 166; Sheffield: Sheffield, 1994); M, BLACK, *An Aramaic Approach to the Gospels and Acts* (3d ed.; Oxford: Clarendon, 1967; repr., with introduction by C. A. Evans, Peabody, Mass.: Hendrickson, 1998); M. BLACK and G. FOHRER, eds., *In Memoriam Paul Kahle* (BZAW 103; Berlin: A. Töpelmann, 1968); J. BOWKER, *The Targums and Rabbinic Literature: An Introduction to Jewish Interpretation of Scripture* (Cambridge: Cambridge University Press, 1969); K. J. CATHCART and M. MAHER, eds., *Targumic and Cognate Studies* (M. J. McNamara FS; JSOTSup 230; Sheffield: Sheffield, 1996); B. D. CHILTON, *The Glory of Israel: The Theology and Provenience of the Isaiah Targum* (JSOTSup 23; Sheffield: JSOT Press, 1982); IDEM, "Rabbinic Literature: Targumim," *DNTB* 902–9; J. W. ETHERIDGE, *The Targum of Onkelos and Jonathan ben Uzziel on the Pentateuch with the Fragments of the Jerusalem Targum* (2 vols.; London: Green, Longman & Roberts, 1862–1865;

repr., 2 vols. in 1; New York: Ktav, 1968) (unreliable in places); C. A. EVANS, "The Aramaic Psalter and the New Testament: Praising the Lord in History and Prophecy," in *From Prophecy to Testament: The Function of the Old Testament in the New* (ed. C. A. Evans; Peabody, Mass.: Hendrickson, 2004), 44–91; IDEM, ed., *The Interpretation of Scripture in Early Judaism and Christianity: Studies in Language and Tradition* (JSPSup 33; SSEJC 7; Sheffield: Sheffield, 2000); P. V. M. FLESHER, ed., *Targum Studies* (SFSHJ 55; Atlanta: Scholars Press, 1992–); J. T. FORESTELL, *Targumic Traditions and the New Testament* (SBLAS 4; Chico, Calif.: Scholars Press, 1979); F. GARCÍA MARTÍNEZ and E. J. C. TIGCHELAAR, *The Dead Sea Scrolls Study Edition* (2 vols.; Leiden: Brill, 1997); R. P. GORDON, *Studies in the Targum to the Twelve Prophets: From Nahum to Malachi* (VTSup 51; Leiden: Brill, 1994); P. GRELOT, *What Are the Targums?* (OTS 7; Wilmington, Del.: Glazier, 1992); B. GROSSFELD, "Bible: Translations, Aramaic (Targumim)," *EncJud* 4:841–51; IDEM, *A Bibliography of Targum Literature* (3 vols.; vols. 1–2; Bibliographica judaica 3, 8; Cincinnati: Hebrew Union College; vol. 3, New York: Sepher-Hermon, 1972–1990) [see the review and supplement by W. BAARS, *VT* 25 (1975): 124–28]; M. JASTROW, *A Dictionary of the Targumim, the Talmud Babli and Yerushalmi, and the Midrashic Literature* (2 vols.; New York: Putnam, 1886–1894; repr., New York: Pardes, 1950); R. LE DÉAUT, "The Current State of Targumic Studies," *BTB* 4 (1974): 3–32; IDEM, "Targumic Literature and New Testament Interpretation," *BTB* 4 (1974): 243–89; E. LEVINE, *The Aramaic Version of the Bible: Contents and Context* (BZAW 174; New York: de Gruyter, 1988); C. MANGAN, J. F. HEALEY, and P. S. KNOBEL, *The Targums of Job, Proverbs, Qohelet* (ArBib 15; Wilmington, Del.: Glazier, 1991); M. MCNAMARA, "Interpretation of Scripture in the Targumim," in *The Ancient Period* (vol. 1 of *A History of Biblical Interpretation;* ed. A. J. Hauser and D. F. Watson; Grand Rapids: Eerdmans, 2003), 167–97 (very helpful bibliography); IDEM, *The New Testament and the Palestinian Targum to the Pentateuch* (2d ed.; AnBib 27A; Rome: Pontifical Biblical Institute, 1978); IDEM, *Targum and Testament: Aramaic Paraphrases of the Hebrew Bible–a Light on the New Testament* (Grand Rapids: Eerdmans, 1972); IDEM, "Targumic Studies," *CBQ* 28 (1966): 1–19; IDEM, "Targums," *IDBSup* 856–61; P. NICKELS, *Targum and New Testament: A Bibliography Together with a New Testament Index* (Rome: Pontifical Biblical Institute, 1967); J. L. TEICHER, "A Sixth-Century Fragment of the Palestinian Targum," *VT* 1 (1951): 125–29; R. DE VAUX and J. T. MILIK, *Qumrân grotte 4.II: I. Archéologie; II. Tefillin, mezuzot, et targums (4Q128–4Q157)* (DJD 6; Oxford: Clarendon, 1977); A. P. WIKGREN, "The Targums and the New Testament," *JR* 24 (1944): 89–95.

CHAPTER SEVEN

Rabbinic Literature

Selected Rabbinic Literature

TALMUDIC LITERATURE
Mishna
Tosefta
Jerusalem Talmud
Babylonian Talmud
Minor Tractates of the Talmud
  ʾAbot de Rabbi Nathan
  Kalla Rabbati
  Soperim
  Semaḥot
  Kalla
  Derek Ereṣ Rabba
  Derek Ereṣ Zuṭa
  Pereq ha-Šalom
  Gerim
  Kutim
  ʿAbadim
  Seper Torah
  Tepillin
  Zizit
  Mezuzah

TANNAIC MIDRASHIC LITERATURE
Mekilta
Sipra Leviticus
Sipre Numbers
Sipre Deuteronomy
Seder ʿOlam Rabbah
Megillat Taʿanit

AMORAIC MIDRASHIC LITERATURE
Midrash Rabbah
  Genesis Rabbah

Exodus Rabbah
Leviticus Rabbah
Numbers Rabbah
Deuteronomy Rabbah
Lamentations Rabbah
Ruth Rabbah
Ecclesiastes Rabbah
Esther Rabbah
Song of Songs Rabbah
Seder Elijah Rabbah
Pesiqta de Rab Kahana
Pesiqta Rabbati
Midrash Tanḥuma
Midrash Tehillin
Pirqe Rabbi Eliezer
Seder ʿOlam Zuṭa
Chronicle of Jerahmeel

LATER MIDRASHIM
Midrash ʾAggadah
ʾAggadat Bereshit
Midrash Megillot Zuṭa
Bereshit Rabbati
Midrash Shemuel
Midrash Mishle
Midrash Yob
Midrash Šir haŠir
Midrash Haggadol
Yalqut Šimeoni
ʾAggadat Esther

(continued on next page)

SELECTED RABBINIC LITERATURE, CONT'D

MEDIEVAL COMMENTATORS
Saadya ben Joseph
Solomon ben Isaac
Abraham Ibn Ezra
Joseph Kimhi

Moses Maimonides
David Kimhi
Moses Kimhi
Moses Nahmanides

As John Townsend has pointed out, rabbinic writings that are used to aid in the interpretation of early Christianity fall into three categories: Targum, Talmud, and midrash (*midraš*). The first category is treated in another chapter; the latter two are considered in this chapter. The writings that fall into the category of Talmud are the first four listed above: Mishna, Tosefta, the Jerusalem (or Palestinian) Talmud, and the Babylonian Talmud, along with its several minor tractates. Of these only a few will be discussed. The remaining writings, from *Mekilta* to *ʾAggadat Esther,* fall into the category of midrash.

These rabbinic writings also fall into two broad periods of time: Tannaic (or Tannaitic) and Amoraic. The Tannaic period extends roughly from 50 B.C.E. to 200 C.E., that is, from the establishment of the early academies, Bet Shammai ("House of Shammai") and Bet Hillel ("House of Hillel"), to the compiling and editing of the Mishna under Rabbi Judah ha-Nasi ("the Prince" or "Patriarch"; 135–217 C.E.) in the first decade or so of the third century C.E. The teachers or sages of this period are called the Tannaim ("teachers," from the Aramaic word *tenāʾ*, which literally means "to repeat"). Midway through this period, probably following Yavne (or Jamnia; late first century C.E.), ordained sages were given the title "Rabbi," which literally means "my master." Informal use of "rabbi," of course, was earlier, as seen in the NT Gospels. Babylonian scholars were called "Rab." The achievement of the Tannaic period was the production of the Mishna (Mishnah). Tannaic sayings found in later writings outside of Mishna are called *baraitot* (an Aramaic word which literally means "standing outside"; sg. *baraita*). The Amoraic period is from 220 C.E. to 500 C.E. Rabbis of this period are called the Amoraim ("expounders" or "spokesmen," from the Aramaic word *ʾamar,* which literally means "to say"). The achievement of the Amoraic period was the production of the two Talmuds and several of the midrashim.

There are two later rabbinic periods. The first is the saboraic (500–650 C.E.). The rabbis of this period are called Saboraim ("reasoners," from Aramaic, *sebar,* "to reason"). The Saboraim edited the Babylonian Talmud. The second period is the geonic (650–1050 C.E.). The major Babylonian rabbis of this period are called the Geonim ("excellent," from Hebrew, *gāʾôn,* "majesty," "pride"). "Gaon" was a title of honor reserved for the chief rabbis, e.g., Saadya Gaon (see below).

Principal Tannaim of the Mishnaic Period*

First Generation (80–120 C.E.)	Second Generation (120–140 C.E.)	Third Generation (140–165 C.E.)
Eleazar ben Arak	Aqiba (ben Joseph)	Abba Saul
Eleazar ben Azaria	Elai	Eleazar ben Shammua
Eliezer (ben Hyrcanus)	Eleazar ben Judah	Eliezer ben Jacob II
Eliezer ben Jacob I	Ishmael (ben Elisha)	Judah ben Elai
Gamaliel (II), the Patriarch	Judah ben Baba	Meir
Joshua (ben Hananiah)	Yohanan ben Nuri	Nehemiah
Judah ben Bathyra	Yose the Galilean	Sim(e)on ben Gamaliel II
Yohanan ben Zakkai	Sim(e)on ben Azzai	Sim(e)on (ben Yohai)
Yose the Priest	Tarfon	Yose (ben Halafta)

Fourth Generation (165–200 C.E.)	Fifth Generation (200–220 C.E.)	Post-Tannaic (220–240 C.E.)
Eleazar ben Sim(e)on (ben Yohai)	Gamaliel III	Joshua ben Levi

Judah the Patriarch
   (or "Rabbi")
	Sim(e)on ben Judah
	   (the Patriarch)
		Yannai

Nathan the Babylonian		
Sim(e)on ben Eleazar		
Yose ben Judah (ben Elai)		

*(Adapted from A. Goldberg, "Mishnah," *LS* 236–38; H. Danby, *Mishnah*, 799–800. Goldberg's "first generation" is Danby's "second," and so forth. Note: The names that begin with "J" are sometimes spelled with "Y," e.g., Yoshua, instead of Joshua, Yehudah, instead of Judah, etc.)

The exegesis of the rabbis is called midrash. This word comes from the Hebrew verb *dāraš* ("to search"). Midrash, therefore, literally means a "search" or the activity of "searching" (cf. John 5:39: "You search the scriptures"; cf. 7:52). In the context of the rabbinic writings, the word means interpretation of Scripture. Midrash is often broken down into two categories: Halakic midrash and haggadic midrash (see below). Rabbinic interpretation is in large measure founded on the assumption that Scripture contains potentially unlimited meaning. One rabbi explained it this way: "'Is not my word like a hammer that breaks the rock in pieces?' [Jer 23:29]. As the hammer causes numerous sparks to flash forth, so is a verse of Scripture capable of many interpretations" (*b. Sanh.* 34a). According to Ben Bag Bag, a student of Hillel: "Turn it [Scripture] and turn it again, for everything is in it; and contemplate it and grow grey and old over it and stir not from it, for thou canst have no better rule than it" (*m. ʾAbot* 5:22). A single exegesis is called a midrash (pl. *midrašim*). Commentaries on Scripture are called midrashim, although the Mishna, the Tosefta, and the two Talmuds are themselves filled with midrash.

The word *midrash*, as well as its Greek equivalent *ereunan* ("to search"), was associated with biblical interpretation in the first century. This is shown by the Qumran materials: "This is the study [*midraš*] of the Law" (1QS 8:15); "The interpretation [*midraš*] of 'Blessed is the man . . .' [cf. Ps 1:1]" (4QFlor 1:14). Indeed, Qumran's leader, the Teacher of Righteousness, is called the "searcher of the Law" (CD 6:7). Philo, the Greek-speaking Jew of Alexandria, urges his readers to join him in searching (*ereunan*) Scripture (*Worse* 17 §57; 39 §141; *Cherubim* 5 §14). John 5:39, cited above, also uses the Greek equivalent *ereunan*.

According to early rabbinic tradition Hillel the Elder articulated seven rules (or *middot*) by which Scripture was to be interpreted. Evidently they were practiced in the first century, for all of these rules are found in the NT. They are as follows (cf. *t. Sanh.* 7.11; *ʾAbot R. Nat.* A 37.10):

1. *Qal wa-homer* (lit. "light and heavy"). According to this rule, what is true or applicable in a "light" (or less important) instance is surely true or applicable in a "heavy" (or more important) instance. This rule is at work when Jesus assures his disciples (cf. Matt 6:26; Luke 12:24) that because God cares for the birds (light), they can be sure that he cares for them (heavy). See also John 10:31–38; 2 Cor 3:6–11; Heb 9:13–14.

2. *Gezera shawa* (lit. "an equivalent regulation"). According to this rule one passage may be explained by another, if similar words or phrases are present. Comparing himself to David, who on one occasion violated the law in eating consecrated bread (1 Sam 21:6), Jesus justified his apparent violation of the Sabbath (Mark 2:23–28). See also Rom 4:3–7; Heb 7:1–28; Jas 2:21–24.

3. *Binyan ʿab mikkatub ʿehad* (lit. "constructing a father [i.e., principal rule] from one [passage]"). Since God is not the God of the dead, but of the living, the revelation at the burning bush, "I am the God of Abraham" (Exod 3:14–15), implies that Abraham is to be resurrected. From this one text and its inference one may further infer, as Jesus did (Mark 12:26), the truth of the general resurrection. See also Jas 5:16–18.

4. *Binyan ʿab mishshene ketubim* (lit. "constructing a father [i.e., principal rule] from two writings [or passages]"). From the commands to unmuzzle the ox (Deut 25:4) and share sacrifices with the priests (Deut 18:1–8) it is inferred that those who preach are entitled to support (Matt 10:10; Luke 10:7; 1 Cor 9:9, 13; 1 Tim 5:18). See also Rom 4:1–25; Jas 2:22–26.

5. *Kelal uperat uperat ukelal* (lit. "General and particular, and particular and general"). When Jesus replies that the greatest commandment (the "general") is to love the Lord with all one's heart (Deut 6:4–5) and to love one's neighbor as one's self (Lev 19:18), he has summed up all of the "particular" commandments (Mark 12:28–34). See also Rom 13:9–10.

6. *Kayotze bo mi–maqom ʿaher* (lit. "To which something [is] similar in another place [or passage]"). If the Son of Man (or Messiah) is to sit on one of the thrones set up before the Ancient of Days (Dan 7:9, which is how Rabbi Aqiba interprets Daniel's plural reference to "thrones," cf. *b. Ḥag.* 14a; *b. Sanh.* 38b), and if Messiah is to sit at God's right hand (Ps 110:1), it may be inferred that when the Son of Man comes with the clouds (Dan 7:13–14), he will be seated at the right hand of God and will judge his enemies. This is evidently what Jesus implied in his reply to Caiaphas (Mark 14:62; see further discussion below). See also Gal 3:8–16; Heb 4:7–9; 8:7–13.

7. *Dabar halamed meʾinyano* (lit. "word of instruction from the context"). This rule is exemplified in Jesus' teaching against divorce (Matt 19:4–8). Although it is true that Moses allowed divorce (Deut 24:1–3), it is also true that

God never intended the marriage union to be broken, as implied in Gen 1:27 and 2:24. See also Rom 4:10–11; Heb 11:1–13, 35–40.

Tradition holds that these rules were expanded to thirteen by Ishmael, a rabbi of the second century (cf. *Baraita R. Ishmael* §1 in the prologue to *Sipra*). Rabbi Eliezer ben Yose the Galilean is credited with expanding the rules of midrash, particularly as they relate to the interpretation of narrative. He is evidently the author of the tractate *Thirty-Two Rules for Interpreting the Torah*, often called the *Baraita of Thirty-Two Rules* (cf. the beginning of *Midr. Mishnat R. Eliezer* and the beginning of *Midr. Haggadol* to Genesis). Many of these rules are atomistic (e.g., finding significance in the numerical value of the letters themselves) and have little or nothing to do with the literary or historical context of the scriptural passage under consideration. Most of these thirty-two rules, rules which made it possible to enjoy the "savory dishes of wisdom" (*m. ʾAbot* 3:19), were applied to homiletical midrash, not legal.

The distinction between homiletical midrash and legal interpretation also requires explanation. Legal midrash is halakic, from the word *hālak* ("to walk"), i.e., how one should walk or conduct himself or herself in life. A legal opinion is called a *halakah* (pl. *halakot*). Homiletical interpretation is haggadic, from the word *nāgad* ("to draw"), i.e., how one narrates a story or explains a problem in the text. A homiletical interpretation is called a *haggadah* (pl. *haggadot;* note that sometimes it is spelled *ʾAggadah*). Best known is the *Passover Haggadah* (cf. *b. Pesaḥ.* 115b, 116b). Haggadic midrash was much more imaginative in its attempts to fill in the gaps in Scripture and to explain away apparent discrepancies, difficulties, and unanswered questions. Legal rulings were not to be derived from haggadic interpretation (cf. *y. Peʾah* 2.6).

The following summaries are chronological in their respective categories to the best of our knowledge. Rabbinic literature is notoriously difficult to date. Part of the problem is that a given work, which may have been edited in the Middle Ages, may contain a great deal of Tannaic tradition. What then is being dated? If the sayings are genuine, the work could be considered Tannaic. If the sayings are not, or at least have been heavily edited, or inaccurately transmitted, then the work should be considered Amoraic (or later). There is also the problem of pseudonymity. Sayings may be credited to a famous Tanna (such as Aqiba or Ishmael), but in reality they derive from a much later Amora.

Bibliography: H. MACCOBY, *ERW;* J. NEUSNER, *IRL;* H. L. STRACK and G. STEMBERGER, *ITM*.

Summaries of Talmudic Literature

The word *mishna(h)* (lit. "repetition") comes from the Hebrew verb *šānāh,* "to repeat." It later came to connote learning by repetition, perhaps under the influence of the Aramaic word *tenāʾ,* which has this meaning. The Mishna was edited and published under the direction of Rabbi Judah ha-Nasi, about 200–220

C.E. Rabbi Aqiba and his pupils were the most influential contributors to this corpus, especially at Usha (ca. 150 C.E.), following the defeat of Simon Bar Kokhba. Representing a large portion of Tannaic oral tradition, the themes of Mishna are organized into six major divisions (i.e., *sedarim,* "orders"), each containing several tractates *(massektot),* whose names are either Hebrew or Aramaic:

MISHNA

1. *Zeraʾim* ("seeds")	2. *Moʾed* ("set [feasts]")	3. *Našim* ("women")
Berakot ("benedictions")	*Šabbat* ("Sabbath")	*Yebamot* ("sisters-in-law")
Peʾah ("corner [for gleaning]")	*ʿErubin* ("mixtures")	*Ketubbot* ("marriage deeds")
Demai ("doubtful [produce]")	*Pesaḥim* ("Passovers")	*Nedarim* ("vows")
KilPayim ("diverse kinds")	*Šeqalim* ("shekels")	*Nazir* ("the Nazirite vow")
Šebiʿit ("seventh [year]")	*Yoma* ("the day	*Sotah* ("the suspected adulteress")
Terumot ("heave-offerings")	[of atonement]")	*Giṭṭin* ("bills of divorce")
Maʿaśerot ("tithes")	*Sukkah* ("tabernacle")	*Qiddušin* ("betrothals")
Maʿaśer Šeni ("second tithe")	*Beṣah = Yom Ṭob*	
Ḥallah ("dough-offering")	("good day"/"egg")	
ʿOrlah ("uncut [young trees]")	*Roš Haššanah* ("New Year")	
Bikkurim ("firstfruits")	*Taʿanit* ("fast day")	
	Megillah ("the Scroll [of Esther]")	
	Moʾed Qaṭan ("lesser set [feasts]")	
	Ḥagigah ("the festal offering")	

4. *Neziqin* ("damages")	5. *Qodašim* ("sacred things")	6. *Tohorot* ("cleannesses")
Baba Qamma ("first gate")	*Zebaḥim* ("sacrifices")	*Kelim* ("vessels")
Baba Meṣiʿa ("middle gate")	*Menaḥot* ("meal offerings")	*ʾOhalot* ("tents")
Baba Batra ("last gate")	*Ḥullin* ("non-holy things")	*Negaʿim* ("plagues")
Sanhedrin ("the council")	*Bekorot* ("firstlings")	*Parah* ("cow")
Makkot ("stripes")	*ʿArakin* ("vows of valuation")	*Tohorot* ("cleannesses")
Šebuʿot ("oaths")	*Temurah* ("exchange")	*Miqwaʾot* ("ritual baths")
ʿEduyyot ("testimonies")	*Kerithot* ("uprootings")	*Niddah* ("the menstruant")
ʿAbodah Zarah ("idolatry")	*Meʿilah* ("sacrilege")	*Makširin* ("defilers")
(Pirqe) ʾAbot ("the fathers")	*Tamid* ("always")	*Zabim* ("those with flux")
Horayot ("instructions")	*Middot* ("measurements")	*Tebul Yom* ("immersed
	Qinnim ("birds' nests")	that day")
		Yadayim ("hands")
		ʿUqṣin ("stalks")

Mishna represents a codification of the oral tradition of the Tannaic sages and rabbis. As the table of contents above shows, these materials have been arranged according to topic. For example, the order *Neziqin* contains tractates concerned with civil and criminal law. (*Pirqe ʾAbot,* it should be noted, is not really a mishnaic tractate, but a collection of the sayings of Tannaic sages and rabbis that is more akin to wisdom literature than the halakic materials one encounters in the Mishna.) The "gate" tractates, once originally combined, primarily treat civil law. *Baba Qamma* deals with personal injury. *Baba Meṣiʿa* deals with lost property, questions of guardianship, usury, and the hire of laborers. *Baba Batra* deals with problems relating to the ownership of real estate and other immovable property. *Sanhedrin* deals primarily with criminal law, especially as it pertains to capital punishment, while *Makkot*, originally part of *Sanhedrin*, deals with the question of punishment for false witnesses. Below are sample passages from *Sanhedrin* (6:4; 7:5) that could have some relevance for NT interpretation:

> "All that have been stoned must be hanged." So Rabbi Eliezer [late first, early second century C.E.]. But the Sages [first century C.E.] say: "None is hanged save the blasphemer and idolator." "A man is hanged with his face to the people and a woman with her face towards the gallows." So Rabbi Eliezer. But the Sages say: "A man is hanged but a woman is not hanged." Rabbi Eliezer said to them: "Did not Simeon ben Shetah [first century B.C.E.] hang women in Askelon?" They answered: "He hanged eighty women, whereas two ought not to be judged in the one day." How did they hang a man? They put a beam into the ground and a piece of wood jutted from it. The two hands [of the body] were brought together and [in this fashion] it was hanged. Rabbi Yose [early second century C.E.] says: "The beam was made to lean against a wall and one hanged the corpse thereon as butchers do. And they let it down at once: if it remained there overnight a negative command is thereby transgressed, for it is written, 'His body shall not remain all night upon the tree, but you shall surely bury him the same day; for he that is hanged is a curse of God' [Deut 21:23]; as if to say: 'Why was this one hanged? Because he blessed [euphemism for cursed] the Name, and the Name of Heaven was found profaned.'"

> "The blasphemer" [Lev 24:10–23] is not culpable unless he pronounces the Name itself. Rabbi Joshua ben Karha [second century C.E.] says: "On every day [of the trial] they examined the witnesses with a substituted name, [such as] 'May Yose strike Yose.' When sentence was to be given they did not declare him guilty of death [on the grounds of the evidence given] with the substituted name, but they sent out all the people and asked the chief among the witnesses and said to him, 'Say expressly what you heard,' and he says it; and the judges stand up on their feet and tear their garments, and they may not mend them again. And the second witness says, 'I also heard the like,' and the third says, 'I also heard the like.'"

These passages may clarify certain features of Jesus' trial before Caiaphas the high priest and the Sanhedrin (Mark 14:53–65). Caiaphas asked Jesus if he was the Messiah, the Son of the Blessed (v. 61). When Jesus affirmed the question and alluded to Ps 110:1 and Dan 7:13–14 (v. 62), Caiaphas tore his garments and accused Jesus of blasphemy (vv. 63–64). The Sanhedrin agreed that Jesus deserved death (v. 64). Some think that the mishnaic rules do not apply, at least not exactly, since Jesus did not pronounce the Divine Name, but employed a circumlocution ("You will see the Son of Man seated at the right hand of Power"). But it is possible that what we have in Mark is the public report of what Jesus said. This report would not have used the Divine Name. What Jesus may have said before Caiaphas and the Sanhedrin was, "You will see the Son of Man seated at the right hand of Yahweh." Jesus' claim to be seated at God's right hand and someday to come with clouds of heaven as the Son of Man would have been blasphemous in itself (see discussion below). Pronouncing the Divine Name would have allowed the Sanhedrin to sentence him to death. The use of Deut 21:23 could explain why Jesus was taken down from the cross the same day of his crucifixion (Mark 15:42–46). Note also the theological use of the verse in Paul (Gal 3:13; cf. 2 Cor 5:21).

Although most of this material arose after the destruction of the Jewish temple in 70 C.E., some of it does derive from the time of Jesus and his disciples. The criticisms leveled at Jesus for associating with "sinners" (Mark 2:15–17), failing to fast (Mark 2:18–20), gleaning on the Sabbath (Mark 2:23–27), healing on the Sabbath (Mark 3:1–6), and eating with unwashed hands (Mark 7:1–13) are all based on the oral tradition current in the early first century that was developed further, collected, edited, and eventually published as the Mishna.

Deserving of comment is Jacob Neusner's controversial view of the Mishna as an ahistorical, even antihistorical philosophy, which is interested in neither eschatology nor messianology and which as such represents the essence of Judaism (*Judaism: The Evidence of the Mishnah* [Chicago: University of Chicago Press, 1981); cf. idem, *Messiah in Context: Israel's History and Destiny in Formative Judaism* (Philadelphia: Fortress, 1984); idem, *Judaism as Philosophy: The Method and Message of the Mishnah* (Columbia: University of South Carolina, 1991). E. P. Sanders (*Jewish Law from Jesus to the Mishnah* [Philadelphia: Trinity Press International, 1990], 309–31) has argued that this assessment founders on the question of genre. Mishna, says Sanders, is a compendium of law; it is not a philosophy of history, nor an apocalypse. Since its concern is primarily legal (i.e., how to obey the commandments of Torah), one should expect to find in it little historical narrative and little eschatology. Neusner's assessment may also be vulnerable for assuming that what is not in the Mishna was therefore of no interest to the rabbis. Sanders comments that this is a false use of the argument from silence. (See the related discussion below on Messiah in rabbinic literature.)

References to Mishna are usually cited with an *m.* followed by the name of the tractate, its chapter (or *pereq*) and its paragraph (or *mishnah*). For example, the two passages from *Sanhedrin* cited above would appear as *m. Sanh.* 6:4; 7:5. For the SBL's recommended abbreviations of mishnaic tractates, see P. H. Alexander et al., eds., *The SBL Handbook of Style for Ancient Near Eastern, Biblical, and Early Christian Studies* (Peabody, Mass.: Hendrickson, 1999), 79–80.

Text: P. BLACKMAN, *Mishnayoth* (6 vols.; 2d ed.; New York: Judaica, 1990) (includes some notes, English translation, and commentary); J. RABBINOWITZ, *Mishnah Megillah* (Oxford: Oxford University Press, 1931) (includes some notes and commentary). *Translations:* H. DANBY, *The Mishnah* (Oxford: Clarendon, 1933); J. NEUSNER, *The Mishnah: A New Translation* (New Haven: Yale University Press, 1988). *Introduction:* H. MACCOBY, *ERW* 30–35, 49–133; J. NEUSNER, *IRL* 97–128; IDEM, *The Mishnah: An Introduction* (Northvale, N.J.: Aronson, 1989); IDEM, "Rabbinic Literature: Mishnah and Tosefta," *DNTB* 893–97; H. L. STRACK and G. STEMBERGER, *ITM* 119–66. *Commentary:* J. NEUSNER, *A History of the Mishnaic Law of Appointed Times* (5 vols.; SJLA 34; Leiden: Brill, 1981–1983); IDEM, *A History of the Mishnaic Law of Damages* (5 vols.; SJLA 35; Leiden: Brill, 1983–1985); IDEM, *A History of the Mishnaic Law of Holy Things* (6 vols.; SJLA 30; Leiden: Brill, 1978–1980); IDEM, *A History of the Mishnaic Law of Purities* (22 vols.; SJLA 6; Leiden: Brill, 1974–1977); IDEM, *A History of the Mishnaic Law of Women* (5 vols.; SJLA 33; Leiden: Brill, 1979–1980) (these commentaries include the Tosefta; a 10-vol. commentary by Neusner on *Zeraim* ["Seeds"] is projected [Brill]). *Critical Study:* A. GOLDBERG, "The Mishna—a Study Book of Halakha," *LS* 211–62; J. NEUSNER, *Judaism: The Evidence of the Mishnah* (Chicago:

University of Chicago Press, 1981); IDEM, *Form Analysis and Exegesis: A Fresh Approach to the Interpretation of Mishnah* (Minneapolis: University of Minnesota Press, 1980); IDEM, *The Mishnah before 70* (BJS 51; Atlanta: Scholars Press, 1987); IDEM, *The Modern Study of the Mishnah* (SPB 23; Leiden: Brill, 1973); IDEM, *The Comparative Hermeneutics of Rabbinic Judaism* (Binghamton, N.Y.: Global, 2000), esp. vols. 1–6.

PRINCIPAL AMORAIM OF THE TALMUDIC PERIOD*

First Generation (220–250 C.E.)	*Second Generation* (250–290 C.E.)	*Third Generation* (290–320 C.E.)
Hanina ben Hama	Eleazar ben Pedat	Abbahu
Joshua ben Levi	Hamnuna	Hisda
Oshaya Rabbah	Huna	Joseph ben Hiyya
Rab (Abba ben Aibu)	Judah ben Ezekiel	Rabbah ben Huna
Samuel	Simeon ben Lakish	Rabbah ben Nahmani
Yannai	Yohanan	Zeira

Fourth Generation (320–350 C.E.)	*Fifth Generation* (350–375 C.E.)	*Sixth Generation* (375–425 C.E.)
Abbaye	Huna ben Joshua	Ameimar
Haggai	Mana ben Jonah	Mar Zutra
Jeremiah	Pappa	Rab Ashi
Jonah	Tanhuma ben Abba	Rabina
Raba ben Joseph	Yose ben Abin	
Yose	Zevid	

Seventh Generation (425–460 C.E.)	*Eighth Generation* (460–500 C.E.)
Geviha of Bet-Katil	Ahai ben Huna
Mar ben Rab Ashi	Rabina II ben Huna
Yeimar	Yose

*(Adapted from *EncJud* 1:866. For a convenient compilation of the rabbis in the rabbinic literature, see J. Neusner, ed., *Dictionary of Ancient Rabbis: Selections from the Jewish Encyclopaedia* [Peabody, Mass.: Hendrickson, 2003].)

Tosefta. Tosefta ("supplement") was probably published about one generation after Mishna (220–230 C.E.), though some, such as Jacob Neusner, have argued for a later date (e.g., 300 C.E.). Tosefta contains mostly Tannaic traditions, but adds the next two generations of rabbis. It is thus an admixture of Tannaic and early Amoraic materials. The major contributor of the new material is Rabbi Judah ha-Nasi, the compiler of Mishna. The editor of Tosefta was Rabbi Judah's pupil Rabbi Hiya the Elder. Tosefta complements, explains, expands upon, identifies anonymous sayings, and at times explicitly comments on the Mishna. (One could say that its relationship to Mishna is somewhat analogous to Matthew's and Luke's respective relationships to Mark.) As a result, it is more than twice the length of the Mishna. In a very real sense it is the forerunner of Talmud itself.

Tosefta follows the same format and structure as the Mishna and has the same basic contents. There are some differences, however. In the first order, *Zera'im*, a few of the tractates are in different positions. The fourth order, *Neziqin*, does not contain *Pirqe 'Abot*. The fifth order, *Qodašim*, lacks the tractates *Tamid*,

Middot, and *Qinnim*. The sixth order, *Ṭohorot*, arranges *Kelim* differently. In both *Qodašim* and *Ṭohorot* some tractates are in different positions.

There is material in Tosefta that may shed light on the NT. Supplementing and commenting on the last part of *m. Menaḥ.* 13:10, the Tosefta has this to say about activities of the last two generations of the ruling priests (*t. Menaḥ.* 13.18–22; cf. *t. Zebaḥ.* 11.16–17; *b. Pesaḥ.* 57a):

> At first [the lower-ranking priests] brought the hides of Holy Things to the room of *bet happarvah* and divided them in the evening to each household which had served on that day. But the powerful men of the [ruling] priesthood would come and take them by force. [Then] they ordained that they should divide [them] on Fridays to each and every watch [of lower-ranking priests]. But still violent men of the [ruling] priesthood came and took [them] away by force. [Therefore,] the owners went and dedicated them to Heaven.

> Abba Saul [ca. 140 C.E.] says, "Beams of sycamore were in Jericho. And strong-fisted men would come and take them by force. The owners went and dedicated them to Heaven." [The Sages said,] "The owners dedicated to Heaven only beams of sycamore alone." Concerning these and people like them and people who do deeds like their deeds Abba Saul ben Batnit [ca. 80 C.E.] and Yose ben Yohanan of Jerusalem [ca. 10 C.E.] say, "Woe is me because of the House of Boethus. Woe is me because of their clubs. Woe is me because of the house of Qadros. Woe is me because of their pen. Woe is me because of the House of Hanin. Woe is me because of their whispering. Woe is me because of the House of Ishmael ben Phiabi. For they are High Priests, and their sons [are] treasurers, and their sons-in-law [are] supervisors, and their servants come and beat us with clubs." Yohanan ben Torta [ca. 120 C.E.] said, "On what account was Shiloh [cf. Jer 7:12] destroyed? Because of the disgraceful disposition of the Holy Things which were there. As to Jerusalem's first [temple], on what account was it destroyed? Because of idolatry and licentiousness and bloodshed which was in it. But [as to] the latter [temple] we know that they devoted themselves to Torah and were meticulous about tithes. On what account did they go into exile? Because they love money and hate one another."

These passages describe the last two generations of the ruling priests of Jerusalem. In the "woes" of Abba Saul ben Batnit and Yose ben Yohanan of Jerusalem we find criticism leveled at three of the four principal ruling families during the period of the Herodian temple. "Boethus" was the lower-ranking priest whose son Simon Herod the Great made high priest (22–5 B.C.E.) in return for the hand of his daughter (cf. Josephus, *Ant.* 15.9.3 §320). "Qadros" is probably "Simon Cantheras," another son of Boethus (*Ant.* 19.6.2 §297; 19.6.4 §313), who served less than one year as high priest (41 C.E.). The House of Boethus is remembered for its clubs and for its pen, by which they wrote their oppressive and unfair decrees. "Hanin" is the Annas of the NT (Luke 3:2; John 18:13, 14; Acts 4:6), who served as high priest (6–15 C.E.) and whose five sons, a grandson, and son-in-law Caiaphas at various times served as high priest (*Ant.* 18.2.1 §26; 20.9.1 §198, where he is called Ananus). Ben Batnit and ben Yohanan lament their "whispering," by which they probably mean their conspiracies. Tosefta does not tell us specifically why "Phiabi" and his son Ishmael (*Ant.* 18.2.2 §34) were a cause for lamentation. The Talmud (*b. Pesaḥ.* 57a) tells us it was "because of their fists." In reference to all of these priestly families, the woes are summed up: "they are High Priests, and their sons [are] treasurers, and their sons-in-law [are] supervisors, and their servants come and beat us with clubs."

Tosefta also explains why the Herodian temple was destroyed. Because of greed, avarice, and nepotism, the second temple, like the sanctuary at Shiloh and the first temple of Jerusalem, was destroyed. The "powerful men of the [ruling] priesthood" stole the tithes that rightfully belonged to the lower-ranking priests. With the profits they were able to cover the temple with gold (part of *t. Menaḥ.* 13.19 omitted in the quotation). If any one opposed them, they had their servants beat them with clubs.

The tradition is apparently very ancient. The "woes" originated with Yose ben Yohanan of Jerusalem, a sage from the turn of the era, and probably reached the form we now have them in Abba Saul ben Batnit. Yohanan ben Torta adds later moralizing commentary. His statement that it was because of hatred and the love of money is quite significant. The tradition enjoys a measure of confirmation from Josephus. He specifically mentions another Ishmael, part of the Phiabi family, who served as high priest (59–61 C.E.), whose servants beat the lower-ranking priests and stole their tithes (*Ant.* 20.8.8 §§179–181; 20.9.2 §207).

These passages may clarify several aspects of Jesus' relationship to the temple establishment and why he was arrested. First, it could help us understand Jesus' criticism of the economic policies of the temple establishment. This is seen in Jesus' statement that the sons of the king are free from the obligation to pay the annual half-shekel temple tax (Matt 17:24–27). It is clearly seen in his Vineyard parable (Mark 12:1–12), in which the priestly aristocracy is threatened with the loss of their position. Jesus' warning of the scribes who "devour widows' houses" (Mark 12:38–40), his lament (not praise!) over the poor widow's offering (Mark 12:41–44), and his prediction of the destruction of the "wonderful buildings" (Mark 13:1–2) should be understood as criticisms of the economic policies and practices of the first-century ruling priesthood.

Second, Jesus' action in the temple (Mark 11:15–17) is now clarified. His action was no protest against "external" religion or against the sacrificial system itself. He protested against the profit-motivated policies of Caiaphas the high priest and his aristocratic supporters. By alluding to Jeremiah 7 Jesus implied that his contemporaries were guilty of some of the same practices of the priests of Jeremiah's time. Some scholars have doubted the authenticity of the saying in Mark 11:17, because Jeremiah's reference to "robbers" implies violence, taking by force, not thievery or swindling. But according to Josephus and the Tosefta's version of *Menaḥot*, violence perpetrated by the first-century ruling priesthood *was* a problem. Of course, Jesus did not imply that people were being mugged in the temple precincts, any more than they were in the days of Jeremiah. But the ruling priesthood was avaricious and at times violent, just as in the days of Jeremiah. Calling them robbers would not have been unintelligible. Jesus' action would have been understood as a prophetic condemnation of temple polity. Since the high priest is directly responsible for temple polity, this action would have been keenly felt by Caiaphas.

Third, details of Jesus' arrest cohere with Tosefta's picture. Judas, bribed by the ruling priests (Mark 14:10–11), assisted Caiaphas in his conspiracy to take Jesus by stealth. Thus far, he has lived up to Tosefta's picture of the family that "whispers." While alone in Gethsemane, Jesus was approached by "a crowd with swords and clubs, from the ruling priests and the scribes and elders" (Mark 14:32, 43). Again we are reminded of Tosefta's *Menaḥot*. In the minor scuffle that ensued the "slave of the high priest" is struck (v. 47). It is interesting that the only person of the arresting party to be mentioned is the servant of the *high priest*. His presence and violent involvement suggest that Caiaphas had taken a personal interest in seeing Jesus arrested.

Finally, Caiaphas's interest in the case is further documented by his personal appearance at Jesus' hearing before the Sanhedrin (Mark 14:53–65). Indeed, the proceedings apparently took place in his home (v. 54). When Jesus was charged with blasphemy and condemned to death he was slapped and spat upon (v. 65). Thus we find at several points coherence between the Gospels' portrayal of Jesus' criticisms of the ruling priesthood and the traditions and reminiscences preserved in one of the Tosefta tractates.

References to Tosefta, as in the case of Mishna, are usually cited with a *t.* followed by the name of the tractate, its chapter, and its paragraph (or halakah), e.g., *t. Soṭah* 9.15. In his translation Jacob Neusner has very helpfully outlined the logical flow of the topics and arguments. The abbreviations of Tosefta's tractates are the same as those of Mishna.

Text: S. LIEBERMAN, *Tosefot Rishonim* (4 vols.; Jerusalem: Bamberger & Wahrmann, 1936–1939) [Hebrew; includes some notes and commentary]; M. S. ZUCKERMANDEL, *Tosephta: Based on the Erfurt and Vienna Codices* (2d ed.; Jerusalem: Bamberger & Wahrmann, 1937) (Hebrew). *Translation:* J. NEUSNER, ed., *The Tosefta: Translated from the Hebrew* (6 vols.; New York: Ktav, 1977–1986), repr., *The Tosefta in English* (6 vols. in 2; Peabody, Mass.: Hendrickson, 2002) (with a new introduction). *Introduction:* H. MAC-COBY, *ERL*, 35–36, 133–47; J. NEUSNER, *IRL* 129–52; IDEM, "Rabbinic Literature: Mishnah and Tosefta," *DNTB* 893–97; IDEM, *The Tosefta: An Introduction* (SFSHJ 47; Atlanta: Scholars Press, 1992); H. L. STRACK and G. STEMBERGER, *ITM* 167–81. *Commentary:* See Neusner's 2002 translation with commentary on Mishna, cited above. *Critical Study:* A. GOLDBERG, with M. KRUPP, "The Tosefta—Companion to the Mishna," *LS* 283–302; J. NEUSNER, *The Tosefta: Its Structures and Its Sources* (BJS 112; Atlanta: Scholars Press, 1986); P. R. WEIS, "The Controversies of Rab and Samuel and the Tosefta," *JSS* 3 (1958): 288–97; S. ZEITLIN, "The Tosefta," *JQR* 47 (1956–1957): 382–99.

Jerusalem Talmud. The Hebrew name of the Jerusalem Talmud is *Talmud Yeru-shalmi.* In English it is usually referred to as the Jerusalem or Palestinian Talmud. "Jerusalem" is a misnomer, since this version of the Talmud took shape in Galilee. In his new translation Jacob Neusner calls it the Talmud of the Land of Israel, which actually reflects the earliest name given to it. The word *talmud* means "learning" or "study," from *lāmad* "to learn" or "study." (A disciple is a *talmid*, i.e., a "learner." These are the same words, only in Greek, used in the NT.) The Talmud is made up of Mishna (and Tosefta) plus interpretive expansions called gemara (from the Hebrew word *gāmar,* "to complete"). The Palestinian Talmud was completed about 400–425 C.E. The first published edition made its appearance in 1522 (Venice). Not every tractate of Mishna is commented upon. Thirty-nine of the sixty-three tractates have gemara. Most of them are the tractates of the first three orders. Not all of the gemara is commentary on the given *mishnah;* some of it is related discussion; some of this discussion derives from the Tannaic period (i.e., *baraitot*). The best known MS is in the University Library of Leiden. In the seventies E. S. Rosenthal discovered that the Escorial MS (Spain) contains the Jerusalem Talmud. Jacob Neusner has completed an English translation of thirty-five volumes. Another English translation, including pointed text, is being prepared by A. Ehrman.

When citing a passage from the Jerusalem Talmud it is customary to use a *y.* (for *Yerushalmi*) followed by tractate name and chapter and paragraph, e.g., *y. Taʿan.* 4.5. Since these are the names of the mishnaic tractates they are abbreviated the same way as the Mishna tractates.

Text: *Talmud Yerushalmi* (New York: Shulsinger, 1948); *Talmud Yerushalmi* (4 vols.; Jerusalem: Kedem, 1971); A. EHRMAN, ed., *The Talmud with English Translation and Commentary* (Jerusalem: El-'Am, 1965–). **Translation:** J. NEUSNER, *The Talmud of the Land of Israel* (35 vols.; Chicago: University of Chicago Press, 1982–1994). **Introduction:** B. M. BOKSER, "An Annotated Bibliographical Guide to the Study of the Palestinian Talmud," *ANRW* 19.2:139–256, repr. in *The Study of Ancient Judaism* (ed. Neusner), 2:1–119; H. MACCOBY, "Rabbinic Literature: Talmud," *DNTB* 897–902; J. NEUSNER, *IRL* 153–81; IDEM, *The Yerushalmi—the Talmud of the Land of Israel: An Introduction* (Northvale, N.J.: Aronson, 1993); H. L. STRACK and G. STEMBERGER, *ITM* 208–44. **Commentary:** J. NEUSNER, *The Talmud of the Land of Israel: An Academic Commentary to the Second, Third, and Fourth Divisions* (SFACS 108–36, 138; Atlanta: Scholars Press; continuing publication, Lanham, Md.: University Press of America, 1995–1998); IDEM, *The Talmud of the Land of Israel: A Complete Outline of the Second, Third, and Fourth Divisions* (3 vols. in 8; SFACS 45–52; Atlanta: Scholars Press, 1995–1996). **Critical Study:** A. GOLDBERG, with M. KRUPP, "The Palestinian Talmud," *LS* 303–22; M. S. JAFFEE, "Oral Torah in Theory and Practice: Aspects of Mishnah-Exegesis in the Palestinian Talmud," *Religion* 15 (1985): 387–410; S. LIEBERMAN, "A Tragedy or a Comedy?" *JAOS* 104 (1984): 315–19 (criticizes Neusner's translation); J. NEUSNER, *Introduction: Taxonomy* (vol. 35 of *The Talmud of the Land of Israel: A Preliminary Translation and Explanation;* Chicago: University of Chicago Press, 1985).

Babylonian Talmud. Like the shorter Palestinian Talmud, the Babylonian Talmud (or Talmud Babli) combines Mishna (and some Tosefta—less than in the case of the Palestinian Talmud) with gemara. There is gemara on thirty-six of the mishnaic tractates, most from the second, third, fourth, and fifth orders. The Babylonian Talmud was probably completed about 500–550 C.E. Unlike its Palestinian counterpart, the Babylonian Talmud underwent a later editing which has left it smoother and much more polished. During this later editing some of the sayings of the Saboraim were added (on the question of editing, see Kalmin). The Babylonian Talmud is longer than the Palestinian, primarily because the former contains much more haggadic material than the latter (though, ironically, much of the haggadic material of the Babylonian Talmud is Palestinian in origin).

Whereas the Babylonian Talmud is about one-third haggadah, the Palestinian is one-sixth. The first published edition appeared in 1484 (Soncino, near Milan). The oldest complete MS is in Munich.

The Mishna used by the Babylonian Talmud is not identical to that used in the Palestinian Talmud. The Babylonian Mishna is the official version of Mishna. But scholars think that the Palestinian Talmud is closer to the original edition of Mishna produced by Rabbi Judah ha-Nasi. When citing a passage from the Babylonian Talmud it is customary to use a *b.* (for *Babli*) followed by tractate name and folio, front side ("a") or backside ("b"), e.g., *b. B. Bat.* 14a. Since these are the names of the mishnaic tractates, they are abbreviated the same way as the Mishna tractates.

Text: *Talmud Babli* (Vilna: Romm, 1886); I. EPSTEIN, ed., *Hebrew-English Edition of the Babylonian Talmud* (30 vols.; London: Soncino, 1960–1990). **Translation:** I. EPSTEIN, *The Babylonian Talmud* (35 vols.; London: Soncino, 1935–1948); J. NEUSNER, *The Talmud of Babylonia: An American Translation* (75 vols.; BJS; Missoula, Mont., Chico, Calif., and Atlanta: Scholars Press, 1984–1995). **Introduction:** H. MACCOBY, *ERL,* 182–85; IDEM, "Rabbinic Literature: Talmud," *DNTB* 897–902; J. NEUSNER, *The Bavli: An Introduction* (SFSHJ 42; Atlanta: Scholars Press, 1992); IDEM, *IRL* 182–220; H. L. STRACK and G. STEMBERGER, *ITM* 208–44. **Commentary:** J. NEUSNER, *The Talmud of Babylonia: An Academic Commentary* (SFACS 1–26, 28–30, 32–36, 43–44, 67–74, 139–40; Atlanta: Scholars Press; continuing publication, Lanham, Md.: University Press of America, 1994–) (the work will total 46 vols.); IDEM, *The Talmud of Babylonia: A Complete Outline* (4 vols. in 8; SFACS 27, 31, 37–42; Atlanta: Scholars Press, 1995–1996). **Critical Study:** A. GOLDBERG, with M. KRUPP, "The Babylonian Talmud," *LS* 323–66; D. GOODBLATT, "The Babylonian Talmud," *ANRW* 19.2:257–336, repr. in *The Study of Ancient Judaism* (ed. J. Neusner), 2:120–99; L. JACOBS, "How Much of the Babylonian Talmud Is Pseudepigraphic?" *JJS* 28 (1977): 46–59; R. L. KALMIN, *The Redaction of the Babylonian Talmud: Amoraic or Saboraic?* (MHUC 12; Cincinnati: Hebrew Union College Press, 1989); J. KAPLAN, *The Redaction of the Babylonian Talmud* (New York: Bloch, 1933); H. MACCOBY, *The Philosophy of the Talmud* (Richmond, Eng.: Curzon, 2002); J. NEUSNER, *The Formation of the Babylonian Talmud* (SPB 17; Leiden: Brill, 1970); IDEM, *The Rules of Composition of the Talmud of Babylonia: The Cogency of the Bavli's Composite* (SFSHJ 13; Atlanta: Scholars Press, 1991); IDEM, *Sources and Traditions: Types of Composition in the Talmud of Babylonia* (SFSHJ 36; Atlanta: Scholars Press, 1992); IDEM, *The Two Talmuds Compared* (3 vols. in 14; SFACS 53–66; Atlanta: Scholars Press, 1995–1996).

The "Minor" Tractates. Gathered at the end of the Babylonian Talmud are fifteen tractates largely comprising Tannaic traditions, though in many cases edited and augmented well into the Amoraic period and even later. They are as follows:

MINOR TRACTATES
ʾAbot de Rabbi Nathan ("The Fathers according to Rabbi Nathan")
Kalla Rabbati ("The Long [Version of] Kalla")
Soperim ("Scribes")
Semaḥot ("Rejoicings")
Kalla ("A Bride")

Derek Ereṣ Rabba ("The Major Way of the Land")
Derek Ereṣ Zuṭa ("The Minor Way of the Land")
Pereq ha-Šalom ("The Chapter of Peace")
Gerim ("Proselytes")
Kutim ("Cutheans [i.e., Samaritans]")
ᶜAbadim ("Slaves")
Seper Torah ("The Book of Torah")
Tepillin ("Phylacteries")
Zizit ("Fringes")
Mezuzah ("Doorpost")

For NT interpretation perhaps the most important is *ʾAbot de Rabbi Nathan* (late third century C.E.). This work is an expansion of *Pirqe ʾAbot* ("Chapters of the Fathers"; see discussion of Mishna above) and is preserved in two versions (A and B). It is not clear why this tractate is associated with the name of Rabbi Nathan. Perhaps he was the editor. Pereq §4 of version A contains several items of interest. The chapter opens with a discussion of Hos 6:6: "I desire mercy and not sacrifice, and the knowledge of God rather than burnt offerings," a passage that the Matthean Jesus had appealed to in halakic disputes (Matt 9:13; 12:7). A sage infers from the passage that "the study of Torah is more beloved by God than burnt offerings." After a few paragraphs concerning the temple service, the discussion returns to Hos 6:6. Taken up now is the story of Yohanan ben Zakkai and the destruction of the Herodian temple:

> "Woe unto us!" Rabbi Joshua cried, "that this, the place where the iniquities of Israel were atoned for, is laid waste!"

> "My son," Rabban Yohanan said to him, "be not grieved; we have another atonement as effective as this. And what is? It is acts of loving-kindness, as it is said, 'For I desire mercy and not sacrifice' [Hos 6:6]."

In the next paragraph the story is told of ben Zakkai's opposition to the rebellion, the plot against his life, and his escape to the Romans via concealment in a coffin carried outside of the walls of Jerusalem. When he later heard that the temple had been destroyed, he tore his clothes and wept. The final paragraph of pereq §4 begins with a quotation of Zech 11:1, where "Lebanon" is understood as an allusion to the temple, and an interpretation: "This refers to the High Priests who were in the Temple, who took their keys in their hands and threw them up to the sky, saying to the Holy One, blessed be He: 'Master of the Universe, here are your keys which you gave us, for we have not been trustworthy custodians to do the King's work and to eat of the King's table.'" The interpretation of Hos 6:6 and the recognition of improper stewardship of the temple service align with Jesus' earlier criticisms.

The minor tractates are usually cited by name, followed by chapter and paragraph, e.g., *Semaḥot* 2.1, or simply the chapter, §2. In the case of *ʾAbot de Rabbi Nathan* it is necessary to indicate which version is being cited, e.g., *ʾAbot de Rabbi Nathan* B §9. The SBL has recommended abbreviations for many of these tractates, for example, *'Abot R. Nat., Kallah Rab., Sop., Sem., Der. Er. Rab., Der. Er. Zuṭ.*

Text and Translations of Minor Tractates: A. COHEN, *The Minor Tractates of the Talmud* (2d ed.; 2 vols.; London: Soncino, 1971); J. GOLDIN, *The Fathers according to Rabbi Nathan* (YJS 10; New Haven: Yale University Press, 1955) (version A, including H. Danby's translation of *Pirqe 'Abot*). *Introduction:* L. FINKELSTEIN, "Introductory Study to Pirke Abot," *JBL* 57 (1938): 13–50; J. NEUSNER, *IRL* 591–608 (on *'Abot de Rabbi Nathan*); H. L. STRACK and G. STEMBERGER, *ITM* 245–53. *Commentary:* J. NEUSNER, *The Fathers according to Rabbi Nathan* (vol. 6 of *The Components of the Rabbinic Documents: From the Whole the Parts;* SFACS 84; Atlanta: Scholars Press, 1997); IDEM, *The Fathers according to Rabbi Nathan: An Analytical Translation and Explanation* (BJS 114; Atlanta: Scholars Press, 1986); A. J. SALDARINI, *The Fathers according to Rabbi Nathan* (SJLA 13; Leiden: Brill, 1975) (translation and commentary on version B). *Critical Study:* J. GOLDIN, "The Third Chapter of Abot De-Rabbi Nathan," *HTR* 58 (1965): 365–86; IDEM, "The Two Versions of Abot de Rabbi Nathan," *HUCA* 19 (1945–1946): 97–120; M. B. LERNER, "The External Tractates," *LS* 367–409; M. VAN LOOPIK, *The Ways of the Sages and the Way of the World: The Minor Tractates of the Babylonian Talmud* (TSAJ 26; Tübingen: Mohr [Siebeck], 1991); J. NEUSNER, *Judaism and Story: The Evidence of the Fathers according to Rabbi Nathan* (Chicago: University of Chicago Press, 1992); A. J. SALDARINI, *Scholastic Rabbinism: A Literary Study of the Fathers according to Rabbi Nathan* (BJS 14; Chico, Calif.: Scholars Press, 1982).

Summaries of Tannaic Midrashic Literature

Chronologically, the midrashim are categorized as Tannaic or Amoraic (or later). Thematically the midrashim are categorized as halakic (i.e., having to do with legal matters) or haggadic (or homiletical). The oldest midrashim are Tannaic, and they fall in the halakic category. They comprise *Mekilta* (on Exodus), *Sipra* (or Leviticus), and the *Sipre* (on Numbers and Deuteronomy). Unlike the talmudic literature (Mishna, Tosefta, and Talmud), the midrashim are focused on and guided by the scriptural text. The Tannaic midrashim do not themselves date to the Tannaic period (i.e., up to the beginning of the third century C.E.); rather, they contain Tannaic material. Exactly when these midrashim were compiled and edited is not known.

Bibliography: D. BOYARIN, *Intertextuality and the Reading of Midrash* (Bloomington: Indiana University Press, 1990); IDEM, "Voices in the Text: Midrash and the Inner Tension of Biblical Narrative," *RB* 93 (1986): 581–97; G. L. BRUNS, "The Hermeneutics of Midrash," in *The Book and the Text: The Bible and Literary Theory* (ed. R. Schwartz; Oxford: Blackwell, 1990), 189–213; M. FISHBANE, *The Midrashic Imagination: Jewish Exegesis, Thought, and History* (Albany: State University of New York Press, 1993); L. HAAS, "Bibliography on Midrash," in *The Study of Ancient Judaism* (ed. J. Neusner), 1:93–106; H. MACCOBY, *ERW* 22–25, 147–48; J. NEUSNER, *Invitation to Midrash: The Working of Rabbinic Bible Interpretation—a Teaching Book* (San Francisco: Harper & Row, 1988); IDEM, *IRL* 221–45; IDEM, *The Midrash: An Introduction* (Northvale, N.J.: Aronson, 1990); IDEM, *Midrash in Context* (Philadelphia: Fortress, 1983); IDEM, *What is Midrash?* (Philadelphia: Fortress, 1987);

IDEM, *The Workings of Midrash: Major Trends in Rabbinic Bible Interpretation* (San Francisco: Harper & Row, 1987); G. G. PORTON, "Defining Midrash," in *The Study of Ancient Judaism* (ed. J. Neusner), 1:55–92; IDEM, "Midrash: Palestinian Jews and the Hebrew Bible in the Greco-Roman Period," *ANRW* 19.2:103–38; IDEM, "Rabbinic Literature: Midrashim," *DNTB* 889–93; IDEM, "Rabbinic Midrash," in *The Ancient Period* (vol. 1 of *A History of Biblical Interpretation;* ed. A. J. Hauser and D. F. Watson; Grand Rapids: Eerdmans, 2003), 198–224 (very helpful bibliography); IDEM, *Understanding Rabbinic Midrash: Text and Commentary* (Hoboken, N.J.: Ktav, 1985); A. SHINAN and Y. ZAKOVITCH, "Midrash on Scripture and Midrash within Scripture," in *Studies in Bible: 1986* (ed. S. Japhet; ScrHier 31; Jerusalem: Magnes Press, 1986), 257–78; H. L. STRACK and G. STEMBERGER, *ITM* 254–68; G. VERMES, "Bible and Midrash: Early Old Testament Exegesis," in *From the Beginnings to Jerome* (vol. 1 of *Cambridge History of the Bible;* ed. P. R. Ackroyd et al.; Cambridge: Cambridge University Press, 1970), 199–231.

Mekilta. The *Mekilta* (Aramaic for "measure" or "form") is a collection of Tannaic commentary related to portions of Exodus (Exod 12:1–23:19; 31:12–17; 35:1–3). The best known and most fully preserved version is the *Mekilta of Rabbi Ishmael* (ca. 60–140 C.E.), possibly named after this great Tanna because a large portion of the material derives from him. Compiled sometime in the mid to late fourth century C.E. (but see the debate between Stemberger and Wacholder) and published in 1515 (Constantinople), this work is divided into nine tractates named after key words (Hebrew or Aramaic) from the text of Exodus:

Pisha (Aramaic for "the Passover")	Exod 12:1–13:16
Beshallah ("when he had let go")	Exod 13:17–14:31
Širata (Aramaic for "the Song")	Exod 15:1–21
Vayassa' ("and he led")	Exod 15:22–17:7
'Amalek ("Amalek")	Exod 17:8–18:27
Bahodesh ("in the [third] month")	Exod 19:1–20:23
Neziqin (Aramaic for "damages")	Exod 21:1–22:23
Kaspa (Aramaic for "the money")	Exod 22:24–23:19
Šabbata (Aramaic for "the Sabbath")	Exod 31:12–35:3

There is also a *Mekilta de Rabbi Simeon ben Yohai* (compiled ca. 400–450 C.E.), extant as fragments from the Cairo Genizah and also contained in *Midraš Haggadol* ("the Great Midrash"), a thirteenth-century compilation of midrash on the Pentateuch (see Epstein and Melamed).

Let us consider the opening midrash in *Širata* 1.1–10 on Exod 15:1: "Then Moses sang." The midrash begins with a word study, after a fashion, on *'āz* ("then"). It is observed that *'āz* is used in contexts referring to the past ("Then men began to call upon the name of the Lord" [Gen 4:26], etc.) and to the future ("Then shall the eyes of the blind be opened" [Isa 35:5], etc.). The implication of this observation is that *'āz* in Exod 15:1 may be referring to the future, and not only to the past. The midrash makes a second observation concerning the verb. Although Exod 15:1 reads *yāšîr*, which as a consecutive and in context should probably be read as a preterite ("he sang"), it is also the form of the future tense. Therefore, with the futuristic possibilities of *'āz* in mind, Exod 15:1 can be read:

"Then Moses *will* sing." If Moses, who died centuries ago, will someday sing again, then, in the words of the midrashist, "we find that we can derive the resurrection of the dead from the Torah."

This interesting piece of midrashic exegesis closely resembles the approach Jesus took in answering the Sadducees' question about levirate marriage, which "Moses wrote for us" (cf. Deut 25:5; Gen 38:8), and the resurrection (cf. Mark 12:18–27). The Sadducees did not believe in the resurrection. References to Isa 26:19 or Dan 12:2 would have been pointless, since they only accepted the Books of Moses, the Torah, as authoritative (cf. Josephus, *Ant.* 18.1.4 §16). Therefore, if they are to be answered in a manner that they would find compelling, it must be from Torah, as *Mekilta*'s exegesis had been. Jesus argued that since God, centuries after the Patriarchs had died, identified himself to Moses as "the God of Abraham, and the God of Isaac, and the God of Jacob" (Exod 3:6), the implication is that these persons will live again, or why would God, the living God (cf. Num 14:28), identify himself with the dead? By appealing explicitly to Exodus 3, one of the passages of Torah most treasured by Jewish interpreters, and implicitly to texts such as Num 14:28 which speak of God as living, Jesus has answered the Sadducees on their own ground. He has, as has the midrashist of the *Mekilta*, derived the resurrection from the Torah.

Mekilta is sometimes cited in this manner: "*Mekilta* on Exod 12:2." Sometimes it is cited by tractate, chapter, and the line number(s) according to Lauterbach's edition, e.g., "*Mekilta, Pisha* 2.1–4." For the sake of clarity I recommend combining both: "*Mekilta* on Exod 12:2 (*Pisha* 2.1–4)." The SBL abbreviation for *Mekilta* is *Mek.* There are no recommended abbreviations for the tractates (except *Nez.* for *Neziqin*).

Critical Text: H. S. HOROVITZ and A. RABIN, *Mechilta d'Rabbi Ismael* (Frankfurt am Main: J. Kauffmann, 1928–1931; repr., Jerusalem: Bamberger & Wahrmann, 1960). *Texts and Translations:* Y. N. EPSTEIN and E. Z. MELAMED, *Mekilta De-Rabbi Shimeon Ben Yohai* (Jerusalem: Mekize Nirdamim, 1955; repr., Jerusalem: Hillel, 1980) (Hebrew, no English translation available; based on fragments from the Cairo Genizah); J. Z. LAUTERBACH, *Mekilta De-Rabbi Ishmael* (3 vols.; Philadelphia: Jewish Publication Society of America, 1933–1935; repr., 1976) (Hebrew text with English translation); J. NEUSNER, *Mekhilta according to Rabbi Ishmael: An Analytical Translation* (2 vols.; BJS 148, 154; Atlanta: Scholars Press, 1988). *Introduction:* J. NEUSNER, *IRL* 249–70; IDEM, *Mekhilta according to Rabbi Ishmael: An Introduction to Judaism's First Scriptural Encyclopaedia* (BJS 152; Atlanta: Scholars Press, 1988); G. G. PORTON, "Rabbinic Literature: Midrashim," *DNTB* 891; H. L. STRACK and G. STEMBERGER, *ITM* 274–83. *Commentary:* H. MACCOBY, *ERW* 148–72 (selections); J. NEUSNER, *Mekhilta Attributed to Rabbi Ishmael* (1 vol. in 3; vol. 8 of *The Components of the Rabbinic Documents: From the Whole to the Parts;* SFACS 88–90; Atlanta: Scholars Press, 1997); IDEM, *A Theological Commentary to the Midrash,* vol. 9. *Critical Study:* J. Z. LAUTERBACH, "The Arrangement and the Divisions of the Mekilta," *HUCA* 1 (1924): 427–66; IDEM, "The Name of the Mekilta," *JQR* 11 (1920–1921): 169–95; G. STEMBERGER, "Die Datierung der Mekhilta," *Kairos* 21 (1979): 81–118 (argues against Wacholder's late dating of *Mekilta*); W. S. TOWNER, *The Rabbinic "Enumeration of Scriptural Examples": A Study of a Rabbinic Pattern of Discourse with Special Reference to Mekhilta d'Rabbi Ishmael*

(SPB 22; Leiden: Brill, 1973); B. Z. WACHOLDER, "The Date of the Mekilta de-Rabbi Ishmael," *HUCA* 39 (1968): 117–44 (argues for a medieval date).

Sipra (Sifra) (on Leviticus). Sipra (Aramaic, "the book"), or *Torat Kohanin* ("The Law of Priests"), is a compendium of Tannaic halakot devoted to the interpretation of Leviticus. It originated in the late second and early third centuries, possibly under the leadership of the school of Aqiba, and was completed sometime around 400 C.E. The first published edition appeared in 1552 (Constantinople). Portions of Mishna and Tosefta appear in *Sipra.* Jacob Neusner has observed that *Sipra* and Mishna "cover the same ground, sharing something like 90–95 percent of the same themes and ideas, not to mention laws" (*Sifra*, 1:32). Neusner believes that *Sipra* is an integrated, unified document (contrary to James Kugel, *Early Biblical Interpretation* [Philadelphia: Westminster, 1986], who tends to view *Sipra* and other midrashim as loose collections of unrelated midrashic traditions).

Sipra is made up of some 277 "chapters" and "explanations" extended over thirteen thematic sections (e.g., *Negaᶜim* ["plagues," i.e., leprosy], *Zabim* ["those with flux"], *'Aḥarê Mot* ["after death"], *Qiddušin* ["holy things"]). A prologue entitled *Baraita de Rabbi Ishmael* ("Rabbi's Ishmael's [teachings that] stand outside [of Mishna]") prefaces the work and explains the Rabbi's famous thirteen rules (*middot*) of exegesis.

Sipra is usually cited by referring to the passage in Leviticus, e.g., "*Sipra* on Lev 2:14–16," though including reference to section and chapter (*pereq*) or explanation (*parashah*) would be more helpful, e.g., "*Sipra* on Lev 2:14–16 (*Dibura Denedabah* §13)." This manner of citation is analogous to that recommended for citing *Mekilta.* Since the letter *p* is aspirated, the work is often spelled *Sifra*, but in citations it is often spelled *Sipra*. The same holds for *Sipre on Numbers* and *on Deuteronomy.* Unlike *Sipre on Numbers* and *on Deuteronomy*, the name *Sipra* can stand alone; everyone knows that it refers to Leviticus ("*the* Book").

Text: L. FINKELSTEIN, *Sifra or Torat Kohanim according to Codex Assemani LXVI* (New York: Jewish Theological Seminary of America, 1956) (facsimile); IDEM, *Text of Sifra according to Vatican Manuscript Assemani 66* (New York: Jewish Theological Seminary of America, 1983). *Translation:* J. NEUSNER, with G. G. PORTON, *Sifra.* *Introduction:* H. MACCOBY, *ERW* 172–77; J. NEUSNER, *IRL* 271–304; G. G. PORTON, "Rabbinic Literature: Midrashim," *DNTB* 891; H. L. STRACK and G. STEMBERGER, *ITM* 283–89. *Commentary:* J. NEUSNER, *Sifra* (1 vol. in 4; vol. 1 of *The Components of the Rabbinic Documents: From the Whole to the Parts*; SFACS 75–78; Atlanta: Scholars Press, 1997); IDEM, *A Theological Commentary to the Midrash*, vol. 7. *Critical Study:* J. NEUSNER, "The Primacy of Documentary Discourse: The Case of Sifra, Its Plan and Program," in *Understanding Seeking Faith: Essays on the Case of Judaism* (ed. J. Neusner; 3 vols.; BJS 73, 116, 153; Atlanta: Scholars Press, 1986–1987), 2:15–41; IDEM, *Sifra in Perspective: The Documentary Comparison of the Midrashim of Ancient Judaism* (BJS 146; Atlanta: Scholars Press, 1988); IDEM, *Uniting the Dual Torah: Sifra and the Problem of the Mishnah* (Cambridge: Cambridge University Press, 1990); J. NEUSNER, with G. G. PORTON, *Sifra*, 1:1–53.

Sipre on Numbers. Sipre (Hebrew, "book") *on* (or to) *Numbers* was compiled about 350–400 C.E. and published in 1545 (Venice). It is associated with the school of Rabbi Ishmael. Like *Sipra,* it is made up of Tannaic traditions. There is also a *Sipre Zuṭa* ("Minor Book") on Numbers.

Sipre on Numbers is divided into 161 sections or *pisqaot* (Aramaic, "[biblical] verses" or "sections"; sg. *pisqa* [lit. "cut"]). Each *pisqa* begins with a passage from Numbers, e.g., *pisqa* §1 treats Num 5:1–4, *pisqaot* §§2–6 treat Num 5:5–10, *pisqaot* §§7–21 treat Num 5:11–10. Exegetical discussion then ensues, often prompted by leading questions.

Sipre on Numbers is normally cited by reference to the *pisqa*, with the biblical passage in parentheses, e.g., *"Sipre Num.* §12 (on Num 5:15–22)."

Text: H. S. HOROVITZ, *Sipre 'al Bemidbar we-Sipre Zuṭa* (Jerusalem: Wahrmann, 1966) (Hebrew); S. LIEBERMAN, *Sipre Zuṭa* (New York: Jewish Theological Seminary of America, 1968) (Hebrew). *Translation:* P. P. LEVERTOFF, *Midrash Sifre on Numbers* (TED III: Palestinian-Jewish and Cognate Texts (Rabbinic); London: SPCK, 1926) (selections, with an introduction by G. H. Box). *Introduction:* J. NEUSNER, *IRL* 305–27; G. G. PORTON, "Rabbinic Literature: Midrashim," *DNTB* 891; H. L. STRACK and G. STEMBERGER, *ITM* 290–93. *Commentary:* K. G. KUHN, *Der tannaitische Midrasch Sifre zu Numeri* (Rabbinische Texte, 2: Tannaitische Midraschim 3; Stuttgart: Kohlhammer, 1959) (German translation, with notes); J. NEUSNER, *Sifré to Numbers* (1 vol. in 3; vol. 12 of *The Components of the Rabbinic Documents: From the Whole to the Parts;* SFACS 104–7; Atlanta: Scholars Press, 1998); IDEM, *A Theological Commentary to the Midrash,* vol. 8. *Critical Study:* D. BÖRNER-KLEIN, *Midrasch Sifre Numeri: Voruntersuchungen zur Redaktionsgeschichte* (Judentum und Umwelt 39; Frankfurt am Main: Peter Lang, 1993); IDEM, *Der Midrasch Sifre zu Numeri* (new ed.; Rabbinische Texte, 2: Tannaitische Midraschim 3 [bis]; Stuttgart: Kohlhammer, 1997).

Sipre on Deuteronomy. *Sipre on Deuteronomy* was completed about 350–400 C.E. It is traditionally associated with the school of Rabbi Aqiba. Like *Sipra* and like *Sipre on Numbers,* with which there is a close relationship, *Sipre on Deuteronomy* is made up of Tannaic traditions and may have been compiled shortly after *Sipre on Numbers.* It has been pointed out that *Sipre Deuteronomy* resembles *Mekilta de Rabbi Simeon ben Yohai.* There have been discovered genizah fragments of a *Mekilta to Deuteronomy* (or *Midraš Tannaim on Deuteronomy*) from the school of Rabbi Ishmael.

Sipre on Deuteronomy is divided into 357 *pisqaot* and covers ten lessons, e.g., *Debarim* ("words," §1–25), *Wa-'etḥannan* ("and I besought," §§26–36), *'Eqeb* ("because," §§37–52), etc. The names for these lessons come from the verses that open the new sections. Thus, *Debarim* is taken from Deut 1:1 ("These are the *words* which Moses spoke to all Israel"), *Wa-'etḥannan* from Deut 3:23 ("*And I besought* the Lord"), and *'Eqeb* from Deut 7:12 ("And it was *because* you hearken to these ordinances"). These are the standard lections noted in most Hebrew Bibles.

As an example of how *Sipre Deuteronomy* can be of value for NT interpretation let us consider the latter part of *pisqa* §105 (on Deut 14:22, "Thou shalt surely tithe all the increase of thy seed," and 14:23, "and thou shalt eat before the Lord thy God"). The midrash concludes that the commandment to tithe applies not only to what is grown, but also to stored produce. Then comes an interesting and very old Tannaic tradition (also found in *y. Pe²ah* 2.16):

> The Sages said: "The (produce) stores of the children of Hanan [= Annas] were destroyed three years before the rest of the Land of Israel because they failed to set aside tithes from their produce, for they interpreted 'Thou shalt surely tithe . . . and thou shalt eat' as excluding the seller, and 'The increase of thy seed' as excluding the buyer."

The Sages are talking about the house of high priest Annas, the same priestly family discussed above in *t. Menaḥ.* 13. The reference to the destruction of their property three years before the destruction of the rest of the land of Israel (70 C.E.) is to some extent clarified by Josephus. He tells us that Ananias the high priest was caught and killed by the zealots (*J.W.* 2.16.9 §441) and that his house was burned (*J.W.* 2.17.6 §426). This was in 66 C.E. Later Josephus describes the Zealot-Idumean coalition that looted and murdered many of the aristocracy, including Ananus the son of Annas the high priest and the former high priest, Jesus the son of Gamalas the high priest (*J.W.* 4.5.2 §§314–317). This probably took place in late 67 or early 68 C.E. It is in reference to these murders and acts of looting committed against high priests that the comment of the Sages should be understood.

The failure of the high priests, at least those of the family of Annas, to tithe on the wealth that they accumulated from the temple offerings may shed light on one aspect of Jesus' parable of the Wicked Vineyard Tenants (Mark 12:1–12). In the parable, the vineyard tenants represent the ruling priests and the owner represents God. When the owner sends for "some of the fruit of the vineyard," the tenants refuse to give it. Their failure to pay what is owed will lead to their destruction. This is very similar to the point made in *Sipre on Deuteronomy*. Through a clever interpretation of Deut 14:22–23 the family of Annas justified their failure to pay tithes on the profits of their trade in sacrificial commodities. For this reason they suffered the loss of their wealth three years before the Romans crushed the Jewish rebellion. This parable will be discussed at greater length in chapter 12 below.

Sipre on Deuteronomy is normally cited in the same manner as *Sipre on Numbers*, e.g., "*Sipre Deut.* §251 (on Deut 27:7)."

Text: L. FINKELSTEIN, *Sipre Debarim* (New York: Jewish Theological Seminary of America, 1969) (Hebrew); D. HOFFMANN, *Midrash Tannaim zum Deuteronomium* (Berlin: M. Poppelaver, 1908–1909). *Translation:* H. BIETENHARD, *Der tannaitische Midrasch Sifre Deuteronomium* (Judaica et christiana 8; New York: Peter Lang, 1984) (German translation with notes); R. HAMMER, *Sifre: A Tannaitic Commentary on the Book of Deuteronomy* (YJS 24; New Haven: Yale University Press, 1986); G. KITTEL, *Sifre zu Deuteronomium*

(Stuttgart: Kohlhammer, 1922) (German translation); H. LJUNGMAN, *Der tannaitische Midrasch Sifré zu Deuteronomium* (Rabbinische Texte, 2: Tannaitische Midraschim 4; Stuttgart: Kohlhammer, 1964) (German translation with notes); J. NEUSNER, *Sifré to Deuteronomy: An Analytical Translation* (2 vols.; BJS 122–23; Atlanta: Scholars Press, 1987). **Introduction:** H. MACCOBY, *ERW* 177–81; J. NEUSNER, *IRL* 328–51; G. G. PORTON, "Rabbinic Literature: Midrashim," *DNTB* 891–92; H. L. STRACK and G. STEMBERGER, *ITM* 294–98. **Commentary:** J. NEUSNER, *Sifré to Deuteronomy* (1 vol. in 3; vol. 7 of *The Components of the Rabbinic Documents: From the Whole the Parts;* SFACS 85–87; Atlanta: Scholars Press, 1997); IDEM, *A Theological Commentary to the Midrash*, vol. 8. **Critical Study:** S. D. FRAADE, "Sifre Deuteronomy 26 (ad Deut. 3:23): How Conscious the Composition?" *HUCA* 54 (1983): 245–301; R. HAMMER, "Section 38 of Sifre Deuteronomy: An Example of the Use of the Independent Sources to Create a Literary Unit," *HUCA* 50 (1979): 165–78; T. MARTÍNEZ SAÍZ, "La muerte de Moisés en Sifré Deuteronomio," in *Salvación en la palabra—Targum–Derash–Berith: En memoria del profesor Alejandro Díez Macho* (ed. D. Muñoz León; Madrid: Consejo Superior de Investigaciones Científicas, 1986), 205–14; J. NEUSNER, *Sifré to Deuteronomy: An Introduction to the Rhetorical, Logical, and Topical Program* (BJS 124; Atlanta: Scholars Press, 1987).

Seder ʿOlam Rabbah. Seder ʿOlam Rabbah ("The Long Order of the World") is mentioned in the Talmud (*b. Šabb.* 88a). According to Rabbi Yohanan (a third-century amora) the work was produced by Rabbi Yose ben Halafta (a second-century tanna) (*b. Yebam.* 82b; *Nid.* 46b). The work is divided into three major parts, each consisting of ten chapters. Part one is concerned with biblical events from the creation to the crossing of the Jordan under the leadership of Joshua. Part two is concerned with the conquest of the promised land to the murder of Zechariah. Part three is concerned with the destruction of the temple by Nebuchadnezzar to the defeat of Simon Bar Kokhba. This history is embellished with haggadic traditions and in places may depend on Demetrius the Chronographer (see ch. 2). The work has been translated into Latin (1577 and 1692) and recently has become available in English (see Guggenheimer). See *Seder ʿOlam Zuṭa* below. The SBL abbreviation is *S. ʿOlam Rab.*

Text and Critical Study: C. J. MILIKOWSKY, *Seder Olam*, 2:209–448 (critical text with apparatus); B. RATNER, *Seder ʿOlam Rabba (Die grosse Weltchronik)* (2 vols.; Vilna: Romm, 1894–1897; repr., ed. S. K. Mirksy; New York: Talmudical Research Institute, 1966); M. J. WEINSTOCK, *Seder Olam Rabbah ha-shalem* (3 vols.; Jerusalem: Metivta Torat, 1956–1962) (Hebrew). **Translation:** H. W. GUGGENHEIMER, *Seder Olam: The Rabbinic View of Biblical Chronology* (Northvale, N.J.: Aronson, 1998); C. J. MILIKOWSKY, *Seder Olam*, 449–550. **Introduction:** H. L. STRACK and G. STEMBERGER, *ITM* 354–55. **Critical Study:** S. GANDZ, "The Calendar of the Seder ʿOlam," *JQR* 43 (1952–1953): 177–92; A. MARX, *Seder Olam (Cap. 1–10) nach Handschriften und Druckwerken herausgegeben, übersetzt, und erklärt* (Berlin: H. Itzkowski, 1903); C. J. MILIKOWSKY, *Seder Olam*, 1:1–208.

Megillat Taʿanit. Megillat Taʿanit ("Scroll of Fasts") is principally concerned with noting the days on which fasting was forbidden. It may have some value for chronological studies. Since the document is mentioned in the Mishna (cf.

m. Ta'an. 2:8), it apparently originated, at least in part, in the second century. The abbreviation is *Meg. Ta'an.*

Text: H. LICHTENSTEIN, "Megillath Taanith," *HUCA* 8–9 (1931–1932): 257–51. *Translation:* A. EDERSHEIM, *The Life and Times of Jesus the Messiah* (2 vols.; 3d ed.; London: Longmans, 1886; repr., Peabody, Mass.: Hendrickson), 2:698–700. *Introduction:* H. L. STRACK and G. STEMBERGER, *ITM* 39–40. *Critical Study:* W. R. FARMER, *Maccabees, Zealots, and Josephus* (New York: Columbia University Press, 1956), 151–58; S. ZEITLIN, "Megillath Taanith as a Source," *JQR* 9 (1918–1919): 71–102; 10 (1919–1920): 49–80.

Summaries of Amoraic Midrashic Literature

Midrash Rabbah. *Midrash Rabbah* ("The Long Midrash") consists of commentary on the five books of Moses (*Berešit [Genesis] Rabbah, Šemot [Exodus] Rabbah, Vayyiqra' [Leviticus] Rabbah, Bemidbar [Numbers] Rabbah,* and *Debarim [Deuteronomy] Rabbah*), and commentary on the five Megilloth, or "Scrolls" (*Šir hašir [Song of Songs] Rabbah, Ruth Rabbah, 'Ekah [Lamentations] Rabbah, Qohelet [Ecclesiastes] Rabbah,* and *Esther Rabbah*). The work as a whole ranges from about 450 to about 1100 C.E. with Genesis being the oldest (ca. 425–450), followed closely by Lamentations (ca. 450) and Leviticus (550). The Middle Age midrashim include Song of Songs (ca. 600–650), Qohelet (ca. 650), and Ruth (ca. 750). The late midrashim are Deuteronomy (ca. 900), Exodus (ca. 1000), and Numbers (ca. 1100). Esther presents special problems. There are indications that the work is quite old, perhaps as early as 500 C.E., but there are portions that are quite late, such as material from the tenth-century *Yosippon* (e.g., Mordecai's dream in ch. 8). The younger elements, however, may represent late interpolations, in which case the original form of *Esther Rabbah* is much older.

Although much of the material is Tannaic and Amoraic, there is material from later authorities and there are numerous glosses (and late interpolations). Moreover, much of this material has been taken from other midrashim and talmudic writings. Study of these midrashim should bear this in mind, especially if these works are being used in conjunction with NT study.

These midrashim are cited in two ways. All but *Song Rabbah, Lamentations Rabbah,* and *Qohelet Rabbah* are cited in this way: "*Gen. Rab.* 28.4 (on Gen 6:7)" or "*Lev. Rab.* 12.1 (on Lev 10:9)." Sometimes the Hebrew names of the books are used, e.g., "*Ber. Rab.* 28.4 (on Gen 6:7)." In these examples the chapter and paragraph of the midrash is cited, with the chapter and verse of the biblical book noted in parentheses. Song, Lamentations, and Qohelet are cited in this manner: "*Song Rab.* 5:15 §2" or "*Lam. Rab.* 1:9 §37." In these examples the chapter and verse of the biblical book is cited, followed by the paragraph number of the midrash. These two systems of citation reflect the different ways the midrashim of *Midrash Rabbah* have been compiled.

Text and Commentary: M. MIRKIN, *Midrash Rabbah* (11 vols.; Tel Aviv: Yavneh, 1977) (Hebrew; the text of *Midrash Rabbah* has vowel pointing). *Translation:* H. FREEDMAN and

M. SIMON, eds., *Midrash Rabbah* (10 vols.; London: Soncino, 1983); J. NEUSNER, *Esther Rabbah Part One: An Analytical Translation* (BJS 182; Atlanta: Scholars Press, 1989); IDEM, *Genesis Rabbah, the Judaic Commentary to the Book of Genesis: A New American Translation* (3 vols.; BJS 104–6; Atlanta: Scholars Press, 1985); IDEM, *Lamentations Rabbah: An Analytical Translation* (BJS 193; Atlanta: Scholars Press, 1989); IDEM, *Ruth Rabbah: An Analytical Translation* (BJS 183; Atlanta: Scholars Press, 1989); IDEM, *Song of Songs Rabbah: An Analytical Translation* (2 vols.; BJS 197–98; Atlanta: Scholars Press, 1989). **Introduction:** H. MACCOBY, *ERW* 226–29; J. NEUSNER, *IRL* 355–410 (on *Genesis* and *Leviticus*), 467–546 (on *Song of Songs, Ruth, Lamentations,* and *Esther*); G. G. PORTON, "Rabbinic Literature: Midrashim," *DNTB* 892; H. L. STRACK and G. STEMBERGER, *ITM* 300–317, 333–39. **Commentary:** J. NEUSNER, *The Components of the Rabbinic Documents: From the Whole the Parts* (Atlanta: Scholars Press): vol. 2, *Esther Rabbah I* (SFACS 79 [1997]); vol. 3, *Ruth Rabbah* (SFACS 80 [1997]); vol. 4, *Lamentations Rabbah* (SFACS 81 [1997]); vol. 5, *Song of Songs Rabbah* (1 vol. in 2; SFACS 82–83 [1997]); vol. 9, *Genesis Rabbah* (1 vol. in 6; SFACS 92–94, 101–3 [1998]); vol. 10, *Leviticus Rabbah* (1 vol. in 3; SFACS 95–97 [1998]); IDEM, *A Theological Commentary to the Midrash,* vols. 1–6. **Critical Study:** T. BAARDA, "A Graecism in Midrash Echa Rabba I,5," *JSJ* 18 (1987): 69–80; L. L. LYKE, "What Does Ruth Have to Do with Rahab? Midrash *Ruth Rabbah* and the Matthean Genealogy of Jesus," in *The Function of Scripture in Early Jewish and Christian Tradition* (ed. C. A. Evans and J. A. Sanders; JSNTSup 154; SSEJC 6; Sheffield: Sheffield, 1998), 262–84; J. NEUSNER, *Comparative Midrash: The Plan and Program of Genesis Rabbah and Leviticus Rabbah* (BJS 111; Atlanta: Scholars Press, 1986); IDEM, *The Integrity of Leviticus Rabbah: The Problem of the Autonomy of a Rabbinic Document* (BJS 93; Chico, Calif.: Scholars Press, 1985); IDEM, *Judaism and Scripture: The Evidence of Leviticus Rabbah* (Chicago: University of Chicago Press, 1986); IDEM, *The Midrash Compilations of the Sixth and Seventh Centuries: An Introduction to the Rhetorical, Logical, and Topical Program* (4 vols.; BJS 187–90; Atlanta: Scholars Press, 1990); H. ODEBERG, *The Aramaic Portions of Bereshit Rabba: With Grammar of Galilean Aramaic* (2 vols.; Lunds universitets årsskrift 36/3–4; Lund, Swed.: Gleerup, 1939).

Seder Eliyahu Rabbah. According to an old rabbinic legend, *Seder Eliyahu* (or *Elijah) Rabbah* ("The Major Work of Elijah"), also called *Tanna debe Elijah* ("The Lore of Elijah"), represents material revealed by Elijah the prophet to Rabbi Anan, a late third-century Amora (cf. *b. Ketub.* 106a). Although many modern scholars dismiss this legend out of hand, Meir Friedmann has accepted it. William Braude and Israel Kapstein think that there may be an element of truth behind the legend. They reason that since mystical experiences were not uncommon, it is entirely possible that Rabbi Anan had some sort of vision or experience, which he assumed was given by the prophet Elijah, the patron of heavenly revelations. (On Jewish mysticism, see G. Scholem, *Major Trends in Jewish Mysticism* [Jerusalem: Schocken, 1941]; idem, *Jewish Gnosticism, Merkabah Mysticism, and Talmudic Tradition* [New York: Jewish Theological Seminary of America, 1960].) Braude and Kapstein also point out that the work may derive from Rabbi Elijah and that through later confusion a legend grew up involving the prophet Elijah. Whatever the circumstances of the work's origin, on internal grounds there is no reason why the work could not have been compiled about 300 C.E. Other scholars, however, have argued that the work could be as late as 850 C.E. The first printed edition appeared in 1598 (Venice). It is referred to as *Teni Elijah* in *Gen. Rab.* 54.4 (on Gen 21:28) and simply as Elijah in *Num. Rab.* 4.20 (on Num 4:16).

Seder Eliyahu Rabbah accompanies a smaller work entitled *Seder Eliyahu Zuta* ("The Minor Work of Elijah"). One cites the chapter of *Seder Eliyahu Rabbah* or Zuta and in parentheses the page number of Friedmann's text (which are noted in the margins of the translation by Braude and Kapstein), e.g., "*S. Eli. Rab.* §17 (83)."

Text: M. FRIEDMANN, *Seder Eliahu Rabba und Seder Eliahu Zuta (Tanna d'be Eliahu); Pseudo-Seder Eliahu* (Jerusalem: Bamberger & Wahrmann, 1960; repr., Jerusalem: Wahrmann, 1969) (Friedmann's two earlier editions combined in one volume). *Translation:* W. G. BRAUDE and I. KAPSTEIN, *Tanna Debe Eliyyahu: The Lore of the School of Elijah* (Philadelphia: Jewish Publication Society of America, 1981). *Introduction:* H. L. STRACK and G. STEMBERGER, *ITM* 369–71. *Critical Study:* W. G. BRAUDE, "'Conjecture' and Interpolation in Translating Rabbinic Texts: Illustrated by a Chapter from Tanna debe Eliyyahu," in *Christianity, Judaism, and Other Greco-Roman Cults* (ed. J. Neusner; 4 vols.; SJLA 12; Leiden: Brill, 1975), 4:77–92; IDEM, "*Novellae* in Eliyahu Rabbah's Exegesis," in *Studies in Aggadah, Targum, and Jewish Liturgy in Memory of Joseph Heinemann* (ed. E. Fleischer and J. J. Petuchowski; Jerusalem: Magnes Press, 1981), 11–22; M. KADUSHIN, *The Theology of Seder Eliahu* (New York: Bloch, 1932); R. J. Z. WERBLOWSKY, "A Note on the Text of Seder Eliyahu," *JJS* 6 (1955): 210–11.

Pesiqta de Rab Kahana. *Pesiqta de Rab Kahana* ("Lessons of Rab Kahana") is a compilation of Rab Kahana's discourses or lessons for Sabbaths and holidays. It was compiled in Palestine about 500 C.E. The authorities, therefore, are Tannaic and Amoraic. Although several rabbis of the geonic period (650–1050 C.E.) refer to or cite *Pesiqta de Rab Kahana*, it was not published until 1832. The work consists of twenty-eight *pisqaot*, with seven supplementary *pisqaot* added later. Each *pisqa* begins with a citation of Scripture, which is then tied into the ensuing discussion concerned with a holiday.

It is customary to cite *pisqa* and paragraph, e.g., "*Pesiq. Rab Kah.* 11.18." It is not necessary to cite the Scripture passage that heads the *pisqa*. The recommended SBL abbreviation is *Pesiq. Rab Kah.*

Text: B. MANDELBAUM, *Pesikta de Rav Kahana* (2 vols.; 2d ed.; New York: Jewish Theological Seminary of America, 1987) (Hebrew and Aramaic). *Translation:* W. G. BRAUDE and I. J. KAPSTEIN, *Pesikta de-Rab Kahana: R. Kahana's Compilation of Discourses for Sabbaths and Festal Days* (Philadelphia: Jewish Publication Society of America, 1975) (contains several helpful indexes); J. NEUSNER, *Pesiqta deRab Kahana: An Analytical Translation and Explanation* (2 vols.; BJS 122–23; Atlanta: Scholars Press, 1987). *Introduction:* J. NEUSNER, *IRL* 411–33; H. L. STRACK and G. STEMBERGER, *ITM* 317–22. *Commentary:* J. NEUSNER, *Pesiqta deRab Kahana* (1 vol. in 3; vol. 11 of *The Components of the Rabbinic Documents: From the Whole the Parts*; SFACS 98–100; Atlanta: Scholars Press, 1998). *Critical Study:* J. NEUSNER, *From Tradition to Imitation*; G. SVEDLUND, *The Aramaic Portions of the Pesiqta de Rab Kahana according to MS Marshall Or. 24: The Oldest Known Manuscript of the Pesiqta de Rab Kahana, with English Translation, Commentary, and Introduction* (Stockholm: Almqvist & Wiksell, 1974); Z. ZINGER, "The Bible Quotations in the Pesikta de Rav Kahana," *Text* 5 (1966): 114–24.

Pesiqta Rabbati. *Pesiqta Rabbati* ("The Long Lessons") was compiled in Palestine about 550–650 C.E. It is simply called "Pesiqta" in *b. Yebam.* 81b. Over one half of the homilies begin in the name of Rabbi Tanhuma, an Amora who flourished at the end of the fourth and the beginning of the fifth centuries. *Pesiqta Rabbati* bears a close relationship to *Pesiqta de Rab Kahana.* Ten *pisqaot* of the former parallel *pisqaot* in the latter. It is possible that it was called *Pesiqta Rabbati* in order to distinguish it from the shorter version of Rab Kahana. *Pesiqta Rabbati* is made up of 53 *pisqaot* devoted to holidays, seasons, feasts, fasts, and special Sabbaths. The first printed edition appeared in 1654 (Prague).

It is customary to cite *pisqa* and paragraph, e.g., "*Pesiq. Rab.* 5.2." It is not necessary to cite the Scripture passage that heads the *pisqa.*

Text: M. FRIEDMANN, *Pesikta Rabbati: Midrasch für den Fest-Cyclus und die ausgezeichneten Sabbathe* (Vienna: [self-published], 1880; repr., Tel Aviv: Esther, 1963). *Translation:* W. G. BRAUDE, *Pesikta Rabbati: Discourses for Feasts, Fasts, and Special Sabbaths* (2 vols.; YJS 18; New Haven: Yale University Press, 1968) (contains several very helpful indexes). *Introduction:* J. NEUSNER, *IRL* 434–63; H. L. STRACK and G. STEMBERGER, *ITM* 322–29. *Critical Study:* N. J. COHEN, "The London Manuscript of Midrash Pesiqta Rabbati: A Key Text-Witness Comes to Light," *JQR* 73 (1982–1983): 209–37; J. NEUSNER, *From Tradition to Imitation* (includes a translation of *pisqaot* §§1–5 and §15); R. ULMER, ed., *Pesiqta Rabbati: A Synoptic Edition of Pesiqta Rabbati Based upon All Extant Manuscripts and the editio princeps* (3 vols.; vols. 1–2, SFSHJ 155, 200; Atlanta: Scholars Press, 1997–2000; vol. 3, Studies in Judaism; Lanham, Md.: University Press of America, 2002).

Midrash Tanhuma. A commentary on the Pentateuch, *Midrash Tanhuma* ("The Exegesis of Rabbi Tanhuma") was compiled about 800 C.E., possibly in Italy. Solomon Buber, however, argued for a fourth-century date because all of the authorities cited in the work date from the fourth century or earlier (*see* Strack and Stemberger, *ITM* 332). John Townsend believes that the Buber recension cannot be much earlier than the ninth century, since it quotes a chapter from Rabbi Ahai's Aramaic *She'iltot* (ca. 750 C.E.). Since *Tanhuma* is otherwise a Hebrew document (with a sprinkling of Latin and Greek loan words—a fact that argues for an Italian provenance), it is more likely that *Tanhuma* borrowed from the *Se'iltot* than the reverse. Nevertheless, although the recension itself may be late, the traditions it contains are early, originally Palestinian for the most part, and potentially of value for NT study. Whichever date is accepted, *Midrash Tanhuma* is the oldest commentary on the whole Pentateuch.

There are three recensions of *Midrash Tanhuma.* The first two, A and B, were known to the author of *Yalqut,* a thirteenth-century compilation of midrashic traditions. He called recension A *Tanhuma* and recension B *Yelammedenu* ("Let [our Master] teach us"). Recension A is the recension that Buber edited and published in 1885. Other than fragments (see the bibliography), recension B is lost. Recension C apparently drew upon the earlier recensions. Nevertheless, the exact nature of the relationship of *Tanḥuma* and *Yelammedenu* continues to be debated (see Strack and Stemberger, *ITM* 331–33).

The structure of *Tanḥuma* is based on a triennial lectionary cycle, though most printed editions structure it on the basis of the traditional one-year cycle of readings. Each lesson has a name, e.g., the first is *Berešit*, which comments on Gen 1:1–6:4; the second is *Noah*, which comments on Gen 6:9–11:7; the third is *Lek-Leka*, which comments on Gen 12:1–17:3; and so forth.

I suggest citing *Tanḥuma* (Buber) as follows: "*Tanḥ*. (B) on Gen 18:2 (*Way-yera* §5)." See Townsend (p. xiii) for his recommendation. Beyond using *Midr.* as the abbreviation for *Midrash*, there is no SBL abbreviation for *Midrash Tanḥuma*.

Text: S. BUBER, *Midrash Tanchuma: Ein agadischer Commentar zum Pentateuch von Rabbi Tanchuma ben Rabbi Abba* (Vilna: Romm, 1885; repr., Jerusalem: Ortsel, 1963–1964). **Published Fragments:** L. GINZBERG, *Midrash and Haggadah* (vol. 1 of *Genizah Studies in Memory of Doctor Solomon Schecter;* TSJTS 7; New York: Jewish Theological Seminary of America, 1928; repr., New York: P. Feldheim, 1969); L. GRÜNHUT, *Sefer Haliqqutim* (6 vols.; Frankfurt am Main: J. Kauffmann, 1900–1903), vols. 4–6; A. JELLINEK, *Bet ha-Midrasch* (6 vols.; Leipzig: C. W. Vollrath, 1853–1877; repr., Jerusalem: Wahrmann, 1967), 6:79–105; A. NEUBAUER, "Le Midrasch Tanchuma et extraits du Yélammdénu et petits midraschim," *REJ* 13 (1886): 224–38; 14 (1887): 92–113. **Translation:** H. BIETENHARD, *Midrasch Tanhuma B: R. Tanhuma über die Tora, genannt Midrasch Jelammedenu* (2 vols.; Judaica et christiana 5–6; Bern: Peter Lang, 1980–82) (German translation of Codex Vat. Ebr. 34); J. T. TOWNSEND, *Midrash Tanhuma* (Hoboken, N.J.: Ktav): vol. 1, *Genesis* (1989); vol. 2, *Exodus and Leviticus* (1997); vol. 3, *Numbers and Deuteronomy* (2003). **Introduction:** H. L. STRACK and G. STEMBERGER, *ITM* 329–33.

Midrash Tehillin. *Midrash Tehillin* (also called *Midrash I Psalms,* "Exegesis on the Psalms") or *Šoḥer Ṭob* (from Prov 11:27, "he that seeks good") was compiled about 750–800 C.E. Most of the authorities are Palestinian Tannaim and Amoraim. The earliest quoted authorities are Hillel and Shammai. No post-talmudic authorities are quoted by name. In the midrashim on certain psalms, nearly every verse is commented upon, in others only a few selected verses are treated. Sometimes *Midrash Tehillin* is printed with *Midrash Mišle* and *Midrash Šemuel.*

This work is normally cited by psalm and paragraph of exegesis, followed by the psalm's chapter and verse in parentheses, e.g., "*Midr. Pss.* 18.36 (on Ps 18:51)" or "*Midr. Pss.* 18 §36 (on Ps 18:51)."

Text: S. BUBER, *Midrasch Tehillim (Schocher Tob): Sammlung agadischer Abhandlungen über die 150 Psalmen* (Vilna: Romm, 1891; repr., Jerusalem, 1965–1966) (Hebrew and Aramaic). **Translation:** W. G. BRAUDE, *The Midrash on Psalms* (2 vols.; YJS 13; New Haven: Yale University Press, 1959) (contains several helpful indexes); A. WÜNSCHE, *Midrasch Tehillim* (2 vols.; Trier: Sigmund Mayer, 1892–1893; repr., Hildesheim: Olms, 1967) (German translation). **Introduction:** H. L. STRACK and G. STEMBERGER, *ITM* 350–52. **Critical Study:** A. CORDES, T. HANSBERGER, and E. ZENGER, "Die Verwüstung des Tempels—Krise der Religion? Beobachtungen zum Volksklagepsalm 74 und seiner Rezeption in der Septuaginta und im Midrasch Tehillim," in *Zerstörungen des Jerusalemer Tempels: Geschehen-Wahrnehmung-Bewältigung* (ed. J. Hahn; WUNT 147; Tübingen: Mohr Siebeck, 2002), 61–91; E. M. MENN,

"Praying King and Sanctuary of Prayer, Part I: David and the Temple's Origins in Rabbinic Psalms Commentary (Midrash Tehillim)," *JJS* 52 (2001): 1–26; IDEM, "Praying King and Sanctuary of Prayer, Part II: David's Deferment and the Temple's Dedication in Rabbinic Psalms Commentary (Midrash Tehillim)," *JJS* 53 (2002): 298–323; L. RABINOWITZ, "Does Midrash Tillim Reflect the Triennial Cycle of Psalms?" *JQR* 26 (1935–1936): 349–68 (Rabinowitz thinks it does).

Pirqe Rabbi Eliezer. Pirqe Rabbi Eliezer ("Chapters of Rabbi Eliezer") was compiled about 750–850 C.E., probably in Palestine. The work consists of fifty-three chapters devoted to various scriptural themes or personalities, e.g., *pereq* §3 treats the first day of creation, *pereq* §10 treats Jonah, *pereq* §24 treats Nimrod and the Tower of Babel, and so forth. Scholars suspect that this work may be an example of a rabbinic pseudepigraphon (see also *3 Enoch,* a pseudepigraphon credited to Rabbi Ishmael).

The work is usually cited in this manner: "*Pirqe R. El. §7.*" The SBL abbreviation is *Pirqe R. El.*

Text: M. HIGGER, "Pirqe Rabbi Eli'ezer," *Horeb* 8 (1944): 82–98; 9 (1946): 94–166; 10 (1948): 185–294. *Translation:* G. FRIEDLANDER, *Pirke de-Rabbi Eliezer* (1916; repr., New York: Sepher-Hermon, 1981). *Introduction:* H. L. STRACK and G. STEMBERGER, *ITM* 356–58. *Critical Study:* L. M. BARTH, "The Ban and the 'Golden Plate': Interpretation in *Pirqe d'Rabbi Eliezer* 38," in *The Quest for Context and Meaning: Studies in Biblical Intertextuality in Honor of James A. Sanders* (ed. C. A. Evans and S. Talmon; BIS 28; Leiden: Brill, 1997), 625–40; R. HAYWARD, "Pirqe de Rabbi Eliezer and Targum Pseudo-Jonathan," *JJS* 42 (1991): 215–46; A. UROWITZ-FREUDENSTEIN, "Pseudepigraphic Support of Pseudepigraphical Sources: The Case of Pirqe de Rabbi Eliezer," in *Tracing the Threads: Studies in the Vitality of Jewish Pseudepigrapha* (ed. J. C. Reeves; SBLEJL 6; Atlanta: Scholars Press, 1994), 35–53.

Seder ʿOlam Zuṭa. On the basis of a date given in the De Rossi MS many think that *Seder ʿOlam Zuṭa* ("The Short Order of the World") was composed in 804 C.E. Others have contended that this date is a gloss and that the work was composed in the sixth century. It is made up of ten chapters. The first six cover the period from Adam to Jehoiachin. Chapters 7–10 cover the period from Jehoiachin to the collapse of the Sassanid dynasty about 640 C.E. For the biblical period the author made use of *Seder ʿOlam Rabbah.* For the later period the author drew on chronological materials available in the Babylonian academies. A Latin translation was published in Paris in 1572. There is no English translation. The abbreviation is *S. ʿOlam Zuṭ.* See the older, related text *Seder ʿOlam Rabbah* above.

Text: M. GROSSBERG, *Seder ʿOlam Zuta* (London: Y. Neroditsi, 1910); M. J. WEINSTOCK, *Seder ʿOlam Zuta ha-Shalem* (Jerusalem: Metivta Torat, 1957). *Introduction:* H. L. STRACK and G. STEMBERGER, *ITM* 355. *Critical Study:* A. D. GOODE, "The Exilarchate in the Eastern Caliphate, 637–1258," *JQR* 31 (1940–1941): 149–69; S. SCHEICHTER, "Seder Olam Suta," *MGWJ* 39 (1895): 23–28.

Midrash Shemuel (on Samuel). This midrash is also called *Agadat Shemuel* ("narrative of Samuel") or, in Aramaic, *Agadata' d' Šemuel.* There has been little critical work done with this midrashic compilation. The text as we have it probably dates to the eleventh century, but its contents are mostly Tannaic and Palestinian. Indeed, where it parallels the Talmud, it is usually Yerushalmi and evidently in a less polished, edited form. This midrash begs for more scholarly attention. Those interested in eschatology will want to compare *parashah* §4 (on 1 Sam 2:1–10) with *Tg. 1 Sam.* 2:1–10. August Wünsche's translation of the text into German is at times very paraphrastic. There is no English translation. Buber's text is divided into thirty-two *parashot,* and each *parashah* is divided into paragraphs. It may be cited this way: *Midr. Šem.* 4.1 (on 1 Sam 2:1).

Text: S. BUBER, *Midraš Šemuel* (Cracow: Joseph Peshar, 1893; repr., Jerusalem: n.p., 1965). *Translation:* A. WÜNSCHE, *Der Midrasch Samuel,* 6–169 (provides notes identifying parallels with talmudic and midrashic literature). *Introduction:* H. L. STRACK and G. STEMBERGER, *ITM* 390–91; A. WÜNSCHE, *Der Midrasch Samuel,* 3–5. *Critical Study:* M. HIGGER, "Beraitoth in Midrash Samuel and Midrash Mishle," *Talpioth* 5 (1952): 669–82 (Hebrew).

Midrash Mishle (on Proverbs). The midrash on Proverbs probably dates to the ninth or tenth centuries, though much of the material within it is older and is Palestinian in character. Gospel interpreters will be interested in this midrash. Although several of the parables are found in other sources, some of parables here, or their forms, are distinctive. It is recommended to cite it according to the scriptural passage, e.g., *Midr. Mish* on Prov 10:1. Vistotzky's translation is based on his own critical edition of the text.

Text: S. BUBER, *Midraš Mišlei* (Vilna: Romm, 1893; repr., Jerusalem: n.p., 1965) (combined with the midrash on Samuel). *Translation:* B. L. VISOTZKY, *The Midrash on Proverbs* (YJS 27; New Haven: Yale University Press, 1992); A. WÜNSCHE, *Der Midrasch Mischle* (vol. 5, part 3 of *Bibliotheca rabbinica;* Leipzig: O. Schulze, 1885; repr., Hildesheim: Olms, 1967) (German translation). *Introduction:* H. L. STRACK and G. STEMBERGER, *ITM* 352–53. *Critical Study:* M. HIGGER, "Beraitoth in Midrash Samuel and Midrash Mishle," *Talpioth* 5 (1952): 669–82 (Hebrew); B. L. VISOTZKY, *Midrash Mishle* (New York: Jewish Theological Seminary of America, 1990).

Chronicle of Jerahmeel. Jerahmeel ben Solomon (ca. 1150) lived in southern Italy and produced a work called *Megillat Yerahme'el* ("The Scroll of Jerahmeel") or *Seper ha-Yerahme'el* ("The Book of Jerahmeel"). The work is a compilation of Jewish legend and lore. In two places the author identifies himself: "I, Jerahmeel, have found in the Book of Strabo of Caphtor that Nimrod was the son of Shem . . ." (32:1); "And I, Jerahmeel, have discovered in the Book of Nicholas of Damascus . . ." (35:2). As is clear from these statements, Jerahmeel used many authors (e.g., in addition to Strabo and Nicholas, he drew upon Josephus, Philo, and various apocryphal works and midrashim, such as *Pirqe Rabbi Eliezer).* Portions of the *Chronicle of Jerahmeel* were incorporated by Eleazar ben Asher ha-Levi (ca. 1325) in his work *Seper ha-Zikronot* ("The Book of Records"). Moses Gaster believes that most of Jerahmeel's materials are no later than the seventh century. Many dispute this claim, however. The use of *Pirqe Rabbi Eliezer* (Jerahmeel's first seven chapters are copied from this work), which dates from the eighth or ninth century, tells against Gaster's view.

Translation: M. GASTER, *The Chronicles of Jerahmeel; or, the Hebrew Bible Historiale* (Oxford: Oxford University Press, 1899; repr., New York: Ktav, 1971). *Critical Study:* P. COLELLA, "Baruch lo scriba e Jerahmeel il figlio del re," *BeO* 23 (1981): 87–96; H. JACOBSON, "Thoughts on the Chronicles of Jerahmeel, Ps-Philo's Liber antiquitatum biblicarum, and Their Relationship," *Studia philonica Annual* 9 (1997): 239–63; J. REINER, "The Original Hebrew Yosippon in the Chronicle of Jerahmeel," *JQR* 60 (1969–1970): 128–46.

Later Midrashim

Midrash ʾAggadah [on the Pentateuch]—(10th century)
ʾAggadat Berešit [on Genesis]—(10th century)
Midrash Megillot Zuṭa [on the Song of Songs]—(10th century)
Berešit Rabbati [on Genesis]—(11th century)
Midrash Yob [on Job]—(date unknown, only fragments extant)
Midrash Šir haŠir [on the Song of Songs]—(12th century)
Midrash Haggadol [on the Pentateuch]—(13th century)
Yalqut Šimeoni [on Tanak]—(13th century)
ʾAggadat Esther [on Esther]—(14th century)

Medieval Commentators

Rabbi Saadya ben Joseph ["Saadya Gaon"]—(882–942)
Rabbi Solomon ben Isaac ["Rashi"]—(1040–1105)
Rabbi Abraham Ibn Ezra—(1089–1164)
Rabbi Joseph Kimhi [father of David and Moses Kimhi]—(ca. 1105–1170)
Rabbi Moses ben Maimon/Maimonides ["Rambam"]—(1135–1204)
Rabbi David Kimhi ["Radak"]—(ca. 1160–1235)
Rabbi Moses Kimhi ["Ramak"]—(date unknown)
Rabbi Moses ben Nahman/Nahmanides ["Ramban"]—(1194–1270)

Bibliography: V. APTOWITZER, *Das Schriftwort in der rabbinischen Literatur* (5 vols.; Vienna: Alfred Holder, 1906–15; repr., with prolegomenon by S. Loewinger; 5 vols. in 1; New York: Ktav, 1970) (an assessment of variants in quotations of Scripture in rabbinic literature); A. DAVIS and A. KLEINKAUFMAN, eds., *The Metsudah Chumash Rashi: A New Linear Translation* (5 vols.; Brooklyn: B. Walzer, 1991–1997) (Hebrew, with English translation; one volume per book of the Pentateuch); P. DORON, *Rashi's Torah Commentary: Religious, Philosophical, Ethical, and Educational Insights* (Northvale, N.J.: Aronson, 2000); I. ELBOGEN, *Jewish Liturgy: A Comprehensive History* (Philadelphia: Jewish Publication Society, 1993); R. G. FINCH, trans., with introduction by G. H. Box, *The Longer Commentary of R. David Kimhi on the First Book of Psalms (I–X, XV–XVII, XIX, XXII, XXIV)* (TED III: - Palestinian-Jewish and Cognate Texts [Rabbinic] 6; London: SPCK, 1919); L. FINKELSTEIN, *The Commentary of David Kimhi on Isaiah* (Columbia University Oriental Studies 19;

New York: Columbia University Press, 1926; repr., New York: AMS Press, 1966); E. L. GREENSTEIN, "Medieval Bible Commentaries," in *Back to the Sources: Reading the Classic Jewish Texts* (ed. B. W. Holtz; New York: Summit, 1984), 213–59; M. I. GRUBER, *Rashi's Commentary on Psalms* (Brill Reference Library of Judaism 18; Boston: Brill, 2004) (text and analysis); M. MAIMONIDES, *Commentary to the Mishnah* (7 vols.; Jerusalem: Mossad Harav Kook, 1963–1968) (Arabic original, with Hebrew translation by J. Kafih); E. I. J. ROSENTHAL, ed., *Saadya Studies in Commemoration of the One Thousandth Anniversary of the Death of R. Saadya Gaon* (Publications of the University of Manchester 282; Manchester, Eng.: Manchester University Press, 1943).

Special Themes

Messianic Ideas in the Rabbinic Literature. Messianic ideas are quite diverse in the rabbinic literature. There was fervent messianic expectation even after the two disastrous wars with Rome in 66–70 and 132–135 C.E. Some of it coheres at points with the messianic ideas in the NT. The following is a sample of the early traditions:

Yohanan ben Zakkai predicted the destruction of the temple (ca. 60 C.E.): "O Temple, why do you frighten us? We know that you will be destroyed" (*y. Soṭah* 6.3; *b. Yoma* 39b). According to another tradition, he hailed Vespasian, the general in command of the Roman forces that were trying to put down the first Jewish rebellion, as "Lord Emperor." When Vespasian objected (since he was not emperor), Yohanan prophesied: "If you are not the king, you will be eventually, because the Temple will only be destroyed by a king's hand" (*Lam. Rab.* 1:5 §31). Rabbi Zadok, Yohanan's disciple, also anticipated the temple's destruction (*b. Giṭ.* 56a). These traditions are not necessarily messianic, at least not explicitly, but there may have been a relationship between Messiah and the temple (viz., that he will build a new temple) in first-century thinking. In any case, these predictions have relevance for NT messianism.

Just before his death (ca. 80 C.E.) Yohanan also predicted the coming of Messiah: "Remove all vessels lest they be rendered unclean, and prepare a throne for Hezekiah, king of Judea, who is come" (*b. Ber.* 28b). Evidently the aged Sage felt that "Hezekiah," that is, Israel's Messiah, had arrived. Whether ben Zakkai had in mind a recently born infant or an adult is not clear. According to later tradition King Messiah, whose name is Menahem son of Hezekiah, was born on the day that the temple was destroyed (*y. Ber.* 2.4; cf. *b. Sanh.* 98b, 99a). Although it is possible that this tradition had something to do with Menahem the zealot and apparent messianic claimant who, as a "veritable king," entered Jerusalem in 66 C.E. (cf. Josephus, *J.W.* 2.17.8–10 §§433–448), I do not think that it is too probable.

Aqiba was one of many rabbis who predicted the appearance of the Messiah (*b. Sanh.* 97b). Apparently shortly after the destruction of the temple he predicted that Messiah would come in forty years, by analogy of Israel's forty-year period of wandering in the wilderness (*Pesiq. Rab.* 1.7). The forty-year expectation may have had something to do with the Jewish revolt in Judea, Egypt, and Cyrene in 114 or 115 C.E. According to Eusebius, the Jewish people rallied to one Lukuas, "their king" (*Hist. eccl.* 4.2.1–4). Rabbis Eleazar ben Azariah, Yose the Galilean, Ishmael, Nathan, and Simeon ben Yohai predicted the approach of Messiah (*b. Sanh.* 99a, 97b; *Midr. Pss.* 90.17 [on Ps 90:15]; *Song Rab.* 8:9 §3). Calculations of the Messiah's appearance continued on into and through the Middle Ages (see Silver).

Aqiba also taught that the plural "thrones" of Dan 7:9 implied that Messiah would sit next to God, an interpretation that shocked his contemporaries Yose the Galilean and Eleazar ben Azariah (*b. Ḥag.* 14a; *b. Sanh.* 38b). Aqiba also proclaimed Simon Bar Kokhba Messiah (*y. Taʿan.* 4.5; cf. *Lam. Rab.* 2:2 §4). Aqiba's identification of Bar Kokhba had to do with a wordplay by which he was identified with the star of Num 24:17, a passage that was understood in a messianic sense in the first century, if not earlier (cf. Philo, *Rewards* 16 §95; Josephus, *J.W.* 6.5.4 §§312–313; cf. 3.8.9 §§400–402; Matt 2:2; 4QTest 9–13; CD 7:18–21; cf. *Tgs.* Num 24:17).

Finally, a late Tannaic commentary should be noted: "With the footprints of the Messiah presumption shall increase and dearth reach its height; the vine shall yield its fruit but the vine shall be costly. . . . Galilee shall be laid waste and Gablan shall be made desolate. . . . The wisdom of the Scribes shall become insipid. . . . Children shall shame the elders, and the elders shall rise up before the children, 'for the son dishonors the father, the daughter rises up against her mother, the daughter-in-law against her mother-in-law; a man's enemies are the men of his own house' [Mic 7:6]" (*m. Soṭah* 9:15; cf. *Pesiq. Rab Kah.* §5.9; *Song Rab.* 2:13 §4).

The NT parallels these messianic traditions at four points.

1. Jesus also predicted the destruction of the temple: "Do you see these great buildings? There will not be left here one stone upon another, that will not be thrown down" (Mark 13:2 par.). Jesus is later accused of threatening to destroy the temple: "We heard him say, 'I will destroy this temple that is made with hands, and in three days I will build another, not made with hands'" (Mark 14:58; cf. John 2:19: "Destroy this temple and in three days I will raise it up").

2. The NT witnesses fervent messianic expectation. There are warnings to beware of false prophets and false christs who claim that the end is at hand (Matt 24:5, 11; Mark 13:5–6; Luke 21:8–9). Not all of those who made false predictions of the end were necessarily non-Christians. It is quite likely that Christians, too, predicted the end and the appearance of the glorified Christ (cf. 2 Thess 2:1–3).

3. Aqiba's exegesis of Dan 7:9 coheres with Jesus' response to Caiaphas in Mark 14:64. Jesus says that he will be "seated at the right hand" and will be "coming on the clouds of heaven" (cf. Ps 110:1; Dan 7:13–14). Some commentators have wondered how Jesus could be both stationary (i.e., seated) and moving (i.e., coming on the clouds). Because of the apparent discrepancy, it has been suggested that two separate traditions have been combined. (The juxtaposition of Ps 110:1 and

Dan 7:13–14 occurs several times in the rabbis; cf. *b. Sanh.* 96b–97a, 98a; *Num. Rab.* 13.14 [on Num 7:13]; *Midr. Pss.* 21.5 [on Ps 21:7]; 93.1 [on Ps 93:1].) What has been overlooked, however, is that the throne that is being alluded to is the divine chariot throne (Dan 7:9: "thrones were placed and one what was ancient of days took his seat . . . his throne was fiery flames, its *wheels* were burning fire"; cf. Ezek 1). Jesus can speak of sitting and coming because he will be seated next to God on his chariot throne and will, with him, come thundering from heaven in judgment. The saying in Mark 14:64 is, therefore, intelligible. Moreover, the idea is not without parallel. According to *1 En.* 51:3, the "Elect One shall sit on [God's] throne." According to Rev 3:12, the risen Christ says, "He who conquers, I will grant him to sit with me on my throne, as I myself conquered and sat down with my father on his throne." Caiaphas's outrage, "You have heard his blasphemy" (Mark 14:65) parallels the responses of Yose the Galilean and Eleazar ben Azariah: "Aqiba, how long will you profane the Divine Presence!"

4. Mishna's reference to the "footprints of the Messiah" and the fulfillment of Mic 7:6 parallels NT Gospel tradition. Jesus also spoke of approaching times of trouble: "Brother will deliver up brother to death, and the father his child, and children will rise against parents and have them put to death; and you will be hated by all" (Mark 13:12–13). The allusion to Mic 7:6 is unmistakable. In Q (Matt 13:35–36; Luke 12:52–53) it is explicit. All of this social turmoil is in reference to Jesus as Israel's Messiah. The use of Mic 7:6 in *m. Soṭah* 9:15 clarifies the exegetical background against which these synoptic traditions should be studied.

What precisely were the messianic hopes of the framers of the Mishna is not easy to determine, but it is unlikely that they held to a noneschatological, nonmessianic ahistoricism, as Jacob Neusner has recently argued. Neusner is correct to insist that every document (in this case, the Mishna) be taken on its own terms. He is also correct in supposing that the one major passage that speaks of the Messiah (*Soṭah* 9:15) should not be viewed as central to the primary concerns of the Mishna. At the same time, it is to argue beyond the evidence to conclude that because there is no other significant messianic teaching in the Mishna, its framers had no interest in the subject. We have every reason to believe that the rabbis who composed the Mishna attended synagogue regularly and, indeed, may even have contributed to its order of service, including prayers in which the hope of the Messiah's speedy appearance was emphatically articulated (as seen esp. in the Kaddish and the Amidah).

Because the focus of the Mishha is law, eschatology and messianism play little role. The same can be said regarding the Tosefta, which supplements the Mishna. In the Talmud, which comments upon and elaborates both Tosefta and Mishna, the focus widens to all things Jewish—law, legend, eschatology, and all. In these later compilations, messianism and the haggadic midrash that provides the grist for the mill are openly and critically explored. We do not have here a shift in worldview (i.e., from ahistoricism and nonmessianism). Rather, we see the emergence of a Jewish encyclopedia, in which all aspects of the Jewish worldview are taken into account—the halakic concerns of daily life and the haggadic ruminations of the world to come.

Bibliography: P. S. ALEXANDER, "The King Messiah in Rabbinic Judaism," in *King and Messiah in Israel and the Ancient Near East: Proceedings of the Oxford Old Testament Seminar* (ed. J. Day; JSOTSup 270; Sheffield: Sheffield, 1998), 456–73; C. A. EVANS, "Mishna and Messiah 'in Context': Some Comments on Jacob Neusner's Proposals," *JBL* 112 (1993): 267–89 (with a response by Neusner on pp. 291–304); M. HADAS-LEBEL, "Hezekiah as King Messiah: Traces of an Early Jewish-Christian Polemic in the Tannaitic Tradition," in *Jewish Studies at the Turn of the Twentieth Century* (ed. J. Targarona Borrás and A. Sáenz-Badillos; 2 vols.; Leiden: Brill, 1999), 1:275–81; W. HORBURY, *Messianism among Jews and Christians* (New York: T&T Clark, 2003), 275–327; R. KASHER, "Eschatological Ideas in the Toseftot Targum to the Prophets," *JAB* 2 (2000): 22–59; R. KIMELMAN, "The Messiah of the Amidah: A Study in Comparative Messianism," *JBL* 116 (1997): 313–24; J. KLAUSNER, *The Messianic Idea in Israel: From Its Beginning to the Completion of the Mishnah* (New York: Macmillan, 1955), 388–517; J. NEUSNER, *Messiah in Context: Israel's History and Destiny in Formative Judaism* (Philadelphia: Fortress, 1984); J. NEUSNER and W. S. GREEN, eds., *Judaisms and Their Messiahs at the Turn of the Christian Era* (Cambridge: Cambridge University Press, 1987); A. OPPENHEIMER, "Leadership and Messianism in the Time of the Mishnah," in *Eschatology in the Bible and in Jewish and Christian Tradition* (ed. H. G. Reventlow; JSOTSup 243; Sheffield: Sheffield, 1997), 152–68; P. SCHÄFER, "Die messianischen Hoffnungen des rabbinischen Judentums zwischen Naherwartung und religiösen Pragmatismus," in *Zukunft in der Gegenwart: Wegweisungen in Judentum und Christentum* (ed. C. Thoma; Judaica et christiana 1; Bern: Lang, 1976), 95–125, repr. in P. Schäfer, *Studien zur Geschichte und Theologie des rabbinischen Judentums* (AGJU 15; Leiden: Brill, 1978), 214–43; G. SCHOLEM, *The Messianic Idea in Judaism and Other Essays on Jewish Spirituality* (New York: Schocken, 1971), 1–36; A. H. SILVER, *A History of Messianic Speculation in Israel* (New York: Macmillan, 1927; repr., Gloucester, Mass.: Peter Smith, 1978).

References to Jesus. There are some references to Jesus in the writings of the rabbis. Because of the fear of persecution during the Middle Ages, scribes omitted or altered several explicit references to Jesus. In place of the name "Jesus" (*Yeshu*) or "Jesus the Nazarene" (*Yeshu ha-Noṣri*) were inserted various other names (e.g., "ben Stada" or "ben Pantera") and disparaging terms (e.g., "so-and-so"). Therefore, it is not always easy to determine which passages actually refer to Jesus and which do not. The following is a sampling of passages that have from time to time been identified as having to do with Jesus.

1. *On Jesus' parents and birth.* "She who was the descendant of princes and governors [i.e., Mary], played the harlot with carpenters [i.e., Joseph]" (*b. Sanh.* 106a). "[The angel of death] said to his messenger, 'Go, bring me Miriam [Mary] the Women's hairdresser!' He went and brought him Miriam" (*b. Ḥag.* 4b; "hairdresser" is *megaddelā'*, which probably refers to Mary Magdalene, who was sometimes confused with Mary the mother of Jesus).

2. *On the life of Jesus.* Stories are told of Jesus' being rejected by various rabbis: "When King Janneus [104–78 B.C.E.] slew our Rabbis [ca. 87 B.C.E.], Rabbi Joshua [ben Perahiah] and Jesus fled to Alexandria of Egypt" where Jesus was

later excommunicated and condemned for worshipping an idol (*b. Sanh.* 107b; *b. Soṭah* 47a; cf. *y. Ḥag.* 2.2; *y. Sanh.* 6.6). The association of Jesus with a flight to Egypt may have been suggested by Matt 2:13–15. The anachronism of the rabbinic tradition is obvious, but does not offer a serious difficulty to the identification of the character with Jesus of Nazareth.

3. *On the ministry of Jesus.* We are told that "Jesus had five disciples: Matthai, Nakai, Nezer, Buni, and Todah" (*b. Sanh.* 107b). Although the first name does resemble one of the disciples' names (i.e., Matthew), and the last possibly that of another (Thaddeus), these names are only meant to serve the purpose of creating word-plays, as seen in the subsequent paragraph of *Sanhedrin*, that, casting aspersions against Jesus and his disciples, justify their deaths. Jesus' ministry of miracles was explained as sorcery: "Jesus the Nazarene practiced magic and led Israel astray" (*b. Sanh.* 107b; cf. *t. Šabb.* 11.15; *b. Sanh.* 43a; *b. Šabb.* 104b; *b. Soṭah* 47a). The charge of practicing magic parallels the accusation in the Gospels that Jesus cast out demons by the power of Satan (cf. Mark 3:22). Celsus held similar views (cf. Origen *Cels.* 1.6, 38, 71).

4. *On the teaching of Jesus.* The rabbis expressed the hope that they will "not have a son or a disciple who burns his food in public [i.e., teaches heresy], like Jesus the Nazarene" (*b. Sanh.* 103a; *b. Ber.* 17a–b). "One of the disciples of Jesus . . . told me, 'Thus did Jesus the Nazarene teach me: "For of the hire of a harlot has she gathered them, and to the hire of a harlot shall they return" [cf. Deut 23:18]'" (*b. ʿAbod. Zar.* 16b–17a; *t. Ḥul.* 2.24 [" . . . Jesus ben Pantera . . ."]; cf. *Qoh. Rab.* 1:8 §3; *Yal. Šimeoni* on Mic 1 and Prov 5:8). "The disciples of Balaam the wicked shall inherit Gehenna and go down to the pit of destruction" (*m. ʾAbot* 5:19). "He [a judge] said to them: 'I looked at the end of the book, in which it is written, "I am not come to take away the Law of Moses and I am not come to add to the Law of Moses" [cf. Matt 5:17], and it is written, "Where there is a son, a daughter does not inherit" [cf. Num 27:8].' She said to him: 'Let your light shine forth as a lamp' [cf. Matt 5:16]. Rabbi Gamaliel said to her: 'The ass came and kicked the lamp over'" (*b. Šabb.* 116b). From the same tradition we find a proverbial statement that probably sums up very well the rabbinic view of Jesus' teaching: "Since the day that you were exiled from your land [i.e., the destruction of Jerusalem in 70 C.E.] the Law of Moses has been abrogated, and the law of the *euangelion* has been given" (*b. Šabb.* 116a). In fact, by playing on the Greek word *euangelion*, the rabbis sometimes referred to it as the *ʾāwen-gillāyôn* ("falsehood of the scroll") or the *ʾawôn-gillāyôn* ("perversion of the scroll"). Most offensive to the rabbis was Jesus' claim to be God and Son of Man (cf. Mark 14:61–62; John 19:7), who would ascend to heaven (cf. John 20:17). Rabbi Abbahu (late third, early fourth century) is reported to have said: "If a man says to you, 'I am God,' he is a liar; [or] 'I am the son of man,' in the end he will regret it; [or] 'I will go up to heaven'—he that says it will not perform it" (*y. Taʿan.* 2.1). Again from Abbahu: "[God] says . . . '"I am the first"—I have no father; "I am the last"—I have no son'" (*Exod. Rab.* 29.5 [on Exod 20:2]). Similarly Rabbi Aha (fourth century) declares: "There is One that is alone, and he has not a second; indeed, he has neither

son nor brother—but: 'Hear O Israel, the Lord our God, the Lord is One'" (*Deut. Rab.* 2.33 [on Deut 6:4]). "There was a man, the son of a woman, who would rise up and seek to make himself God, and cause the entire world to err. . . . If he says that he is God, he lies; and in the future he will cause to err—that he departs and returns in the end. He says, but will not do. . . . Alas, who shall live of that people that listens to that man who makes himself God?" (*Yal. Šimeoni* on Num 23:7). Elsewhere we are told that Moses warns Israel not to expect "another Moses" who will "arise and bring another Law from heaven" (*Deut. Rab.* 8.6 [on Deut 30:11–12]). The rabbis predict that "the 'servant' [i.e., Jesus] will bow down to the [real] Messiah" (*b. Sanh.* 61b). Lying behind this statement is the Christian view of Jesus as the Lord's Servant.

5. *On the crucifixion of Jesus.* "On the eve of Passover they hanged Jesus the Nazarene. And a herald went out before him for forty days, saying: 'He is going to be stoned, because he practiced sorcery and enticed and led Israel astray. Anyone who knows anything in his favor, let him come and plead in his behalf.' But, not having found anything in his favor, they hanged him on the eve of Passover" (*b. Sanh.* 43a; cf. *t. Sanh.* 10.11; *y. Sanh.* 7.12; *Tg. Esth. I* 7:9). "They brought him to the Beth Din [i.e., "House of Judgment," perhaps the Sanhedrin] and stoned him . . . and they hanged him on the eve of Passover" (*b. Sanh.* 67a;. *y. Sanh.* 7.16). Jesus' execution "on the eve of Passover" agrees with Johannine chronology (cf. John 18–19). "Balaam the lame was thirty-three years (old) when Phineas the brigand killed him" (*b. Sanh.* 106b). Although it is disputed, "Phineas the brigand" may refer to Pontius Pilate. If this is correct, then the thirty-three year old "Balaam" must be Jesus. "The robber was caught and they hanged him on the gallows, and all passersby say: 'It seems that the ruler is hanged.' Thus, it is said, 'He that is hanged is a reproach to God' [cf. Deut 21:23]" (*t. Sanh.* 9.7). Excluded from the "World to Come" (*m. Sanh.* 10:2), Jesus will be boiled in filth in Gehenna (*b. Giṭ.* 56b–57a).

6. *On the resurrection of Jesus.* "He then went and raised Jesus by incantation" (*b. Giṭ.* 57a, MS M). "Woe to him who makes himself alive by the name of God" (*b. Sanh.* 106a). Jesus' resurrection is probably viewed here as part of the general accusation that Jesus was a magician.

7. *On healing in the name of Jesus.* "It once happened that [Eliezer] ben Dama, the son of Rabbi Ishmael's sister, was bitten by a snake; and Jacob [James? cf. Jas 5:14–15], a native of Kefar Sekaniah, came to him in the name of Jesus ben Pantera. But Rabbi Ishmael did not permit him." Ishmael goes on to say that it is better to die in peace than to be healed in the name of Jesus (*t. Ḥul.* 2.22–23; cf. *y. Šabb.* 14.4; *y. ʿAbod. Zar.* 2.2; *b. ʿAbod. Zar.* 27b; *Qoh. Rab.* 10:5 §1).

8. *Seper Toledot Yeshu.* In the Middle Ages, perhaps as early as the eighth century, many of these traditions were compiled into a small book known as the *Seper Toledot Yeshu* ("The Book of the Generations of Jesus"). This title is taken from the opening words of Matt 1:1. Alternate titles are *Maʾase Talui* ("The Deeds of the Hanged One"), *Maʾase deʾoto we-ʾet Beno* ("The Deeds of That One and His Son"), or *Maʾase Yeshu* ("The Deeds of Jesus"). The earliest references to this

writing date from the ninth century. In places it is dependent upon the *Yosippon* (see ch. 5). For an edited version see Goldstein, 148–54.

9. *The Gospels.* The Gospels are sometimes alluded to: "The books of the evangelists and the books of the *minim* [heretics] they do not save from the fire. But they are allowed to burn" (*t. Šabb.* 13:5). The rabbis discuss whether or not it is required to cut out references to the Divine Name before the heretical books are burned.

Bibliography: E. BAMMEL, "Eine übersehene Angabe zu den Toledoth Jeschu," *NTS* 35 (1989): 479–80; R. E. BROWN, "The Babylonian Talmud on the Execution of Jesus," *NTS* 43 (1997): 158–59; F. F. BRUCE, *Jesus and Christian Origins outside the New Testament* (Grand Rapids: Eerdmans, 1974), 54–65; G. H. DALMAN, with H. LAIBLE, *Jesus Christ in the Talmud, Midrash, Zohar, and the Liturgy of the Synagogue* (Cambridge: Deighton, Bell, 1893; repr., New York: Arno, 1973); C. A. EVANS, "Jesus in Non-Christian Sources," in *Studying the Historical Jesus: Evaluations of the State of Current Research* (ed. C. A. Evans and B. Chilton; NTTS 19; Leiden: Brill, 1994), 443–78, esp. 443–50; M. GOLDSTEIN, *Jesus in the Jewish Tradition* (New York: Macmillan, 1950); R. T. HERFORD, *Christianity in Talmud and Midrash* (London: Williams & Norgate, 1903; repr., New York: Ktav, 1975); W. HORBURY, "The Trial of Jesus in Jewish Tradition," in *The Trial of Jesus* (ed. E. Bammel; SBT 13; London: SCM Press, 1970), 103–16; J. KLAUSNER, *Jesus of Nazareth: His Life, Times, and Teaching* (London: George Allen & Unwin, 1925), 18–54; S. KRAUSS, *Das Leben Jesu nach jüdische Quellen* (Berlin: S. Calvary, 1902), 181–94; J. Z. LAUTERBACH, "Jesus in the Talmud," in *Rabbinic Essays* (Cincinnati: Hebrew Union College Press, 1951), 473–570; J. MAIER, *Jesus von Nazareth in der talmudischen Überlieferung* (Erträge der Forschung 82; Darmstadt: Wissenschaftliche Buchgesellschaft, 1978); J. P. MEIER, *The Roots of the Problem and the Person* (vol. 1 of *A Marginal Jew: Rethinking the Historical Jesus;* ABRL; New York: Doubleday, 1991), 93–98; H. I. NEWMAN, "The Death of Jesus in the *Toledot Yeshu* Literature," *JTS* 50 (1999): 59–79; D. ROKEAH, "Ben Stada Is Ben Pantera—towards the Clarification of a Philological-Historical Problem," *Tarbiz* 39 (1969–1970): 9–18 (Hebrew; Rokeah doubts that Jesus should be identified with either ben Stada or ben Pantera); G. N. STANTON, "Jesus of Nazareth: A Magician and a False Prophet Who Deceived God's People," in *Jesus of Nazareth: Lord and Christ* (ed. J. B. Green and M. Turner; I. H. Marshall FS; Grand Rapids: Eerdmans, 1994), 164–80; G. H. TWELFTREE, "Jesus in Jewish Traditions," in *Jesus Traditions outside the Gospels* (ed. D. Wenham; Gospel Perspectives 5; Sheffield: JSOT Press, 1982), 290–325; R. E. VAN VOORST, *Jesus outside the New Testament: An Introduction to the Ancient Evidence* (Studying the Historical Jesus; Grand Rapids: Eerdmans, 2000), 104–34; H. J. ZIMMELS, "Jesus and 'Putting Up a Brick,'" *JQR* 43 (1952–1953): 225–28.

The Halakah of Jesus. Did the teaching of Jesus influence rabbinic Judaism? In a recent investigation into this interesting question Phillip Sigal has concluded that Jesus probably did have an impact on rabbinic halakah. He believes that some of Jesus' views entered the Tannaic stream of tradition, but either anonymously or under the names of other authorities. One of his most compelling examples is Jesus' teaching on the priority of the human being over the Sabbath:

> One sabbath he was going through the grainfields; and as they made their way his disciples began to pluck heads of grain. And the Pharisees said to him, "Look, why are they doing what is not lawful on the sabbath?" And he said to them, "Have you

not read what David did, when he was in need and was hungry, he and those who were with him: how he entered the house of God, when Abiathar was high priest, and ate the bread of the Presence, which it is not lawful for any but the priests to eat, and also gave it to those who were with him?" And he said to them, "The sabbath was made for man, not man for the sabbath; so the Son of Man is lord even of the sabbath." (Mark 2:23–28 par.)

Sigal draws our attention to the parallel saying attributed to Rabbi Simon ben Menasya, who said: "Behold, it says: 'And you shall keep the sabbath, for it is holy unto you' [Exod 31:14]. This means: The sabbath is given to you but you are not surrendered to the sabbath" (*Mek.* on Exod 31:12–17 [*Šabb.* 1.25–28]; Lauterbach, *Mekilta De-Rabbi Ishmael* [3 vols.; Philadelphia: Jewish Publication Society of America, 1933–1935; repr., 1976], 3:198). Sigal reasons that since this parallel is too close to be regarded as nothing more than a coincidence, and since Jesus, who antedates Simon ben Menasya by more than 200 years, is the first to have articulated this halakah, it is most likely that what is credited to Menasya originated with Jesus. Sigal suspects that in other areas, such as in his stricter views of personal piety and more lenient views of cultic requirements, Jesus influenced Tannaic Judaism. As an example of the latter one thinks of Jesus' citation of Hos 6:6 (Matt 9:13; 12:7) and the parallel saying of Yohanan ben Zakkai about 75–80 C.E. (*ʾAbot R. Nat. A* §4; see the discussion above).

Haggadah in Paul. Arguing that God's promise to Abraham included the coming of Christ, Paul explains to the Christians of the churches of Galatia, "Now the promises were made to Abraham and to his seed. It does not say, 'And to seeds,' as of many; but it says, 'And to your seed,' that is, to one person, who is Christ" (Gal 3:16). Paul infers the reference to the Messiah from the singular "seed" of Gen 12:7, 13:15, 17:7, and 24:7 (*sperma* in the LXX; *zeraʾ* in the Hebrew). Paul's argument strikes most moderns as somewhat odd. After all, is not the singular *seed* a collective, referring to Abraham's descendants as a whole? It is probable that Paul understood this dimension, but in true rabbinic fashion he sees in the grammatical singularity an interesting exegetical possibility: a reference to a single person—the Messiah.

Rabbinic parallels to Paul's reasoning are not hard to find. We read in *m. Šabb.* 9:2, "How do we know of a garden bed, six handbreadths square, that five different kinds of seed may be sown in it, four on the sides and one in the middle? Since it says, 'For as the earth brings forth her bud and as the garden causes seeds sown in it to spring forth' (Isa 61:11). 'Its seed' is not said, but 'Its seeds.'" In this case, the plurality of *zeraʾ* in Isa 61:1 justifies the conclusion that more than one type of seed may be sown in a small garden plot. The plural "bloods" in Gen 4:10 ("What have you done? Listen, your brother's blood [lit. 'bloods' (*damim*)] is crying out to me from the ground!") implies that Abel's many *descendants* are in view, not simply the death of Abel himself—at least according to the Targum: "What is this that you have done? The voice of the blood *of the righteous multitudes that were to arise from Abel* your brother is crying *against you before me* from the earth" (*Neofiti*). This Aramaic paraphrase is spelled out more fully in the Mishna: "In the case of a trial for property cases, a person (who gives false testimony) pays money and achieves atonement for himself. In capital cases (the accused's) blood [*dam*] and the blood [*dam*] of all those who were destined to be born from him (who was wrongfully convicted and sentenced to death) are held against him (who testifies falsely) to the end of time, for so we find in the case of Cain who slew his brother, as it is said, 'The bloods of your brother cry out' (Gen 4:10). It does not say, 'The blood of your brother,' but, 'The bloods of your brother'—his blood and the blood of all those who were destined to be born from him" (*m. Sanh.* 4:5). The form and logic of this argument—"It does not say . . . but"—match exactly what we see in Galatians.

Bibliography: I. ABRAHAMS, *Studies in Pharisaism and the Gospels* (2 vols.; Cambridge: Cambridge University Press, 1917–1924; repr., with prolegomenon by M. S. Enslin; 2 vols. in 1; New York: Ktav, 1967); E. BISCHOFF, *Jesus und die Rabbinen: Jesu Bergpredigt und "Himmelreich" in ihrer Unabhängigkeit vom Rabbinismus* (Leipzig: Hinrichs, 1905); J. H. CHARLESWORTH and L. L. JOHNS, eds., *Hillel and Jesus: Comparisons of Two Major Religious Leaders* (Minneapolis: Fortress, 1997); D. DAUBE, "The Interpretation of a Generic Singular," in *The New Testament and Rabbinic Judaism* (London: Athlone, 1956), 438–44; P. FIEBIG, *Jesu Bergpredigt: Rabbinische Texte zum Verständnis der Bergpredigt* (FRLANT 20; Göttingen: Vandenhoeck & Ruprecht, 1924); A. FINKEL, *The Pharisees and the Teacher of Nazareth* (AGSU 4; Leiden: Brill, 1964); S. T. LACHS, *A Rabbinic Commentary on the New Testament: The Gospels of Matthew, Mark, and Luke* (Hoboken, N.J.: Ktav, 1987); W. R. G. LOADER, *Jesus' Attitude towards the Law: A Study of the Gospels* (WUNT 2.97; Tübingen: Mohr [Siebeck], 1997); C. G. MONTEFIORE, *The Synoptic Gospels: Edited with an Introduction and a Commentary* (2 vols.; 2d ed.; London: Macmillan, 1927); E. P. SANDERS, *Jewish Law from Jesus to the Mishnah* (Philadelphia: Trinity Press International, 1990), 19–23; P. SIGAL, *The Halakah of Jesus of Nazareth according to the Gospel of Matthew* (Lanham, Md.: University Press of America, 1986); F. VOUGA, *Jésus et la loi selon la tradition synoptique* (MdB 563; Paris: Labor et Fides, 1988).

General Bibliography

J. M. DAVIS, "Bibliography on the Story in Ancient Judaism," in *New Perspectives on Ancient Judaism* (ed. J. Neusner; Lanham: University Press of America, 1987); E. E. ELLIS, "Biblical Interpretation in the New Testament Church," *SJWSTP* 699–709; B. GERHARDSSON, *Memory and Manuscript: Oral Tradition and Written Transmission in Rabbinic Judaism and Early Christianity* (ASNU 22; Uppsala: Almqvist & Wiksells, 1961); L. HAAS, "Bibliography on Midrash," in *The Study of Ancient Judaism* (ed. J. Neusner; 2 vols.; New York: Ktav, 1972), 1:93–106; D. W. HALIVNI, *Midrash, Mishnah, and Gemara: The Jewish Predilection for Justified Law* (Cambridge: Harvard University Press, 1986); A. HYMAN, *Torah HaKetuba VeHaMessurah: A Reference Book of the Scriptural Passages Quoted in Talmudic, Midrashic, and Early Rabbinic Literature* (3 vols.; 2d ed.; Tel Aviv: Dvir, 1979); M. JASTROW, *A Dictionary of the Targumim, the Talmud Babli and Yerushalmi, and the Midrashic Literature* (2 vols.; New York: Putnam, 1886–1894; repr., New York: Pardes, 1950); S. KRAUSS, *Griechische und lateinische Lehnwörter im Talmud, Midrasch, und Targum* (2 vols.; Berlin: S. Calvary, 1898–1899; repr., Hildesheim, Ger.: Olms, 1987); C. J. MILIKOWSKY, *Seder Olam: A Rabbinic Chronography* (2 vols. in 1; Ann Arbor, Mich.: University Microfilms, 1981); G. F. MOORE, *Judaism in the First Centuries of the Christian Era: The Age of the Tannaim* (3 vols.; Cambridge: Harvard, 1927); R. C. MUSAPH-ANDRIESSE, *From Torah to Kabbalah* (New York: Oxford University Press, 1982); J. NEUSNER, *From Tradition to Imitation: The Plan and Program of Pesiqta Rabbati and Pesiqta deRab Kahana* (BJS 80; Atlanta: Scholars Press, 1987); IDEM, *The Peripatetic Saying: The Problem of the Thrice-Told Tale in Talmudic Literature* (BJS 89; Chico, Calif.: Scholars Press, 1985); IDEM, *The Study of Ancient Judaism* (2 vols.; New York: Ktav, 1981); IDEM, *A Theological Commentary to the Midrash* (9 vols.; Studies in Ancient Judaism; Lanham, Md.: University Press of America, 2001); J. NEUSNER, with G. G. PORTON, *Sifra: An Analytical Translation* (3 vols.; BJS 138–40; Atlanta: Scholars Press, 1988); A. J. SALDARINI, "Reconstructions of Rabbinic Judaism," *EJMI* 437–77; E. P. SANDERS, *Jewish Law from Jesus to the Mishnah* (Philadelphia: Trinity Press International, 1990); S. SCHECHTER, *Aspects of Rabbinic Theology: Major Concepts of the Talmud* (London: Macmillan, 1909; repr., Peabody, Mass.: Hendrickson, 1998); D. SPERBER, *A Dictionary of Greek and Latin Terms in Rabbinic Literature* (Ramat-Gan: Bar-Ilan University Press, 1984); J. T. TOWNSEND, "Rabbinic Sources," in *The Study of Judaism* (ed. J. Neusner; New York: Ktav, 1972), 35–80; E. E. URBACH, *The Sages: Their Concepts and Beliefs* (2d ed., Jerusalem: Magnes Press, 1979); A. WÜNSCHE, *Der Midrasch Samuel* (vol. 5, part 1, of *Aus Israels Lehrhallen;* Leipzig: E. Pfeiffer, 1910; repr., Hildesheim: Olms, 1967); S. ZEITLIN, "Hillel and the Hermeneutical Rules," *JQR* 54 (1963–1964): 161–73.

CHAPTER EIGHT

The New Testament Apocrypha and Pseudepigrapha

Agrapha
Abbaton, Angel of Death
Apostolic Histories of Pseudo-Abdias
Gospel of the Adversary of the Law and the Prophets
Acts of Andrew
Acts of Andrew and Matthias
Acts of Andrew and Paul
Epistle of the Apostles
Memoria of Apostles
Acts of Barnabas
Gospel of Barnabas
Book of the Resurrection of Christ by Bartholomew
Martyrdom of Bartholomew
Letters of Christ and Abgarus
Letter of Christ from Heaven
Pseudo-Clementines
Coptic Narratives of the Ministry and the Passion
Testamentum Domini ("Testament of the Lord")
Gospel of the Ebionites
Gospel of the Egyptians
Book of Elchasai
Gospel of Eve
Gospel of Gamaliel
Gospel of the Hebrews
Arabic Gospel of the Infancy

Armenian Gospel of the Infancy
Latin Gospel of the Infancy
Acts of James (the Greater)
Ascent of James (the Greater)
Protevangelium of James
Acts of John
Acts of John by Procurus
Apocryphal Gospel of John
Book of John
1 Revelation of John
2 Revelation of John
3 Revelation of John
Syriac History of John
John the Baptist
Narrative of Joseph in Arimathea
History of Joseph the Carpenter
Letter of Lentulus
Acts of Mark
Birth of Mary
Gospel of the Birth of Mary
Passing of Mary
Questions of Mary
Gospel of Pseudo-Matthew
Martyrdom of Matthew
Gospel and Traditions of Matthias
Gospel of the Nazoreans
Gospel of Nicodemus
Acts of Paul
Greek Acts of Peter and Paul

(continued on next page)

Apocalypse of Paul	Letters of Pilate and Herod
Correspondence between Seneca and Paul	Letter of Pilate to Tiberius
	Letter of Tiberius to Pilate
Epistle of Paul to the Alexandrians	Report and Paradosis of Pilate
Paul's Third Letter to the Corinthians	The Avenging of the Savior
Epistle to the Laodiceans	Sibylline Oracles
Martyrdom of Paul	Revelation of Stephen
Vision of Paul	Acts of Thaddeus
Acts of Peter	Acts of Thomas
(Slavonic) Acts of Peter	Minor Acts of Thomas
Acts of Andrew and Peter	Apocalypse of Thomas
Apocalypse of Peter	Consumption of Thomas
Gospel of Peter	Gospel of Thomas
Martyrdom of Peter	Infancy Gospel of Thomas
Passions of Peter and Paul	Martyrdom of Thomas
Preaching of Peter	The Dialogue of Timothy and Aquila
Acts of Philip	Epistle of Titus
(Syriac) Acts of Philip	Gospel of the Twelve Apostles
Gospel of Philip	Apocalypse of the Virgin
Martyrdom of Philip	Assumption of the Virgin
Translation of Philip	Coptic Lives of the Virgin
Acts of Pilate	Acts of Xanthippe and Polyxena
Death of Pilate	Apocalypse of Zechariah
Letter of Pilate to Claudius	

The title "New Testament Apocrypha and Pseudepigrapha" is a misnomer, since it implies that these are writings of the NT itself. In reality these are post-NT Christian apocryphal and pseudepigraphal writings, some of which date from the Middle Ages. Portions of this large corpus are translated in James; in the updated version by Elliott, *ANT;* and in Hennecke and Schneemelcher. Because most of these documents are quite late and secondary and therefore do not assist NT interpretation, this chapter treats only a few of the items listed in the box above. In recent years, several apocryphal—or, less pejoratively, extracanonical—gospels have received a great deal of attention, with some scholars arguing that they may contain ancient, independent, and possibly superior traditions and forms of Jesus' sayings. These items are treated in the summaries.

Summaries of Selected Writings

Gospel of Thomas. For the NT, the most important tractate of the Nag Hammadi library is the *Gospel of Thomas* (not to be confused with the various pseudepigraphal infancy gospels of Thomas). Parts of *Thomas,* in Greek, had already been known from the Oxyrhynchus Papyri, discovered in Egypt at the end of the nineteenth century (P.Oxy. 1 [= §§26–33], 654 [= Prologue + §§1–7], 655 [§§24, 36–39, 77]). Subsequently the whole of the *Gospel of Thomas* in Coptic was found among the Nag Hammadi codices. These leather-bound books were discovered along the Nile River in Upper Egypt in 1945.

Coptic *Thomas*, comprising 114 sayings or logia, has answered at least one vital question relating to the origins of the Synoptic Gospels. One of the major objections raised against the Two Document Hypothesis (i.e., that Matthew and Luke made use of two "documents"—Mark and "Q") is that there was no evidence that a gospel devoid of a narrative framework, but rather consisting only of sayings, ever existed or would have been desirable. With the discovery of the *Gospel of Thomas*, that objection has been met. Although not in itself a version of Q, the *Gospel of Thomas* is certainly an example of the Q genre. *Thomas* may also make a second important contribution to Synoptic studies. Some think this gospel may contain authentic sayings of Jesus not already found in the NT Gospels and that it may also contain more primitive forms of sayings than are found in the NT Gospels. This is, however, certainly debatable.

Quoting or alluding to more than half of the writings of the NT (Matthew, Mark, Luke, John, Acts, Romans, 1–2 Corinthians, Galatians, Ephesians, Colossians, 1 Thessalonians, 1 Timothy, Hebrews, 1 John, and Revelation; on this, see Evans, Webb, and Wiebe), *Thomas* could very well be a collage of NT and apocryphal materials that have been interpreted, often allegorically, in such a way as to advance second- and third-century gnostic ideas. Another problem with viewing *Thomas* as early and independent of the NT Gospels is the presence of a significant amount of material distinctive to Matthew (what is usually called "M"), Luke ("L"), and John. Moreover, there is evidence in *Thomas* of contact with second-century Syriac traditions, including Tatian's *Diatessaron* (see Perrin). Finally, Matthean and Lukan redaction is also present in *Thomas* (cf., e.g., Mark 4:22; Luke 8:17; P.Oxy. 655 = *Gos. Thom.* §5). Accordingly, assumptions that *Thomas* contains a significant amount of material reaching back to the middle of the first century are risky at best.

Bibliography: J. B. BAUER, "The Synoptic Tradition in the Gospel of Thomas," *SE* 3 (1961): 314–17; C. L. BLOMBERG, "Tradition and Redaction in the Parables of the Gospel of Thomas," in *The Jesus Tradition outside the Gospels* (ed. D. Wenham; Gospel Perspectives 5; Sheffield: JSOT Press, 1984), 177–205; J. H. CHARLESWORTH and C. A. EVANS, "Jesus in the Agrapha and Apocryphal Gospels," esp. 496–503; C. A. EVANS, R. L. WEBB, and R. A. WIEBE, eds., *Nag Hammadi Texts and the Bible: A Synopsis and Index* (NTTS 18; Leiden: Brill, 1993), 88–144; J. A. FITZMYER, "The Oxyrhynchus logoi of Jesus and the Coptic Gospel according to Thomas," in Fitzmyer, *ESBNT* 355–433; O. HOFIUS, "Das koptische Thomasevangelium und die Oxyrhynchus-Papyri Nr. 1, 654 und 655," *EvT* 20 (1960): 21–41, 182–92; F. LAPHAM, *An Introduction to the New Testament Apocrypha*, 113–31 (locates *Thomas* and other pseudepigrapha of the Thomas cycle in the "Church in Mesopotamia"); N. PERRIN, *Thomas and Tatian: The Relationship between the Gospel of Thomas and the Diatessaron* (Academia Biblica 5; Atlanta, Ga.: Society of Biblical Literature, 2002); W. R. SCHOEDEL, "Parables in the Gospel of Thomas: Oral Tradition or Gnostic Exegesis?"

CTM 43 (1972): 548–60; K. R. SNODGRASS, "The Gospel of Thomas: A Secondary Gospel," *SecCent* 7 (1989–1990): 19–38; C. M. TUCKETT, "Thomas and the Synoptics," *NovT* 30 (1988): 132–57; R. URO, *Thomas: Seeking the Historical Context of the Gospel of Thomas* (New York: T&T Clark International, 2003). For additional bibliography, see J. H. CHARLESWORTH, *NTAP* 374–402; W. SCHNEEMELCHER, *NTApoc*² 110.

Egerton Papyrus 2. Egerton Papyrus 2, which is housed in the British Museum, consists of four fragments. The fourth fragment yields nothing more than one illegible letter, and the third fragment yields little more than a few scattered words. The first and second fragments offer four (or perhaps five) stories that parallel Johannine and Synoptic materials. Papyrus Köln 255 constitutes a related fragment that overlaps with, and adds about another three lines to, Egerton 2 fragment 1 recto.

J. D. Crossan has argued not only that the material in Egerton 2 is primitive but that the Markan evangelist made use of it as a source. Helmut Koester does not go that far, but he too thinks Egerton 2 preserves early, pre-Synoptic and pre-Johannine traditions. Indeed, Koester thinks the Synoptic-Johannine material in Egerton 2 represents a very early stage, a stage antedating the bifurcation of this material into two separate streams—one Synoptic and one Johannine. The hypotheses of Crossan and Koester, however, are very problematic, and not many have followed them.

The Synoptic and Johannine elements in Egerton 2 are more plausibly explained as second-century conflation, as we see in other second-century Christian works (e.g., Justin Martyr, *1 Apol.* 16.9–13, where elements from Matthew, Luke, and John are conflated and presented as a unified dominical discourse). As in the case of *Thomas*, Lukan and Matthean redaction is present in Egerton 2. Moreover, the poorly preserved fourth story (frg. 2 verso) appears to relate a fantastic story, similar to one preserved in the second-century *Infancy Gospel of Thomas*. All of these factors tell against a first-century origin of Egerton 2 (for the papyrus itself and the tradition it preserves).

Bibliography: K. ALAND, *Synopsis quattuor evangeliorum*, 60, 323, 332, 340, 422; H. I. BELL and T. C. SKEAT, *Fragments of an Unknown Gospel and Other Early Christian Papyri* (London: British Museum, 1935), 8–15; J. H. CHARLESWORTH and C. A. EVANS, "Jesus in the Agrapha and Apocryphal Gospels," esp. 514–25; D. LÜHRMANN, "Das neue Fragment des PEgerton 2 (PKöln 255)," in *The Four Gospels, 1992* (ed. F. Van Segbroeck et al.; F. Neirynck FS; 3 vols.; BETL 100; Leuven: Peeters, 1992), 3:2239–55; D. LÜHRMANN, with E. SCHLARB, *Fragmente apokryph gewordener Evangelien in griechischer und lateinischer Sprache*, 142–53. For additional bibliography, see W. SCHNEEMELCHER, *NTApoc*² 98.

Secret Gospel of Mark. What is probably the strangest case involving an alleged gospel source is the controversy of the Clementine letter that the late Morton Smith claims to have found written in the back of a seventeenth-century book containing the letters of Ignatius. Smith says he found the letter during a visit to the Mar Saba Monastery in 1958. (Mar Saba is located in the Kidron Valley, on the south side, about halfway between Jerusalem to the west and the Dead Sea to the east.) In 1973 Smith published a learned version of the text, complete with introduction, notes, commentary, and photographic plates (*Clement of Alexandria*), and a popular version (*Secret Gospel*). For thirty years the authenticity of this Clementine letter has been disputed. Charles Hedrick and a few others have continued to defend Smith and the authenticity of the letter, in which Clement of Alexandria speaks of a longer, secret version of the Gospel of Mark in which Jesus imparts esoteric secrets to a youthful disciple. Other scholars have expressed grave doubts about Smith's claims, even suggesting that Smith himself penned the Clementine letter (and in one of the photographs one can even see Smith's name on the page, leaving one critic to wonder if Smith has "signed his own work?"). The mystery only deepens. Robert Price (2004) has identified a novel, published and reprinted several times in the 1940s, that tells a tale in which the discovery of the letter of Nicodemus at the Mar Saba Monastery leads to controversy and intrigue. Price wonders if this work of fiction—which parallels the present case in an obvious and uncanny way—inspired Smith to adopt a similar strategy. Regrettably, the pages of the seventeenth-century book have not been subjected to the usual battery of tests to determine, among other things, the age of the ink (which according to Smith's testimony, would have to be eighteenth century, and certainly not mid–twentieth century). But such testing may never take place, for, alas, the pages seem to have gone missing.

Whatever position one takes regarding the authenticity of the Clementine letter, extreme caution is in order. Clement was notorious for accepting pseudepigraphical materials at face value. Accordingly, even if the letter is accepted as genuine, we are not able to make firm judgments about the historicity of an alleged secret version of the Gospel of Mark. Developing complicated theories of Synoptic origins and relationships on the basis of such a source—unverified and possibly even a modern hoax—is precarious scholarship at best.

Bibliography: J. H. CHARLESWORTH and C. A. EVANS, "Jesus in the Agrapha and Apocryphal Gospels," esp. 526–32; C. W. HEDRICK, "The Secret Gospel of Mark: Stalemate in the Academy," *JECS* 11 (2003): 133–45; C. W. HEDRICK, with N. Olympiou, "Secret Mark: New Photographs, New Witnesses," *The Fourth R* 13/5 (2000): 3–16; D. LÜHRMANN, with E. SCHLARB, *Fragmente apokryph gewordener Evangelien in griechischer und lateinischer Sprache*, 182–85; R. M. PRICE, "Second Thoughts on the Secret Gospel," *BBR* 14 (2004): 127–32; Q. QUESNELL, "The Mar Saba Clementine: A Question of Evidence," *CBQ* 37 (1975): 48–67; M. SMITH, *Clement of Alexandria and a Secret Gospel of Mark* (Cambridge: Harvard University Press, 1973); IDEM, *The Secret Gospel* (New York: Harper & Row, 1973) (a popular version of the former). For more bibliography and critical assessment of *Secret Mark*, see H. MERKEL, "Appendix: The 'Secret Gospel' of Mark," in W. SCHNEEMELCHER, *NTApoc*[2] 106–9.

Gospel of Peter. Until its discovery in the winter of 1886–1887, the *Gospel of Peter* was known only through one clear reference in Eusebius (*Hist. eccl.* 6.12.2–6). Five years later the ninth-century Greek text was published (see Bouriant). Since then P.Oxy. 2949 has been identified as a late-second-century Greek fragment of the *Gospel of Peter* (see Lührman 1981). Papyrus Oxyrhynchus 4009 may also be a fragment of *Peter,* but this identification is tenuous (see Lührman and Parsons).

The surviving text of the *Gospel of Peter* narrates the story of the passion, from Pilate washing his hands to a greatly embellished account of the resurrection—complete with angels whose heads reach the heavens and a walking-talking cross who replies to a heavenly question. Despite the many secondary characteristics of this gospel, a few scholars (e.g., Crossan) argue that at the core of *Peter* is an early source on which the NT Gospels themselves are based. It is far more probable, however, that *Peter*—at every stage of its composition—derives from the NT Gospels, particularly the Gospel of Matthew (on this point, see Green). On the dubiousness of the thesis that *Peter* is early and is the passion source on which the NT Gospels are based, D. Moody Smith (p. 150) asks rhetorically, "[I]s it thinkable that the tradition began with the legendary, the mythological, the anti-Jewish, and indeed the fantastic, and moved in the direction of the historically restrained and sober?" Prudence demands a negative response to Smith's question.

Bibliography: K. ALAND, *Synopsis quattuor evangeliorum*, 479–80, 484, 489, 493–94, 498, 500, 507; U. BOURIANT, "Fragments du texte grec du livre d'Enoch et de quelques écrits attribués à Saint Pierre," in J. BAILLET, *Le papyrus mathématique de Akhmim* (Mémoires publiés par les membres de la mission archéologique française au Caire 9/1; Paris: Libraire de la Société Asiatique, 1892), 137–42; R. E. BROWN, "The Gospel of Peter and Canonical Gospel Priority," *NTS* 33 (1987): 321–43; J. H. CHARLESWORTH and C. A. EVANS, "Jesus in the Agrapha and Apocryphal Gospels," esp. 503–14; J. D. CROSSAN, *The Cross That Spoke: The Origins of the Passion Narrative* (San Francisco: Harper & Row, 1988); J. B. GREEN, "The Gospel of Peter: Source for a Pre-canonical Passion Narrative?" *ZNW* 78 (1987): 293–301; F. LAPHAM, *An Introduction to the New Testament Apocrypha*, 88–112 (locates the *Gospel of Peter* and other Petrine pseudepigrapha in the "Church in Syria"); D. LÜHR-MANN, "POx 2949: EvPt 3–5 in einer Handschrift des 2./3. Jahrhunderts," *ZNW* 72 (1981): 216–22; D. LÜHRMANN and P. J. PARSONS, "4009: Gospel of Peter?" in *The Oxyrhynchus Papyri* (ed. B. P. Grenfell et al.; London: Egypt Exploration Fund, 1898–), 60:1–5 and pl. 1; D. LÜHRMANN, with E. SCHLARB, *Fragmente apokryph gewordener Evangelien in griechischer und lateinischer Sprache*, 72–95; M. G. MARA, *Evangile de Pierre* (SC 201; Paris: Cerf, 1973); J. A. ROBINSON and M. R. JAMES, *The Gospel according to Peter* (London: C. J. Clay, 1892); D. M. SMITH, "The Problem of John and the Synoptics in Light of the Relation between Apocryphal and Canonical Gospels," in *John and the Synoptics* (ed. A. Denaux; BETL 101; Leuven: Peeters and Leuven University Press, 1992), 147–62; T. ZAHN, *Das Evangelium des Petrus* (Erlangen: Deichert, 1893). For additional bibliography, see J. H. CHARLESWORTH, *NTAP* 321–27; W. SCHNEEMELCHER, *NTApoc*[2] 216.

The Jewish Gospels. With one or two notable dissenters, most scholars in the last century have followed Philipp Vielhauer and Georg Strecker (in Hennecke and Schneemelcher *NTApoc*), and more recently A. F. J. Klijn (1992), in extrapolating from the church fathers three distinct extracanonical Jewish gospels: the *Gospel of the Nazarenes*, the *Gospel of the Ebionites*, and the *Gospel of the Hebrews*. A recent study by Peter Lebrecht Schmidt (1998), however, has called this near consensus into question. Critically assessing the discussion from Schmidtke to Klijn, Schmidt thinks that originally there was only one Jewish gospel, probably written in Aramaic about 100 C.E., called the "Gospel according to the Hebrews," which was subsequently translated into Greek and Latin. In this theory, it is to this gospel, in its various forms and versions, that the church fathers refer when they speak of a *Gospel of the Ebionites*, or a *Gospel of the Nazarenes*. This is a complicated question, however, that cannot be adjudicated here.

If we have little confidence in the traditional identification of the three Jewish gospels (*Nazarenes, Ebionites*, and *Hebrews*), then perhaps we should work with the sources we have: (1) the Jewish gospel known to Origen, (2) the Jewish gospel known to Epiphanius, and (3) the Jewish gospel known to Jerome. By taking this approach we do not have to decide the question of how many Jewish gospels there were and, if more than one, how they related to one another and which one(s) the church fathers were citing. As it so happens, there is some correspondence with the traditionally identified three gospels. The quotations and traditions provided by Origen roughly correspond to what has been called the *Gospel of the Hebrews;* those provided by Epiphanius, to the *Gospel of the Ebionites;* and those provided by Jerome, to the *Gospel of the Nazarenes*.

Possibly related to this difficult question are the various Hebrew versions of the Gospel of Matthew; among these, the text of Shem Tob does not appear to be simply a Hebrew translation of Greek or Latin Matthew (see Howard). One should also take into account the recently published Coptic version of Matthew, which in places appears to be independent of Greek Matthew, in ways that could suggest a relationship to a variant tradition, perhaps even related to a Hebrew Matthew (see Schencke).

Bibliography: C. A. EVANS, "Jewish Versions of the Gospel of Matthew," *Mishkan* 38 (2003): 70–79; G. HOWARD, *The Gospel of Matthew according to a Primitive Hebrew Text* (rev. ed.; Macon, Ga.: Mercer University Press, 1995); A. F. J. KLIJN, *Jewish-Christian Gospel Tradition* (VCSup 17; Leiden: Brill, 1992); F. LAPHAM, *An Introduction to the New Testament Apocrypha,* 66–87 (places the Jewish Gospels in the context of the "Church in Samaria"); D. LÜHRMANN, with E. SCHLARB, *Fragmente apokryph gewordener Evangelien in griechischer und lateinischer Sprache,* 32–55; H.-M. SCHENKE, *Das Matthäus-Evangelium im mittelägyptischen Dialekt des Koptischen (Codex Schøyen)* (Manuscripts in the Schøyen Collection 2: Coptic Papyri 1; Oslo: Hermes, 2001); P. L. SCHMIDT, " 'Und es war geschrieben auf Hebräisch, Griechisch, und Lateinisch': Hieronymus, das Hebräer-Evangelium, und seine mittelalterliche Rezeption," *Filologia mediolatina* 5 (1998): 49–93; A. SCHMIDTKE, *Neue Fragmente und Untersuchungen zu den juden-christlichen Evangelien: Ein Beitrag zur Literatur und Geschichte der Judenchristen* (TU 37/1; Leipzig: Hinrichs, 1911).

Other Gospel Fragments. There are several fragments of other gospels. These include P.Merton 51, P.Oxy. 210, P.Oxy. 840, and P.Oxy. 1224. Of these the most interesting is P.Oxy. 840, in which we read of Jesus quarreling with a Pharisaical priest within the temple precincts over ritual purity. Published in 1908, this text touched off a firestorm of debate. It comprises a single page of parchment (not papyrus), with twenty-two lines of text on one side and twenty-three lines on the other. Its small size suggests that it could have been an amulet. The fact that we have two stories, the conclusion of one in lines 1–7 and most of a second in lines 7–45, encourages us to view this parchment as a leaf from a codex, albeit a small one, whether or not it was used as an amulet.

Although some scholars think the author of this story was unfamiliar with Jewish temple and ritual customs (see Bovon), recent investigation of P.Oxy. 840 and advances in archaeology in the land of Israel may be tipping the balance in favor of viewing the story as true to first-century Jewish practices, though not necessarily as deriving from an actual event in the life of Jesus. The alleged inaccuracies can in most instances be satisfactorily explained. The story may in fact provide us with an important glimpse into temple practices (see Schwartz).

Bibliography: F. BOVON, "Fragment Oxyrhynchus 840, Fragment of a Lost Gospel, Witness of an Early Christian Controversy over Purity," *JBL* 119 (2000): 705–28; C. A. EVANS, "Jewish Versions of the Gospel of Matthew," *Mishkan* 38 (2003): 70–79; D. LÜHRMANN, with E. SCHLARB, *Fragmente apokryph gewordener Evangelien in griechischer und lateinischer Sprache,* 139–79; D. R. SCHWARTZ, " 'Viewing the Holy Utensils' (P. Ox. V, 840)," *NTS* 32 (1986): 153–59.

SECTION BIBLIOGRAPHY: K. ALAND, ed., *Synopsis quattuor evangeliorum* (Stuttgart: Deutsche Bibelgesellschaft, 1985); R. CAMERON, ed., *OG* (English translations with brief introductions); J. H. CHARLESWORTH and C. A. EVANS, "Jesus in the Agrapha and Apocryphal Gospels," in *Studying the Historical Jesus: Evaluations of the State of Current Research* (ed. B. D. Chilton and C. A. Evans; NTTS 19; Leiden: Brill, 1994), 479–533; J. D. CROSSAN, *Four Other Gospels: Shadows on the Contours of Canon* (New York: Harper & Row, 1985; repr., Sonoma, Calif.: Polebridge, 1992) (exegetical studies of *Thomas,* Egerton, *Secret Mark,* and *Peter*); J. K. ELLIOTT, *ANT* (English translation, introductions, and bibliography); C. W. HEDRICK, ed., *The Historical Jesus and the Rejected Gospels* (Semeia 44; Atlanta: Scholars Press, 1988); H. KOESTER, *Ancient Christian Gospels: Their History and Development* (Philadelphia: Trinity Press International, 1990); F. LAPHAM, *An Introduction to the New Testament Apocrypha* (New York: T&T Clark International, 2003); D. LÜHRMANN, with E. SCHLARB, *Fragmente apokryph gewordener Evangelien in griechischer und lateinischer Sprache* (MTS 59; Marburg: N. G. Elwert, 2000) (Greek and Latin text and German translation of all extracanonical gospels and fragments); R. J. MILLER, *CG* (English translation with brief introductions); W. SCHNEEMELCHER, *NTApoc*[2] (English translation, introductions, and bibliography).

Studies

Agrapha. Genuine sayings of Jesus? According to Eusebius (*Hist. eccl.* 3.39.11), Papias "adduces other accounts, as though they came to him from unwritten [*agrapha*] tradition, and some strange parables and teachings of the Savior, and some other more mythical accounts." An example of a NT agraphon is Acts 20:35: "Always I have shown you that by so laboring one must help the weak, remembering the words of the Lord Jesus, that he said, 'It is more blessed to give than to receive' " (from Jeremias, 49–87):

> On the same day he saw a man performing a work on the Sabbath. Then he said to him: "Man! If you know what you are doing, you are blessed. But if you do not know, you are cursed and a transgressor of the Law" (from Codex D, following Luke 6:5).

He who is near me is near the fire; he who is far from me is far from the Kingdom (from Origen, *Homilies on Jeremiah* 20.3; also found in Didymus, *Commentary on the Psalms* 88.8 and *Gos. Thom.* §82).

No one can obtain the kingdom of heaven who has not passed through temptation (from Tertullian *On Baptism* 20).

You have rejected the Living One who is before your eyes, and talk idly of the dead (from Augustine *Against the Enemy of the Law and the Prophets* 2.4.14).

There will be dissensions and squabbles (Justin *Dialogue with Trypho* 35.3).

The Kingdom is like a wise fisherman who cast his net into the sea; he drew it up from the sea full of small fish; among them he found a large (and) good fish; that wise fisherman threw all the small fish down into the sea; he chose the large fish without regret (*Gos. Thom.* §8).

Ask for the great things, and God will add to you the little things (first quoted by Clement of Alexandria, *Stromateis* 1.24.158).

Hofius is less sanguine. He tentatively accepts two of the above and recommends the following two:

And never be joyful, save when you look upon your brother in love (*Gos. Heb.* §5; cf. Jerome *Commentary On Ephesians* 5.4).

[He that] stands far off [today] will tomorrow be [near you] (POxy 1224 §2).

Hofius believes that only nine agrapha are worth serious attention. Of these only four have a reasonable chance of being authentic: (1) the addition to Luke 6:5 in Codex D; (2) Origen, *Hom. Jer.* 20.3; Didymus, *On the Psalms* 88.8; *Gos. Thom.* §82; (3) *Gos. Heb.* §5; cf. Jerome, *Comm. Eph.* 5.4; (4) P.Oxy. 1224 §2. From this he concludes that the canonical Gospels preserve virtually all of the dominical tradition that the church of the second half of the first century had retained. He thinks therefore that assumptions that there was a vast amount of genuine material in circulation outside of the NT Gospels are unfounded.

Bibliography: J. D. CROSSAN, *Sayings Parallels: A Workbook for the Jesus Tradition* (FF: New Testament; Philadelphia: Fortress, 1986) (limited to "units which could or did exist in the tradition as isolated segments passed on in different contexts"; given this limitation, cites all instances of sayings in canonical and early extracanonical sources); O. HOFIUS, "Unknown Sayings of Jesus," in *The Gospel and the Gospels* (ed. P. Stuhlmacher; Grand Rapids: Eerdmans, 1991), 336–60; J. JEREMIAS, *Unknown Sayings of Jesus* (London: SPCK, 1958); W. D. STROKER, *Extracanonical Sayings of Jesus* (SBLRBS 18; Atlanta: Scholars Press, 1989) (extremely valuable tool that provides texts [Coptic, Greek, and Latin], translations, and helpful indexes; excellent bibliography).

The Early Church's Awareness of Pseudepigraphy. The early church was aware of pseudepigraphy and did not approve of it. The Muratorian Canon rejects the "forged" letters of Paul to the Laodiceans and Alexandrians (§§63–67). Tertullian defrocked an elder for writing the *Acts of Paul* and possibly also *3 Corinthians* (*Bapt.* 17). Eusebius avers:

> Among the books which are not genuine must be reckoned the Acts of Paul, the work entitled the Shepherd, the Apocalypse of Peter, and in addition to them the letter called of Barnabas and the so-called Teachings of the Apostles. And in addition, as I said, the Revelation of John, if this view prevail. For as I said, some reject it, but others count it among the Recognized Books. Some have also counted the Gospel according to the Hebrews, in which those of the Hebrews who have accepted Christ take a special pleasure. These would all belong to the disputed books, but we have nevertheless been obliged to make a list of them distinguishing between those writings which, according to the tradition of the Church are true, genuine, and recognized, and those which differ from them in that they are not canonical but disputed, yet nevertheless are known to most of the writers of the Church, in order that we might know them and the writings that are put forward by heretics under the name of the apostles containing gospels such as those of Peter, and Thomas, and Matthias, and some others besides, or Acts such as those of Andrew and John and the other apostles. To none of these has any who belonged to the succession of the orthodox ever thought it right to refer in his writings. Moreover, the type of phraseology differs from apostolic style, and the opinion and tendency of their contents are widely dissonant from true orthodoxy and clearly show that they are the forgeries of heretics. They ought, therefore, to be reckoned not even among spurious books but shunned as altogether wicked and impious. (Eusebius, *Hist. eccl.* 3.25.4–7 [Lake, in K. Lake and J. Oulton, *Eusebius* (2 vols.; LCL; Cambridge: Harvard University Press), 1:257–59])

According to Eusebius, Serapion, bishop of Antioch, condemned the *Gospel of Peter:*

> Another book has been composed by him [Serapion (d. 211 C.E.) entitled,] *Concerning what is known as the Gospel of Peter,* which he has written refuting the false statements in it, because of certain [people] in the community of Rhossus, who on the ground of the said writing turned aside into heterodox teachings. It will not be unreasonable to quote a short passage from this work, in which he puts forward the view he held about the book, writing as follows: "For our part, brethren, we receive both Peter and the other apostles as Christ, but the writings which falsely [*pseudepigrapha*] bear their names we reject, as men of experience, knowing that such were not handed down to us." (Eusebius, *Hist. eccl.* 6.12.2–3 [Oulton, LCL 2:41])

To this a general word of condemnation of all "poisonous books" is added by the *Apostolic Constitutions and Canons,* itself a pseudepigraphon:

> We [i.e., the Apostles] have sent all things to you, that you may know what our opinion is; and that you may not receive those books which obtain in our name, but are written by the ungodly. For you are not to attend to the names of the apostles, but to the nature of the things, and their settled opinions. For we know that Simon and Cleobius, and their followers, have compiled poisonous books under the name of Christ and of his disciples, and carry them about in order to deceive you who love Christ, and us his servants. (*Apos. Con.* 6:16)

For a concise discussion of the criteria of canonicity in the early church, see Lee McDonald. For studies concerned with the problem of pseudonymity, see Meade; Metzger.

Bibliography: J. D. G. DUNN, "The Problem of Pseudonymity," in *The Living Word* (London: SCM Press, 1987), 65–88; E. E. ELLIS, "Pseudonymity and Canonicity of New Testament Documents," in *History and Interpretation in New Testament Perspective* (BIS 54; Leiden: Brill, 2001), 17–29; L. M. MCDONALD, *The Formation of the Christian Biblical Canon* (rev. ed.; Peabody, Mass.: Hendrickson, 1995) [a third edition is forthcoming]; D. G. MEADE, *Pseudonymity and Canon: An Investigation into the Relationship of Authorship and Authority in Jewish and Earliest Christian Tradition* (Grand Rapids: Eerdmans, 1986); B. M. METZGER, "Literary Forgeries and Canonical Pseudepigrapha," *JBL* 91 (1972): 3–24; T. L. WILDER, "New Testament Pseudonymity and Deception," *TynBul* 50 (1999): 156–58.

Apocryphal Gospels and the Historical Jesus. But what of the Synoptic parallels in the apocryphal gospels? The extracanonical gospels discussed above have in recent years found a place in the scholarly discussion of the historical Jesus. Could some of these parallels represent more primitive tradition? In recent studies John Dominic Crossan argued that some of the apocryphal gospels (e.g., *Gospel of Thomas,* Papyrus Egerton 2, *Secret Gospel of Mark,* and *Gospel of Peter*) have retained primitive, perhaps even pre-Synoptic traditions. He argues, for example, that the *Gospel of Peter* offers evidence for a "Cross Gospel," which was the "single known source for the Passion and Resurrection narrative. It flowed into Mark, flowed along with him into Matthew and Luke, flowed along with the three synoptics into John, and finally flowed along with the intracanonical tradition into the pseudepigraphal *Gospel of Peter*" (1988, 404). But for the reasons briefly stated above, it is improbable that these extracanonical sources can provide us with early, independent, and reliable data.

For descriptions, parallels with NT Gospels, and principal bibliography, see appendix 3 below. For a more detailed discussion of a passage which may be significantly clarified by appeal to an apocryphal gospel, see chapter 12.

Bibliography: P. BESKOW, *Strange Tales about Jesus: A Survey of Unfamiliar Gospels* (Philadelphia: Fortress, 1983); R. CAMERON, ed., *OG;* J. D. CROSSAN, *The Cross That Spoke: The Origins of the Passion Narrative* (San Francisco: Harper & Row, 1988); IDEM, *Four Other Gospels: Shadows on the Contours of Canon* (Minneapolis: Winston, 1985); A. A. T. EHRHARDT, "Judaeo-Christians in Egypt, the Epistula apostolorum, and the Gospel to the Hebrews," *SE* 3 (1961): 360–82; J. K. ELLIOTT, *The Apocryphal Jesus: Legends of the Early Church* (Oxford: Oxford University Press, 1996); J. HILLS, *Tradition and Composition in the Epistula apostolorum* (HDR 24; Minneapolis: Fortress, 1990); L. L. KLINE, *The Sayings of Jesus in the Pseudo-Clementine Homilies* (SBLDS 14; Missoula, Mont.: Scholars Press, 1975); H. KOESTER, "Apocryphal and Canonical Gospels," *HTR* 73 (1980): 105–30; J. P. MEIER, *A Marginal Jew: Rethinking the Historical Jesus* (3 vols.; ABRL; New York: Doubleday, 1991–2001), 112–66 (questions the independence and authenticity of the Jesus tradition in the noncanonical gospels); R. J. MILLER, *CG;* M. SMITH, *Clement of Alexandria and a Secret Gospel of Mark* (Cambridge: Harvard University Press, 1973); IDEM, *The Secret Gospel: The Discovery and Interpretation of the Secret Gospel according to Mark* (New York:

Harper & Row, 1973) (a popular version of the former); W. D. STROKER, *Extracanonical Sayings of Jesus* (SBLRBS 18; Atlanta: Scholars Press, 1989); D. WENHAM, ed., *The Jesus Tradition outside the Gospels* (Gospel Perspectives 5; Sheffield: JSOT Press, 1985) (several essays examine Jesus tradition in Paul, James, 1 Peter, *Gospel of Thomas,* the Apostolic Fathers, apocryphal gospels, early Jewish and classical authors; bibliography); R. McL. WILSON, "The New Passion of Jesus in the Light of the New Testament," in *Neotestamentica et semitica* (ed. E. E. Ellis and M. Wilcox; M. Black FS; Edinburgh: T&T Clark, 1969), 264–72.

General Bibliography

J. H. CHARLESWORTH, *NTAP;* J. K. ELLIOTT, *ANT;* C. A. EVANS, "The Interpretation of Scripture in the New Testament Apocrypha and Gnostic Writings," in *The Ancient Period* (vol. 1 of *A History of Biblical Interpretation;* ed. A. J. Hauser and D. F. Watson; Grand Rapids: Eerdmans, 2003), 430–56 (bibliography); M. R. JAMES, *Apocrypha anecdota: A Collection of Thirteen Apocryphal Books and Fragments* (Texts and Studies 2/3; Cambridge: Cambridge University Press, 1893); IDEM, *Apocrypha anecdota: Second Series* (Texts and Studies 5/1; Cambridge: Cambridge University Press, 1897); IDEM, *The Apocryphal New Testament* (Oxford: Clarendon, 1924; corrected ed., 1953) [see the further updated version in J. K. Elliott, *ANT*]; H. KOESTER, *Ancient Christian Gospels: Their History and Development* (Philadelphia: Trinity Press International, 1990); F. LAPHAM, *An Introduction to the New Testament Apocrypha* (New York: T&T Clark International, 2003); D. R. MACDONALD, "Apocryphal New Testament," *HBD* 38–39; W. SCHNEEMELCHER, *NTApoc*[2].

CHAPTER NINE

Early Church Fathers

Only a select number of early apologists, exegetes, and theologians are listed in this chapter. Those that are listed are those who were early and interpret Scripture, both OT and NT, and preserve early traditions. The major contributions that these writers make to NT interpretation are enumerated in the following paragraphs. Most of the attention is given to the Apostolic Fathers.

Summaries

Apostolic Fathers. The so-called Apostolic Fathers is, in reality, a collection of postapostolic writings that were revered and, in some cases, rivaled the very writings that now make up the canon of the NT. This corpus represents a collection of early writings, mostly epistles, of late first- and early- to mid-second century church leaders. This collection contributes to NT studies in at least five important areas: (1) OT text types with which the early church was familiar; (2) dominical traditions parallel to and in some instances outside of the NT Gospels; (3) early interpretations of NT books and passages; (4) traditions relating to early church history; and (5) traditions regarding the authorship of NT books. For the Greek text and English translation on facing pages, see K. Lake, *The Apostolic Fathers.*

Bibliography: J. V. BARTLET et al., *The New Testament in the Apostolic Fathers* (Oxford: Clarendon, 1905); B. D. EHRMAN, trans., *The Apostolic Fathers* (2 vols.; LCL 24–25; Cambridge: Harvard University Press, 2003); R. M. GRANT, *An Introduction* (vol. 1 of *The Apostolic Fathers;* ed. R. M. Grant; 1964); K. LAKE, trans., *The Apostolic Fathers* (2 vols.; LCL 24–25; Cambridge: Harvard University Press, 1912–1913); J. B. LIGHTFOOT, *The Apostolic Fathers: Clement, Ignatius, and Polycarp* (5 vols.; London: Macmillan, 1889–1890; repr., Peabody, Mass.: Hendrickson, 1989); IDEM, *S. Clement of Rome* (2 vols. London: Macmillan, 1869–1877): vol. 1, *The Two Epistles to the Corinthians,* vol. 2, *Appendix Containing the Newly Recovered Portions, with Introductions, Notes, and Translations;* J. B. LIGHTFOOT and J. R. HARMER, *The Apostolic Fathers* (New York: Macmillan, 1891) (Greek text and English translation, edited and completed by Harmer); IDEM, *The Apostolic Fathers* (ed. M. W. Holmes; rev. ed.; Grand Rapids: Baker, 1989).

1 Clement. First Clement is a letter to the church at Corinth that was commissioned by a small group of presbyters of the church at Rome. Clement was one of these presbyters and may very well have been the leader of the group; hence his name's association with the letter. The letter, penned in either 95 or 96 C.E., urges the Corinthians to settle their disputes peaceably. The writer sometimes appeals to Paul's Corinthian correspondence (cf. 13:27; 35:8; 37:3). The SBL abbreviation is *1 Clem.*

Bibliography: L. W. BARNARD, "St. Clement of Rome and the Persecution of Domitian," in *Studies in the Apostolic Fathers and Their Background* (Oxford: Blackwell, 1966), 5–18; B. E. BOWE, "Prayer Rendered for Caesar? 1 Clement 59.3–61.3," in *The Lord's Prayer and Other Prayer Texts from the Greco-Roman Era* (ed. J. H. Charlesworth and M. Kiley; Philadelphia: Trinity Press, 1994), 85–99; IDEM, "The Rhetoric of Love in Corinth: From Paul to Clement of Rome," in *Common Life in the Early Church: Essays Honoring Graydon F. Snyder* (ed. J. V. Hills; Harrisburg, Pa.: Trinity Press International, 1998), 244–57; G. L. COCKERILL, "Heb 1:1–14, 1 Clem 36:1–6, and the High Priest Title," *JBL* 97 (1978): 437–40; P. ELLINGWORTH, "Hebrews and 1 Clement: Literary Dependence or Common Tradition?" *BZ* 23 (1979): 262–69; R. M. GRANT and H. H. GRAHAM, *First and Second Clement* (vol. 2 of *The Apostolic Fathers;* ed. R. M. Grant; 1965), 3–106; D. A. HAGNER, *The Use of the Old and New Testaments in Clement of Rome* (NovTSup 34; Leiden: Brill, 1973); A. VAN DEN HOEK, "Techniques of Quotation in Clement of Alexandria: A View of Ancient Literary Working

Methods," *VC* 50 (1996): 223–43; D. G. HORRELL, *The Social Ethos of the Corinthian Correspondence: Interests and Ideology from 1 Corinthians to 1 Clement* (Studies of the New Testament and Its World; Edinburgh: T&T Clark, 1996); M. KALAMBA, "Spiritualité de Clement de Rome dans la lettre aux Corinthiens," *Revue africaine de théologie* 22 (1998): 21–48; D. PETERLIN, "Clement's Answer to the Corinthian Conflict in A. D. 96," *JETS* 39 (1996): 57–69; C. C. TARELLI, "Clement of Rome and the Fourth Gospel," *JTS* 48 (1947): 208–9; C. TREVETT, "Ignatius 'To the Romans' and I Clement LIV–LVI," *VC* 43 (1989): 35–52; L. L. WELBORN, "On the Date of First Clement," *BR* 29 (1984): 35–54; A. E. WILHELM-HOOIJBERGH, "A Different View of Clemens Romanus," *HeyJ* 16 (1975): 266–88; F. W. YOUNG, "The Relation of 1 Clement to the Epistle of James," *JBL* 67 (1948): 339–45.

2 Clement. From antiquity the writing that is called *2 Clement* was associated with *1 Clement.* However, its authorship, date, place of writing, and occasion are unknown. Moreover, it is not a letter, but a sermon based on Isa 54:1 (cf. *2 Clem.* 2:1). Only three MSS are extant, the earliest in Codex Alexandrinus (fifth century C.E.). The SBL abbreviation is *2 Clem.*

Bibliography: K. P. DONFRIED, *The Setting of Second Clement in Early Christianity* (NovTSup 38; Leiden: Brill, 1974); IDEM, "The Theology of Second Clement," *HTR* 66 (1973): 487–501; R. M. GRANT and H. H. GRAHAM, *First and Second Clement* (vol. 2 of *The Apostolic Fathers;* ed. R. M. Grant; 1965), 109–32; R. KNOPF, *Lehre der zwölf Apostel: Zwei Clemensbriefe* (Tübingen: Mohr [Siebeck], 1920); C. C. RICHARDSON, "An Anonymous Sermon, Commonly Called Clement's Second Letter," in *Early Christian Fathers* (ed. Richardson), 183–202; J. D. THOMPSON and J. A. BAIRD, eds., *A Critical Concordance to the Second Epistle of Clement to the Corinthians* (Wooster, Ohio: Biblical Research Associates, 1996); W. C. VAN UNNIK, "The Interpretation of 2 Clement 15,5," *VC* 27 (1973): 29–34; R. WARNS, *Untersuchungen zum 2. Clemens-Brief* (Marburg: Rüdiger Warns, 1985).

Ignatius. After his arrest in Syrian Antioch, Ignatius was sent to Rome, where he presumably was martyred. While on his journey he penned seven letters (six to churches [*Ephesians, Magnesians, Philadelphians, Romans, Smyrnaeans, Trallians*], one to Polycarp), though the authenticity of a few of them from time to time has been doubted. The matter has been complicated by the preservation of three recensions (short, middle, and long). Most scholars now accept the authenticity of all seven letters (see the discussion in William Schoedel's commentary). The letters are dated broadly to 100–118 C.E., though some narrow the span to 107–110. Ignatius wrote to encourage and promote harmony, especially in his home church of Antioch. The SBL abbreviations are Ign. *Eph.*, Ign. *Magn.*, etc.

Bibliography: L. W. BARNARD, "The Background of St. Ignatius of Antioch," *VC* 17 (1963): 193–206; C. K. BARRETT, "Jews and Judaizers in the Epistles of Ignatius," in *Jews, Greeks, and Christians: Religious Cultures in Late Antiquity* (ed. R. Hamerton-Kelly and R. Scroggs; SJLA 21; Leiden: Brill, 1976), 220–44; R. BULTMANN, "Ignatius and Paul," in *Existence and Faith: Shorter Writings of Rudolf Bultmann* (ed. S. M. Ogden; New York: Meridian, 1960), 267–77; P. J. DONAHUE, "Jewish Christianity in the Letters of Ignatius of Antioch," *VC* 32 (1978): 81–93; R. M. GRANT, *Ignatius of Antioch* (vol. 4 of *The Apostolic Fathers;* ed. R. M. Grant; 1966); R. M. HÜBNER, "Thesen zur Echtheit und Datierung der sieben Briefe des Ignatius von Antiochien," *ZAC* 1 (1997): 44–72; A. LINDEMANN, "Antwort auf die 'Thesen zur Echtheit und Datierung der sieben Briefe des Ignatius von Antiochien,'" *ZAC* 1 (1997): 185–94; W. R. SCHOEDEL, "Are the Letters of Ignatius of Antioch Authentic?" *RelSRev* 6 (1980): 196–201; IDEM, *Ignatius of Antioch* (Hermeneia; Philadelphia: Fortress, 1985); IDEM, "Polycarp of Smyrna and Ignatius of Antioch," *ANRW* 27.1:272–358; G. F. SNYDER, "The Historical Jesus in the Letters of Ignatius of Antioch," *BR* 8 (1963): 3–12; G. N. STANTON, "Other Early Christian Writings: 'Didache,' Ignatius, 'Barnabas,' Justin Martyr," in *Early Christian Thought in its Jewish Context* (ed. J. Barclay and J. Sweet; Cambridge: Cambridge University Press, 1996), 174–90.

Polycarp to the Philippians. Polycarp's letter to the Philippians was apparently written shortly after the martyrdom of Ignatius, since Polycarp evidently assumes that the bishop is dead (1:1; 9:1) but has received no final word (13:2). In response to a written request (cf. 3:1), Polycarp offers encouragement and admonition to the Philippians. Percy Harrison's hypothesis that this writing is actually a conflation of two letters has not won acceptance. The SBL abbreviation is Pol. *Phil.*

Bibliography: L. W. BARNARD, "The Problem of St. Polycarp's Epistle to the Philippians," in *Studies in the Apostolic Fathers and Their Background* (Oxford: Blackwell, 1967), 31–40; K. BERDING, *Polycarp and Paul: An Analysis of Their Literary and Theological Relationship in Light of Polycarp's Use of Biblical and Extra-biblical Literature* (VCSup 62; Leiden: Brill, 2002); R. GARRISON, "The Love of Money in Polycarp's Letter to the Philippians," in *The Graeco-Roman Context of Early Christian Literature* (JSNTSup 137; Sheffield: Sheffield, 1997), 74–79; P. N. HARRISON, *Polycarp's Two Epistles to the Philippians* (Cambridge: Cambridge University Press, 1936); P. HARTOG, *Polycarp and the New Testament: The Occasion, Rhetoric, Theme, and Unity of the Epistle to the Philippians and Its Allusions to New Testament Literature* (WUNT 2.134; Tübingen: Mohr [Siebeck], 2002); M. W. HOLMES, "A Note on the Text of Polycarp Philippians 11.3" *VC* 51 (1997): 207–10; W. R. SCHOEDEL, *Polycarp, Martyrdom of Polycarp, Papias* (vol. 5 of *The Apostolic Fathers;* ed. R. M. Grant; 1967); IDEM, "Polycarp of Smyrna and Ignatius of Antioch," *ANRW* 27.1:272–358; IDEM, "Polycarp's Witness to Ignatius of Antioch," *VC* 41 (1987): 1–10.

Martyrdom of Polycarp. This writing offers itself as an eyewitness account ("from the papers of Irenaeus"; 22:2) of the martyrdom of Polycarp (cf. 15:1; 18:1), bishop of the church of Smyrna. Polycarp, who was 86 years old at the time of his death (cf. 9:3), was martyred sometime after 160 C.E. The purpose of the writing seems to have been to set up Polycarp as an example of piety and faithfulness in the face of torture and death. The SBL abbreviation is *Mart. Pol.*

Bibliography: J. DEN BOEFT and J. BREMMER, "Notiunculae martyrologicae III: Some Observations on the Martyria of Polycarp and Pionius," *VC* 39 (1985): 110–30; M. H. SHEPHERD Jr., "The Martyrdom of Polycarp, as Told in the Letter of the Church of Smyrna to the Church of Philomelium," in *Early Christian Fathers* (ed. Richardson), 141–58; W. TELFER, "The Date of the Martyrdom of Polycarp," *JTS* 3 (1952): 79–83; F. W. WEIDMANN, "Polycarp's Final Prayer (Martyrdom of Polycarp 14)," in *Prayer from Alexander to Constantine: A Critical Anthology* (ed. M. Kiley et al.; New York: Routledge, 1997), 285–90.

The Didache. The *Didache,* or *Teaching of the Twelve Apostles,* may have been written as early as 70–80 C.E. Its purpose is to underscore the "Two Ways," that is, the
way of life and the way of death (1:1–6:2), and to provide instruction in church
order and practice (6:3–16:8). The SBL abbreviation is *Did.*

Bibliography: J. DRAPER, "The Jesus Tradition in the Didache," in *The Jesus Tradition outside the Gospels* (ed. D. Wenham; Gospel Perspectives 5; Sheffield: JSOT Press, 1985),
269–87; R. GLOVER, "The Didache's Quotations and the Synoptic Gospels," *NTS* 5 (1958):
12–29; C. N. JEFFORD, ed., *The Didache in Context: Essays on Its Text, History, and Transmission* (NovTSup 77; Leiden: Brill, 1995); IDEM, *The Sayings of Jesus in the Teaching of the
Twelve Apostles* (VCSup 11; Leiden: Brill, 1989); J. S. KLOPPENBORG, "Didache 16 6–8 and
Special Matthean Tradition," *ZNW* 70 (1979): 54–67; R. A. KRAFT, *Barnabas and the
Didache* (vol. 3 of *The Apostolic Fathers;* ed. R. M. Grant; 1965), 1–12, 57–77, 134–77;
B. LAYTON, "The Source, Date, and Transmission of Didache 1.3b–2.1," *HTR* 61 (1968):
343–83; K. NIEDERWIMMER, *The Didache* (Hermeneia; Minneapolis: Fortress, 1998); C. C.
RICHARDSON, "The Teaching of the Twelve Apostles, Commonly Called the Didache," in
Early Christian Fathers (ed. Richardson), 161–70; P. SCHAFF, *The Oldest Church Manual
Called the Teaching of the Twelve Apostles* (New York: Funk & Wagnalls, 1885); F. E. VOKES,
"The Didache and the Canon of the New Testament," *SE* 3 (1964): 427–36.

Barnabas. The *Epistle of Barnabas,* written either in the late first century or in the
early second, is concerned with the question of how Christians are to interpret
the Jewish Scriptures. (In reality this writing is not a letter, and it was not penned
by Barnabas.) The author's approach, like the Jewish interpreter Philo before him
and the Christian interpreter Origen after him, was to allegorize the Scriptures.
The SBL abbreviation is *Barn.*

Bibliography: L. W. BARNARD, "The Epistle of Barnabas and the Tannaitic Catechism,"
AThR 41 (1959): 177–90; IDEM, "The Testimonium concerning the Stone in the New Testa-
ment and in the Epistle of Barnabas," *SE* 3 (1961): 306–13; M. DACY, "The Epistle to Bar-
nabas and the Dead Sea Scrolls," in *The Dead Sea Scrolls: Fifty Years after Their Discovery:
Proceedings of the Jerusalem Congress, July 20–25, 1997* (ed. L. H. Schiffman, E. Tov, and J. C.
VanderKam; Jerusalem: Israel Exploration Society and Israel Antiquities Authority, 2000),
139–47; Y. Z. ELIAV, " 'Interpretative Citation' in the Epistle of Barnabas and the Early
Christian Attitude towards the Temple Mount," in *The Interpretation of Scripture in Early
Judaism and Christianity: Studies in Language and Tradition* (ed. C. A. Evans; JSPSup 33;
SSEJC 7; Sheffield: Sheffield, 2000), 353–62; E. FERGUSON, "Christian and Jewish Baptism
according to the Epistle of Barnabas," in *Dimensions of Baptism: Biblical and Theological
Studies* (ed. S. E. Porter and A. R. Cross; JSNTSup 234; New York: Sheffield, 2002), 207–23;
R. A. KRAFT, *Barnabas and the Didache* (vol. 3 of *The Apostolic Fathers;* ed. R. M. Grant;
1965), 1–56, 78–162; IDEM, "Barnabas' Isaiah Text and the 'Testimony Book' Hypothesis,"
JBL 79 (1960): 336–50; IDEM, "An Unnoticed Papyrus Fragment of Barnabas," *VC* 21
(1967): 150–63.

Shepherd of Hermas. The Shepherd of Hermas is the longest writing of the
Apostolic Fathers. It appears in three major sections: (five) *Visions,* (twelve)
Mandates, and (ten) *Similitudes* (or *Parables*). The work, which was composed
sometime in the first half of the second century, is a Christian apocalypse com-

parable to *1 Enoch*. It may have originally been two parts (*Visions* 1–4 and *Vision* 5–*Similitude* 10). The SBL abbreviations are Herm. *Vis.*, Herm. *Man.*, Herm. *Sim.*

Bibliography: D. E. AUNE, "Herm. Man. 11.2: Christian False Prophets Who Say What People Wish to Hear," *JBL* 97 (1978): 103–4; L. W. BARNARD, "Hermas and Judaism," *StPatr* 8 (1966): 3–9; IDEM, "The Shepherd of Hermas in Recent Study," *HeyJ* 9 (1968): 29–36; N. BROX, *Der Hirt des Hermas* (Kommentar zu den Apostolischen Vätern 7; Göttingen: Vandenhoeck & Ruprecht, 1991); G. D. KILPATRICK, "A New Papyrus of the Shepherd of Hermas," *JTS* 48 (1947): 204–5; C. OSIEK, "The Genre and Function of the Shepherd of Hermas," in *Early Christian Apocalypticism: Genre and Social Setting* (ed. A. Y. Collins; Semeia 36; Atlanta: Scholars Press, 1986), 113–21; IDEM, "The Oral World of Early Christianity in Rome: The Case of Hermas," in *Judaism and Christianity in First-Century Rome* (ed. K. P. Donfried and P. Richardson; Grand Rapids: Eerdmans, 1998), 151–72; IDEM, *Rich and Poor in the Shepherd of Hermas: An Exegetical-Social Investigation* (CBQMS 15; Washington, D.C.: Catholic Biblical Association, 1983); IDEM, *The Shepherd of Hermas: A Commentary* (Hermeneia; Minneapolis: Fortress, 1999); J. REILING, *Hermas and Christian Prophecy: A Study of the Eleventh Mandate* (NovTSup 37; Leiden: Brill, 1973); O. J. F. SEITZ, "Relationship of the Shepherd to the Epistle of James," *JBL* 63 (1944): 131–40; G. F. SNYDER, *The Shepherd of Hermas* (vol. 6 of *The Apostolic Fathers;* ed. R. M. Grant; 1968).

Diognetus. The *Epistle to Diognetus* is in reality an apologetic tract in the form of an open letter. It is not written to Christians, but to non-Christians. As such, it is an invitation to embrace the Christian faith. The writing likely originated in the late second or early third century. The SBL abbreviation is *Diogn.*

Bibliography: P. ANDRIESSEN, "The Authorship of the Epistula ad Diognetum," *VC* 1 (1947): 129–36; E. CATTANEO, "L'enigma dell' Ad Diognetum," *Rassegna di teologia* 32 (1991): 327–32; E. R. FAIRWEATHER, "The So-Called Letter to Diognetus," in *Early Christian Fathers* (ed. Richardson), 205–24; H. G. MEECHAM, *The Epistle to Diognetus: The Greek Text with Introduction, Translation, and Notes* (Manchester, Eng.: Manchester University Press, 1949); R. NOORMANN, "Himmelsbürger auf Erden: Anmerkungen zum Weltverhältnis und zum 'Paulinismus' des Auctor ad Diognetum," in *Die Weltlichkeit des Glaubens in der Alten Kirche* (ed. D. Wyra; U. Wickert FS; BZNW 85; Berlin: de Gruyter, 1997), 199–229; P.-H. POIRIER, "Éléments de polémique anti-juive dans l'Ad Diognetum," *VC* 40 (1986): 218–25.

Papias. Some two dozen fragments of Papias's five-volume work, *Expositions of the Sayings of the Lord*, are preserved in Eusebius and other church theologians and historians. This early Father (ca. 70–160 C.E.) is well known for his statements regarding the transmission of the dominical tradition and the authorship of the Gospels.

Bibliography: R. ANNAND, "Papias and the Four Gospels," *SJT* 9 (1956): 46–62; A. D. BAUM, "Papias als Kommentator evangelischer Aussprüche Jesu: Erwägungen zur Art seines Werkes," *NovT* 38 (1996): 257–76; IDEM, "Papias und der Presbyter Johannes: Martin Hengel und die johanneische Frage," *JET* 9 (1995): 21–42; M. BLACK, "The Use of Rhetorical Terminology in Papias on Mark and Matthew," *JSNT* 37 (1989): 31–41; J. F. BLIGH, "The Prologue of Papias," *TS* 13 (1952): 234–40; D. D. DEEKS, "Papias Revisited," *ExpTim* 88 (1977): 296–301, 324–29; D. FARKASFALVY, "The Papias Fragments on Mark and

Matthew and their Relationship to Luke's Prologue: An Essay on the Pre-history of the Synoptic Problem," in *The Early Church in Its Context* (ed. A. J. Malherbe et al.; E. Ferguson FS; NovTSup 90; Leiden: Brill, 1998), 92–106; R. M. GRANT, "Papias and the Gospels," *AThR* 25 (1943): 218–22; R. G. HEARD, "Papias' Quotations from the New Testament," *NTS* 1 (1954): 122–29; C. E. HILL, "What Papias Said about John (and Luke): A 'New' Papian Fragment," *JTS* 49 (1998): 582–629; T. MULLINS, "Papias and Clement and Mark's Two Gospels," *VC* 30 (1976): 189–92; IDEM, "Papias and the Oral Tradition," *VC* 21 (1967): 137–40; IDEM, "Papias on Mark's Gospel," *VC* 14 (1960): 216–24; M. OBERWEIS, "Das Papias-Zeugnis vom Tode des Johannes Zebedäi," *NovT* 38 (1996): 277–95; J. TRIGG, "The Apostolic Fathers and the Apologists," in *The Ancient Period* (vol. 1 of *A History of Biblical Interpretation;* ed. A. J. Hauser and D. F. Watson; Grand Rapids: Eerdmans, 2003), 304–33 (very helpful bibliography).

Early Apologists, Exegetes, and Theologians. The writings of several other early apologists, exegetes, and theologians are worth examining in doing NT interpretation. Most of these writers quoted the OT and NT, often preserving older interpretations. Comparative study, therefore, can sometimes aid the interpreter in appreciating the full range of ancient interpretive traditions and may, in some instances, clarify a tradition that is only hinted at in the NT. One such example is treated in chapter 12 below. These writers will be treated quite briefly.

Among the earliest apologists are Aristides (ca. 145), Athenagoras (ca. 170–180), Justin Martyr (d. 165), Melito of Sardis (d. ca. 190), Tatian (d. 180?), and Theophilus of Antioch (ca. 180–185). Justin is famous for his *Apologia* (*Apology*) and his *Dialogus cum Tryphone* (*Dialogue with Trypho*), while Tatian is best known for the *Diatessaron* ("Fourfold book"), a work in which he wove together the four NT Gospels into a unified narrative. (He sometimes made use of a fifth— the *Gospel according to the Hebrews.*) This work remained popular in the Eastern church, displacing the canonical Gospels for nearly three centuries. Melito's best-known surviving work is his *Homily on the Passover (De pascha).* Clement of Alexandria (ca. 150–215) is well known for his *Protreptikos pros Hellenas* (*Exhortation to the Greeks*), the *Paedagogus* (*Pedagogue* or *Tutor*), and the *Stromata* (or *Stromateis, Miscellanies*). All of his works are replete with quotations of and allusions to the OT and NT. One of the most influential early Christian apologists and exegetes was Origen of Alexandria (ca. 185–254). He is best known for his allegorical interpretation of Scripture, as seen in his numerous commentaries (e.g., Matthew, John, Romans, Psalms), his *Hexapla* (a work containing the Hebrew, LXX, and the recensions in parallel columns), and his polemical work *Contra Celsum* (*Against Celsum*). Other early apologists and theologians include Irenaeus (ca. 140–202) and Tertullian (ca. 160–220). The former is best known for his *Adversus Haereses* (*Against Heresies*), while the latter authored *Adversus Marcionem* (*Against Marcion*), *Apologia* (*Apology*), and various tracts on Christian doctrines. Hippolytus (ca. 170–235) was an early heresiologist who authored *Refutation of All Heresies.* Cyprian (d. 258) authored the *Testimonies to Quirinus.*

Later Major Writers. Other Fathers whose writings are worth consulting include Ambrose, Athanasius, Augustine, Cassiodorus, John Chrysostom, Commodian,

Cyril of Jerusalem, Didymus the Blind, Epiphanius, Eusebius, Jerome, Methodius, and others. First we may consider some of Greek fathers. Athanasius (ca. 296–373), who became bishop of Alexandria, wrote a great number of works, many of them attacking Arianism and defending the Nicene Creed, particularly relating to the *homoiousios/homoousios* controversy. Didymus the Blind (ca. 313–398) of Alexandria gave direction to the catechetical school of Alexandria, whose pupils included Jerome, Gregory of Nazianzus, and Rufinus. Influenced by Origen, Didymus authored treatises and exegetical works. John Chrysostom (ca. 347–407) (not to be confused with Dio Chrysostom), who became bishop of Constantinople and is one of the preeminent doctors of the Eastern Church, authored homilies on books of the Bible and vigorously contested the allegorical approach. Eusebius (ca. 260–339) is well known for his *Historia ecclesiastica* (*Ecclesiastical History*), which contains many early and valuable traditions (such as the fragments of Papias), and for his *Praeparatio evangelica* (*Preparation of the Gospel*) and *Demonstratio evangelica* (*Demonstration of the Gospel*), which are extant only in fragments. Eusebius also authored a commentary and several homilies on the Psalms.

There were many influential Latin fathers. Lactantius (ca. 240–ca. 320), who converted to the Christian faith late in life (ca. 300), authored *Divinarum institutionum libri VII (Divine Institutes)* and was tutor to Constantine's son Crispus. Jerome (ca. 342–420) is probably best known for his Latin translation of the Bible (ca. 390) that became known as the Vulgate. This late fourth-century translation is based on the Hebrew for the OT and as such is an early witness to the text of the OT. (Outside of Qumran, no extant Hebrew manuscript is earlier than the ninth century C.E.) Several of Jerome's letters and commentaries are extant. These also contain significant exegetical traditions (Jewish as well as Christian), some of which derive from early times. Ambrose (ca. 339–397), who became bishop of Milan, wrote works against paganism and Arianism, as well as works on Christian ethics. Augustine (354–430), a Manichaen who converted to the Christian faith under the influence of Ambrose and became bishop of Hippo, North Africa, authored many classic and influential works, including *Confessions, City of God*, and *On the Trinity*. Ambrose, Augustine, and Jerome are the greatest Latin theologians and exegetes of this period. Lesser-known Latin fathers include Julius Firmicus Maternus (died after 360) and Aurelius Clemens Prudentius (ca. 348–410). The former was author of *De errore profanarum religionum* (*On the Error of the Pagan Religions*), which urged the emperors Constantius and Constans to destroy pagan idols. The latter authored *Cathemerinon* (lit. "Daily [Hymns]") and *Peristephanon* (lit. "Concerning Crowns [of Martyrs]").

In citing the Fathers it is customary to follow the volume and column numbers of J. Migne's Patrologia graeca and Patrologia latina. (Some journals require that Migne be followed.) The SBL abbreviations are PG and PL, respectively. The new series Ancient Christian Commentary on Scripture, edited by Thomas C. Oden (InterVarsity), several volumes of which have already appeared, deserves special mention. This important resource will greatly assist comparative interpretive work. Its volumes provide selections of patristic commentary—often from

works never before translated into English—on all OT and NT writings. See also
J. G. Cook, *The Interpretation of the New Testament in Greco-Roman Paganism*
(Studies and Texts in Antiquity and Christianity 3; Tübingen: Mohr [Siebeck],
2000; repr., Peabody, Mass.: Hendrickson, 2002).

For a convenient compendium of the Christian fathers in English translation, see Roberts and Donaldson for the pre-Nicene fathers, and Schaff and Wace
for the Nicene and post-Nicene fathers.

General Bibliography

B. ALTANER, *Patrology* (New York: Herder and Herder, 1961); L. W. BARNARD,
Studies in the Apostolic Fathers and Their Background (Oxford: Blackwell, 1966);
A. BENOIT et al., *Biblia patristica: Index des citations et allusions bibliques dans la
littérature patristique* (5 vols.; Paris: Centre National de la Recherche Scientifique,
1975–1982) (vol. 5 indexes the writings of Philo of Alexandria); L. BERKOWITZ
and K. A. SQUITIER, *The Thesaurus linguae graecae Canon of Greek Authors and
Works* (2d ed.; New York: Oxford University Press, 1986); R. E. BROWN, *The
Churches the Apostles Left Behind* (Mahwah, N.J.: Paulist, 1984); F. L. CROSS and
E. A. LIVINGSTONE, *ODCC;* H. R. DROBNER, *The Fathers of the Church: A Compre-
hensive Introduction* (trans. S. Schatzmann; Peabody, Mass.: Hendrickson, 2005);
C. A. EVANS, "Isaiah 6:9–10 in Rabbinic and Patristic Writings," *VC* 36 (1982):
275–81; IDEM, "Jerome's Translation of Isaiah 6:9–10," *VC* 38 (1984): 202–4;
F. FIELD, *Origenis Hexapla* (2 vols.; Hildesheim: Olms, 1964) (a compilation of the
fragments of Origen's *Hexapla*); R. GLOVER, "Patristic Quotations and Gospel
Sources," *NTS* 31 (1985): 234–51; E. J. GOODSPEED, *Index patristicus* (Naperville,
Ill.: Allenson, 1907; repr., 1960) (Greek concordance); R. M. GRANT, *After the New
Testament* (Philadelphia: Fortress, 1967); IDEM, ed., *The Apostolic Fathers: A New
Translation and Commentary* (6 vols.; New York: Nelson, 1964–1968); D. A.
HAGNER, "The Sayings of Jesus in the Apostolic Fathers and Justin Martyr," in *The
Jesus Tradition outside the Gospels* (ed. D. Wenham; Gospel Perspectives 5; Shef-
field: JSOT Press, 1985), 233–68; N. G. L. HAMMOND and H. H. SCULLARD, eds.,
The Oxford Classical Dictionary (2d ed.; Oxford: Clarendon, 1970); T. J. HORNER,
Listening to Trypho: Justin Martyr's Dialogue Reconsidered (CBET 28; Leuven:
Peeters, 2001); H. J. DE JONGE, "On the Origin of the Term 'Apostolic Fathers,'"
JTS 29 (1978): 503–5; H. KOESTER, *Synoptische Überlieferung bei den apostolischen
Vätern* (TU 65; Berlin: Akademie, 1957); K. LAKE, *Apostolic Fathers* (2 vols.; LCL;
Cambridge: Harvard University Press, 1912–1913) (Greek text and English trans-
lation); G. W. H. LAMPE, ed., *A Patristic Greek Lexicon* (Oxford: Clarendon,
1961–1968); É. MASSAUX, *The Influence of the Gospel of Saint Matthew on Chris-
tian Literature before Saint Irenaeus* (ed. A. J. Bellinzoni; 3 vols.; NGS 5/1–3;
Macon, Ga.: Mercer University Press, 1990–1993); L. M. MCDONALD, *The Formation of the Christian Biblical Canon* (rev. ed.; Peabody, Mass.: Hendrickson, 1995)
[provides quotations of all the pertinent primary literature]; C. MORESCHINI and
E. NORELLI, *Early Christian Greek and Latin Literature: A Literary History* (trans.

M. O'Connell; Peabody, Mass.: Hendrickson, 2005); R. A. NORRIS Jr., "Augustine and the Close of the Ancient Period," in *The Ancient Period* (vol. 1 of *A History of Biblical Interpretation;* ed. A. J. Hauser and D. F. Watson; Grand Rapids: Eerdmans, 2003), 380–408 (bibliography); J. QUASTEN, *Patrology* (4 vols.; Utrecht: Spectrum, 1950; repr., Westminster, Md.: Newman, 1983); W. REBELL, *Neutestamentliche Apokryphen und Apostolische Väter* (Munich: Kaiser, 1992); C. C. RICHARDSON, *The Early Christian Fathers* (LCC 1; New York: Macmillan, 1970); A. ROBERTS and J. DONALDSON, eds., *The Ante-Nicene Christian Library: Translations of the Writings of the Fathers Down to A.D. 325* (24 vols.; Edinburgh: T&T Clark, 1867–1872), repr. as *The Ante-Nicene Fathers* (10 vols.; Buffalo: Christian Literature Publishing Co., 1887–1896; repr., Peabody, Mass.: Hendrickson, 1994); P. SCHAFF, ed., *A Select Library of the Nicene and Post-Nicene Fathers of the Christian Church* (14 vols.; New York: Christian Literature Co., 1886–1990; repr., Peabody, Mass.: Hendrickson, 1994) (later referred to as the First Series); P. SCHAFF and H. WACE, eds., *A Select Library of Nicene and Post-Nicene Fathers of the Christian Church: Second Series* (14 vols.; New York: Christian Literature Co., 1890– 1900; repr., Peabody, Mass.: Hendrickson, 1994); W. R. SCHOEDEL, "The Apostolic Fathers," in *The New Testament and Its Modern Interpreters* (ed. E. J. Epp and G. W. MacRae; Atlanta: Scholars Press, 1989) [excellent bibliography]; O. SKARSAUNE, *The Proof from Prophecy: A Study in Justin Martyr's Proof-Text Tradition—Text-Type, Provenance, Theological Profile* (NovTSup 56; Leiden: Brill, 1987); D. TRAKATELLIS, *The Pre-existence of Christ in Justin Martyr: An Exegetical Study with Reference to the Humiliation and Exaltation Christology* (HDR 6; Missoula, Mont.: Scholars Press, 1976); F. YOUNG, "Alexandrian and Antiochene Exegesis," in *The Ancient Period* (vol. 1 of *A History of Biblical Interpretation;* ed. A. J. Hauser and D. F. Watson; Grand Rapids: Eerdmans, 2003), 334–54 [bibliography].

CHAPTER TEN

Gnostic Writings

NAG HAMMADI LIBRARY

Until the twentieth century, Gnosticism was believed to have been a Christian heresy that emerged in the late first and early second centuries. It was assumed, for example, that the Johannine writings and the Pastorals were composed in part to counter a gnosticizing tendency in certain circles which tended to deemphasize the incarnation and the need of repentance and faith. Rather than a Jesus who came as Israel's Messiah, physically suffered, and rose bodily from the grave, gnostics taught that Jesus only "appeared" to be physical (the basic tenet of docetism), or perhaps only temporarily inhabited a physical body (adoptionism), and that, instead, it was very important to possess knowledge (*gnōsis*) about the cosmos and how to defeat the evil spiritual powers. Because of the emphasis placed on knowledge, these people were called gnostics (i.e., "knowers" [of ultimate truths]). Just as the apostles John and Paul combatted this heresy, so the heirs (such as Justin Martyr, Epiphanius, Irenaeus, and Hippolytus) of the apostolic gospel combatted it. This was the impression left us by the Fathers of the church.

In the twentieth century scholars came to doubt this portrait as idealistic and inaccurate. Most now believe that the picture was much more complicated. There may very well be more to Gnosticism than just an aberration within the early church. Its roots are probably diverse, geographically, culturally, and religiously, with some of these roots reaching back to the first century C.E. and even further. Moreover, the assumption about how certain NT writings actually relate to Gnosticism is not nearly as simple as the Fathers would have us believe. For example, if John was written to combat early Gnosticism, why did the gnostics of the second century find this Gospel so attractive? See the convenient collection of the fragments of gnostic exegesis of this book in Elaine Pagels, *The Johannine Gospel in Gnostic Exegesis* (New York: Abingdon, 1973). One might raise the same question with respect to Paul; see idem, *The Gnostic Paul* (Philadelphia: Fortress, 1975). Moreover, since the publication of W. Bauer, *Rechtgläubigkeit und Ketzerei im ältesten Christentum* (Tübingen: Mohr, 1934), ET *Orthodoxy and Heresy in Earliest Christianity* (ed. R. A. Kraft and G. Krodel; Philadelphia: Fortress, 1971), scholars have come to recognize that making sharp distinctions between "orthodoxy" and "heresy" in the first two or three centuries of Christianity tends to be anachronistic and misleading in that it obscures the theological pluralism of this period. Perhaps the most hotly debated question is whether or not gnostic mythology played a significant role in the formation of NT Christology. This issue is addressed in the studies below.

The most important collection of gnostic writings are the Nag Hammadi Codices (NHC). Thirteen codices, containing fifty-two tractates, were discovered in upper Egypt in 1945. Six of these tractates were duplicates; six others were already extant; and the remaining forty represented wholly new finds. The complete English translation is J. M. Robinson, ed., *The Nag Hammadi Library in English* (4th rev. ed.; New York: Brill, 1996). Robinson also supervised *The Facsimile Edition of the Nag Hammadi Codices* (12 vols.; Leiden: Brill, 1972–1984), the contents of whose volumes and the dates of publication are listed below. (See now also J. M. Robinson, ed., *The Coptic Gnostic Library: A Complete Edition of the Nag Hammadi Codices* (5 vols.; Boston: Brill, 2000).

Coptic Gnostic Library: Text, Translation, and Commentary

NHC I: H. W. Attridge, ed., *Nag Hammadi Codex I (The Jung Codex)* (2 vols.; NHS 22–23; Leiden: Brill, 1985)

D. Rouleau, *L'Épître apocryphe de Jacques (NH I, 2)* (BCNH: Textes 18; Laval, Que.: Presses de l'Université Laval, 1987)

J. Helderman, *Die Anapausis im Evangelium veritatis: Eine vergleichende Untersuchung des valentinianisch-gnostischen Heilsgutes der Ruhe im Evangelium veritatis und in anderen Schriften der Nag Hammadi Bibliothek* (NHS 18; Leiden: Brill, 1984)

J.-E. Ménard, *L'Evangile de vérité* (NHS 2; Leiden: Brill, 1972)

J.-E. Ménard, *Le Traité sur la résurrection (NH I, 4)* (BCNH: Textes 12; Laval, Que.: Presses de l'Université Laval, 1983)

E. Thomassen and L. Painchaud, *Le Traité tripartite (NH I, 5)* (BCNH: Textes 19; Laval, Que.: Presses de l'Université Laval, 1989)

NHC II: S. Giversen, *Apocryphon Johannis: The Coptic Text of the Apocryphon Johannis in the Nag Hammadi Codex II* (AtDan 5; Leiden: Brill, 1963)

M. Waldstein and F. Wisse, eds., *The Apocryphon of John: Synopsis of Nag Hammadi Codices II, 1, III, 1, and IV, 1 with BG 8502, 2* (NHS 33; Leiden: Brill, 1995)

M. Fieger, *Das Thomasevangelium: Einleitung, Kommentar, und Systematik* (NTAbh 22; Münster: Aschendorff, 1991)

A. Guillaumont et al., *The Gospel according to Thomas: Coptic Text, Established and Translated* (2d ed.; Leiden: Brill, 1976)

M. Lelyveld, *Les logia de la vie dans l'Évangile selon Thomas: A la recherche d'une tradition et d'une rédaction* (NHS 34; Leiden: Brill, 1988)

J.-E. Ménard, *L'Évangile selon Thomas* (NHS 5; Leiden: Brill, 1975)

T. Zöckler, *Jesu Lehren im Thomasevangelium* (NHS 47; Leiden: Brill, 1999)

B. Layton, ed., *Nag Hammadi Codices II, 2–7, Together with XIII, 2*, Brit. Lib. Or. 4926 (1) and P. Oxy. 1, 654, 655* (2 vols.; NHS 20–21; Leiden: Brill, 1989)

H.–M. Schenke, *Das Philippus-Evangelium (Nag Hammadi Codex II, 3)* (TUGAL 143; Berlin: Akademie, 1997)

M. L. Turner, *The Gospel according to Philip: The Sources and Coherence of an Early Christian Collection* (NHS 38; Leiden: Brill, 1996)

B. Barc and M. Roberge, *L'Hypostase des archontes: Traité gnostique sur l'origine de l'homme, du monde, et des archontes (NH II, 4), suivi de Noréa (NH IX, 2)* (BCNH: Textes 5; Laval, Que.: Presses de l'Université Laval, 1980)

L. Painchaud, with W.-P. Funk, *L'écrit sans titre: Traité sur l'origine du monde (NH II, 5 et XIII, 2 et Brit. Lib. Or. 4926[1])* (BCNH: Textes 21; Laval, Que.: Presses de l'Université Laval, 1995)

M. Scopello, *L'Exégèse de l'âme: Nag Hammadi Codex II, 6* (NHS 25; Leiden: Brill, 1985)

J.-M. Sevrin, *L'Exégèse de l'âme (NH II, 6)* (BCNH: Textes 9; Laval, Que.: Presses de l'Université Laval, 1983)

R. Kuntzmann, *Le Livre de Thomas (NH II, 7)* (BCNH: Textes 16; Laval, Que.: Presses de l'Université Laval, 1986)

NHC III: M. Waldstein and F. Wisse, eds., *The Apocryphon of John: Synopsis of Nag Hammadi Codices II, 1, III, 1, and IV, 1 with BG 8502, 2* (NHS 33; Leiden: Brill, 1995)

A. Böhlig and F. Wisse, with P. Labib, eds., *Nag Hammadi Codices III, 2 and IV, 2: The Gospel of the Egyptians (The Holy Book of the Great Invisible Spirit)* (NHS 4; Leiden: Brill, 1975)

D. M. Parrott, ed., *Nag Hammadi Codices III, 3–4 and V, 1 with Papyrus Berolinensis 8502, 3 and Oxyrhynchus Papyrus 1081: Eugnostos and the Sophia of Jesus Christ* (NHS 27; Leiden: Brill, 1991)

A. Pasquier, *Eugnoste (NH III, 3 et V, 1): Lettre sur le Dieu transcendant* (BCNH: Textes 26; Laval, Que.: Presses de l'Université Laval, 2000)

C. Barry, *La Sagesse de Jésus-Christ (BG, 3; NH III, 4)* (BCNH: Textes 20; Laval, Que.: Presses de l'Université Laval, 1993)

S. Emmel, ed., *Nag Hammadi Codex III, 5: The Dialogue of the Savior* (NHS 26; Leiden: Brill, 1984)

NHC IV: M. Waldstein and F. Wisse, eds., *The Apocryphon of John: Synopsis of Nag Hammadi Codices II, 1, III, 1, and IV, 1 with BG 8502, 2* (NHS 33; Leiden: Brill, 1995)

NHC V: A. Pasquier, *Eugnoste (NH III, 3 et V, 1): Lettre sur le Dieu transcendant* (BCNH: Textes 26; Laval, Que.: Presses de l'Université Laval, 2000)

D. M. Parrott, ed., *Nag Hammadi Codices V, 2–5 and VI with Papyrus Berolinensis 8502, 1 and 4* (NHS 11; Leiden: Brill, 1979)

A. Veilleux, *La Première apocalypse de Jacques (NH V, 3); la Seconde apocalypse de Jacques (NH V,4)* (BCNH: Textes 17; Laval, Que.: Presses de l'Université Laval, 1986)

F. Morard, *L'Apocalypse d'Adam (NH V, 5)* (BCNH: Textes 15; Laval, Que.: Presses de l'Université Laval, 1985)

NHC VI: D. M. Parrott, ed., *Nag Hammadi Codices V, 2–5 and VI with Papyrus Berolinensis 8502, 1 and 4* (NHS 11; Leiden: Brill, 1979)

P.-H. Poirier, with W.-P. Funk, *Le Tonnerre, intellect parfait (NH VI, 2)* (BCNH: Textes 22; Laval, Que.: Presses de l'Université Laval, 1995)

P.-H. Poirier and L. Painchaud, *Les Sentences de Sextus (NH XII, 1); fragments (NH XII, 3); fragment de la République de Platon (NH VI, 5)* (BCNH: Textes 11; Laval, Que.: Presses de l'Université Laval, 1983)

NHC VII: B. A. Pearson et al., eds., *Nag Hammadi Codex VII* (NHS 30; Leiden: Brill, 1996)

M. Roberge, *La Paraphrase de Sem (NH VII, 1)* (BCNH: Textes 25; Laval, Que.: Presses de l'Université Laval, 2000)

L. Painchaud, *Le Deuxième traité du Grand Seth (NH VII, 2)* (BCNH: Textes 6; Laval, Que.: Presses de l'Université Laval, 1982)

Y. Janssens, *Les Leçons de Silvanos (NH VII, 4)* (BCNH: Textes 13; Laval, Que.: Presses de l'Université Laval, 1983)

P. Claude, *Les Trois stèles de Seth: Hymne gnostique à la triade (NH VII, 5)* (BCNH: Textes 8; Laval, Que.: Presses de l'Université Laval, 1983)

NHC VIII: C. Barry et al., *Zostrien (NH VIII, 1)* (BCNH: Textes 24; Laval, Que.: Presses de l'Université Laval, 2000)

J.-E. Ménard, *La Lettre de Pierre à Philippe (NH VIII, 2)* (BCNH: Textes 1; Laval, Que.: Presses de l'Université Laval, 1977)

J. Sieber, ed., *Nag Hammadi Codex VIII* (NHS 31; Leiden: Brill, 1991)

NHC IX: J.-P. Mahé, C. Gianotto, and W.-P. Funk, *Melchisédek (NH IX, 1): Oblation, baptême, et vision dans la gnose séthienne* (BCNH: Textes 28; Laval, Que.: Presses de l'Université Laval, 2001)

B. Barc and M. Roberge, *L'Hypostase des archontes: Traité gnostique sur l'origine de l'homme, du monde, et des archontes (NH II, 4), suivi de Noréa (NH IX, 2)* (BCNH: Textes 5; Laval, Que.: Presses de l'Université Laval, 1980)

A. Mahé and J.-P. Mahé, *Le Témoignage véritable (NH IX, 3): Gnose et martyre* (BCNH: Textes 23; Laval, Que.: Presses de l'Université Laval, 1996)

B. A. Pearson, ed., *Nag Hammadi Codices IX and X* (NHS 15; Leiden: Brill, 1981)

NHC X: W.-P. Funk, P.-H. Poirier, and J. D. Turner, *Marsanès (NH X)* (BCNH: Textes 27; Laval, Que.: Presses de l'Université Laval, 2000)

B. A. Pearson, ed., *Nag Hammadi Codices IX and X* (NHS 15; Leiden: Brill, 1981)

NHC XI: C. W. Hedrick, ed., *Nag Hammadi Codices XI, XII, and XIII* (NHS 28; Leiden: Brill, 1990)

J.-E. Ménard, *L'Exposé valentinien, les fragments sur le baptême et sur l'eucharistie (NH XI, 2)* (BCNH: Textes 14; Laval, Que.: Presses de l'Université Laval, 1985)

NHC XII: C. W. Hedrick, ed., *Nag Hammadi Codices XI, XII, and XIII* (NHS 28; Leiden: Brill, 1990)

P.-H. Poirier and L. Painchaud, *Les Sentences de Sextus (NH XII, 1); fragments (NH XII, 3); fragment de la République de Platon (NH VI, 5)* (BCNH: Textes 11; Laval, Que.: Presses de l'Université Laval, 1983)

NHC XIII: C. W. Hedrick, ed., *Nag Hammadi Codices XI, XII, and XIII* (NHS 28; Leiden: Brill, 1990)

Y. Janssens, *La Prôtennoia trimorphe (NH XIII, 1)* (BCNH: Textes 4; Laval, Que.: Presses de l'Université Laval, 1978)

B. Layton, ed., *Nag Hammadi Codices II, 2–7, Together with XIII, 2*, Brit. Lib. Or. 4926 (1) and P. Oxy. 1, 654, 655* (2 vols.; NHS 20–21; Leiden: Brill, 1989)

L. Painchaud, with W.-P. Funk, *L'écrit sans titre: Traité sur l'origine du monde (NH II, 5 et XIII, 2 et Brit. Lib. Or. 4926[1])* (BCNH: Textes 21; Laval, Que.: Presses de l'Université Laval, 1995)

J.-E. Ménard, *L'Évangile de vérité* (NHS 2; Leiden: Brill, 1972)

Studies on Related Texts:

A. Pasquier, *L'Évangile selon Marie (BG 1)* (BCNH: Textes 10; Laval, Que.: Presses de l'Université Laval, 1983)

M. Tardieu, *Écrits gnostiques: Codex de Berlin* (SGM 1; Paris: Cerf, 1984)

C. Schmidt, V. MacDermot, and R. McL. Wilson, *Pistis Sophia* (NHS 9; Leiden: Brill, 1978)

C. Schmidt and V. MacDermot, *The Books of Jeu and the Untitled Text in the Bruce Codex* (NHS 13; Leiden: Brill, 1978)

C. W. Hedrick and P. A. Mirecki, *Gospel of the Savior: A New Ancient Gospel* (Sonoma, Calif.: Polebridge, 1999)

Studies

Gnostic Gospels and the Jesus Tradition. In the Nag Hammadi codices, several writings are identified as gospels: *Gospel of Truth, Gospel of Thomas* (discussed above in ch. 8), *Gospel of Philip, Gospel of the Egyptians,* and (in the Berlin codex 8502) *Gospel of Mary.* There are also dialogue, or Q-like, writings, including *Dialogue of the Savior, Apocryphon* (or *Secret Book*) *of James,* and the *Sophia of Jesus Christ.* Indeed, most of the documents found at Nag Hammadi comprise dialogues (or constitute a "rambling treatise," as one scholar has put it), either of Jesus or of some other heavenly revealer. Although some scholars have claimed that these writings contain early and independent tradition, most think that they originated in the second century or later and that it is improbable reliable tradition can be gleaned from them.

Bibliography: C. A. EVANS, "Jesus in Gnostic Literature," *Bib* 62 (1981): 406–12; H. KOESTER, *Ancient Christian Gospels: Their History and Development* (Philadelphia: Trinity Press International, 1990), 173–200; G. W. MACRAE, *Studies in the New Testament and Gnosticism* (ed. D. J. Harrington and S. B. Marrow; GNS 26; Wilmington, Del.: Glazier, 1987), 163–217; R. J. MILLER, *CG* 247–360; P. PERKINS, *Gnosticism and the New Testament* (Minneapolis: Fortress, 1993), 53–73; J. M. ROBINSON, "LOGOI SOPHON: On the *Gattung* of Q," in J. M. Robinson and H. Koester, *Trajectories through Early Christianity* (Philadelphia: Fortress, 1971), 71–113; T. SÄVE-SÖDERBERGH, "Gnostic and Canonical Gospel Tradition," in *Le origini dello gnosticismo: Colloquio di Messina, 13–18 aprile 1966* (ed. U. Bianchi; Leiden: Brill, 1967), 552–59; W. D. STROKER, *Extracanonical Sayings of Jesus* (SBLRBS 18; Atlanta: Scholars Press, 1989) (provides English translation and original language); R. McL. WILSON, *Gnosis and the New Testament* (Philadelphia: Fortress, 1968), 85–99.

Pre-Christian Gnosticism (?) and New Testament Christology. The major issue that scholars have debated is whether or not Gnosticism, in its earliest forms, contributed to NT theology, particularly Christology, in any significant way. Specifically, attention has focused on the question of whether or not there existed a myth of a descending and ascending redeemer and whether or not if such a myth existed, it existed early enough to have influenced NT Christology. A few scholars answer these questions in the affirmative. Most, it would appear, have grave reservations. Edwin Yamauchi has reviewed all of the proposed evidence and finds little that suggests that Gnosticism existed prior to Christian origins. Charles Talbert finds no reason to believe that Christianity derived its Christology of a descending/

ascending heavenly savior from anything other than its Jewish roots. I think that his position is essentially correct. Moreover, the recent assertions of Gesine Robinson and Jack Sanders that the Prologue of the Fourth Gospel has more in common with the mythology of a gnostic work like the *Trimorphic Protennoia* than it has with anything else are wholly unjustified. Pheme Perkins is much closer to the truth when she concludes that the gnostic writings of Nag Hammadi "developed their picture of the Savior from traditions quite different from those which underlie NT christological assertions" (p. 606). Martin Hengel adds: "In reality there is no gnostic redeemer myth in the sources which can be demonstrated chronologically to be pre-Christian" (p. 33). The basic problem with the views of Robinson and Sanders is that those gnostic writings that bear the closest affinities with John contain allusions to, and sometimes explicit quotations of, the writings of the NT. A. D. Nock was right when he commented: "Certainly it is an unsound proceeding to take Manichaean and other texts [viz. Mandaean and Coptic gnostic texts], full of echoes of the New Testament, and reconstruct from them something supposedly lying back of the New Testament" (2:958).

Bibliography: C. K. BARRETT, "The Theological Vocabulary of the Fourth Gospel and of the Gospel of Truth," in *Current Issues in New Testament Interpretation* (ed. W. Klassen and G. F. Snyder; O. Piper FS; New York: Harper & Row, 1962), 210–23; C. A. EVANS, "On the Prologue of John and the *Trimorphic Protennoia*," *NTS* 27 (1981): 395–401; IDEM, *Word and Glory: On the Exegetical and Theological Background of John's Prologue* (JSNTSup 89; Sheffield: JSOT Press, 1993), 13–76 (reviews problems associated with proposals of a gnostic background for the Fourth Gospel); C. W. HEDRICK and R. HODGSON Jr., eds., *Nag Hammadi, Gnosticism, and Early Christianity* (Peabody, Mass.: Hendrickson, 1986); M. HENGEL, *Son of God* (Philadelphia: Fortress, 1976); A. D. NOCK, *Essays on Religion and the Ancient World* (2 vols.; Cambridge: Harvard University Press, 1972); P. PERKINS, "Gnostic Christologies and the New Testament," *CBQ* 43 (1981): 590–606; G. ROBINSON, "The Trimorphic Protennoia and the Prologue of the Fourth Gospel," in *Gnosticism and the Early Christian World* (ed. Goehring et al.), 37–50; J. M. ROBINSON, "Jesus: From Easter to Valentinus (or to the Apostles' Creed)," *JBL* 101 (1982): 5–37; J. T. SANDERS, "Nag Hammadi, Odes of Solomon, and NT Christological Hymns," in *Gnosticism and the Early Christian World* (ed. Goehring et al.), 51–66; C. H. TALBERT, "The Myth of the Descending-Ascending Redeemer in Mediterranean Antiquity," *NTS* 22 (1976): 418–40; E. M. YAMAUCHI, "The Issue of Pre-Christian Gnosticism Reviewed in the Light of the Nag Hammadi Texts," in *The Nag Hammadi Library after Fifty Years: Proceedings of the 1995 Society of Biblical Literature Commemoration* (ed. J. D. Turner and A. McGuire; NHS 44; Leiden: Brill, 1997), 72–88; IDEM, *Pre-Christian Gnosticism: A Survey of the Proposed Evidences* (2d ed.; Grand Rapids: Baker, 1983), 163–69, 243–45 (doubts existence of pre-Christian Gnosticism).

Mandaean Materials

There are also various gnostic writings produced by the Mandaeans, a small sect that survives in southern Iraq. Their primary works from antiquity (i.e., from the sixth to eighth centuries) consist of the *Book of John*, which extols

John the Baptist as a Mandaean and Jesus as a false Messiah, and the *Ginza*, which treats the origin and nature of the cosmos. Scholars who think that these materials may contain traditions that predate NT Christology have attempted to find traces of Mandaean ideas in earlier writings, such as the *Odes of Solomon* or the *Acts of Thomas*. The best known attempt to explain the origins of NT Christology along such lines was that by Rudolf Bultmann in his commentary on John. Although some scholars, such as Kurt Rudolph and James Robinson, still think that Mandaeanism and other forms of Gnosticism help explain the origins of NT Christology, most are doubtful.

Bibliography: R. BULTMANN, *The Gospel of John* (trans. G. R. Beasley-Murray; Philadelphia: Westminster, 1971) (1st German ed., 1941); E. S. DROWER, *The Canonical Prayer-Book of the Mandaeans* (Leiden: Brill, 1959); C. A. EVANS, *Word and Glory: On the Exegetical and Theological Background of John's Prologue* (JSNTSup 89; Sheffield: JSOT Press, 1993); M. LIDZBARSKI, *Ginzā, der Schatz, oder das grosse Buch der Mandäer* (Göttingen: Vandenhoeck & Ruprecht, 1925; repr., 1978); IDEM, *Das Johannesbuch der Mandäer* (2 vols.; Giessen: Töpelmann, 1905–1915; repr., Berlin: Töpelmann, 1966); IDEM, *Mandäische Liturgien* (Göttingen: Vandenhoeck & Ruprecht, 1920; repr., Hildesheim: Olms, 1962) (parts of this work were translated by G. R. S. Mead, *The Gnostic John the Baptizer* [London: Watkins, 1924]); K. RUDOLPH, *Mandaeism* (Leiden: Brill, 1978); E. M. YAMAUCHI, *Mandaic Incantation Texts* (AOS 49; New Haven: Yale University Press, 1967); IDEM, *Pre-Christian Gnosticism: A Survey of the Proposed Evidences* (Grand Rapids: Eerdmans, 1973), 117–42; IDEM, "The Present Status of Mandaean Studies," *JNES* 25 (1966): 88–96.

General Bibliography

A. ATIYA et al., eds., *Coptic Encyclopedia* (8 vols.; New York: Macmillan, 1991); W. E. CRUM, ed., *A Coptic Dictionary* (Oxford: Clarendon, 1939) (the standard Coptic lexicon); E. S. DROWER and R. MACUCH, *A Mandaic Dictionary* (Oxford: Clarendon, 1963); C. A. EVANS, "Current Issues in Coptic Gnosticism for New Testament Study," *Studia biblica et theologica* 9, no. 2 (1979): 95–129; IDEM, "The Interpretation of Scripture in the New Testament Apocrpha and Gnostic Writings," in *The Ancient Period* (vol. 1 of *A History of Biblical Interpretation*; ed. A. J. Hauser and D. F. Watson; Grand Rapids: Eerdmans, 2003), 430–56 (bibliography); J. E. GOEHRING et al., eds., *Gnosticism and the Early Christian World* (J. M. Robinson FS; Sonoma, Calif.: Polebridge, 1990); J. M. ROBINSON, "Gnosticism and the New Testament," in *Gnosis* (ed. B. Aland; H. Jonas FS; Göttingen: Vandenhoeck & Ruprecht, 1978), 125–43; K. RUDOLPH, *Gnosis* (San Francisco: Harper & Row, 1980); D. M. SCHOLER, *Nag Hammadi Bibliography, 1948–1969* (NHS 1; Leiden: Brill, 1971); IDEM, *Nag Hammadi Bibliography, 1970–1994* (NHS 32; Leiden: Brill, 1997) (annual updates continue in *Novum Testamentum*); R. McL. WILSON, *Gnosis and the New Testament* (Philadelphia: Fortress, 1968); E. M. YAMAUCHI, "Jewish Gnosticism? The Prologue of John, Mandaean Parallels, and the Trimorphic Protennoia," in *Studies in Gnosticism and Hellenistic Religions* (ed. R. van den Broek and M. J. Vermaseren; G. Quispel FS; EPRO 91; Leiden: Brill, 1981), 467–97.

CHAPTER ELEVEN

Other Writings

Greco-Roman Authors	Corpus Hermeticum
Tacitus	
Suetonius	Samaritan Writings
Pliny the Younger	Memar Marqah
Celsus	The Chronicles
Thallus the Samaritan	The Liturgy
Mara bar Serapion	Magical Papyri
Plutarch	
Lucian of Samosata	

This chapter will only briefly touch on some of the miscellaneous writings that have some bearing on NT study. Some of these writings may contain parallels to ideas in the NT. All contribute to our understanding of the diverse and pluralistic context in which the NT emerged.

Greco-Roman Authors

Many Greco-Roman writers provide important background information and parallels to events, customs, institutions, terminology, and concepts found in the NT. Many of these writers are famous philosophers, poets, and statesmen. Others are less known. All in the list below are cited at least once in appendix 2, which lists parallels to the NT. The following list provides only the briefest thumbnail sketches of these writers.

Achilles Tatius (late first to middle second century C.E.) was the author of *Leucippe and Cleitophon,* among others.

Aelian (165/170–230/235 C.E.), or Claudius Aelianus, was the author of *Varia historia* (or *Miscellany*), among others.

Aelius Aristides, Publius (117–after 181 C.E.), was the author of *Orationes (Sacred Speeches* [or *Discourses*]).

Aeschylus (ca. 525–ca. 456 B.C.E.), an Athenian tragedian, was the author of *Oedipus, Persians, Seven against Thebes, Prometheus Bound,* and many other plays.

Aetius (late first to middle second century C.E.) was the author of *De placita philosophorum,* which later came to be included in Plutarch's *Moralia* and in Stobaeus's *Eclogae*.

Alciphron (second or third century C.E.), a Sophist, was the author of *Letters*.

Ammianus Marcellinus (ca. 330–395 C.E.), a Latin historian, was the author of *Res gestae (Roman History)*.

Anaxagoras of Clazomenai (ca. 500–428 B.C.E.) was an early philosopher who settled in Athens; his philosophical work survives as fragments (quotations), mostly in the work of Simplicius.

Apollonius of Tyana (first–second centuries C.E.) was the author of letters and treatises, of which no authentic letter survives and only a fragment of one treatise, *On Sacrifices,* is extant; he was the subject of a tendentious and greatly embellished biography by Philostratus, designed, in part, as an attack on Christianity.

Apollonius Paradoxographus (second century B.C.E.) was the author of a paradoxical work, *Mirabilia* (or *Historiae mirabiles*) compiled from earlier writers.

Appian (ca. 90s–160s C.E.), a Greek historian, was the author of *Historia romana (Roman History)* and *Bella civilia (Civil Wars)*.

Apuleius (ca. 125–after 170 C.E.), a writer and orator educated in Carthage and Athens, was the author of the *Apologia, Metamorphoses* (*The Golden Ass*), *Florida,* and other works, most of which are lost; several spurious works have been attributed to him.

Aratus (ca. 315–before 240 B.C.E.), a poet who studied at Athens, was the author of *Phaenomena,* his best-known and only surviving work, quoted in Acts 17:28 (in Paul's speech to the Athenians).

Archilochus (seventh century B.C.E.) was a Greek poet; only fragments of his work survive.

Aristophanes (ca. 450–shortly before 386 B.C.E.) was the greatest of the Attic Greek comedians; eleven plays are extant (e.g., *Lysistrata, Plutus, Birds, Frogs*), and fragments or titles of another 32 are known.

Aristotle (384–322 B.C.E.), the famous philosopher, was a pupil of Plato, instructed Alexander the Great, son of Philip II, and established the Lyceum in Athens, a school of philosophy later left to his successor Theophrastus; author of *Categories, Metaphysics, Eudemian Ethics, De anima* (*On the Soul*), and many others.

Arrian (ca. 86–160 C.E.), or Lucius Flavius Arrianus, was the author of *Anabasis of Alexander*, among others, and published the *Discourses* of Epictetus and its summarizing "handbook," or *Enchiridion.*

Aurelius Victor, Sextus (fourth century C.E.), a politician, historian, was the author of *De Caesaribus* (*On the Caesars*).

Bacchylides (ca. 520–450 B.C.E.), a lyric poet, was a contemporary of Pindar; only fragments of the poetry survive.

Callimachus of Cyrene (third century B.C.E.), a Greek scholar and poet, was the author of *Aetia* (*Causes*), *Epigrammata* (*Epigrams*), and several hymns, such as *Hymn to Apollo, Hymn to Zeus, Hymn to Ceres or Demeter* (*Hymnus in Cererem*), *Hymn to Delos,* and *Hymn to Artemis* (or *Diana*).

Catullus, Gaius Valerius (ca. 84–54 B.C.E.), a Latin poet, was the author of 114 poems.

Cebes (fourth century B.C.E.) of Thebes, a colleague of Plato, appears frequently in *Phaedo* as dialogue partner; he apparently was the author of *Pinax, Hebdome,* and *Phrynichus,* of which only a few brief quotations survive.

Celsus (second century C.E.), a critic of Christianity, was the author of *True Doctrine,* of which fragments are preserved, primarily in Origin, who replies in his treatise *Against Celsus* (*Contra Celsum*).

Chariton of Aphrodisias (second century C.E.), a novelist, was the author of *Chaereas and Callirhoe,* an eight-book novel of romance, adventure, danger, and happy ending.

Cicero, Marcus Tullius (106–43 B.C.E.), a soldier, jurist, politician, and orator, was the author of numerous letters as well as speeches and treatises, such as *In Verrem* (*Against Verres*), *Philippics, Pro Milone* (*In Defense of Milo*), *Pro Roscio Amerino Sexto* (*In Defense of Sextus Roscius of Ameria*), *Pro Flacco* (*In Defense of Flaccus*), and *De officiis* (*On Duties*).

Cleanthes of Assos (331–232 B.C.E.), a student of Zeno and successor of the Stoa, was the author of *Hymn to Zeus*, of which a lengthy fragment survives.

Cornutus, Lucius Annaeus (first century C.E.), a Stoic philosopher, grammarian, and rhetorician, was the author of *Satires*, he was later exiled by Nero.

Crates (ca. 365–285 B.C.E.), an influential Cynic, disciple of Diogenes, was the author of a collection of *Epistles;* his life is briefly summarized in Diogenes Laertius, *Vit. phil.* 6.85–93.

Curtius Rufus Quintus (early first century–second century C.E.) was the author of a ten-book history of Alexander the Great, the first two books of which are lost.

Democritus (ca. 460–380 B.C.E.) was the author of dozens of treatises on ethics, mathematics, music, physics (on which rested his greatest claim to fame in antiquity); only fragments survive, mostly maxims.

Demosthenes (384–322 B.C.E.), the greatest Athenian orator, politically active (to the cost of his life), was the author of several juridical pieces of apologetic and rhetoric, such as *Against Timocrates, For the Megalopolitans, Against Arisocrates, Against Aristogeiton, On the Liberty of the Rhodians,* and the four *Philippics*.

Dio Cassius (174–after 229 C.E.), or Cassius Dio, a Greek senator, was the author of the eighty-book *Historia romana* (*Roman History*) (from the founding to 229 C.E.), of which portions are no longer extant.

Dio Chrysostom (40/50–after 110 C.E.), or Dio Cocceianus (not to be confused with the church father John Chrysostom), a rhetorician, orator, Stoic philosopher, was the author of numerous speeches, compiled as *Discourses*. According to his biographer, Synesius, Dio Chrysostom (3.2) makes reference to the Essenes.

Diodorus Siculus (first century B.C.E.), or Diodorus of Sicily, was the author of *Bibliotheca historica* (*Library of History*), a universal history from mythological times to 60 B.C.E. Only fifteen of the original forty volumes are extant.

Diogenes Laertius (third century C.E.) was the author of compendium of the lives and teachings of the great philosophers, from Thales (sixth century B.C.E.) to Epicurus (third century B.C.E.), called *Vitae philosophorum* (*Lives of Eminent Philosophers*).

Diogenes of Sinope (ca. 403–324 B.C.E.), the founder of the Cynic way of life, who spent most of his life in Athens and Corinth, was the author of a collection of *Epistles;* Diogenes Laertius (*Vit. phil.* 6.70–73) sums up his teaching.

Empedocles (ca. 492–432 B.C.E.), of Sicily, was the author of *On Nature* and *Purifications,* of which only fragments remain.

Epictetus (first to second century C.E.) was a Stoic philosopher from Hierapolis of Asia Minor; his *Dissertationes* (*Discourses*) and *Enchiridion* (*Handbook* or *Manual*), were published by Arrian and influenced the Roman emperor Marcus Aurelius.

Epimenides (sixth or seventh century B.C.E.) was a holy man from Crete; various works, including *De oraculis* (*On Oracles*) and *Theogony,* were credited to him. The former may be cited in Titus 1:12.

Eratosthenes (ca. 285–294 B.C.E.), a pupil of Callimachus and Lysanias, studied at Athens and was invited by Ptolemy III Euergetes to succeed Apollonius Rhodius as head of the library at Alexandria; he was the author of works in literary criticism, mathematics, chronology, philosophy, and poetry, of which only several small fragments survive.

Eunapius (345–after 396 C.E.), a Greek Sophist and historian who opposed Christianity, was the author of a *History,* much of which is lost, and *Lives of the Sophists,* featuring his favorite, Iamblichus.

Euripides (ca. 480s–407 B.C.E.), an Athenian tragedian, was the author of about ninety plays, including *Alcestis, Helen, Electra, Bacchae, Heraclidae, Ion,* and *Cyclops;* many others are lost.

Florus (second century C.E.), or Lucius (or Publius) Annaeus Florus (and these may be different people), was the author of *Vergilius orator an poeta* (*Was Virgil an Orator or a Poet?*) and *Epitome bellorum omnium annorum DCC* (*Epitome of Roman History*), among other works.

Gaius (second century C.E.), a teacher of law, was the author of *Institutiones* (*Institutes*) and other works.

Galen (ca. 129–199 or 216 C.E.) went from gladiator physician to court physician under Marcus Aurelius, made major advances in medical theory and practice, and authored numerous medical and philosophical writings, such as *On the Natural Faculties, On the Use of Parts, On Cohesive Causes, Commentaries on Epidemics,* and *On the Opinions of Hippocrates and Plato.*

Heliodorus (fourth century C.E.), a Greek novelist, was the author of *Aethiopica* (or *Ethiopian Story of Theagenes and Chariclea*).

Heraclitus of Ephesus (sixth century B.C.E.), an aristocrat interested in concept of *psychē* (soul) and *logos* (word), is said to have authored a book that he placed in the temple of Artemis; only fragments of his work have survived.

Herodotus of Halicarnassus (fifth century B.C.E.), an historian and traveler, was the author of the *Histories*.

Hesiod (eighth/seventh century B.C.E.), a Greek poet, is believed to be the author of *Theogony, Works and Days,* and, less probably, *Shield* and *Catalogue of Women;* numerous poems are lost.

Homer (eighth century B.C.E.) is the legendary author of the poetic epics *Iliad* (750 B.C.E.?), comprising about 15,600 lines, and *Odyssey* (725 B.C.E.?), comprising about 12,000 lines. The *Iliad* relates the legend of Achilles, his quarrel with Agamemnon, and the Trojan War. The *Odyssey* tells the romantic tale of the nautical adventures of Odysseus. These classics functioned as sacred literature in the Greek world.

Horace (65–8 B.C.E.), or Quintus Horatius Flaccus, was the author of the *Epodes* (or *Iambi*), comprising seventeen poems; two books of *Satires;* three books of *Odes* (*Carmina*), comprising eighty-eight lyric poems, to which a fourth book was added, comprising another fifteen poems; and a collection of *Epistles*. In *Epodes* and *Odes* Horace praises Augustus for his achievements.

Iamblichus (ca. 245–325 C.E.), a neoplatonist philosopher and founder of a school in Syria, was the author of several treatises, of which only a few survive: *On the Life of Pythagoras, Protrepticus, On General Mathematical Science, On Nichomachus's Arithmetical Introduction,* and *On the Mysteries*. Fragments are extant in various authors (such as Macrobius and Stobaeus).

Isocrates (436–338 B.C.E.), a speech writer and Athenian orator, politically active, was the author of numerous letters and treatises, including *Philippus, Against the Sophists, Antidosis, On the Peace, Areopagiticus, Against Callimachus, To Demonicus, To Nicocles,* and many others.

Justinian (ca. 482–565 C.E.), an eastern emperor (527–565 C.E.), was the author of a major attempt to codify Roman law, in three works: *Codex, Digesta,* and *Institutiones*.

Juvenal (second century C.E.), or Decimus Iunius Iuvenalis, was a Roman satirist whose five books of *Satires* set the tone for this genre for centuries.

Leonidas of Tarentum (third century B.C.E.) was an epigrammist and anthologist whose work survives in the *Anthologia palatina* (or *latina*).

Livy (59 B.C.E.–12 C.E.), or Titus Livius, was the author of *Ab urbe condita libri* (*Books from the Foundation of the City* or *Roman History*). The work originally comprised 142 books, of which today only books 1–10 and 21–45 (with portions missing in books 41 and 43–45) survive. An epitaph at Padua, Italy, may be his (cf. *ILS* 2919).

Lucan (39–65 C.E.), or Marcus Annaeus Lucanus, a nephew to Seneca, studied philosophy under (Lucius Annaeus) Cornutus, was forced to commit suicide for taking part in a plot against Nero in 65, and was the author of *De bello civili* (*On the Civil War*), sometimes mistakenly called *Pharsalia;* fragments of other works survive, such as *Catacthonia, Iliaca,* and *Orpheus.*

Lucian of Samosata (ca. 120–after 180 C.E.), or Lucianus, who spoke Greek but whose mother tongue may have been Aramaic, was the author of numerous works, including *Lover of Lies, Passing of Peregrinus, Philosophies for Sale, Alexander the False Prophet, How to Write History, On Funerals, Saturnalia, Concerning the Sects, Imagines* (*Essays in Portraiture*), and many others.

Lysias (ca. 459–380 B.C.E.), an Attic orator who appears as a character in Plato's *Phaedrus* and *Republic,* was the author of numerous speeches, of which about one-fifth are extant, including *Pro milite.*

Macrobius (fifth century C.E.) was the author of *On the Difference of the Greek and Latin Verbs, Commentaries on Dreams,* and *Saturnalia.* In the last work, Macrobius relates a famous remark attributed to Augustus, who said in reference to Herod the Great, "I would rather be Herod's pig than his son" (*Sat.* 2.4.11). Although this passage is in Latin, the emperor's witticism must originally have been uttered in Greek, where *hys* ("pig") played on *huios* ("son").

Marcus Aurelius (121–180 C.E.), or Marcus Aurelius Antoninus, educated by the statesman Marcus Cornelius Fronto (95–166 C.E.), with whom in later years he corresponded frequently, was the author of the private journal that in modern times came to be called *Meditations.*

Martial (38/41–after 101 C.E.), or Marcus Valerius Martialis, a Latin poet, was the author of *Liber de spectaculis,* of which thirty-three poems have survived; *Epigrammaton libri XII* (*Epigrams*), consisting of more than a thousand poems; and the smaller *Xenia* and *Apophoreta.*

Maximus of Tyre (second century C.E.) was the author of forty-one extant *Dissertationes* (Greek *Dialexeis*), delivered in Rome during the reign of Commodus.

Menander (ca. 344–292 B.C.E.), a comic playwright, was the author of many plays. *Dyskolos* is almost fully extant; only fragments of the rest, including *Epitrepontes, Aspis, Thais, Georgos, Heros,* and *Kolax,* survive.

Moschus (second century B.C.E.), a poet, was the author of *Europa, Megara, Idylls,* and a few minor works.

Musonius (before 30–before 101 C.E.), or Gaius Musonius Rufus, a Roman Stoic, was the author of many epigrams and apophthegms, several of which have been preserved by his pupils, including Epictetus.

Oenomaus (second century C.E.), a Cynic philosopher, was the author of *Against the Oracles,* frequently quoted by the church historian Eusebius.

Oppian (second century C.E.), or Oppianus, was the author of *Halieutica* (on fishing) and *Cynegetica* (on animals), both poetic, symbolic works.

Ovid (43 B.C.E.–17 C.E.), a Roman poet, was the author of numerous poems, including *Heroides, Amores, Ars amatoria* (*Remedies for Love*), *Metamorphoses,* and *Tristia, Fasti.*

Pausanias (second century C.E.) was the author of *Description of Greece,* a guide with a special interest in monuments.

Petronius (first century C.E.), or Petronius Arbiter, was the author of *Satyrica* (sometimes *Satyricon*), a satirical novel that may have originally consisted of twenty books but of which only fragments of books 14, 15, and 16 survive.

Philostratus (third century), or L. Flavius Philostratus, was the author of *Life of Apollonius of Tyana, Lives of the Sophists,* and a few other minor works.

Phocylides (sixth century B.C.E.) was perhaps a fictitious personage associated with a gnomic poem, to which additions were made and of which only fragments are extant; it probably inspired the late-first-century B.C.E. Jewish work referred to as Ps.-Phocylides (see ch. 2 above).

Pindar (ca. 518–? B.C.E.), a lyric poet, was regarded by some ancients as the greatest of the nine poets of the lyric canon. The Alexandria editors arranged Pindar's work into seventeen volumes, of which only portions survive. These include some of the victory songs (*epinicia*), such as *Olympian Odes, Nemean Odes,* and *Pythian Odes.*

Plato (ca. 429–347 B.C.E.), an Athenian philosopher and student of Socrates, was the founder of the Academy, whose greatest student was Aristotle. Plato's works are presented in the form of dialogues, in which the great philosopher himself does not appear and never asserts views as his own. A considerable body of material has survived, including *Crito, Phaedo, Gorgias, Phaedrus, Protagoras, Symposium, Meno, Timaeus, Cleitophon,* and *Theaetetus.* His major works are *Laws* (twelve books) and the *Republic* (ten books). Pseudo-Plato, the author of *Axiochus,* dates to the first century C.E.

Plautus (flourished 205–184 B.C.E.), or Titus Maccius Plautus, a comic play-wright, was the author of *Bacchides, Carbonaria, Cistellaria, Mercator, Pseudolus,* and *Miles gloriosus,* among others. Little of the Greek plays upon which he based his own survive.

Pliny the Elder (23–79 C.E.), or Gaius Plinius Secundus, an uncle of Pliny the Younger, a Roman equestrian, and a commander of the fleet at Misenum, was the author of the thirty-seven-book *Naturalis historia,* an encyclopedic anthology of all natural subjects studied in late antiquity, including fauna, flora, and geog-raphy among others. Of special interest is his description of Palestine and men-tion of the Essenes (*Nat.* 5.17.4).

Pliny the Younger (ca. 61–112 C.E.), or Gaius Plinius Caecilius Secundus, whose name appears in inscriptions (e.g., *ILS* 2927), was raised by his uncle Pliny the Elder; studied rhetoric under Quintilian; served in the Roman Senate, on the bench, and in various political capacities as praetor, consul, and prefect; and was the author of numerous letters (*Epistles*) and the speech *Panegyricus.* His tenth book of letters includes his correspondence with the emperor Trajan (reigned 98–117 C.E.). In *Ep.* 10.96 he describes Christian worship (see below).

Plutarch (before 50–after 120 C.E.), or Mestrius Plutarchus, who held various ad-ministrative posts, including procurator in Greece during the reign of Hadrian (reigned 117–138 C.E.), was the author of numerous essays and biographies (*Lives*). The former, mostly gathered under the general heading *Moralia,* include *Education of Children, On Love of Wealth,* and *On Superstition.* The latter include *Alexander and Caesar, Pericles and Favius, Tiberius and Gaius Gracchus, Aratus,* and *Artaxerxes.*

Polybius (ca. 200–118 B.C.E.), a Greek historian of the rise of Rome, was the au-thor of *Histories,* much of which survives.

Porphyry (234–305 C.E.), a philosopher and student of religions, studied at Ath-ens, became a disciple of Plotinus, and authored commentaries on Plato and Ar-istotle, biographies (such as *Life of Pythagoras*), historical and chronological work, a treatise on vegetarianism (*On Abstinence*), and a treatise against Chris-tianity (*Against the Christians*).

Posidonius (ca. 135–51 B.C.E.), a Stoic philosopher, scientist, and historian, was the author of many works covering a broad range of subjects; only fragments sur-vive, many of them as quotations in Galen.

Propertius, Sextus (ca. 54–15 B.C.E.), was a Latin poet; his love poems were gath-ered into four books.

Publilius Syrus (not Publius Syrus) was brought to Rome in the first century B.C.E. as a slave. Although none of his works survive, many of his aphorisms and epigrams have been gathered under the title *Sententiae* (*Sentences*).

Quintilian (ca. 35–90s C.E.), or Marcus Fabius Quintilianus, a Roman rhetorician, was the author of *On the Causes of Corruption of Eloquence, In Defense of Naevius Arpinianus*, both lost, and two works on rhetoric, also lost. His *Institutio oratoria* (*Training in Oratory*) is extant.

Seneca, Lucius Annaeus (ca. 4 B.C.E.–65 C.E.), a politician, advisor to Nero, and philosopher, was the author of ten ethical treatises, or *dialogi*—including *De ira* (*On Anger*), *De providentia* (*On Providence*), *Ad Marciam de consolatione* (*To Marcia, on Consolation*), *De beneficiis* (*On Benefits*), *De vita beata* (*On the Happy Life*)—and other writings, including his numerous *Epistulae morales* (*Moral Epistles*).

Sextus Empiricus (second century C.E.), a physician and skeptic, was the author of *Against the Professors* and *Outlines of Pyrrhonism*.

Simonides (sixth–fifth century B.C.E.) was a Greek elegiac poet; only fragments of his work survive.

Sophocles (fifth century B.C.E.) is said to have written about 120 plays, of which 7 are extant, including *Ajax, Electra, Oedipus tyrannus, Antigone*, and *Trachiniae* (*Women of Trachis*).

Stobaeus (fifth century C.E.), or John of Stobi, was the author of *Eclogae* (Greek *Eklogai*, "Selections") and *Anthologium* (*Anthology*), handbooks consisting of extracts from philosophers and moralists from Homer to Themistius. The absence of Christian material suggests that Stobaeus was not a Christian.

Strabo (64 B.C.E.–after 21 C.E.) was the author of the seventeen-book *Geographica*, an important source for ancient geography and quotations from otherwise lost works.

Suetonius (ca. 70–130 C.E.), or Gaius Suetonius Tranquillus, briefly a military tribune in Britain, joined the retinue of the governor of Bithynia (ca. 110 C.E.). He was the author of *De viris illustribus* (*On Illustrious Men*), of which only portions survive, and *De vita Caesarum* (*On the Lives of the Caesars*), comprising biographies of twelve emperors, from Julius Caesar (reigned 48–44 B.C.E.) to Domitian (reigned 81–96 C.E.). His other works are lost. He may refer to Christ (see below).

Tacitus (ca. 56–after 118 C.E.), or Cornelius Tacitus, a Latin historian who became praetor in 88 C.E. and held various government posts, was the author of *Agricola* (a biography of his father-in-law, Julius Agricola), *Germania* (on German history and beliefs), the *Dialogues* (on the decline of oratory), and *Histories* and *Annals,* both of which are only partially extant (and whose titles were assigned in the sixteenth century). He refers to Christians (see below).

Themistius (317–388 C.E.), a politician and admirer of Plato and Aristotle, was the author of several works; of these, thirty-four of his *Speeches* and portions of his paraphrases of Aristotle's works survive.

Theocritus (third century B.C.E.) was a bucolic poet of Syracuse whose surviving works include *Thalysia* and others later grouped under the somewhat misleading title *Idylls.*

Theognis (sixth century B.C.E., perhaps seventh?), was an elegiac poet; about 1,400 verses (*Elegi*) survive.

Theophrastus (fourth century B.C.E.), an associate and successor of Aristotle's Lyceum, was the author of many works (*apud* Diogenes Laertius 5.36–57), of which only a few are extant, including *History of Plants, Metaphysics,* and *Characters.*

Thucydides (ca. 460–400 B.C.E.), a soldier and historian, was the author of the incomplete *History of the War* (i.e., the Peloponnesian War).

Valerius Harpocration of Alexandria (second century C.E.), a Greek lexicographer and possibly one of the tutors of Lucius Verus (emperor, 161–169 C.E.), was the author of *Collection of Fine Passages* (not extant), *Lexicon of the Ten Orators* (extant in abridged form), and *On the Powers of Nature.*

Valerius Maximus (flourished first half of the first century C.E.), a politician and ethicist, was the author of *Factorum ac dictorum memorabilium libri IX* (*Memorable Deeds and Sayings*).

Velleius Paterculus (ca. 19–after 31 C.E.), a Roman politician and political writer, was the author of an untitled two-volume historical work, published in 30 C.E., that begins with Greek mythology and ends with Roman history to 29 C.E. Most of the first volume is lost.

Vettius Valens (second century C.E.), a Greek astrologer, was the author of the nine-volume *Anthologies,* which preserves, among other things, a collection of Greek horoscopes.

Virgil (70–19 B.C.E.), or Publius Vergilius Maro (originally spelled Vergil, but early on, the name was spelled with an *i,* as seen in an inscription; cf. *ILS* 2949), was the author of *Eclogues, Georgics,* and *Aeneid* (twelve books). *Georgics,* written at the time of the clash between Octavian (later Augustus) and his brother-in-law Marc Antony, extols the great emperor.

Xenophon (ca. 430–354 B.C.E.), an adventurer, soldier, mercenary, and statesman, was the author of numerous works, including *Hellenica* (seven books), *Anabasis* (seven books), *Apologia, Memorabilia, Oeconomicus, Symposium, Cyropaedia* (eight books), and various minor writings. Best known is the *Anabasis*, which recounts the march of the ten thousand Greek mercenaries in support of Cyrus's attempt to defeat and overthrow his brother Artaxerxes (battle was joined at Cunaxa in 401 B.C.E.). A brief biography by Diogenes Laertius (*Vit. phil.* 6.2) tells of Xenophon's first meeting with Socrates.

Zosimus (fifth–sixth century C.E.), a Greek historian, was the author of *Historia nova*.

Bibliography: S. HORNBLOWER and A. SPAWFORTH, eds., *The Oxford Classical Dictionary* (3d ed.; New York: Oxford University Press, 1996). Many of the works of the above authors are presented in the Loeb Classical Library (LCL) in the Greek or Latin, with English on facing pages.

Greco-Roman Authors on Jesus and Early Christianity

Much of the importance of the first six Greco-Roman authors listed below lies in the fact that they refer to Jesus and/or early Christianity. Their comments give us some idea, as limited as it is, as to how those outside of the church viewed Christianity in its earliest stages. The last two writers, Plutarch and Lucian, are included because some think that their writings are helpful for understanding various theological, philosophical, and ethical ideas in the NT.

Tacitus. In his *Annals* (15.44) Tacitus (110–120 C.E.) states:

> This name [i.e., "Christian"] originates from "Christus" who was sentenced to death by the procurator, Pontius Pilate, during the reign of Tiberius. This detestable superstition, which had been suppressed for a while, spread anew not only in Judea where the evil had started, but also in Rome, where everything that is horrid and wicked in the world gathers and finds numerous followers.

Tacitus's knowledge is at best thirdhand. It would be interesting to know precisely what he means by saying that Christianity "had been suppressed for a while." Could he be referring to the active opposition and persecution of the Jewish religious authorities, as described in Acts and alluded to in places in Paul's letters?

Suetonius. In his *Divus Claudius* (*Life of Emperor Claudius*) (25.4) Suetonius (110–120 C.E.) states that "Claudius expelled the Jews from Rome who, instigated by Chrestus, never ceased to cause unrest." By "Jews" Suetonius means Christians, though Christianity, at that time still in its infancy, was probably predominantly Jewish, even toward the beginning of the second century C.E. "Chrestus" is an error, probably from confusing the word *chrestus* (sometimes used as a personal name, especially for slaves) with the Jewish title *christus*, a title with which a Roman might not be familiar.

Pliny the Younger. In his tenth epistle (*Ep.* 10.96 [to Emperor Trajan]) Pliny the Younger (110 C.E.) seeks Trajan's advice in dealing with Christians. His description of Christian beliefs and practices is interesting:

> They [the Christians] assured me that the sum total of their guilt or their error consisted in the fact that they regularly assembled on a certain day before daybreak. They recited a hymn antiphonally to Christ as (their) God and bound themselves with an oath not to commit any crime, but to abstain from theft, robbery, adultery, breach of faith, and embezzlement of property entrusted to them. After this it was their custom to separate, and then to come together again to partake of a meal, but an ordinary and innocent one.

Celsus. According to Origen, Celsus claimed that Jesus performed his miracles by the power of magic (*Cels.* 1.6), a power that he had acquired while living in Egypt (1.38). When he returned to Palestine he dazzled people and called himself God (1.38). The charges of Celsus are similar to those found in the rabbinic writings.

Thallus the Samaritan Chronicler. In reference to the darkness at the time of Jesus' crucifixion (see Mark 15:33), Julius Africanus (d. after 240 C.E.) reports (according to frg. 18 of Africanus's five-volume *Chronography,* preserved in Georgius Syncellus, *Chronology*) that "this darkness Thallus, in the third book of his *History,* calls, as appears to me without reason, an eclipse of the sun."

Mara bar Serapion. In a letter to his son (perhaps late first century), Mara bar Serapion asks: "For what advantage did . . . the Jews [gain] by the death of their wise king, because from that same time their kingdom was taken away?"

Bibliography: T. D. BARNES, "Legislation against the Christians," *JRS* 58 (1968): 32–50 (on Tacitus); S. BENKO, "The Edict of Claudius of A.D. 49 and the Instigator Chrestus," *TZ* 25 (1969): 406–18; F. F. BRUCE, *Jesus and Christian Origins outside the New Testament* (Grand Rapids: Eerdmans, 1974); H. CHADWICK, *Origen: Contra Celsum* (Cambridge: Cambridge University Press, 1953; repr., 1965) (on Celsus); H. CONZELMANN, *History of Primitive Christianity* (Nashville: Abingdon, 1973), 163–78 (on Tacitus, Suetonius, Pliny the Younger); W. CURETON, *Spicilegium syriacum* (London: Rivington, 1855), 73 (on Mara bar Serapion); M. DALY-DENTON, "Singing Hymns to Christ as to a God (Cf. Pliny Ep. X, 96)," in *The Jewish Roots of Christological Monotheism: Papers from the St. Andrews Conference on the Historical Origins of the Worship of Jesus* (ed. C. C. Newman, J. R. Davila, and G. Lewis; JSJSup 63; Leiden: Brill, 1999), 277–92; C. A. EVANS, "Jesus in Non-Christian Sources," in *Studying the Historical Jesus: Evaluations of the State of Current Research* (ed. C. A. Evans and B. D. Chilton; NTTS 19; Leiden: Brill, 1994), 443–78, esp. 454–66 (on Thallus, Mara bar Serapion, Suetonius, Pliny the Younger, Lucian of Samosata, Tacitus); H. FUCHS, "Tacitus über die Christen," *VC* 4 (1950): 65–93; M. J. HARRIS, "References to Jesus in Early Classical Authors," in *The Jesus Tradition outside the Gospels* (ed. D. Wenham; Gospel Perspectives 5; Sheffield: JSOT Press, 1985), 343–68; H. HOMMEL, "Tacitus und die Christen,"

in *Sebasmata: Studien zur antiken Religionsgeschichte und zum frühen Christentum* (2 vols.;
WUNT 31–32; Tübingen: Mohr [Siebeck], 1983–1984), 2:174–99; A. KURFESS, "Tacitus
über die Christen," *VC* 5 (1951): 148–49; E. LAUPOT, "Tacitus' Fragment 2: The Anti-
Roman Movement of the Christiani and the Nazoreans," *VC* 54 (2000): 233–47; A. ROB-
ERTS and J. DONALDSON, eds., *The Ante-Nicene Fathers* (10 vols.; Buffalo: Christian Litera-
ture Publishing Co., 1887–1896; repr., Peabody, Mass.: Hendrickson, 1994), 6:136 (on
Thallus); D. SLINGERLAND, "Suetonius *Claudius* 25.4, Acts 18, and Paulus Orosius'
Historiarum adversum paganos libri vii: Dating the Claudian Explosion(s) of Roman Jews,"
JQR 83 (1992): 127–44; R. E. VAN VOORST, *Jesus outside the New Testament: An Introduc-
tion to the Ancient Evidence* (Studying the Historical Jesus; Grand Rapids: Eerdmans,
2000), 19–74 (on Thallus, Pliny the Younger, Suetonius, Tacitus, Mara bar Serapion,
Lucian of Samosata, Celsus).

Plutarch. Plutarch of Chaeronea (ca. 49–119 C.E.) was associated with the sanctuary of Apollo at Delphi and in his later years served as a priest of Apollo. Plutarch's principal works are *Moralia* and *Lives*. Both of these writings are Greek
and are in F. C. Babbitt et al., trans., *Plutarch's Moralia* (16 vols. in 17; LCL; Cambridge: Harvard University Press, 1927–2004). Hans Dieter Betz and members of
the Corpus Hellenisticum Novi Testamenti have prepared critical editions that
investigate Plutarch's theological and ethical themes, subject by subject, as found
in the *Moralia*.

Bibliography: H. D. BETZ, ed., *Plutarch's Ethical Writings and Early Christian Literature*
(SCHNT 4; Leiden: Brill, 1978); IDEM, ed., *Plutarch's Theological Writings and Early Christian Literature* (SCHNT 3; Leiden: Brill, 1975); V. K. ROBBINS, "Laudation Stories in the
Gospel of Luke and Plutarch's Alexander," in *SBL Seminar Papers, 1981* (ed. K. H. Rich-
ards; SBLSP 20; Chico, Calif.: Scholars Press, 1981), 293–308.

Lucian of Samosata. Lucian, who called himself a Syrian, was born sometime before 125 C.E. at Samosata in Commagene. He died sometime after 180. His Greek
writings, with English translation, are found in A. M. Harmon, K. Kilburn, and
M. D. Macleod, trans., *Lucian* (8 vols.; LCL; Cambridge: Harvard University
Press, 1953–1967). For a study that considers the significance of Lucian's writings
for the NT, see Betz. In one of the most important passages in Lucian's writings,
he refers to Peregrinus, who, as a Christian, at one time worshiped "the man who
was crucified in Palestine" (*Peregr.* §11; cf. §13: "that crucified sophist").

Bibliography: H. D. BETZ, "Lukian von Samosata und das Christentum," *NovT* 3 (1959):
226–37, repr. in *Hellenismus und Urchristentum* (Gesammelte Aufsätze 1; Tübingen: Mohr
[Siebeck], 1990), 10–21; IDEM, *Lukian von Samosata und das Neue Testament: Religions-
geschichtliche und paränetische Parallelen* (TU 76; Berlin: Akademie, 1961).

Corpus Hermeticum

Corpus hermeticum, named after the mythical Hermes Trismegistus (lit. the
"Thrice-Greatest Hermes"), is an interesting collection of Greek theosophical

writings. The Hermetica are eclectic, lacking a coherent philosophy. In some ways they resemble the *Sibylline Oracles* (see ch. 2). Parts of the collection are monotheistic, but others are polytheistic (esp. *Asclepius*). There is interest in God, the human race, and the cosmos. With regard to its literary form, the Hermetica are arranged as didactic conversations, with six figures portrayed as teachers and/ or pupils: (1) Hermes Trismegistus, (2) Hermes' son Tat (or Thot), (3) Asclepius, (4) Agathos Daimon (lit. "Good Demon"), also known as the Egyptian god Kneph, (5) Hammon, and (6) Poimandres (lit. "Shepherd of Men"), whose name is also associated with the whole collection. Even the great Hermes, normally himself the master-teacher, is instructed by Nous (lit. "Mind").

Following G. R. S. Mead, *Thrice-Greatest Hermes: Studies in Hellenistic Theosophy and Gnosis* (3 vols.; London: John M. Watkins, 1949), who provides text and commentary, the sources of *Corpus hermeticum* may be outlined as follows:

1. *Corpus hermeticum graecum,* which includes Poimandres and Asclepius (18 tractates in all, with Tractate I on Poimandres, Tractate II on Asclepius)

2. Latin Asclepius, also known as the "Perfect Sermon" (41 chapters)

3. Excerpts by John Stobaeus, a pagan writer from the late fifth or early sixth century (27 excerpts in all)

4. References, allusions, and fragments in the church fathers (some 25 fragments from Justin Martyr, Clement of Alexandria, Tertullian, Cyprian, Arnobius, Lactantius, Augustine, and Cyril of Alexandria)

5. References, allusions, and fragments in the Philosophers (from Zosimus, Fulgentius, Iamblichus, and Julian the Emperor-Philosopher)

Various writers of antiquity exhibit dependence upon or close parallels to hermetic ideas (e.g., Philo of Alexandria, the Naassenes [early Jewish and Christian mystics], Zosimus, Plutarch, various gnostic sects).

Bibliography: For texts, see B. P. COPENHAVER, *Hermetica: The Greek Corpus hermeticum and the Latin Asclepius in a New English Translation, with Notes and Introduction* (Cambridge: Cambridge University Press, 1992) [English translation, notes, and introduction]. A. D. NOCK and A.-J. FESTUGIÈRE, *Hermès Trismégiste: Corpus hermeticum* (4 vols.; Paris: Belles Lettres, 1946–1954; repr., 1981) [Greek text and French translation and commentary]. R. REITZENSTEIN, *Poimandres: Studien zur griechisch-ägyptischen und frühchristlichen Literatur* (Leipzig: Teubner, 1904) [Greek text of *Corp. herm.* 1, 13, 16–18]. W. SCOTT, *Hermetica* (4 vols.; Oxford: Clarendon, 1924–1936) [Greek and Latin text, English translation, commentary, and introduction]. For parallels with the NT, see J. BÜCHLI, *Der Poimandres: Ein paganisiertes Evangelium* (WUNT 2.27; Tübingen: Mohr [Siebeck], 1987); W. C. GRESE, *Corpus hermeticum XIII and Early Christian Literature* (SCHNT 5; Leiden: Brill, 1979); IDEM, "The Hermetica and New Testament Research," *BR* 28 (1983): 37–54; K.-W. TRÖGER, *Mysterienglaube und Gnosis in Corpus hermeticum XIII* (TU 110; Berlin: Akademie, 1971). For general discussion, see A. D. NOCK, "Diatribe Form in the Hermetica," in *Essays on Religion and the Ancient World* (ed. Z. Stewart; 2 vols.; Oxford: Clarendon, 1986), 1:26–32. For studies, see A.-J. FESTUGIÈRE, *L'hermétisme* (Lund, Swed.: Gleerup, 1948); J.-P. MAHÉ, "PALINGENESIA et structure du monde supérieur dans les Hermetica et le Traité d'Eugnoste de Nag Hammadi," in *Deuxième journée d'études coptes: Strasbourg, 25 Mai 1984* (ed. J.-E. Ménard; Cahiers de la Bibliothèque copte 3; Paris:

Peeters, 1986), 137–49; IDEM, "Preliminary Remarks on the Demotic Book of Thoth the Greek Hermetica," *VC* 50 (1996): 353–63; IDEM, "La voie d'immortalité à la lumière des Hermetica de Nag Hammadi et de découvertes plus récentes," *VC* 45 (1991): 347–75; G. VAN MOORSEL, *The Mysteries of Hermes Trismegistus* (Utrecht: Kemink, 1955); B. A. PEARSON, "Jewish Elements in Corpus hermeticum I (Poimandres)," in *Studies in Gnosticism and Hellenistic Religions* (ed. R. van den Broek and M. J. Vermaseren; G. Quispel FS; EPRO 91; Leiden: Brill, 1981), 336–48, repr. in B. A. Pearson, *Gnosticism, Judaism, and Egyptian Christiantiy* (SAC; Minneapolis: Fortress, 1990), 136–47; IDEM, "Jewish Sources in Gnostic Literature," *SJWSTP* 474–75; P. SELLEW, "A Secret Hymn about Rebirth: Corpus hermeticum XIII.17–20," in *Prayer from Alexander to Constantine: A Critical Anthology* (ed. M. Kiley et al.; New York: Routledge, 1997), 165–70; F. SIEGERT, ed., *Das Corpus hermeticum einschliesslich der Fragmente des Stobaeus* (Münsteraner judaistische Studien 3; Münster: Lit, 1999).

Corpus hermeticum and the Johannine Writings. C. H. Dodd (*The Interpretation of the Fourth Gospel* [Cambridge: Cambridge University Press, 1953], 34–35, 50–51) offers several parallels. Here are those that appear to be the most promising:

Corpus Hermeticum	Johannine Writings
"I am that light . . . your God" (1.6)	"I am the light of the world" (John 8:12)
	"God is light" (1 John 1:5)
	"in order that every one who believes in
"This one remains in darkness	me should not remain in darkness"
deceived" (1.19)	(John 12:46)
"They ascend to the Father" (1.26)	"I ascend to my Father" (John 20:17)
"Holy God the Father" (1.31)	"Holy Father" (John 17:11)
"I shall enlighten my brothers who are	"the true light which enlightens every
in ignorance" (1.32)	man" (John 1:9)
"I believe and I bear witness" (1.32)	"he came for a witness . . . that all should
	believe through him" (John 1:7)
"I advance unto life and light" (1.32)	"he will have the light of life" (John 8:12)
"none can be saved before regeneration"	"except one be born again, he cannot see
(13.1)	the kingdom of God" (John 3:4)
"The true seed is good" (13.2)	"His seed abides forever" (1 John 3:9)
"the begetting by God" (13.6)	"they were begotten of God" (John 1:13)
"cleanse yourself" (13.7)	"He cleanses every one bearing fruit"
	(John 15:2)
"knowledge of God came to us" (13.8)	"that they should know you, the only true
	God" (John 17:3)
"no longer no punishment of darkness	"lest darkness overcome you" (John 12:35;
came upon you" (13.9)	cf. John 1:5)
"a child of that One" (13.14)	"We have one Father, God" (John 8:41)
"I rejoice in the joy of my mind" (13.18)	"in order that my joy might be in you"
	(John 15:11)
"The Powers which are in me . . . complete	"in order that I should do the will of the
your will" (13.19)	One who sent me" (John 4:34)
"The mind shepherds . . ." (13.19)	"I am the Good Shepherd" (John 10:11)

Samaritan Writings

In addition to the Samaritan Pentateuch (see ch. 4) and the *Samaritan Targum* (see ch. 6) there are several writings that contain various biblical traditions and legends. These writings fall into three broad categories: midrash, chronicles, and liturgy. The origin of the Samaritan sect is disputed. The Samaritans themselves claim that they are the descendants of the ten northern tribes that were exiled by the Assyrian Empire in the eighth century B.C.E. Jewish Scripture and tradition, however, tell a different story. According to them, the Samaritans are at best part Jewish, having intermarried with people from Cuthea, one of the regions of the old Assyrian Empire. For this reason they are called "Cutheans" or Kutim. (One of the minor tractates of the Babylonian Talmud treats Jewish laws pertaining to the Kutim.) Scholars today are inclined to think that the Samaritans, as a distinct movement separated from Judah, emerged in the second century, especially after the destruction of their temple at Gerizim.

Samaritans awaited a *Taheb* (lit. "returning one"), who is expected to be a descendant of either Jacob, Seth, Phineas, Moses, or Noah. His name is unknown. He will be like Moses (cf. Deut 18:18). Repentance must precede his coming. He will come from the east, to Mount Gerizim. He will bring the staff of Aaron, manna, and the holy tabernacle. He is not a priest; he is a prophet and king. He will reign over the whole world.

The Dosithean sect was founded by Dosithius, a man who may have been the leader of a Samaritan group, though who this person was and what his teachings were is disputed. He may have applied Deut 18:15–19 to himself. After his death an aretalogy (i.e., a legendary account of one's virtues and accomplishments) developed. His following awaited his return, perhaps as the *Taheb*. The sect died out (or was assimilated into mainstream Samaritan culture) by the fourteenth century.

Bibliography: R. T. ANDERSON, "Samaritans," *ABD* 5:940–47; A. D. CROWN, *A Bibliography of the Samaritans* (2d ed.; ATLA Bibliography Series 32; [Philadelphia]: American Theological Library Association and Scarecrow, 1993); IDEM, ed., *New Samaritan Studies* (Sydney, Australia: University of Sydney Press, 1995); F. DEXINGER, "Limits of Tolerance in Judaism: The Samaritan Example," in *Aspects of Judaism in the Graeco-Roman Period* (vol. 2 of *Jewish and Christian Self-Definition*; ed. E. P. Sanders; Philadelphia: Fortress, 1981), 88–114; IDEM, "Samaritan Eschatology," in *The Samaritans* (ed. A. D. Crown; Tübingen: Mohr [Siebeck], 1989), 266–92, esp. 272–76; IDEM, *Der Taheb: Ein "messianischer" Heilsbringer der Samaritaner* (Salzburg: Müller, 1986); M. GASTER, *The Samaritans: Their History, Doctrines, and Literature* (London: British Academy, 1925); S. J. ISSER, *The Dositheans: A Samaritan Sect in Late Antiquity* (SJLA 17; Leiden: Brill, 1976); J. MACDONALD, *The Theology of the Samaritans* (London: SCM Press, 1964); L. A. MAYER, *Bibliography of the Samaritans* (ed. D. Broadriff; Leiden: Brill, 1964); J. D. PURVIS, *The Samaritan Pentateuch and the Origin of the Samaritan Sect* (HSM 2; Cambridge: Harvard University Press, 1968); N. SCHUR, *History of the Samaritans* (BEATAJ 18; New York: Peter Lang, 1989); A. TAL, "Samaritan Literature," in *The Samaritans* (ed. A. D. Crown; Tübingen: Mohr [Siebeck],

1989), 413–67; J. E. H. THOMSON, *The Samaritans: Their Testimony to the Religion of Israel* (London: Oliver & Boyd, 1919).

Memar Marqah. The *Memar Marqah* (or *Marqe*) is the "sayings of Marqah." This work, which has also been called *Seper Peli'ata* ("Book of Wonders")—which has more to do with book 1 than with the rest of the work—dates roughly to the second, third, and fourth centuries. Outside of the Samaritan Pentateuch and the *Samaritan Targum,* it is the most important of the Samaritan writings. It comprises six books, written in Hebrew and Aramaic. The themes of these books are as follows:

> Book 1: Moses and the burning bush, Moses and Pharaoh, the Exodus (parallels Exod 3–14)
>
> Book 2: how God defeated the Egyptians, commentary on Exodus 15
>
> Book 3: on priests, elders, princes, judges, teachers, and leaders of Israel
>
> Book 4: theology (how God deals with humanity, humanity's duty to God), commentary on Exodus 32, the promise that the *Taheb* will arise (4:12)
>
> Book 5: on Moses' death, ascension, and glorification
>
> Book 6: on creation, wisdom, Word of God, alphabet

The following excerpts could have some relevance for NT interpretation (the page numbers refer to Macdonald, vol. 2):

> "To Mount Gerizim, the House of God, which I have desired, I shall go before I die" (5:2; p. 198).
>
> "The great prophet Moses ascended Mount Nebo with great majesty, crowned with light. All the hosts of the heavenly angels gathered to meet him" (5:3; p. 202).
>
> "The Glory drew near to him and embraced him, while all the hosts of the hidden regions and of the revealed ones came to do honour to Moses the man" (5:3; p. 203).
>
> "He ascended from human status to that of the angels" (5:3; p. 206 [recalling Moses receiving the Ten Commandments]).
>
> "The great prophet Moses went up Mount Nebo to see six hundred thousand [Israelites below] and all the angels [above] waiting to meet him. When he reached the top of the mountain, the cloud came down and lifted him up from the sight of all the congregation of Israel" (5:4; p. 208; cf. Acts 1:9).

Several of these excerpts are reminiscent of Moses and Samaritan traditions in the book of Acts, and especially in the Fourth Gospel. For further discussion see W. A. Meeks, *The Prophet-King: Moses Traditions and the Johannine Christology* (NovTSup 14; Leiden: Brill, 1967).

Bibliography: A. BROADIE, *A Samaritan Philosophy: A Study of the Hellenistic Cultural Ethos of the Memar Marqah* (SPB 31; Leiden: Brill, 1981); S. LOWY, *The Principles of Samaritan Bible Exegesis* (SPB 28; Leiden: Brill, 1977); J. MACDONALD, *Memar Marqah: The Teaching of Marqah* (2 vols.; BZAW 84; Berlin: Töpelmann, 1963) (vol. 1 provides text; vol. 2, an English translation); D. RETTIG, *Memar Marqa: Ein samaritischer Midrasch zum Pentateuch* (Bonner orientalistische Studien 8; Stuttgart: Kohlhammer, 1934).

The Samaritan Chronicles. A few of the *Samaritan Chronicles* may date to the early centuries of the church and so are worth mentioning briefly. Moses Gaster thinks that the Aramaic Chronicle I (*Asatir*), which relates the teachings of Moses, derives from the third century. Other scholars disagree. Z. Ben-Hayyim thinks that the work derives from the tenth century. It is not clear why Gaster calls it the "Book of the Secrets of Moses," for nowhere in Samaritan literature is it ever called this. Chronicle II (*Seper he-Yamim*), which may have been a "Book of Joshua," is written entirely in Hebrew and may derive from the third century C.E. Among other things, it retells the story of Samuel and David, with the focus on the ark of the covenant. According to the Samaritan version, Samuel the prophet-priest is evil, like Eli and his sons. Saul and Jesse fight the northern tribes because they (the tribes) have remained loyal to Mount Gerizim. Saul and Jesse, under Samuel's influence, worship at Shiloh. But the Samaritan chronicler likes David, because he opposed Saul. In fact, David used to send offerings to Mount Gerizim. Unfortunately, the Judahites persuaded David to build a temple in Jerusalem, an act which angered the Samaritans. However, because of the displeasure of the Samaritan high priest Jair the son of Jehonathan, David stopped building and said, "My son Solomon shall build the house for the Ark, for I have shed much blood" (Macdonald, 135). Nathan's oracle (2 Sam 7) is omitted, but David's sins (e.g., the affair with Bathsheba) are emphasized. Chronicle IV (*Sepher Yehoshua*) is an embellished retelling of the story of Joshua and subsequent Samaritan history. The compiler claims that his Arabic chronicle is a translation from the Hebrew, but John Bowman doubts this. Contents: Chapters 1–25 concern Joshua son of Nun, paralleling the biblical book of Joshua. Chapters 26–37 tell of war of war between Joshua and Shaubak, king of Persia. Chapters 38–44 tell of Joshua's death and burial. Chapters 45–50 continue the story right on through the intertestamental period. Chapter 46 recounts the exploits of Alexander the Great. Chapter 47 tells of the reign of the Roman Emperor Hadrian. Chapters 48–50 tell of various Samaritan high priests during Roman persecution. Some of this material may be early. Some of it was available in Hebrew, but some is known only from Arabic sources.

Bibliography: Z. BEN-HAYYIM, "The Book of Asatir," *Tarbiz* 14 (1944): 104–25, 174–90; 15 (1945): 71–87; J. BOWMAN, *Samaritan Documents Relating to Their History, Religion, and Life* (Pittsburgh: Pickwick, 1977); J. M. COHEN, *A Samaritan Chronicle: A Source-Critical Analysis of the Life and Times of the Great Samaritan Reformer, Baba Rabbah* (SPB 30; Leiden: Brill, 1981) (discusses the nonbiblical portions of *Chronicle II*); A. D. CROWN, "New Light on the Interrelationships of Samaritan Chronicles from Some Manuscripts in the John Rylands University Library of Manchester," *BJRL* 55 (1972): 1–58; M. GASTER,

The Asatir, the Book of the Secrets of Moses (Oriental Translation Fund 26; London: Royal Asiatic Society, 1927); H. G. KIPPENBERG, *Garizim und Synagogue* (Berlin: de Gruyter, 1971); J. MACDONALD, *The Samaritan Chronicle No. II; or, Sepher Ha-Yamim: From Joshua to Nebuchadnezzar* (BZAW 107; Berlin: de Gruyter, 1969) (provides an English translation of the biblical portions of the chronicle); Y. MAGEN, "Mount Gerizim and the Samaritans," in *Early Christianity in Context: Monuments and Documents* (ed. F. Manns and E. Alliata; Jerusalem: Franciscan Printing Press, 1993), 91–147; P. STENHOUSE, "Samaritan Chronicles," in *The Samaritans* (ed. A. D. Crown; Tübingen: Mohr [Siebeck], 1989), 218–65.

Samaritan Liturgy. Two items from the Samaritan liturgy, both dating from the fourth century, should be mentioned. The first is the *Defter*. The name is from a Greek loan word (*diphthera,* meaning "skin" or "parchment"). The *Defter* represents the oldest collection of Samaritan prayers and poems for weekly religious services and for holidays. This collection remained in use until the fourteenth century. The second item is the *Durran,* which receives its name from the Arabic (*bit durran,* meaning a "string of pearls"). The *Durran* is made up of the poems of *Amram Dare,* which, like the *Defter,* played an important role in the Samaritan liturgy.

Bibliography: R. T. ANDERSON and T. GILES, *The Keepers: An Introduction to the History and Culture of the Samaritans* (Peabody, Mass.: Hendrickson, 2002); J. BOWMAN, *Samaritan Documents Relating to Their History, Religion, and Life* (Pittsburgh: Pickwick, 1977); A. E. COWLEY, *The Samaritan Liturgy* (Oxford: Oxford University Press, 1909); Y. MAGEN, "Samaritan Synagogues" in *Early Christianity in Context: Monuments and Documents* (ed. F. Manns and E. Alliata; Jerusalem: Franciscan Printing Press, 1993), 193–230; R. PUMMER, "Samaritan Synagogues and Jewish Synagogues," in *Jews, Christians, and Polytheists in the Ancient Synagogue* (ed. S. Fine; New York: Routledge, 1999), 118–60; H. WEISS, "The Sabbath among the Samaritans," *JSJ* 25 (1994): 252–73.

Papyri, Inscriptions, Coins, and Ostraca

Very little that falls under the present heading is literature. Yet these items contribute important written material that in various ways illuminates the world of early Christianity and sometimes clarifies specific passages and themes in the NT. Papyri (sg. papyrus, from which the modern word *paper* derives) do preserve literature such as the NT itself and most of the writings considered in the several chapters above. The nonliterary papyri are meant here, however.

Papyri

Under the general heading of nonliterary papyri are legal documents, imperial documents (decrees, proclamations, and the like), personal letters, business papers (agenda, minutes, contracts, agreements), military correspondence, and religious and quasi-religious documents (see the magical papyri below).

Personal letters and business correspondence provide us with significant insight into the details of everyday life in late antiquity. In the Zenon collection of papyri, we have business papers, contracts, and correspondence dealing with Egypt and Palestine of the third century B.C. We read of labor disputes, legal complaints, and agents intending to collect a debt being "cast out" (*egballein*) of town (P.Cair.Zen 59018; cf. Mark 12:8: *ekballein*). A second-century letter from a wayward son implores reconciliation with his mother, who confesses, "I know that I have sinned" (BGU 846; cf. Luke 15:18, 21; Deissmann, 187–92). In a turn-of-the-era letter, a man advises his pregnant wife, "If you bear a boy, keep it; if a girl, throw it out" (P.Oxy. 744; 1 B.C.E.). A woman petitions a judge for justice, reminding him, "I am a widow woman" (P.Mich. 29; cf. Luke 18:1–8; White, 46).

Public documents also have features of interest. The following letter of the newly enthroned emperor Claudius to the people of Alexandria was, by order of the Roman prefect, to be posted publicly for all to read (41 C.E.). Part of this letter speaks to how the emperor is or is not to be honored:

> Wherefore I gladly accepted the honors given to me by you, though I have no weakness for such things. And first I permit you to keep my birthday as a *dies Augustus* as you have yourselves proposed, and I agree to the erection in their several places of the statues of myself and my family; for I see that you were anxious to establish on every side memorials of your reverence for my house. Of the two golden statues the one made to represent the Pax Augusta Claudiana, as my most honored Barbillus suggested and entreated when I wished to refuse for fear of being thought too offensive, shall be erected at Rome, and the other according to your request shall be carried in procession on name-days in your city; and it shall be accompanied by a throne, adorned with whatever trappings you chose. (P.Lond. 1912; cf. Hunt and Edgar, 2:81, 83)

The following proclamation of an Egyptian prefect in 104 C.E. invites comparison with the census mentioned in Luke 2:1–5:

> Proclamation of Gaius Vibius Maximus, prefect of Egypt. The house-to-house census having started, it is essential that all persons who for any reason whatsoever are absent from their homes be summoned to return to their own hearths, in order that they may perform the customary business of registration and apply themselves to the cultivation which concerns them. (P.Lond. 904; cf. Hunt and Edgar, 2:109)

Papyri (Greek and Latin) relating to the Roman military also convey interesting data about recruitment, rosters, everyday life, issues of discipline, wages, receipts, reports, and personal correspondence. One account enumerates the sacrifices and celebrations throughout the year for several deified emperors, including Augustus, Trajan, Hadrian, and Marcus Antoninus (P.Dur. 54; cf. Fink, 422–29).

For selections of papyri that illuminate the world of late antiquity and the world of the NT, see W. H. Davis, *Greek Papyri of the First Century* (New York: Harper, 1933); R. O. Fink, *Roman Military Records on Papyrus* (Philological Monographs of the American Philological Association 26; Cleveland: Case Western

Reserve University Press, 1971); G. H. R. Horsley and S. R. Llewelyn, *NewDocs* [a very helpful series]; A. S. Hunt and C. C. Edgar, *Select Papyri* (LCL 266, 282; Cambridge: Harvard University Press): vol. 1, *Non-literary Papyri: Private Affairs* (1932), vol. 2, *Non-literary Papyri: Public Documents* (1934); H. G. Meecham, *Light from Ancient Letters: Private Correspondence in the Non-literary Papyri of Oxyrhynchus of the First Four Centuries and Its Bearing on New Testament Language and Thought* (New York: Macmillan, 1923); G. Milligan, *Here and There among the Papyri* (London: Hodder & Stoughton, 1923); idem, *Selections from the Greek Papyri* (Cambridge: Cambridge University Press, 1912); J. H. Moulton, *From Egyptian Rubbish Heaps* (London: Charles H. Kelly, 1916); P. J. Parsons and J. R. Rea, eds., *Papyri: Greek and Egyptian* (E. G. Turner FS; Graeco-Roman Memoirs 68; London: British Academy and Egypt Exploration Society, 1981); S. K. Stowers, *Letter Writing in Greco-Roman Antiquity* (LEC; Philadelphia: Westminster, 1986); J. L. White, *Light from Ancient Letters* (FF; Philadelphia: Fortress Press, 1986) (highlights important parallels with NT letters).

Certain sites in Egypt, such as Antinoopolis, Hibeh, Oxyrhynchus, and Tebtunis, have yielded large and important quantities of papyri, including papyri of the Greek NT and the LXX. Many of these documents have been published, but many have not. The bibliography below provides a selection of publications. For an introduction to Greek papyri, see F. G. Kenyon, *The Paleography of Greek Papyri* (Oxford: Clarendon, 1899; repr., Chicago: Ares, 1998); E. G. Turner, *Greek Papyri, an Introduction* (2d ed.; Oxford: Oxford University Press, 1980). For checklists, see R. A. Coles, *Location-List of the Oxyrhynchus Papyri and of Other Greek Papyri Published by the Egypt Exploration Society* (Graeco-Roman Memoirs 59; London: Egypt Exploration Society, 1974); J. F. Oates et al., *Checklist of Editions of Greek, Latin, Demotic and Coptic Papyri, Ostraca, and tablets* (5th ed.; BASPSup 9; [Oakville, Conn.]: American Society of Papyrologists, 2001); C. H. Roberts and E. G. Turner, eds., *Catalogue of the Greek Papyri in the John Rylands Library Manchester* (4 vols.; Manchester, Eng.: Manchester University Press, 1911–1952).

Bibliography: For *Antinoopolis,* see C. H. ROBERTS et al., eds., *The Antinoopolis Papyri* (3 vols.; Graeco-Roman Memoirs 28, 37, 47; London: Egypt Exploration Society, 1950–1967) (P.Ant. 7–214). For *Hibeh,* see B. P. GRENFELL et al., eds., *The Hibeh Papyri* (2 vols., Graeco-Roman Memoirs 7, 32; London: Egypt Exploration Society, 1906–1955) (vol. 1, P.Hib. 1–171; vol. 2, 172–284). For *Oxyrhynchus,* see B. P. GRENFELL et al., eds., *The Oxyrhynchus Papyri* (London: Egypt Exploration Fund, 1898–) (P.Oxy. 1–; it is estimated that only one-half of the papyri found at Oxyrhynchus have been published to date). For *Tebtunis,* see B. P. GRENFELL et al., eds., *The Tebtunis Papyri* (4 vols.; University of California Publications: Graeco-Roman Archaeology 1–4; Graeco-Roman Memoirs 4, 25, 32, 52, 64; vols. 1–2, London: H. Frowde; vol. 3, parts 1–2, New York: Oxford University Press; vol. 4, London: British Academy and the Egypt Exploration Society, 1902–1976) (vol. 1, P.Tebt. 1–264; vol. 2, 265–689; vol. 3, part 1, 690–825; vol. 3, part 2, 826–1093; vol. 4, 1094–1150); W. J. TAIT, ed., *Papyri from Tebtunis in Egyptian and in Greek (P.Tebt.)* (Texts from Excavations 3; London: Egypt Exploration Society, 1977). For an important series devoted to Zenon, see C. C. EDGAR, *Zenon papyri* (5 vols.; Catalogue général des antiquités égyptiennes du Musée du Caire 79, 82, 85, 90; Cairo: L'Institut Française d'Archéologie Orientale, 1925–1931) (P.Cair.Zen. 59001–59800); IDEM, "Selected Papyri from the Archives of Zenon," *Annales du Service des antiquités* 18 (1918): 159–82, 225–44 (P.Edg. 1–20); 19 (1919–1920): 13–36, 81–104 (22–48); 20 (1920): 19–40, 181–206 (49–64); 21 (1921): 89–109 (65–66); 22 (1922): 209–31 (67–72); 23 (1923): 73–98, 187–209 (73–88); 24 (1924): 17–52 (89–111).

Jewish papyri outside Israel (i.e., the region of the Dead Sea) have also been collected. Aramaic Jewish papyri have been recovered from ancient Elephantine (modern Aswan), Egypt. Greek Jewish papyri have been recovered from various locations in Egypt (see Tcherikover and Fuks).

The Aramaic papyri mention several Persian kings, ranging from Cambyses (530–522 B.C.E.) to Amyrtaeus (ca. 405–399 B.C.E.), including the famous Artaxerxes II (404–358 B.C.E.), who survived the revolt of his brother and his ten thousand Greek mercenaries (immortalized in Xenophon's *Anabasis*). The bulk of the datable correspondence falls between 494 and 400 B.C.E., overlapping with the time of Ezra the priest. Although it has been suggested that this correspondence derives from Samaritans, most today think it is Jewish, as seen to references to the *Yehudia* ("the Jews") and *Chila Yehudia* ("the Jewish force"). The Jewish colony in Elephantine may have originated as an encampment of Jewish mercenaries (as in *Let. Aris.* 13). The (principal) Jewish God is called Yahu, probably a derivation of the Tetragrammaton (YHWH). There are references to swearing "by the God Yahu" (e.g., no. 6), though other gods are also mentioned. One letter orders a Jewish garrison to keep the Passover and the Feast of Unleavened Bread: "To my brothers, Yedoniah and his colleagues the Jewish garrison, your brother Hananiah. May the gods seek the welfare of my brothers. Now this year, the 5th year of King Darius [419 B.C.E.), word was sent from the king to Arsames, saying: 'In the month of Tybi let there be a Passover for the Jewish garrison . . . Be clean and take heed. Do no work on the 15th day and on the 21st day. Also drink no beer, and anything at all in which there is leaven" (no. 21; cf. Cowley 1923, 63). Another, lengthy letter, probably the most important in the collection, written in the seventeenth year of Darius II (408 B.C.E.), petitions the governor of Judea to take action against certain Egyptians and one Waidrang, a Persian governor, who destroyed the Jewish temple at Yeb. Yedoniah, probably the leading priest, writes,

To our lord Bigvai, governor of Judea, your servants Yedoniah and his colleagues, the priests who are in Yeb the fortress. May the God of heaven seek after the health of your lordship exceedingly at all times and give you favor before Darius the king and the princes of the palace more than now a thousand times, and may he grant you long life, and may you be happy and prosperous at all times. Now your servant Yedoniah and his colleagues depose as follows: In the month of Tammuz in the 14th year of Darius the king, when Arsames departed and went to the king, the priests of the god Khnub, who is in the fortress of Yeb, were in league with Waidrang, who was governor there, saying, "Let them remove from there the Temple of Yahu the God, which is in the fortress of Yeb." Then that Waidrang, the reprobate, sent a letter to his son Nephayan, who was commander of the garrison in the fortress of Syene, saying, "Let them destroy the temple that is in Yeb the fortress." Then Nephayan led out the Egyptians with the other forces. They came to the fortress of Yeb with their weapons, they entered that temple, they destroyed it to the ground, and the pillars of stone which were there they broke. . . . When this was done, we with our wives and our children put on sack-cloth and fasted and prayed to Yahu the Lord of Heaven . . . till this day we wear sack-cloth and fast. Our wives are made widow-like, we do not anoint ourselves with oil and we drink no wine. . . . If it seem good to your lordship, take thought for that temple to build it, since they do not allow us to build it. (no. 30; cf. Cowley 1923, 113–14 [adapted])

Bibliography: A. E. COWLEY, *Jewish Documents of the Time of Ezra Translated from the Aramaic* (TED I: Palestinian Jewish Texts 1; London: SPCK, 1919) (popular presentation); IDEM, ed., *Aramaic Papyri of the Fifth Century B.C.* (Oxford: Clarendon, 1923) (Elephantine papyri); G. R. DRIVER, *Aramaic Documents of the Fifth Century B.C.* (Oxford: Clarendon, 1957) (exegesis of several texts); E. G. KRAELING, ed., *The Brooklyn Museum Aramaic Papyri: New Documents of the Fifth Century B.C. from the Jewish Colony at Elephantine* (Publications of the Department of Egyptian Art; New Haven: Yale University Press, 1953); B. PORTEN et al., *The Elephantine Papyri in English: Three Millennia of Cross-Cultural Continuity and Change* (DMOA 22; Leiden: Brill, 1996); A. H. SAYCE and A. E. COWLEY, eds., *Aramaic Papyri Discovered at Assuan* (London: A. Moring, 1906); V. A. TCHERIKOVER and A. FUKS, eds., *Corpus papyrorum judaicarum* (2 vols.; Cambridge: Harvard University Press, 1957–1960); J. C. VANDERKAM, *An Introduction to Early Judaism* (Grand Rapids: Eerdmans, 2001), 147–50 (comments on the significance of the Jewish Elephantine papyri).

Greek Magical Papyri. The Greek Magical Papyri, mostly dating from the NT period and later, contain a variety of formulas, oaths, spells, charms, and religious concepts. Some of these interesting traditions may be of some use in NT research. This corpus of material is usually abbreviated *PGM* (*Papyri graecae magicae*).

Some of the exorcistic papyri make use of Jewish and Christian material, invoking the names of Solomon, Jesus, and others and providing instructions for attempting the exorcism. As a prophylactic, a magical papyrus could be worn around the neck as an amulet. Here is an interesting example:

A tested charm of Pibechis for those possessed by demons: Take oil of unripe olives with the herb mastigia and the fruit pulp of the lotus, and boil them with colorless marjoram while saying, " . . . come out from—(add the victim's name)." . . . This is the conjuration: "I conjure you by the god of the Hebrews, Jesus . . . who appears in fire, who is in the midst of land, snow, and fog . . . let your angel, the implacable, descend and let him assign the demon flying around this form, which god formed in his holy paradise, because I pray to the holy god . . . I conjure you by the one who appeared to Osrael in a shining pillar and a cloud by day, who saved his people from the Pharaoh and brought upon Pharaoh the ten plagues because of his disobedience. I conjure you by the seal that Solomon placed on the tongue of Jeremiah . . . I conjure you by the great god Sabaoth, through whom the Jordan River drew back and the Red Sea, which Israel crossed, became impassable . . ." (*PGM* IV. 3007–56; trans. W. C. Grese [adapted], in Betz 1996, 96–97; see commentary in Deissmann, 256–64; Sperber)

Bibliography: For Greek texts, see A. DEISSMANN, *Light from the Ancient East* (New York: George H. Doran, 1927; repr., Peabody, Mass.: Hendrickson, 1995) [not limited to magical papyri; shows relevance to the NT]; F. L. GRIFFITH and H. THOMPSON, *The Leyden Papyrus: An Egyptian Magical Book* (3 vols.; London: Grevel, 1904; repr., New York: Dover, 1974) [also contains translation and commentary]; R. D. KOTANSKY, *Greek Magical Amulets: The Inscribed Gold, Silver, Copper, and Bronze "Lemellai": Text and Commentary* (Abhandlungen der Nordhein-Westfällischen Akademie der Wissenschaften: Sonderreihe Papyrologica coloniensia 22; Opladen: Westdeutscher Verlag, 1994); K. PREISENDANZ, *PGM*. For an introduction and English translation of the papyri, see H. D. BETZ, ed., *The Greek Magical Papyri in Translation, Including the Demotic Spells* (2d ed.; Chicago: University of Chicago Press, 1996–) [brief notes; comparison is made with the NT; very helpful bibliography]; W. M. BRASHEAR, "The Greek Magical Papyri—an Introduction and Survey: Annotated Bibliography (1928–1994)," *ANRW* 18.5:3380–3684. For additional sources, see C. BONNER, *Studies in Magical Amulets Chiefly Graeco-Egyptian* (Ann Arbor: University of Michigan Press, 1950); O. KERN, ed., *Orphicorum fragmenta* (2d ed.; Dublin: Weidmann, 1972); E. A. W. BUDGE, *Amulets and Talismans* (New York: Dover, 1978). For recent critical studies, see H. D. BETZ, "Magic and Mystery in the Greek Magical Papyri," in *Magika hiera: Ancient Greek Magic and Religion* (ed. C. A. Faraone and D. Obbink; New York: Oxford University Press, 1991), 244–59; IDEM, "Secrecy in the Greek Magical Papyri," in *Secrecy and Concealment: Studies in the History of Mediterranean and Near Eastern Religions* (ed. H. G. Kippenberg and G. G. Stroumsa; SHR 64; Leiden: Brill, 1995), 153–75; L. J. CIRAOLO, "Supernatural Assistants in the Greek Magical Papyri," in *Ancient Magic and Ritual Power* (ed. M. Meyer and P. Mirecki; Religions in the Graeco-Roman World 129; Leiden: Brill, 1995), 279–95; R. D. KOTANSKY, "Greek Exorcistic Amulets," in *Ancient Magic and Ritual Power* (ed. M. Meyer and P. Mirecki; Religions in the Graeco-Roman World 129; Leiden: Brill, 1995), 243–77; D. SPERBER, "Some Rabbinic Themes in Magical Papyri," *JSJ* 16 (1985): 95–99 (treats *PGM* IV. 3040–60).

Inscriptions

Greco-Roman Regal Inscriptions. The Greek kings and despots and the later Roman emperors are routinely described as "gods" and "sons of god" in the inscriptions. Most inscriptions, like coin legends, are public. They convey political propaganda as well as regulations, policies, and decrees pertaining to holidays and celebrations. References to the rulers as gods constitute more than mere flattery; they are meant to underscore the legitimacy of absolute rule.

Most of the following quotations are from inscriptions, but parallels from a few papyri are also cited. The parallels to the language and titulature of NT Christology are obvious. The collections of Dittenberger and Bureth are indispensable.

Ptolemy V Epiphanes (210–180 B.C.E.): "Inasmuch as King Ptolemy, the everliving . . . being a god born of a god and a goddess—even like Horus, the son of Isis and Osiris . . ." (Rosetta Stone, Greek text [= *OGIS* no. 90], lines 9–10 [196 B.C.E.]).

Antiochus IV Epiphanes (175–164 B.C.E.): "From King Antiochus, god, savior of Asia and founder of the city . . . to king Antiochus, God Epiphanes" (*OGIS* no. 253; *SEG* XX no. 324a).

Ptolemy XIII (80–51 B.C.E.): "the Lord king God, a new Dionysius" (*OGIS* no. 186).

Ptolemy XIV (59–44 B.C.E.) and *Cleopatra VII* (69–30 B.C.E.): "to the lords, the greatest of the gods" (Deissmann, 352).

Julius Caesar (48–44 B.C.E.): "The manifest god from Mars and Aphrodite, and universal savior of human life" (*SIG* no. 760); "The Carthaean people honor the god and emperor and savior of the inhabited world Gaius Julius Caesar son of Gaius Caesar" (*IG* no. 12.5, 556–57).

Augustus (31 B.C.E.–14 C.E.): "Emperor Caesar Augustus, son of god" (*SB* no. 401; BGU no. 628); "Emperor Caesar, god from god" (*SB* no. 8895; *OGIS* no. 655; P.Oxy. 1453).

Tiberius (14–37 C.E.): "Emperor Tiberius Caesar Augustus, son of god" (*SB* no. 8317); "Emperor Tiberius Caesar, new Augustus, son of Zeus the liberator" (P.Oxy. 240); "Tiberius Caesar, a new Augustus, emperor, son of the god Augustus" (*SB* no. 7174; P.Mich. 233; cf. *SB* nos. 8329 and 8330).

Caligula (37–41 C.E.): The people of Halasarna erect an altar in honor of Gaius Caligula as to a "new god" (*IGR* no. 4.1094); "Son of Augustus, a new Ares" (*CIA* no. 3.444); "Gaius Caesar Germanicus, a new Augustus, emperor" (P.Oxy. 267).

Claudius (41–54 C.E.): "Tiberius Claudius lord" (*SB* no. 4331; cf. P.Oxy. 37); "Claudius god" (*PSI* no. 1235; P.Oxy. 713; *SB* nos. 8245 and 8444); "God Claudius Caesar Augustus Germanicus, emperor" (*OGIS* no. 668).

Nero (54–68 C.E.): "Nero the lord" (O.Berl. no. 25); "Nero Caesar the lord" (*SB* no. 9604; P.Oxy. 246); "Nero Claudius Caesar . . . the savior and benefactor of the inhabited world" (*OGIS* no. 668); "The good god of the inhabited world, the beginning of all good things" (P.Oxy. 1021); "good god" (*OGIS* no. 666).

Vespasian (69–79 C.E.): "Vespasian the lord" (P.Oxy. 1439; *SB* no. 1927); "Emperor Vespasian the lord" (*SB* no. 4586); "Vespasian god" (P.Oxy. 257, 1112, 1266, 1452, and 2186; P.Oxy. 1112); "Divine Vespasian" (*Divus Vespasianus*) (P.Mich. 432).

Titus (79–81 C.E.): "Titus the lord" (P.Fay. 67; O.Theb. no. 45; *SB* no. 1016); "Titus Caesar the lord" (*SB* no. 9604; O.Theb. no. 46); "God Titus" (BGU no. 5; *SB* no. 7193; P.Oxy. 369 and 1028; P.Tebt. 298).

Domitian (81–96 C.E.): "Domitian the lord" (P.Oxy. 1028; P.Lond. 1265; *SB* no. 2084); "Domitian Caesar the lord" (O.Bodl. no. 675; P.Flor. 86); "Emperor Domitian the lord" (O.Bodl. no. 985; *SB* no. 4592); "God Domitian" (P.Oxy. 2186).

Bibliography: P. BURETH, *Les titulatures impériales dans les papyrus, les ostraca, et les inscriptions d'Égypte (30 a.C.–284 p.C.)* (Brussels: Fondation Égyptologique Reine Élisabeth, 1964); A. DEISSMANN, *Light from the Ancient East* (New York: George H. Doran, 1927; repr., Peabody, Mass.: Hendrickson, 1995); W. DITTENBERGER, ed., *Orientis Graeci Inscriptiones Selectae: Supplementum Sylloges Inscriptionum Graecarum* (3d ed.; 2 vols.; Leipzig: S. Hirzel, 1903–1905; repr., Hildesheim: Olms, 1960, 1970, 1986).

The Gospel and the Roman Imperial Cult. The Priene/Apamea Calendar Inscription in honor of Augustus provides a very important parallel to Mark 1:1 ("The beginning [*archē*] of the good news [*euangelion*] of Jesus Christ, the Son of God [*theos*]"), clarifying the significance that Christian proclamation would have had for inhabitants of the Roman Empire. The Priene Inscription is restored in places by parallels in similar inscriptions found in Apamea, Eumeneia, Dorylaeum. The inscription records the letter of the proconsul Paulus Fabius Maximus and the decrees of the province of Asia. Its dates to 9 B.C.E. What follows is taken from the proem of the second part of the document:

> It seemed good to the Greeks of Asia, in the opinion of the high priest Apollonius of Menophilus Azanitus: "Since Providence, which has ordered all things and is deeply interested in our life, has set in most perfect order by giving us Augustus, whom she filled with virtue that he might benefit humankind, sending him as a savior [*sōtēr*], both for us and for our descendants, that he might end war and arrange all things, and since he, Caesar, by his appearance [*epiphanein*] (excelled even our anticipations), surpassing all previous benefactors, and not even leaving to posterity any hope of surpassing what he has done, and since the birthday of the god [*theos*] Augustus was the beginning [*archein*] of the good news [*euangelia*] for the world that came by reason of him," which Asia resolved in Smyrna. (*OGIS* 458 = *SEG* IV no. 490)

The imperial cult, which promises good news for the world through the advent of Caesar, son of God, is also echoed in a papyrus reference to Nero cited above: "The good god of the inhabited world, the beginning of all good things" (P.Oxy. 1021). Christian claims that Jesus of Nazareth is the true "Son of God," "Savior," "Lord," and "beginning of the good news" flew in the face of the imperial doctrine and would have been viewed as a direct challenge to the legitimacy of the emperors.

Jews and the earliest Christians knew full well the implications of this language. When word spread of Vespasian's accession to the throne, "every city celebrated the good news [*euangelia*] and offered sacrifices on his behalf" (Josephus, *J.W.* 4.10.6 §618). Josephus later relates, "On reaching Alexandria Vespasian was greeted by the good news [*euangelia*] from Rome and by embassies of congratulation from every quarter of the world, now his own. . . . The whole empire being now secured and the Roman state saved [*sōzein*] beyond expectation, Vespasian turned his thoughts to what remained in Judaea" (*J.W.* 4.11.5 §656–657).

Bibliography: W. DITTENBERGER, ed., *Orientis graecae inscriptiones selectae: Supplementum sylloges inscriptionum graecarum* (2 vols.; Leipzig: S. Hirzel, 1903–1905; repr., Hildesheim: Olms, 1960), 2:48–60 (= *OGIS* no. 458); V. EHRENBERG and A. H. M. JONES, *Documents Illustrating the Reigns of Augustus and Tiberius* (2d ed.; Oxford: Clarendon, 1955), 81–83 (no. 98); J. SCHNIEWIND, *Euangelion: Ursprung und erste Gestalt des Begriffs Evangelium* (2 vols.; BFCT 2 .25; Gütersloh: Bertelsmann, 1927–1931); L. R. TAYLOR, *The Divinity of the Roman Emperor* (APAMS 1; New York: Arno, 1931; repr., Chico, Calif.: Scholars Press, 1975), 273.

Proconsul Gallio and the Apostle Paul. At the time Paul visited Corinth, we are told, "Gallio was proconsul of Achaia" (Acts 18:12). Although some difficulties remain, this reference and the discovery of a fragmentary inscription at Delphi, in Greece, have greatly assisted scholars in establishing Pauline chronology. Part of this inscription reads (*SIG* no. 801),

> [1]Tiberius Claudius Caesar Augustus Germanicus, Pontifex Maximus, of tribunician authority [2]for the twelfth time, imperator for the twenty-sixth time, father of his country, consul for the fifth time, censor, greetings to the city of the Delphians. [3]Long ago I was eager for the city of the Delphians . . . and benevolent from the beginning, [4]but I have observed the worship of Apollo of the Python . . . but as much as [5]it is now said those citizens's rivalries . . . just as Lucius Junius [6]Gallio, my friend, and the proconsul of Achaia wrote . . .

On the basis of the reference to the "twelfth time" that the "tribunician authority" of Claudius has been recognized, the year of the inscription is put at or shortly after 52 C.E., suggesting that Gallio served from 50 to 51, overlapping with Paul's stay in Corinth (see Murphy-O'Connor).

Bibliography: C. J. HEMER, "Observations on Pauline Chronology," in *Pauline Studies* (ed. D. A. Hagner and M. Harris; F. F. Bruce FS; Grand Rapids: Eerdmans, 1980), 3–18, esp. 6–9; J. MURPHY-O'CONNOR, "Paul and Gallio," *JBL* 112 (1993): 315–17; A. PLASSART, "Lettre de l'empereur Claude au gouverneur d'Achaie (en 52)," in *Les inscriptions du temple du iv siècle* (École française d'Athènes: Fouilles de Delphes 3/4; Paris: Boccard, 1970), 26–33 (no. 286); D. SLINGERLAND, "Acts 18:1–18, the Gallio Inscription, and Absolute Pauline Chronology," *JBL* 110 (1991): 439–49.

Greco-Roman Miracle Inscriptions. Another interesting genre of inscriptions is the accounts of miracles, usually healing. Just as Delphi was famous for its oracles (many of which are inscribed), so Epidaurus was famous for its miracles. Many of the healings, some of which are quite strange, are inscribed. The principal god of healing is Asklepios. On Stele A, one inscription reads (no. A1),

> Kleo was pregnant for five years. After the fifth year of pregnancy, she came as a suppliant to the god (Asklepios) and slept in the Abaton. As soon as she had left it and was outside the sacred area, she gave birth to a son who, as soon as he was born, washed himself at the fountain and walked about with his mother. After this success, she inscribed upon an offering . . .

Here is another (A5):

> A mute boy. He came to the sanctuary for a voice. He performed the opening sacrifices and did the required things; and then the boy who carries fire for the god, looking over at the boy's father, bid him to promise to sacrifice within a year, if what he came for occurred. Suddenly the boy said, "I promise." The father was amazed and told him to repeat it. The boy spoke again and from this he became well.

Bibliography: L. EDELSTEIN and E. EDELSTEIN, *Asclepius: A Collection and Interpretation of the Testimonies* (2 vols.; Baltimore: Johns Hopkins University Press, 1945); L. R. LIDONNICI,

The Epidaurian Miracle Inscriptions: Text, Translation, and Commentary (SBLTT 36; GRR 11; Atlanta: Scholars Press, 1995).

Greco-Roman Burial Inscriptions. According to Hesychius (cf. Lattimore, 21 n. 1), death is the "separation of the soul from the body." Similarly, Iamblichus opines that the soul "goes forth from the body, and upon going forth is separated and scattered" (*apud* Stobaeus, *Ecl.* 1). Some likened the body to a house in which the soul is imprisoned (e.g., Plato, *Cratylus* 400c; *Phaedo* 81d; cf. Toynbee, 33–39). In keeping with these ideas, many people in late antiquity hoped for or assumed some sort of life beyond the grave, though on what form it may take there was much doubt. We see this concept expressed in the following epitaphs:

EG 21b (= Thucydides 1.63; cf. Lattimore, 31):

Air has taken their souls, but earth their bodies.

IG 9.2.641.6 (cf. Lattimore, 32):

The soul given to the air, the body concealed in dust.

EG 288.2–3 (cf. Lattimore, 32):

Earth hides your body,
taking back the gift that she gave long ago.

EG 90 (cf. Lattimore, 33):

Earth keeps the bones and flesh of the dear child,
but his soul has gone to the house of the blessed.

IG 12.7123.5–6 (cf. Lattimore, 35):

Mother, do not weep for me. What is the use? Instead, revere me.
For I have become an evening star, among the gods.

Bibliography: R. A. LATTIMORE, *Themes in Greek and Latin Epitaphs* (Illinois Studies in Language and Literature 28/1–2; Urbana: University of Illinois Press, 1942; repr., 1962); P. SHORE, *Rest Lightly: An Anthology of Latin and Greek Tomb Inscriptions* (Wauconda, Ill.: Bolchazy-Carducci, 1997); J. M. C. TOYNBEE, *Death and Burial in the Roman World* (Aspects of Greek and Roman Life; Ithaca, N.Y.: Cornell University Press, 1971). For introductions to Latin epigraphy, see A. E. GORDON, *Illustrated Introduction to Latin Epigraphy* (Berkeley: University of California Press, 1983); L. J. F. KEPPIE, *Understanding Roman Inscriptions* (Baltimore: Johns Hopkins University Press, 1991); J. E. SANDYS, *Latin Epigraphy: An Introduction to the Study of Latin Inscriptions* (rev. S. G. Campbell; 2d ed.; Cambridge: Cambridge University Press, 1927); M. N. TOD, *Sidelights on Greek History: Three Lectures on the Light Thrown by Greek Inscriptions on the Life and Thought of the Ancient World* (Oxford: Blackwell, 1932) (with interesting observations on how inscriptions augment literary sources).

Jewish Inscriptions. Several inscriptions, many of them Jewish, have a direct bearing on the NT and the world of early Christianity. They are listed here in the order of their discovery. For a treatment of most of these inscriptions and others, with full bibliography, see L. Boffo, *Iscrizioni greche e latine per lo studio della Bibbia* (Brescia: Paideia, 1994), 47–60 (Samaritan inscriptions at Delos), 104–12 (an inscription dedicated by Antiochus IV Epiphanes), 217–33 (a Pontius Pilate inscription), 247–56 (a Delphi inscription with the name of the proconsul Gallio), 302–10 (a Flavius Silva inscription), 311–14 (the arch of Titus), 315–18 (a Jerusalem inscription that mentions Legion X Fretensis), 319–33 (an imperial edict against the violation of sepulchers), 338–42 (a dedication of Queen Berenice and of King Agrippa II), 343–48 (a Jerusalem inscription with the name of Nicanor), 349–52 (an inscription of the aedile of Corinth).

The Jewish Temple Warning Inscription (1871). In 1871 Charles Clermont-Ganneau found a limestone block (ca. 85 cm in length, ca. 57 cm in height, and ca. 37 cm thick), on which was inscribed a warning to Gentiles to stay out of the perimeter surrounding the sanctuary. A fragment of a second inscription was found in 1935 outside the wall around Jerusalem's Old City. The inscription reads (*OGIS* no. 598; *CII* no. 1400; *SEG* VIII no. 169),

> Let no Gentile enter
> within the partition and barrier
> surrounding the temple; whosoever
>   is caught shall be responsible
>   for his subsequent
> death.

This inscription is almost certainly one of the inscribed warnings mentioned by Josephus. For example, he states, "Upon [the partition wall of the temple court] stood pillars, at equal distances from one another, declaring the law of purity, some in Greek, and some in Roman letters, that 'no foreigner should go within that holy place'" (*J.W.* 5.5.2 §§ 193–194; cf. 6.2.4 §§ 124–128; *Ant.* 15.2.5 §417; *Ag. Ap.* 2.8 §103).

The temple's warning inscriptions may clarify various NT passages—for example, Mark 11:15–18, where appeal is made to Isa 56:7, evidently as an encouragement of a Gentile presence in the temple precincts; Acts 21:27–36, especially verse 28, where the accusation is leveled against Paul that "he has actually brought Greeks into the temple and has defiled this holy place"; and Eph 2:14–15, whose author declares that Jesus "has broken down the dividing wall, that is, the hostility between us. He has abolished the law with its commandments and ordinances."

Bibliography: E. J. BICKERMAN, "The Warning Inscriptions of Herod's Temple," *JQR* 37 (1946–1947): 387–405; C. S. CLERMONT-GANNEAU, "Une stèle du temple de Jérusalem," *RAr* 28 (1872): 214–34, 290–96 and pl. X; J. H. ILIFFE, "The θανατος Inscription from Herod's Temple: Fragment of a Second Copy," *QDAP* 6 (1936): 1–3 and pls. I-II.

Caesar's Edict against Grave Robbery Inscription (1878). In 1878 a marble slab, 61 cm high, 38 cm wide, and 8 cm thick, on which was inscribed an imperial edict forbidding robbing and vandalizing graves, came to light. It is believed that the stone came from Nazareth (though the provenance of this discovery has not been confirmed; it may well have come from one of the cities of the Decapolis). In 1925 it was sent to the Paris Bibliothèque nationale and was published in 1930 by Franz Cumont. The text reads (*SEG* VIII no. 13),

> 1Ordinance of Caesar: 2It is my pleasure that graves and tombs—3whoever has made them as a pious service for ancestors 4or children or members of their house—5that these remain unmolested 6in perpetuity. But if any person lay information that 7another either has destroyed them, or has in any other 8way cast out the bodies 9which have been buried there, or 10with malicious deception has 11transferred them to other places, to the dishonor of those 12buried there, or has removed the headstones or other 13stones, in such a case 14I command that a trial 15be instituted, just as if they were concerned with the gods 16for the pious services of mortals. 17For beyond all else it shall be obligatory 18to honor those who have been buried. 19Let no one remove them for any reason. 20If not, however (i.e., if anyone does so), 21capital punishment on the charge of 22tomb robbery I will to take place. (Metzger, 77 [adapted])

Most interesting is the warning in lines 10 and 11 not to transfer bodies from one grave to another. This part of the ordinance is especially relevant to the Gospels' stories about the visit of the women to the tomb and, especially, the story in Matthew about Pilate sealing the tomb and the claim that the disciples stole the body of Jesus (Matt 27:62–66; 28:11–15).

Bibliography: F. E. BROWN, "Violation of Sepulture in Palestine," *AJP* 52 (1931): 1–29; S. A. COOK, "A Nazareth Inscription on the Violation of Tombs," *PEFQS* (1932): 85–87; F. CUMONT, "Les ossuaires juifs et le Διάταγμα Καίσαρος," *Syria* 14 (1933): 223–24; IDEM, "Un rescrit impérial sur la violation de sépulture," *RH* 163 (1930): 241–66; P. W. VAN DER HORST, *Ancient Jewish Epitaphs: An Introductory Survey of a Millennium of Jewish Funerary Epigraphy (300 B.C.E.–700 CE)* (Kampen, Neth.: Kok Pharos, 1991), 159–60; B. M. METZGER, "The Nazareth Inscription Once Again," in *New Testament Studies: Philological, Versional, and Patristic* (NTTS 10; Leiden: Brill), 75–92; F. DE ZULUETA, "Violation of Sepulture in Palestine at the Beginning of the Christian Era," *JRS* 22 (1932): 184–97.

Theodotos Synagogue Inscription (1913). During excavations in and around Mount Ophel, or the "City of David," in 1913 Raimund Weill discovered a stone slab (75 cm by 41 cm), which probably had served as a foundation stone, bearing what is now usually called the Theodotos Inscription. The stone is now housed in the Rockefeller Archaeological Museum in East Jerusalem. This Greek inscription may provide evidence of the existence of buildings prior to 70 C.E. specifically designated as "synagogues." The inscription moreover attests the rank of "synagogue ruler" (*archisynagōgos*). The inscription reads (cf. *CII* no. 1404),

> Theodotos, (son) of Vettenus, priest and synagogue ruler, son of a synagogue ruler, (and) grandson of a synagogue ruler, built the synagogue for the reading of the law and the teaching of the commandments, and the guest room, and the chambers,

and the water fixtures, as an inn for those in need from foreign parts, (the synagogue) which his fathers and the elders and Simonides founded.

Bibliography: J. S. KLOPPENBORG VERBIN, "Dating Theodotos (*CII* 1404)," *JJS* 51 (2000): 243–80; R. RIESNER, "Synagogues in Jerusalem," in *The Book of Acts in Its Palestinian Setting* (ed. R. Baukham; vol. 4 of *The Book of Acts in Its First Century Setting;* Grand Rapids: Eerdmans, 1995), 179–211, esp. 192–200.

The Pilate Inscription (1961). During excavations in and around the theater at Caesarea Maritima, a stone was unearthed bearing an inscription that referred to Pontius Pilate:

[   ]S TIBERIÉVM
[PON]TIVS PILATVS
[PRAEF]ECTVS IVDA[EA]E
[   ]É[ ]

Restoration of the second and third lines is not difficult. Most believe that the fourth line contained the word *dédit* ("has given") or *refécit* ("has restored"). The missing word in the first line has been more contentious. Recently it has been suggested that it may have read *nautis* ("seamen"). If so, the inscription originally read, "The Seamen's Tiberieum Pontius Pilate, prefect of Judea, has restored" (so Alföldy). In any case, the inscription settles the question of Pilate's rank (i.e., either procurator or prefect; He was a prefect.), and it may also suggest that one of the governor's principal occupations was the restoration of Herod's harbor at Caesarea Maritima.

Bibliography: G. ALFÖLDY, "Pontius Pilatus und das Tiberieum von Caesarea Maritima," *SCI* 18 (1999): 85–108; A. FROVA, "L'iscrizione di Ponzio Pilato a Cesarea," *RenIL* 95 (1961): 419–34 (the first to publish the inscription); E. J. VARDAMAN, "A New Inscription Which Mentions Pilate as 'Prefect,'" *JBL* 81 (1962): 70–71.

Burial Inscriptions. Numerous Jewish inscriptions on ossuaries and on walls of tombs have been found. Ossuaries are small bone chests used in the Jewish practice of secondary burial, wherein, one year after primary burial, the bones of the deceased are collected and placed in an ossuary. Jewish burial inscriptions on ossuaries, sarcophagi, and the walls of tombs provide us with a wealth of information, touching questions of language, religious customs and beliefs, social status, rank, and occupation. The inscriptions also provide us with an important sampling of names that were used in late antiquity. On this, see T. Ilan, *Palestine, 330 B.C.E.–200 C.E.* (vol. 1 of *Lexicon of Jewish Names in Late Antiquity;* TSAJ 91; Tübingen: Mohr Siebeck, 2002). L. Y. Rahmani has produced the most important reference work on ossuaries. Bagatti and Milik have given us an important work on the ossuaries and inscriptions at Dominus Flevit (on the Mount of Olives), and Avigad, Lifshitz, Mazar, and Schwabe have given us three volumes of work relating to the inscriptions found at Beth She'arim in Galilee. These works and others are cited in the bibliography below. Some of the most interesting ossuary inscriptions follow.

Temple builders. Two ossuaries are of particular interest in that they refer to building the temple of Jerusalem. A third mentions contributing to the building of a synagogue. In 1902 a crypt consisting of four separate chambers was discovered on the Mount of Olives. In these chambers were seven ossuaries, on the end of one of which were inscribed three lines of Greek and one line of Hebrew/Aramaic. The inscription seems to read (*CII* no. 1256),

> Bones of the [sons] of Nicanor of Alexandria, who built the doors—Nicanor the Alexa(ndrian)

It is also possible that the inscription reads:

> Bone receptacle of Nicanor of Alexandria, who built the doors—Nicanor the Alexa(ndrian)

In any case, this Nicanor of Alexandria may be the person who built the "Nicanor Gate," mentioned in the Talmud: "There were seven gates in the temple court, three to the north, three to the south, and one to the east. . . . . To the east the Nicanor Gate" (*b. Yoma* 19a). Commentators have also wondered if the "Beautiful Gate" mentioned in Acts (cf. 3:2, 10) is in fact the Nicanor Gate.

Another interesting ossuary inscription reads (Rahmani no. 200),

> Simon, builder of the temple
> Simon,
> builder of the temple

The first line is Hebrew; the third line is Aramaic. Although it has been suggested that "builder of the temple" be taken in a metaphorical sense (i.e., in that Simon was a priest or religious teacher; cf. the way Paul speaks of "building" the church in Rom 15:20 and 1 Cor 3:10), it is probably better to take the words of the inscription literally. Simon, along with thousands of others, over a period of many years, was a "builder of the (Herodian) temple" (cf. John 2:20: "This temple has been under construction for forty-six years").

At Dabbura in the Golan, we have a bilingual inscription that acknowledges the contributions two men made to the building of the synagogue (Gregg and Urman, 126):

> Eleazar, son of Eliezer the Great, made the columns above
> the arches and beams. May he be blessed. Rusticus built (it).

Most of the inscription is in Hebrew; the last two words are Greek. There are other fragmentary Hebrew inscriptions at this location, reading, "They made the house of . . . May he be blessed," and, "Made the gate."

Simon of Cyrene? Among the ossuaries found by Eleazar Sukenik in the Kidron Valley in 1941, one bears what appear to be inscriptions referring to a certain Alexander the Cyrene, son of Simon. The inscription was published twenty years later. We find on the front and back sides of ossuary no. 9 clumsy attempts to inscribe in Greek, "Alexander (son) of Simon," and on the lid we find in Greek "(bones) of Alexander" and in Hebrew "Alexander (the) Cyrene." The inscription on the lid of the ossuary reads (Avigad, 9–11, no. 9 + pl. 4),

> of Alexander
> Alexander QRNYT

The first line is Greek; the second is Hebrew (or Aramaic). The word "QRNYT" is taken by most to refer to Cyrene (North Africa). If so, Alexander, the son of Simon, was known as the "Cyrene" (or Cyrenite). Given this constellation of agreements with the person mentioned in the NT Gospels (viz., his name is Alexander, his father is Simon, he died in Jerusalem, but he was from Cyrene), we may indeed have the ossuary of Alexander, son of Simon, the man mentioned in Mark's Gospel: "They compelled a passer-by, who was coming in from the country, to carry his cross; it was Simon of Cyrene, the father of Alexander and Rufus" (Mark 15:21; cf. Matt 27:32; Luke 23:26).

Corban. In Mark 7:9–13 Jesus makes critical reference to the Corban (*qorban*) tradition, whereby assets and property are consecrated, or "given," to God, and are therefore no longer available for profane or secular use. In some cases, Pharisaic application of this tradition could have negative consequences. As Jesus puts it, "But you say that if anyone tells father or mother, 'Whatever support you might have had from me is Corban' (that is, an offering to God)—then you no longer permit doing anything for a father or mother" (vv. 11–12).

The following inscription is very important:

> Everything that a man will find to his profit in this ossuary (is)
> an offering to God from the one within it.

Joseph Fitzmyer sees this inscription as a close parallel to Mark 7:11. The Corban inscription thus provides a valuable parallel to part of Jesus' teaching, which in this instance stands in tension with Pharisaic halakah.

House of David. In 1971 Amos Kloner excavated a burial cave at Giv'at Ha-Mivtar in which were found sixteen ossuaries. The inscription on ossuary M, in burial niche no. 6, reads (Rahmani no. 430),

> belonging to the house of David

This inscription seems to corroborate literary evidence that in the time of Jesus there were Jews who believed that they were indeed descendants of Israel's famous king. See, for example, *y. Ber.* 2.4 and Eusebius, who reports that various Roman emperors persecuted Davidic descendants in *Hist. eccl.* 3.12–13

("Vespasian . . . ordered a search to be made for all who were of the family of David"); 3.19–20 ("Domitian gave orders for the execution of those of the family of David. . . . He asked them if they were of the house of David and they admitted it"); 3.32.3–4 (certain heretics "accused Simon the son of Clopas of being descended from David . . . when Trajan was emperor"). See also *m. Ta'an.* 4.5 ("The wood-offering of the priests and the people was brought nine times . . . on the 20th of Tammuz by the family of David of the tribe of Judah").

High Priest Caiaphas? In November 1990, while working in Jerusalem's Peace Forest (North Talpiyot), which is a mile south of the Old City, a crew inadvertently uncovered a crypt with four loculi, in which twelve ossuaries were discovered. Happily, most of the ossuaries were found intact, unmolested by grave robbers. Coins and the style of writing seen in the inscriptions have dated these ossuaries to the first century C.E. On one of the ornate ossuaries (ossuary no. 6, measuring 74 cm long, 29 cm wide, and 38 cm high, now on display in the Israel National Museum in Jerusalem), two very interesting inscriptions were found. The inscriptions have been transcribed as follows (cf. Reich):

side of ossuary:	Yehoseph bar
	Qyph'
end of ossuary:	Yehoseph bar Qph'

This ossuary, containing the bones of a sixty-year-old man, two infants, a toddler, a young boy, and a woman, is thought by some (including the authorities of the Israel National Museum) to be the ossuary of Caiaphas the high priest, to whom Josephus refers as Joseph Caiaphas (cf. *Ant.* 18.2.2 §35, "Joseph Caiaphas"; and 18.4.3 §95, "the High Priest Joseph, called Caiaphas") and whom the Gospels and Acts call more simply Caiaphas (cf. Matt 26:3, 57; Luke 3:2; John 11:49; 18:13, 14, 24, 28; Acts 4:6). Those who think the ossuary belonged to Caiaphas vocalize the inscribed name as *Qayapha* (or *Qayyapha*), the Hebrew or Aramaic equivalent of the Greek name Caiaphas. Others question this vocalization, suggesting instead *Qopha* or *Qupha* (see Horbury for objections to the Caiaphas identification).

Whatever the case may be regarding the so-called Caiaphas inscription, we may indeed have inscriptions referring to four other Jewish high priests.

Theophilus the High Priest? The name of Theophilus, son of Annas (or Ananus) and brother-in-law of Caiaphas, appears on the ossuary of Yehohanah, granddaughter of the high priest. The ossuary made its appearance in the antiquities market in 1983 and almost certainly was looted from a crypt either in Jerusalem or in nearby Hizma. The inscription is found on the decorated side of the ossuary, within the middle arch of three arches. It reads (Rahmani no. 871),

Yehohanah
Yehohanah, daughter of Yehohanan,
son of Theophilus the high priest

Vitellius, who ordered Pontius Pilate to return to Rome after the Samaritan incident in late 36 C.E., appointed Theophilus to the office of high priest in 37 C.E. According to Josephus, Vitellius "deposed Jonathan [immediate successor to Caiaphas] from his office as high priest and conferred it on Jonathan's brother Theophilus" (*Ant.* 18.5.3 §123).

Annas the High Priest? On an ostracon found at Masada (Mas no. 461) were inked these words:

A[nani]as the high priest, 'Aqavia his son

The inscription may refer to Ananias, son of Nedebaeus, who served as high priest from 47 to 59 C.E. According to Josephus, "Herod, king of Chalcis, now removed Joseph, the son of Camei, from the high priesthood and assigned the office to Ananias, the son of Nedebaeus, as successor" (*Ant.* 20.5.2 §103). This may be the man mentioned in the NT, who orders that Paul be struck (Acts 23:2–5).

Qatros the High Priest? We may have attested the name of yet another high priest. On a circular stone weight found in the ruins of the "Burnt House" (70 C.E.) in the Old City of Jerusalem (not too far from the southwest corner of the Temple Mount), we find this inscribed:

[of] the son of
Qatros

The name may also be found inked on an ostracon from Masada (Mas no. 405). It reads, "daughter of Qatra."

Boethus the High Priest? Finally, we have an inscription that may refer to the high priest Boethos. On an ossuary found on the western slope of Mount Scopus, Jerusalem, we find this inscribed (Rahmani no. 41):

Boethos
Shim'on, of (the family of) Boethos

Sukenik (1934) links this inscription and ossuary to the family of Simon, son of Boethos of Alexandria, whom Herod appointed to the high priesthood in order to marry his daughter (Josephus, *Ant.* 15.9.3 §§320–322). The Qatros, or Canteras, mentioned above, may have been his son. The form (*Boton*), Sukenik suggests, represents the genitive plural (*Boethon*) of *Boethos*. Accordingly, the inscription literally means "Simon, of the Boethians."

We may have inscriptional evidence of yet another member of this family. On an ossuary is "Yoezer, son of Simon" (*CII* no. 1354), and on ostraca from Masada are "Yoezer" (*SEG* no. 383) and "Simeon ben Yoezer" (*SEG* no. 466). The affiliation of Yoezer and Simeon is significant in light of what Josephus relates: "Jozar [= Yoezer], also a Pharisee, came of a priestly family; the youngest, Simon, was descended from high priests" (*Life* 39 §197). This Jozar may be the same person as Joazar, son of Boethos (cf. Josephus, *Ant.* 17.6.4 §164; 18.1.1 §3), who himself served as high priest briefly in 4 B.C.E.

James Ossuary? In the fall of 2002, it was announced that an ossuary long in private hands was discovered with an inscription possibly referring to James, the brother of Jesus. The authenticity of this inscription is still hotly debated. The inscription in Aramaic reads (Lemaire),

> Jacob son of Joseph, brother of Yeshuᶜa

With the names in their familiar NT forms, this would be

> James son of Joseph, brother of Jesus

The ossuary is about 50 cm in length, at the base, widening to 56 cm at the top, about 30 cm in width at one end, about 26 cm in width at the other, and about 30 cm high. (Thus the ossuary is not perfectly rectangular in form.) Written along the long side of the ossuary the inscription, which is made up of five words, is 19 cm in length. The lid is flat and rests on a ledge inside the rim. One corner of the lid is chipped away. Badly weathered, the ossuary reveals faint traces of rosettes on one side. It is also reported that the ossuary contained several small bone fragments.

If this inscription proves to be authentic, it will corroborate and clarify a few important contextual issues relating to research in Jesus and James: (1) James and his family probably spoke Aramaic, which scholars have long recognized as Jesus' first language. The James ossuary lends an important measure of support to this hypothesis. (2) James, originally of Galilee, continued to live in or near Jerusalem. We are left with this impression in the NT (particularly in Acts and Paul's letter to the churches of Galatia). If James's family and home were still in Galilee, we would not expect his ossuary to be found in Jerusalem. Its discovery in Jerusalem would show that in all probability his home had become Jerusalem. (3) The James ossuary may also suggest that James died in or near Jerusalem, as early church traditions maintain. If the ossuary was discovered in a burial vault near the Temple Mount, perhaps in the Kidron Valley, as has been conjectured, this may offer a measure of support to the tradition that James was closely associated with the temple, even if at odds with the powerful priestly family of Annas. (4) Secondary burial, according to Jewish burial custom, would imply that James, though a follower of Jesus and part of a movement that was beginning to drift away from its Jewish heritage, continued to live as a Jew and so was buried as a Jew. The Christianity of James, we may infer, was not understood as separate from, or opposed to, Jewish faith.

Bibliography: N. AVIGAD, "A Depository of Inscribed Ossuaries in the Kidron Valley," *IEJ* 12 (1962): 1–12 and pls. 1–4; C. A. EVANS, *Jesus and the Ossuaries: What Jewish Burial Practices Reveal about the Beginning of Christianity* (Waco, Tex.: Baylor University Press, 2003); P. FIGUERAS, *Decorated Jewish Ossuaries* (DMOA 20; Leiden: Brill, 1983); J. A. FITZMYER, "The Aramaic Qorbân Inscription from Jebel Hallet et-Tûrî and Mk 7:11/Mt 15:5," *JBL* 78

(1959): 60–65, repr. in *Essays on the Semitic Background of the New Testament* (London: Geoffrey Chapman, 1971; repr., SBLSBS 5; Missoula, Mont.: Scholars Press, 1974), 93–100; R. C. GREGG and D. URMAN, *Jews, Pagans, and Christians in the Golan Heights: Greek and Other Inscriptions of the Roman and Byzantine Eras* (SFSHJ 140; Atlanta: Scholars Press, 1996); R. HACHLILI, "The Goliath Family in Jericho: Funerary Inscriptions from a First Century A.D. Jewish Monumental Tomb," *BASOR* 235 (1979): 31–66; W. HORBURY, "The 'Caiaphas' Ossuaries and Joseph Caiaphas," *PEQ* 126 (1994): 32–48; W. HORBURY and D. NOY, *Jewish Inscriptions of Graeco-Roman Egypt* (Cambridge: Cambridge University Press, 1992); A. KLONER, "A Burial Cave of the Second Temple Period at Giv'at Ha-Mivtar, Jerusalem," *Qad* 19–20 (1972): 108–9 (Hebrew; on the House of David inscription); A. LEMAIRE, "Burial Box of James the Brother of Jesus," *BAR* 28, no. 6 (2002): 24–33, 70; IDEM, "Ossuary Update: Israel Antiquities Authority's Report Deeply Flawed," *BAR* 29, no. 6 (2003): 50–59, 67, 70; E. M. MEYERS, *Jewish Ossuaries: Reburial and Rebirth* (BibOr 24; Rome: Pontifical Biblical Institute, 1971) (a critical point of departure for the study of Jewish ossuaries); R. REICH, "Ossuary Inscriptions from the Caiaphas Tomb," *Jerusalem Perspective* 4, nos. 4–5 (1991): 13–21; IDEM, "Ossuary Inscriptions from the 'Caiaphas' Tomb," *ʿAtiqot* 21 (1992): 72–77; H. SHANKS and B. WITHERINGTON, *The Brother of Jesus* (San Francisco: HarperCollins, 2003) (a popular recounting of the discovery of the James ossuary); E. L. SUKENIK, "A Jewish Tomb Cave on the Slope of Mount Scopus," *Qovetz* 3 (1934): 62–73 (Hebrew; on the Boethos inscription). Collections: For a catalogue of ossuaries and inscriptions, see L. Y. RAHMANI, *A Catalogue of Jewish Ossuaries in the Collections of the State of Israel* (Jerusalem: Israel Antiquities Authority, 1994) (descriptions, plates, inscription texts, translations, notes, and bibliography). For burial inscriptions of Beth Sheʿarim, see B. MAZAR et al., *Beth Sheʿarim: Report on the Excavations during 1936–1940* (New Brunswick, N.J.: Rutgers University Press): vol. 1, *Catacombs 1–4* (1973); vol. 2, *The Greek Inscriptions* (1974); vol. 3, *Catacombs 12–23: Report on the Excavations during 1953–1958* (1976). For burial inscriptions of Dominus Flevit (Mount of Olives), see B. BAGATTI and J. T. MILIK, *La necropoli del periodo romano* (vol. 1 of *Gli scavi del "Dominus Flevit" [Monte Oliveto–Gerusalemme]*; Jerusalem: Tip. dei PP. Francescani, 1958). For ostraca of Masada, see H. M. COTTON and J. GEIGER, *Masada II: The Yigael Yadin Excavations, 1963–1965, Final Reports: The Latin and Greek Documents* (Jerusalem: Israel Exploration Society, 1989) (*SEG* nos. 721–951); Y. YADIN, J. NAVEH, and Y. MESHORER, *Masada I: The Yigael Yadin Excavations, 1963–1965, Final Reports: The Aramaic and Hebrew Ostraca and Jar Inscriptions, the Coins of Masada* (Jerusalem: Israel Exploration Society, 1989) (*SEG* nos. 1–701). For Aramaic texts, including ossuary inscriptions, see J. A. FITZMYER and D. J. HARRINGTON, *A Manual of Palestinian Aramaic Texts (Second Century B.C.–Second Century A.D.)* (BibOr 34; Rome: Pontifical Biblical Institute, 1978).

Coins

The study of coins (numismatics) reveals much about a culture. Coin legends and imagery convey what society, especially government, wants the world to believe about itself. Accordingly, coins play an important role in political propaganda, somewhat analogous to public inscriptions. In the case of coins, limitations of space require a brief legend and a tiny portrait that make a precise and important point. Coins are also invaluable to the archaeologist in that they help date the various strata of an excavation.

Greek Coins. One of the most offensive coins in Jewish intertestamental history was that of Antiochus IV Epiphanes. This pompous ruler called himself Epiphanes (lit. "divine manifestation"), though the Jews whom he had so greatly irritated called him Epimanes, which means "madman." More explicitly, he also called himself "God" (*theos*). One of the coins that he minted in 166 B.C.E. (one year after he defiled the Jewish temple) reflects these conceits, reading, "(A coin) of King Antiochus—God, Epiphany, Conqueror." Revolt was inevitable.

Bibliography: I. CARRADICE, *Greek Coins* (London: British Museum, 1995) (helpful introductory survey, sixth–first centuries B.C.E.); I. CARRADICE and M. PRICE, *Coinage in the Greek World* (London: B. T. Batsford, 1988); G. F. HILL, *Catalogue of the Greek Coins of Palestine (Galilee, Samaria, and Judaea)* (Catalogue of the Greek Coins in the British Museum 27; London: Longmans, 1914; repr., 1965); G. K. JENKINS, *Ancient Greek Coins* (2d ed.; Coins in History; London: Seaby, 1990).

Greco-Roman Coins. The declarations of the Roman coins that Caesar is "son of God" or "savior" made the point that coins in antiquity were supposed to make. Roman power, with the blessing and aid of the gods, was emphasized. In the aftermath of the conquest of Jerusalem in 70 C.E., Rome issued coins whose legends read *Iudaea capta* ("Judea captured"), illustrated by a portrait of a woman kneeling before her conqueror, thus underscoring the empire's continuing domination.

Bibliography: H. K. BOND, "The Coins of Pontius Pilate: Part of an Attempt to Provoke the People or to Integrate them into the Empire?" *JSJ* 27 (1996): 241–62; J. P. C. KENT, *Roman Coins* (London: Thames & Hudson, 1978); A. KINDLER, "More Dates on the Coins of the Procurators," *IEJ* 6 (1956): 54–57; H. MATTINGLY, *Augustus to Vitellius* (vol. 1 of *Coins of the Roman Empire in the British Museum;* London: British Museum, 1965); B. OESTREICHER, "A New Interpretation of Dates on the Coins of the Procurators," *IEJ* 9 (1959): 193–95; C. H. V. SUTHERLAND, *Roman Coins: Illustrated by Photographs of Coins from the Collection of the British Museum* (World of Numismatics; London: Barrie & Jenkins, 1974).

Jewish Coins. During the intertestamental period, the Hasmonean rulers variously referred to themselves as "high priest." Alexander Jannaeus (or Yehonathan; ruled 103–76 B.C.E.) evidently was the first to call himself "king." Some of the legends on his coins read, "Yehonathan the High Priest," "Yehonathan the king," and "King Alexander" (in Hebrew and in Greek, the latter usually in reference to "king"). Mattathias Antigonus (40–37 B.C.E.) called himself "Mattithya the High Priest" and "King Antigonus" (with the former in Hebrew and the latter in Greek).

Coins of Rebellion. During the first revolt against Rome (66–73 C.E.), Jewish insurgents overstruck Roman coins to read, "Shekel of Israel," "Jerusalem Is Holy," "Freedom of Zion," and "For the Redemption of Zion." These legends clarify the goals and rationale of the rebellion. During the Bar Kokhba rebellion, Roman coins were again overstruck, with legends reading, "Year One of the Redemption of Israel," "Simeon Prince of Israel" (in reference to Simon Bar Kokhba, leader of the rebellion), "Eleazar the Priest," "Year 2 of the Freedom of Israel," "Jerusalem," and various combinations of the like.

Bibliography: D. BARAG, "A Note on the Geographical Distribution of the Bar Kokhba Coins," *Israel Numismatic Journal* 4 (1980): 30–33; B. KANAEL, "The Historical Background of the Coins 'Year Four . . . of the Redemption of Zion,'" *BASOR* 129 (1953): 18–20; A. KINDLER, "Some Unpublished Coins of King Herod," *IEJ* 3 (1953): 239–41; Y. MESHORER, *Ancient Jewish Coinage* (2 vols.; Dix Hills, NY: Amphora Books, 1982): vol. 1, *Persian Period through the Hasmoneans;* vol. 2: *Herod the Great through Bar Cokhba;* L. MILDENBERG, "Bar Kokhba Coins and Documents," *HSCP* 84 (1980): 311–35; L. Y. RAHMANI, "The Coins from the Cave of Horror," *IEJ* 12 (1962): 200; E. SCHÜRER, *The History of the Jewish People in the Age of Jesus Christ* (rev. and ed. G. Vermes, F. Millar, and M. Black; 3 vols. in 4; Edinburgh: T&T Clark, 1973–1987), 1:602–606 (a succinct summary of Jewish coin legends); Y. YADIN, J. NAVEH, and Y. MESHORER, *Masada I: The Yigael Yadin Excavations, 1963–1965, Final Reports: The Aramaic and Hebrew Ostraca and Jar Inscriptions, the Coins of Masada* (Jerusalem: Israel Exploration Society, 1989).

Ostraca

Greco-Roman. Although neither as personal nor as lengthy (usually), the ostraca (or ostraka) provide insight into the everyday life of late antiquity. An ostracon is piece of broken pottery (or potsherd) on which one wrote a name, a brief list of items, a brief message, or perhaps a promissory note or a receipt, much as we moderns might jot something down on a scrap of paper or on the back of an envelope. Given the relative scarcity and expense of papyrus (not to mention vellum), people of late antiquity frequently utilized potsherds, often for significant matters, such as important messages, replies, tax receipts, and other items of business and finance. Ostraca, even more than inscriptions, provide us with precise details, not rounded, exaggerated figures (as is often the case in literature). They fill in the gaps of detail often left in the literary accounts.

Ostraca in large quantity in a given location assist archaeologists and historians to identify families, their occupations, and their length of stay (up to several generations) in a given village. Ostraca also list goods, foods, rosters of soldiers, workers, slaves, and wagon drivers. They thus provide candid snapshots of real life in late antiquity.

Bibliography: L. AMUNDSEN, ed., *Greek Ostraca in the University of Michigan Collection* (University of Michigan Studies: Humanistic Series 34; Ann Arbor: University of Michigan Press, 1935) (= O.Mich.); R. S. BAGNALL, ed., *The Florida Ostraka (O. Florida): Documents from the Roman Army in Upper Egypt* (Greek, Roman, and Byzantine Monographs 7; Durham, N.C.: Duke University Press, 1976) (= O.Florida); R. S. BAGNALL et al., eds., *Greek Ostraka: A Catalogue of the Collection of Greek Ostraka in the National Museum of Antiquities at Leiden, with a Chapter on the Greek Ostraka in the Papyrological Institute of the University of Leiden* (2 vols.; Collections of the National Museum of Antiquities at Leiden 4; Zutphen, Neth.: Terra, 1980) (= O.Leid.); IDEM, eds., *Ostraka in Amsterdam Collections* (Studia amstelodamensia ad epigraphicam 9; Zutphen, Neth.: Terra, 1976) (= O.Amst.); A. H. GARDINER et al., eds., *Theban Ostraca* (University of Toronto Studies: Philological Series 1; [Toronto]: University of Toronto Library, 1913) (= O.Theb.); A. E. SAMUEL et al., eds., *Ostraka in the Royal Ontario Museum* (2 vols.; ASP 10, 15; Toronto: A. M. Hakkert, 1971–1976) (= O.Ont.Mus.); J. G. TAIT and C. PRÉAUX, eds., *Greek Ostraca in the Bodleian Library at Oxford and Various Other Collections* (3 vols.; Graeco-Roman Memoirs 21, 33, 43; London: Egypt Exploration Society, 1930–1964) (= O.Bodl.); P. VIE-RECK, ed., *Griechische und griechisch-demotische Ostraka der Universitäts-und Landes-bibliothek zu Strassburg im Elsass* (Berlin: Weidmann, 1923) (= O.Stras.); S. P. VLEEMING, ed., *Ostraka varia: Tax Receipts and Legal Documents on Demotic, Greek, and Greek-Demotic Ostraka, Chiefly of the Early Ptolemaic Period from Various Collections* (Papyrologica Lugduno-Batavia 26; Leiden: Brill, 1994) (= O.L.Bat.); U. WILCKEN, ed., *Griechische Ostraka aus Ägypten und Nubien* (2 vols.; Leipzig: Gieseke & Devrient, 1899; repr., with addenda compiled by P. J. Sijpesteijn; Amsterdam: Hakkert, 1970; repr., ed. C. Gallazzi; Cairo: Service des Antiquités de l'Égypte, 1983) (= O.Wilck.).

Ostraca of Masada. The largest single corpus of Jewish ostraca comes from Masada, which has yielded about seven hundred Hebrew and Aramaic ostraca and another two hundred Greek and Latin ostraca. We have dozens of names, not all Jewish. There are lists of priests and priestly shares of tithes and offerings, letters, instructions, and inventories. One letter begs (*SEG* no. 554),

> . . . son of Ma'uzi, Peace. Have pity (*raham*) on me [and please] pay (me) the silver, five denarii . . . that you owe me. [Have p]ity, because I am [. . .] and I do not possess [. . .]

The language of the petitioner is reminiscent of the debtors in Jesus' parable of the Unforgiving Servant: "Should you not have had mercy [or pity] on your fellow servant, as I had mercy on you?" (Matt 18:33); or the cries of the blind man: "Jesus, Son of David, have mercy [or pity] on me!" (Mark 10:47).

Among the most interesting Latin ostraca are references to Herod the Great, whose title "king of the Jews," bestowed upon him by Marc Antony and the Roman Senate (cf. Josephus, *J.W.* 1.12.5 §244; cf. 1.14.4 §282), is attested in Latin on several wine amphorae imported from Rome: *Regi Herodi iudaico* "for King Herod, of the Jews," or "for Herod, king of the Jews" (*SEG* nos. 804–10, 812–13, and 815–16). On the Latin form of Herod's name and title, one finds the more precise form *Herodes rex Iudaeorum* ("Herod, king of the Jews") in fifth-century Macrobius (cf. *Sat.* 2.4.11).

Bibliography: H. M. COTTON and J. GEIGER, *Masada II: The Yigael Yadin Excavations, 1963–1965, Final Reports: The Latin and Greek Documents* (Jerusalem: Israel Exploration Society, 1989) (*SEG* nos. 721–951); Y. YADIN, J. NAVEH, and Y. MESHORER, *Masada I: The Yigael Yadin Excavations, 1963–1965, Final Reports: The Aramaic and Hebrew Ostraca and Jar Inscriptions, the Coins of Masada* (Jerusalem: Israel Exploration Society, 1989) (*SEG* nos. 1–701).

General Bibliography

R. T. ANDERSON and T. Giles, *The Keepers: An Introduction to the History and Culture of the Samaritans* (Peabody, Mass.: Hendrickson, 2002); IDEM, *The Tradition Kept* (Peabody, Mass.: Hendrickson, 2005); J. BOWMAN, *Samaritan Documents*

Relating to Their History, Religion, and Life (Pittsburgh: Pickwick, 1977); R. J. COGGINS, *Samaritans and Jews: The Origins of Samaritanism Reconsidered* (Atlanta: John Knox, 1975); J. M. COHEN, *A Samaritan Chronicle: A Source-Critical Analysis of the Life and Times of the Great Samaritan Reformer, Baba Rabbah* (SPB 30; Leiden: Brill, 1981); A. DEISSMANN, *Light from the Ancient East* (New York: George H. Doran, 1927; repr., Peabody, Mass.: Hendrickson, 1995); F. MANNS and E. ALLIATA, *Early Christianity in Context: Monuments and Documents* (Jerusalem: Franciscan Printing Press, 1993); M. MEYER and P. MIRECKI, eds., *Ancient Magic and Ritual Power* (Religions in the Graeco-Roman World 129; Leiden: Brill, 1995).

CHAPTER TWELVE

Examples of New Testament Exegesis

This final chapter offers a few examples to illustrate the value of the various literatures surveyed for NT interpretation. The examples are taken from the Gospels and the Epistles. These examples do not represent attempts to deal with all of the questions that the interpreter is expected normally to address. The point here will be simply to show how the noncanonical writings at times significantly contribute to the exegetical task.

The Nazareth Sermon

When Jesus preached in the synagogue of Nazareth he touched off an outburst that nearly resulted in his being cast down a cliff, possibly as a prelude to stoning (Luke 4:16–30). Commentators have often wondered what it was that so angered the audience. The suggestion that it was the realization that Jesus was Joseph's son (v. 22) and therefore, as the son of a humble carpenter, he had no right to make great claims for himself is probably not the reason. The audience's recognition that it was indeed Jesus who stood before them should be interpreted as a joyful and expectant discovery. The proverb that Jesus quotes in the next verse and the interpretation that he gives it confirm this. The real turning point in the sermon comes when Jesus cites the examples of Elijah and Elisha and by doing so suggests that the blessings and benefits of his messianic ministry will be shared with Israel's traditional enemies.

The reason for the audience's angry reaction may have been clarified through the discovery and publication of 11QMelchizedek. In this Dead Sea Scroll, portions of Isa 61:1–2, the very passage with which Jesus began his Nazareth sermon (cf. Luke 4:18–19), are cited and linked with Isa 52:7 in order to expound upon the meaning of Lev 25:13, a passage understood to promise the coming of an eschatological era of jubilee. Indeed, 4Q521, a passage that makes explicit reference to God's Messiah, alludes to words and phrases from Isa 61:1–2 and related passages. It is therefore very probable that many Jews of Jesus' time understood Isaiah 61 as not only eschatological but also messianic.

In understanding Isa 61:1–2 in an eschatological sense the author of 11QMelchizedek agrees with Jesus, who had proclaimed to his audience: "Today this scripture has been fulfilled in your hearing" (Luke 4:21). But in emphasizing the judgmental nature of the passage the author of 11QMelchizedek moves in a completely different direction. The very line that Jesus had omitted from his quotation, "and the day of vengeance of our God" (cf. Isa 61:2), seems to hold the key to Qumran's understanding, not only of the jubilee of Lev 25:13, but even of the "good news" passage, Isa 52:7. The Hebrew text, which consists of consonants, not vowels, has been revocalized, so that it not only promises "peace" (šālôm) to the faithful, but "retribution" (šillûm) to Qumran's enemies.

If Qumran's understanding of Isa 61:1–2 approximated the understanding of the audience of the Nazareth synagogue, we are able to appreciate much better the dynamics at work. When Jesus quoted Isa 61:1–2 and announced that it was fulfilled, he and his audience would have drawn two opposing conclusions. For Jesus the eschatological jubilee meant forgiveness and mercy for all, but for his kinsmen and long-time friends it meant blessings for them and judgment for their enemies. Jesus' omission of the line, "and the day of vengeance of our God," might have initially slipped by unnoticed. But when he illustrated his understanding of the prophetic passage by appealing to the examples of mercy Elijah and Elisha showed Israel's enemies, his audience clearly understood his position and they did not like it. They viewed Jesus' interpretation as a betrayal of their messianic hopes.

Bibliography: M. P. MILLER, "The Function of Isa. 61, 1–2 in Melchizedek," *JBL* 88 (1969): 467–69; P. RAINBOW, "Melchizedek as a Messiah at Qumran," *BBR* 7 (1997): 179–94; J. A. SANDERS, "From Isaiah 61 to Luke 4," in *Christianity, Judaism, and Other Greco-Roman Cults* (ed. J. Neusner; M. Smith FS; Leiden: Brill, 1975), 75–106.

The Parable of the Talents

Can the apocryphal gospels (cf. ch. 8 and appendix 3) shed light on the NT Gospels? Sometimes. Consider the parable of the Talents (Matt 25:14–30; roughly paralleled by Luke 19:11–27). Commentators have usually assumed that Jesus intended his hearers to understand that the heroes of the parable are the servants who doubled their master's money. These servants are models for Jesus' followers: "All of this constitutes an appeal to good works as demonstrating the reality of professed discipleship" (Gundry, 505). The servant who hid his master's money, and did not even lend to bankers for interest, is understood to be a poor model: "Thus the parable closes on a threatening note concerning the punishment Jesus will mete out to disciples who falsify their profession by failing to do good works" (Gundry, 510).

The traditional interpretation runs into problems when we are mindful of the biblical principles and economical realities by which the majority of Palestinians in Jesus' day lived. The first problem has to do with the master. He expects exorbitant profits, he is a "hard" man, he reaps the fields of others, gathers the grain that others have threshed, and has no difficulty with usury (Matt 25:24–27). Moreover, he is merciless (Matt 25:30). At the very least this is a hard-nosed businessman who does not observe the law's express prohibition against the practice of usury (cf. Exod 22:25; Ps 15:5). But it is more probable that the picture is worse. This man may be an oppressive gouger and a thief. In any case, it is hard to imagine how an agrarian audience, for the most part peasants, could have heard this parable and understood the master in a favorable sense. This observation has been made recently by Richard Rohrbaugh (Rohrbaugh 1993).

The second problem has to do with the actions of the servants. The first two double their master's money. In the minds of first-century peasants such margins of profit were not fair, but could take place only through high interest rates, excessive returns from tenant farmers, taxation, or outright theft. However these profits were obtained, the peasants knew that it would be at their expense. (For a recent study that treats this subject, see Oakman.) The third servant neither cheated anyone, nor made a profit at anyone's expense. He kept his master's money safe and returned it to him. Although guiltless in the eyes of the peasants, this servant is "worthless" in the eyes of his master and is punished.

For these reasons one may well wonder if the parable as we now have it in the canonical Gospels has been misunderstood. Eusebius wondered this also. Commenting on the Matthean version of the parable he discusses the different perspective of the *Gospel of the Nazarenes* (*Gos. Naz.* §18; cf. Eusebius, *Theoph.* 22 [on Matt 25:14–15]):

> But since the Gospel in Hebrew characters which has come into our hands enters the threat not against the man who had hid [the talent], but against him who had lived dissolutely—for he [the master] had three servants: one who squandered his master's substance with harlots and flute-girls, one who multiplied the gain, and one who hid the talent; and accordingly one was accepted (with joy), another merely rebuked, and another cast into prison—I wonder whether in Matthew the threat which is uttered after the word against the man who did nothing may refer not to him, but by epanalepsis to the first who had feasted and drunk with the drunken.

The parable of the *Gospel of the Nazarenes* seems to be a combination of the parable of the Talents (Matt 25:14–30) and the parable of the Wicked Servant (Matt 24:45–51; Luke 12:45–48). But what is interesting is Eusebius's thought that perhaps the word of rebuke was originally uttered against the man who made huge profits.

Additional problems arise when we consider the Lukan form of the parable (Luke 19:11–27), the so-called parable of the Pounds (or Minas). Not only is the man (called a "nobleman") harsh and demanding, but he is hated by his subjects who do not want him to reign as king over them (Luke 19:14). After his return, he settles with his servants, much as in the Matthean version. But he appears even more harsh, for he demands that those who did not want him to be king be brought before him and be slain in his very presence (Luke 19:27). The traditional interpretation of this form of the parable is not unlike the interpretation of the Matthean version (e.g., Fitzmyer, 2:1232–33; C. A. Evans, 284–87). The evangelist Luke, as the evangelist Matthew, probably understood the parable along the lines that modern commentators interpret it.

There is a second problem with the Lukan version. It appears that the unique parts of the parable, that of the nobleman's quest to receive a kingdom and the citizens' sending a delegation in the hope of frustrating this goal, are based upon the experience of the hated Archelaus not too many years before. (He ruled Judea from 4 B.C.E. to 6 C.E.) This is suggested by the numerous parallels between the parable's nobleman and Archelaus (whose experience is recounted in Josephus): The nobleman went to a far country (v. 12), just as Archelaus went to Rome (*Ant.* 17.9.3 §219); the nobleman hoped to receive a kingdom (*basileia*) and to return (v. 12), just as Archelaus hoped (*Ant.* 17.9.3 §220: *basileia*); the nobleman left household instructions to his servants (v. 13), just as Archelaus did (*Ant.* 17.9.3 §219, 223); the nobleman's citizens hated (*misein*) him (v. 14), just as Archelaus's subjects hated him (*Ant.* 17.9.4 §227: *misos*); an embassy (*presbeia*) is sent after the nobleman (v. 14), as one was sent after Archelaus (*Ant.* 17.11.1 §300: *presbeia*); the citizens petitioned the foreign country against the nobleman's rule (v. 14), just as the envoys petitioned against Archelaus (*Ant.* 17.11.1 §302); the nobleman slaughtered (*katasphazein*) his citizens who opposed him (v. 27), just as Archelaus had done before his journey (*Ant.* 17.9.5 §237, 239: *sphazein*); when the nobleman returned as ruler, he collected his revenues (vv. 15–19), just as Josephus notes that Archelaus was to receive 600 talents as his yearly tribute (*Ant.* 17.11.4 §320); and finally, when the nobleman returned, he settled accounts with those who had opposed him (v. 27), which parallels Archelaus's settling with Joazar the high priest for having supported the rebels (*Ant.* 17.13.1 §339). Since Herod Antipas also traveled to Rome to press his claim to the throne, and was also opposed, his experience loosely fits the experience of the parable's nobleman. But it is Archelaus who offers the closest match.

Why would Jesus tell a parable whose hero is supposed to be law-breaking, despised tyrant? In what sense does such a man model Jesus? In what sense are the servants who work for this man and assist him in his oppressive activities models for Jesus' followers? But perhaps this is not what Jesus originally intended. Following the lead of Eusebius's discussion of the form of the parable in the *Gospel of the Nazarenes,* it is possible, if not probable, that Jesus originally told his parable(s) to illustrate how *not* to be a master and how *not* to be servants. This idea coheres with his teaching elsewhere (Mark 10:42–44):

> You know that those who are supposed to rule over the Gentiles lord it over them, and their great men exercise authority over them. But it shall not be so among you;

but whoever would be great among you must be your servant, and whoever would be first among you must be slave of all.

In its original context, the parable may have presented a contrast between Jesus' style of kingship and that of the Herodian dynasty. The latter was known for its oppression and ruthlessness. But Jesus wished to present a new way and expected his followers to practice it as well.

It is easy to see how the original point of the parable(s) came to be confused with teaching concerned with stewardship and responsibility (cf. Matt 24:45–47; Luke 12:35–38; 17:7–10). The servant that is wise and faithful, doing what he is expected to do, such as treating the members of the master's household properly (not profiteering at his neighbors' expense) will be rewarded. It is possible, then, that the theme of reward drew these parables together, so that the servants of the oppressive master and nobleman came to be interpreted much as the servants of the other parables. But whereas the latter were held up as worthy models, the former were not.

Bibliography: C. A. EVANS, *Luke* (NIBC 3; Peabody, Mass.: Hendrickson, 1990); J. A. FITZMYER, *The Gospel according to Luke X–XXIV* (2 vols.; AB 18, 28A; Garden City, N.Y.: Doubleday, 1981–1985); R. H. GUNDRY, *Matthew: A Commentary on His Literary and Theological Art* (Grand Rapids: Eerdmans, 1982); D. E. OAKMAN, *Jesus and the Economic Questions of His Day* (Lewiston, N.Y.: Mellen, 1986); R. ROHRBAUGH, "A Peasant Reading of the Parable of the Talents/Pounds: A Text of Terror?" *BTB* 23 (1993): 32–39.

The Parable of the Wicked Vineyard Tenants

The parable of the Wicked Tenants (Mark 12:1–11=Matt. 21:33–46=Luke 20:9–19) is clearly based on Isaiah's Song [or Parable] of the Vineyard (Isa 5:1–7, esp. 5:1–2; cf. Mark 12:1). Whereas Isaiah's parable is directed against the "house of Israel and the men of Judah" (Isa 5:7), Jesus' parable is directed against the religious authorities: "they perceived that he had told the parable against them" (Mark 12:12). How could the chief priests (cf. Mark 11:27) so readily perceive that the parable was directed against them? If Isaiah's parable was aimed against the people as a whole, why should Jesus' allusion to it be perceived as a threat against one particular group within Jewish society? The explanation is suggested by *Targum Isaiah*, which inserts "sanctuary" and "altar" in place of tower and wine vat. This would seem to indicate that in the time of Jesus (for *Targum Isaiah* clearly contains traditions that derive from the first century) Isaiah's Song of the Vineyard had come to be understood as directed against the temple establishment. Tosefta's explicit identification of the tower with the temple, and the wine vat with the altar (cf. *t. Meʿil.* 1.16 and *t. Sukkah* 3.15) shows that this interpretation was not limited to the synagogue, where the Targum evolved, but seems to have been known in the rabbinic academies as well.

The Targum plays a further role when Jesus quotes Ps 118:22: "The stone which the builders rejected has become the head of the corner." According to the

Targum the builders rejected "the son" (or child). If this was how Ps 118:22 was understood, then the association of this verse with the rejected son of the parable becomes understandable. When we note further that the religious authorities referred to themselves as "builders" (cf. *y. Yoma* 3.5; *b. Šabb.* 114a; *b. Ber.* 64a; *Exod. Rab.* 23.10 [on 15:1]; *Song Rab.* 1.5 §3; cf. Paul's usage in 1 Cor 3:10), and in fact were called "builders of a rickety wall" by their critics (cf. CD 4:19; 8:12, 18), then the appropriateness of Ps 118:22 for this context becomes even clearer.

The realism of the parable is demonstrated when one makes comparison with Cicero's account of one Marcus Brutus, a landlord, who had difficulty collecting a debt from his tenants (cf. Cicero, *Ad Atticum* 5.21; 6.1). The authenticity of the parable, moreover, is not undermined by its appearance in the Coptic *Gospel of Thomas* (see log. §65 and §66). It has sometimes been asserted that the quotation of Ps 118:22 represents a later, inauthentic addition to the parable. Thomas, it is believed, supports this view. On the contrary, the fact that the parable (log. §65) is followed immediately by the quotation of Ps 118:22 (log. §66) could just as easily argue that the quotation was an original component of the parable. In any case, *Thomas*'s habit of introducing statements with "he said" or "Jesus said" (within logia and not just at the beginning) does not provide conclusive grounds for making certain judgments. Note that Matthew, who has probably followed Mark, inserts "Jesus said" (Matt 21:42), which is without parallel in Mark. *Thomas*'s reading may reflect Matthew's redaction and not an earlier tradition which contained the parable minus the OT quotation.

Bibliography: M. BLACK, "The Christological Use of the Old Testament in the New Testament," *NTS* 18 (1971): 1–14, esp. 11–14; G. J. BROOKE, "4Q500 1 and the Use of Scripture in the Parable of the Vineyard," *DSD* 2 (1995): 268–94; B. D. CHILTON, *A Galilean Rabbi and His Bible: Jesus' Use of the Interpreted Scripture of His Time* (GNS 8; Wilmington, Del.: Glazier, 1984), 111–14; C. A. EVANS, "How Septuagintal is Isa. 5:1–7 in Mark 12:1–9?" *NovT* 45 (2003): 105–10; IDEM, "On the Vineyard Parables of Isaiah 5 and Mark 12," *BZ* 28 (1984): 82–86; K. R. SNODGRASS, *The Parable of the Wicked Tenants: An Inquiry into Parable Interpretation* (WUNT 27; Tübingen: Mohr [Siebeck], 1983).

"I Said, 'You Are Gods'"

When Jesus claims that he and the Father are "one" (John 10:3), his countrymen are ready to put him to death (John 10:31). Jesus then defends his extraordinary claim by appealing to his good works. For which of these will they stone him? His accusers retort:

> "It is not for a good work that we stone you but for blasphemy; because you, being a man, make yourself God." Jesus answered them, "Is it not written in your law, 'I said, you are gods' [Ps 82:6]? If he called them gods to whom the word of God came . . . do you say of him whom the Father consecrated and sent into the world, 'You are blaspheming,' because I said, 'I am the Son of God'?" (John 10:33–36)

This remarkable passage raises several questions. First, how did Jesus understand Ps 82:6 and, therefore, how did he imagine that by appealing to it he had answered his critics? Second, how was Ps 82:6 interpreted in late antiquity? Third, what is meant by "gods"? Fourth, what did Jesus mean by being "one" with the Father? By claiming this did he make himself God?

The fourth question can be answered easily. When Jesus claimed that he was "one" with the Father he was in fact claiming to be equal to God (John 5:18). In many places Jesus claims the prerogatives normally associated with God himself. Jesus will raise and judge the dead (5:28–29). He is able to grant eternal life (5:21; 10:28). No one but God can do these things. Accordingly, when Jesus says, "I and the Father are one," he surely means that he is equal to God. His accusers, therefore, are at least partially correct; Jesus has made himself God.

The first three questions cannot be understood until we have studied the ancient interpretations and applications of Ps 82:6. Recently Jerome Neyrey has undertaken this task. He finds Ps 82:6 interpreted in several Jewish midrashim: *Mek.* on Exod 20:18–19 (*Bahodesh* 9); *b. ʿAbod. Zar.* 5a; *Sipre Deut.* §320 (on Deut 32:20); and *Num. Rab.* 16.24 (on Num 14:11). Neyrey observes that Ps 82:6 is applied to passages which discuss Sinai, when Israel received the law. On that occasion they were immortal, as Adam had been. Hence, they could be called "gods," because like God, they were immortal. But when they sinned (the golden calf), they were subject to death, just as Adam's sin led to his mortality. Therefore, though once called "gods" (because the Word of God came to them), they nevertheless died like mere men.

How then has Jesus applied the passage to himself? Because he has been consecrated, that is, made holy, he too is immortal. Who can convict him of sin (John 8:46)? Because of his sinlessness he will not die. Because of his immortality, he has every right to claim divinity, just as Psalm 82 had called the generation of the exodus "gods."

Bibliography: J. H. NEYREY, "I Said 'You Are Gods': Psalm 82:6 and John 10," *JBL* 108 (1989): 647–63.

"The Word Is Near You"

In Rom 10:5–10 Paul contrasts righteousness based on law with righteousness based on faith. To make his case he paraphrases parts of Deut 30:11–14. In applying Deuteronomy 30, which speaks of the law, to Christ, Paul is doing something similar to what has been done before. This same OT passage had been applied earlier to personified Wisdom: "Who has gone up into heaven, and taken her, and brought her down from the clouds? Who has gone over the sea and found her . . . ?" (Bar 3:29–30). For Paul, of course, Christ is the "wisdom of God" (cf. 1 Cor 1:24). Baruch provides the bridge between speaking of the law and speaking of Christ.

But Paul's paraphrase of Deut 30:12–13 is at variance with both Greek and Hebrew versions of the OT. His paraphrase and commentary read as follows:

> Do not say in your heart, "Who will ascend into heaven?" (that is, to bring Christ down) or "Who will descend into the abyss?" (that is, to bring Christ up from the dead). But what does it say? The word is near you. . . .

The relevant lines of the MT read this way:

> "Who will go up for us to heaven, and bring it to us . . . ?"
> "Who will go over the sea for us, and bring it to us . . . ?"

The relevant lines of the LXX read this way:

> "Who will ascend into heaven for us and receive it for us . . . ?"
> "Who will cross for us to the other side of the sea and receive it for us . . . ?"

In contrast to the Greek and Hebrew versions, Paul's paraphrase speaks of descending into the sea, not of crossing it. He prefers this reading, of course, in order to complement the picture of Jesus descending into the grave and being raised up. But did this variant reading originate with Paul? No, probably not. It is likely that it reflects an Aramaic paraphrase of the synagogue, since a similar reading is found in *Targum Neofiti*. The relevant lines read as follows:

> "Would that we had one like the prophet Moses, who would ascend to heaven and fetch it for us. . . ."

> "Would that we had one like the prophet Jonah, who would descend into the depths of the Great Sea and bring it up for us. . . ."

The point of Deut 30:11–14 is that the law has been given once and for all. There is no need for a prophet to ascend to heaven or to traverse the sea to obtain it. The Aramaic paraphrase illustrates this with two biblical characters whose experiences roughly match the language of the passage. Moses, it was believed, had ascended to heaven when he received the law from God. For example, in *Tg. Ps.-J.* Deut 34:5 we are told that Moses "brought it [the law] from heaven"; and in *Pesiq. Rab.* 4.2 we read: "Moses went up to heaven" (see also *L.A.B.* 15:6; 2 Esdr 3:17–18). These traditions are based on Exod 19:3 and 20, where God summons Moses to meet him on the mountain. The reference to the sea, of course, provides the link to Jonah. In fact, the Targum's "descend into the depths" draws the OT passage into closer alignment with Jonah's experience, for the prophet did not go *across* the sea, but *down into* it (see the reference to "abyss" in Jonah 2:3).

In the NT, of course, Christ is compared to both Moses and Jonah, specifically at points that are relevant to the traditions just reviewed. Like Moses, Jesus brought a new law from heaven (Mark 9:2–8; John 1:17; 3:13–14); like Jonah, Jesus descended into the abyss (Matt 12:39–40; 16:4; Luke 11:29–30).

Bibliography: M. McNamara, *The New Testament and the Palestinian Targum to the Pentateuch* (2d ed.; AnBib 27A; Rome: Pontifical Biblical Institute, 1978), 70–78.

Ascending and Descending with a Shout

By way of consolation to the bereaved of the church at Thessalonica Paul repeats a tradition "by the word of the Lord" (1 Thess 4:15–17a):

> . . . we who are alive and remain until the coming of the Lord will not precede those who sleep; because the Lord himself will descend from heaven with a shout, with the voice of the archangel, and with the trumpet of God, and the dead in Christ will rise first. . . .

The apocalyptic elements in this passage and its context echo many texts, both in the NT (Matt 24:31; 1 Cor 15:51–52) and outside it (Isa 27:13; Zech 9:14; Joel 2:1). Although these passages and others like them parallel various details of 1 Thess 4:16, none can be said specifically to lie behind Paul's "word of the Lord."

A few years ago C. F. D. Moule suggested that Paul's statement might be an echo of Ps 47:5 (47:6 in the MT; 46:6 in the LXX). The suggestion has merit. The reading of the LXX compares as follows:

LXX Ps 46:6	1 Thess 4:16
God has ascended [*anabainein*] with a shout, the Lord with the sound of a trumpet.	The Lord himself with a shout with the sound of an archangel and with the trumpet of God will descend [*katabainein*] from heaven.

Seven of the LXX's (Greek) words appear in 1 Thess 4:16. The major difference, however, is that whereas the LXX speaks of the Lord's ascent, Paul speaks of the Lord's descent. But could the passages be related, nonetheless? And, if 1 Thess 4:16 is based on Ps 46:6 [LXX], what does that tell us about Paul's "word of the Lord"?

Patristic interpretation of Ps 47:5 proves to be very interesting. Justin Martyr (*Dial.* 37), John Chrysostom (*Expositions in the Psalms* on Ps 47:5 [46:6 LXX]), Eusebius (*Commentaries on the Psalms* on Ps 47:5 [46:6 LXX]), and other Fathers interpret Ps 47:5 as fulfilled in Christ's ascension. In fact, they often cite Acts 1:11, noting that Jesus will return the same way that he departed. The most crucial exegesis for our purposes comes from Origen (*Selections on the Psalms* on Ps 47:5 [46:6 LXX]):

> "God went up with a shout, etc." Even as the Lord will come "with the voice of an angel, and with the trumpet of God he will descend from heaven," so "God went up with a shout." But the Lord "with the sound of a trumpet" (went up) meaning possibly with the shout of all the nations clapping their hands, shouting to God with the sound of rejoicing. To these ones I expect God to ascend. But if some one should praise him with the sound of a trumpet, even the one who ascends will himself ascend with the sound of a trumpet.

Not only has Origen interpreted Ps 47:5 [46:6 LXX] in terms of the ascension of Christ, something that several Greek and Latin Fathers did, but he explicitly relates the verse from the psalm to 1 Thess 4:16: "Even as the Lord . . . 'will descend [*katabainein*] from heaven,' so 'God ascended [*anabainein*] with a shout.'" Apparently what has drawn the two passages together is their common language, especially *anabainein/katabainein*.

Is it possible that early patristic exegesis has preserved an interpretive tradition presupposed by Paul, but only partially presented? Just as "God ascended with a shout," so Jesus "will descend with a shout." Or, as Acts 1:11 promises, "This Jesus, who was taken up from you into heaven, will come in the same way as you saw him go into heaven."

Jewish interpretation coheres with the eschatological interpretation that Paul and the Fathers have given Ps 47:5. This is an important point to observe, for in its original ancient setting Psalm 47 was not understood in an eschatological sense. Several Tannaic and Amoraic rabbis believe that the passage will be fulfilled in the day of judgment (cf. *Mek.* on Exod 19:19 [*Bahodesh* §4]; *Lev. Rab.* 29.3 [on Lev 23:24]; *Pesiq. Rab.* 40.5; *Pesiq. Rab Kah.* 1.4). In one midrash Ps 47:5 may even be related to the Messiah (cf. *Num. Rab.* 15.13 [on 10:1]).

If we are correct in concluding that lying behind the words of 1 Thess 4:16 is Ps 47:5, we are left with a striking implication. This NT passage has applied to Christ an OT verse that speaks of God. What we could have here is a fragment of early, but remarkably advanced Christology. Consider this very different rabbinic interpretation of Ps 47:5: "'Who has ascended into heaven (and descended?)' [Prov 30:4] alludes to the Holy One, blessed be he, of whom it is [also] written, 'God has ascended with a shout' [Ps 47:5]" (*Num. Rab.* 12.11 [on 7:1]). Psalm 47 speaks of *God* ascending, as this rabbinic interpretation understands. The early Christian interpretation of 1 Thessalonians has applied the text to the risen and returning *Christ*.

Bibliography: F. F. BRUCE, *1 and 2 Thessalonians* (WBC 45; Dallas: Word, 1982), 101; C. A. EVANS, "Ascending and Descending with a Shout: Psalm 47.6 and 1 Thessalonians 4.16," in *Paul and the Scriptures of Israel* (ed. Evans and J. A. Sanders; JSNTSup 83; SSEJC 1; Sheffield: JSOT Press, 1993), 238–53; B. LINDARS, "The Sound of the Trumpet: Paul and Eschatology," *BJRL* 65 (1984–1985): 766–82; C. F. D. MOULE, *The Origin of Christology* (Cambridge: Cambridge University Press, 1977), 42.

Paul and the First Adam

In the context of a polemical defense of the resurrection, the Apostle Paul compares Jesus, the "last Adam," with the "first Adam."

> Thus it is written, "The first man, Adam, became a living being"; the last Adam became a life-giving spirit. But it is not the spiritual that is first, but the physical, and then the spiritual. The first man was from the earth, a man of dust; the second man is from heaven. (1 Cor 15:45–47; cf. Gen 2:7)

Paul has quoted a portion of Gen 2:7, adding the words "first" and the proper name "Adam." This manner of referring to Adam occurs at least five times in

Targum Psalms (i.e., *adam qedema;* cf. 49:2; 69:32; 92:1; 94:10). All of these references are to the Adam of the creation story, who offered sacrifice (*Tg. Pss.* 69:32), uttered a song concerning the Sabbath (*Tg. Pss.* 92:1), and was taught knowledge by the Lord (*Tg. Pss.* 94:10). Paul's contrast between the first man, who is physical, and the second man, who is heavenly, has its counterpart in Philo (cf. *Alleg. Interp.* 1.31–32 [commenting on Gen 2:7]), but the locution "first Adam" is distinctly targumic.

Bibliography: C. A. EVANS, "The Aramaic Psalter and the New Testament: Praising the Lord in History and Prophecy," in *From Prophecy to Testament: The Function of the Old Testament in the New* (ed. C. A. Evans; Peabody, Mass.: Hendrickson, 2004), 44–91, here 90.

APPENDIX ONE

Canons of Scripture that Include the Apocrypha

Books of the Apocrypha	Roman Catholic Canon	Greek Orthodox Canon	Russian Orthodox Canon	Coptic Canon
1 Esdras		X	X	
2 Esdras			X	
Tobit	X	X	X	X
Judith	X	X	X	X
Add Esther	X	X	X	X
Wisdom	X	X	X	X
Sirach	X	X	X	X
Baruch	X	X	X	X
Ep Jeremiah	X	X	X	X
Song of Three	X	X	X	X
Susanna	X	X	X	X
Bel	X	X	X	X
Pr Man		X	X	
1 Macc	X	X	X	X
2 Macc	X	X	X	X
3 Macc		X	X	
4 Macc		X*		
Psalm 151		X	X	

*Contained in an appendix

Third and Fourth Maccabees and Psalm 151 are usually included among the Pseudepigrapha.

Numerous Eastern groups, such as the Syrians, Nestorians, Melchites, Armenians, and Jacobites, accept most, if not all, of the apocryphal books (and in some cases more besides). The Apocrypha is viewed as having semi-canonical status in the Anglican Church.

Even with regard to the canon of the NT, there is some diversity. The Coptic Church includes the *Apostolic Constitutions and Canons* and *1* and *2 Clement*. The Armenian Church accepts an apocryphal letter *to* the Corinthians and two others *from* the Corinthians. The Nestorians, however, exclude the four smaller catholic epistles (2 Peter, 2 and 3 John, Jude), part of the "antilegomena."

APPENDIX TWO

Quotations, Allusions, and Parallels to the New Testament

This appendix contains a list of NT passages that quote, allude to, or contain ideas that closely parallel the OT and/or the writings surveyed in this book. This list is not comprehensive; it is illustrative only. For an index of OT passages in the Dead Sea Scrolls, see J. A. Fitzmyer, *DSS* 205–37; D. L. Washburn, *A Catalog of Biblical Passages in the Dead Sea Scrolls* (SBL Text-Critical Studies 2; Atlanta: Society of Biblical Literature, 2002); M. O. Wise, M. G. Abegg Jr., and E. M. Cook, *The Dead Sea Scrolls: A New Translation* (San Francisco: HarperCollins, 1996), 506–13. For parallels with rabbinic and related literature, see J. Lightfoot, *A Commentary on the New Testament from the Talmud and Hebraica* (4 vols., Peabody: Hendrickson, 1989 [orig. *Horae Hebraicae et Talmudicae,* 1658–74; ET Oxford: Oxford University Press, 1859]); H. L. Strack and P. Billerbeck, *Kommentar zum Neuen Testament aus Talmud und Midrasch* (6 vols.; Munich: C. H. Beck, 1922–1961). For parallels with Greco-Roman literature, see M. E. Boring, K. Berger, and C. Colpe, *Hellenistic Commentary to the New Testament* (Nashville: Abingdon, 1995); C. T. Ramage, *Scripture Parallels in Ancient Classics* (London: A. & C. Black, 1878). For specific passages challenged by pagan authors in late antiquity, see J. G. Cook, *The Interpretation of the New Testament in Greco-Roman Paganism* (Studies and Texts in Antiquity and Christianity 3; Tübingen: Mohr [Siebeck], 2000; repr., Peabody, Mass.: Hendrickson, 2002).

Matthew

Matt 1:1	Gen 5:1
Matt 1:11	1 Esdr 1:32
Matt 1:21	Suetonius, *Aug.* 94
Matt 1:21–23	Virgil, *Ecl.* 4.48; Suetonius, *Vesp.* 1.4
Matt 1:23	LXX Isa 7:14
Matt 2:1	Strabo, *Geogr.* 15.1.68; Xenophon, *Cyr.* 8.1.23–24

Matt 2:2	Jer 23:5; Num 24:17; Philo, *Rewards* 16 §95; Josephus, *J.W.* 6.5.3 §289; 6.5.4 §§312–313; cf. 3.8.9 §§400–402; 4QTest 9–13; CD 7:18–21; *Tgs.* Num 24:17; *Aristobulus* frg. 4:5; *Orphica* 31
Matt 2:5–6	Mic 5:2; *Tg. Mic.* 5:1–3
Matt 2:9	Josephus, *J.W.* 6.5.3 §289; Tacitus, *Hist.* 2.78; Ammianus Marcellinus, *Res gest.* 22.9
Matt 2:15	Hos 11:1; 4 Ezra 6:58; cf. LXX Num 24:7–8a; *Frg. Tg.* Num 24:7
Matt 2:18	Jer 31:15
Matt 2:23	Isa 11:1; Isa 4:2; Jer 23:5; 33:15; Zech 3:8; 6:12; cf. Judg 13:5–7; *Tg. Isa.* 11:1; *Tg. Zech.* 3:8; 6:12
Matt 3:4	Diodorus Siculus 19.94
Matt 3:7	Zeph 1:15; 1QH 11:28
Matt 3:7–10	*Ap. Jas.* (NHC I) 9:24–10:6
Matt 3:8–9	Pr Man 8; *Tg. Isa.* 33:11–14
Matt 3:11	*1 En.* 67:13; *T. Isaac* 5:21
Matt 3:12	*Tg. Isa.* 33:11–12
Matt 3:16	*2 Bar.* 22:2; Homer, *Od.* 1.320
Matt 4:1	*2 Bar.* 10:8; *Tg. Ps.-J.* Deut 32:10
Matt 4:2	*L.A.E.* 6:3
Matt 4:4	Wis 16:26
Matt 4:4–10	Deut 8:3; 6:16, 13
Matt 4:6	Ps 91:11–12; *Tg. Pss.* 91; 11QPsApa 4:4–5:14
Matt 4:15	1 Macc 5:15
Matt 4:15–16	Isa 9:1–2; cf. *Tg. Isa.* 9:1–6
Matt 5:2–3	Sir 25:7–12
Matt 5:3	Isa 61:1; 1QSb 5:21; 1QM 14:7; *Der. Er. Rab.* 2.14; *Gos. Thom.* §54
Matt 5:3–12	4Q525 frgs. 2+3 ii 1–9
Matt 5:4	Isa 61:2; *y. Ber.* 2.4; *Lam. Rab.* 1:16 §51
Matt 5:5	Isa 61:5; Gen 15:7; Ps 37:11; 4QpPs 37 (frg. 1) 1:8–10; *Tg. Pss.* 37:11; *1 En.* 5:7; *m. Qidd.* 1:10
Matt 5:6	Isa 61:3, 6, 8, 11; *4 Bar.* 9:21; *Gos. Thom.* §69b
Matt 5:7	*t. B. Qam.* 9.30; *Tg. Ps.-J.* Lev 22:28
Matt 5:8	Isa 61:1; Ps 24:3–4; 4 Ezra 7:98; *2 En.* 45:3; *Der. Er. Rab.* 2.19; Plato, *Phaedo* 67A, 80D, 108C, 114C
Matt 5:9	*2 En.* 52:9; *m. Pe'ah* 1:1; *'Abot* 1:12
Matt 5:10	Isa 61:3, 8, 11; *1 En.* 96:7; *T. Levi* 16:2; *T. Jud.* 21:9
Matt 5:11	LXX Ps 34:7; LXX Ps 108:20; *Gos. Thom.* §68
Matt 5:12	Isa 61:10; LXX Isa 61:10; *4 Bar.* 6:20; *Tg. Isa.* 28:11–12; Livy 29.17
Matt 5:13	*Sop.* 15.8; *b. Ber.* 8b
Matt 5:14	Isa 49:6; *Apoc. Ab.* 9:3; *b. B. Batr.* 4a; Cicero, *In Catilinam* 4.6
Matt 5:15	Bar 4:1
Matt 5:16	Ps 66:5; *T. Benj.* 5:3; *'Abot* 5:23
Matt 5:17	2 Macc 2:22; 7:19; 4 Macc 5:19, 33; *b. Šabb.* 116a–b
Matt 5:18	LXX Ps 148:6; 4 Ezra 9:37; Bar 4:1; *2 Bar.* 77:15; Philo, *Moses* 214; *Gen. Rab.* 10.1 (on Gen 1:1)

Matt 5:19	*T. Levi* 13:9; *T. Mos.* 12:10–12; Dio Chrysostom, *Disc.* 31.86
Matt 5:20	*1 En.* 15:1
Matt 5:21	Exod 20:13; Deut 5:17; *t. Šebu.* 3.6; *Mek.* on Exod 20:13 (*Bahodesh* §8); *Tg. Onq.* Gen 9:6; *Tg. Ps.-J.* Gen 9:6; *Gen. Rab.* 34.14 (on Gen 9:6)
Matt 5:21–22	Sir 28:7
Matt 5:22	*2 En.* 46:1
Matt 5:23–24	Valerius Maximus, *Fact. dict.* 2.1.6
Matt 5:25–26	*Ahiqar* 142; Sir 8:1
Matt 5:26	*Sent. Sextus* 39
Matt 5:27	Exod 20:14; Deut 5:18; *t. Šebu.* 3.6
Matt 5:27–28	Cicero, *Sen.* 12; Seneca, *Ira* 1.3; Plutarch, *Life of Pericles* 8.5; Suetonius, *Nero* 29; Publilius Syrus, *Sent.* 789; Aelian, *Var. hist.* 14.28, 42
Matt 5:28	Sir 9:8; *T. Benj.* 8:2; *Sent. Sextus* 233; Ps.-Phocylides, *Sent.* 52
Matt 5:29	Plato, *Symp.* 204C
Matt 5:29–30	*1 En.* 27:2
Matt 5:31	Deut 24:1–4; *m. Soṭah* 6:3; *m. Giṭ.* 3:2; 9:10; *t. Soṭah* 5.9; *t. Giṭ.* 2.4–10
Matt 5:33	Lev 19:12; Ps 50:14
Matt 5:34	Epictetus, *Ench.* 33.5
Matt 5:34–35	Isa 66:1; Ps 11:4; *2 En.* 49:1; *m. 'Abot* 6:10; *Barn.* 16:2
Matt 5:35	Ps 48:2; *m. Tamid* 7:4
Matt 5:36	*m. Sanh.* 3:2; *Lev. Rab.* 19.2 (on Lev 15:25)
Matt 5:37	Epictetus, *Ench.* 33.5
Matt 5:38	Exod 21:23–25; Lev 24:19–20; Deut 19:21; *m. Mak.* 1:6
Matt 5:38–42	Musonius 10; Seneca, *Ira* 2.34.1, 5; Epictetus, *Ench.* 5; *Sent. Sextus* 17
Matt 5:39	Plato, *Gorg.* 509C; Cicero, *Tusc.* 5.19; Epictetus *Diatr.* 3.22.54; Suetonius, *Divus Titus* 9
Matt 5:42	Sir 4:4; *Gos. Thom.* §95; Seneca, *Ben.* 2.5
Matt 5:43	Lev 19:17–18; *m. Ned.* 9:4; *t. Šebu.* 3.8
Matt 5:44	*Sent. Sextus* 105, 213; P.Oxy. 1224 §2; Valerius Maximus, *Fact. dict.* 4.2.4; Epictetus, *Ench.* 10; Marcus Aurelius, *Med.* 7.26; Diogenes Laertius 1.4.4
Matt 5:45	Sir 4:10; Diogenes Laertius 8.1.23; Epictetus 4.5.2; *Sent. Sextus* 135, 371–372; Seneca, *Ot.* 1.4
Matt 5:48	Deut 18:13; Epictetus, *Ench.* 5
Matt 6:1–18	Tob 12:8
Matt 6:2	CD 11:21–22; *m. Taʿan.* 2:5; Demosthenes, *Against Aristogeiton* 502
Matt 6:3–4	Quintilian, *Institutio oratoria;* Publilius Syrus, *Sent.* 78; Seneca, *Ben.* 2.10; Martial, *Epigr.* 5.52
Matt 6:4	Epictetus 2.8.14; 2.14.11
Matt 6:5	Amidah
Matt 6:6	Isa 26:20; Homer, *Od.* 12.333; Seneca, *Ben.* 6.38.5
Matt 6:7	1 Kgs 18:26–29; Sir 7:14; Marcus Aurelius, *Med.* 5.7
Matt 6:8	Dio Cassius, *Hist. rom.* 39.8

Matt 6:9	1 Kgs 9:7; LXX Ezek 36:23; Sir 23:1, 4; *1 En.* 61:12; *Sent. Sextus* 59; Epictetus 1.3.1; 1.6.40; 1.9.7
Matt 6:9–13	Kaddish
Matt 6:10	1 Macc 3:60; *t. Ber.* 3.11; Epictetus 2.17.22; Seneca, *Ep.* 76.23
Matt 6:12	Sir 28:2
Matt 6:13	Sir 23:1; 33:1; Jas 1:13; *b. Ber.* 60b; Euripides, *Andromache* 880
Matt 6:14–15	Sir 28:2–4
Matt 6:16	1 Macc 3:47; Bar 1:5; *T. Zeb.* 8:6; *T. Jos.* 3:4; *Did.* 8:1; Suetonius, *Aug.* 76.2; Aristophanes, *Lysistrata* 7; idem, *Plutus* 756; Aelian, *Var. hist.* 14.22
Matt 6:17	Ps 104:15; Ruth 3:3; Jdt 16:8
Matt 6:19	LXX Mic 6:10; Diogenes Laertius 6.1.11; 10.1.11; Plutarch, *Mor.* 5D: *[Lib. ed.]* 8; *Mor.* 523C–528B: *On Love of Wealth* 1–10; *Tg. Neof.* Gen 15:1
Matt 6:19–20	Sir 29:9–12; *2 Bar.* 14:13
Matt 6:20	Sir 29:10–11; *Pss. Sol.* 9:5; 4 Ezra 7:77; *Sent. Sextus* 77, 118; Lucian, *Timon* 36
Matt 6:20–21	*T. Levi* 13:5
Matt 6:21	Epictetus 2.22.19; *Sent. Sextus* 316
Matt 6:22	Sir 23:19; *T. Iss.* 4:6; *T. Job* 18:3
Matt 6:22–23	*T. Iss.* 3:4; *Dialog. Sav.* 125.18–126.1
Matt 6:23	Sir 14:8, 10; 26:11; Tob 4:7; *T. Benj.* 4:2; *ʾAbot* 2:9
Matt 6:24	*Tg. Isa.* 5:23; Epictetus 4.10.24; *C.Tg.* (C) Gen 34:23
Matt 6:25	Horace, *Carm.* 2.11.4–5; *Sent. Sextus* 15; *Pesiq. Rab. Kah.* 8.1
Matt 6:26	Ps 147:9; *Pss. Sol.* 5:9–11; *m. Qidd.* 4:14; *Sent. Sextus* 32
Matt 6:27	*Sent. Sextus* 255
Matt 6:28	P.Oxy. 655 1.9–10; *Pesiq. Rab. Kah.* 8.1
Matt 6:29	2 Chr 9:22; Sir 47:18
Matt 6:30	Isa 5:24; Ps 103:15–16; *Sent. Sextus* 1–2, 6; *Midr. Tanḥ.* on Exod 13:17ff (*Beshallah* 117b)
Matt 6:33	Wis 7:11; *Sent. Sextus* 14, 311; Seneca, *Ep.* 18.12
Matt 6:34	Prov 27:1; *b. Ber.* 9b; *b. Sanh.* 100b
Matt 7:1–5	Aristotle, *Eth. nic.* 3.2; Musonius 23, 32; Ps.-Diogenes 50; Seneca, *Ira* 2.28.5–8; Petronius, *Sat.* 57.7; *Sent. Sextus* 183–184
Matt 7:2	*T. Zeb.* 5:3; 8:3; *2 En.* 44:5; Ps.-Phocylides, *Sent.* 11; *m. Soṭah* 1:7; *t. Soṭah* 3.1, 2; *b. Soṭah* 8b; *Sipre Num.* §106 (on Num 12:1–6); *C.Tg.* (D) Gen 38:26; *Tg. Neof.* Num 12:15; *Frg. Tg.* Num 12:15; *Tg. Ps.-J.* Num 12:14; *Tg. Isa.* 27:8; cf. *b. Šabb.* 127b; *b. Meg.* 28a; *b. Roš Haš.* 16b; *b. Sanh.* 100b
Matt 7:4–5	Epictetus 3.22.98; Seneca, *Vit. beat.* 27.4; *b. Qidd.* 70a; *b. ʿArak.* 16b; *b. B. Bat.* 15b
Matt 7:6	*m. Temurah* 6:5; *Did.* 9:5; 1QS 9:16–20; *Sent. Sextus* 354
Matt 7:7	Pss 2:8; 21:4; 27:4; Prov 8:17; 4 Ezra 4:42; Wis 6:12; *b. Meg.* 12b; Sophocles, *Oed. tyr.* 110
Matt 7:9	Seneca, *Ben.* 2.7.1
Matt 7:11	*Lev. Rab.* 34.14 (on Lev 25:25)

Matt 7:12	Tob 4:15; Sir 31:15; *Let. Aris.* 207; Isocrates, *Demon.* 4; idem, *Aeginet.* 23; Seneca, *Ep.* 9.6; 94.43; 103.3; *2 En.* 61:2; *Sent. Sextus* 89, 90, 179; *Syr. Men.* 250–251; *'Abot* 2:11; *Tg. Ps.-J.* Lev 19:18
Matt 7:13	Prov 16:25; Sir 21:10; *2 Bar.* 85:13; Diogenes Laertius 4.49
Matt 7:13–14	Deut 11:26; 30:15; Jer 21:8; *T. Ash.* 1:3–5; *T. Ab.* (A) 11:2–3; *2 En.* 30:15; *Sipre Deut.* §53 (on Deut 11:26); *b. Ber.* 28b; *Ceb. Tab.* 270; Ps.-Diogenes 30.2
Matt 7:14	Jer 21:8; *Ps.-Clem. Homilies* 3.52.2
Matt 7:15	CD 6:1–2; *T. Jud.* 21:9; *2 Bar.* 66:4; *Mart. Isa.* 5:2, 12
Matt 7:16	Sir 27:6; *b. Ber.* 48a; Epictetus 2.20.18; Seneca, *Ep.* 87.25; *Song Rab.* 1:1 §6
Matt 7:17–18	*2 En.* 42:14; Horace, *Carm.* 4.4.29; Seneca, *Ep.* 87.25; idem, *Ira* 2.10.6; *Gos. Thom.* §45
Matt 7:19	Jer 22:7
Matt 7:21	LXX Ps 108:21; 1 Esdr 8:16
Matt 7:22	Ezra 5:1; Zech 13:3; Acts 19:13–16
Matt 7:23	Ps 6:8
Matt 7:24–27	*'Abot* 3:18; *'Abot R. Nat.* (A) 24.3; Seneca, *Ep.* 52.5
Matt 7:28	Deut 31:24; 32:45
Matt 8:4	Lev 14:2–20; *m. Neg.* 3:1
Matt 8:11	Ps 107:3; Bar 4:37; 2 Macc 1:27–29; 4 Macc 13:17; *Tg. Isa.* 53:8; *Tg. Hos.* 14:8; *Tg. Mic.* 5:1–3
Matt 8:12	1QSb 5:21; 4Q252 5:4; *1 En.* 104a; 1QS 4:12–13; Plutarch, *Mor.* 167A: *Superst.* 4
Matt 8:13	*b. Ber.* 34b
Matt 8:17	Isa 53:4; *Tg. Isa.* 52:13–53:12
Matt 8:19–20	Plutarch, *Lives of Tiberius et Caius Gracchus* 9.5; Epictetus 3.22.9–11
Matt 8:20	Dio Cassius, *Hist. rom.* 40.2; Ps.-Anacharsis 5
Matt 8:21	Tob 4:3
Matt 8:22	*Sent. Sextus* 7b; *Exod. Rab.* 5.14 (on Exod 5:2)
Matt 8:23–27	Ps 65:5–8
Matt 8:26	*Sent. Sextus* 6
Matt 8:29	*1 En.* 16:1
Matt 9:13	Hos 6:6; *'Abot R. Nat.* §4; *b. Šabb.* 31a; *Num. Rab.* 8.4 (on Num 5:6)
Matt 9:17	Sir 9:10
Matt 9:20	*b. Ta'an.* 23b
Matt 9:23	*m. Ketub.* 4:4
Matt 9:27–31	Suetonius, *Vesp.* 7.2–3; Dio Cassius, *Hist. rom.* 65.8; Tacitus, *Hist.* 4.81
Matt 9:32	*T. Sol.* 12:2
Matt 9:36	Num 27:16–17; 1 Kgs 22:17; Zech 10:2; Jdt 11:19
Matt 9:37	*'Abot* 2:15
Matt 9:38	1 Macc 12:17; 4 Ezra 4:26–37; *2 Bar.* 70:1–2
Matt 10:1	*Pss. Sol.* 17:26–28
Matt 10:6	*Pss. Sol.* 17:26–28
Matt 10:9	*Sent. Sextus* 242; *b. Bek.* 29a; *Derek Ereṣ Zuṭa* 2.4

Matt 10:10	Crates, *Ep.* 16, 23, 33; Diogenes, *Ep.* 7, 13, 15, 19, 26, 30, 34, 38, 46; Diogenes Laertius 4.51; 6.13, 33; *PGM* IV. 2381
Matt 10:15	Gen 19:24, 28; *Jub.* 13:17; *T. Levi* 14:6; *T. Naph.* 3:4; *T. Ash.* 7:1; *T. Benj.* 9:1
Matt 10:16	Sir 13:17; *Song Rab.* 2:14 §1
Matt 10:19	*Ahiqar* 32
Matt 10:21	Mic 7:6; *m. Soṭah* 9:15; *b. Soṭah* 49b; *3 Bar.* 4:17
Matt 10:22	4 Macc 1:11
Matt 10:24	Philo, *Cherubim* 107
Matt 10:25	*T. Sol.* 3:6
Matt 10:26	Ep Jer 29 (= Bar 6:29); *2 Bar.* 83:2–3; Pindar, *Ol.* 1.53; 10.65; Sophocles, *Ajax* 646–647; Seneca, *Ira* 2.22.2–3; idem, *Ep.* 79.14
Matt 10:28	4 Macc 13:14–15; *Sent. Sextus* 363; Ps.-Heraclitus 5.2
Matt 10:29	Amos 3:5; *Gen. Rab.* 79.6 (on Gen 33:18)
Matt 10:30	*Apoc. Sedr.* 8:6–7
Matt 10:34–36	Mic 7:6; *m. Soṭah* 9:15; *b. Soṭah* 49b; *3 Bar.* 4:17
Matt 10:39	*b. Tamid* 32a; *'Abot R. Nat.* (B) §32; Epictetus 4.1.164–165
Matt 10:40	*Mek.* on Exod 14:32 (*Beshallah* §7); *Sipre Num.* §103 (on Num 12:8); *Mek.* on Exod 18:12 (*Amalek* §3)
Matt 10:42	Suetonius, *Claud.* 40.2; *T. Isaac* 6:21; *T. Jacob* 2:23; *2 Bar.* 48:19; *Gen. Rab.* 58.8 (on Gen 23:17)
Matt 11:1	Deut 32:45
Matt 11:2	Josephus, *Ant.* 18.5.2 §§118–119
Matt 11:3	4Q252 5:3
Matt 11:5	Isa 26:19; 35:5–6; 53:8; 61:1; 4Q521 frgs. 2+4 ii 1–12; Sir 48:5; *Apoc. El. (C)* 3:9
Matt 11:7	3 Macc 2:22
Matt 11:10	Mal 3:1; 4:5; *m. ʿEd.* 8:7
Matt 11:11	*Frg. Tg.* (Paris MS) Exod 14:29
Matt 11:14	Sir 48:10
Matt 11:16	Josephus, *J.W.* 6.8.5 §408
Matt 11:17	*b. Sanh.* 103a; *Lam. Rab.* proem §12; Aesop, *Fables* 39; Herodotus, *Hist.* 1.141
Matt 11:18	Sophocles, *Ajax* 243
Matt 11:19	Deut 21:20
Matt 11:21	Diodorus Siculus 19.106; Plutarch, *Mor.* 168D: *Superst.* 7
Matt 11:22	Jdt 16:17
Matt 11:23	Isa 14:13, 15; *Pss. Sol.* 1:5; *t. Soṭah* 3.19
Matt 11:25	Dan 2:21, 23; Tob 7:17; Sir 51:1; *Tg. Isa.* 48:6
Matt 11:27	John 10:15; Tob 5:2
Matt 11:28–29	Sir 6:24–25; 24:19; 51:23–27; Jer 6:16; *m. Ber.* 2:2
Matt 11:29	Sir 6:24–29; *2 En.* 34:1
Matt 11:30	*m. 'Abot* 3:5; *b. Ber.* 2:2; Diogenes Laertius, *Vit. phil.* 7.170
Matt 12:1	Deut 23:25
Matt 12:2	Exod 20:10; Deut 5:14

Matt 12:3–4	1 Sam 21:1–6
Matt 12:4	2 Macc 10:3
Matt 12:5	*b. Šabb.* 132b
Matt 12:7	Hos 6:6; *ʾAbot R. Nat.* §4
Matt 12:11	Deut 22:4; Prov 12:10; CD 11:13–14; *m. Beṣah* 3:4
Matt 12:18–21	Isa 42:1–4; *Tg. Isa.* 42:1–6; 1QH 13:18–19; *Barn.* 14:7
Matt 12:22	*T. Sol.* 12:2
Matt 12:23	Josephus, *J.W.* 7.6.3 §§180–185; *Ant.* 8.2.5 §§45–49; *T. Sol.* 1:7
Matt 12:24	*T. Sol.* 2:9–3:6; 6:1–11
Matt 12:28	*T. Ezek.* 7:3
Matt 12:30	*Pss. Sol.* 4:10; 17:26; *Tg. Isa.* 53:6, 8; *t. Ber.* 6.24; *y. Ber.* 9.5
Matt 12:33	*b. Ber.* 48a
Matt 12:34	1 Sam 24:13; *b. Pesaḥ.* 63a; *Midr. Pss.* 28.4 (on Ps 28:3); *Eccl. Rab.* 7:2 §1; Diogenes Laertius, *Vit. phil.* 9.7.5
Matt 12:35	Deut 28:12; *T. Ash.* 1:9
Matt 12:37	Ps 51:4
Matt 12:38–42	Isa 7:11; Josephus, *Ant.* 20.5.1 §§97–98; 20.8.6 §§169–170
Matt 12:39	*Tg. Isa.* 57:3; *b. Sanh.* 98a
Matt 12:39–40	3 Macc 6:8; *m. Taʿan.* 2:4; *Tg. Neof.* Deut 30:13; *Liv. Pro.* 10:10–11
Matt 12:40	*T. Zeb.* 4:4
Matt 12:41	Jonah 3:5
Matt 12:42	1 Kgs 10:1–13; Sir 47:17
Matt 12:43	*T. Sol.* 5:11–12; 20:16
Matt 12:44	Josephus, *Ant.* 8.2.5 §47; Philostratus, *Vit. Apoll.* 4.20
Matt 12:45	Gen 4:15; *T. Reu.* 2:2
Matt 13:5	Sir 40:15
Matt 13:6	*Pss. Sol.* 18:6–7
Matt 13:16–17	*Pss. Sol.* 17:44; *Mek.* on Exod 15:2 (*Shirata'* §3); *b. Ḥag.* 14b
Matt 13:17	*2 Bar.* 85:2; *Tg. Isa.* 48:6
Matt 13:22	Phocylides, frg. 39
Matt 13:24–30	*Gos. Thom.* §57; Diogenes Laertius, *Vit. phil.* 6.6; Seneca, *Ep.* 73.16
Matt 13:26	LXX Gen 1:11
Matt 13:30	Mal 4:1
Matt 13:32	Dan 4:20–22
Matt 13:33	Gen 18:6; *Gos. Thom.* §96
Matt 13:35	LXX Ps 77:2; 4Q427 frg. 7 i 18–19; 1QH 20:13
Matt 13:39	Jer 51:33; Joel 3:13; *1 En.* 16:1; 54:6; 63:1; *2 Bar.* 70:2
Matt 13:42	Dan 3:6
Matt 13:43	Dan 12:3; *T. Levi* 4:2; 4 Ezra 7:97; *2 En.* 22:10; 65:8, 11
Matt 13:44	Sir 20:30–31; Josephus, *J.W.* 7.5.2 §§114–115; *m. B. Bat.* 4:8; *Midr. Tanḥ.* (B) on Lev 22:26–27 (*Emor* 8.9); *Gos. Thom.* §109; Virgil, *Aen.* 1.358–359
Matt 13:45–46	*b. Šabb.* 119a; *b. Sanh.* 119a; *T. Job* 18:6–8; *Mek. R. Sim. Yoh.* 14.5; *Gos. Phil.* 2.29–32; 3.11–13; *Acts Pet. 12 Apos.* 4.15–5.1; *Gos. Thom.* §76; Epictetus 2.12.21–22

Matt 13:47	*b. ʿAbod. Zar.* 3b–4a; *ʾAbot R. Nat.* (A) 40.9
Matt 13:48	*b. Ḥul.* 63b; *Gos. Thom.* §8
Matt 13:49	Dan 12:13
Matt 13:52	Sir 1:25; 39:1–3; Epictetus 3.22.4
Matt 14:19–20	*4 Bar.* 9:21
Matt 14:27	*2 En.* 1:7
Matt 14:30	Virgil, *Aen.* 6.370
Matt 14:31	*Sent. Sextus* 6
Matt 15:13	*m. Sanh.* 10:1
Matt 15:14	Aristophanes, *Plutus* 13; Cicero, *Tusc.* 5.38
Matt 15:31	Isa 35:5–6; 61:1–2; *Mek.* on Exod 20:15–19 (*Bahodesh* §9)
Matt 16:1–4	3 Macc 6:8; *m. Taʿan.* 2:4; *Tg. Neof.* Deut 30:13; *Liv. Pro.* 10:10–11
Matt 16:2–3	*b. Yoma* 21b; *b. B. Bat.* 84a; *b. Taʿan.* 9b; *Gos. Thom.* §91
Matt 16:8	*Sent. Sextus* 6
Matt 16:17	Gal 1:16; Ignatius, *Phil.* 7:2
Matt 16:18	Isa 51:1–2; Jer 31:4; Wis 7:11; 16:13; Homer, *Il.* 23.70; Lucian, *Men.* 6
Matt 16:19	Isa 22:22; *m. Terumot* 5:4; Diodorus Siculus 1.27
Matt 16:22	1 Macc 2:21
Matt 16:26	*2 Bar.* 51:16; Plato, *Phaedo* 107C
Matt 16:27	LXX Ps 61:13; Prov 24:12; Sir 35:19, 22
Matt 16:28	4 Ezra 6:26
Matt 17:2	*T. Levi* 18:40; *2 Bar.* 51:3; *L.A.B.* 12:1; *Sipre Num.* §140 (on Num 27:1–11); Plutarch, *Mor.* 323C: *Fort. Rom.* 3
Matt 17:5	*2 En.* 14:8; *2 Bar.* 22:2; *T. Ab.* (A) 9:8
Matt 17:11	Sir 48:10
Matt 17:24	4Q159 frg. 1 ii 6–7
Matt 17:27	*b. Sanh.* 119a; *b. B. Bat.* 133b; *Pesiq. Rab.* 23.6; Jerome, *Comm. Matt.* 3.17.26 (on Matt 17:24–27)
Matt 18:6, 10	*2 Bar.* 48:19; *Pr. Jos.* frg. A
Matt 18:10	Tob 12:15; *1 En.* 104:1; Plutarch, *Mor.* 361BC: *Is. Os.* 26
Matt 18:12–14	Isa 40:11; 53:6; Ezek 34:11–16; Pss 23:1; 119:176; *Pss. Sol.* 17:40; Epictetus 3.22.23; Seneca, *Ira* 1.14.3; idem, *Ep.* 34.1
Matt 18:15	Lev 19:16–17; Prov 3:12; 25:9; CD 9:6–8; *T. Gad* 6:3, 6; Aristotle, *Eth. nic.* 9.3
Matt 18:16	Deut 19:15; CD 9:16–10:3; *T. Ab.* (A) 13:8; *m. Soṭah* 6:3; *t. Šeb.* 3.8; 5.4
Matt 18:17	LXX Deut 4:10; LXX 1 Chr 28:2; Sir 33:18
Matt 18:19	*b. Ber.* 8a
Matt 18:20	*ʾAbot* 3:2; *Frg. Tg.* (Vatican MS) Exod 20:21
Matt 18:21	Gen 4:15; Lev 16:14; 26:18; Prov 24:16; 4Q511 frg. 35, lines 1–3; Epictetus, *Ench.* 43
Matt 18:23–35	Sir 28:1–5
Matt 18:25	Exod 22:1; 1 Sam 22:2; Diogenes Laertius, *Vit. phil.* 4.46–58
Matt 18:34	Livy 3.13.8; 25.4.8–10; Appian, *Hist. rom.* 2.8.2; *b. Roš Haš.* 17b–18a
Matt 18:35	*T. Gad* 6:7

Matt 19:5	Gen 2:24; CD 4:19–5:2
Matt 19:6	Ps.-Quintilian, *Decl.* 376
Matt 19:10	Josephus, *Ant.* 18.1.5 §21; idem, *J.W.* 2.8.2 §120; Epictetus 3.22.37, 47
Matt 19:28	4 Ezra 7:75
Matt 19:28–30	*T. Benj.* 10:7; *Pss. Sol.* 17:26–28; *T. Ab.* (A) 13:6
Matt 19:29	*T. Zeb.* 6:6
Matt 20:1–16	*y. Ber.* 2.8
Matt 20:2	Tob 4:6; 5:15
Matt 21:5	Isa 62:11; Zech 9:9
Matt 21:12	*Pss. Sol.* 17:30
Matt 21:14	*Tg. 2 Sam.* 5:8
Matt 21:16	LXX Ps 8:3; Wis 10:18–21; *Mek.* on Exod 15:1 (*Shirata'* §1)
Matt 21:28–32	*Exod. Rab.* 27.9 (on Exod 18:1); *Deut. Rab.* 7.4 (on Deut 28:1)
Matt 21:40	2 Esdr 1:24
Matt 21:43	2 Esdr 1:24
Matt 22:7	Josephus, *J.W.* 6.5.1 §275; *y. Soṭah* 6.3
Matt 22:11–12	*b. Šabb.* 153b
Matt 22:13	Wis 17:2; *1 En.* 10:4; Diogenes Laertius, *Vit. phil.* 8.1.19; Virgil, *Aen.* 6.557
Matt 22:14	4 Ezra 8:3; 9:15
Matt 22:15	*T. Jos.* 7:1
Matt 22:32	4 Macc 7:19; 16:25; *T. Jud.* 25:1
Matt 22:37–39	*T. Dan* 5:3
Matt 23:2	*Exod. Rab.* 43.4 (on Exod 32:22); *Pesiq. Rab. Kah.* 1.7
Matt 23:3	Deut 17:10; *Sipre Deut.* §154 (on Deut 17:10); *Pesiq. Rab.* 3.1; *Lev. Rab.* 35.7 (on Lev 26:3); Epictetus 3.7.17
Matt 23:4	*b. ʿAbod. Zar.* 36a; *b. Sanh.* 94b; *ʾAbot R. Nat.* (A) 2.2
Matt 23:5	Num 15:38; *b. Ned.* 62a
Matt 23:9	Dio Chrysostom, *Disc.* 1.22
Matt 23:10	Josephus, *Ant.* 18.1.6 §23; Epictetus 1.19.9
Matt 23:11	*Sipre Deut.* §38 (on Deut 11:10)
Matt 23:15	*Gen. Rab.* 39.14 (on Gen 12:5); *b. Yebam.* 47a; Justin Martyr, *Dial.* 122
Matt 23:16	Philo, *Virtues* 7
Matt 23:16–22	*m. Ned.* 1:3; *m. Šebu.* 4:13
Matt 23:20	Exod 29:37; *m. Zebaḥ.* 9:1
Matt 23:22	Isa 66:1; *Mek.* on Exod 17:16 (*Amalek* §2)
Matt 23:23	Hos 6:6; *Tg. Isa.* 28:25; *m. Demai* 2:1; *b. Yebam.* 47a
Matt 23:26	*b. Ber.* 28a; *b. Yoma* 72b; *Gos. Thom.* §22
Matt 23:29	1 Macc 13:27–30; Josephus, *Ant.* 7.15.3 §§392–394; 13.8.4 §249; 18.4.6 §108; 20.4.3 §95; *J.W.* 5.12.2 §506
Matt 23:34	*Tg. Jer.* 18:18; *T. Ezek.* 7:26
Matt 23:34–35	Gen 4:10; 2 Chr 24:20–22; 2 Esdr 1:32
Matt 23:35	Gen 4:8; 2 Chr 24:20–21; *Liv. Pro.* 23:1; Zech 1:1
Matt 23:37	Deut 32:11; Isa 31:5

Matt 23:37–38	2 Esdr 1:30, 33; *Tg. Isa.* 28:11–12; 32:14
Matt 23:38	Jer 12:7; 22:5; Tob 14:4
Matt 23:39	Ps 118:26
Matt 24:1	4 Ezra 5:2
Matt 24:4	*Apoc. Elijah* 1:14
Matt 24:5	*Apoc. Elijah* 3:1
Matt 24:6	*2 Bar.* 48:34, 37
Matt 24:6–7	*Sib. Or.* 3:636–637
Matt 24:7	4 Ezra 13:31; 15:15; *2 En.* 70:23; *2 Bar.* 27:9
Matt 24:8	*2 Bar.* 27:3
Matt 24:11	*2 Bar.* 48:34; Tacitus, *Ann.* 15.44
Matt 24:12	*m. Soṭah* 9:15
Matt 24:15	1 Macc 1:54; 6:7; 2 Macc 8:17; *2 Bar.* 28:1
Matt 24:16	1 Macc 2:28
Matt 24:17	*2 Bar.* 53:9
Matt 24:19	*2 Bar.* 10:14
Matt 24:20	*m. ʿErub.* 4:3; 5:7
Matt 24:21	*T. Mos.* 8:1
Matt 24:24	*2 Bar.* 48:34
Matt 24:26	LXX Deut 32:25
Matt 24:27	Zech 9:14; 4Q246 2:1–2; *Apoc. Elijah* 3:4; Suetonius, *Dom.* 16.1
Matt 24:28	Job 39:30; Hab 1:8; 1QpHab 3:8–12; Cornutus, *De natura deorum* 21; Seneca, *Ep.* 95.43
Matt 24:29	*Apoc. Elijah* 3:6
Matt 24:30	Zech 12:10; *2 Bar.* 25:3
Matt 24:31	Isa 27:13; *1 En.* 22:3; *Apoc. Mos.* 22:3; *Apoc. Ab.* 31:1
Matt 24:37–39	Gen 7:6–10; *Sib. Or.* 3:815–818, 823–827; Ovid, *Metam.* 8.618–724
Matt 24:38	Gen 7:6–10
Matt 24:40–41	*Apoc. Zeph.* 2:2
Matt 24:51	Jdt 16:17
Matt 25:14–30	*Ahiqar* 192
Matt 25:23	*3 Bar.* 15:4
Matt 25:24	Sir 13:4; 26:29
Matt 25:30	1QS 4:12–13
Matt 25:31	*1 En.* 61:8; 62:2–3; 69:27
Matt 25:31–46	*T. Jos.* 1:5
Matt 25:33–34	*T. Benj.* 10:6
Matt 25:34	*2 En.* 9:1; 23:5; 42:3
Matt 25:35	Tob 4:17; *T. Isaac* 6:21; *2 En.* 9:1
Matt 25:35–36	*T. Jos.* 1:5–6; *Der. Er. Rab.* 2.21
Matt 25:36	Sir 7:32–35
Matt 25:41	*1 En.* 10:13; *2 En.* 10:4; Virgil, *Aen.* 6.741; Plutarch, *Mor.* 167A: *Superst.* 4
Matt 25:46	Dan 12:2; Plato, *Phaedo* 113D
Matt 26:13	*1 En.* 103:4

Matt 26:15	Zech 11:12–13; LXX Exod 9:12; Jer 18:1–3; 19:11; 32:6–15
Matt 26:24	*1 En.* 38:2; *2 Bar.* 10:6
Matt 26:38	Sir 37:2
Matt 26:39	*Jos. Asen.* 14:3; *Sib. Or.* 3:655
Matt 26:52	*Tg. Isa.* 50:11; *Jos. Asen.* 29:4
Matt 26:53	*2 Bar.* 63:5–11
Matt 26:57	Josephus, *Ant.* 18.2.2 §35; 18.4.3 §95
Matt 26:64	*1 En.* 69:27
Matt 26:70	*T. Jos.* 13:2
Matt 26:73	*b. Ber.* 32a; *b. Meg.* 24b; *b. ᶜErub.* 53b
Matt 27:3–8	Zech 11:12–13; LXX Exod 9:12; Jer 18:1–3; 19:11; 32:6–15
Matt 27:4	Deut 27:25; *T. Zeb.* 2:2
Matt 27:5	Zech 11:13; 2 Sam 17:23
Matt 27:6	Deut 23:18; *T. Zeb.* 3:3
Matt 27:7	Zech 11:13; cf. Gen 23:17–20
Matt 27:9–10	Zech 11:12–13; Jer 18:2–3; 32:6–15
Matt 27:19	Suetonius, *Divus Julius* 81.1–3
Matt 27:24	Deut 21:6–8; Pss 26:6; 73:13; Sus 44, 46; Herodotus, *Hist.* 1.35; Virgil, *Aen.* 2.719; Sophocles, *Ajax* 654
Matt 27:24–25	*T. Levi* 16:3
Matt 27:25	Deut 19:10; 2 Sam 1:16
Matt 27:43	Ps 22:8; Wis 2:13, 18–20
Matt 27:50	*2 En.* 70:16
Matt 27:51	*T. Lev.* 3:9; 4:1; 10:3
Matt 27:52–53	Ezek 37:12; Dan 12:2
Matt 27:55–56	Ps 38:11
Matt 27:60	Josh 10:18, 27
Matt 27:62–66	*SEG* 13; cf. 1 Kgs 13:21–22; *m. Sanh.* 6:5; *Sem.* 2.7
Matt 28:3	Dan 7:9
Matt 28:4	*CIL* VI.3
Matt 28:11–15	*Acts of Pilate* 13:1–3
Matt 28:12	Josephus, *Ant.* 20.9.2 §205
Matt 28:13	Arrian, *Anab.* 6.29.4; Plutarch, *Mor.* 173B: *Sayings of Kings and Commanders: Semiramis;* Euripides, *Rhes.* 812–819, 825–827; Tacitus, *Hist.* 5.22
Matt 28:18	Dan 7:13–14
Matt 28:20	LXX Exod 7:2; Dan 12:13

Mark

Mark 1:1	*OGIS* 458.31–42; P.Oxy. 1021.1–13
Mark 1:2–3	Mal 3:1; Exod 23:20; LXX Isa 40:3; 1QS 8:12–14; 9:17–20; Bar 5:7; *Barn.* 9:3
Mark 1:4–5	Josephus, *Ant.* 18.5.2 §117; *Sib. Or.* 4:165
Mark 1:6	Josephus, *Life* 2 §11; Lev 11:22; *m. Ḥul.* 8:1

Mark 1:10	*T. Jud.* 24:2; cf. *T. Levi* 18:6–7; Mal 3:10; Homer, *Od.* 1.320
Mark 1:11	Ps 2:7; cf. Gen 22:2; Isa 42:1; 2 Esdr 7:28–29; 1QSa 2:11–12; 4QFlor 1:10–12 (on 2 Sam 7:11–16); *b. Sukkah* 52a; *Midr. Pss.* 2.9 (on Ps 2:7); *Tg. Isa.* 41:8–9; 42:1; 43:10; Theocritus, *Id.* 17.71
Mark 1:12–13	*T. Naph.* 8:4; *T. Benj.* 5:2; 2 *Bar.* 10:8; *Tg. Ps.-J.* Deut 32:10
Mark 1:14–15	*Tg. Isa.* 40:9; 52:7
Mark 1:15	Tob 14:5
Mark 1:17	*Jos. Asen.* 21:21
Mark 1:20	Epictetus, *Ench.* 7
Mark 1:23	11QPs[a] 19:15
Mark 1:25	*PGM* IV. 3013; Josephus, *Ant.* 8.2.5 §§46–49; *T. Sol.* 6:11
Mark 1:26	11QPs[a] 19:15
Mark 1:30	*b. Ned.* 41a
Mark 1:31	*b. Ber.* 5b
Mark 1:32	4Q242 (= Prayer of Nabonidus) 2–4
Mark 1:34	*T. Sol.* 6:11
Mark 1:40	Num 12:10; 2 Kgs 5:27; Herodotus, *Hist.* 1.138; Epictetus 3.10.15
Mark 1:40–45	P.Eger. 2 (frg. 1 recto, lines 32–41) + P.Köln 22
Mark 1:41	2 Kgs 5:13
Mark 1:44	*PGM* I. 130–32
Mark 2:5	*Tg. Isa.* 53:11–12
Mark 2:7	*b. Ned.* 41a
Mark 2:10	Dan 7:9–14; 4Q242 (= Prayer of Nabonidus) frgs.1–3, lines 4–5 + frg. 4, line 1; *Tg. Isa.* 53:5, 6, 11, 12; Horace, *Carm.* 4.15
Mark 2:11–12	Lucian, *Philops.* 11
Mark 2:17	Diogenes Laertius, *Vit. phil.* 6.6; Ps.-Diogenes 40.1
Mark 2:22	Sir 9:10
Mark 2:23	Exod 20:10; 34:21; Deut 5:14; CD 10:14–11:18; *m. Šabb.* 7:2
Mark 2:25–26	1 Sam 21:1–6
Mark 2:27	*Mek.* on Exod 31:13 (*Shabbata* §1); 2 Macc 5:19; 2 *Bar.* 14:17
Mark 3:1–6	*Gos. Naz.* §10 (*apud* Jerome, *Comm. Matt.* 2 [on Matt 12:13])
Mark 3:3	*m. Yoma* 8:6; *b. Šabb.* 132a
Mark 3:12	*T. Sol.* 6:11
Mark 3:21	Acts 26:24; *Sib. Or.* 3:811–818; Alciphron, *Letters of Courtesans:* Thais to Euthydemus, 1.34.1–2
Mark 3:22	*Jub.* 10:7; *T. Sol.* 2:9; 3:3–6; 6:1–11; Justin Martyr, *Dial.* 69.7; Origen, *Cels.* 1.6, 38
Mark 3:24	LXX Dan 5:28; 11:4; *T. Sol.* 5:5
Mark 3:25	LXX Prov 14:11; Job 8:15; Dio Cassius, *Hist. rom.* 38.16
Mark 3:26	*T. Mos.* 10:1, 3; *T. Dan* 6:4
Mark 3:27	*1 En.* 10:4; *T. Sol.* 5:5; *Pss. Sol.* 5:3
Mark 3:29	*ʾAbot R. Nat.* (A) 39.1; *Sent. Sextus* 85
Mark 3:34	Epictetus 3.22.81–82; Diogenes Laertius, *Vit. phil.* 6.63, 88
Mark 4:3–9	Isa 55:10–11; Jer 4:3; 4 Ezra 8:41; *Gos. Thom.* §9; *ʾAbot* 5:15; *ʾAbot R. Nat.* (A) 29.3; 40.6–11

Mark 4:5	Sir 40:15
Mark 4:6	2 Kgs 19:26
Mark 4:7	*m. Šeb.* 4:2
Mark 4:8	Gen 26:12; Ezek 17:8; *Jub.* 24:15; *Sib. Or.* 3:264–265; Josephus, *Ag. Ap.* 1.22 §195
Mark 4:11	Wis 2:22
Mark 4:11–12	*Tg. Isa.* 6:9–10; *Mek.* on Exod 19:2; *b. Roš Haš.* 17b; *b. Meg.* 17b; *y. Ber.* 2:3; *S. Eli. Rab.* §16 (82–83); *Gen. Rab.* 81.6 (on Gen 42:1); *Ap. John* 22:25–29; *Testim. Truth* 48.8–13; *Ap. Jas.* 7:1–10
Mark 4:14	4 Ezra 9:31; *b. Ber.* 63a; Seneca, *Ep.* 38.2
Mark 4:15	*Jub.* 11:11; 4 Ezra 8:41
Mark 4:16–17	Isa 40:24; Hos 9:16; Sir 40:15; Wis 4:3
Mark 4:18	Jer 4:3
Mark 4:19	Gen 3:18; *Jub.* 3:25; Phocylides, frg. 39
Mark 4:20	4 Ezra 3:20; 9:31–32; 2 Kgs 19:30; Isa 37:31; Prov 12:12
Mark 4:21	Exod 40:4; 1 Macc 4:50; *Gos. Thom.* §33
Mark 4:22	*2 Bar.* 83:2–3; 2 Esdr 16:63–66; *Gos. Thom.* §5; Sophocles, *Ajax* 646–647
Mark 4:24	*m. Soṭah* 1:7; *Mek.* on Exod 13:19 (*Beshallah* §1); *Tg. Isa.* 27:8; cf. *b. Šabb.* 127b; *b. Meg.* 28a; *b. Roš Haš.* 16b
Mark 4:25	*ʾAbot* 1:13; *t. Soṭah* 4.17; *Gen. Rab.* 20.5 (on Gen 3:14)
Mark 4:28	LXX Lev 25:5, 11
Mark 4:29	Isa 18:5; LXX Joel 3:13; *b. Sanh.* 95b; *Gos. Thom.* §21
Mark 4:30	*m. Nid.* 5:2; *m. Ṭohor.* 8:8; *b. Ber.* 31a
Mark 4:30–32	Ezek 17:23; Dan 4:20–22; *Gos. Thom.* §20; Cicero, *Sen.* 15
Mark 4:32	Theophrastus, *History of Plants* 7.1.1–3; Pliny the Elder, *Nat.* 19.170–171
Mark 4:33	1 Kgs 4:32; Eccl 12:9; Sir 47:15; 11QPs[a] 27:2, 5, 11
Mark 4:35–41	Pss 65:7; 89:9; 104:6–7; 107:23–30; *T. Naph.* 6:3–9; *y. Ber.* 9.1; *b. B. Meṣiᶜa* 59b
Mark 4:39	Theocritus, *Id.* 22.15; Virgil, *Aen.* 1.154; Horace, *Carm.* 1.12.27; Statius, *Silvae* 2.2.25
Mark 4:41	2 Macc 9:8
Mark 5:2–3	*b. Ḥag.* 3b; *b. Sanh.* 65b; *b. Ḥul.* 74b
Mark 5:3	*1 En.* 69:28; 103:8
Mark 5:4	*Sib. Or.* 1:153–154
Mark 5:5	LXX Ps 87:2
Mark 5:7	*1 En.* 10:1, 13
Mark 5:9	*b. Ber.* 6a; *b. Pesaḥ.* 111b
Mark 5:12	Isa 65:4; *b. Pesaḥ.* 112b
Mark 5:13	*T. Sol.* 5:11
Mark 5:15	Philostratus, *Vit. Apoll.* 4.20
Mark 5:28	Arrian, *Anab.* 6.13.3; Plutarch, *Life of Sulla* 35
Mark 5:34	Jdt 8:35
Mark 6:3	Justin Martyr, *Dial.* 88; Qur'an 3.45; 5.112

Mark 6:4	*Gos. Thom.* §31; Apollonius of Tyana, *Letters to Hestiaeus* 44; Dio Cassius, *Hist. rom.* 47.2, 5–6; Epictetus 3.16.11
Mark 6:8	Crates, *Ep.* 16, 23, 33; Diogenes, *Ep.* 7, 13, 15, 19, 26, 30, 34, 38, 46; Diogenes Laertius 4.51; 6.13, 33; *PGM* IV. 2381
Mark 6:8–10	Josephus, *J.W.* 2.8.4 §§124–127
Mark 6:11	*2 Bar.* 13:4; *m. Ber.* 9:5; *Sipre Deut.* §258 (on Deut 23:15); *b. Sanh.* 12a
Mark 6:17–29	Josephus, *Ant.* 18.5.2 §§116–119; 18.5.4 §136
Mark 6:18	Lev 18:16; 20:21; *m. Yeb.* 3:10
Mark 6:23	Aelian, *Var. hist.* 9.26
Mark 6:34	Num 27:17; cf. 1 Kgs 22:17; Ezek 34:5; Jdt 11:19
Mark 6:35–42	2 Kgs 4:42–44; Isa 25:6; *2 Bar.* 29:1–8
Mark 6:39–40	4Q378 frg. 3 ii 6–7
Mark 6:48	LXX Job 9:8; *Apoc. Elijah* 3:8; Eratosthenes, frg. 182 (*apud* Hesiod, *Astronomy* 4)
Mark 6:49	Wis 17:15
Mark 7:3–5	*m. Yad.* 1:1–2:3
Mark 7:5	ʾAbot 1:1; ʾAbot R. Nat. (A) 15.3
Mark 7:6–7	LXX Isa 29:13; P.Eger. 2 §3; *2 Clem.* 3:5
Mark 7:10–11	Exod 20:12; 21:17; Lev 20:9; Deut 5:16
Mark 7:11–12	*m. Ned.* 1:2–2:2, 5; 3:2, 5; 5:6; 9:7; 11:5; *m. Naz.* 2:1–3; Philo, *Spec. Laws* 2.16–17; Josephus, *Ant.* 4.4.4 §73; idem, *Ag. Ap.* 1.22 §167
Mark 7:15	Ps.-Phocylides, *Sent.* 228; *Sent. Sextus* 110–111; Menander, frg. 540; *Gos. Thom.* §14
Mark 7:27–28	Diogenes Laertius, *Vit. phil.* 6.46; Philostratus, *Vit. Apoll.* 1.19
Mark 7:32	1QapGenᵃʳ 20:28–29
Mark 7:33	Suetonius, *Vesp.* 7.2–3; Tacitus, *Hist.* 4.81
Mark 7:35	Isa 35:5–6
Mark 8:11–13	3 Macc 6:8; *m. Taʿan.* 2:4; *Tg. Neof.* Deut 30:13; *Liv. Pro.* 10:10–11
Mark 8:18	Jer 5:21; cf. Isa 6:9–10; Ezek 12:2
Mark 8:24	*SIG* 1168–69 (Epidaurus)
Mark 8:27–30	*Gos. Thom.* §13
Mark 8:29	*1 En.* 48:10; 52:4; 4Q252 frg. 1 v 3–4; 4Q285 frg. 5 i 1–6
Mark 8:31	*Tg. Hos.* 6:2
Mark 8:33	*Ap. Jas.* 5.33–6.4
Mark 8:34	Epictetus 2.2.10; ʾAbot 3:5; *m. Ber.* 2:2
Mark 8:35	ʾAbot R. Nat. (B) §35
Mark 8:36	Ps 49:7–9; *2 Bar.* 51:15
Mark 8:37	Sir 26:14; Menander, *Sent.* 843; *Interp. Know.* 9.33–35
Mark 9:1	4 Ezra 6:26
Mark 9:2–3	4 Ezra 7:97, 125; *1 En.* 37:7; 51:5; 62:15; *Liv. Pro.* 21:2; *Homeric Hymns* 2.275–280
Mark 9:2–8	*Ep. Pet. Phil.* 134.9–16; *Treat. Res.* 48.3–11
Mark 9:4	*Deut. Rab.* 3.17 (on Deut 10:1); *Pesiq. Rab.* 4.2
Mark 9:7	Ps 2:7; Gen 22:2; Deut 18:15

Mark 9:9	*Corp. herm.* 13.1, 22
Mark 9:11	Mal 4:5–6; Sir 48:10; 4Q558; *m. ʿEd.* 8:7; *Mek.* on Exod 16:32 (*Vayassaʾ* §6)
Mark 9:12	*Sib. Or.* 2:187–188; *m. Soṭah* 9:15; *b. Sanh.* 113a
Mark 9:14	Josephus, *Ant.* 8.2.5 §§45–49; *PGM* IV. 3007–14
Mark 9:17–18	*T. Sol.* 12:2
Mark 9:22	Philostratus, *Vit. Apoll.* 3.38
Mark 9:25	*T. Sol.* 13:1–3
Mark 9:26	Josephus, *Ant.* 8.2.5 §48; Philostratus, *Vit. Apoll.* 4.20
Mark 9:31	Ep Jer 2:18
Mark 9:35	4 Ezra 5:42
Mark 9:38	Josephus, *J.W.* 7.6.3 §§180–185; idem, *Ant.* 8.2.5 §§46–49; *PGM* IV. 1229–49
Mark 9:40	Cicero, *Pro Ligario* 11; P.Oxy. 1224
Mark 9:42	*b. Sanh.* 55a
Mark 9:43–47	Sir 9:5; 23:8; *Pss. Sol.* 16:7; Plato, *Symp.* 204C; Aristotle, *Eth. eud.* 7.1.14; *Sent. Sextus* 12–13, 273
Mark 9:48	Isa 66:24; *Tg. Isa.* 66:24; Jdt 16:17; Sir 7:17; *t. Ber.* 5.31; *t. Sanh.* 13.5; *Pesiq. Rab. Kah.* 10:4; *Midr. Pss.* 12.5 (on Ps 12:8); *2 Clem.* 7:6; 17:5
Mark 9:49	Lev 2:13; Num 18:19; Ezek 43:24; *Jub.* 21:11; *T. Levi* 9:14; 11QTemple 20
Mark 9:50	*m. Soṭah* 9:15
Mark 10:2–12	Josephus, *Ant.* 18.5.4 §136; CD 4:20–5:2; 11QTemple 57:15–19
Mark 10:4	Deut 24:1–4; *m. Giṭ.* 9:10; *b. Giṭ.* 90a–b
Mark 10:5	Mal 2:16; *b. Giṭ.* 90b
Mark 10:6	Gen 1:27; CD 4:20–5:2; *m. Yebam.* 6:6
Mark 10:7–8	Gen 2:24
Mark 10:9	*Tg. Ps.-J.* Gen 2:24; *Tg. Ps.-J.* Deut 34:6; cf. *Tg. Neof.* Deut 32:4; *SIG* II.1267
Mark 10:11	Exod 20:14; Deut 5:18
Mark 10:12	Josephus, *Ant.* 15.7.10 §§259–260; *m. Ketub.* 7:10
Mark 10:14	*b. Sanh.* 110b; *b. Yoma* 22b; *b. Nid.* 30b; *Kallah Rab.* 2.9
Mark 10:19	Exod 20:12–16; Deut 5:16–20; Sir 4:1; *m. Mak.* 1:3
Mark 10:20	*2 Bar.* 38:4
Mark 10:21	Josephus, *J.W.* 2.8.3 §122; 1QS 6:17–22; Tob 4:8–9; *Pss. Sol.* 9:5; Sir 29:10–12; *2 Bar.* 24:1
Mark 10:22	LXX Dan 2:12
Mark 10:25	*b. Ber.* 55b; *Song Rab.* 5:2 §2
Mark 10:27	Philo, *Moses* 1.174; idem, *Virtues* 27
Mark 10:30	*T. Job* 4:6–9; *ʾAbot R. Nat.* (A) 28.5
Mark 10:31	*Ruth Rab.* 3.1 (on Ruth 1:17)
Mark 10:38	*Tg. Neof.* Gen 40:23; *Tg. Neof.* Deut 32:1; Isa 51:22; Jer 25:15; *Pss. Sol.* 8:14; *Mart. Isa.* 5:13
Mark 10:41–45	Eusebius, *Hist. eccl.* 2.1.3
Mark 10:43–44	*Mek.* on Exod 18:12 (*Amalek* §3); Cicero, *Off.* 1.90

Mark 10:45	Dan 7:13–14; Isa 52:13–53:12; *Tg. Isa.* 53:12; LXX Exod 21:30; 1 Macc 2:50
Mark 10:47	LXX Isa 30:19; LXX Pss 6:3; 9:14; CBS 9012; *Pss. Sol.* 17:21; 20:1–2
Mark 11:1–11	Josephus, *Ant.* 11.8.4–5 §§325–339; 12.7.4 §312; 12.8.5 §§348–349; 13.11.1 §§304–306; 16.2.1 §§12–15; 17.8.2 §§194–239; 1 Macc 4:19–25; 5:45–54; 13:43–51; 2 Macc 4:21–22
Mark 11:2	1 Kgs 1:32–48; Zech 9:9; *m. Sanh.* 2:5; Horace, *Epodes* 9.22
Mark 11:8	2 Kgs 9:12–13; 2 Macc 10:7; Herodianus 1:16
Mark 11:9–10	1 Kgs 1:32–40; Ps 118:25–26; *Tg. Pss.* 118:19–27; *Midr. Pss.* 118.22 (on Ps 118:24–29)
Mark 11:15	Josephus, *Ag. Ap.* 2.8 §104; idem, *Ant.* 20.5.3 §§106–107; idem, *J.W.* 2.12.1 §§24–27; Zech 14:20–21
Mark 11:16	Josephus, *Ag. Ap.* 2.8 §§106, 109; *m. Ber.* 9:5
Mark 11:17	Isa 56:7; Jer 7:11; *Tg. Jer.* 7:11; Josephus, *J.W.* 6.5.3 §§300–309
Mark 11:18	*T. Levi* 16:3
Mark 11:20	Suetonius, *Galba* 1.1
Mark 11:23	*T. Sol.* 23:1; *b. Ber.* 64a; *b. B. Bat.* 3b
Mark 11:25	Sir 28:2; Amidah
Mark 12:1–9	*Sipre Deut.* §312 (on Deut 32:9); *Midr. Tanḥ.* (B) on Lev 19:1 (*Qedoshin* 7.6); *S. Eli. Rab.* §28 (150); *Exod. Rab.* 30.17 (on Exod 21:18); *Gos. Thom.* §§65–66; Isa 5:1–7; *Tg. Isa.* 5:1–7; 4Q500; *t. Me*ᶜ*il.* 1.16; *Sukkah* 3.15; *Sipre Deut.* §312 (on Deut 32:9)
Mark 12:8	P.Cair.Zen. 59.018
Mark 12:10–12	Ps 118:22–23; *Tg. Pss.* 118:22; CD 4:19; 8:12, 8; Acts 4:11; *b. Ber.* 64a; *b. Šabb.* 114a
Mark 12:13	Josephus, *Ant.* 18.1.1 §§1–10; *J.W.* 2.8.1 §§117–118
Mark 12:13–17	P.Eger. 2 frg. 2 recto; *Gos. Thom.* §100
Mark 12:16	Epictetus 4.5.16–17
Mark 12:17	Justin Martyr, *1 Apol.* 17.2; *Sent. Sextus* 20
Mark 12:18–27	Gen 38:8; Deut 25:5–6; Ruth 4; Josephus, *Ant.* 4.8.23 §§254–256; 18.1.4 §16
Mark 12:19	Gen 38:8; Deut 25:5–6; *m. Yebam.* 3:9
Mark 12:20	Tob 3:7–15
Mark 12:25	*1 En.* 15:6–7; 51:4; 104:4, 6; *2 Bar.* 51:5, 10; 4Q511 frg. 35, lines 3–4; Philo, *Sacrifices* 5
Mark 12:26–27	Exod 3:6; 4 Macc 7:18–19; 16:25; *T. Jud.* 25:1; Philo, *On the Life of Abraham* 50–55; *Sipre Num.* §112 (on Num 15:27–31); *y. Ber.* 2.3; *Midrash Mishle* on Prov 17:1
Mark 12:29–30	Deut 6:4–5; *m. Ber.* 2:2; 9:5; *m. Soṭah* 7:8; *t. Roš Haš.* 2.13; *t. Soṭah* 7.17
Mark 12:29–31	*T. Dan* 5:3; *T. Iss.* 5:2; 7:6; Philo, *Spec. Laws* 2.63; *Sipra Lev.* §200 (on Lev 19:15–20); *b. Šabb.* 31a
Mark 12:31	Lev 19:18; *m. Ned.* 9:4; *t. Soṭah* 5.11; *t. Sanh.* 9.11
Mark 12:32	Deut 6:4b + 4:35
Mark 12:33	1 Sam 15:22; Hos 6:6

Mark 12:36	Ps 110:1; *Midr. Pss.* 110.4 (on Ps 110:1); *b. Sanh.* 38b; *Gen. Rab.* 85.9 (on Gen 38:18); *Num. Rab.* 18.23 (on Ps 17:21); cf. *Pss. Sol.* 17:21; *Apoc. Elijah* 4:28; *Barn.* 12:10–11
Mark 12:38	Philo, *Embassy* 296; Josephus, *Ant.* 3.7.1 §151; 11.4.2 §80; *y. Ber.* 2.1; *b. Ber.* 24b
Mark 12:41	Neh 12:44; Josephus, *J.W.* 5.5.2 §200; 6.5.2 §282; 1 Macc 14:49; 2 Macc 3:6, 24, 28, 40; *m. Šeqal.* 6:5
Mark 12:44	*Lev. Rab.* 3.5 (on Lev 1:17)
Mark 13:1	Josephus, *J.W.* 5.5.1–8 §§184–247; *Ant.* 15.11.3 §§391–402
Mark 13:1–2	*T. Levi* 16:4; *T. Jud.* 23:3; *Sib. Or.* 3:665; *Liv. Pro.* 10:10–11; 12:11; Josephus, *J.W.* 3.8.3 §§351–352; 6.2.1 §109; 6.5.3 §§301–309; 6.5.4 §311; *y. Soṭah* 6.3
Mark 13:2	2 Sam 17:13; Ezek 26:12; Hag 2:15; Josephus, *J.W.* 7.1.1 §§1–4; *y. Yoma* 1.1
Mark 13:4	*2 Bar.* 25:3
Mark 13:5	*Apoc. Elijah* 1:14
Mark 13:6	*Apoc. Elijah* 1:13; Josephus, *J.W.* 4.9.3–8 §§503–544; 4.9.10 §§556–565; Tacitus, *Hist.* 2.8; Suetonius, *Nero* 57.2
Mark 13:7	Jer 51:46; Dan 11:44; *2 Bar.* 27:3, 5; *Apoc. Elijah* 2:2; *m. Soṭah* 9:15; *Pesiq. Rab. Kah.* 5.9
Mark 13:8	2 Chr 15:6; Isa 19:2; 4 Ezra 6:13–15; 9:3; 13:31; *T. Mos.* 10:4; *2 Bar.* 27:2, 6, 8, 9; *Sib. Or.* 3:363–364, 635–636; Ovid, *Metam.* 15.798; Livy 32.8.3; Appian, *Bell. civ.* 1.9.83; *Mek.* on Exod 16:28–36 (*Vayassaʾ* §6); *Pesiq. Rab. Kah.* 5.9
Mark 13:9	Acts 4:1–22; 5:27–41; 6:12; 22:30; 23:1; 24:20; Josephus, *Ant.* 20.9.1 §200; *2 Bar.* 13:4
Mark 13:11	Exod 4:12; *Ahiqar* 115
Mark 13:12	Isa 19:2; Mic 7:6; *1 En.* 100:1–2; *3 Bar.* 4:17
Mark 13:13	4 Ezra 6:25
Mark 13:14	Dan 9:27; 11:31; 12:11; 1 Macc 1:54; Josephus, *Ant.* 12.5.4 §253; 2 Thess 2:3–4
Mark 13:15–16	Gen 19:17
Mark 13:17	4 Ezra 6:21
Mark 13:19	Dan 12:1; *T. Mos.* 8:1
Mark 13:20	Isa 60:21–22; 4Q385 frg. 3, lines 3–5
Mark 13:22	Deut 13:1–3; *Tg. Neof.* Deut 13:1–3; *Sib. Or.* 3:63–69; Josephus, *J.W.* 2.13.4 §259
Mark 13:24–25	Isa 8:22; 13:10; 34:4; Jer 10:18; LXX Mic 2:12; Hab 3:16; *T. Mos.* 10:1–4; *Sib. Or.* 3:796–803; Virgil, *Aen.* 1.463; Suetonius, *Dom.* 16.1
Mark 13:26	Dan 7:13–14; *b. Sanh.* 96b–97a, 98a; *Num. Rab.* 13.14 (on Num 7:13); *Midr. Pss.* 21.5 (on Ps 21:7); 93.1 (on Ps 93:1); *Frg. Tg.* Exod 12:42
Mark 13:27	*1 En.* 62:13–14; *Pss. Sol.* 8:28; 11:1–4; 17:21–28; *Tg. Isa.* 53:8; *Tg. Hos.* 14:8; *Tg. Mic.* 5:1–3

Mark 13:32	Isa 46:10; Zech 14:7; 4 Ezra 4:51–52; *2 Bar.* 21:8; *Mek.* on Exod 16:28–36 (*Vayassa'* §6)
Mark 13:35	Josephus, *Ant.* 5.6.5 §223
Mark 13:37	Homer, *Il.* 18.299
Mark 14:1	*T. Levi* 16:3
Mark 14:2	Josephus, *Ant.* 17.9.3 §§213–215
Mark 14:3	Pliny the Elder, *Nat.* 13.3.9
Mark 14:3–9	Pss 23:5; 141:5; *b. Ḥul.* 94a
Mark 14:4–5	*m. Pesaḥ.* 9:11
Mark 14:7	*b. Šabb.* 63a
Mark 14:9	*Jos. Asen.* 19:8; *b. B. Bat.* 21a; *m. Yoma* 3:9
Mark 14:12	Deut 16:7; *Sipre Num.* §69 (on Num 9:10); *t. Pesaḥ.* 8.2
Mark 14:13	1 Sam 10:1–5
Mark 14:18	Ps 41:9; 1QH 13:23–25 (formerly 5:23–25); *Syr. Men.* 215–216
Mark 14:21	*1 En.* 38:2; *2 En.* 41:2; *m. Ḥag.* 2:1; Bacchylides, frg. 3
Mark 14:22	*m. Ber.* 6:1; Josephus, *Ant.* 3.6.6 §§142–143; Melito of Sardis, *De pascha* 642
Mark 14:22–25	1 Macc 6:44; 2 Macc 7:33, 37–38; 4 Macc 1:11; 17:21–22; 18:3–4; 1QS 8:3–4; *L.A.B.* 18:5; *T. Mos.* 9:6–10:1; *Mek.* on Exod 12:1 (*Pesaḥ.* §1); *Sipre Deut.* §333 (on Deut 32:43); *y. Sanh.* 11.5
Mark 14:23	*m. Ber.* 6:1; *Jos. Asen.* 8:5, 11; 16:16
Mark 14:24	Jer 31:31; Zech 9:11; cf. Exod 24:8; Isa 53:12
Mark 14:25	Isa 25:6; 4 Ezra 6:52; *1 En.* 60:7; 62:14; *2 Bar.* 29:5–8
Mark 14:26	Psalm 136; *m. Pesaḥ.* 10:7
Mark 14:27	Zech 13:7; CD 19:5–11
Mark 14:28	*Tg. Song* 8:5
Mark 14:30	*m. Yoma* 1:8; *m. Tamid* 1:2
Mark 14:31	4 Macc 10:15; *T. Job* 5:1
Mark 14:34	LXX Jonah 4:9; Sir 37:2
Mark 14:36	Sir 23:1; 4Q372 frg. 1, line 16; 4Q460 frg. 5, line 6; *b. Taʿan.* 23b; Isa 51:22; Epictetus 2.17.22; 4.1.89–90; idem, *Ench.* 53.3; Catullus 11.13
Mark 14:37	Epictetus 3.22.95
Mark 14:41	LXX Ps 139:9 (140:8)
Mark 14:43	Josephus, *Ant.* 20.8.8 §181; 20.9.2 §§206–207; *t. Menaḥ.* 13.19–21; *t. Zebaḥ.* 11.16–17; *b. Pesaḥ.* 57a; *b. Yebam.* 86a–b; *b. Ketub.* 26a
Mark 14:45	2 Sam 20:9–10; 1 Esdr 4:47; *t. Ḥag.* 2.1
Mark 14:52	*T. Jos.* 8:3
Mark 14:58	Dan 2:44–45; Zech 6:12; *Tg. Zech.* 6:12; John 2:19; *2 Bar.* 4:2
Mark 14:59	Sus 36–62
Mark 14:61	Ps 2:2–7; 1QSa 2:11–12
Mark 14:62	*T. Job* 29:3–4; Ps 110:1; Dan 7:13 (cf. Mark 13:26 above); *Midr. Pss.* 2.9 (on Ps 2:7); Rev 3:21
Mark 14:63	*m. Sanh.* 7:5; Job 1:20
Mark 14:64	LXX Gen 26:11; Lev 24:16
Mark 14:65	Num 12:14; Deut 25:9; 4 Ezra 6:56; *2 Bar.* 82:5; *L.A.B.* 7:3

Mark 14:66	*t. Menaḥ.* 13.21
Mark 14:68	*T. Jos.* 13:2
Mark 15:1	Tacitus, *Ann.* 15.44; Philo, *Embassy* 301–302; Josephus, *J.W.* 2.9.2–3 §§171–174; 2.9.4 §175
Mark 15:2	Josephus, *J.W.* 1.14.4 §282
Mark 15:4	Isa 53:7; Plato, *Resp.* 362A; Plutarch, *Mor.* 498DE: *An vit.* 2
Mark 15:6–15	P.Flor. 61; *m. Pesaḥ.* 8:6; Josephus, *Ant.* 17.8.4 §204; 20.9.5 §215; Pliny the Younger, *Ep.* 10.31; Livy 5.13.8
Mark 15:14–15	Josephus, *Ant.* 18.3.3 §§63–64
Mark 15:15	*Dig.* 48.19.8.3; Josephus, *J.W.* 2.14.9 §306; 6.5.3 §304; 5.11.1 §449; 7.6.4 §203; Philo, *Posterity* 61; idem, *Dreams* 2.213; Juvenal, *Sat.* 14.77–78; Horace, *Ep.* 1.16.48; Pliny the Elder, *Nat.* 28.41, 46; Seneca, *De consolatione* 20.3; idem, *Ira* 3.3.6; idem, *Vit. beat.* 19.3; idem, *Ep.* 101.11–14; Lucan, *De bello civili* 6.543–547; Suetonius, *Aug.* 13.1–2; Plutarch, *Mor.* 499D: *An vit.* 3; Achilles Tatius 2.37.3; Ps.-Quintilian, *Decl.* 274; Galen, *On the Use of Parts* 12.11; Apuleius, *Metam.* 3.17.4
Mark 15:16–20	Philo, *Flaccus* 36–39; Dio Cassius, *Hist. rom.* 64.20–21; 4 Macc 6:1–30; P.Louvre 68 1.1–7; Plutarch, *Life of Pompey* 24.7–8
Mark 15:17	Suetonius, *Tiberius* 17.2
Mark 15:18	Suetonius, *Claud.* 21.6
Mark 15:20–21	Plautus, *Carbonaria* 2; idem, *Miles gloriosus* 2.4.6–7 §§359–360; Plutarch, *Mor.* 554AB: *Sera* 9; Seneca, *Ira* 3.2.2; 6.20.3; Josephus, *J.W.* 5.11.1 §§449–451
Mark 15:23	Prov 31:6; *b. Sanh.* 43a; *Sem.* 2.9; Pliny the Elder, *Nat.* 14.15.92; 14.19.107
Mark 15:24	Ps 22:18; *Dig.* 48.20.1; Tacitus, *Ann.* 6.29
Mark 15:26	Suetonius, *Cal.* 32.2; Dio Cassius, *Hist. rom.* 54.3.6–7
Mark 15:29	Ps 22:7; Wis 2:17–18; *Mart. Isa.* 5:2–3
Mark 15:33	Exod 10:22; Jer 15:9; Amos 8:9; Joel 2:10; Diogenes Laertius 4.64; Plutarch, *Life of Caesar* 69.3–5; Virgil, *Georgics* 1.463–468; *b. Moʾed Qaṭan* 25b
Mark 15:34	Ps 22:1
Mark 15:35	Sir 48:10; *b. ʿAbod. Zar.* 17b; *b. Taʿan.* 21a
Mark 15:36	Ps 69:2
Mark 15:37	Josephus, *Ant.* 12.9.1 §357
Mark 15:38	Josephus, *J.W.* 5.5.4 §214
Mark 15:42–46	Deut 21:22–23; *t. Sanh.* 9.7
Mark 15:43	*Dig.* 48.24.1–2; 48.16.15; Tacitus, *Ann.* 6.29
Mark 15:44–45	Seneca, *Ira* 3.2.2; Juvenal, *Sat.* 14.77–78; Petronius, *Sat.* 111
Mark 16:5	2 Macc 3:26, 33; Josephus, *Ant.* 5.8.2 §277; *L.A.B.* 9:10
Mark 16:6	*T. Job* 39:11–12
Mark 16:8	Chariton of Aphrodisias, *Chaereas and Callirhoe* 3.3.1–7
Mark 16:9	Luke 8:2
Mark 16:10	Matt 9:15
Mark 16:11	Luke 24:11

Mark 16:12	Luke 24:13–35
Mark 16:14	John 20:19, 26
Mark 16:14–15	W (Codex Washington)
Mark 16:15	Matt 28:19
Mark 16:16	John 3:18, 36
Mark 16:17	Acts 2:4; 10:46
Mark 16:18a	Acts 28:3–5; *T. Jos.* 6:2, 7; *T. Benj.* 3:5; 5:2; Apollonius Paradoxographus, *Mirabilia* 6; *m. Ber.* 5:1; *t. Ber.* 3.20; *b. Ber.* 33a
Mark 16:18b	Acts 9:17; 28:8
Mark 16:19	Luke 24:51; Acts 1:2, 9
Mark 16:20	Book of Acts

Luke

Luke 1:1–4	*Let. Aris.* 1–2; Josephus, *Ag. Ap.* 1.1 §§1–3; 2.1 §1
Luke 1:6	*2 En.* 9:1; *Apoc. Zeph.* 3:4
Luke 1:7–23	Judg 13:2–21
Luke 1:13	Gen 17:19
Luke 1:15	Num 6:3; Judg 13:4; *m. Naz.* 9:5
Luke 1:17	Mal 4:5–6; Sir 48:10; 3 Macc 48:10; *m. ʿEd.* 8:7
Luke 1:18	Gen 15:8
Luke 1:19	Tob 12:15
Luke 1:25	LXX Gen 30:23
Luke 1:31	Isa 7:14
Luke 1:32–35	2 Sam 7:12, 13, 16; Isa 9:6–7; *Tg. Isa.* 9:6–7; Mic 4:7; Dan 2:44; 7:14; 1QSa 2:11–12; 4QFlor 1:1–13; 4Q246 1:7–2:4; 4Q252 5
Luke 1:34–38	*T. Isaac* 3:17
Luke 1:37	Aetius, *Plac. phil.* 1.7
Luke 1:42	Jdt 13:18; *2 Bar.* 54:11
Luke 1:46–55	1 Sam 2:1–10; *Tg. 1 Sam.* 2:1–10
Luke 1:47	Hab 3:18
Luke 1:48	LXX 1 Sam 1:11; Ps 113:5–6
Luke 1:49	Deut 10:21; Ps 111:9
Luke 1:50	Ps 103:17
Luke 1:51	Ps 89:11
Luke 1:52	1 Sam 2:4, 7; Sir 10:14; Ovid, *Tristia* 3.7.41
Luke 1:53	Ps 107:9; 1 Sam 2:5; Job 22:9
Luke 1:54–55	Isa 41:8–9; Ps 98:3; Gen 12:1–3; 17:6–8; Mic 7:20
Luke 1:59	Lev 12:3
Luke 1:68	Pss 41:3; 111:9
Luke 1:69	Pss 18:2; 132:17
Luke 1:70	1QS 1:3
Luke 1:71	Ps 18:71; 2 Sam 22:18; Ps 106:10
Luke 1:72	Gen 24:12; Mic 7:2; Pss 105:8; 106:45
Luke 1:73	Gen 26:3; Jer 11:5

Luke 1:75	Josh 24:14; Isa 38:20
Luke 1:76	Mal 3:1; Isa 40:3
Luke 1:78	*T. Zeb.* 7:3; 8:2
Luke 1:79	Ps 107:10; Isa 9:2; 59:8
Luke 2:1–2	Josephus, *J.W.* 7.8.1 §§253–255
Luke 2:7	Wis 7:4
Luke 2:11	*Pss. Sol.* 17:32
Luke 2:14	*Pss. Sol.* 18:10; *1 Clem.* 60:4; 1QH 19:9; 4Q545 frg. 3, line 5
Luke 2:19	LXX Dan 4:28; *T. Levi* 6:2; *Apoc. Mos.* 3:3; Homer, *Od.* 1.230; Aeschylus, *Prom.* 705
Luke 2:22	Lev 12:6; *m. Ker.* 6:9
Luke 2:23	Exod 13:2, 12, 15
Luke 2:24	Lev 12:8
Luke 2:25	Isa 40:1; 49:13; *2 Bar.* 44:8; *Lam. Rab.* 1:16 §51
Luke 2:29	Tob 11:9
Luke 2:30	Isa 40:5
Luke 2:31	Isa 52:10
Luke 2:32	Isa 42:6; 49:6; *1 En.* 48:4; *Tg. Isa.* 42:6; cf. Isa 40:5; LXX Isa 46:13; *Barn.* 14:8
Luke 2:34	Isa 8:14
Luke 2:35	*Sib. Or.* 3:316
Luke 2:37	Jdt 8:6; *T. Jos.* 4:8
Luke 2:42	Josephus, *Ant.* 5.10.4 §348
Luke 2:51	*Apoc. Mos.* 3:3; Homer, *Od.* 1.230; Aeschylus, *Prom.* 705
Luke 2:52	1 Sam 2:26; Prov 3:4; *T. Reu.* 4:8
Luke 3:2	Josephus, *Ant.* 18.2.2 §35; 20.9.1 §198
Luke 3:3–4	*Sib. Or.* 4:165
Luke 3:4–6	Exod 40:3–5; 4Q174 3:15
Luke 3:7	Zeph 1:15; 1QH 11:28
Luke 3:8	Pr Man 8; *Tg. Isa.* 33:11–14
Luke 3:14	Plato, *Tim.* 17D–18B
Luke 3:16	*1 En.* 67:13; *T. Isaac* 5:21
Luke 3:17	*Tg. Isa.* 33:11–12
Luke 3:23	1QSa 1:13
Luke 3:36	*Jub.* 8:2
Luke 4:1–2	*2 Bar.* 10:8; *Tg. Ps.-J.* Deut 32:10
Luke 4:4–12	Deut 8:3; 6:16, 13
Luke 4:13	*L.A.E.* 17:2
Luke 4:18–19	LXX Isa 61:1–2; 58:6; cf. LXX Lev 25:10–13; 11QMelch 2:9–16
Luke 4:23	Euripides, frg. 1086; Plutarch, *Mor.* 71F: *How to Recognize a Flatterer* 32; *Gen. Rab.* 23.4 (on Gen 4:23–25); *Gos. Thom.* §31
Luke 4:25–27	1 Kgs 17:8–16; 2 Kgs 5:1–14
Luke 5:1	Josephus, *J.W.* 3.10.7 §506
Luke 5:31	Seneca, *Ep.* 50.4; Plutarch, *Life of Demosthenes* 3.2
Luke 5:37–39	Sir 9:10

Luke 6:1	*m. Šabb.* 7:2; *b. Šabb.* 73a–b
Luke 6:10	*T. Sim.* 2:13
Luke 6:12	4 Macc 3:13–19
Luke 6:18	Heliodorus, *Aeth.* 4.174
Luke 6:20	*Pss. Sol.* 10:7; *b. Ber.* 6b
Luke 6:20–23	4Q525 2+3 ii 1–9
Luke 6:21	*Gos. Thom.* §69b
Luke 6:23	*Tg. Isa.* 28:11–12
Luke 6:24	Isa 3:11; Jer 22:13; Hab 2:6, 9, 12, 15, 19; *1 En.* 94:8
Luke 6:25	Sir 7:34; 21:20
Luke 6:27	Lysias, *Pro milite* 20; Diogenes Laertius 8.1.23
Luke 6:28	Herodotus, *Hist.* 7.160; *Der. Er. Rab.* 2.13
Luke 6:29	Job 16:10; Lam 3:30
Luke 6:30	Tob 4:7
Luke 6:31	Tob 4:15
Luke 6:33	Cicero, *Off.* 1.15; idem, *De provinciis consularibus* 17
Luke 6:35	Wis 15:1; 16:29; 4 Macc 9:10
Luke 6:36	*Tg. Ps.-J.* Lev 22:28; Juvenal, *Sat.* 15.131, 149
Luke 6:37	Velleius Paterculus 2.56; Ammianus Marcellinus, *Res gest.* 19.12
Luke 6:38	*2 En.* 44:4; 50:5; Ps.-Phocylides, *Sent.* 12–13; Hesiod, *Op.* 349; Lucian, *Imag.* 12; *m. Soṭah* 1:7; *t. Soṭah* 3.1, 2; *Sipre Num.* §106 (on Num 12:1–16)
Luke 6:39	Plato, *Resp.* 554B; Philo, *Virtues* 7; Dio Cassius, *Hist. rom.* 62.7; Plutarch, *Mor.* 139A: *Conj. praec.* 6; Curtius Rufus Quintus 7.4.10
Luke 6:40	*Sipra Lev.* §251 (on Lev 25:18–24)
Luke 6:44	Sir 27:6; *b. Ber.* 48a; Seneca, *Ep.* 87.25
Luke 6:45	Sir 13:25; Bar 1:21; *Gos. Thom.* §45
Luke 6:48	*PSI* 672.3; P.Magd. 27.4
Luke 6:49	Epictetus 2.15.9
Luke 7:3	*Let. Aris.* 46
Luke 7:10	*b. Ber.* 34b
Luke 7:11–17	1 Kgs 17:17–24; 2 Kgs 4:8–37; Sir 48:1–14; *Liv. Pro.* 21–22; Philostratus, *Vit. Apoll.* 4.45
Luke 7:22	Isa 26:19; 35:5–6; 53:8; 61:1; 4Q521 frgs. 2+4 ii 1–12; Sir 48:5; *Apoc. Elijah* 3:9
Luke 7:27	Mal 3:1; 4:5; *m. ᶜEd.* 8:7
Luke 7:39, 41, 47	*Tg. Neof.* Exod 32:31
Luke 8:29	Lucian, *Philops.* 16
Luke 9:3	Crates, *Ep.* 16, 23, 33; Diogenes, *Ep.* 7, 13, 15, 19, 26, 30, 34, 38, 46; Diogenes Laertius 4.51; 6.13, 33; *PGM* IV. 2381
Luke 9:8	Sir 48:10
Luke 9:27	4 Ezra 6:26
Luke 9:51	Gen 5:24; 2 Kgs 2:9–16; LXX Ezek 21:1–3
Luke 9:52	Mal 3:1; Josephus, *Ant.* 20.6.1 §118
Luke 9:54	LXX 2 Kgs 1:10, 12; *T. Ab.* (A) 10:11

Luke 9:60	*Sent. Sextus* 7b; *Exod. Rab.* 5.14 (on Exod 5:2)
Luke 9:61–62	1 Kgs 19:19–21; Hesiod, *Op.* 443; Epictetus 3.5.2–3; Ps.-Crates 28
Luke 10:1–2	Gen 10:2–31; 46:27; *1 En.* 89–90
Luke 10:3	*1 En.* 89; Diogenes Laertius, *Vit. phil.* 6.92; Epictetus 3.22.35
Luke 10:4	Crates, *Ep.* 16, 23, 33; Diogenes, *Ep.* 7, 13, 15, 19, 26, 30, 34, 38, 46; Musonius 19; Diogenes Laertius 4.51; 6.13, 33; *PGM* IV. 2381
Luke 10:5	1 Sam 25:6; Job 21:9; Aristophanes, *Birds* 959; Lucian, *Philosophies for Sale* 10
Luke 10:7	Epictetus 3.26.27–28
Luke 10:15	Isa 14:13, 15; *Pss. Sol.* 1:5; *t. Soṭah* 3.19
Luke 10:17	Tob 6:17
Luke 10:18	*T. Sol.* 20:16–17; *Tg. Isa.* 14:12; *L.A.E.* 12:1; *2 En.* 29:5; 31:4
Luke 10:19	Sir 11:19
Luke 10:19–20	Ps 91:13; *T. Sim.* 6:6; *T. Levi* 18:12; *T. Zeb.* 9:8
Luke 10:20	Mal 3:16–17; *1 En.* 47:3; 104:1; 1QM 12:2; Phil 4:3; Rev 3:5; 21:27
Luke 10:21	Sir 51:1
Luke 10:24	*Tg. Isa.* 48:6
Luke 10:27	Deut 6:5; Lev 19:18; *T. Iss.* 5:2; *T. Iss.* 5:2; *T. Dan* 5:3; Philo, *Decalogue* 109–100; idem, *Spec. Laws* 2.63; *Sipra Lev.* §200 (on Lev 19:15–20)
Luke 10:28	CD 3:14–20; *Tg. Onq.* Lev 18:5
Luke 10:30–35	2 Chr 28:8–15
Luke 10:36–37	Seneca, *Vit. beat.* 24
Luke 10:37	Deut 7:2; *t. ʿAbod. Zar.* 3.11–15; LXX 1 Kgs 2:31; *2 Bar.* 5:4
Luke 10:42	*ʾAbot* 2:8; 3:2
Luke 11:5	Diogenes Laertius, *Vit. phil.* 6.56
Luke 11:8	Josephus, *Ag. Ap.* 2.23 §197
Luke 11:20	Exod 31:18; Deut 9:10
Luke 11:21–22	Isa 53:12; *Pss. Sol.* 5:4
Luke 11:25	*2 Bar.* 25:3
Luke 11:27	Prov 23:24–25; *ʾAbot* 2:8; *Tg. Neof.* Gen 49:25; *Gos. Thom.* §79; Virgil, *Aen.* 1.605; Ovid, *Metam.* 4.322
Luke 11:27–28	*Tg. Neof.* Gen 49:25; *Tg. Ps.-J.* Gen 49:25; *Gen. Rab.* 98.20 (on Gen 49:25)
Luke 11:38	*Num. Rab.* 20.21 (on Num 24:3)
Luke 11:39	Euripides, *Orest.* 1606; idem, *Hipp.* 317
Luke 11:52	*Gos. Thom.* §39
Luke 12:11–12	*Ahiqar* 114
Luke 12:13–21	*Ahiqar* 137
Luke 12:14	*PSI* 452; Epictetus 3.3.9; *Gos. Thom.* §72 (cf. Exod 2:14)
Luke 12:15	Sir 11:18–19; Seneca, *Ad Helviam* 9.9
Luke 12:16–20	*Gos. Thom.* §63
Luke 12:18	P.Cair.Zen. 59.509
Luke 12:19	Isa 22:13; Tob 7:10; *1 En.* 97:8–10; *T. Mos.* 7:4, 8; Aeschylus, *Pers.* 840; Horace, *Carm.* 1.9.14; Rufinus, in *Anth. pal.* 5.12; *EG* 362;

	Publilius Syrus, *Sent.* 359; Seneca, *Ep.* 101.4–5; Valerius Maximus, *Fact. dict.* 2.9.1
Luke 12:19–20	Sir 11:18–19
Luke 12:20	Wis 15:8; Philo, *Alleg. Interp.* 3.227; Josephus, *Ant.* 1.13.2 §227; Dio Cassius, *Hist. rom.* 16.8; Virgil, *Aen.* 10.739–741
Luke 12:33	Sir 29:9–12
Luke 12:33–34	Tob 4:8–10
Luke 12:45	*T. Jos.* 3:5
Luke 12:54	1 Kgs 18:44
Luke 13:1	Philo, *Embassy* 38; Josephus, *Ant.* 18.3.1–2 §§55–62; idem, *J.W.* 2.9.2–4 §§169–177
Luke 13:4	*ʾAbot R. Nat.* (A) 35.1
Luke 13:6	Mic 4:4; Pliny the Elder, *Nat.* 17.35.200
Luke 13:24	4 Ezra 7:11–14; *Sipre Deut.* §53 (on Deut 11:26)
Luke 13:27	LXX Ps 6:9; 1 Macc 3:6
Luke 13:28–29	*2 En.* 42:5
Luke 13:29	Bar 4:37
Luke 13:32	*ʾAbot* 4:15; *b. Ber.* 61b; Pindar, *Pyth.* 2.77–78; Plutarch, *Life of Solon* 30.2; Epictetus 1.3.8–9
Luke 13:33	Diogenes Laertius, *Vit. phil.* 2.35
Luke 13:34	Deut 32:11; Isa 31:5
Luke 13:34–35	*Tg. Isa.* 28:11–12; 32:14
Luke 13:35	Jer 12:7; 22:5; Ps 118:26; Tob 14:4
Luke 14:2	*b. ʿErub.* 41b; *b. Šabb.* 33a
Luke 14:5	CD 11:13–14
Luke 14:7–11	Prov 25:6–7; Sir 3:18, 20; *b. ʿErub.* 13b; *Lev. Rab.* 1.5 (on Lev 1:1); Plutarch, *Mor.* 148E–149A: *Sept. sap. conv.* 3; *Mor.* 615CD: *Quaest. conv.* 1.2.1; Dio Chrysostom, *Disc.* 30.41–44
Luke 14:11	Ezek 21:26; Sir 3:17–20
Luke 14:12–14	Tob 2:2; Plato, *Phaedo* 233E; Dio Chrysostom, *Disc.* 7.88
Luke 14:14	*2 En.* 50:5
Luke 14:15	Isa 25:6; 1QSa 2:11–22
Luke 14:16	*2 En.* 42:5
Luke 14:28	Cicero, *Off.* 1.21; Juvenal, *Sat.* 11.35
Luke 14:31–32	2 Sam 8:10
Luke 15:1–2	Sir 12:4; *Mek.* on Exod 18:1 (*Amalek* §3)
Luke 15:3–7	Isa 40:11; Ezek 34:11–16; *Gos. Thom.* §107; *Exod. Rab.* 2.2 (on Exod 3:1)
Luke 15:4	1 Sam 17:28
Luke 15:5	Job 31:36; Sir 6:25
Luke 15:7	*Jos. Asen.* 15:8; *ʾAbot* 4:22
Luke 15:8–10	Prov 2:4; *Song Rab.* 1:1 §9
Luke 15:11–12	Deut 21:15–17
Luke 15:11–24	*Sipre Deut.* §345 (on Deut 33:4); *Deut. Rab.* 2.24 (on Deut 4:30); *Pesiq. Rab.* 44.9; Ps.-Quintilian, *Decl.* 5; *Apoc. Sedr.* 6:4–6

Luke 15:12	Deut 21:17; Tob 3:17; 1 Macc 10:29–30; Sir 33:19, 23
Luke 15:13	Sir 3:12; Dio Chrysostom, *Disc.* 4.103–104
Luke 15:15–16	Lev 11:7; Deut 14:8
Luke 15:16	*Lev. Rab.* 13.4 (on Lev 11:2); *Lam. Rab.* proem §17; 3:14 §5; *Sipre Num.* §89 (on Num 11:7–9)
Luke 15:17	*T. Jos.* 3:9; *Lam. Rab.* 1:7 §34
Luke 15:18	Exod 10:16; BGU 846.12
Luke 15:20	Gen 29:13; Tob 11:9
Luke 15:24	*Lev. Rab.* 6.6 (on Lev 5:1)
Luke 15:30	Philo, *Providence* 2.4–5
Luke 15:32	*Lev. Rab.* 6.6 (on Lev 5:1)
Luke 16:1–9	Deut 15:7–8; 23:20–21; Dio Cassius, *Hist. rom.* 52.37.5–6; Seneca, *Ben.* 4.27.5
Luke 16:2	*T. Jos.* 13:1
Luke 16:3	Ps.-Phocylides, *Sent.* 158
Luke 16:8	1QS 1:9; 2:16; 3:13; 1QM 1:3, 9, 11, 13
Luke 16:9	*1 En.* 39:4; 63:10; *Tg. Isa.* 5:23; 33:15; *Tg. 1 Sam.* 12:3; *T. Ezek.* 22:27; *Tg. Hos.* 5:11
Luke 16:10	*Sent. Sextus* 9–10
Luke 16:11	*1 En.* 39:4; 63:10; *Tg. Isa.* 5:23; 33:15; *Tg. 1 Sam.* 12:3; *T. Ezek.* 22:27; *Tg. Hos.* 5:11
Luke 16:13	*Pythagorean Sentences* 110; Dio Chrysostom, *Disc.* 66.13; Seneca, *Ep.* 18.13
Luke 16:19	Prov 31:22
Luke 16:19–31	Tob 4:10; *Sent. Sextus* 73
Luke 16:21	Callimachus, *Hymn. Cer.* 113
Luke 16:23	4 Ezra 7:36; 4 Macc 13:15; *1 En.* 22:9–11
Luke 16:24	4 Ezra 8:59
Luke 16:26	*1 En.* 18:11–12; Plato, *Resp.* 615D–617D; 4 Ezra 7:36; 4 Macc 13:15; *1 En.* 22:9–11
Luke 17:3	*T. Gad* 6:3
Luke 17:10	ʾAbot 2:8
Luke 17:20	*b. Sanh.* 98a
Luke 17:21	*Gos. Thom.* §3
Luke 17:24	*Apoc. Elijah* 3:4
Luke 17:28–29	Gen 7:6–23; 18:20–21; 19:1–14
Luke 17:34–35	*Apoc. Zeph.* 2:2
Luke 18:1–8	P.Mich. 29; P.Ryl. 2; Plutarch, *Mor.* 179CD: *Sayings of Kings and Commanders: Philip the Father of Alexander* 31; idem, *Life of Demetrius* 42; Stobaeus, *Flor.* 13.28
Luke 18:7	Sir 35:22
Luke 18:8	Philo, *Moses* 1.47; *CII* 2
Luke 18:11	Horace, *Sat.* 2.7.72
Luke 18:11–12	*b. Ber.* 28b
Luke 18:12	Suetonius, *Aug.* 76.2

Luke 18:13	*1 En.* 13:5; 4 Ezra 8:47b–50
Luke 18:21	*2 Bar.* 38:4
Luke 18:22	Sir 29:11; Tob 4:8–10
Luke 19:8	Exod 22:1
Luke 19:9	*ʾAbot* 5:19; Gal 3:29
Luke 19:10	Ezek 34:16
Luke 19:12–27	*Ahiqar* 193; Josephus, *Ant.* 17.9.3–11.4 §§219–320; 17.13.1 §339; *J.W.* 2.2.1–2.6.3 §§14–100 (on Archelaus's bid for kingship)
Luke 19:13	*Gen. Rab.* 100.10 (on Gen 50:22); *Midr. Tanḥ.* (B) on Exod 21:1–24:18 (*Mishpatim* 6.9)
Luke 19:20	*m. B. Meṣiʿa* 3:10; *b. Ketub.* 67b
Luke 19:22	*Num. Rab.* 16.21 (on Num 14:2)
Luke 19:23	Deut 23:19–20; Exod 22:25; Lev 25:36–37
Luke 19:39–40	Hab 2:11; *Tg. Hab.* 2:11; 1QpHab 9:14–10:1; *b. Taʿan.* 11a; *b. Ḥag.* 16a; *Midr. Pss.* 73.4 (on Ps 73:10)
Luke 19:40	4 Ezra 5:5
Luke 19:41	Jer 8:23 (9:1)
Luke 19:42	Jer 6:8; cf. Isa 48:18; *Gen. Rab.* 56.10 (on Gen 22:14)
Luke 19:43	2 Kgs 20:17; cf. Jer 7:32; Jer 6:6; Ezek 4:2; Isa 29:3
Luke 19:44	2 Sam 17:13; 2 Kgs 8:12; Jer 6:15; Hos 10:14; Wis 3:7; Josephus, *J.W.* 4.9.11 §573
Luke 19:46	Plutarch, *Life of Tiberius Gracchus* 15.6
Luke 20:18	Isa 8:14–15; Dan 2:34–35, 44–45; *Esth. Rab.* 7.10 (on Esth 3:6)
Luke 20:23	Sir 19:25
Luke 20:36	*2 Bar.* 51:9
Luke 20:37	4 Macc 7:19; 16:25
Luke 20:37–38	*T. Jud.* 25:1; 4 Macc 7:18–19
Luke 21:5–6	Josephus, *Ant.* 15.1.3 §395; Tacitus, *Hist.* 5.8.1
Luke 21:7	*2 Bar.* 25:3
Luke 21:10	*Sib. Or.* 636–637
Luke 21:11	2 Macc 5:2–3; *Sib. Or.* 3:796–808; *T. Jud.* 23:3; *2 Bar.* 27:9
Luke 21:19	*2 En.* 50:2
Luke 21:20	LXX Jer 41:1 (34:1); Dan 12:11
Luke 21:21	Jer 50:8; 51:6, 45; cf. Eusebius, *Hist. eccl.* 3.5.3; Epiphanius, *Pan.* 29.7.8; idem, *Treatise on Weights and Measures* §15
Luke 21:22	Hos 9:7; LXX Jer 28:6 (51:6); Isa 61:2
Luke 21:23	2 Kgs 8:12; Zeph 1:15–16
Luke 21:24	Sir 28:18; Deut 28:41, 64; Jer 15:2; Zech 12:1–3; 2 Kgs 3:27; Tob 1:10; LXX Ezra 9:7; Zech 12:3; *Pss. Sol.* 17:22, 25; 1 Macc 3:45, 51; Dan 12:7; Tob 14:5
Luke 21:25	Isa 13:10; 17:12; 34:4; Joel 2:10; Wis 5:22; *1 En.* 80:4–7; *T. Mos.* 10:5
Luke 21:25–26	*2 Bar.* 25:4
Luke 21:26	Isa 24:18–19; Joel 2:10; *T. Levi* 4:1
Luke 21:28	Isa 63:4; LXX Dan 4:34; *1 En.* 51:2
Luke 21:34	Cicero, *Philippics* 2.19

Luke 21:34–35   Isa 24:17; CD 4:12–19

Luke 22:25   *OGIS* 458.39–42; 666.3–9; P.Lond. 177.24; P.Oxy. 486.27; *IG* 978; *CIG* 5041

Luke 22:27   *T. Jos.* 17:8

Luke 22:28–30   *T. Ab.* (A) 13:6

Luke 22:31   Job 1:6–7; *T. Benj.* 3:3

Luke 22:33   John 21:18–19; Eusebius, *Hist. eccl.* 2.25.5; Valerius Maximus, *Fact. dict.* 4.6.3

Luke 22:37   Isa 53:12; cf. *Tg. Isa.* 52:13–53:12; *Pss. Sol.* 16:5

Luke 22:42   Epictetus 2.17.22; 4.1.89–90; idem, *Ench.* 53.3; Catullus 11.13

Luke 22:43–44   𝔓⁷⁵ ℵ A B; *Jos. Asen.* 4:9

Luke 22:44   Diodorus Siculus 17.90

Luke 22:45   Isa 38:15; Dan 2:1; 6:18; Prov 3:24; Homer, *Od.* 12.310; 16.450; Propertius 1.3.45

Luke 22:48   Homer, *Il.* 24.759

Luke 23:12   Livy 1.46; Ammianus Marcellinus, *Res gest.* 28.1

Luke 23:17   𝔓⁷⁵ ℵ A B

Luke 23:28   Jer 9:20

Luke 23:29   2 Kgs 20:17; Jer 7:32; Isa 54:1; *2 Bar.* 10:14; *Apoc. Elijah* 2:38; *Gen. Rab.* 5.9 (on Gen 1:13)

Luke 23:30   Hos 10:8; cf. Rev 6:16; Jer 7:32; 16:14; *Apoc. Elijah* 2:34

Luke 23:34   Lev 4:2; Num 15:25–30; Isa 2:6, 9; Plato, *Apol.* 41D

Luke 23:39–43   *Ruth Rab.* 3.3 (on Ruth 1:17)

Luke 23:45   Josephus, *Ant.* 14.12.3 §309; Diogenes Laertius, *Vit. phil.* 4.64

Luke 23:46   Ps 31:5; cf. *Num. Rab.* 20.20 (on Num 23:24); *Midr. Pss.* 25.2 (on Ps 25:1); *b. Ber.* 5a; *Apoc. Mos.* 42:8

Luke 23:48   Josephus, *Ant.* 7.10.5 §252; Arrian, *Anab.* 7.24.3

Luke 24:4   2 Macc 3:26

Luke 24:5   *Exod. Rab.* 5.14 (on Exod 5:2); *Lev. Rab.* 6.6 (on Lev 5:1)

Luke 24:16   2 Kgs 6:15–17

Luke 24:18   Cicero, *Pro Milone* 12.33

Luke 24:31   2 Macc 3:34

Luke 24:32   *T. Naph.* 7:4

Luke 24:44   4Q397 (= MMT) frgs. 14–21 ii 10–12 ("the Book of Moses, and the words of the Prophets, and David"); Sir 39:1

Luke 24:46   Isaiah 53; Hos 6:2; Joel 2:32; *b. Sanh.* 97b

Luke 24:50   Sir 50:20–21

Luke 24:53   Sir 50:22

John

John 1:1   LXX Ps 118:89; Prov 8:23, 27, 30; *Jub.* 2:1; Sir 1:1; 24:3, 9; Wis 8:3; 9:4; 18:15; Anaxagoras of Clazomenai, frg. 1 (*apud* Aetius, *Plac. phil.* 1.3); *2 En.* 33:4; *Corp. herm.* frg. 27; *Odes Sol.* 16:18

John 1:1–2	Gen 1:1; *Tg. Neof.* Gen 1:1; Prov 8:23, 27, 30; Wis 18:15; Philo, *Confusion* 62–63, 146–147; idem, *Flight* 97, 101; idem, *Dreams* 1.228–230; idem, *QE* 2.68 (on Exod 25:22); Iamblichus, *On the Mysteries* 8.2
John 1:1–3	*Tg. Neof.* Gen 1:1–2:3; Philo, *Heir* 205–206
John 1:1–5	*Tg. Neof.* Exod 12:42
John 1:3	LXX Ps 32:6 (33:6); Prov 3:19; Sir 24:8; 42:15; Wis 9:1–2, 9; 4 Ezra 6:38; 1QS 11:11; Philo, *Cherubim* 127; idem, *Creation* 20; *Odes Sol.* 12:8, 10; 16:18–19; *Tg. Neof.* Gen 1:26–27; *Frg. Tg.* Exod 3:14; *Tg. Isa.* 44:24
John 1:4	LXX Ps 118:25; Prov 8:35; Sir 24:27; Wis 18:3–4, 13; Bar 4:1–2; Philo, *Creation* 30; *Odes Sol.* 12:8, 10; 41:14; *Tg. Ps.-J.* Gen 3:24
John 1:5	Gen 1:2–5, 15; *Tg. Neof.* Exod 12:24; *Frg. Tg.* Gen 1:3; Isa 45:7; 1Q27 5–6; Wis 7:29–30; Philo, *Creation* 33–34; 4 Ezra 14:20; *L.A.B.* 60:2; *2 Bar.* 59:2; *Odes Sol.* 18:6; 21:3; *Corp. herm.* 13.9
John 1:7	*Corp. herm.* 1.32
John 1:8	*2 En.* 46:3
John 1:9	Job 33:30b; Sir 24:27, 32; *T. Levi* 14:4; *2 Bar.* 18:2; *Tg. Ps.-J.* Gen 1:3; *Odes Sol.* 36:3; *Corp. herm.* 1.32; 13.19
John 1:10	Sir 24:28; Bar 3:12; Philo, *Creation* 24; *Odes Sol.* 24:12
John 1:10–11	LXX Ps 147:15; Wis 9:10
John 1:11	Prov 1:29; Sir 24:12; *Odes Sol.* 7:12; 8:12
John 1:12	Sir 24:11; Wis 7:14, 27; *Odes Sol.* 7:4; 12:13; 42:4; *Frg. Tg.* Gen 40:23; Exod 14:31
John 1:13	Prov 8:25; *Corp. herm.* 13.6
John 1:14	Sir 1:10; 24:8–10, 16, 26; Wis 7:22, 25; 18:15; Bar 3:37; Exod 25:8; 29:46; 40:34; Joel 3:17; Zech 2:10(14); *Pss. Sol.* 7:6; *Pr. Jos.* frg. A; *Jub.* 7:6; *1 En.* 42:1–3; 1QS 4:4–5; *Odes Sol.* 12:12; Plato, *Tim.* 92C; Diodorus Siculus, *Bib. hist.* 6.1; Philo, *Embassy* 118; idem, *Confusion* 146; idem, *QG* 2.62 (on Gen 9:6); *Tg. Ps.-J.* Exod 29:42–46; *Tg. Zech.* 2:9
John 1:14–18	Exod 33:18–34:6; Philo *Confusion* 146; Wis 1:4; Sir 1:10; *1 En.* 4:1–3
John 1:16	Sir 24:26, 29; Philo, *Alleg. Interp.* 1.44
John 1:17	Exod 34:6; Sir 24:23
John 1:18	Exod 33:20; Sir 43:31; Prov 8:25, 30; Philo, *Posterity* 169; idem, *Flight* 101; *ʾAbot R. Nat.* (A) 31.3; *Gen. Rab.* 8.2 (on Gen 1:26); *Tg. Onq.* Exod 33:20–23; Cicero, *Tusc.* 1.28; Seneca, *Nat.* 7.30.3
John 1:23	Isa 40:3 (see Mark 1:3 above)
John 1:26	*Tg. Mic.* 4:8; cf. *Tg. Zech.* 4:7; 6:12
John 1:29	*2 En.* 64:5
John 1:38	Sirach, prologue
John 1:51	Gen 28:12; *Frg. Tg.* Gen 28:12; *Tg. Ps.-J.* Gen 28:12
John 2:1–11	Pausanias, *Descr.* 6.26.1–2; Pliny the Elder, *Nat.* 2.231; Philostratus, *Vit. Apoll.* 6.10; *2 Bar.* 29:1–8; Lucian, *A True Story* 1.7
John 2:4	Eunapius, *Life of Iamblichus* 549

John 2:17	Ps 69:9
John 2:24–25	*Tg. Ps.-J.* Gen 3:9
John 2:25	*3 En.* 10:3–11:3
John 3:3–5	Plato, *Phaedo* 70C, 71E; Philo, *QE* 2.46; idem, *Moses* 1.279; Marcus Aurelius, *Med.* 10.8; Apuleius, *Metam.* 11.23–24; Clement of Alexandria, *Exc.* 78.2; Hippolytus, *Haer.* 5.8.40–41; *Mithras Liturgy* (*apud* P.Paris 574); *Corp. herm.* 13.1–2; *b. Yebam.* 48b
John 3:4	*Corp. herm.* 13.1
John 3:5	Isa 44:4; 1QS 4:19–21
John 3:8	Sir 16:21; *Corp. herm.* 13.3
John 3:10–12	Wis 9:14, 16–17
John 3:12	Wis 9:16; 18:15–16
John 3:13	Prov 30:4; Bar 3:29; 4 Ezra 4:8; *Mek.* on Exod 19:8 (*Bahodesh* §2)
John 3:14	Ps.-Callisthenes, *Life and Works of Alexander* 2.21.7–11
John 3:14–15	Num 21:4–9; Wis 16:7; *Frg. Tg.* Num 21:9
John 3:15–16	1QS 4:7
John 3:17	Philo, *On God* (Armenian) frg. 7; *Apoc. Elijah* 1:6
John 3:18	Josephus, *J.W.* 2.8.6 §135
John 3:19	*T. Naph.* 2:10; 1QS 4:10, 20; *2 Bar.* 18:2
John 3:19–21	*2 En.* 46:3
John 3:20	Ammianus Marcellinus, *Res gest.* 15.7
John 3:21	Tob 4:6; 1QS 1:5; 5:3; 8:2
John 3:27	*Jub.* 5:3–4
John 3:29	1 Macc 9:39
John 3:31	Sir 24:4
John 3:36	1QS 4:7, 12
John 4:2	Josephus, *Ant.* 20.6.1 §118; idem, *Life* 52 §269
John 4:4–15	Macrobius, *Sat.* 1.12.28
John 4:9	Sir 50:25
John 4:10	*Memar Marqah* 2:1–2; 6:3
John 4:12–13	*Tg. Neof.* Gen 28:10; *Frg. Tg.* Gen 28:10
John 4:14	*1 En.* 42:1–3; *Memar Marqah* 2:1–2; 6:3; 1QS 4:7; CD 19:33–34
John 4:19	SP Exod 20:21b; *Memar Marqah* 2:1–2; 6:3
John 4:22–24	*Corp. herm.* 5.10
John 4:24	Epictetus 2.8.1; Stobaeus, *Ecl.* 1.29, 38
John 4:25	SP Exod 20:21b; *Memar Marqah* 3:6; 4:12
John 4:34	*Corp. herm.* 13.19
John 4:36	1QS 4:7
John 4:42	*Memar Marqah* 4:12
John 4:46–54	*b. Ber.* 34b
John 4:48	Wis 8:8
John 5:17	Maximus of Tyre, *Diss.* 15.16.2; Suetonius, *Cal.* 22
John 5:18	Wis 2:16; Philo, *Alleg. Interp.* 1.49
John 5:19	Plutarch, *Mor.* 550AB, 550DE: *Sera* 4, 5
John 5:21	*Jos. Asen.* 8:10–11

John 5:22	*Jub.* 69:27; *1 En.* 69:27; *T. Levi* 2:3 (*apud* MS e)
John 5:24	*Jos. Asen.* 8:10–11; 1QS 4:7; *Corp. herm.* 1.21
John 5:27	*T. Ab.* (A) 13:2–7
John 5:31–32	Cicero, *Pro Roscio Amerino* 36.103
John 5:33	1QS 8:6
John 5:35	*2 Bar.* 18:2; *2 En.* 46:3
John 5:41	*T. Benj.* 6:4
John 5:44	*T. Benj.* 6:4
John 5:46	*Mek.* on Exod 14:31 (*Beshallah* §7)
John 6:12	Sir 24:19
John 6:26–65	Philo, *Alleg. Interp.* 3.173
John 6:28	1QS 4:4
John 6:31	Ps 78:24; cf. Exod 16:4, 15; Neh 9:15; *2 Bar.* 29:8; *t. Soṭah* 4.3
John 6:35	Sir 24:21–22; *Jos. Asen.* 8:5
John 6:38	*Sib. Or.* 3:655; *Pr. Jos.* frg. A
John 6:45	LXX Isa 54:13; cf. Jer 31:33–34
John 6:46	Epictetus, *Ench.* 29
John 6:48	*T. Ab.* (A) 16:10–12; *Jos. Asen.* 8:5; P.Lond. 46.145–155
John 6:51	*T. Ab.* (A) 16:10–12; P.Lond. 46.145–155
John 6:52–58	*Jos. Asen.* 16:14, 16
John 6:53	Sir 24:21–22; *Corp. herm.* 1.29
John 7:27	Justin Martyr, *Dial.* 8.4
John 7:37–38	Prov 18:4; Zech 14:8; Isa 55:1; 58:11; Sir 24:30–31, 40, 43; 1QS 4:19–21; *Odes Sol.* 30:1–7; cf. *m.* ʾ*Abot* 6:1; *Tg. Ps.-J.* Gen 35:14
John 7:42	*Jub.* 17:21
John 7:53–8:11	*m. Sanh.* 6:1–4
John 8:7	Seneca, *Ira* 1.14.2
John 8:12	*Sipre Num.* §41 (on Num 6:25); *b. B. Bat.* 4a; *Deut. Rab.* 7.3 (on Deut 28:1); *Exod. Rab.* 36.3 (on Exod 27:20); *2 En.* 46:3; 1QS 3:7, 21; 4:11; Plato, *Resp.* 514A–530C; *Corp. herm.* 1.6, 32
John 8:31–34	Cicero, *De Finibus* 3.75; Stobaeus, *Hypothetica* 2.101.14–18
John 8:31–36	Epictetus 4.1–3
John 8:33	*Tg. Isa.* 34:12; *m. B. Qam.* 8:6
John 8:34	Tacitus, *Ann.* 3.65
John 8:41	Seneca, *Ben.* 4.7–8; *Corp. herm.* 13.14
John 8:44	Wis 2:23b–24; Porphyry, *On Abstinence* 2.42
John 8:53	Sir 44:19
John 8:56	*Gen. Rab.* 14.22 (on Gen 15:10–11); cf. *Pirqe R. El.* §28
John 8:58	*Pr. Jos.* frg. A
John 9:2–3	Bar 3:4, 7–8
John 9:3	1QS 4:4
John 9:5	*b. B. Bat.* 4a; *Deut. Rab.* 7.3 (on Deut 28:1); *2 En.* 46:3
John 9:6	*SIG* 1173; Suetonius, *Vesp.* 7.2–3; Dio Cassius, *Hist. rom.* 65.8; Tacitus, *Hist.* 4.81
John 9:22	*b. Ber.* 28b–29a; Amidah §12; cf. John 12:42; 16:2

John 9:39–41	1QS 4:11
John 10:1–15	Themistius, *Speeches* 1.9D–10D
John 10:11	*Corp. herm.* 13.19
John 10:14	*Odes Sol.* 9:12–14; cf. Aristotle, *Rhet.* 1371B
John 10:16	Plutarch, *Mor.* 329AB: *Alex. fort.* 6
John 10:20	Wis 5:4; cf. Plato, *Phaedr.* 249CD
John 10:21	1QS 4:11
John 10:22	1 Macc 4:59; *m. Moʾed Qaṭ.* 3:9
John 10:27	*Odes Sol.* 9:12–14; cf. Aristotle, *Rhet.* 1371B
John 10:34	Ps 82:6; *Exod. Rab.* 32.1, 7 (on Exod 23:20); *Lev. Rab.* 4.1 (on Lev 4:2); 11.3 (on Lev 9:1); *Num. Rab.* 7.4 (on Num 5:2); 16.24 (on Num 14:11); *Deut. Rab.* 7.12 (on Deut 29:5 [4]); *Song Rab.* 1:2 §5; *Eccl. Rab.* 3:16 §1
John 11:1–44	*EG* 48.6–7; 298; 304; 433
John 11:39	*Eccl. Rab.* 12:6 §1
John 11:50	Dio Cassius, *Hist. rom.* 63.13; Epictetus 3.24.64
John 11:51	Josephus, *J.W.* 1.2.8 §§68–69; Philo, *Spec. Laws* 4.192; *t. Soṭah* 13.5–6
John 12:3	Sir 24:15
John 12:26	4 Macc 17:20
John 12:27	*Tg. Ps.-J.* Gen 38:25
John 12:29	Homer, *Od.* 20.97–104
John 12:31	*L.A.E.* 12:1
John 12:32	*Tg. Isa.* 52:13; 53:2, 10
John 12:34	Ps 89:36 (LXX 88:37); 89:4–5; 110:4; Isa 9:7; Ezek 37:25; Dan 7:13–14; Sir 24:9; *Tg. Isa.* 52:13; 53:2, 10; Justin Martyr, *Dial.* 32.1
John 12:35	1QS 3:21; 4:11; *Corp. herm.* 13.9
John 12:36	1QS 3:24–4:1
John 12:38	LXX Isa 53:1
John 12:40	Isa 6:10 (see Mark 4:12 above)
John 12:41	*Tg. Isa.* 6:1, 5
John 12:46	*Corp. herm.* 1.19
John 12:50	Epictetus 3.1.36
John 13:15	Xenophon, *Mem.* 4.3.17–18; Epictetus 4.8.30–31
John 13:17	Hesiod, *Op.* 826–827; Seneca, *Ep.* 75.7
John 13:18	Ps 41:9; *Ahiqar* 139
John 13:27	*T. Sim.* 2:7
John 13:35	Iamblichus, *Life of Pythagoras* 33.230
John 13:37	Seneca, *Ben.* 2.14.4
John 14:2	*2 Bar.* 48:6; *2 En.* 39:3–4; 61:2
John 14:5–6	Epictetus 1.4.23–30
John 14:15–16	Wis 6:18–19
John 14:16–17	Philo, *Moses* 2.134
John 14:17	*Jub.* 25:14; 1QS 3:18–19; 4:21, 23
John 14:19	*Corp. herm.* 13.3
John 14:21	Sir 1:10

John 14:23	*1 En.* 45:3
John 14:26	*Jub.* 32:24–26; 1QS 4:21; *Corp. herm.* 13.2; Herm. *Vis.* 2.1.3–4
John 15:1	Sir 24:17; LXX Jer 2:21; *2 Bar.* 39:7
John 15:1–5	Sir 24:16–17
John 15:2	Sir 24:17; *Corp. herm.* 13.7
John 15:5	Sir 24:16–17; Aelius Aristides, *Or.* 37.10
John 15:9–10	Wis 3:9
John 15:11	*Corp. herm.* 13.18
John 15:15	Philo, *Migration* 45; idem, *Sobriety,* 55–56
John 15:25	Ps 69:4; cf. Ps 35:19; *Jub.* 7:1
John 15:26	*T. Jud.* 20:1, 5; 1QS 3:18–19; 4:21, 23
John 16:2	Amidah 12
John 16:7–13	*T. Jud.* 20:5
John 16:13	1QS 3:18–19; 4:21, 23
John 16:20	*Corp. herm.* 13.8
John 16:28	*1 En.* 42:1–3
John 17:1	*PGM* VII. 500–504
John 17:3	Wis 15:3; *Corp. herm.* 13.8
John 17:5	*PGM* VII. 500–504
John 17:6	*PGM* XII. 92–94; Epictetus 4.10.16
John 17:11	*Corp. herm.* 1.31
John 17:12	*Apoc. Elijah* 2:40
John 17:19	*Corp. herm.* 1.32
John 17:22	*T. Jud.* 25:3
John 18:37	Herodotus, *Hist.* 1.126; 1QS 8:6
John 19:2–3	Philo, *Flaccus* 36–39
John 19:9	Philostratus, *Vit. Apoll.* 8.2
John 19:10–11	Epictetus 1.2.19–20
John 19:30	*L.A.E.* 45:3
John 19:36	Exod 12:46; cf. Num 9:12; Ps 34:20; cf. *m. Pesaḥ.* 7:10, 11
John 19:37	Zech 12:10
John 20:17	*Corp. herm.* 1.26
John 20:22	Wis 15:11; 1QS 4:21
John 20:25	*Exod. Rab.* 46.1 (on Exod 34:1)
John 20:29	Plato, *Theaet.* 155E; *b. B. Bat.* 75a
John 20:30	Aelius Aristides, *Or.* 45
John 21:25	1 Macc 9:22; Philo, *Posterity* 144; Valerius Harpocration of Alexandria, *On the Powers of Nature; Sopherim* 16.8

Acts of the Apostles

Acts 1:1–2	Josephus, *Ag. Ap.* 1.1 §§1–3; 2.1 §1
Acts 1:8	*Pss. Sol.* 8:15
Acts 1:9	*2 En.* 3:1
Acts 1:9–11	Dio Cassius, *Hist. rom.* 56.46

Acts 1:10	2 Macc 3:26
Acts 1:11–12	*4 Bar.* 9:20
Acts 1:18	Wis 3:17
Acts 1:20	Pss 69:25; 109:8
Acts 2:3	*Frg. Tg.* Num 11:26
Acts 2:4	Sir 48:12
Acts 2:6	Plutarch, *Mor.* 370B: *Is. Os.* 47
Acts 2:11	Sir 36:7; *2 En.* 54:1
Acts 2:11–13	Philo, *Decalogue* 33, 46–47; Lucian, *Alex.* 13
Acts 2:15	*2 En.* 51:5
Acts 2:17–21	LXX Joel 3:1–5 = ET 2:28–32; Num 11:29; *Midr. Pss.* 14.6 (on Ps 14:7); *Num. Rab.* 15.25 (on Num 11:17)
Acts 2:25–28	LXX Ps 15:8–11 (16:8–11); *Midr. Pss.* 16.4, 10–11 (on Ps 16:4, 9–10)
Acts 2:30	Pss 132:11; 89:3–4; 2 Sam 7:12–13; *Tg. Pss.* 132:10–18, esp. v. 17
Acts 2:31	LXX Ps 15:8–11 (16:8–11); *Midr. Pss.* 16.4, 10–11 (on Ps 16:4, 9–10)
Acts 2:34–35	Ps 110:1 (see Mark 12:36 above)
Acts 2:39	Sir 24:32
Acts 2:44	Josephus, *J.W.* 2.8.3 §122; Aristotle, *Eth. nic.* 8.9; Diogenes Laertius, *Vit. phil.* 8.10; Lucian, *Peregr.* 13
Acts 3:1	*2 En.* 51:5
Acts 3:13	*2 Bar.* 70:10; Pr Man 1
Acts 3:21	Tacitus, *Ann.* 1.43
Acts 3:22–23	Deut 18:15–16, 19; Lev 23:29; cf. 1 Macc 4:46; 14:41; *T. Benj.* 9:2; *T. Levi* 8:15; 1QS 9:11; 4QTest 5–8; Josephus, *Ant.* 18.4.1 §§85–86
Acts 3:25	Gen 22:18; cf. Gen 12:3; 17:4, 5; 18:18; 26:4; 28:14
Acts 3:26	*2 Bar.* 70:10; Pr Man 1
Acts 4:11	Ps 118:22 (see Mark 12:10 above)
Acts 4:19	Plato, *Apol.* 29D
Acts 4:24	Jdt 9:12
Acts 4:25–26	Ps 2:1–2; 4QFlor 1:18–19; *Midr. Pss.* 2.2–3 (on Ps 2:1–2); *b. Ber.* 7b; *ʿAbod. Zar.* 3b
Acts 4:27	*2 Bar.* 70:10
Acts 4:31	Virgil, *Aen.* 3.84–89
Acts 5:1–11	1QS 6:24–25
Acts 5:2	2 Macc 4:32
Acts 5:7	3 Macc 4:17
Acts 5:21	1 Macc 12:6; 2 Macc 1:10
Acts 5:29	Plato, *Apol.* 29D
Acts 5:34	Homer, *Od.* 10.38
Acts 5:38	Aeschylus, *Ag.* 1466
Acts 5:39	Wis 12:13–14; 2 Macc 7:19
Acts 6:1	*T. of Job* 10:1–11:4
Acts 6:9	*CII* 1404
Acts 7:2	LXX Gen 12:7; 1QapGen^ar 22:27 (on Gen 15:1); *Apoc. Elijah* 1:5
Acts 7:3	Gen 12:1; *Tg. Ps.-J.* Gen 12:1

Acts 7:4	Gen 11:26–12:4; SP Gen 11:32; Philo, *Migration* 177
Acts 7:5	Gen 17:8; SP Deut 2:5
Acts 7:6–7	Gen 15:13–14; Exod 2:22; 3:12
Acts 7:8	Gen 17:10–14; 21:4
Acts 7:9	Gen 37:11, 28; 39:21
Acts 7:10	Gen 41:37–39, 40–44; *Tg. Ps.-J.* Gen 41:40–41; LXX Ps 104:21 (105:21); *T. Reu.* 4:8, 10
Acts 7:11	Gen 41:54–57; 42:5; LXX Ps 36:19 (37:19)
Acts 7:12	Gen 42:1–2
Acts 7:13	Gen 45:3–4, 16
Acts 7:14	Gen 45:9–11, 18–19; LXX 46:27; cf. LXX Exod 1:4–5; 4QExod^a
Acts 7:15	Gen 46:5–6; 49:33; Exod 1:6
Acts 7:15–16	*Jub.* 46:10
Acts 7:16	Gen 23:16–17; *T. Reu.* 7:2; *Tg. Onq.* Gen 33:19; *Tg. Neof.* Gen 33:19; *Tg. Ps.-J.* Gen 33:19; *Tg. Josh.* 24:32
Acts 7:17–18	LXX Exod 1:7–8
Acts 7:19	Exod 1:10–11, 22
Acts 7:20–28	Exod 2:2–14; Sir 45:3
Acts 7:22	Lucian, *Philops.* 34
Acts 7:23	*Jub.* 47:10
Acts 7:29	Exod 2:15, 21–22; 18:3–4
Acts 7:30	*Jub.* 48:2
Acts 7:30–34	Exod 3:2–10
Acts 7:31–32	SP Exod 3:6
Acts 7:35	Exod 2:14; 3:2
Acts 7:36	Exod 7:3; 14:21; Num 14:33; *T. Mos.* 3:11
Acts 7:36–41	*T. Mos.* 3:11
Acts 7:37	LXX Deut 18:15 (see Acts 3:22–23 above)
Acts 7:38	Exod 19:1–6; 20:1–17; Deut 5:4–22; 9:10
Acts 7:39	Num 14:3
Acts 7:40	Exod 32:1, 23
Acts 7:41	Exod 32:4–6; cf. Wis 13:10; Ep Jer 50
Acts 7:42–43	LXX Jer 7:18; Amos 5:25–27
Acts 7:44	Exod 27:21; Num 1:50; Exod 25:9, 40; *Sib. Or.* 4:10
Acts 7:45	Josh 3:14–17; 18:1; 23:9; 24:18
Acts 7:45–46	2 Sam 7:2–16; 1 Kgs 8:17–18
Acts 7:47	1 Kgs 6:1, 14; 8:19–20
Acts 7:48–49	*Sib. Or.* 4:8; Clement of Alexandria, *Strom.* 5.1.76
Acts 7:48–50	Strabo, *Geogr.* 16.35–37; Seneca, *Ben.* 7.6; *L.A.B.* 22:5–6
Acts 7:49–50	Isa 66:1–2; *m. ʾAbot* 6:10; *Barn.* 16:2
Acts 7:51	Exod 32:9; 33:3, 5; Lev 26:41; Jer 9:26; 6:10; Isa 63:10; *m. Ned.* 3:11
Acts 7:53	*Jub.* 1:28
Acts 7:55	*Apoc. Mos.* 33:1
Acts 7:57	*2 Bar.* 22:1
Acts 7:58	*m. Sanh.* 6:1–6; 7:4–5

Acts 8:10	*Sam. Tg.* SP Gen 17:1; *PGM* IV. 1275–77
Acts 8:22	*Frg. Tg.* Gen 18:21; 19:24; *Frg. Tg.* Exod 10:28; 14:29
Acts 8:23	*T. Naph.* 2:8
Acts 8:26–40	Wis 3:14
Acts 8:32–33	LXX Isa 53:7–8; *Tg. Isa.* 52:13–53:12; *Barn.* 5:2
Acts 8:38	*2 Bar.* 6:4
Acts 9:1–29	2 Macc 3:24–40; 4 Macc 4:1–14
Acts 9:2	1 Macc 15:21
Acts 9:7	Wis 18:1; Euripides, *Hipp.* 85; *Tg. Ps.-J.* Gen 22:10
Acts 10:2	Tob 12:8; Juvenal, *Sat.* 14.96–106; *CII* 748; *IEph* III.690.8–12 (*NewDocs* 4.128); Aphrodisias Stele a.19–20 (*NewDocs* 9.73)
Acts 10:9	*2 En.* 51:5
Acts 10:13–14	*m. Ḥul.* 1:1–2:3
Acts 10:22	1 Macc 10:25; 11:30, 33
Acts 10:26	Wis 7:1
Acts 10:30	2 Macc 11:8
Acts 10:34	Sir 35:12–13
Acts 10:36	Wis 8:3
Acts 11:15–18	*Tg. Ps.-J.* Exod 33:16
Acts 11:18	Wis 12:19
Acts 12:5	Jdt 4:9
Acts 12:10	Sir 19:26
Acts 12:11	*T. Sim.* 2:8
Acts 12:22	Ammianus Marcellinus, *Res gest.* 15.8
Acts 12:23	1 Macc 7:41; 2 Macc 9:9; Jdt 16:17; Sir 28:7; Hesiod, *Op.* 137; Herodotus, *Hist.* 4.205; Pausanias, *Descr.* 9.7.2; 9.33.6; Pliny the Elder, *Nat.* 11.38; Diogenes Laertius, *Vit. phil.* 3.41; Lucian, *Alex.* 59; *m. Soṭah* 7:8; *t. Soṭah* 7.16; cf. *m. Bik.* 3:4
Acts 13:10	Sir 1:30
Acts 13:11	*Tg. Pss.* 58:9
Acts 13:17	Wis 19:10
Acts 13:22	*Tg. 1 Sam.* 13:14
Acts 13:33	LXX Ps 2:7 (see Mark 1:11 above)
Acts 13:34	LXX Isa 55:3
Acts 13:35	LXX Ps 15:10 (16:10) (see Acts 2:25–28 above)
Acts 13:41	LXX Hab 1:5
Acts 13:47	LXX Isa 49:6 (see Luke 2:32 above)
Acts 14:11–13	Ovid, *Metam.* 8.610–700; Catullus 64.385; Heliodorus, *Aeth.* 3
Acts 14:14	Jdt 14:16–17
Acts 14:15	4 Macc 12:13; Wis 3:17
Acts 14:17	Herodotus, *Hist.* 3.117
Acts 14:23	*T. Benj.* 1:4
Acts 15:4	Jdt 8:26
Acts 15:14	*Tg. Zech.* 2:15(11)

Acts 15:16–18	LXX Amos 9:11–12; Isa 45:21; Jer 12:15; 4QFlor 1:11–13; CD 7:13–21; *Tg. Amos* 9:11; *b. Sanh.* 96b–97a; *Midr. Pss.* 76.3 (on Ps 76:3); *Gen. Rab.* 88.7 (on Gen 40:23)
Acts 15:19–21	*b. Sanh.* 56a
Acts 15:20	*1 En.* 7:5; *m. Yoma* 5:6; *m. Mak.* 3:2; *m. Ḥul.* 1:1; 2:1, 4; 3:1–4; 8:3; *m. Ker.* 1:1; 5:1; *m. Ṭohor.* 1:1
Acts 15:28	*IG* 12.3, 178
Acts 15:29	4 Macc 5:2
Acts 16:9	Strabo, *Geogr.* 4.1.4
Acts 16:13	*IGA* 2.11 (*NewDocs* 3.121); *OGIS* 96, 101, 129
Acts 16:14	2 Macc 1:4
Acts 16:17	*SEG* 1355, 1356 (*NewDocs* 1.25–29); *OGIS* 96 (*NewDocs* 4.201); *IGA* 2.116 (*NewDocs* 3.121); cf. Gen 14:18, 19–20, 22; Num 24:16; Deut 32:8; 2 Sam 22:14; Ps 82:6; Isa 14:14; Dan 3:26; Mark 5:7; Luke 1:32, 35; 4Q246 2:1
Acts 16:21	Cicero, *Nat. d.* 3.2.5
Acts 16:23	*T. Jos.* 8:5
Acts 16:25	*T. Jos.* 8:5
Acts 17:21	Homer, *Od.* 1.351; Thucydides 3.38.5; Demosthenes, *1 Philippic* 1.10; Pindar, *Ol.* 9.72; Pliny the Younger, *Ep.* 8.18; Lucian, *Slander* 21
Acts 17:22	Sophocles, *Oed. col.* 260; Polybius, *Hist.* 6.56; Pausanias, *Descr.* 1.17.1; Josephus, *Ag. Ap.* 2.11 §130
Acts 17:22–31	Cleanthes, *Hymn to Zeus;* Apuleius, *Metam.* 11.4
Acts 17:23	Wis 14:20; 15:17; Pausanias, *Descr.* 1.1.4; Cicero, *Tusc.* 1.16; Diogenes Laertius, *Vit. phil.* 1.110; Philostratus, *Vit. Apoll.* 6.3.5
Acts 17:24	Wis 9:9; Tob 7:17; Plato, *Phaedo* 97C; idem, *Tim.* 28C; Horace, *Carm.* 1.12–13
Acts 17:24–25	Wis 9:1
Acts 17:25	Cicero, *Rosc. Amer.* 45; Seneca, *Ep.* 95.47
Acts 17:26	Wis 7:18
Acts 17:27	Wis 13:6
Acts 17:28	Aratus, *Phaen.* 5 (cf. Clement of Alexandria, *Strom.* 5.14); Cleanthes, *Hymn to Zeus* 3; Aristobulus frg. 4 (*apud* Eusebius, *Praep. ev.* 13.12.6–7)
Acts 17:29	Wis 13:10
Acts 17:30	Sir 28:7
Acts 17:31	Ps 9:8; cf. Pss 96:13; 98:9
Acts 17:32	Aeschylus, *Eumenides* 647–48; Lucian, *Peregr.* 13
Acts 17:34	Eusebius, *Hist. eccl.* 3.4.11
Acts 18:2	Suetonius, *Claud.* 25.4; Dio Cassius, *Hist. rom.* 60.6.6
Acts 18:12	*SIG* 801 (Gallio Inscription of Delphi); Seneca, *Ep.* 104.1; Pliny the Elder, *Nat.* 31.62; Dio Cassius, *Hist. rom.* 61.20.1
Acts 18:18	Arrian, *Anab.* 7.14
Acts 19:13	Mark 9:38; *PGM* IV. 3020
Acts 19:15	Mark 1:24; 3:11

Acts 19:19	Ps.-Phocylides, *Sent.* 149; Suetonius, *Aug.* 31.1
Acts 19:27	Wis 3:17
Acts 19:28	Bel 18, 41
Acts 19:34	Achilles Tatius 8.9
Acts 20:26	Sus 46
Acts 20:32	Wis 5:5
Acts 20:35	Sir 4:31
Acts 21:26	1 Macc 3:49
Acts 21:27–28	*OGIS* 598 (= *CII* 1400); Philo, *Embassy* 212; Josephus, *J.W.* 5.5.2 §§193–194; idem, *Ant.* 12.3.4 §145; cf. Lev 16:2; Num 1:51
Acts 22:9	Wis 18:1; *Tg. Ps.-J.* Gen 22:10
Acts 23:6–10	Josephus, *J.W.* 2.8.14 §§162–166
Acts 23:9	Euripides, *Bacch.* 325; Pindar, *Pyth.* 2.162
Acts 23:11	*2 En.* 1:7
Acts 24:2	2 Macc 4:6
Acts 24:14	4 Macc 12:17
Acts 26:14	Aeschylus, *Ag.* 1623; Pindar, *Pyth.* 2.94–95, 161; Euripides, *Bacch.* 795
Acts 26:18	Wis 5:5
Acts 26:23	Isa 42:6; 49:6 (see Luke 2:32 above)
Acts 26:24	*Tg. Ps.-J.* Num 22:5
Acts 26:25	Jdt 10:13
Acts 27:18	Curtius Rufus Quintus 5.9.3; cf. Jonah 1:5
Acts 28:1–6	*Mek.* on Exod 23:6–12 (*Kaspa* §3)
Acts 28:4	Hesiod, *Op.* 256; Sophocles, *Oed. col.* 1377; Arrian, *Anab.* 4.9
Acts 28:26–27	LXX Isa 6:9–10
Acts 28:28	LXX Ps 66:3 (67:2)

Romans

Rom 1:3	4Q246 1:7–2:4
Rom 1:4	*T. Levi* 18:7
Rom 1:7	*2 Bar.* 78:3
Rom 1:9	*2 Bar.* 86:1
Rom 1:17	Hab 2:4; 1QpHab 7:17–8:3; 8ḤevXIIgr 17:30; 1QS 11:2–22; *Tg. Hab.* 2:4; *Tg. Zech.* 2:17 (MS Parma 555); *b. Mak.* 24a; *2 Bar.* 54:17
Rom 1:18	*1 En.* 91:7
Rom 1:18–32	Wis 13:5–10; 14:22–27
Rom 1:19	*2 Bar.* 54:17–18; Cicero, *Nat. d.* 1.17; 2.4; idem, *Tusc.* 1.13; Seneca, *Ep.* 117.5
Rom 1:19–21	Ps.-Aristotle, *On the Cosmos* 399B
Rom 1:19–32	Wisdom 13–15
Rom 1:20	Diodorus Siculus 12.84
Rom 1:20–21	Wis 13:5, 8; *2 Bar.* 54:18
Rom 1:20–23	*m. Sanh.* 7:6; *m. ʿAbod. Zar.* 4:7
Rom 1:21	4 Ezra 8:60; Wis 13:1; *1 En.* 99:8; *T. Reu.* 3:8

Rom 1:22	Plato, *Laws* 732A
Rom 1:22–23	Wis 12:24
Rom 1:23	Wis 11:15; 12:12
Rom 1:25	*T. Mos.* 5:4
Rom 1:26	Wis 14:24; *T. Jos.* 7:8; *Sib. Or.* 3:185
Rom 1:26–27	Plato, *Laws* 836ABC; Philo, *Spec. Laws* 3.37–39; Ps.-Lucian, *Affairs of the Heart* 19–20
Rom 1:28	2 Macc 6:4; 3 Macc 4:16
Rom 1:29	Ps.-Phocylides, *Sent.* 71
Rom 1:29–31	Wis 14:24–27; 4 Macc 1:26; 2:15; Seneca, *Ben.* 1.10.4
Rom 1:32	*T. Ash.* 6:2; *2 En.* 10:4
Rom 2:1	Tacitus, *Hist.* 3.25
Rom 2:3	*Jub.* 15:8
Rom 2:4	Wis 11:23; 12:19–20; Pr Man 8; Plutarch, *Mor.* 551DE: *Sera* 6; *Tg. Neof.* Gen 6:3; *Frg. Tg.* Gen 6:3; *Tg. Onq.* Gen 6:3
Rom 2:5	*Jub.* 9:5; *T. Levi* 3:2; *Apoc. Elijah* 1:19; Euripides, *Ion* 923; Plautus, *Mercator* 56
Rom 2:6	Sir 16:14
Rom 2:10	Aelian, *Var. hist.* 12.59
Rom 2:11	Sir 35:12–13
Rom 2:14–15	*2 Bar.* 48:40; Xenophon, *Mem.* 4.4; Sophocles, *Oed. tyr.* 863; Aristotle, *Rhet.* 1.15.3–8; idem, *Eth. nic.* 4.8.8–10
Rom 2:15	*T. Reu.* 4:3; *T. Jud.* 20:5; Wis 17:11; *2 Bar.* 57:2; Seneca, *Lucil.* 3.28.10
Rom 2:17	*Jub.* 17:1; *2 Bar.* 48:22
Rom 2:17–24	Plutarch, *Mor.* 88D–89B: *Inim. util.* 4–5; Seneca, *Ira* 2.28.5–8
Rom 2:22	*T. Levi* 14:4
Rom 2:23	*T. Naph.* 8:4, 6
Rom 2:24	Isa 52:5; Ezek 36:20; Ign. *Rom.* 8:2; Pol. *Phil.* 10:3; *2 Clem.* 13:2
Rom 2:28	Philo, *QE* 2.2
Rom 2:29	*Jub.* 1:23
Rom 3:1	*2 Bar.* 14:4
Rom 3:3	*Jub.* 8:28
Rom 3:4	LXX Pss 115:2 (116:11); 50:6 (51:4); 1QH 9:26–27
Rom 3:9–25	1QH 17:14–15
Rom 3:10–18	LXX Pss 13:2–3 (14:1–3); LXX 52:2–6 (53:1–3); Eccl 7:20; LXX Pss 5:9–10 (5:9); 139:4 (140:3); 9:28 (10:7); Isa 59:7–8; Prov 1:16; Ps LXX 35:2 (36:1)
Rom 3:13	Ovid, *Am.* 1.8.104
Rom 3:20	LXX Ps 142:2 (143:2); Seneca, *Ira* 2.281–284
Rom 3:21–24	Philo, *Heir* 6; idem, *Spec. Laws* 2.264–265; Plutarch, *Mor.* 321B–324D: *Fort. Rom.* 9–11; *Corp. herm.* 13.9–10
Rom 3:21–4:25	1QS 11
Rom 3:23	Seneca, *Ben.* 1.10.3; Diogenes Laertius, *Vit. phil.* 1.88; *Apoc. Mos.* 21:5–6
Rom 3:25	LXX Lev 17:11; 4 Macc 6:29; 17:22

Rom 3:28	2 Esdr 8:32
Rom 4:3	Gen 15:6; *1 Clem.* 10:6; *Barn.* 13:7; *Jub.* 31:12–25
Rom 4:7–8	Ps 32:1–2; Wis 11:17
Rom 4:9	Gen 15:6; *1 Clem.* 10:6; *Barn.* 13:7
Rom 4:10–11	Gen 17:10; *t. Ned.* 2.5
Rom 4:13	Sir 44:21; *Jub.* 19:21; *2 Bar.* 14:13; 51:3
Rom 4:15	*2 Bar.* 15:2; *Jub.* 33:16
Rom 4:17	Gen 17:5; *2 Bar.* 21:5; 48:8; *t. Ber.* 1.12–14
Rom 4:18	Isa 48:13; Gen 15:5
Rom 4:20	*Tg. Neof.* Gen 22:14
Rom 4:22	Gen 15:6; *1 Clem.* 10:6; *Barn.* 13:7
Rom 5:1–10	Plutarch, *Life of Themistocles* 28.1–2
Rom 5:1–11	Apuleius, *Metam.* 11.2, 24–25
Rom 5:3	*T. Jos.* 10:1
Rom 5:3–4	Homer, *Od.* 5.222; Publilius Syrus, *Sent.* 149
Rom 5:5	Sir 18:11
Rom 5:7	Aristotle, *Eth. nic.* 8.9
Rom 5:12	Wis 2:24; 4 Ezra 3:6–8, 21–22, 26; *2 Bar.* 17:3; 23:4; 54:15; *1 Clem.* 3:4
Rom 5:12–21	*Apoc. Mos.* 14:2; *Corp. herm.* 1.12–15
Rom 5:16	4 Ezra 7:118–19
Rom 6:1	Sir 5:4–6; *T. Levi* 4:1
Rom 6:1–10	Apuleius, *Metam.* 11.21–24; Plutarch, *Mor.* 107F–110D *Cons. Apoll.* 13–15; Firmicus Maternus, *On the Error of the Pagan Religions* 22.1–3; Prudentius, *Peristephanon* §10
Rom 6:7	*T. Sim.* 6:1; Sophocles, frg. 940; Cicero, *Tusc.* 1.74; *IG* 2534; *EG* 463.2; *SEG* 612.4
Rom 6:10	4 Macc 7:19; Philo, *Worse* 49; idem, *Heir* 82
Rom 6:12	Cicero, *Off.* 1.29; Horace, *Ep.* 1.18.98; idem, *Sat.* 2.7.93; Seneca, *Ep.* 123.3
Rom 6:12–23	Dio Chrysostom, *Disc.* 14.17–18; Plutarch, *Mor.* 166CDE: *Superst.* 4; idem, *Mor.* 125BC: *Advice about Keeping Well* 7
Rom 6:23	*2 En.* 30:16; Archilochus, frg. 57
Rom 7:2–3	Gaius, *Inst.* 1.63
Rom 7:7	Exod 20:17; Deut 5:21; 4 Macc 2:5–6; *Apoc. Mos.* 19:3; Philo, *Spec. Laws* 4.84–85
Rom 7:7–11	4 Macc 2:1–6
Rom 7:7–23	Ovid, *Am.* 3.4.17
Rom 7:12	4 Ezra 9:37; *Tg. Neof.* Gen 3:24b
Rom 7:13	*Sipre Deut.* §45 (on Deut 11:18)
Rom 7:14–17	Euripides, *Hipp.* 379; Xenophon, *Cyr.* 6.1.21; Ovid, *Am.* 2.4.7; Plutarch, *Mor.* 566A: *Sera* 27
Rom 7:15	Epictetus 2.26.1, 4; Seneca, *Lucil.* 51.13
Rom 7:19–21	Epictetus 2.26.1, 4; Seneca, *Lucil.* 51.13
Rom 7:22–23	Plato, *Phaedo* 83D; idem, *Resp.* 588D–589B; *Corp. herm.* 13.7
Rom 7:23	4 Ezra 7:72

Rom 7:24	Epictetus 1.3.5; 1.4.23; idem, *Ench.* 26
Rom 8:2	Plutarch, *Cato the Younger* 65; Ps.-Cicero, *Rhetorica ad Herennium* 4.17
Rom 8:3–4	2 Esdr 3:22; 9:36
Rom 8:10	*Corp. herm.* 1.15
Rom 8:12	Philo, *Heir* 57
Rom 8:14–17	*Sipre Num.* §115 (on Num 15:37–41)
Rom 8:16	Seneca, *De providentia* 1.5
Rom 8:18	*2 Bar.* 15:8; 32:6
Rom 8:19	4 Ezra 7:11, 75
Rom 8:22	4 Ezra 10:9
Rom 8:28	*Pss. Sol.* 4:25; Plato, *Resp.* 612E
Rom 8:35	*2 En.* 66:6
Rom 8:36	LXX Ps 43:23 (44:22)
Rom 8:38	*L.A.E.* 28:2
Rom 8:38–39	*3 En.* 4:6–9
Rom 9:1–2	4 Ezra 7:47–61
Rom 9:3	Plutarch, *Life of Antony* 44.2–5
Rom 9:4	Sir 44:12, 18; 2 Macc 6:23
Rom 9:7	Gen 21:12; *t. Soṭah* 5.12
Rom 9:7–13	Philo, *Alleg. Interp.* 3.75–88
Rom 9:9	Gen 18:10, 14
Rom 9:12	Gen 25:23
Rom 9:13	Mal 1:2–3
Rom 9:14	Deut 32:4
Rom 9:15	Exod 33:19
Rom 9:16	*T. Mos.* 12:7
Rom 9:17	Exod 9:16
Rom 9:18	Exod 4:21; 7:3; 9:12; 14:4, 17
Rom 9:19	Wis 12:12; *2 Bar.* 3:7; Hesiod, *Op.* 105; Aeschylus, *Pers.* 93; Oenomaus, *apud* Eusebius, *Praep. ev.* 6.7.36
Rom 9:20	Isa 29:16; 45:9; Wis 12:12
Rom 9:21	Jer 18:6; Sir 33:10–13; Wis 15:7; *T. Naph.* 2:2
Rom 9:22	Jer 50:25; *2 Bar.* 24:2; 59:6
Rom 9:22–23	Wis 12:20
Rom 9:24	*Jub.* 2:19
Rom 9:25	Hos 2:23
Rom 9:26	Hos 1:10
Rom 9:27–28	Isa 10:22–23; Hos 1:10
Rom 9:29	Isa 1:9
Rom 9:31	Wis 2:11; Sir 27:8
Rom 9:32	Isa 8:14; 28:16
Rom 10:5	Lev 18:5; *Tg. Onq.* Lev 18:5; *2 Bar.* 67:6; *m. Mak.* 3:15; *t. Šabb.* 15.17
Rom 10:6–8	Deut 9:4; 30:12–14; Bar 3:29–31; 4 Ezra 3:17–18; 4:8; *Tg. Neof.* Deut 30:12–14; *Frg. Tg.* Deut 30:12–14; *L.A.B.* 15:6; *Pesiq. Rab.* 4.2

Rom 10:7	Wis 16:13
Rom 10:11	Isa 28:16
Rom 10:13	Joel 3:5 (ET 2:32)
Rom 10:15	Isa 52:7; Nah 1:15; 11QMelch 2:9–16
Rom 10:16	Isa 53:1
Rom 10:18	LXX Ps 18:5 (19:4)
Rom 10:19	Deut 32:21; *3 Bar.* 16:3
Rom 10:20	Isa 65:1
Rom 10:21	Isa 65:2
Rom 11:2	1 Sam 12:22; LXX Ps 93:14 (94:14)
Rom 11:3	1 Kgs 19:10, 14
Rom 11:4	1 Kgs 19:18; 2 Macc 2:4
Rom 11:8	Deut 29:3 (4); Isa 29:10
Rom 11:9–10	Pss 68:23–24 (69:22–23); 34:8 (35:8)
Rom 11:15	Sir 10:20–21
Rom 11:16	Num 15:17–21; Neh 10:37; Ezek 44:30
Rom 11:21	*2 Bar.* 13:10
Rom 11:25	4 Ezra 4:35–36; *T. Zeb.* 9; *2 Bar.* 23:5
Rom 11:26–27	Isa 59:20; LXX Ps 13:7 (14:7); Isa 27:9; Jer 31:33–34; *T. Benj.* 10:11; 4 Ezra 13:3–8, 35–37
Rom 11:33	Isa 45:15; 55:8; Wis 17:1; *2 Bar.* 14:8–10
Rom 11:34	*2 En.* 33:4; Xenophon, *Oec.* 2.5; Hesiod, *Op.* 483; idem, frg. (*apud* Clement of Alexandria, *Strom.* 5.14); Solon, frg. 149 (*apud* Clement of Alexandria, *Strom.* 5.14); Cicero, *Nat. d.* 1.22
Rom 11:34–35	Isa 40:13; Job 15:8; Jer 23:18; Job 41:11
Rom 11:36	Marcus Aurelius, *Med.* 4.23
Rom 12:1	*T. Levi* 3:6; Philo, *Spec. Laws* 1.277; Epictetus 1.16.20–21; *Corp. herm.* 1.30–32; 13.18; Isocrates, *Ad Nic.* 6
Rom 12:3	Aurelius Victor, *De Caesaribus: Aurelius* 35
Rom 12:4–5	Seneca, *Ep.* 95.52
Rom 12:8	*T. Iss.* 3:8
Rom 12:9	Amos 5:15
Rom 12:11	Crates, *Ep.* 4
Rom 12:15	Sir 7:34
Rom 12:15–16	Seneca, *Ag.* 664; idem, *Ep.* 103.3; Pliny the Younger, *Ep.* 8.16; Curtius Rufus Quintus 4.10.21
Rom 12:17	LXX Prov 3:4; Aelian, *Var. hist.* 12.49; Marcus Aurelius, *Med.* 4.44
Rom 12:17–20	1QS 10:17–21
Rom 12:18	Seneca, *Ben.* 7.31.1; idem, *Ira* 2.34.5
Rom 12:19	Deut 32:35; *Tg. Neof.* Deut 32:35; *T. Gad* 6:6; *2 En.* 50:4; Seneca, *Ira* 2.32.2–3; Plutarch, *Mor.* 551C: *Sera* 5
Rom 12:20	Prov 25:21–22; Sophocles, *Ajax* 660; idem, *Oed. col.* 1189; Diogenes Laertius 1.91
Rom 12:21	*T. Benj.* 4:3–4
Rom 13:1	*T. Benj.* 4:27; Sir 10:4; Wis 6:3–4; Josephus, *J.W.* 2.8.7 §140

Rom 13:1–2	Ammianus Marcellinus, *Res gest.* 19.12; Dio Chrysostom, *Disc.* 1.45
Rom 13:2	Sir 4:27
Rom 13:4	Tacitus, *Hist.* 3.68; Dio Cassius, *Hist. rom.* 42.27; Plutarch, *Life of Numa* 6.2; Philostratus, *Lives of the Sophists* 1.25.3; P.Mich. 577.7–8
Rom 13:7	Cicero, *Fin.* 5.23
Rom 13:9	Exod 20:13–15, 17; Deut 5:17–19, 21; Lev 19:18; 4 Macc 2:6; *t. Šebu.* 3.7
Rom 13:10	Lev 19:18; Sir 10:6; Wis 6:18; *Let. Aris.* 168, 207
Rom 13:12	*T. Naph.* 2:10; Homer, *Il.* 10.251
Rom 13:13	Ps.-Phocylides, *Sent.* 69
Rom 13:16–18	Ps.-Phocylides, *Sent.* 69
Rom 14:2–3	*T. Reu.* 1:8–10; Philo, *Providence* 2.69–70
Rom 14:8	4 Macc 7:19
Rom 14:11	Isa 49:18; 45:23
Rom 14:19	Cicero, *Off.* 1.41
Rom 15:3	LXX Ps 68:10 (69:9)
Rom 15:4	1 Macc 12:9
Rom 15:8	Mic 7:20; Sir 36:20
Rom 15:9	LXX Ps 17:50 (18:49); 2 Sam 22:50
Rom 15:10	Deut 32:43
Rom 15:11	LXX Ps 116:1 (117:1)
Rom 15:12	Isa 11:10
Rom 15:13	Xenophon, *Hellenica* 3.4.18
Rom 15:21	Isa 52:15
Rom 15:33	*T. Dan* 5:2
Rom 16:20	Gen 3:15; *Frg. Tg., Tg. Ps.-J.* Gen 3:15; cf. *T. Levi* 18:12
Rom 16:27	4 Macc 18:24; Ps.-Phocylides, *Sent.* 54; Plato, *Phaedr.* 278D; Stobaeus, *Anth.* 2.279

1 Corinthians

1 Cor 1:3	*2 Bar.* 78:3
1 Cor 1:18–25	Plato, *Apol.* 20D, 23A
1 Cor 1:19	Isa 29:14
1 Cor 1:26–31	Celsus, *True Doctrine* (*apud* Origen, *Cels.* 3.44, 59, 64)
1 Cor 1:30	Jer 23:5–6
1 Cor 1:31	Jer 9:24; *1 Clem.* 13:1
1 Cor 2:4	Plato, *Apol.* 17C; Polybius, *Hist.* 2.56; Maximus of Tyre, *Diss.* 15
1 Cor 2:7–12	Wis 9:13, 17
1 Cor 2:9	Isa 52:15; 64:4; 65:17; Sir 1:10; *L.A.B.* 26:13; 4 Ezra 7:15; *1 Clem.* 34:8; *2 Clem.* 11:7; 14:5; Plato, *Phaedr.* 247C; Empedocles, frg. 1.2
1 Cor 2:10	Seneca, *Ot.* 5.6; idem, *Nat.* 6.5
1 Cor 2:10–11	Jdt 8:14
1 Cor 2:11	Prov 20:27; Seneca, *Nat.* praef. 1; Stobaeus, *Ecl.* 1.94; Maximus of Tyre, *Diss.* 1.13

1 Cor 2:14	Plato, *Tim.* 40DE; Posidonius, *apud* Galen, *Plac. Hip. Plat.* 4.7; Seneca, *Nat.* praef. 1; Stobaeus, *Ecl.* 1.94; Maximus of Tyre, *Diss.* 1.13
1 Cor 2:16	Isa 40:13; Jdt 8:14
1 Cor 3:10	Aristotle, *Eth. nic.* 6.7
1 Cor 3:11	Isa 28:16
1 Cor 3:13–15	*T. Ab.* (A) 3:13–15; Oracle of Hystaspes, *apud* Lactantius, *Inst.* 7.21.3–6; Florus 2.2.22
1 Cor 3:14	4 Ezra 7:99
1 Cor 3:16	Epictetus 1.14.12–14; Marcus Aurelius, *Med.* 5.27
1 Cor 3:16–17	1QS 8:5–9; Epictetus 2.8.9–14
1 Cor 3:19	Job 5:13
1 Cor 3:20	LXX Ps 93:11 (94:11)
1 Cor 4:4	Ps 143:2; *T. Iss.* 7:1; *T. Zeb.* 1:4
1 Cor 4:5	*2 Bar.* 83:3
1 Cor 4:9	4 Macc 17:14
1 Cor 4:12	Ps 109:28
1 Cor 4:13	Lam 3:45
1 Cor 5:1	Lev 18:7–8; Deut 22:30; 27:20; Ps.-Phocylides, *Sent.* 179; Josephus, *Ant.* 3.12.1 §274
1 Cor 5:4–5	1QS 2:4–10
1 Cor 5:11	Ps.-Phocylides, *Sent.* 69
1 Cor 5:12–13	Deut 17:7; 19:19; 22:21, 24; 24:7; *m. Sanh.* 11:2
1 Cor 6:1–11	Epictetus 3.22.55–56; Musonius 10.15–23
1 Cor 6:2	Dan 7:22; Wis 3:8
1 Cor 6:3	*1 En.* 14:3
1 Cor 6:9	Plato, *Laws* 841DE; Martial, *Epigr.* 1.90; Seneca, *Ep.* 95.23–24; Sextus Empiricus, *Outlines of Pyrrhonism* 3.198–200
1 Cor 6:9–10	*Sib. Or.* 3:185
1 Cor 6:10	Ps.-Phocylides, *Sent.* 69
1 Cor 6:12	Sir 37:28; Plutarch, *Mor.* 236BC: *Apoph. lac.* 65; Epictetus 4.4.1
1 Cor 6:15–20	Strabo, *Geogr.* 8.20–23
1 Cor 6:16	Gen 2:24
1 Cor 6:19–20	Epictetus 2.8.9–14
1 Cor 7:1	Diogenes, *Ep.* 47; *SIG* 982
1 Cor 7:1–9	Philo, *Moses* 2.13.68
1 Cor 7:3	Tacitus, *Agricola* 6
1 Cor 7:3–5	*Tg. Neof.* Exod 21:10
1 Cor 7:5	*T. Naph.* 8:8; *m. Ketub.* 5:6
1 Cor 7:7	*Let. Aris.* 236–238; Pindar, *Nem.* 1.36; idem, *Ol.* 9.160; Virgil, *Ecl.* 8.63
1 Cor 7:11	Valerius Maximus, *Fact. dict.* 2.1.3
1 Cor 7:12–16	Plutarch, *Mor.* 140D: *Conj. praec.* 19
1 Cor 7:19	Josephus, *Ant.* 20.2.4 §41
1 Cor 7:21–23	Crates, *Ep.* 34
1 Cor 7:29–31	2 Esdr 16:40–46; Epictetus 2.16.28; 3.24.4–5, 59–60

1 Cor 7:32–35	Epictetus 3.22.69–71
1 Cor 7:37	Ps.-Phocylides, *Sent.* 215–217
1 Cor 8:4	Deut 6:4; Plutarch, *Mor.* 420AB: *Def. orac.* 19
1 Cor 8:6	*Orphic Fragments* 6.10, *apud* Plutarch, *Mor.* 436D: *Def. orac.* 48; Diogenes Laertius 7.1.135–136; Maximus of Tyre, *Diss.* 8.6
1 Cor 8:7–13	Galen, *Plac. Hip. Plat.* 4.6.1–2; Horace, *Sat.* 1.9.60–72
1 Cor 8:10	P.Oxy. 110
1 Cor 9:9	Deut 25:4
1 Cor 9:10	Seneca, *Ep.* 13.16
1 Cor 9:13–23	Plutarch, *Mor.* 613F–614A: *Quaest. conv.* 1.1.3
1 Cor 9:25	*2 Bar.* 15:8; Plato, *Laws* 647D; Publilius Syrus, *Sent.* 295
1 Cor 10:1	*Tg. Ps.-J.* Exod 13:20
1 Cor 10:3	*Tg. Ps.-J.* Exod 16:4a
1 Cor 10:4	*Tg. Neof.* Num 21:16–19; *Tg. Ps.-J.* Num 21:16–19
1 Cor 10:5	*Tg. Ps.-J.* Num 11:7
1 Cor 10:7	Exod 32:6; *Tg. Neof.* Exod 32:6
1 Cor 10:8	Num 25:1, 9
1 Cor 10:9	Num 25:5–6
1 Cor 10:10	Num 14:2, 36; 16:41–49; Ps 106:25–27
1 Cor 10:20	Deut 32:17; Ps 106:37; Bar 4:7
1 Cor 10:23	Plutarch, *Mor.* 236BC: *Apoph. lac.* 65; Epictetus 4.4.1
1 Cor 10:23–33	Galen, *Plac. Hip. Plat.* 4.6.1–2; Horace, *Sat.* 1.9.60–72
1 Cor 10:26	LXX Ps 23:1 (24:1)
1 Cor 11:1	Cicero, *Fam.* 1.7; Pliny the Younger, *Pan.* 45.6
1 Cor 11:3	*Corp. herm.* 11.15
1 Cor 11:4–16	Plutarch, *Mor.* 266C–267C: *Roman Questions* 10–14
1 Cor 11:7	Gen 1:27; 5:1; Wis 2:23; *T. Naph.* 2:5
1 Cor 11:8	Gen 2:21–23
1 Cor 11:9	Gen 2:18
1 Cor 11:10	4Q403 frg. 1 i 30–46; Philo, *Virtues* 73–74
1 Cor 11:14	Ps.-Phocylides, *Sent.* 210–212; Epictetus 1.16.10–14
1 Cor 11:17–34	Plutarch, *Mor.* 226F–227A: *[Apoph. lac.]*, *Lycurgus* 6–7; Lucian, *Saturnalia* 3.32
1 Cor 11:25	Exod 24:8; Jer 31:31; 32:40; Exod 24:6–8; Zech 9:11
1 Cor 11:26	Homer, *Il.* 24.305
1 Cor 11:27–29	Epictetus 3.21.14
1 Cor 11:31–32	*T. Benj.* 6:7
1 Cor 12:2	Hab 2:18–19
1 Cor 12:12–27	Plato, *Resp.* 462B–E; Livy 2.32.9–12; Seneca, *Ira* 2.31.7; Marcus Aurelius, *Med.* 12.35–36
1 Cor 13:1	*T. Job* 48–50
1 Cor 13:1–13	Plato, *Symp.* 197A–E
1 Cor 13:5	*T. Zeb.* 8:5
1 Cor 13:6	*T. Sim.* 4:8
1 Cor 13:9–12	Plutarch, *Mor.* 5D: *[Lib. ed.]* 8

1 Cor 13:11	Aristotle, *Eth. nic.* 10.2
1 Cor 13:12	4 Ezra 7:33–34; Cicero, *Fin.* 5.15
1 Cor 13:13	Virgil, *Ecl.* 10.69; Pliny the Younger, *Ep.* 4.19
1 Cor 14:1–2	*T. Job* 48–50
1 Cor 14:5	Num 11:29 (see Acts 2:17–21 above)
1 Cor 14:21	Isa 28:11–12; Deut 28:49
1 Cor 14:25	Isa 45:14; Dan 2:47; Zech 8:23; *Tg. Isa.* 45:14; *2 Bar.* 83:3
1 Cor 14:26–28	Philo, *Moses* 2.191
1 Cor 14:34	Aeschylus, *Sept.* 230–32; Democritus, frgs. 110–111, 274; Sophocles, *Ajax* 292–293; Euripides, *Heracles* 474–477; *Phoenician Maidens* 198–201; *Daughters of Troy* 651–656; Plutarch, *Mor.* 142CD: *Conj. praec.* 31–32; *b. Meg.* 23a; *Sipre Deut.* §235 (on Deut 22:13)
1 Cor 15:3	Isa 53:8–9; *Tg. Isa.* 52:13–53:12
1 Cor 15:4	Ps 16:10; Hos 6:2; Jonah 1:17
1 Cor 15:9	*2 Bar.* 21:13
1 Cor 15:18	Sophocles, frg. 837; Pindar, frg. 121; *EG* 101; 236.8; 459.7–8; 646; 720; *SEG* 571.3–4; *CLE* 185.2; 1495; 1170.14; 2071.2
1 Cor 15:21	Gen 3:17–19; *2 Bar.* 17:3
1 Cor 15:22	4 Ezra 6:23; Seneca, *Ep.* 99.8
1 Cor 15:24	Dan 2:44
1 Cor 15:24–25	*2 Bar.* 73:1
1 Cor 15:25	Ps 110:1
1 Cor 15:27	LXX Ps 8:7 (8:6)
1 Cor 15:28	*Corp. herm.* 13.2
1 Cor 15:29	2 Macc 12:38–45
1 Cor 15:32	Isa 22:13; 56:12
1 Cor 15:33	Menander, *Thais* 218; Theognis, *Elegi* 305; Aeschylus, *Sept.* 605; *MAMA* VIII.569; Seneca, *Ira* 3.8.1–2; idem, *Ep.* 7.7; Diodorus Siculus 12.12; Plutarch, *Mor.* 4A: *[Lib. ed.]* 6; *Anthologia latina* 1.13
1 Cor 15:35–54	Philo, *Moses* 2.288; Euripides, frg. 839
1 Cor 15:38	Gen 1:11; *Apoc. Zeph.* 10:14
1 Cor 15:41	*2 Bar.* 51:1
1 Cor 15:44	2 Macc 7:10–11, 22–23; 14:46
1 Cor 15:45	Gen 2:7; Philo, *Virtues* 203–204; idem, *Confusion* 62–63, 146–147; idem, *QG* 1.4 (on Gen 2:7); *Tg. Neof.* Gen 2:8
1 Cor 15:45–49	1QS 4:20–23; CD 3:20; Philo, *Alleg. Interp.* 1.31–32
1 Cor 15:47	Gen 2:7; Philo, *Virtues* 203–204; idem, *Confusion* 62–63, 146–147; idem, *QG* 1.4 (on Gen 2:7); *Tg. Neof.* Gen 2:8
1 Cor 15:49	Gen 5:3
1 Cor 15:51	*T. Benj.* 10:8; *2 Bar.* 49:3; 51:1
1 Cor 15:52	4 Ezra 6:23; *2 Bar.* 30:2; *Apoc. Mos.* 22:3
1 Cor 15:54	Isa 25:8; *Tg. Isa.* 25:8
1 Cor 15:55	Hos 13:14; *Tg. Hos.* 13:14b

2 Corinthians

2 Cor 1:2	*2 Bar.* 78:3
2 Cor 1:3–11	BGU 423
2 Cor 2:14	BGU 1061; Seneca, *Ben.* 2.11.1; Josephus, *J.W.* 7.5.4–7 §§123–162; Plutarch, *Life of Antony* 84; Dio Cassius, *Hist. rom.* 6
2 Cor 2:14–16	*T. Ab.* (A) 16:7–8; 17:16–18
2 Cor 3:3	Exod 24:12; 31:18; 34:1; Deut 9:10, 11; Prov 3:3; 7:3; Jer 31:33; Ezek 11:19; 36:26; Thucydides 2.43.2
2 Cor 3:6	Exod 24:8; Jer 31:31; 32:40
2 Cor 3:7	Exod 34:29–30; Philo, *Moses* 2.70; *L.A.B.* 12:1
2 Cor 3:7–4:6	*Tg. Onq.* Exod 34:29–30; *Tg. Neof.* Exod 34:29–30
2 Cor 3:9	Deut 27:26
2 Cor 3:10	Exod 34:29–30; Philo, *Moses* 2.70; *L.A.B.* 12:1
2 Cor 3:13	Exod 34:33, 35
2 Cor 3:14	*Tg. Ps.-J.* Exod 33:5–7, 16; *Tg. Ps.-J.* Num 7:89
2 Cor 3:16	Exod 34:34
2 Cor 3:18	Exod 16:7; 24:17; Philo, *Moses* 2.69
2 Cor 4:2	Epictetus 3.22.13–15
2 Cor 4:4	*Corp. herm.* 7:2–3
2 Cor 4:5	Dio Chrysostom, *Disc.* 13.11–12
2 Cor 4:6	Gen 1:3; Isa 9:2; *Corp. herm.* 7:2–3; Cicero, *Tusc.* 1.26; Seneca, *Ep.* 44.2
2 Cor 4:8	Epictetus 2.24.24
2 Cor 4:10–12	Plato, *Phaedo* 66DE, 67E
2 Cor 4:13	Ps 116:10
2 Cor 4:16	Seneca, *Ep.* 24.19–20
2 Cor 4:17	*2 Bar.* 15:8; 48:50; Seneca, *Tranq.* 16.4
2 Cor 4:18	Plato, *Phaedo* 79A–C
2 Cor 5:1	Job 4:19; Wis 9:15
2 Cor 5:1–2	*2 Bar.* 48:6
2 Cor 5:1–4	Wis 9:15
2 Cor 5:1–5	*Apoc. Mos.* 31:1; Philo, *Virtues* 76
2 Cor 5:1–8	Plato, *[Ax.]* 365E–366A
2 Cor 5:2–4	*Corp. herm.* 10.17–18
2 Cor 5:3	*Corp. herm.* 1.24–26
2 Cor 5:3–4	*2 En.* 22:8
2 Cor 5:4	4 Ezra 14:15; Wis 9:15
2 Cor 5:10	Plato, *Phaedr.* 249AB; idem, *Crito* 54B; idem, *Gorg.* 526B; Virgil, *Aen.* 6.540, 566
2 Cor 5:17	Isa 43:18; Polybius. *Hist.* 4.2.4–5
2 Cor 5:20	Isa 52:7
2 Cor 6:2	Isa 49:8
2 Cor 6:10	Crates, *Ep.* 7
2 Cor 6:14	*2 En.* 34:1

2 Cor 6:14–15	*T. Levi* 19:1
2 Cor 6:14–7:1	4QMMT C 6–15 (= 4Q397 frgs. 14–21, lines 6–15)
2 Cor 6:15	1QM 1:1
2 Cor 6:16	Lev 26:12; Jer 32:38; Ezek 37:27
2 Cor 6:17	Isa 52:11; Ezek 20:34, 41
2 Cor 6:18	2 Sam 7:8, 14; Isa 43:6; Jer 31:9; LXX Amos 3:13; 4:13
2 Cor 7:3	Euripides, *Orest.* 307; Horace, *Carm.* 3.9.24
2 Cor 7:4	Epictetus 2.16.42
2 Cor 7:6	Isa 49:13
2 Cor 7:10	3 Macc 38:18; Sir 38:18; *T. Gad* 5:7
2 Cor 8:9	Plutarch, *Mor.* 374CD: *Is. Os.* 57
2 Cor 8:12	Prov 3:27–28; Tob 4:8
2 Cor 8:15	Exod 16:18
2 Cor 8:21	LXX Prov 3:4
2 Cor 9:6	Prov 11:24; 22:9
2 Cor 9:7	LXX Prov 22:8; Tob 4:16; *T. Reu.* 1:9; *2 En.* 61:5; Publilius Syrus, *Sent.* 326; Seneca, *Ben.* 2.1.3
2 Cor 9:9	LXX Ps 111:9 (112:9)
2 Cor 9:10	LXX Hos 10:12
2 Cor 9:15	Xenophon, *Mem.* 4.2
2 Cor 10:4	Epictetus 3.24.34
2 Cor 10:17	Jer 9:24
2 Cor 11:3	*2 En.* 31:6; *Apoc. Mos.* 14:2
2 Cor 11:3–14	*Tg. Ps.-J.* Gen 3:1, 5–6; *Tg. Neof.* Gen 3:5
2 Cor 11:14	*Apoc. Mos.* 17:1; *L.A.E.* 9:1; Publilius Syrus, *Sent.* 403
2 Cor 11:24–27	Cicero, *Acad.* 2.8
2 Cor 11:27	*2 En.* 66:6
2 Cor 12:1–10	Philo, *Migration* 34–35; *m. Ḥag.* 2:1
2 Cor 12:2	*2 En.* 8:1; 42:3; *Apoc. Mos.* 37:5
2 Cor 12:4	*2 Bar.* 4:7; *2 En.* 8:1
2 Cor 12:10	Epictetus 1.6.40
2 Cor 13:1	Deut 19:15

Galatians

Gal 1:1	Plato, *Ion* 534E; Epictetus 1.6.40
Gal 1:4	Epictetus 1.9.7
Gal 1:5	4 Macc 18:24
Gal 1:10	Epictetus, *Ench.* 23
Gal 1:15	Isa 49:1; Jer 1:5
Gal 2:6	Deut 10:17; Sir 35:13
Gal 2:9	*Tg. Ps.-J.* Num 20:29
Gal 2:12	*Jub.* 22:16
Gal 2:13	Epictetus 2.9.19–22
Gal 2:15	*Jub.* 23:24

Gal 2:16	Ps 143:2
Gal 2:19	4 Macc 7:19; *Pythagorean Sentences* 30
Gal 2:21	2 Esdr 3:22; 9:36
Gal 3:8	Gen 12:3; 18:18; Sir 44:21; 3 Macc 44:21
Gal 3:10	Deut 27:26; 4 Macc 5:20
Gal 3:10–13	11QTemple 64:6–13
Gal 3:11	Hab 2:4 (see Rom 1:17 above)
Gal 3:12	Lev 18:5
Gal 3:13	Deut 21:23; *t. Sanh.* 9.7; *Tg. Neof.* Gen 40:19; 41:13; 4QpNah (or 4Q169) 3+4 i 6–8 (cf. Nah 2:23); Josephus, *J.W.* 1.4.5 §§93–97
Gal 3:16	Gen 12:7; 13:15; 17:7; 24:7
Gal 3:17	Exod 12:40
Gal 3:19	*Jub.* 1:28
Gal 3:22	Polybius, *Hist.* 3.63.3–4
Gal 3:24	Xenophon, *Lac.* 3.1
Gal 3:28	Plato, *Symp.* 189DE; Aristotle, *Pol.* 1.2.3; Diogenes Laertius, *Vit. phil.* 1.33
Gal 4:1–2	Plato, *Lysis* 208C; Justinian, *Inst.* 1.22
Gal 4:4	Tob 14:5; *2 Bar.* 40:4
Gal 4:8	2 Chr 13:9; Isa 37:19; Jer 2:11; Ep Jer 16, 23, 29, 40, 44, 56, 65, 69
Gal 4:10	*1 En.* 72–82
Gal 4:16	Amos 5:10
Gal 4:22	Gen 16:15; 21:2
Gal 4:26	4 Ezra 10:7; *4 Bar.* 5:35
Gal 4:27	Isa 54:1
Gal 4:29	Gen 21:9; *Tg. Ps.-J.* Gen 21:9–12; *Tg. Neof.* Gen 16:5; *Tg. Ps.-J.* Gen 16:5
Gal 4:30	Gen 21:10
Gal 5:14	Lev 19:18
Gal 5:15	Plutarch, *Mor.* 1124DE: *Reply to Colotes* 30
Gal 5:16	Plato, *Phaedo* 80A
Gal 5:17	Plato, *Phaedr.* 237DE; Cicero, *Tusc.* 4.5
Gal 5:19–20	Ps.-Phocylides, *Sent.* 71
Gal 5:19–23	1QS 4:2–11; *Corp. herm.* 9.3–4; Diogenes Laertius 7.87–103
Gal 5:24	Lucian, *Men.* 4
Gal 6:1	Wis 17:17
Gal 6:4	Seneca, *Ep.* 81.17
Gal 6:6	*2 En.* 42:11
Gal 6:7	Euripides, *Hecuba* 331, 903; Callimachus, *Hymn. Cer.* 137
Gal 6:7–8	*T. Levi* 13:6
Gal 6:10	Tob 4:6–7
Gal 6:16	LXX Pss 124:5 (125:5); 127:6 (128:6)
Gal 6:17	3 Macc 2:29

Ephesians

Eph 1:4	CD 2:4b–13
Eph 1:5	*T. Benj.* 11:2; Cicero, *Acad.* 1.7; Seneca, *Ep.* 77.10; 101.7
Eph 1:6	Sir 45:1; 46:13
Eph 1:17	Isa 11:2; Wis 7:7
Eph 1:20	Ps 110:1
Eph 1:21	*Pr. Jos.* frg. A
Eph 1:22	Ps 8:6
Eph 2:2	*T. Benj.* 3:4; *2 En.* 29:4; *4 Bar.* 9:17
Eph 2:3	*Apoc. Mos.* 3:2
Eph 2:12	*Apoc. Elijah* 1:14
Eph 2:13	Isa 57:19
Eph 2:14	*2 Bar.* 54:5; *OGIS* 598
Eph 2:14–17	Plutarch, *Mor.* 329A–C: *Alex. fort.* 6
Eph 2:17	Isa 57:19; 52:7; Zech 9:10
Eph 2:20	Isa 28:16
Eph 3:9	3 Macc 2:3
Eph 3:9–10	LXX Prov 8:21
Eph 3:14	Aeschylus, *Ag.* 922
Eph 3:16	Tacitus, *Ann.* 3.54
Eph 3:20	Juvenal, *Sat.* 10.346
Eph 4:2	Plutarch, *Mor.* 90EF: *Inim. util.* 9
Eph 4:4	*T. Jud.* 25:3
Eph 4:4–6	*2 Bar.* 48:24
Eph 4:8	LXX Ps 67:19 (68:18); *Tg. Pss.* 68:19; *Apoc. Elijah* 1:4; Tertullian, *Marc.* 5.8.5
Eph 4:9–10	*Pr. Jos.* frg. A
Eph 4:14	Sir 5:9; Oppian, *Halieutica* 3.501
Eph 4:18	*T. Reu.* 3:8; Plutarch, *Life of Artaxerxes* 28.3
Eph 4:24	Gen 1:26; Wis 9:3
Eph 4:25	Zech 8:16; *T. Reu.* 6:9; *T. Dan* 5:2; *2 En.* 42:12; Ps.-Phocylides, *Sent.* 6–7
Eph 4:26	LXX Ps 4:5 (4:4)
Eph 4:29	Publilius Syrus, *Sent.* 665
Eph 4:30	Isa 63:10
Eph 5:2	LXX Ps 39:7 (40:6)
Eph 5:5	*T. Jud.* 19:1
Eph 5:6	*T. Naph.* 3:1
Eph 5:8–9	*T. Naph.* 2:10
Eph 5:12	*2 En.* 34:1
Eph 5:14	Isa 26:19; 51:17; 52:1; 60:1
Eph 5:18	LXX Prov 23:31; *T. Jud.* 14:1; 16:1; *Hist. Rech.* 1:4
Eph 5:20	Epictetus 1.16.16; 4.7.9
Eph 5:27	Plautus, *Persae* 4.4.6

Eph 5:31	Gen 2:24
Eph 6:1–2	Valerius Maximus, *Fact. dict.* 4.1.2
Eph 6:2–3	Exod 20:12; Deut 5:16
Eph 6:4	Deut 6:7, 20–25; Ps.-Phocylides, *Sent.* 207
Eph 6:5	*2 En.* 66:2
Eph 6:9	Deut 10:17; 2 Chr 19:17
Eph 6:10–20	*Apoc. Mos.* 20:2
Eph 6:11–17	Isa 59:17; Wis 5:17–20
Eph 6:12	*T. Levi* 3:10; *Apoc. Mos.* 28:2
Eph 6:13	*T. Levi* 8:2; Wis 5:17
Eph 6:14	Isa 11:5; 59:17; Wis 5:18
Eph 6:15	Isa 52:7; Nah 1:17
Eph 6:16	LXX Ps 7:14 (7:13); Wis 5:19, 21
Eph 6:17	Isa 59:17; 11:4; 49:2; Hos 6:5

Philippians

Phil 1:19	Job 13:16
Phil 1:21	Plato, *Apol.* 40CD; Sophocles, *Ant.* 461
Phil 1:23	Seneca, *Ep.* 65.16–18
Phil 1:24	Seneca, *Ep.* 98.15, 17; 104.4
Phil 2:6–8	*Apoc. Elijah* 1:6
Phil 2:6–11	*Corp. herm.* 1.12–15; *Ascen. Isa.* 2:33–36
Phil 2:8–9	Seneca, *Ep.* 13.14; 67.9
Phil 2:9	*Pr. Jos.* frg. A
Phil 2:10–11	Gen 41:43; Isa 45:23; *Sib. Or.* 3:290; 4:106; *Jub.* 22:11; 26:2, 23–24; *T. Reu.* 6:12; *2 En.* 20:4; Pr Man 11
Phil 2:12	Ps 2:11; *2 En.* 66:2
Phil 2:15	Deut 32:5; *T. Levi* 14:3
Phil 2:16	Isa 49:4; 65:23
Phil 3:2	*Tg. Neof.* Exod 22:30
Phil 3:6	*2 Bar.* 67:6
Phil 3:12–13	Epictetus 4.12.19
Phil 3:19	*T. Jud.* 14:8; *Apoc. Elijah* 1:13; Ps.-Phocylides, *Sent.* 69
Phil 3:21	*2 Bar.* 51:3
Phil 4:1	*Tg. Isa.* 28:5
Phil 4:3	Dan 12:1
Phil 4:4	*T. Benj.* 6:4
Phil 4:5	Wis 2:19
Phil 4:6	Valerius Maximus, *Fact. dict.* 1.1; 7.2
Phil 4:11	Xenophon, *Mem.* 3.2; Aristotle, *Eth. nic.* 1.7; Seneca, *Tranq.* 10.4
Phil 4:11–13	Vettius Valens, *Anthologies* 5.9.2
Phil 4:13	Wis 7:23
Phil 4:18	Gen 8:21; Exod 29:18; Ezek 20:41; Sir 35:6; Epictetus 3.24.2–3, 17

Colossians

Col 1:13	*1 En.* 58:5–6; 89:8; *T. Levi* 18:4; *T. Gad* 5:7; *T. Ash.* 5:2; *T. Jos.* 19:3; *T. Benj.* 5:3; *2 En.* 67:2; *2 Bar.* 59:2
Col 1:14	*1 En.* 5:6; 12:5
Col 1:15	Wis 7:26; *Pr. Jos.* frg. A
Col 1:15–17	Wis 7:22, 24–27; 8:1, 4–5; 9:1–2
Col 1:16	*T. Levi* 3:8; *Apoc. Elijah* 1:8; 4:10; *2 En.* 20:1
Col 1:17	*Pr. Jos.* frg. A; Seneca, *Ep.* 76.17
Col 1:18	"Orphic Hymn," *apud* Eusebius, *Praep. ev.* 3.9.2
Col 1:22	*1 En.* 102:5
Col 2:3	Isa 45:3; Sir 1:24–25; *1 En.* 46:3; Prov 2:3–4
Col 2:6–19	*Kerygma Petrou, apud* Clement of Alexandria, *Strom.* 6.5.41
Col 2:14	Plutarch, *Mor.* 499D: *An vit.* 3; Philo, *Posterity* 61; Seneca, *Vit. beat.* 19.3
Col 2:18	4QS 4:22–26; 11:7–9; 1QSa 2:8–9; 1QSb 1:5; 3:5–6; 4:24–27; 1QM 10:9–12; 12:1–6; 1QH 14:12–13; 4Q491 frg. 11 i 10–18; *Ascen. Isa.* 7:13–9:33
Col 2:22	Isa 29:13
Col 3:1	Ps 110:1
Col 3:2	Euripides, *Cyclops* 210
Col 3:5	*T. Jud.* 19:1
Col 3:10	Gen 1:26–27
Col 3:16	*Corp. herm.* 13:15
Col 3:18–4:1	Aristotle, *Pol.* 1.2.1–4; P.Oxy. 744
Col 3:21	Ps.-Phocylides, *Sent.* 207
Col 4:1	Lev 25:43, 53
Col 4:16	*2 Bar.* 86:1

1 Thessalonians

1 Thess 1:3	4 Macc 17:4
1 Thess 1:8	4 Macc 16:12
1 Thess 1:10	*Sib. Or.* 3:555–562
1 Thess 2:4	Jer 11:20
1 Thess 2:5	Tacitus, *Hist.* 1.15
1 Thess 2:5–6	Aelius Aristides, *Or.* 4
1 Thess 2:15	Tacitus, *Hist.* 5.5
1 Thess 2:15–16	1QM 4:2
1 Thess 2:16	*T. Levi* 6:11
1 Thess 3:11	Jdt 12:8
1 Thess 3:13	Zech 14:5
1 Thess 4:5	Ps 79:6; Jer 10:25
1 Thess 4:6	Ps 94:1; Sir 5:3; *2 En.* 60:1; Diogenes, *Ep.* 45
1 Thess 4:8	Ezek 36:27; 37:14
1 Thess 4:9	Jer 31:33–34; Homer, *Il.* 304–308

1 Thess 4:11	Seneca, *Brev. vit.* 19.3; idem, *Ep.* 72.12
1 Thess 4:13	Wis 3:18; *CIG* 1973; Ammianus Marcellinus, *Res gest.* 25.3
1 Thess 4:13–18	4 Ezra 5:41–42; 13:16–24; P.Oxy. 115
1 Thess 4:16	LXX Ps 46:6 (47:5); 4 Ezra 6:23; *Apoc. Mos.* 22:3
1 Thess 5:1	Wis 8:8
1 Thess 5:2	Wis 18:14–15
1 Thess 5:2–3	*Apoc. Elijah* 2:40
1 Thess 5:3	Jer 6:14; 8:11; Ezek 13:10; *1 En.* 62:4; Wis 17:14
1 Thess 5:4–9	1QS 3:13–15, 20–21; 4:18–19, 22–23
1 Thess 5:8	Isa 59:17; Wis 5:18; *Apoc. Elijah* 4:31
1 Thess 5:15	Prov 20:22
1 Thess 5:18	Seneca, *Ben.* 2.31.3
1 Thess 5:22	Job 1:1, 8; 2:3
1 Thess 5:23	*T. Dan* 5:2

2 Thessalonians

2 Thess 1:7	Zech 14:5; *Apoc. Elijah* 3:3
2 Thess 1:8	Ps 79:6; Isa 66:15; Jer 10:25
2 Thess 1:9	Isa 2:10, 19, 21
2 Thess 1:10	LXX Ps 67:36
2 Thess 1:12	Isa 24:15; 66:5; Mal 1:11
2 Thess 2:1	2 Macc 2:7
2 Thess 2:3	*Jub.* 10:3; *Sib. Or.* 3:570–571; *Apoc. Elijah* 1:10; 2:40
2 Thess 2:3–4	*Ascen. Isa.* 4:2–3
2 Thess 2:4	Dan 11:36; Ezek 28:2; Josephus, *J.W.* 2.10.1 §§184–186; 2.10.3–4 §§192–197
2 Thess 2:6–7	1Q27 frg. 1 i 2–8
2 Thess 2:8	Job 4:9; Isa 11:4; *Apoc. Elijah* 2:41
2 Thess 2:13	Deut 33:12
2 Thess 3:10	Ps.-Phocylides, *Sent.* 153

1 Timothy

1 Tim 1:10	Maximus of Tyre, *Diss.* 16.3
1 Tim 1:13	*T. Jud.* 19:3
1 Tim 1:17	Tob 13:7, 11; Diogenes Laertius, *Vit. phil.* 10.123
1 Tim 2:1–2	Aelius Aristides, *Or.* 46.42; Livy 3.7; Seneca, *Ep.* 73.1; Pliny the Younger, *Pan.* 1.45.5; 1.67.3
1 Tim 2:2	2 Macc 3:11; Bar 1:11–12
1 Tim 2:4	Ezek 18:23
1 Tim 2:5	*T. Dan* 6:2
1 Tim 2:8	*Tg. Mal.* 1:11; *Tg. Isa.* 49:8
1 Tim 2:12	Philo, *Moses* 1.180
1 Tim 2:14	Gen 3:6, 13; *2 En.* 30:17
1 Tim 3:4	Homer, *Od.* 9.114; Aristotle, *Eth. nic.* 10.9; idem, *Pol.* 1.4

1 Tim 3:4–5	Isocrates, *Demon.* 35
1 Tim 3:16	4 Macc 6:31; 7:16; 16:1; Virgil, *Ecl.* 4.15–17
1 Tim 4:2	Plato, *Gorg.* 313C
1 Tim 4:3	Gen 9:3
1 Tim 4:4	Gen 1:31
1 Tim 5:1	Lev 19:32; Juvenal, *Sat.* 13.54; Valerius Maximus, *Fact. dict.* 2.1.9
1 Tim 5:5	Jer 49:11
1 Tim 5:18	Deut 25:4; *Tg. Ps.-J.* Deut 25:4; Homer, *Od.* 14.58; Euripides, *Rhes.* 161
1 Tim 5:19	Deut 17:6; 19:15
1 Tim 5:24	2 Esdr 16:64–66
1 Tim 6:3	Maximus of Tyre, *Diss.* 16.3
1 Tim 6:7	Eccl 5:15; Job 1:21; Ps.-Phocylides, *Sent.* 110–11; Propertius 4.4.13
1 Tim 6:8	Prov 30:8; Lucan, *Pharsalia* 4.377
1 Tim 6:9	Prov 23:4; 28:22
1 Tim 6:10	*Ahiqar* 137; Plato, *Laws* 743A; Stobaeus, *Anth.* 3.417.37
1 Tim 6:15	Deut 10:17; 2 Macc 12:15; 13:4; 3 Macc 5:35; Sir 46:5; Homer, *Od.* 5.7; Aeschylus, *Suppl.* 524
1 Tim 6:16	Ps 104:2; Exod 33:20; Seneca, *Nat.* 7.30
1 Tim 6:17	Ps.-Phocylides, *Sent.* 62
1 Tim 6:18–19	Tob 12:8

2 Timothy

2 Tim 2:13	Num 23:19
2 Tim 2:16	*T. Jud.* 21:8
2 Tim 2:19	Num 16:5, 26; LXX Joel 3:5; Sir 17:26; 23:10; 35:3
2 Tim 2:22	Valerius Maximus, *Fact. dict.* 6.1
2 Tim 3:1–5	*T. Dan* 5:4
2 Tim 3:2	Aristotle, *Ethica* 9.8
2 Tim 3:5	Livy 39.16
2 Tim 3:8–9	Exod 7:11, 22; *Tg. Ps.-J.* Exod 7:11; 1:15; Num 22:22; *Tg. Ps.-J.* Num 22:22; CD 5:17–19; *L.A.B.* 47:1; *Jannes and Jambres* (frgs.); Numenius of Apamea, *apud* Eusebius, *Praep. ev.* 9.8; Pliny the Elder, *Nat.* 30.2.11
2 Tim 3:11	Ps 34:19; *Pss. Sol.* 4:23
2 Tim 3:16	Philo, *Moses* 2.36–40; 4 Ezra 14:23–26, 37–48
2 Tim 4:1–5	*Apoc. Elijah* 1:13
2 Tim 4:3	Maximus of Tyre, *Diss.* 16.3
2 Tim 4:5	*2 En.* 50:3–4
2 Tim 4:8	Wis 5:16; *T. Levi* 8:2; *2 Bar.* 15:8
2 Tim 4:14	2 Sam 3:39; Pss 28:4; 62:12; Prov 24:12
2 Tim 4:17	Ps 22:21; Dan 6:21; 1 Macc 2:60

Titus

Titus 1:9	Maximus of Tyre, *Diss.* 16.3
Titus 1:12	Callimachus, *Hymn to Zeus* 8; Epimenides, *De oraculis;* Leonidas, *Anth. lat.* 3.369; Polybius, *Hist.* 6.47
Titus 2:1–8	Maximus of Tyre, *Diss.* 16.3
Titus 2:5	Euripides, *Orest.* 108; Theocritus, *Id.* 28.14
Titus 2:6	Homer, *Il.* 3.108
Titus 2:9–10	Publilius Syrus, *Sent.* 707
Titus 2:11	2 Macc 3:30; 3 Macc 6:9
Titus 2:12	*Aristobulus* frg. 4:8
Titus 2:14	Ps 130:8; Exod 19:5; Deut 4:20; 7:6; 14:2; Ezek 37:23
Titus 3:2	Justinian, *Inst.* 12.1, 9
Titus 3:4	Wis 1:6
Titus 3:6	Joel 3:1 (2:28)

Philemon

Phlm	P.Colon. 7921; Philo, *Good Person* 79
Phlm 10–18	Philo, *Alleg. Interp.* 3.194; CD 12:10–11; *m. Giṭ.* 4:6; *t.* ʿ*Abod. Zar.* 3.16, 18–19; *Tg. Ps.-J.* Deut 23:16–17

Hebrews

Heb 1:2	Philo, *Confusion* 146
Heb 1:2–3	Wis 7:22, 25–26; 8:4
Heb 1:3	Ps 110:1; Wis 7:25–26
Heb 1:4	*Pr. Jos.* frg. A
Heb 1:5	LXX Ps 2:7; 2 Sam 7:14; 1 Chr 17:13
Heb 1:6	LXX Deut 32:43; LXX Ps 96:7 (97:7)
Heb 1:7	LXX Ps 103:4 (104:4); 4 Ezra 8:22; *2 En.* 29:1
Heb 1:8–9	LXX Ps 44:7–8 (45:6–7)
Heb 1:9	Epictetus 2.16.44
Heb 1:10–12	LXX 101:26–28 (102:25–26)
Heb 1:13	LXX Ps 109:1 (110:1)
Heb 1:14	Pss 34:8; 91:11; Plato, *Symp.* 202E
Heb 2:2	*Tg. Neof.* Deut 33:2; *Tg. Neof.* Exod 20:2; *Tg. Ps.-J.* Exod 20:2
Heb 2:5	Sir 17:17
Heb 2:6–8	LXX Ps 8:5–7
Heb 2:9	LXX Ps 8:6
Heb 2:10	*Corp. herm.* 1.26
Heb 2:12	LXX Ps 21:23 (22:22)
Heb 2:13	LXX Isa 8:17–18; LXX 2 Sam 22:3; Isa 12:2
Heb 2:16	Isa 41:8–9
Heb 3:1–6	*Memar Marqah* 3:6; 4:6
Heb 3:2	Num 12:7

Heb 3:5	Num 12:7
Heb 3:7–11	LXX Ps 94:7–11 (95:7–11)
Heb 3:11	Num 14:21–23
Heb 3:12	Exod 17:7; Num 20:2–5
Heb 3:15	LXX Ps 94:7–8 (95:7–8)
Heb 3:16–18	Num 14:1–35
Heb 3:17	Num 14:29
Heb 3:18	Num 14:22–23; LXX Ps 94:11 (95:11)
Heb 4:3	LXX Ps 94:11 (95:11); *2 Bar.* 73:1; *2 En.* 53:3
Heb 4:4	Gen 2:2
Heb 4:5	LXX Ps 94:11 (95:11)
Heb 4:7	LXX Ps 94:7–8 (95:7–8)
Heb 4:8	Deut 31:7; Josh 22:4
Heb 4:10	Gen 2:2
Heb 4:12	Isa 49:2; Wis 7:22–30; 18:15–16; *2 Bar.* 83:3; Phocylides, frg. 118; Ps.-Phocylides, *Sent.* 124
Heb 4:13	*1 En.* 9:5; Plutarch, *Mor.* 161F: *Sept. sap. conv.* 18
Heb 4:15	*Pss. Sol.* 17:36
Heb 5:3	Lev 9:7; 16:6
Heb 5:4	Exod 28:1
Heb 5:5	LXX Ps 2:7
Heb 5:6	LXX Ps 109:4 (110:4); 1 Macc 14:41
Heb 5:7	*Tg. Isa.* 53:4; 3 Macc 5:7–9
Heb 5:8	Philo, *Dreams* 2.107–108
Heb 5:9	Isa 45:17
Heb 5:10	LXX Ps 109:4 (110:4)
Heb 5:12	*1 En.* 61:7
Heb 6:4	*b. B. Bat.* 15b–16a
Heb 6:8	Gen 3:17–18
Heb 6:12	*Pss. Sol.* 12:6
Heb 6:13	Gen 22:16
Heb 6:13–18	*T. Mos.* 3:9
Heb 6:14	Gen 22:17; Sir 44:21; 3 Macc 44:21
Heb 6:16	Exod 22:11
Heb 6:18	Num 23:19; 1 Sam 15:29
Heb 6:19	Lev 16:2–3, 12, 15
Heb 6:20	LXX Ps 109:4 (110:4)
Heb 7:1–2	Gen 14:17–20
Heb 7:1–10	11QMelchizedek
Heb 7:2	Thucydides 3.50.1–2
Heb 7:3	LXX Ps 109:4 (110:4)
Heb 7:5	Num 18:21
Heb 7:14	Gen 49:10; Isa 11:1; 4QpIsa (on Isa 11:1–5); *Tgs.* Gen 49:10; *Tg. Isa.* 11:1
Heb 7:17	LXX Ps 109:4 (110:4)

Heb 7:21	LXX Ps 109:4 (110:4)
Heb 7:22	Sir 29:14–16
Heb 7:27	Lev 9:7; 16:6, 15
Heb 8:1	LXX Ps 109:1 (110:1)
Heb 8:1–5	*Sib. Or.* 4:10
Heb 8:2	LXX Num 24:6
Heb 8:2–5	Exod 25:40; Wis 9:8
Heb 8:5	Exod 25:40; *2 Bar.* 59:3; Epictetus, *Ench.* 33.1
Heb 8:8–12	Jer 31:31–34
Heb 9:2	Exod 26:1–30; 25:31–40, 23–30
Heb 9:3	Exod 26:31–33
Heb 9:4–5	Exod 30:1–6; 25:10–16; 16:33; Num 17:8–10; Exod 25:16; Deut 10:3–5; Exod 25:18–22
Heb 9:6	Num 18:2–6
Heb 9:7	Exod 30:10; Lev 16:2, 14, 15; Heraclitus, frg. 5
Heb 9:10	Lev 11:2, 25; 15:18; Num 19:13
Heb 9:11–12	*Sib. Or.* 4:10
Heb 9:12	*Tg. Neof.* Gen 49:18; *C.Tg.* (F) Gen 49:18
Heb 9:13	Lev 16:3, 14, 15; Num 19:9, 17–19; Diogenes Laertius, *Vit. phil.* 6.42
Heb 9:19	Exod 24:3, 6–8; Lev 14:4; Num 19:6
Heb 9:20	Exod 24:8; *t. Ned.* 2.6
Heb 9:21	Lev 8:15, 19
Heb 9:22	Lev 17:11
Heb 9:23	*3 Bar.* 8:4–5
Heb 9:26	*T. Levi* 18:9
Heb 9:27	Gen 3:19; Plato, *Ep. 7* 335A; Horace, *Carm.* 1.28.16; 4.7.21; Propertius 3.18.21
Heb 9:28	Isa 53:12; Caesar, *Bell. gall.* 6.16; Velleius Paterculus 2.7
Heb 10:4	Lev 16:15, 21; Plato, *Laws* 906D; Diogenes Laertius, *Vit. phil.* 6.42
Heb 10:5–7	LXX Ps 39:7–9 (40:6–8)
Heb 10:8–9	LXX Ps 39:7–9 (40:6–8)
Heb 10:11	Exod 29:38
Heb 10:12	LXX Ps 109:1 (110:1)
Heb 10:13	LXX Ps 109:1 (110:1)
Heb 10:16–17	Jer 31:33–34
Heb 10:20	*3 En.* 45:1; Clement of Alexandria, *Exc.* 38.1
Heb 10:22	Ezek 36:25
Heb 10:24	Aristotle, *Ethica* 9.9
Heb 10:27	Isa 26:11
Heb 10:28	Deut 17:6; 19:15
Heb 10:29	Exod 24:8
Heb 10:30	Deut 32:35, 36; LXX Ps 134:14 (135:14); *2 En.* 50:4
Heb 10:32	*2 En.* 50:3–4
Heb 10:37–38	LXX Hab 2:3–4 (see Rom 1:17 above); LXX Isa 26:20
Heb 10:38	*2 Bar.* 54:17

Heb 11:1	Cicero, *Nat. d.* 1.31
Heb 11:2	Sir 44:1
Heb 11:3	Gen 1:1; LXX Ps 32:6, 9 (33:6, 9); *2 Bar.* 14:17; *2 En.* 24:2; 25:1; 48:5
Heb 11:4	Gen 4:3–10; *Tg. Neof.* Gen 4:8, 10
Heb 11:5	Gen 5:24; Wis 4:10; Sir 44:16; 3 Macc 44:16; *1 En.* 70:1–4
Heb 11:6	Wis 10:17
Heb 11:7	Gen 6:13–22; 7:1
Heb 11:8	Gen 12:1–5; *1 Clem.* 10:3
Heb 11:9	Gen 23:4; 26:3; 35:12, 27; *T. Ab.* (A) 8:6
Heb 11:10	4 Ezra 10:27; 2 Macc 4:1; Wis 13:1
Heb 11:11	Gen 17:19; 18:11–14; 21:2
Heb 11:12	Gen 15:5–6; 22:17; 32:12; Exod 32:13; Deut 1:10; 10:22; LXX Dan 3:36; Sir 44:21; 3 Macc 44:21; Pindar, *Ol.* 2.178; 13.64
Heb 11:13	Gen 23:4; 47:9; 1 Chr 29:15; LXX Ps 38:13 (39:12); Plutarch, *Mor.* 117F: *[Cons. Apoll.]* 31
Heb 11:16	Exod 3:6, 15; 4:5
Heb 11:17	Gen 22:1–10; 1 Macc 2:52
Heb 11:18	Gen 21:12
Heb 11:20	Gen 27:27–29, 39–40
Heb 11:21	Gen 48:15–16; Exod 1:22
Heb 11:24	Exod 2:10–12
Heb 11:25	4 Macc 15:2, 8
Heb 11:27	Exod 2:15; 12:51; Sir 2:2
Heb 11:28	Exod 12:21–30; Wis 18:25
Heb 11:29	Exod 14:21–31
Heb 11:30	Josh 6:12–21
Heb 11:31	Josh 2:11–12; 6:21–25
Heb 11:32	Isocrates, *Demon.* 3
Heb 11:33	Judg 14:6–7; 1 Sam 17:34–36; Dan 6:1–27
Heb 11:34	Dan 3:23–25
Heb 11:34–35	1 Macc 5:1–7; 6:18–31
Heb 11:35	1 Kgs 17:17–24; 2 Kgs 4:25–37; 2 Macc 6:18–7:42; 4 Macc 9:13–18
Heb 11:36	1 Kgs 22:26–27; 2 Chr 18:25–26; Jer 20:2; 37:15; 38:6
Heb 11:37	2 Chr 24:21; *Ascen. Isa.* 5:11–14
Heb 11:38	Cicero, *Tusc.* 3.26
Heb 12:1	4 Macc 16:16; 17:10–15
Heb 12:2	LXX Ps 109:1 (110:1)
Heb 12:4–11	*2 Bar.* 13:10
Heb 12:5–6	Prov 3:11–12
Heb 12:7	Deut 8:5; 2 Sam 7:14; *Pss. Sol.* 10:2; 14:1
Heb 12:9	Num 16:22; 27:16; 2 Macc 3:24
Heb 12:12	Isa 35:3; Sir 25:23
Heb 12:13	LXX Prov 4:26
Heb 12:14	LXX Ps 33:15 (34:14)
Heb 12:15	LXX Deut 29:27

Heb 12:16	Gen 25:33–34
Heb 12:17	Gen 27:30–40; Wis 12:10
Heb 12:18–19	Exod 19:16–22; 20:18–21; Deut 4:11–12; 5:22–27
Heb 12:20	Exod 19:12–13
Heb 12:21	Deut 9:19; 1 Macc 13:2
Heb 12:22	*4 Bar.* 5:35
Heb 12:23	Gen 18:25; LXX Ps 49:6 (50:6)
Heb 12:24	Gen 4:10
Heb 12:26	Exod 19:18; Judg 5:4; LXX Ps 67:9 (68:8); Hag 2:6
Heb 12:29	Deut 4:24; 9:3; Isa 33:14
Heb 13:1	Xenophon, *Cyr.* 8.7.13
Heb 13:2	Gen 18:1–8; 19:1–3; Plato, *Soph.* 216A; Ps.-Phocylides, *Sent.* 24–25; Plutarch, *Mor.* 307EF: *Parallela graeca et romana* 9
Heb 13:5	Deut 31:6; cf. Gen 28:15; Deut 31:8; Josh 1:5; Ps.-Phocylides, *Sent.* 6–7
Heb 13:6	LXX Ps 117:6–7 (118:6)
Heb 13:7	Sir 33:19; Wis 2:17
Heb 13:11	Lev 16:27
Heb 13:13	*Tg. Ps.-J.* Exod 33:5–7
Heb 13:14	Diodorus Siculus 1.51; Marcus Aurelius, *Med.* 2.17
Heb 13:15	2 Chr 29:31; LXX Ps 49:14, 23 (50:14, 23); Hos 14:2; *Pss. Sol.* 15:2–3
Heb 13:17	Isa 62:6; Ezek 3:17
Heb 13:20	Isa 63:11; Zech 9:11; Isa 55:3; Jer 32:40; Ezek 37:26; *T. Dan* 5:2
Heb 13:22	*2 Bar.* 81:1

James

Jas 1:1	2 Macc 1:27
Jas 1:2	Sir 2:1; Wis 3:4–5; *T. Dan* 4:5
Jas 1:2–4	Sir 2:1–6
Jas 1:3	4 Macc 1:11
Jas 1:4	4 Macc 15:7
Jas 1:5	Prov 2:3–6; Sir 4:17; Wis 7:7; 8:21; Aratus, *Phaen.* 4
Jas 1:6	Isa 57:20; Sir 33:2; Philo, *Migration* 148; idem, *Giants* 51; Virgil, *Aen.* 12.487; Epictetus 1.4.19; Appian, *Bell. civ.* 3.20
Jas 1:7	Sir 5:9; *T. Ash.* 2:5; Plato, *Resp.* 397E, 554D
Jas 1:8	Aristotle, *Ethica* 9.6; Epictetus 2.1.12; Polybius, *Hist.* 7.4.6
Jas 1:10–11	Ps 102:4, 11; Isa 40:6–7; LXX Job 14:2
Jas 1:12	*2 Bar.* 15:8; *2 En.* 50:3–4; *Apoc. Elijah* 1:8, 14
Jas 1:13–14	Sir 15:11–20; 15:20; 16:12; Homer, *Od.* 1.30–35; Philo, *Alleg. Interp.* 2.19; *Teachings of Silvanus* 115; Seneca, *Ep.* 94.54; Plutarch, *Mor.* 117A: *[Cons. Apoll.]* 30
Jas 1:14	*1 En.* 98:4; Aristotle, *Rhet.* 1.10
Jas 1:15	*Apoc. Mos.* 19:3
Jas 1:17	*2 En.* 33:4; Macrobius, *Sat.* 1.15; Maximus of Tyre, *Diss.* 1.11

Jas 1:19	Sir 5:11; Eccl 7:9; Ps.-Phocylides, *Sent.* 57
Jas 1:21	Sir 3:17
Jas 1:22	*Apoc. Zeph.* 10:8
Jas 1:23–24	Plautus, *Pseudolus* 4.2.16
Jas 1:25	Epictetus 4.1.158; *m.* ʾ*Abot* 6:2
Jas 1:26	Pss 34:13; 39:1; 141:3
Jas 1:27	*T. Jos.* 4:6; Marcus Aurelius, *Med.* 2.13.2
Jas 2:1	Job 34:19
Jas 2:2	Seneca, *Nat.* 7.31.5
Jas 2:5	*Apoc. Elijah* 1:14
Jas 2:8	Lev 19:18
Jas 2:9	Deut 1:17
Jas 2:10	Deut 27:26; 4 Macc 5:20; 1QS 8:16; *T. Ash.* 2:5–10; Philo, *Alleg. Interp.* 3.241; *b. Hor.* 8b; *b. Šabb.* 70b; *b. Yebam.* 47b
Jas 2:11	Exod 20:14; Deut 5:18; Exod 20:13; Deut 5:17
Jas 2:13	Tob 4:9–10; Sir 27:30–28:7; *T. Zeb.* 5:3; 8:1–3; Ps.-Phocylides, *Sent.* 11; *b. Šabb.* 15b; Seneca, *Ira* 2.34.4; Curtius Rufus Quintus 5.5.17
Jas 2:18	Epictetus 1.29.56–57; Plato, *Theaet.* 200E; Herodotus, *Hist.* 4.150
Jas 2:21	Gen 22:9, 12
Jas 2:23	Gen 15:6; 2 Chr 20:7; Isa 41:8; Wis 7:27; 1 Macc 2:51–52; *Jub.* 19:9; *Apoc. Ab.* 9:7; *T. Ab.* (A) 15:13; *Apoc. Zeph.* 9:5; Theognis, *Elegi* 653
Jas 2:25	Josh 2:4, 15; 6:17
Jas 3:2	Sir 14:1
Jas 3:5	Philo, *Decalogue* 173; Ovid, *Metam.* 7.79; Aristophanes, *Peace* 609; Ps.-Phocylides, *Sent.* 144; Curtius Rufus Quintus 6.3.11; Florus 3.5.14
Jas 3:6	Sir 22:27; *1 En.* 48:7
Jas 3:6, 10	Sir 5:13; 28:11, 22; *Pss. Sol.* 12:2; Plutarch, *Mor.* 507B: *Concerning Talkativeness* 10
Jas 3:8	Ps 140:3
Jas 3:9	Gen 1:26, 27; Sir 23:1, 4; *2 En.* 44:1
Jas 3:9–12	Sir 28:12; *2 En.* 44:1
Jas 3:10	Sir 28:12; *T. Benj.* 6:5
Jas 3:13	Sir 3:17
Jas 3:15	Plato, *Philebus* 49A
Jas 3:18	Isa 32:17
Jas 4:1	*Apoc. Elijah* 1:16
Jas 4:2	1 Macc 8:16
Jas 4:3	Xenophon, *Cyr.* 1.6
Jas 4:5	Exod 20:5
Jas 4:6	LXX Prov 3:34; Homer, *Il.* 9.254; Theognis, *Elegi* 159; Aeschylus, *Pers.* 827
Jas 4:7	*T. Naph.* 8:4
Jas 4:8	Zech 1:3; Mal 3:7; Isa 1:16; *T. Dan* 4:8; Ovid, *Heroides* 7.129
Jas 4:10	Job 5:11

Jas 4:11	Wis 1:11
Jas 4:13	*1 En.* 97:8–10
Jas 4:13–14	Prov 27:1
Jas 4:14	Prov 27:1; Sir 11:18; Simonides, *Elegi* 69; Pindar, *Nem.* 11.20; idem, *Pyth.* 10.131; Ps.-Phocylides, *Sent.* 116–117; *2 Bar.* 14:10; Plutarch, *Mor.* 107A–C: *[Cons. Apoll.]* 11; Seneca, *Marc.* 10.1–5; idem, *Ep.* 99.10
Jas 5:1	*1 En.* 94:8
Jas 5:3	Ps 21:9; Jdt 16:17; Sir 12:11; 29:9–10; *2 Bar.* 23:7
Jas 5:4	Deut 24:14–15; Mal 3:5; Gen 4:10; Ps 18:6; Isa 5:9; Tob 4:14; Ps.-Phocylides, *Sent.* 19–21
Jas 5:5	Jer 12:3; 25:34
Jas 5:6	Wis 2:10, 12, 19
Jas 5:7	Deut 11:14; Jer 5:24; Joel 2:23
Jas 5:10	4 Macc 9:8
Jas 5:11	Dan 12:12; Exod 34:6; Ps 103:8; 111:4; *T. Job* 1:5
Jas 5:12	*2 En.* 49:1; Diogenes Laertius, *Vit. phil.* 8.22
Jas 5:13	*Pss. Sol.* 3:2
Jas 5:16	Plutarch, *Mor.* 229D: *[Apoph. lac.]* 10; Arrian, *Anab.* 7.29
Jas 5:17	1 Kgs 17:1; Arrian, *Anab.* 7.1
Jas 5:18	1 Kgs 18:42–45
Jas 5:20	Prov 10:12; *Pistis Sophia* 3.104

1 Peter

1 Peter 1:1	Philo, *Cherubim* 120–121
1 Pet 1:3	Sir 16:12
1 Pet 1:6–7	Wis 3:5–6
1 Pet 1:7	Job 23:10; Ps 66:10; Prov 17:3; Isa 48:10; Zech 13:9; Mal 3:3; Sir 2:5
1 Pet 1:11	Psalm 22; Isa 53
1 Pet 1:12	*1 En.* 1:2; 16:3; *2 En.* 24:3; 11QPs[a] 26:11–12 (= vv. 4–5)
1 Pet 1:16	Lev 11:44, 45; 19:2; 20:7
1 Pet 1:17	Ps 89:26; Isa 64:8; Jer 3:19; Wis 14:3; Sir 23:4; 2 Chr 19:7; Pss 28:4; 62:12; Prov 24:12; Isa 59:18; Jer 17:10
1 Pet 1:18–19	LXX Isa 52:3; Caesar, *Bell. gall.* 6.16
1 Pet 1:23	Dan 6:26
1 Pet 1:24–25	Isa 40:6–8; Cicero, *Off.* 1.26; Diodorus Siculus 1.2; Marcus Aurelius, *Med.* 4.50
1 Pet 2:3	LXX Ps 33:9 (34:8)
1 Pet 2:4–8	LXX Ps 117:22 (118:22); Isa 28:16; 8:14
1 Pet 2:5	Exod 19:6; Isa 61:6
1 Pet 2:9	Isa 43:20; Exod 19:5–6; LXX 23:22; Isa 43:21; Deut 4:20; 7:6; 14:2; Isa 43:21; 9:2; *Jub.* 16:19
1 Pet 2:10	Hos 2:23
1 Pet 2:11	Ps 39:12; *Apoc. Elijah* 1:17

1 Pet 2:11–12	Plutarch, *Mor.* 607A–F: *On Exile* 17
1 Pet 2:12	Isa 10:3
1 Pet 2:13–14	Livy 5.9
1 Pet 2:13–3:7	Aristotle, *Pol.* 1.1–14; Arius Didymus, *apud* Stobaeus, *Anth.* 148–151
1 Pet 2:17	Prov 24:21; Plutarch, *Life of Themistocles* 27.3
1 Pet 2:19	*2 En.* 50:3–4; 51:3
1 Pet 2:21	Seneca, *Ep.* 2.6
1 Pet 2:22	Isa 53:9; Xenophon, *Mem.* 1.1.11
1 Pet 2:23	Isa 53:7; Epictetus 2.12.14; Maximus of Tyre, *Diss.* 18.8
1 Pet 2:24	Isa 53:4, 12, 5
1 Pet 2:25	Isa 53:6; Ezek 34:5–6; Wis 1:6
1 Pet 3:1–6	*CIL* VI.10230
1 Pet 3:3–5	*T. Reu.* 5:5
1 Pet 3:6	Gen 18:12; Tacitus, *Ann.* 3.33–34
1 Pet 3:10–12	LXX Ps 33:13–17 (34:12–16)
1 Pet 3:14	*2 En.* 51:3
1 Pet 3:14–15	Isa 8:12–13
1 Pet 3:15	Diodorus Siculus 12.20
1 Pet 3:18–20	*1 En.* 15:2–4
1 Pet 3:19	*1 En.* 9:10; 10:11–15; Ps.-Jeremiah, *apud* Justin Martyr, *Dial.* 72.4; Irenaeus, *Haer.* 4.22.1; 4.33.1, 12; 5.31.1
1 Pet 3:20	Genesis 6–7
1 Pet 3:21	Josephus, *Ant.* 18.5.2 §117
1 Pet 4:6	*1 En.* 9:10; 10:11–15; Ps.-Jeremiah, *apud* Justin Martyr, *Dial.* 72.4; Irenaeus, *Haer.* 4.22.1; 4.33.1, 12; 5.31.1
1 Pet 4:7	*2 Bar.* 23:7
1 Pet 4:8	Prov 10:12
1 Pet 4:14	Ps 89:50–51; Isa 11:2
1 Pet 4:17	Jer 25:29; Ezek 9:6
1 Pet 4:18	LXX Prov 11:31
1 Pet 4:19	Ps 31:5; 2 Macc 1:27
1 Pet 5:4	*2 Bar.* 15:8; *Apoc. Elijah* 2:7
1 Pet 5:5	LXX Prov 3:34
1 Pet 5:6	Job 22:29; Epictetus, *Ench.* 52
1 Pet 5:7	Ps 55:22; Wis 12:13; Xenophon, *Mem.* 4.3

2 Peter

2 Pet 1:4	Epictetus 1.9.4–6
2 Pet 1:5	*m. Soṭah* 9:15
2 Pet 1:14	Plato, *Phaedo* 115CD; Lactantius, *Inst.* 3.3
2 Pet 1:19	4 Ezra 12:43
2 Pet 1:21	Plato, *Ion* 534D–535A; idem, *Phaedr.* 244AB; Horace, *Ars* 391
2 Pet 2:2	Isa 52:5; Wis 5:6
2 Pet 2:3	*T. Reu.* 3:5

2 Pet 2:4	*T. Reu.* 5:5; *T. Gad* 7:5; *1 En.* 10:4–5, 11–14; 91:15; *2 En.* 7:1; *L.A.E.* 12:2; Hesiod, *Theog.* 717; Plato, *Phaedo* 113E
2 Pet 2:5	Gen 8:18; *Jub.* 7:35
2 Pet 2:6	Gen 19:24
2 Pet 2:7	Gen 19:1–16; Wis 10:6; 3 Macc 2:13
2 Pet 2:8	Homer, *Od.* 1.229
2 Pet 2:15	Num 22:7
2 Pet 2:15–16	*Tg. Ps.-J.* Num 22:30; 23:1; 24:1, 14, 25
2 Pet 2:16	Num 22:28
2 Pet 2:22	Prov 26:11
2 Pet 3:3	*T. Dan* 5:4; *1 En.* 72:2
2 Pet 3:5	Gen 1:6–9; *2 En.* 33:4; 47:4
2 Pet 3:5–7	Berossus, *apud* Seneca, *Nat.* 3.29
2 Pet 3:6	Gen 7:11–21; *1 En.* 83:3–5
2 Pet 3:8	Ps 90:4; *Jub.* 4:30; Zosimus, *Hist.* 2.37
2 Pet 3:9	Hab 2:3; Sir 35:19; *2 Bar.* 21:21; 48:40
2 Pet 3:10–12	Cicero, *Acad.* 3.37; Aelian, *Var. hist.* 8.11
2 Pet 3:13	Isa 65:17; 66:22; 60:21; *Jub.* 1:29; *1 En.* 72:2
2 Pet 3:18	Sir 18:10

1 John

1 John 1:1	Gen 1:1; *Tg. Neof.* Gen 1:1–3; *Tg. Ps.-J.* Gen 3:24
1 John 1:3	Epictetus 2.19.26
1 John 1:5	*Corp. herm.* 1.6
1 John 1:6	1QS 1:5; 5:3; 8:2
1 John 1:7	Isa 2:5
1 John 1:8	Plato, *Resp.* 619C
1 John 1:9	Ps 32:5; Prov 28:13; *Pesiq. Rab. Kah.* 24.8
1 John 2:8	1Q27 5–6
1 John 2:9	*CIL* VI.377
1 John 2:10	Ps 119:165
1 John 2:11	*Odes Sol.* 18:6–7
1 John 2:12	Ps 25:11
1 John 2:15	*Apoc. Elijah* 1:2
1 John 2:16	LXX Prov 27:20
1 John 2:17	Wis 5:15; Plato, *Apol.* 41C; Ps.-Quintilian, *Decl.* 4.9
1 John 2:18	*Did.* 16:2–5; *Apoc. Pet.* 2
1 John 2:27	Jer 31:34
1 John 3:1	Epictetus 1.3.1
1 John 3:3	Plato, *Phaedo* 67CD
1 John 3:5	Isa 53:9
1 John 3:9	*Corp. herm.* 13.2
1 John 3:12	Gen 4:8
1 John 3:15	Cicero, *Off.* 2.7

1 John 3:17	Deut 15:7–8
1 John 3:21–22	Sir 14:2
1 John 4:6	*Jub.* 8:14; 1QS 3:18–19; 4:21, 23
1 John 4:12	Epictetus 1.14.14; Seneca, *Ep.* 31.11; 41.2; 73.16
1 John 4:19	Cicero, *Nat. d.* 1.44
1 John 5:3	Deut 30:11
1 John 5:7	Aristotle, *Cael.* 1.1
1 John 5:16	*Jub.* 21:22
1 John 5:16–17	*T. Iss.* 7:1
1 John 5:21	Ep Jer 72

2 John

| 2 John 4 | 1QS 4:6, 15 |

3 John

| 3 John 3 | 1QS 4:6, 15 |
| 3 John 11 | Ps.-Phocylides, *Sent.* 77; Cicero, *Acad.* 4.45 |

Jude

Jude 3	*1 En.* 10:4
Jude 4	*1 En.* 48:10
Jude 5	Exod 12:51; Num 14:29–30, 35
Jude 6	*T. Reu.* 5:5; *T. Gad* 7:5; *1 En.* 10:6, 12; 12:4; 22:11; *2 En.* 7:1
Jude 7	Gen 19:4–25; *T. Naph.* 3:4
Jude 9	*As. Mos.* (according to Clement, Origen, and Didymus); Dan 10:13, 21; 12:1; Zech 3:2; *L.A.E.* 15:3
Jude 11	Gen 4:3–8; Num 22:7; 31:16; 16:19–35
Jude 12	Ezek 34:8
Jude 13	Isa 57:20; Wis 14:1; *1 En.* 18:15–16; 21:5–6; *2 En.* 40:13; Seneca, *Ep.* 82.15
Jude 14	*1 En.* 60:8; 93:3; Deut 33:2; Zech 14:5; *Jub.* 7:39
Jude 14–15	*1 En.* 1:9; *Jub.* 4:16–25
Jude 14–16	*L.A.E.* 51:9
Jude 16	*1 En.* 5:4
Jude 22	*T. Zeb.* 7:2
Jude 22–23	*T. Naph.* 3:3
Jude 23	Amos 4:11; Zech 3:2

Revelation

| Rev 1:1 | Dan 2:28, 29, 45; *1 En.* 1:1–2; *2 Bar.* 10:3 |
| Rev 1:4 | Exod 3:14; Isa 41:4; *Tg. Ps.-J.* Exod 3:14; *Tg. Ps.-J.* Deut 32:39; *Mek.* on Exod 15:3 (*Shirata'* §4); *Exod. Rab.* 3.6 (on Exod 3:14); Apuleius, |

	Metam. 11.1; Plutarch, *Mor.* 153C: *Sept. sap. conv.* 9; Stobaeus, *Ecl.* 1.28; Diogenes Laertius, *Vit. phil.* 1.35–36
Rev 1:5	Pss 89:27; 130:8; Isa 40:2
Rev 1:6	Exod 19:6; Isa 61:6
Rev 1:7	Dan 7:13; Zech 12:10, 12, 14
Rev 1:8	Exod 3:14; Isa 41:4; *Tg. Ps.-J.* Exod 3:14; *Tg. Ps.-J.* Deut 32:39; *Mek.* on Exod 15:3 (*Shirata'* §4); *Exod. Rab.* 3.6 (on Exod 3:14); LXX Amos 3:13; 4:13; *2 Bar.* 21:9; *T. Isaac* 6:34; *Orphica* 39; *Aristobulus* frg. 4:5
Rev 1:9–20	*Corp. herm.* 1.1–9; Apuleius, *Metam.* 11.3–4
Rev 1:12	*Tg. Ps.-J.* Exod 39:37; 40:4
Rev 1:13	Dan 7:13; LXX Ezek 9:2, 11; Dan 10:5
Rev 1:13–15	*Apoc. Zeph.* 6:12
Rev 1:14	Dan 7:9; *2 En.* 1:5; *Apoc. Ab.* 11:3; Moschus, *Idylls* 1.7
Rev 1:14–15	Dan 10:6
Rev 1:15	Ezek 1:24; 43:2
Rev 1:16	Isa 49:2; *2 En.* 1:5; *Tg. Ps.-J.* Exod 39:37; 40:4
Rev 1:17	Isa 44:6; 48:12; 4 Ezra 10:30
Rev 1:18	Sir 18:1
Rev 1:19	LXX Isa 48:6; Dan 2:28, 29, 45; *2 En.* 39:2
Rev 2:7	Gen 2:9; LXX Gen 2:8; LXX Ezek 28:13; 31:8, 9; 4 Ezra 8:52; *2 Bar.* 4:7; *1 En.* 25:5; *2 En.* 8:3
Rev 2:10	2 Macc 13:14; *2 Bar.* 15:8; 3 Macc 7:16
Rev 2:11	*Tg. Onq.* Deut 33:6; *Frg. Tg.* (Paris MS) Deut 33:6; *Tg. Isa.* 22:14; 65:5b–6; *Tg. Jer.* 51:39, 57
Rev 2:12	Wis 18:15–16
Rev 2:17	2 Macc 2:4–8; *2 Bar.* 29:8
Rev 2:18	*Apoc. Zeph.* 6:13
Rev 2:23	Sophocles, *Oed. tyr.* 614
Rev 2:26–27	Ps 2:8, 9; *Pss. Sol.* 17:23–24
Rev 3:4–5	2 Esdr 2:39–40; *2 En.* 22:9
Rev 3:7	Isa 22:22; Job 12:14
Rev 3:12	*T. Dan* 5:12; *Apoc. Elijah* 1:9
Rev 3:18	*Pss. Sol.* 17:43; *2 En.* 22:9
Rev 4:1	*2 Bar.* 10:3; 22:2; 23:7
Rev 4:1–2	*2 En.* 20:1
Rev 4:1–11	*T. Levi* 3:9
Rev 4:2	1 Kgs 22:19; Isa 6:1; Ezek 1:26–27; Sir 1:8; *2 En.* 20:3
Rev 4:2–3	*1 En.* 14:18
Rev 4:4	*2 En.* 4:1; 22:9; *Apoc. Elijah* 4:10
Rev 4:6	*2 En.* 3:3
Rev 4:6–7	Ezek 1:5–10, 22; 10:14
Rev 4:7	*T. Naph.* 5:6
Rev 4:8	Isa 6:2; Ezek 1:18; 10:12; Isa 6:3; LXX Amos 3:13; Isa 41:4; Exod 3:14; *Apoc. Elijah* 5:2
Rev 4:8–11	*CIG* 2715

Rev 4:9	1 Kgs 22:19; Isa 6:1; Ezek 1:26–27; Sir 1:8; *Tg. Neof.* Exod 14:14
Rev 4:10	1 Kgs 22:19; Isa 6:1; Ezek 1:26–27; Sir 1:8
Rev 4:11	3 Macc 2:3; Wis 1:14; Sir 18:1
Rev 5:1	1 Kgs 22:19; Isa 6:1; Ezek 1:26–27; Sir 1:8; *2 En.* 20:3; *4 Bar.* 3:10
Rev 5:1–4	*Jub.* 32:20–22; *1 En.* 81:2–3
Rev 5:1–6	4 Ezra 12:31–33
Rev 5:7	1 Kgs 22:19; Isa 6:1; Ezek 1:26–27; Sir 1:8
Rev 5:8	*T. Levi* 3:7
Rev 5:11	Dan 7:10; *1 En.* 14:22; 40:1; *Apoc. Zeph.* 4:1–2
Rev 5:13	1 Kgs 22:19; Isa 6:1; Ezek 1:26–27; Sir 1:8
Rev 5:20	*Jub.* 16:19
Rev 6–16	*2 Bar.* 26–27
Rev 6:9–11	4 Ezra 4:33–37
Rev 6:10	*Sib. Or.* 3:313
Rev 6:11	*2 Bar.* 23:5; *2 En.* 22:9
Rev 6:12	*Apoc. Elijah* 3:8; *Ap. Ezek.* frg. 2
Rev 6:14	*Sib. Or.* 3:82
Rev 6:16	Hos 10:8; 1 Kgs 22:19; Isa 6:1; Ezek 1:26–27; Sir 1:8; *Apoc. Elijah* 2:34
Rev 6:17	*Apoc. Zeph.* 12:6
Rev 7:3	Ezek 9:4; CD 19:12–13; *Pss. Sol.* 15:6; *Apoc. Elijah* 1:9
Rev 7:4	2 Esdr 2:38
Rev 7:9	2 Macc 10:7; 2 Esdr 2:39–40, 42; *2 En.* 22:9
Rev 7:10	1 Kgs 22:19; Isa 6:1; Ezek 1:26–27; Sir 1:8
Rev 7:13	2 Esdr 2:44; *Apoc. Elijah* 1:9
Rev 7:14	*Apoc. Elijah* 1:9
Rev 7:15	1 Kgs 22:19; Isa 6:1; Ezek 1:26–27; Sir 1:8
Rev 7:16	Isa 49:10; *Apoc. Elijah* 5:6
Rev 7:17	Ps 23:1; Ezek 34:23; Ps 23:2; Isa 49:10; Jer 2:13; Isa 25:8; *T. Ash.* 6:6; *T. Jud.* 24:4
Rev 8:1	Wis 18:14
Rev 8:2	Tob 12:15; *Apoc. Mos.* 22:3
Rev 8:3	Tob 12:12
Rev 8:3–4	*T. Levi* 3:7
Rev 8:7	Exod 9:23–25; Ezek 38:22; Wis 16:22; Sir 39:29
Rev 8:8	*1 En.* 18:13; 21:3
Rev 8:10	*1 En.* 86:1; *Sib. Or.* 5:155
Rev 8:12	*Apoc. Mos.* 36:3
Rev 9:1	*Sib. Or.* 5:155; *2 En.* 42:1
Rev 9:2	4 Ezra 7:36
Rev 9:3	Exod 10:12, 15; Wis 1:14; 16:9
Rev 9:4	Ezek 9:4; CD 19:12–13; *Pss. Sol.* 15:6
Rev 9:6	*Apoc. Elijah* 2:5, 32
Rev 9:13–18	*Sib. Or.* 5:93–94
Rev 9:20	Pss 115:4–7; 135:15–17; Dan 5:23
Rev 10:5–6	Deut 32:40; Dan 12:7; Gen 14:19, 22; Exod 20:11

Rev 11:3–12	*Ascen. Isa.* 2:8–11
Rev 11:8	*Apoc. Elijah* 4:13
Rev 11:15	*2 En.* 1:5
Rev 11:18	Sir 11:26–28
Rev 11:19	2 Macc 2:4–8; *T. Levi* 5:1
Rev 12:1	*T. Naph.* 5:1
Rev 12:1–3	*2 Bar.* 24:4
Rev 12:1–18	Herodotus, *Hist.* 2.156; Euripides, *Iphigenia taurica* 1234–1251
Rev 12:5	Isa 7:14; 66:7; Ps 2:9
Rev 12:7	*Tg. Neof.* Gen 3:15
Rev 12:7–12	*L.A.E.* 14:1
Rev 12:9	*Liv. Pro.* 12:13; *L.A.E.* 12:1
Rev 12:11	*T. Jud.* 25:4
Rev 12:14	*2 Bar.* 28:1
Rev 12:17	*Liv. Pro.* 12:13
Rev 13:1	4 Ezra 11:1
Rev 13:1–18	Tacitus, *Hist.* 15.44
Rev 13:10	Jer 15:2; 43:11
Rev 13:14	*1 En.* 54:6
Rev 13:18	*Sib. Or.* 5:28
Rev 14:1	Ezek 9:4; CD 19:12–13; *Pss. Sol.* 15:6; *Apoc. Elijah* 1:9
Rev 14:10	Gen 19:24; Ps 11:6; Ezek 38:22; 3 Macc 2:5
Rev 14:10–11	4 Ezra 7:61
Rev 14:13	Theognis, *Elegi* 1008; Cicero, *Tusc.* 1.19; Seneca, *Polyb.* 9.8–9
Rev 14:15	*1 En.* 10:13
Rev 14:20	Josephus, *J.W.* 6.8.5 §406
Rev 15:1	*2 Bar.* 27:4
Rev 15:2	*2 En.* 3:3
Rev 15:2–3	*Tg. Neof.* Exod 15:4
Rev 15:3	Jer 10:10 (Theodotion); Tob 13:7, 11; *1 En.* 9:4; 25:5; 27:3
Rev 16:5	*1 En.* 66:2; *2 En.* 19:4
Rev 16:14–16	1QM 1:1–12
Rev 16:16	4 Ezra 13:34
Rev 16:21	Diodorus Siculus 19.45
Rev 17:9	*1 En.* 21:3; 4 Ezra 11
Rev 17:12	*Tg. Neof.* Gen 49:18
Rev 17:14	Deut 10:17; Dan 2:47; 2 Macc 13:4; 3 Macc 5:35; *1 En.* 9:4
Rev 18:2	Isa 13:21; 34:11; Jer 50:39; Bar 4:35
Rev 18:10	*Tg. Neof.* Gen 49:18
Rev 18:11	*Apoc. Elijah* 2:31
Rev 18:17	*Tg. Neof.* Gen 49:18
Rev 18:19	*Tg. Neof.* Gen 49:18
Rev 19–21	*Tg. Ps.-J.* Num 11:26
Rev 19:1	Tob 13:18; *Pss. Sol.* 8:2
Rev 19:4	1 Kgs 22:19; Isa 6:1; Ezek 1:26–27; Sir 1:8; *2 En.* 20:3

Rev 19:10	*Apoc. Zeph.* 6:15
Rev 19:11	2 Macc 3:25; 11:8
Rev 19:11–21	1QM 1:1–12
Rev 19:12	*2 En.* 1:5
Rev 19:13	*Tg. Ps.-J.* Gen 49:10–11
Rev 19:15	Ps 2:9
Rev 19:16	Deut 10:17; Dan 2:47; 2 Macc 13:4; 3 Macc 5:35; *1 En.* 9:4
Rev 19:19	4 Ezra 13:43
Rev 19:20	*1 En.* 10:6; *2 En.* 10:2; *Apoc. Zeph.* 6:2
Rev 20–22	*L.A.B.* 3:9–10; 4 Ezra 7:26–44
Rev 20:1	*2 En.* 42:1
Rev 20:2	*T. Jud.* 25:3
Rev 20:3	*1 En.* 18:16; 21:6
Rev 20:4	*T. Jud.* 25:4; *Apoc. Elijah* 1:9; 5:39
Rev 20:4–6	4Q521 frgs. 7+5 ii
Rev 20:6	*Tg. Onq.* Deut 33:6; *Frg. Tg.* (Paris MS) Deut 33:6; *Tg. Isa.* 22:14; 65:5b–6; *Tg. Jer.* 51:39, 57
Rev 20:7–10	*Sib. Or.* 3:319
Rev 20:8	Ezek 38:2
Rev 20:10	Gen 19:24; Ps 11:6; Ezek 38:22; 3 Macc 2:5; *1 En.* 10:13
Rev 20:10–15	*2 En.* 10:2
Rev 20:11–12	Dan 7:9–10
Rev 20:12	4 Ezra 6:20; *2 Bar.* 24:1
Rev 20:12–13	Ps 28:4; 62:12; Prov 24:12; Isa 59:18; Jer 17:10; Sir 16:12
Rev 20:13	*1 En.* 51:1; 61:5
Rev 20:14	*T. Jud.* 25:3; *Tg. Onq.* Deut 33:6; *Frg. Tg.* (Paris MS) Deut 33:6; *Tg. Isa.* 22:14; 65:5b–6; *Tg. Jer.* 51:39, 57
Rev 21:1	*1 En.* 72:3; *Apoc. Elijah* 5:38
Rev 21:1–22:5	4 Ezra 8:51–55; *Sib. Or.* 3.767–808
Rev 21:3	Lev 26:11–12; 2 Chr 6:18; Ezek 37:27; Zech 2:10; *2 En.* 20:3; *Pr. Jos.* frg. A
Rev 21:4	Isa 25:8; *2 Bar.* 73:2–3; *2 En.* 65:9
Rev 21:5	1 Kgs 22:19; Isa 6:1; Ezek 1:26–27; Sir 1:8
Rev 21:5–22:5	*T. Levi* 5:1
Rev 21:6	Isa 44:6; 48:12; 55:1; Ps 36:9; Jer 2:13
Rev 21:7	2 Sam 7:14
Rev 21:8	Gen 19:24; Ps 11:6; Ezek 38:22; 3 Macc 2:5; *2 En.* 10:2, 5; *Tg. Onq.* Deut 33:6; *Frg. Tg.* (Paris MS) Deut 33:6; *Tg. Isa.* 22:14; 65:5b–6; *Tg. Jer.* 51:39, 57; Aeschylus, *Ag.* 446
Rev 21:9–21	4 Ezra 10:27
Rev 21:12–13	Exod 28:21; Ezek 48:30–35; 4Q554 frg. 1 ii 9–iii 10
Rev 21:15	Ezek 40:3, 5
Rev 21:16–17	Ezek 48:16, 17
Rev 21:19–20	Tob 13:17
Rev 21:24	Isa 60:3, 5; *Pss. Sol.* 17:34

Rev 21:25	Aristophanes, *Frogs* 446
Rev 21:26	Ps 72:10–11; *Pss. Sol.* 17:34
Rev 22:1	*1 En.* 14:19
Rev 22:2	Gen 2:9; 3:22; Ezek 47:12; *T. Levi* 18:11; 4 Ezra 8:52; *Pss. Sol.* 14:3; *1 En.* 25:5; *2 En.* 8:2; *Apoc. Mos.* 9:3
Rev 22:4	*T. Levi* 18:11; 4 Ezra 7:98
Rev 22:6	Dan 2:28, 29, 45
Rev 22:8–9	*Apoc. Zeph.* 6:15
Rev 22:12	4 Ezra 7:99
Rev 22:13	Isa 44:6; 48:12
Rev 22:14	Gen 2:9; 3:22; Ezek 47:12; *1 En.* 25:5
Rev 22:16	Isa 11:1, 10; Num 24:17; *Tgs.* Num 24:17
Rev 22:18–19	Deut 4:2; 12:32; *2 En.* 48:7; *Let. Aris.* 310–311
Rev 22:19	Gen 2:9; 3:22; Ezek 47:12; *T. Levi* 18:11

Parallels between New Testament Gospels and Pseudepigraphal Gospels

This appendix lists parallels between the four NT Gospels and a select number of the pseudepigraphal gospels.

Mark

Mark 1:4–6	*Gos. Eb.* §2 (Epiphanius, *Pan.* 30.13.4–5)
Mark 1:9–11	*Gos. Eb.* §4 (Epiphanius, *Pan.* 30.13.7–8; cf. Matt 3:14–15; Luke 3:22); *Gos. Heb.* §2 (Jerome, *Comm. Isa.* 4 [on Isa 11:2]); *Gos. Naz.* 2 (Jerome, *Pelag.* 3.2)
Mark 1:16–20	*Gos. Eb.* §1 (Epiphanius, *Pan.* 30.13.2–3)
Mark 1:40–45	P.Eger. 2 §2
Mark 2:15–17	P.Oxy. 1224 §1; Justin Martyr *1 Apol.* 15.8
Mark 2:18–10	*Gos. Thom.* §27, §104
Mark 2:21–22	*Gos. Thom.* §47
Mark 3:1–6	*Gos. Naz.* §10 (Jerome *Comm. Matt.* 2 [on Matt 12:13])
Mark 3:23–27	*Gos. Thom.* §35
Mark 3:28–30	*Gos. Thom.* §44
Mark 3:31–35	*Gos. Thom.* §99; *Gos. Eb.* §5 (Epiphanius, *Pan.* 30.13.5)
Mark 4:2–9	*Gos. Thom.* §9
Mark 4:10–12	*Ap. Jas.* 7:1–10
Mark 4:13–20	*Ap. Jas.* 8:10–17
Mark 4:21	*Gos. Thom.* §33
Mark 4:22	P.Oxy. 654 §5; *Gos. Thom.* §5, §6
Mark 4:24–25	*Gos. Thom.* §41

Mark 4:26–29	*Gos. Thom.* §21; *Ap. Jas.* 12:20–31
Mark 4:30–32	*Gos. Thom.* §20
Mark 6:4	P.Oxy. 1 §6; *Gos. Thom.* §31
Mark 7:6–8	P.Eger. 2 §3
Mark 7:14–15	*Gos. Thom.* §14
Mark 8:27–30	*Gos. Thom.* §13
Mark 8:31–33	*Ap. Jas.* 5:31–6:11
Mark 8:34	*Gos. Thom.* §55, §101
Mark 9:40	P.Oxy. 1224 §2
Mark 10:13–16	*Gos. Thom.* §22
Mark 10:17–22	*Gos. Naz.* §16 (Origen, *Comm. Matt.* 15.14 [on Matt 19:16–30])
Mark 10:28–30	*Ap. Jas.* 4:22–37
Mark 10:31	P.Oxy. 654 §4; *Gos. Thom.* §4
Mark 11:22–23	*Gos. Thom.* §48, §106
Mark 12:1–12	*Gos. Thom.* §§65–66
Mark 12:13–17	*Gos. Thom.* §100; P.Eger. 2 §3; *Gos. Thom.* §100
Mark 12:31	*Gos. Thom.* §25
Mark 12:34	*Gos. Thom.* §82
Mark 13:21	*Gos. Thom.* §113
Mark 14:12	*Gos. Eb.* §7 (Epiphanius, *Pan.* 30.22.4)
Mark 14:27–30	Fayyum Fragment
Mark 14:58	*Gos. Thom.* §71
Mark 14:65	*Gos. Pet.* 3.9
Mark 15:1–5	*Acts Pil.* 3:2
Mark 15:6–15	*Acts Pil.* 4:4–5; 9:4–5
Mark 15:7	*Gos. Naz.* §20 (Jerome, *Comm. Matt.* 4 [on Matt 27:16])
Mark 15:16–20	*Gos. Pet.* 2.5–3.9; *Acts Pil.* 10:1
Mark 15:22–32	*Acts Pil.* 10:1
Mark 15:33–39	*Gos. Pet.* 5.15–20; *Acts Pil.* 11:1
Mark 15:38	*Gos. Naz.* §21 (Jerome, *Epistula ad Hedybiam* 120.8)
Mark 15:40–41	*Acts Pil.* 11:2–3a
Mark 15:42–47	*Gos. Pet.* 2.3–5; 6.21–24; *Acts Pil.* 11:3b
Mark 16:1–8	*Gos. Pet.* 9.35–13.57; *Acts Pil.* 13:1–3
Mark 16:14–18	*Acts Pil.* 14:1

Q (Luke/Matthew)

Luke 3:7–9 = Matt 3:7–10	*Ap. Jas.* 9:24–10:6
Luke 4:5 = Matt 4:8	*Gos. Heb.* §3 (Origen, *Comm. Jo.* 2.12.87 [on John 1:3])
Luke 6:20 = Matt 5:3	*Gos. Thom.* §54
Luke 6:21 = Matt 5:6	*Gos. Thom.* §69b
Luke 6:22 = Matt 5:11	*Gos. Thom.* §68

Luke 6:27–28 = Matt 5:44   P.Oxy. 1224 §2
Luke 6:30 = Matt 5:42   *Gos. Thom.* §95
Luke 6:31 = Matt 7:12   P.Oxy. 654 §6; *Gos. Thom.* §6; cf. Tob 4:15
Luke 6:35 = Matt 5:44   P.Oxy. 1224 §2
Luke 6:39 = Matt 15:14   *Gos. Thom.* §34
Luke 6:41–42 = Matt 7:1–5   P.Oxy. 1 §1; *Gos. Thom.* §26
Luke 6:43–45 = Matt 7:16; 12:33–35   *Gos. Thom.* §45, §43
Luke 7:24–25 = Matt 11:7–8   *Gos. Thom.* §78
Luke 7:28 = Matt 11:11   *Gos. Thom.* §46
Luke 8:16–17; 12:2 = Matt 10:26   P.Oxy. 654 §5; *Gos. Thom.* §5, §6
Luke 9:58 = Matt 8:20   *Gos. Thom.* §86
Luke 10:2 = Matt 9:37–38   *Gos. Thom.* §73
Luke 10:3 = Matt 10:16   P.Oxy. 655 §2; *Gos. Thom.* §39; *Gos. Eg.* [?] frg. 3
Luke 10:7–8 = Matt 10:10b–11   *Gos. Thom.* §14b
Luke 10:21 = Matt 11:25   P.Oxy. 654 §3; *Gos. Thom.* §4
Luke 11:3 = Matt 6:11   *Gos. Naz.* §5 (Jerome, *Comm. Matt.* 1 [on Matt 6:11]); *Gos. Heb.* §4

Luke 11:9–13 = Matt 7:7–11   P.Oxy. 654 §2; *Gos. Thom.* §2, §92, §94
Luke 11:33 = Matt 5:15   *Gos. Thom.* §33
Luke 11:34–36 = Matt 6:22–23   *Gos. Thom.* §24
Luke 11:39–40 = Matt 23:25–26   *Gos. Thom.* §89
Luke 12:3 = Matt 10:27   P.Oxy. 1 §8; *Gos. Thom.* §33
Luke 12:12–31 = Matt 6:25–34   P.Oxy. 655 §1a; *Gos. Thom.* §36
Luke 12:33 = Matt 6:19–20   *Gos. Thom.* §76
Luke 12:39–40 = Matt 24:43–44   *Gos. Thom.* §21, §103
Luke 12:49–53; 14:25–27 =   *Gos. Thom.* §10, §16, §55, §101
    Matt 10:34–38
Luke 12:54–56 = Matt 16:2–3   *Gos. Thom.* §91
Luke 13:20–21 = Matt 13:33   *Gos. Thom.* §96
Luke 13:24 = Matt 7:13–14   *T. Ab.* (A) 11:1–12
Luke 14:15–24 = Matt 22:1–14   *Gos. Thom.* §64
Luke 15:3–7 = Matt 18:12–14   *Gos. Thom.* §107
Luke 16:13 = Matt 6:24   *Gos. Thom.* §47
Luke 16:17 = Matt 5:18   *Gos. Thom.* §11
Luke 17:3–4 = Matt 18:15   *Gos. Naz.* §15 (Jerome, *Pelag.* 3.2)
Luke 17:34–35 = Matt 24:40–41   *Gos. Thom.* §61a
Luke 19:11–27 = Matt 25:14–30   *Gos. Naz.* §18 (Eusebius, *Theoph.* 22 [on Matt 25:14–15])

"M" (Material special to Matthew)

Matt 1:18–25   *Prot. Jas.* 14:1–2
Matt 2:1–12   *Prot. Jas.* 21:1–4
Mat 2:13   P.Cairo §1 §2
Matt 2:15   *Gos. Naz.* (Jerome, *Vir. ill.* 3)

Matt 2:16–18	*Prot. Jas.* 22:1–2
Matt 2:23	*Gos. Naz.* (Jerome, *Vir. ill.* 3)
Matt 5:10	*Gos. Thom.* §69a
Matt 5:14	P.Oxy. 1 §7; *Gos. Thom.* §32
Matt 5:17	*Gos. Eb.* §6 (Epiphanius, *Pan.* 30.16.4–5)
Matt 6:2–4	P.Oxy. 654 §6; *Gos. Thom.* §6, §14
Matt 6:3	*Gos. Thom.* §62
Matt 7:6	*Gos. Thom.* §93
Matt 11:30	*Gos. Thom.* §90
Matt 13:24–30	*Gos. Thom.* §57
Matt 13:44	*Gos. Thom.* §109
Matt 13:45–46	*Gos. Thom.* §76
Matt 13:47–50	*Gos. Thom.* §8
Matt 15:13	*Gos. Thom.* §40
Matt 18:20	P.Oxy. 1 §5; *Gos. Thom.* §30
Matt 23:13	P.Oxy. 655 §2; *Gos. Thom.* §39, §102
Matt 27:16	*Gos. Naz.* §20 (Jerome, *Comm. Matt.* 4 [on Matt 27:16])
Matt 27:24–25	*Gos. Pet.* 1.1–2; *Acts Pil.* 9:4–5
Matt 27:62–66	*Gos. Pet.* 8.28–9.34

"L" (Material special to Luke)

Luke 1:5–7	*Gos. Eb.* §3 (Epiphanius, *Pan.* 30.13.6)
Luke 1:8–11	*Prot. Jas.* 8:3
Luke 1:20	*Prot. Jas.* 10:2
Luke 1:21	*Prot. Jas.* 23:1–24:2
Luke 1:26–38	*Prot. Jas.* 11:1–3
Luke 1:36	P.Cairo §2
Luke 1:39–56	*Prot. Jas.* 12:2–3
Luke 1:80	*Inf. Gos. Thom.* 19:5b
Luke 2:1–6	*Prot. Jas.* 17:1–3
Luke 2:7	*Prot. Jas.* 22:2
Luke 2:19	*Inf. Gos. Thom.* 11:2c
Luke 2:26	*Prot. Jas.* 24:4
Luke 2:46–52	*Inf. Gos. Thom.* 19:1–5
Luke 6:46	P.Eger. 2 §3
Luke 11:27–28	*Gos. Thom.* §79
Luke 12:13–14	*Gos. Thom.* §72
Luke 12:16–21	*Gos. Thom.* §63
Luke 17:4	*Gos. Naz.* §15 (Jerome, *Pelag.* 3.2)
Luke 17:21	P.Oxy. 654 §3; *Gos. Thom.* §3
Luke 22:43–44	*Gos. Naz.* §32 (*NTApoc* 1:152)

Luke 23:34	*Acts Pil.* 10:1b; *Gos. Naz.* §24 (Haimo of Auxerre, *Commentarius in Isaiam* [on Isa 53:2]); *Gos. Naz.* §35 (*NTApoc* 1:153)
Luke 23:39–43	*Gos. Pet.* 4.10–14; *Acts Pil.* 10:2
Luke 23:46–48	*Acts Pil.* 11:1
Luke 23:48	*Gos. Pet.* 7.25
Luke 24:30–31	*Gos. Heb.* §7 (Jerome, *Vir. ill.* 2)

John

John 1:9	P.Oxy. 655 §24; *Gos. Thom.* §24
John 1:14	P.Oxy. 1 §28; *Gos. Thom.* §28
John 4:13–15	*Gos. Thom.* §13
John 7:32–36	P.Oxy. 655 §38; *Gos. Thom.* §38
John 8:12; 9:5	*Gos. Thom.* §77
John 18:31	*Acts Pil.* 4:4
John 18:33–38	*Acts Pil.* 3:2
John 19:12	*Acts Pil.* 9:1b
John 19:20	*Acts Pil.* 10:1b
John 20:5, 11–12	*Gos. Pet.* 13.55
John 20:29	*Ap. Jas.* 8:3

Sources and Bibliography

Acts Pil.   *Acts of Pilate*
Composed in the second or third century, it claims to have been written in Hebrew by Nicodemus. Eventually it was incorporated into the *Gospel of Nicodemus.* It is extant in Greek. OG 163–65; *NTApoc* 1:444–70.

Ap. Jas.   *Apocryphon of James*
The *Apocryphon of James* was found at Nag Hammadi as the second tractate in Codex I (NHC I,2). It comprises a series of sayings of the risen Jesus, which, it claims, James wrote down in Hebrew. It was composed in Greek, probably in the second century. *INT* 2:224–25; OG 55–57; *NHL* 29–37; Williams.

Fayum Fragment
This document is a third-century Greek fragment. It is so brief (fewer than twenty legible words) that its derivation is uncertain (an apocryphal gospel?). *NTApoc* 1:115–16.

Gos. Eb.   *Gospel of the Ebionites*
Epiphanius (fourth century) preserves several fragments of a gospel in circulation among Greek-speaking Jewish Christians (second and third century). Epiphanius erroneously calls it the Hebrew Gospel. It may have originated as early as the second century. *INT* 2:202–3; OG 103–4; *NTApoc* 1:153–58.

Gos. Eg.   *Gospel of the Egyptians*
There is one Latin fragment from Ps.-Titus that reads: "The Lord himself said, 'Hear me, you whom I have chosen as lambs, and fear not the wolves.'" This *Gospel of the Egyptians* is not to be confused with the Coptic gnostic *Gospel of the Egyptians* (NHC III,*2* and IV,*2*). Kloppenborg, *Q Parallels*, 67, 239.

Gos. Heb.   *Gospel of the Hebrews*
The *Gospel of the Hebrews* was composed in the second half of the first century or the first half of the second. Only fragments are extant in the church fathers. *INT* 2:223–24; *OG* 83–85; *NTApoc* 1:158–65.

Gos. Naz.   *Gospel of the Nazarenes*
The *Gospel of the Nazarenes* is an expansion of the Gospel of Matthew. Fragments are preserved in the church fathers and in the margins of NT MSS. *INT* 2:201–2; *OG* 97–98; *NTApoc* 1:139–53.

Gos. Pet.   *Gospel of Peter*
The *Gospel of Peter* has survived as a large Greek fragment dating to the eighth century. Other fragments found at Oxyrhynchus, which date to the second or third century, may be related to this apocryphal gospel. The writing has been versified in two ways: chapters 1–14 and verses 1–60. Accordingly, chapter 1 begins with verse 1, but chapter 2 begins with verse 3, chapter 4 with verse 10, etc. *INT* 2:162–63; *OG* 76–78; *NTApoc* 1:179–87.

Gos. Thom.   *Gospel of Thomas*
The *Gospel of Thomas* comprises 114 sayings. It was originally written in Greek, perhaps as early as the late first century. Other than fragments from Oxyrhynchus (P.Oxy. 1, 654, 655) the work survives in the fourth-century Coptic gnostic library found at Nag Hammadi (NHC II,*2*). *INT* 2:150–54; *OG* 23–25; *NHL* 124–38; *NTApoc* 1:278–307.

Inf. Gos. Thom.   *Infancy Gospel of Thomas*
The *Infancy Gospel* tells several imaginative tales of Jesus' boyhood. It may have been written as early as the second century. It is extant in a sixth-century Syriac MS and in several Greek MSS dating from the fourteenth to the sixteenth centuries. It has affinities with the Gospel of Luke. *OG* 122–24; *NTApoc* 1:388–401.

P.Cairo   *Papyrus Cairensis 10735*
This fragment, perhaps originally part of a gospel, describes the flight of the holy family to Egypt. Only a few sentences can be restored with any confidence. *NTApoc* 1:114–15.

P.Eger. 2   *Papyrus Egerton 2*
This papyrus contains a fragment of an unknown gospel, perhaps dating to the early second century. *INT* 2:181–83; *NTApoc* 1:94–97.

P.Oxy. 1   Oxyrhynchus Papyrus 1
P.Oxy. 1 dates to the end of the second century and contains sayings of Jesus that approximate *Gos. Thom.* §§26–33 and a portion of §77; *NTApoc* 1:104–10.

P.Oxy. 654   Oxyrhynchus Papyrus 654
P.Oxy. 654 dates to the third century and contains sayings of Jesus that approximate *Gos. Thom.* §§1–5. *NTApoc* 1:97–104.

P.Oxy. 655   Oxyrhynchus Papyrus 655
P.Oxy. 655 dates to the first half of the third century and contains sayings of Jesus that approximate *Gos. Thom.* §§36–40. *NTApoc* 1:110–13.

P.Oxy. 1224   Oxyrhynchus Papyrus 1224
P.Oxy. 1224 dates to the beginning of the fourth century. It consists of fragments of an unknown apocryphal gospel. *NTApoc* 1:113–14.

Prot. Jas.   Protevangelium of James
The *Protevangelium,* dating from late second century or early third, is an infancy gospel that tells the story of the birth of Mary and the birth of Jesus. It is called "protevangelium" implying that it is the first part of the gospel, the part that precedes the canonical gospel story. *OG* 107–9; *NTApoc* 1:370–88.

Sec. Gos. Mk.   Secret Gospel of Mark
The *Secret Gospel of Mark* appears only in a fragment of a letter of Clement of Alexandria, discovered by Morton Smith in 1958. In the fragment Clement charges that the Carpocratians are misusing and "falsifying" what has been entrusted only to those being perfected. Scholars debate the provenance of the fragment; some think it may be early second century (e.g., Cameron), but others disagree: "It is possible that Clement's letter, along with the quotations of the Secret Gospel of Mark, which it contains, is a forgery, perhaps even [being written by] a twentieth-century forger" (see Quesnell).

T. Ab.   Testament of Abraham
The *Testament of Abraham* is not one of the pseudepigraphal gospels; rather, it is part of the OT Pseudepigrapha. Abraham's vision of the narrow and broad ways parallels Jesus' saying in Q (Luke 13:24 = Matt 7:13–14) so closely that it seemed appropriate to note it. Kloppenborg, 153.

General Bibliography

R. E. BROWN, "The Relation of 'the Secret Gospel of Mark' to the Fourth Gospel," *CBQ* 36 (1974): 466–85; R. CAMERON, ed., *OG;* R. W. FUNK, *New Gospel Parallels* (2 vols.; Philadelphia: Fortress, 1985): vol. 1, *The Synoptic Gospels,* vol. 2, *John and the Other Gospels;* E. HENNECKE and W. SCHNEEMELCHER, *Gospels and Related Writings* (vol. 1 of *NTApoc*); J. S. KLOPPENBORG, *Q Parallels* (Sonoma, Calif.: Polebridge, 1987) (English translation and original languages); H. KOESTER, *INT*; Q. QUESNELL, "The Mar Saba Clementine: A Question of Evidence," *CBQ* 37 (1975): 48–67; J. M. ROBINSON, ed., *NHL;* F. E. WILLIAMS, "NHC I,2: The Apocryphon of James," in *Nag Hammadi Codex I (The Jung Codex): Introduction, Texts, Translations, Indices* (ed. H. W. Attridge; NHS 22; Leiden: Brill, 1985), 13–53.

APPENDIX FOUR

Jesus' Parables and the Parables of the Rabbis

H. K. Mcarthur and R. M. Johnston (1990) have identified more than two dozen parables of Jesus that closely parallel rabbinic parables (most are Tannaic). With some modification and expansion they are as follows:

1. The Sower [or the Four Soils] (Mark 4:3–8; Matt 13:3–8; Luke 8:5–8)
   The Four Types of Students (*m. ʾAbot* 5:15) [anonymous]
2. The Mustard Seed (Mark 4:30–32; Matt 13:31–32; Luke 13:18–19)
   The Seed under Hard Ground (*b. Taʿan.* 4a) [anonymous]
3. The Wicked Tenants (Mark 12:1–11; Matt 21:33–44; Luke 20:9–18)
   The Unworthy Tenants (*Sipre Deut.* §312 [on Deut 32:9]) [anonymous]
4. Paying a Debt and Settling a Dispute (Matt 5:25–26; Luke 12:57–59)
   Paying a Debt and Settling a Dispute (*Pesiq. Rab Kah.* 18.6) [anonymous]
5. Wise Builder and Foolish Builder (Matt 7:24–27; Luke 6:47–49)
   Wise Builder and Foolish Builder (*ʾAbot R. Nat.* A 24:1–4) [R. Elisha ben Abuyah, ca. 120 C.E.]
   The Builder with or without Tools (*ʾAbot R. Nat.* A 22) [R. Yohanan ben Zakkai, ca. 80 C.E.]
6. The Lost Sheep (Matt 18:10–14; Luke 15:3–7)
   On Who Will Seek the Lost Sheep (*Midr. Pss.* 119.3 [on 119:1]; cf. *Exod. Rab.* 2.2 [on Exod 3:1]: "he placed the lamb on his shoulder"; *Gen. Rab.* 86.4 [on Gen 39:2]) [R. Haggai ben Eleazar, ca. 350 C.E.]
7. The Wise and Foolish Maidens (Matt 25:1–13; cf. Matt 22:1–10; Luke 14:15–24)
   The Wise and Foolish Servants (*b. Šabb.* 153a; cf. *Qoh. Rab.* 9.8 §1) [R. Yohanan ben Zakkai, ca. 70–80 C.E.]
8. The Faithful and Unfaithful Servants (Matt 24:45–51; Luke 12:42–46)
   The Wise and Foolish Servants (*Qoh. Rab.* 9.8 §1; cf. *b. Šabb.* 153a) [anonymous, based on parable by R. Yohanan ben Zakkai, ca. 70–80 C.E.]

The King's Ungrateful Servants (*S. Eli. Rab.* §12 [55]) [anonymous]
9. The Watchful Householder (Matt 24:42–44; Luke 12:39–40)
   The Wise and Foolish Servants (*b. Šabb.* 153a) [R. Yohanan ben Zakkai, ca. 70–80 C.E.]
10. The Talents and the Servants' Stewardship (Matt 25:14–30; Luke 19:21–27)
    The Wife's Stewardship (*Song Rab.* 7.14 §1) [anonymous]
    The King's Steward (ʾ*Abot R. Nat.* A 14:6) [R. Eleazar ben Arak, ca. 90 C.E.]
    The Two Administrators (*Mek.* on Exod 20:2 [*Bahodesh* §§5.81–92]) [R. Simon ben Eleazar, ca. 170 C.E.]
    The King's Daughters (*Song Rab.* 4:12 §1) [R. Joshua ben Levi, ca. 220–240 C.E.]
11. The Tares in the Wheat (Matt 13:24–30)
    The Trees of Life and the Trees of Death (*Gen. Rab.* 61.6 [on Gen 25:5]; cf. 83.5 [on 36:39]) [anonymous]
12. The Pearl of Great Price (Matt 13:45–56)
    The Precious Pearl (*Midr. Pss.* 28.6 [on 28:7]; cf. Luke 11:5–8; 18:1–8) [R. Simon, ca. 325 C.E.]
13. The Hidden Treasure (Matt 13:44)
    The Cheaply Sold Field (*Mek.* on Exod 14:5 [*Bešallaḥ* 2.142–48]) [R. Yose the Galilean, ca. 120 C.E.]
    The Cheaply Sold Estate (*Mek.* on Exod 14:5 [*Bešallaḥ* 2.149–55]; cf. *Pesiq. Rab Kah.* 11.7; *Song Rab.* 4.12 §1; *Exod. Rab.* 20.2, 5 [on Exod 13:17]) [R. Simeon ben Yohai, ca. 140 C.E.]
14. The Drag Net (Matt 13:47–50)
    Four Types of Fish (ʾ*Abot R. Nat.* A 40:9) [R. Gamaliel the Elder, ca. 40–50 C.E.]
15. The Unmerciful Servant (Matt 18:23–35)
    The Forgetful Debtor (*Exod. Rab.* 31.1 [on Exod 22:25]) [anonymous]
16. The Generous Employer (Matt 20:1–16)
    The Exceptional Laborer (*Sipra Lev.* §262 [on 26:9]; *Pirqe R. El.* §53) [anonymous]
    The Laborer Paid a Full Day's Wage (*Song Rab.* 6.2 §6; *y. Ber.* 2.8) [R. Zeira, ca. 360–370 C.E.]
17. The Two Sons (Matt 21:28–32)
    The Two Workers (*Exod. Rab.* 27.9 [on Exod 18:1]) [anonymous]
    The Two Tenants (*Deut. Rab.* 7.4 [on Deut 28:1]) [anonymous]
18. The Guest without a Wedding Garment (Matt 22:11–14)
    The Unprepared Guests (*b. Šabb.* 153b; cf. *Qoh. Rab.* 3.9 §1) [R. Yohanan ben Zakkai, ca. 70–80 C.E.]
19. The Friend at Midnight (Luke 11:5–8)
    The Brazen Daughter and the Polite Daughter (*y. Taʿan.* 3.4; cf. *Midr. Pss.* 28.6 [on 28:7]) [R. Aqiba, ca. 95 C.E.]
20. The Insistent Widow (Luke 18:1–8)
    The Brazen Daughter and the Polite Daughter (*y. Taʿan.* 3.4; cf. *Midr. Pss.* 28.6 [on 28:7]) [R. Aqiba, ca. 95 C.E.]
21. The Rich Fool (Luke 12:16–21)
    The Rich Hoarder (*Pesiq. Rab Kah.* 10.3; cf. Sir 11:18–19) [anonymous]

22. The Fruitless Fig Tree (Luke 13:6–9)
The Fruitless Vineyard (*Exod. Rab.* 43.9 [on Exod 32:11]) [R. Simeon ben Yehozadak, ca. 220–230 C.E.]
23. The Closed Door (Luke 13:24–30)
The Closed Door (*Midr. Pss.* 10.2 [on 10:1]) [R. Hanina (ben Hama), ca. 220–230 C.E.]
24. Choosing the Right Place at the Table (Luke 14:7–11)
Choosing the Right Place at the Table (*Lev. Rab.* 1.5 [on Lev 1:1], commenting on Prov 25:6–7 and Ps 113:5–6; cf. Sir 3:17–20) [R. Aqiba and R. Simeon ben Azzai, ca. 120 C.E.]
25. Building a Tower (Luke 14:28–30)
Counting the Cost of *Not* Being Reconciled to God (*Pesiq. Rab Kah.*, Supplement 7.3) [R. Jonathan, ca. 270 C.E.]
26. The King Going to War (Luke 14:31–33)
Counting the Cost of *Not* Being Reconciled to God (*Pesiq. Rab Kah.*, Supplement 7.3) [R. Jonathan, ca. 270 C.E.]
27. The Lost Coin (Luke 15:8–10)
The Lost Coin (*Song Rab.* 1.1 §9) [R. Phineas ben Yair, ca. 165–175 C.E.]
28. The Prodigal Son (Luke 15:11–32)
The Errant Son (*Deut. Rab.* 2.24 [on Deut 4:30]) [R. Meir, ca. 150 C.E.]
The Repatriated Prince (*Sipre Deut.* §345 [on Deut 33:4]) [anonymous]
The Returning Prince (*Pesiq. Rab.* 44.9) [anonymous]
The Favored Son (*Sipre Deut.* §352 [on Deut 33:12]) [anonymous]
29. The Rich Man and Lazarus (Luke 16:19–31)
The Fate of the Two Men (*Ruth Rab.* 3.3 [on Ruth 1:17], commenting on Eccl 1:15; *Qoh. Rab.* 1.15 §1) [anonymous]
The Two Pious Men and the Tax Collector (*y. Sanh.* 6.23; *y. Ḥag.* 2.27) [anonymous]
30. The Servants Who Have Done Their Duty (Luke 17:7–10)
Servants Who Labor for the Fear of Heaven (*m. ʾAbot* 1:3) [Antigonus of Soko, ca. 200? B.C.E.]
Work Claims No Merit (*m. ʾAbot* 2:8) [R. Yohanan ben Zakkai, ca. 80 C.E.]
31. The Log and the Speck (Matt 7:3–5; Luke 6:41–42)
The Log and the Splinter (*b. ʿArak.* 16b) [R. Tarfon, ca. 120 C.E.]
32. The Two Gates (Matt 7:13–14; cf. Luke 13:24)
The Two Ways (*Sipre Deut.* §53 [on Deut 11:26] *Midr. Haggadol* on Deut 11:26) [anonymous]

Other Tannaic parables that resemble the parables of Jesus (in theme, style, or details) include the following (principally based on McArthur and Johnston, 18–24):

1. The Throne and the Footstool (*Gen. Rab.* 1.15 [on Gen 1:1]) [Bet Shammai, ca. 40 C.E.]
2. The Palace (*Gen. Rab.* 1.15 [on Gen 1:1]) [Bet Hillel, ca. 40 C.E.]

3. The Ill-Treated Cupbearer (*m. Sukkah* 2:9) [anonymous]
4. The Well-Rooted Tree (*m. ʾAbot* 3:18; cf. *ʾAbot R. Nat.* A 22:2) [R. Eleazar ben Azariah, ca. 90 C.E.]
5. Ink on Paper (*m. ʾAbot* 4:20; cf. *ʾAbot R. Nat.* A 23:3) [Elisha ben Abuyah, ca. 120 C.E.]
6. The Eater of Ripe Grapes (*m. ʾAbot* 4:20; cf. *ʾAbot R. Nat.* A 23:3 [see Mark 2:22]) [R. Yose ben Judah of Kefar ha-Babli, ca. 190 C.E.]
7. The Inept Servant (*t. Ber.* 6.18) [anonymous]
8. The Lamp Removed (*t. Sukkah* 2.6) [anonymous]
9. The Road between Fire and Snow (*t. Ḥag.* 2.5; cf. *ʾAbot R. Nat.* A 28:10) [anonymous]
10. The Unfortunate Fugitive (*t. Soṭah* 15.7) [anonymous]
11. The Protected Vineyard (*t. Qidd.* 1.11) [R. Gamaliel II, ca. 80 C.E.]
12. The Married Woman (*t. Qidd.* 1.11) [R. Gamaliel II, ca. 80 C.E.]
13. The Fenced Vineyard (*t. Qidd.* 1.11) [R. Gamaliel II, ca. 80 C.E.]
14. The Two Men Who Planned a Wedding Feast (*t. B. Qam.* 7.2) [R. Gamaliel II, ca. 80 C.E.]
15. The Wife Sent Back to Her Father (*t. B. Qam.* 7.3) [R. Yohanan ben Zakkai, ca. 70 C.E.]
16. The King Engaged to a Woman (*t. B. Qam.* 7.4) [R. Yohanan ben Zakkai, ca. 70 C.E.]
17. The Villager Who Smashed Glassware (*Gen. Rab.* 19.6 [on Gen 3:7]) [R. Yohanan ben Zakkai, ca. 70–80 C.E., or R. Aqiba, ca. 120 C.E.]
18. The King's Twin Who Was Executed (*t. Sanh.* 9.7) [R. Meir, ca. 140 C.E.]
19. The Man with a Fine Beard (*b. Ber.* 11a) [R. Eleazar ben Azariah, ca. 80 C.E.]
20. The Fox and the Fishes (*b. Ber.* 61b) [R. Aqiba, ca. 135 C.E.]
21. The King Who Did Not Exempt Himself from Taxes (*b. Sukkah* 30a) [R. Simeon ben Yohai, ca. 140 C.E.]
22. The King Who Forgave a Debt (*b. Roš Haš.* 17b–18a) [R. Yose the Priest, ca. 90 C.E.]
23. Giving Promptly and Slowly (*b. Taʿan.* 25b) [R. Samuel the Younger, ca. 90 C.E.]
24. The Trees with Overhanging Boughs (*b. Qidd.* 40b) [R. Eleazar ben Zadok, ca. 90 C.E.]
25. The Retracted Betrothal (*ʾAbot R. Nat.* A 2:3) [R. Yose the Galilean, ca. 130 C.E.]
26. The Inferior Field (*ʾAbot R. Nat.* A 16:3) [R. Simeon ben Yohai, ca. 140 C.E.]
27. Wise and Foolish Guests at the King's Banquet (*Sem.* 8.10) [R. Meir, ca. 140 C.E.]
28. The Proud Father (*Mek.* on Exod 13:2 [*Pisha* 16.62–67]) [R. Eleazar ben Azariah, ca. 80 C.E.]
29. The King and His Guards (*Mek.* on Exod 15:2 [*Širata* 3.28–39]) [R. Eliezer (ben Hyrcanus?), ca. 90 C.E.]
30. The King Going Out to War (*Mek.* on Exod 20:5 [*Bahodesh* §§6.103–124]) [R. Gamaliel II, ca. 80 C.E.]

31. The King's Images (*Mek.* on Exod 20:16 [*Bahodesh* §§8.69–77]) [R. Hanina
   ben Gamaliel, ca. 85 C.E.]
32. The Foolish Centurion (*Sipre Num.* §131) [R. Aqiba, ca. 130 C.E.]
33. The King Who Repented His Intention to Divorce (*Sipre Num.* §131)
   [R. Aqiba, ca. 130 C.E.]
34. The Unwise Suitor (*Sipre Deut.* §37 [on Deut 11:10]) [R. Simeon ben
   Yohai, ca. 140 C.E.]
35. The King Who Enforced His Will (*Sipre Deut.* §40 [on Deut 11:12])
   [R. Simeon ben Yohai, ca. 140 C.E.]
36. The King's Bird (*Sipre Deut.* §48 [on Deut 11:22]) [R. Simeon ben Yohai,
   ca. 140 C.E.]
37. The Frugal Brother and the Wasteful Brother (*Sipre Deut.* §48 [on Deut
   11:22]) [R. Simeon ben Yohai, ca. 140 C.E.]
38. The Two Wrestlers (*Gen. Rab.* 22.9 [on Gen 4:10]) [R. Simeon ben Yohai,
   ca. 140 C.E.]
39. The King Who Found His Lost Pearl (*Gen. Rab.* 39.10 [on Gen 12:1]; cf.
   Ruth Rab. 8.1 [on Ruth 4:20]) [R. Nehemiah, ca. 150 C.E.]
40. The Foolish Shipmate (*Lev. Rab.* 4.6 [on Lev 4:2]) [R. Simeon ben Yohai,
   ca. 140 C.E.]

Jewish parables from nonrabbinic sources:
1. The Trees and the Bramble (Judg 9:7–21)
2. The Poor Man's Ewe Lamb (2 Sam 12:1–4)
3. The Two Brothers and the Avengers of Blood (2 Sam 14:1–11)
4. The Escaped Prisoner (1 Kgs 20:35–40)
5. The Thistle and the Cedar (2 Kgs 14:9)
6. The Fruitless Vineyard (Isa 5:1–7)
7. The Eagles and the Vine (Ezek 17:3–10)
8. The Lion Whelps (Ezek 19:2–9)
9. The Vine (Ezek 19:10–14)
10. The Forest Fire (Ezek 21:1–5)
11. The Seething Pot (Ezek 24:3–5)
12. The Lame Man and the Blind Man (*Apoc. Ezek.* frg. 1, cited by Epiphanius,
   Pan. 64.70.5–17).

Manson (pp. 61–64) classifies the first and fifth examples above as "fables" rather
than parables.

General Bibliography

A. FELDMAN, *Parables and Similes of the Rabbis: Agricultural and Pastoral* (Cambridge: Cambridge University Press, 1927); D. FLUSSER, *Die rabbinischen Gleich-
nisse und der Gleichniserzähler Jesus* (Bern: Peter Lang, 1981); T. W. MANSON, *The*

Teaching of Jesus: Studies of Its Form and Content (Cambridge: Cambridge University Press, 1948); H. K. MCARTHUR and R. M. JOHNSTON, *They Also Taught in Parables: Rabbinic Parables from the First Centuries of the Christian Era* (Grand Rapids: Zondervan, 1990); W. O. E. OESTERLEY, *The Gospel Parables in the Light of Their Jewish Background* (London: Macmillan, 1936); D. STERN, *Parables in Midrash: Narrative and Exegesis in Rabbinic Literature* (Cambridge: Harvard University Press, 1991); B. H. YOUNG, *Jesus and His Jewish Parables* (New York: Paulist, 1989).

Jesus and Jewish Miracle Stories

The Holy Men

Honi ha-Me ͨaggel ayin (first century B.C.E.)
Abba Hilkiah, grandson of Honi (late first century B.C.E., early first century C.E.)
Hanin ha-Nehba, grandson of Honi (late first century B.C.E., early first century C.E.)
Hanina ben Dosa (first century C.E.)
Eleazar the Exorcist (first century C.E.)
Phineas ben Yair (mid-second century C.E.)
An Anonymous Hasid (first or second century C.E.)

There were several Jewish holy men in the time of Jesus who were well known for mighty acts and remarkable answers to prayer. The lives and activities of seven of them compare in various ways to the life and ministry of Jesus. The principal features of what is known of them will be briefly reviewed, and where appropriate a few comparisons with Jesus have been drawn.

Honi ha-Me ͨaggel

In the rabbinic literature Honi is called ha-Me ͨaggel ("the circle drawer"). Josephus refers to him as "Onias, a righteous man beloved by God." He was remembered for praying for rain during a time of severe drought. When his prayer initially went unheeded, he drew a circle on the ground and told God that he would not leave it until rain came (perhaps following the example of Habakkuk; Hab 2:1). Soon it did rain. The story is found in the Mishna (*m. Ta ͨan.* 3:8; cf. *b. Ta ͨan.* 23a) and is alluded to by Josephus (*Ant.* 14.2.1 §22). A certain Simeon ben Shetah expressed disapprobation over Honi's familiarity with heaven: "Had you not been Honi, I would have pronounced a ban against you! For were these years like those concerning which Elijah said no rain should fall—for the keys to rainfall were in his hands—would not the result of your action have been the desecration of God's name? But what can I do with you, since you importune God and he performs your will, like a son that importunes his father and he performs his will." Simeon's complaint implies comparison between Elijah and Honi. In another tradition the comparison is explicit: "No man has existed comparable to Elijah and Honi the Circle-Drawer, causing mankind to serve God" (*Gen. Rab.* 13.7 [on 2:5]; however, some MSS omit either Elijah or Honi). According to Josephus, Honi was stoned (ca. 65 B.C.E.) when he refused to pronounce a curse on Aristobulus and his supporters (*Ant.* 14.2.1 §§23–24).

Honi's life and activities present a few points of comparison with the life and ministry of Jesus. Honi's persistence in praying for rain parallels Jesus' similar teaching, as seen in the parables of the Persistent Friend (Luke 11:5–8) and the Importunate Widow (Luke 18:1–8). Honi's filial relationship with God is also interesting. Jesus taught his disciples to pray to God as "Father" (Matt 6:9; Mark 14:36). Moreover, Jesus was regarded as God's Son (Mark 1:11; more on this below). Since there are other examples of the weather's being affected through the prayers of the Jewish holy men, this aspect will be discussed below.

Abba Hilkiah, Grandson of Honi

Abba Hilkiah, grandson of Honi (son of Honi's son), a very pious and poor man (worked for hire, wore a borrowed coat, insufficient food for guests), was requested by the rabbis to pray for rain. He and his wife went upstairs and, from opposite corners, prayed. Soon clouds began to form (*b. Taᶜan.* 23a–23b).

Poverty is a feature common to most of the traditions of the holy men. Jesus' lifestyle was also one of poverty: "Foxes have holes, and birds of the air have nests; but the Son of Man has nowhere to lay his head" (Matt 8:20; Luke 9:58).

Hanin ha-Nehba

Hanin ha-Nehba (i.e., "the hidden"), grandson of Honi (son of Honi's daughter), was a modest man who used to hide from public view. When the country needed rain the rabbis would send children to him. On one occasion they came to him and said, "Father, give us rain!" Hanin then prayed to God, "Master of the Universe, give rain for the sake of these children who do not even know enough to distinguish between a Father who gives rain and a father who does not" (*b. Taᶜan.* 23b).

Hanina ben Dosa

Hanina, one of the "men of [great] deeds" (*m. Soṭah* 9:15), lived in the town of Arab, a small Galilean village about ten miles north of Nazareth. He was famous for his prayers that resulted in healing (*m. Ber.* 5:5). On one occasion he prayed for the son of Gamaliel II (or possibly Gamaliel the Elder). Because the words of his prayer in this instance came fluently, he knew he had been answered. Gamaliel's disciples noted the time and returned to their master to discover that the boy had indeed recovered at the very hour Hanina had spoken (*b. Ber.* 34b). On another occasion he prayed for the son of Yohanan ben Zakkai, Hanina's teacher. The son recovered (*b. Ber.* 34b).

Once Hanina was walking at night alone, when he met the "queen of the demons." She claimed that had he not enjoyed heaven's protection, she would have harmed him. Hanina then banned her from passing through inhabited places (*b. Pesaḥ.* 112b).

Once while praying, Hanina was bitten by a poisonous snake (or lizard). The snake was later found dead at the opening of its hole. Hanina, however, was unharmed. This gave rise to the saying, "Woe to the man bitten by a snake, but woe to the snake which has bitten Rabbi Hanina ben Dosa" (*t. Ber.* 3.20; *b. Ber.* 33a). This episode may be alluded to in the Mishna: "Even if a snake was twisted around his heel he may not interrupt his prayer" (*m. Ber.* 5:1). There is also a parallel account where Hanina offers his heel to a poisonous lizard that has been injuring people. The lizard bites Hanina's heel and dies. Then Hanina pronounces: "See, my sons, it is not the lizard that kills, it is sin that kills!" (*b. Ber.* 33a).

Through prayer Hanina caused the rain to stop and later continue (*b. Taʿan.* 24b; *b. Yoma* 53b). So impressed with this story Rabbi Joseph commented: "How could the prayer of even the high priest be compared to that of Rabbi Hanina ben Dosa?" The parallels with the Elijah/Elisha stories (1 Kgs 17:1 [drought]; 18:45 [rain]) should be noted.

Once a neighbor woman was building a house. After erecting the walls she discovered that the beams for the roof were too short. She went to Hanina for help. Playing on her name, Hanina said, "May your beams reach!" One Polemo, supposedly an eyewitness, said: "I saw that house and its beams projected one cubit on either side, and people told me, 'This is the house which Rabbi Hanina ben Dosa covered with beams, through his prayer'" (*b. Taʿan.* 25a).

According to Rab: "Each day a heavenly voice came [from Mount Horeb] and said: 'The whole universe is sustained on account of my son, Hanina'" (*b. Taʿan.* 24b; *b. Ber.* 17b; *b. Ḥul.* 86a). Elsewhere Rab views Ahab (Elijah's contemporary and foe) as representative of evil, while Hanina is representative of good (*b. Ber.* 61b). Such an analogy implies a comparison between Hanina and Elijah. Indeed, it may even suggest that Hanina was thought to have superseded Elijah. Another tradition calls Hanina a "man of rank" (cf. Isa 3:3), who enjoyed the favor of heaven (*b. Ḥag.* 14a).

Hanina's life and activities parallel those of Jesus at many points. In the disputed passage in Josephus (*Ant.* 18.3.3 §63), Jesus is called a "wise man [*sophos anēr*]" and a "doer of amazing deeds [*paradoxon ergon poiētēs*]." Even R. Eisler (*The Messiah Jesus and John the Baptist* [trans. A. H. Krappe; New York: Dial, 1931], 62), who suspects that the passage has been tampered with, accepts the latter phrase as original, but with a different sense ("astonishing tricks"). Recall that Hanina was called a "man of doing [or deeds]."

The healing of Gamaliel's son at the very "hour" that Hanina announced to the disciples that he would recover parallels the Jesus tradition: "The father knew that was the hour when Jesus had said to him, 'Your son will live'" (John 4:46–53; cf. Matt 8:5–13; Luke 7:1–10).

Hanina's encounter with the queen of demons is somewhat analogous to Jesus' encounter with the Gerasene demoniac, who ran up and declared that he knew who Jesus was (Mark 5:1–20). The demoniac recognized that he was no match for God's "holy one." Elsewhere Jesus has encounters with Satan: the temptations (Matt 4:1–11; Luke 4:1–13), the vision of Satan falling from heaven (Luke 10:17–20), and Satan's demand to have Peter to sift like wheat and Jesus' prayer in Peter's behalf (Luke 22:31–32). More will be said on Jesus' exorcisms below.

The stories about Hanina's encounters with poisonous snakes and lizards parallel canonical and noncanonical stories about Jesus. In one place Jesus says: "Behold, I have given you authority to tread upon serpents and scorpions . . . and nothing shall hurt you" (Luke 10:19; cf. Mark 16:18; Acts 28:3–6). Hanina's dictum, "See, my sons, it is not the lizard that kills, it is sin that kills!" coheres with Jesus' forgiving sin as either a prerequisite or at least as a corollary of healing (e.g., Mark 2:1–11). The *Infancy Gospel of Thomas* offers an amusing parallel (Greek *Inf. Gos. Thom.* A 16:1–2; Latin *Inf. Gos. Thom.* 14:1). On one occasion Jesus' younger brother James was bitten by a poisonous viper. Just as he was about to die, Jesus approached and breathed upon the bite. Immediately James recovered and the viper burst.

Because of their miracles and mighty works Honi and Hanina were compared to Elijah, the venerated prophet famous for his mighty deeds (Sir 48:1–16). Jesus was also compared to Elijah (Mark 6:15; 8:28) and may himself have compared his ministry to outcasts and the disenfranchised to the similar ministries of Elijah and Elisha (Luke 4:25–27). On the Mount of Transfiguration he was in Elijah's company (Mark 9:4–5).

The *Infancy Gospel of Thomas* also parallels the story of the stretched beams (Greek *Inf. Gos. Thom.* A 13:1–2; Greek *Inf. Gos. Thom.* B 11:1–3; Latin *Inf. Gos. Thom.* 11:1–2). It seems that Joseph, the father of Jesus, failed to cut two beams precisely the same length. Jesus had him take hold of the short beam and then he stretched it to the proper length.

Just as the heavenly voice declared Hanina to be "my son," so the heavenly voice spoke at the baptism and transfiguration of Jesus: "You are my beloved Son" (Mark 1:11; 9:7; cf. John 12:28).

Eleazar the Exorcist

According to Josephus (*Ant.* 8.2.5 §§46–49), a certain Eleazar, who followed the incantations of Solomon, could draw out demons through a person's nostrils, through use of the Baaras root (further described in *J. W.* 7.6.3 §§180–185). Solomon "composed incantations by which illnesses are relieved, and left behind forms of exorcisms with which those possessed by demons drive them out, never to return" (*Ant.* 8.2.5 §45). The tradition of Solomon as exorcist par excellence was widespread in late antiquity. The tradition begins in the Bible itself where Solomon is described as unsurpassed in knowledge (1 Kgs 4:29–34). His knowledge of proverbs and plants (1 Kgs 4:32–33) contributed to later speculation that he had mastered the secrets of herbs and spells. And with his knowledge of herbs and spells the king had power over spirits. According to the Wisdom of Solomon God gave the monarch knowledge of "the powers of spirits and the reasonings of men, the varieties of plants and the virtues of roots; [he] learned what is both secret and what is manifest" (Wis 7:17–21). Solomon's power over demonic forces was appealed to for protection, as has been shown by Aramaic and Hebrew incantations dating from the early centuries of the Common Era. It is to this tradition that Josephus refers in mentioning Eleazar. The tradition was well known in Christian circles. Origen refers to those who attempted exorcisms according to the spells written by Solomon (*Comm. Matt.* 33 [on Matt 26:63]). The pseudepigraphal *Testament of Solomon*, probably written by a Greek-speaking Christian in the second or third century, is wholly dedicated to this theme.

All of this may have an important bearing on Jesus' ministry and self-understanding.

> Then a blind and dumb demoniac was brought to him, and he healed him, so that he saw. And all the people were amazed, and said, "Can this be the son of David?" But when the Pharisees heard it they said, "It is only by Beelzebul, the prince of demons, that this man casts out demons." . . . [Jesus replied,] "if Satan casts out Satan, he is divided against himself; how then will his kingdom stand? And if I cast out demons by Beelzebul, by whom do your sons cast them out?" . . . Then some of the scribes and Pharisees said to him, "Teacher, we wish to see a sign from you." But he answered them, "An evil and adulterous generation seeks for a sign; but no sign shall be given it except the sign of Jonah. . . . The queen of the South will arise at the judgment with this generation and condemn it; for she came from the ends of the earth to hear the wisdom of Solomon, and behold, something greater than Solomon is here. When the unclean spirit has gone out of a man, he passes through waterless places seeking rest, but he finds none. Then he says, 'I return to my house from which I came.' And when he comes he finds it empty, swept, and put in order. Then he goes and brings with him seven other spirits more evil than himself, and they enter and dwell there; and the last state of that man becomes worse than the first. So shall it be also with this evil generation." (Matt 12:22–45; cf. Luke 11:29–32, 24–26)

When Jesus healed a demonized man, the crowd thought of him as the son of David, i.e., one like Solomon. This is evidence of the close association of exorcism and Solomon. It may also indicate that a messianic figure should possess the powers of David's famous son. The religious leaders, however, cast doubt on this inference by suggesting that Jesus is in league with Satan himself (Beelzebul). Jesus replies pointing out how this is illogical. His reference to the exorcisms of their "sons" (as opposed to David's "son"?) and the demons that could return may suggest that Jesus did not think that these exorcisms were entirely successful. In other words, they were not up to standards associated with Solomon, the son of David. Nor were they, by implication, up to the standards of Jesus who was one "greater than Solomon."

Phineas ben Yair

Phineas ben Yair, son-in-law of R. Simeon ben Yohai and a pious ascetic, lived in the second century. Although later than Hanina ben Dosa, he was compared to his famous predecessor. After the story of Hanina's remarkable donkey, who had outwitted bandits and had safely returned home, Raba ben Zemuna [or Abba ben Zevina] commented: "If the sages of former times were like angels, then we are like men. And if they were like men, then we are like donkeys—but not like the donkey of Rabbi Hanina ben Dosa nor like the donkey of Phineas ben Yair, but like ordinary donkeys" (*b. Šabb.* 112b; *y. Dem.* 1.3; *ʾAbot R. Nat.* A §8).

An Anonymous Hasid

The prayer of a certain pious hasid brought on a flood (*t. Taʿan.* 3.1). To some extent this parallels Honi's prayer for rain. When the rain began as a drizzle, he asked for abundant rain. Then it began to pour with the danger of flooding. Honi's continued petitioning resulted in reducing the rain to moderation.

Five of the seven Jewish holy men considered here were remembered to have had their prayers for rain answered. Hanina's request that the rain stop is particularly noteworthy. In no case does Jesus pray for rain. But on at least one occasion he commands a storm to stop (Mark 4:35–41; cf. 6:47–52; John 6:16–21).

Later Traditions about Famous Rabbis

There are later traditions about several of the better known rabbis. It is said (anonymously) that both Eliezer (late first, early second century C.E.) and Aqiba (late first, early second century C.E.) were successful in praying for rain, though apparently the latter enjoyed greater success than the former (*b. Taʿan.* 25b). Joshua ben Levi (early third century C.E.) also apparently had his prayers for rain answered (*b. Taʿan.* 25a). Evidently there was a tradition of requesting major figures and authorities to pray for rain during periods of drought. According to Rabbi Samuel bar Nahmani (ca. 300 C.E.): "When Israel sins and does evil deeds, the rains are withheld. When they bring an elder, such as Rabbi Yose the Galilean [ca. 130–140 C.E.], to intercede for them, the rains fall again" (*y. Ber.* 5.2; cf. *Meg.*

Ta'an. [on Adar §7]: "On the 20th [of Adar] the people fasted for rain, and it was granted to them"). There may have been other traditions of mighty deeds accomplished through Yose the Galilean. Abba Silver cites a tenth-century prayer of a sick man: "Rabbi Yose the Galilean, heal me!" Such a prayer is evidence of belief that healing could be had through Yose's intercession. Such an idea likely had its origin in some remarkable deeds in Yose's lifetime, or in some remarkable legends in the years following his death.

General Bibliography

C. BROWN, "Synoptic Miracle Stories: A Jewish Religious and Social Setting," *Forum* 2, no. 4 (1986): 55–76; A. GUTTMANN, "The Significance of Miracles for Talmudic Judaism," *HUCA* 20 (1947): 363–406; H. VAN DER LOOS, *The Miracles of Jesus* (NovTSup 9; Leiden: Brill, 1965), 139–50; J. NADICH, *Jewish Legends of the Second Commonwealth* (Philadelphia: Jewish Publication Society of America, 1983), 194–200, 255–59, 296 n. 93, 396 n. 149; J. NEUSNER, *A Life of Yohanan ben Zakkai* (Leiden: Brill, 1970); S. SAFRAI, "The Teaching of the Pietists in Mishnaic Literature," *JJS* 16 (1965): 15–33; A. H. SILVER, *A History of Messianic Speculation in Israel* (Gloucester, Mass.: Peter Smith, 1978), 22–23; G. VERMES, "Hanina ben Dosa," in *Post-biblical Jewish Studies* (SJLA 8; Leiden: Brill, 1975), 178–214; IDEM, *Jesus the Jew: A Historian's Reading of the Gospels* (London: Collins, 1973), 58–82.

Messianic Claimants of the First and Second Centuries

In the first and second centuries of the Common Era several persons claimed some form of messianic status. Review of the claims and activities of these claimants helps clarify the "messianic context" of the time and place in which Jesus lived and the later interpretive backgrounds against which the NT authors wrote. The usefulness of the writings of Josephus and others will become readily apparent.

Biblical and Historical Precedents

Although "messiah" (i.e., "anointed one," from Heb. *māšaḥ*/Gk. *chriein*) is often understood in terms of the royal "son of David," in reality messianic concepts in late antiquity were quite diverse. If we understand "messiah" to mean one who believes himself to be anointed by God in order to play a leading role in the restoration of Israel, a restoration which may or may not involve the Davidic monarchy, then it is correct to speak of anointed kings, anointed prophets, and anointed priests. There is evidence that several individuals in the period of time under consideration qualify for inclusion in one or more of these three categories. All of these categories are rooted in biblical and historical precedents.

Kings. The concept of the "anointed" king derives from early biblical history. Saul was anointed king (1 Sam 15:1); later David was anointed (1 Sam 16:13). David, of course, became the archetype of the anointed king (Pss 18:50; 89:20; 132:17) and the basis for future hope (Isa 9:2–7; 11:1–10; cf. v. 2 in the Targum: "And a king shall come forth from the sons of Jesse, and a Messiah"). Kings were sometimes prophets as well. The spirit of prophecy came upon King Saul (1 Sam 10:6–13; 19:23–24). King David also was able to prophesy (1 Sam 16:13; 2 Sam 23:1–7; cf. Josephus, *Ant.* 6.8.2 §166 [where he also casts out demons]; Acts 2:29–30). At the end of 11QPsalms[a] we are told that "All these [psalms and songs] he [David] spoke through prophecy which was given him from before the Most High." Kings apparently also functioned as priests (1 Sam 14:35 [Saul]; 2 Sam 6:12–19 [David]; 2 Sam 8:18 [David's sons]; 1 Kgs 3:15 [Solomon]; cf. Ps 110:1–4).

The hopes pinned on Zerubbabel may very well have been the earliest instance of post-Davidic messianism (Neh 7:7; 12:1, 47; Hag 1:14; 2:20–23; Zech 3:8; 4:6–10; 6:12–14; Sir 49:11–12). Probably of great influence was the portrait of the expected Messiah in *Pss. Sol.* 17–18, where he is described as a warrior, a wise ruler, and one who will purge Jerusalem. Herod the Great, who had been appointed King of the Jews by the Roman Senate in 40 B.C.E., and whose marriage three years later to Mariamne I, of the Hasmonean family, which was probably intended to strengthen his claim to the throne, may very well have thought of himself as some sort of messiah (Josephus, *J.W.* 1.17.4 §331: "[considered] a man of divine favor"; see also *b. B. Bat.* 3b–4a). The account of Herod's attempt to destroy Jesus may imply that the Matthean evangelist regarded the former as some sort of messianic rival of the latter (Matt 2:1–18).

Prophets. Prophets, as well as kings, were "anointed." This is seen in a variety of texts, biblical and postbiblical: God told Elijah to anoint Hazael as king of Syria, Jehu as king of Israel, and Elisha "to be prophet" in Elijah's place (1 Kgs 19:15–16). It is significant that the anointing of Elisha is parallel to the anointing of the two kings. With reference to the wandering patriarchs God warned gentile kings: "Touch not my anointed ones, do my prophets no harm!" (1 Chr 16:22 = Ps 105:15; cf. Gen 20:7). A particularly instructive example comes from Isa 61:1–2: "The Spirit of the Lord God is upon me, because the Lord has anointed me to bring good tidings to the afflicted." According to the Targum, the anointed one is none other than the prophet himself: "The prophet said: 'The spirit of prophecy is upon me. . . .'" In *Mek.* on Exod 20:21 (*Bahodesh* §9.103) the passage is applied to Moses. At Qumran (11QMelch 4–20; 1QH 17:14) and in the NT (Luke 4:18–19; 7:22 = Matt 11:5) Isa 61:1–2 seems to have been understood in prophetic/messianic terms.

Another central idea was the "prophet-like-Moses" theme, for this idea was as kingly as it was prophetic (Meeks, 1967). At many points in rabbinic tradition Moses was compared with Messiah. Like Messiah (*Pesiq. Rab.* 33.6; *Frg. Tg.* Exod 12:42), so Moses was thought to have come into existence prior to the creation of the universe (*T. Mos.* 1:14; cf. *Pesiq. Rab.* 15.10; and the comparison between the Exodus and Israel's eschatological restoration in *Pesiq. Rab Kah.* 5.8; *Sipre Deut.* §130 [on Deut 16:3]; *Tg. Lam* 2:22). Comparisons between Moses and David may also imply comparison between Moses and Messiah: "You find that whatever Moses did, David did. . . . As Moses became king in Israel and in Judah . . . so David became king in Israel and in Judah" (*Midr. Pss.* 1.2 [on Ps 1:1]). Both Moses and David "gave their lives for Israel" (*Sipre Deut.* §344 [on Deut 33:3]). Although these traditions are late, they probably represent embellishments of earlier comparisons between Moses and Messiah. Christians, of course, made their own comparisons (John 1:14–18; Acts 3:22–23; 7:37; Heb 3:1–6; 8:5–6; *Sib. Or.* 8:250: "Moses prefigured [Christ]").

Undoubtedly the most influential prophetic figure in Jesus' lifetime was his contemporary John the Baptist. His baptizing activity around the Jordan, his disciples, the crowds, his eventual arrest and execution, all suggest that he should be included among the other charismatic prophets of this period (Mark 1:2–9; 6:14–29; Matt 3:7b–12; Luke 3:7b–9, 16–17; John 1:19–28; Acts 19:1–7; Josephus, *Ant.* 18.5.2 §§116–119).

Priests. In very old tradition priests appear as kings. Melchizedek, priest-king of Salem, is an obvious example (Gen 14:18; cf. Ps 110:1–4). As were kings, priests also were anointed. Aaron, the brother of Moses was anointed *and crowned* (cf. Exod 29:6–7; cf. Ps.-Philo, *Biblical Antiquities* 13:1). All priests were to be anointed (Lev 16:32). Zadok, the founder of a high-priestly line, was anointed (1 Chr 29:22; cf. 2 Chr 31:10). After the collapse of the Davidic dynasty, the high priest was often the highest Jewish authority. High priest Onias III ruled Jerusalem (2 Macc 3–4). Jason the priest attempted to gain control of Jerusalem when he thought Antiochus IV had died (2 Macc 5:5–7). After the successful Maccabean revolt, the Hasmonean family not only served as high priests, thus usurping the Zadokite succession, but even regarded themselves as kings (Aristobulus I [104–103 B.C.E.]; cf. Josephus, *J.W.* 1.3.1 §70; *Ant.* 13.11.1 §301; and Janneus [103–76 B.C.E.]; cf. Josephus, *Ant.* 13.12.1 §320; *b. Sanh.* 107b). Reflecting the Hasmonean period, the *Testaments of the Twelve Patriarchs* anticipated a priestly ruler, as well as kingly ruler (*T. Sim.* 7:2; *T. Jud.* 21:2; *T. Jos.* 19:6). Qumran looked for an "anointed [priest] of Aaron," who would serve alongside the "anointed [prince] of Israel" (CD 12:23–13:1, 21; 14:19; 1QS 9:11). Christians believed that Jesus was not only prophet and king, but was also the heavenly high priest (Heb 5:1–6), whose death ended the need for a priesthood or for further sacrifice (Heb 7:27–28; 9:23–26).

Even in later rabbinic tradition the anointed priest plays a part in the messianic era. Commenting on Zech 4:14 ("There are the two anointed ones who stand by the Lord"): "This is in reference to Aaron and the Messiah" (*'Abot R. Nat.* A §34). In *Tg. Ps.-J.* Num 25:12, enriched with phrases from Isa 61:1 and Mal 3:1, Eleazar, Aaron's son, is told that he will be made "the messenger of the covenant . . . to announce redemption at the end of days."

Messianic Kings

Our best historical source for the Herodian-Roman period is Josephus. Unfortunately, because of his bias, it is not always easy to distinguish bona fide messianic claimants from those who were truly no more than criminals. Josephus tended to denigrate these claimants as deceivers, impostors, and brigands. For example, he says: "Judea was filled with brigandage. Anyone might make himself a king [*basileus*] . . . causing trouble to few Romans . . . but bringing the greatest slaughter upon their own people" (*Ant.* 17.10.8 §285). This comment certainly betrays Josephus's cynical attitude toward the liberation movements of the first century. But despite this pejorative assessment, several of these aspirants in all probability were messianic claimants whose goal was the liberation of Israel (Horsley and J. Hanson, 88–134; Witherington, 84–85). The following figures sought to rule Israel and bring about political, if not religious, restoration.

Judas (of Sepphoris, Galilee) son of Hezekiah the "brigand chief." In the wake of Herod's death (4 B.C.E.) Judas plundered the royal arsenals and attacked other kingly aspirants (*Ant.* 17.10.5 §§271–272; *J.W.* 2.4.1 §56). According to Josephus, this man "became a terror to all men by plundering those he came across in his desire for great possessions and in his ambition for royal honor [*zēlosei basileiou timēs*]." Although Josephus does not say explicitly, presumably Judas, as well as many of the other insurrectionists of this period of time, was subdued by Varus, the Roman governor of Syria, who quelled rebellion in Galilee, Samaria, Judea, Jerusalem, and Idumea (cf. *Ant.* 17.10.9–10 §§286–298; *J.W.* 2.5.1–3 §§66–79).

Simon of Perea, a former royal servant. Evidently this Simon was another opportunist who arose after Herod's death. According to Josephus, he was a handsome man of great size and strength, who "was bold enough to place the diadem on his head [*diadēma tē etolmēse perithēsthai*], and having got together a body of men, he was himself also proclaimed king [*autos basileus anangeltheis*] by them in their madness, and he rated himself worthy of this beyond anyone else. After burning the royal palace in Jericho, he plundered and carried off the things seized there. He also set fire to many other royal residences . . ." (*Ant.* 17.10.6 §§273–276; *J.W.* 2.4.2 §§57–59: "he placed the diadem on himself [*peritithēsin men heautou diadēma*]"). His claim to kingship was even noted by Tacitus (*Hist.* 5.9: "After the death of Herod . . . a certain Simon seized the title king"). Simon was eventually slain by Gratus (4 B.C.E.).

Athronges the shepherd of Judea. According to Josephus, one Athronges, "remarkable for his great stature and feats of strength," though a mere shepherd of no special ancestry or character, "dared to (gain) a kingdom [*etolmēsen epi basileia*]." "Having put on the diadem [*ho de diadēma perithēmenos*]," he began giving orders, exercising and retaining "power for a long while [4–2 B.C.E.], for he was called king [*basilei tē keklēmeno*]" (*Ant.* 17.10.7 §§278–284; *J.W.* 2.4.3 §§60–65: "He himself, like a king [*autos de kathaper basileus*], handled matters of graver importance. It was then that he placed the diadem on himself [*heauto peritithēsin diadēma*]"). He and his brothers eventually surrendered to Archelaus.

Judas (of Gamala) the Galilean. Judas the Galilean is regarded as one of the anointed kings, and not simply a bandit, because of his "bid for independence" (*Ant.* 18.1.1 §4) and because of his mention in Acts 5:37, thus putting him in the company of Jesus and Theudas, both prophets and probably both messianic claimants. Furthermore, the fact that Judas's son Menahem claimed to be a messiah could suggest that he had inherited his kingly aspirations from his father (which may be hinted at by Josephus himself in *J.W.* 2.17.8 §§433–434). Probably not the same person as Judas son of Hezekiah, this Judas called on his countrymen not to submit to the census administered by Quirinius, the Roman governor who had replaced the deposed Archelaus (*Ant.* 18.1.1 §4–10; *J.W.* 2.8.1 §118). According to Acts, the Pharisee Gamaliel said that "Judas the Galilean arose in the days of the census and drew away some of the people after him; he also perished, and all who followed him were scattered" (5:37). (This passage is problematic, especially if the "Theudas" of Acts 5:36 is the Theudas of 45 C.E.) It is significant that a parallel is drawn between Judas and Theudas (who will be considered below), at least in that both movements ended in the deaths of their leaders. (Josephus does not tell us what became of Judas.) Josephus describes Judas's movement as a "rebellion" and as a "a bid for (national) independence," as well as a "fourth philosophy." It is perhaps significant that at the mention of Judas's call for civil disobedience Josephus goes on to summarize the disturbances of the first century and to suggest that it was this sort of thinking that led to violence and bloodshed that ultimately culminated in the catastrophe of 66–70 C.E. (*Ant.* 18.1.1 §10: "My reason for giving this brief account of [the events that led up to the war] is chiefly that the zeal which Judas and Saddok inspired in the younger element meant the ruin of our cause"). Therefore, although Judas's personal role seems to have been principally that of a teacher, the effect of his teaching warrants regarding him as yet another founder of a movement that opposed foreign domination and, by implication, that advocated the establishment of an independent kingdom of Israel. The crucifixion of his sons Jacob and Simon under Governor Tiberius Alexander (46–48 C.E.) may also have had something to do with rebellion (*Ant.* 20.5.2 §102).

Menahem (grand)son of Judas the Galilean. Josephus tells us that Menahem (ca. 66 C.E.), either the son or the grandson of Judas the Galilean, plundered Herod's armory at Masada, arming his followers as well as other "brigands," and then "returned like a king [*basileus*] to Jerusalem, became the leader of the revolution, and directed the siege of the palace." His followers occupied the Roman barracks and eventually caught and killed Ananias the high priest. As a result of Menahem's accomplishments, Josephus tells us, Menahem, believing himself unrivaled, became an "insufferable tyrant [*tyrannos*]." Finally, insurgents loyal to Eleazar son of Ananias the high priest rose up against him. Menahem, "arrayed in royal [*basilikē*] apparel," was attacked while in the temple. Although he initially managed to escape and hide, he was eventually caught, dragged out into the open, tortured, and put to death (*J.W.* 2.17.8–10 §§433–448). It is possible, but I think improbable, that he is the Menahem referred to in a tradition that tells of the birth of King Messiah, whose name is Menahem son of Hezekiah, born on the day that the temple was destroyed (*y. Ber.* 2.4; cf. *b. Sanh.* 98b).

John of Gischala son of Levi. Initially John of Gischala was commander of the rebel forces in Gischala (*J.W.* 2.20.6 §575). He later became part of the zealot coalition (*J.W.* 4.1.1–5 §§121–146; 5.3.1 §§104–105; 5.6.1 §§250–251) that, having been forced to retreat into Jerusalem, gained control of most of the city and installed a high priest of its own choosing (*J.W.* 4.3.6 §§147–150; 4.3.8 §§155–161). Although Josephus describes him as little more than a power-hungry brigand (*J.W.* 2.21.1 §§585–589), apparently John did have kingly aspirations. Josephus tells us that he aspired to "tyrannical power [*tyrannionti*]," "issued despotic [*despotikoteron*] orders," and began "laying claim to absolute sovereignty [*monarchias*]" (*J.W.* 4.7.1 §§389–393). Fearing the possibility that John might achieve "monarchical rule [*monarchias*]," many of the zealots opposed him (*J.W.* 4.7.1 §§393–394; see also 4.9.11 §566, where the Idumeans turn against the "tyrant"). When the city was finally overrun, John surrendered and was imprisoned for life (*J.W.* 6.9.4 §433). Later in his account of the Jewish war Josephus evaluates John much in the same terms as he does Simon bar Giora (*J.W.* 7.8.1 §§263–266; in 4.9.10 §§564–565 they are compared as the tyrants "within" and "without" Jerusalem; in 6.9.4 §§433–434 Josephus also compares their respective surrenders). One of John's worst crimes was his "impiety towards God. For he had unlawful food served at his table and abandoned the established rules of purity of our forefathers" (*J.W.* 7.8.1 §264). What apparently was so reprehensible to Josephus the Pharisee, of priestly descent, was probably no more than different halakot, ones which were evidently more lenient and more popular. The disgust that Josephus shows is reminiscent of reactions that Jesus' table manners sometimes evoked (cf. Mark 2:15–17; 7:2; Luke 15:1–2).

Simon bar Giora of Gerasa. The most important leader of the rebellion was Simon bar Giora (Aramaic = "son of the proselyte"), a man from Gerasa (or Jerash). Simon distinguished himself with military prowess and cunning (*J.W.* 2.19.2 §521; 4.6.1 §353; 4.9.4 §510; 4.9.5 §§514–520). He drew a large following by "proclaiming liberty for slaves and rewards for the free" (*J.W.* 4.9.3 §508; 4.9.7 §534 ["forty thousand followers"]). His army was "subservient to his command as to a king [*basilea*]" (*J.W.* 4.9.4 §510). Josephus avers that early in his career Simon had shown signs of being tyrannical (*J.W.* 2.22.2 §652 [*tyrannein*]; 4.9.3 §508 [*ho de tyrannion*]; 5.1.3 §11; 7.2.2 §32 [*etyrannesen*]; 7.8.1 §265 [*tyrannon*]). Simon subjugated the whole of Idumea (*J.W.* 4.9.6 §§521–528). The ruling priests, in consultation with the Idumeans and many of the inhabitants of the city, decided to invite Simon into Jerusalem to protect the city from John of Gischala (*J.W.* 4.9.11 §§570–576). Simon entered the city and took command in the spring of 69 C.E. (*J.W.* 4.9.12 §577). Among the leaders of the rebellion "Simon in particular was regarded with reverence and awe . . . each was quite prepared to take his very own life had he given the order" (*J.W.* 5.7.3 §309). Finally defeated and for a time in hiding, Simon, dressed in white tunics and a purple mantle, made a dramatic appearance before the Romans on the very spot where the temple had stood (*J.W.* 7.1.2 §29). He was placed in chains (*J.W.* 7.2.2 §36), sent to Italy (*J.W.* 7.5.3 §118), put on display as part of the victory celebration in Rome (*J.W.* 7.5.6 §154), and was finally executed (*J.W.* 7.5.6 §155).

Lukuas of Cyrene. During the reign of Trajan the Jewish inhabitants of Judea, Egypt, and Cyrene revolted (114 or 115 C.E.). According to Eusebius they rallied to one Lukuas, "their king" (*Hist. eccl.* 4.2.1–4). Dio Cassius mentions this revolt, but calls the Jewish leader Andreas (*Hist. rom.* 68.32; 69.12–13). Eusebius says that General Marcius Turbo "waged war vigorously against [the Jews] in many battles for a considerable time and killed many thousands" (*Hist. eccl.* 4.2.4). Although Dio's claim that hundreds of thousands perished is probably an exaggeration, the papyri and archaeological evidence confirm that the revolt was widespread and very destructive (see Schürer, 1:530–33).

Simon ben Kosiba (Bar Kokhba). Apparently Simon, either the son of a man named Kosiba or from a village (or valley) by that name, was the principal leader of the second Jewish rebellion against Rome (132–135 C.E.). (The rabbis often spell his name with the letter *z* to make a word play with "lie.") According to rabbinic tradition, Rabbi Aqiba, contrary to other rabbis, regarded Simon as the Messiah (*y. Ta‛an.* 4.5). Another tradition adds: "Bar Koziba reigned two and a half years, and then said to the rabbis, 'I am the Messiah.' They answered, 'Of Messiah it is written that he smells [instead of sees] and judges: let us see if he [Bar Koziba] can do so" (*b. Sanh.* 93b). Administering justice by smelling, instead of seeing, is an allusion to Isa 11:3–5 ("He shall not judge by what his eyes see, or decide by what his ears hear; but with righteousness he shall judge the poor, and decide with equity for the meek of the earth . . ."). The talmudic passage goes on to say that Simon failed and so was slain. According to *y. Ta‛an.* 4.5 (cf. *m. Ta‛an.* 4:6; *b. Giṭ.* 57a–b; *Lam. Rab.* 2.2 §4) Simon was defeated at Bether because of arrogance against heaven ("Lord of the Universe, neither help us nor hinder us!") and violence against Rabbi Eleazar, one of Israel's revered teachers.

No doubt because of his ultimate defeat and the disastrous consequences for Israel, the rabbis were very critical of Simon. The evidence suggests, however, that initially he was quite successful. Legends such as his catching and throwing back Roman siege stones may be remnants of popular stories in which Simon had been depicted in a much more favorable light. (According to Jerome [*Against Rufinus* 3.31], Simon deceived the people with fraudulent miracles.) Obviously Aqiba found something appealing about him. In fact, it was Simon's military success, the tradition tells us, that led the famous rabbi to recognize Simon as the Messiah (*Lam. Rab.* 2.2 §4). According to Moses Maimonides, "Rabbi Aqiba, the greatest of the sages of the Mishna, was a supporter of King Ben Kozeba, saying of him that he was King Messiah. He *and all the contemporary sages* regarded him as the King Messiah, until he was killed for sins which he had committed" (*Mishneh Torah, Melakhim* 11:3, my emphasis). For these reasons, as well as the fact that the Romans subdued Judea only with great difficulty, it is probable that Simon enjoyed widespread popularity and support. It is quite possible that the persecution against Christians described by Justin Martyr had to do with their refusal to acknowledge the messiahship of Simon: "During the Jewish war Bar Kochebas, the leader of the Jewish rebellion, commanded Christians to be led away to terrible punishment, unless they denied Jesus as the Messiah and blasphemed" (*1 Apol.* 31.6). According to Eusebius, "Bar Kochebas . . . claimed to be a luminary who had come down to them from heaven" (*Hist. eccl.* 4.6.2).

Simon became known as Bar Kochba because of a word-play between his name and the star of Num 24:17–19, a passage widely regarded as messianic: "A star [*kôkāb*] shall come out of Jacob, and a scepter shall rise out of Israel; it shall crush the forehead of Moab, and break down all the sons of Sheth. Edom [= Rome] shall be dispossessed. . . ." The earliest messianic interpretation of this verse is apparently found in the *Testament of Judah:* "And after this there shall

arise for you a Star from Jacob. . . . This is the Shoot of God. . . . Then he will illu-
mine the scepter of my kingdom, and from your root will arise the Shoot and
through it will arise the rod of righteousness for the nations, to judge and to save
all that call on the Lord" (24:1–6).

Not only are there allusions to Numbers 24, there are allusions to Isa 11:1–5
as well. At Qumran Num 24:17–19 seems to have been understood in a messianic
sense: "Yours is the battle! From [you] comes the power . . . as you declared to
us in former times, 'A star has journeyed from Jacob, a scepter has arisen from
Israel. . . .' And by the hand of your Anointed Ones . . . you have announced to us
the times of the battles . . . " (1QM 11:4–9); "And the Star [alluding to Amos 9:11
in line 15] is the Seeker of the Law who came to Damascus; as it is written, 'A star
has journeyed out of Jacob and a scepter is risen out of Israel.' The scepter is the
Prince of all the congregation, and at his coming 'he will break down all the sons
of Seth'" (CD 7:18–21; cf. 1QSb 5:27–28; 4QTest 9–13). In the Targumim the
messianic interpretation of Num 24:17 is explicit: ". . . a king shall arise out of
Jacob and be anointed the Messiah out of Israel" *(Onqelos);* ". . . a mighty king of
the house of Jacob shall reign, and shall be anointed Messiah, wielding the mighty
scepter of Israel" *(Ps.-Jonathan);* "A king is destined to arise from the house of
Jacob, a redeemer and ruler from the house of Israel, who shall slay the mighty
ones . . . who shall destroy all that remains of the guilty city, which is Rome" *(Frg.
Tg.* 24:17–19). This messianic interpretation of Numbers 24 is likely what lies behind Matt 2:1–12: the magi have seen the Messiah's "star" and have concluded
that the "king of the Jews" has been born. Philo alluded to the passage: "For 'there
shall come a man,' says the oracle, and leading his host to war he will subdue great
and populous nations, because God has sent to his aid the reinforcement which
befits the godly" *(Rewards* 16 §95). It may also be the passage to which Josephus
alluded a generation later: "But what more than all else incited [the Jews] to [the
first] war was an ambiguous oracle, likewise found in their sacred scriptures, to
the effect that at that time one from their country would become ruler of the
world. This they understood to mean someone of their own race, and many of
their wise men went astray in their interpretation of it. The oracle, however, in reality signified the sovereignty of Vespasian, who was proclaimed emperor on Jewish soil" *(J.W.* 6.5.4 §§312–313; cf. 3.8.9 §§400–402). (The report that a Jewish
oracle had spoken of Vespasian's accession to the throne was known to Tacitus
[*Hist.* 1.10; 5.13], Suetonius [*Vesp.* 4–5], Dio Cassius [*Hist. rom.* 66.1], and
Appian [*Hist. rom.* 22, according to Zonaras, *Annals* 11.16].)

But the messianic kingdom that Simon hoped to establish was crushed by
the Romans. In the wake of this defeat Aqiba undoubtedly reassessed his view of
Simon, as would be seen in J. Neusner's translation of *y. Taᶜan.* 4.5: "A disappoint-
ment shall come forth out of Jacob" *(Messiah,* 95). Aqiba's retraction of his earlier
messianic interpretation of Dan 7:9, and possibly the length of the messianic
reign, may also have had something to do with Simon's defeat. For Aqiba and
many other rabbis the defeat proved costly. The edict of Hadrian forbade Jews to
enter Jerusalem and from possessing or teaching Torah. The period is referred to
as the "age of the edict" (*b. Šabb.* 60a; *m. Taᶜan.* 4:6; *Mek.* on Exod 20:6 [*Bahodesh*

§§6.136–143]; see also Dio Cassius, *Hist. rom.* 69.12.2; Eusebius, *Hist. eccl.* 4.6.4: "Hadrian then commanded that by a legal decree and ordinances the whole nation should be absolutely prevented from entering from thenceforth even the district around Jerusalem"; Eusebius, *Demonstration of the Gospel* 6.18.10). Jerusalem's name was changed to Aeilia Capitolina (cf. Dio Cassius, *Hist. rom.* 69.12.1). Aqiba violated the edict, was imprisoned (*t. Sanh.* 2.8; cf. *t. Ber.* 2.13; *b.* *ʿErub.* 21b; *b. Yebam.* 105b, 108b; *y. Yebam.* 12.5), and was cruelly tortured and put to death (*b. Yebam.* 62b; *Lev. Rab.* 13.5 [on 11:4–7]; *Song Rab.* 2.7 §1; *b. Ber.* 61b; *b. Menaḥ.* 29b).

Messianic Prophets

Even those who claimed to be prophets had intentions not too different from the kingly aspirants. They too wished to liberate Israel and consequently provoked violent response from the Romans. Although their respective understandings of leadership, or messiahship, may have differed from those who attempted to wear the diadem (in that they may have expected a little more of Heaven's aid), their attempts at modeling their leadership after Moses strongly suggest that they too were part of the struggle to restore Israel. Part of Moses typology was the "wilderness summons," an idea probably related to Isa 40:3 ("In the wilderness prepare the way of the Lord"), a passage cited in Christian writings (Mark 1:2–3), Qumran (1QS 8:12–14; 9:19–20), and other (Bar 5:7; *T. Mos.* 10:1–5) sources. In the case of Christians (at least with regard to John the Baptist) and Essenes, the passage was acted upon quite literally: they went out into the wilderness to prepare the way of the Lord. Synoptic warnings about not heeding a summons to the wilderness (cf. Matt 24:26) and various claims of false christs (cf. Mark 13:21–22 par.) surely have in mind the people of whom Josephus wrote. At many points there are suggestive parallels (Mark 13:21–22; Matt 24:26; Luke 17:20–23; 21:8; cf. Josephus, *Ant.* 17.10.7 §§278–284; 20.8.6 §168; 20.8.10 §188; *J.W.* 2.13.5 §§261–263; 6.5.4 §315).

The Anonymous Samaritan. Josephus tells us that during the administration of Pontius Pilate (26–36 C.E.) a certain Samaritan (36 C.E.), whom he calls a liar and demagogue, convinced many of his people to follow him to Mount Gerizim where he would show them the place where their sacred temple vessels were buried. (The Samaritan temple on Mount Gerizim had been destroyed by John Hyrcanus in 128 B.C.E. [Josephus, *Ant.* 13.9.1 §256].) Pilate sent a detachment of troops, which routed the pilgrims before they could ascend the mountain (*Ant.* 18.4.1 §§85–87). This episode, although not a Jewish affair, parallels the type of thinking found in Jewish regions (i.e., Galilee and Judea). This Samaritan "uprising" probably had to do with the Samaritan hope for the appearance of the *Taheb*, the "restorer," whose coming was expected in keeping with the promise of Deut 18:15–18 (cf. *Memar Marqah* 4:12; John 4:20, 25: "Our [Samaritan] fathers worshiped on this mountain [i.e., Mount Gerizim] . . . I know that Messiah is coming . . . when he comes, he will show us all things"). As such, it is another example of the messianic fervor and unrest of the region in this period of time.

Theudas. During the administration of Fadus (44–46 C.E.), Josephus tells us that "a certain impostor named Theudas persuaded the majority of the populace to take up their possessions and follow him to the Jordan River. He stated that he was a prophet and that at his command the river would be parted and would provide easy passage. With this talk he deceived many" (*Ant.* 20.5.1 §§97–98). The Roman governor dispatched the cavalry, which scattered Theudas's following. The would-be prophet was himself decapitated and his head put on display in Jerusalem. Acts 5:36 tells us that he had a following of about four hundred men. Although he regarded himself as a "prophet [*prophētēs*]," Josephus calls Theudas an "impostor [*goēs*]" who "deceived many." (Note the similar description in 2 Tim 3:13: "evil men and impostors will go from bad to worse, deceivers and deceived." Judging by Philo's usage [*Spec. Laws* 1.58 §315], a *goēs* was the precise opposite of the genuine *prophētēs*.) Theudas's claim to be able to part the Jordan River is an unmistakable allusion either to the crossing of the Red Sea (Exod 14:21–22) or to the crossing of the Jordan River (Josh 3:14–17), part of the imagery associated with Israel's redemption (cf. Isa 11:15; 43:16; 51:10; 63:11). In either case, it is probable that Theudas was claiming to be the prophet "like Moses" (Deut 18:15–19; cf. 1 Macc 4:45–46; 9:27; 14:41). As such, he was claiming to be more than a mere prophet; he was claiming to be a messianic figure. Indeed, it is possible that Theudas may have had even more ideas about himself. O. Betz (pp. 22–23) has suggested that Theudas's claim "to be someone" (*einai tina;* Acts 5:36) may allude to a claim to be the "son of man" (*bar 'enāš*) of Dan 7:13, an expression which was understood in a messianic sense in the Similitudes of Enoch (*1 En.* 37–71), material that likely dates from the first half of the first century (cf. 48:10; 52:4). His suggestion is based on the fact that the Aramaic expression, "son of man," is often the equivalent of the indefinite pronoun "someone," which in Greek is *tis*. If Betz is correct, then we have evidence of another first-century messianic claimant who understood himself as Daniel's "son of man."

The Anonymous Egyptian (Jew). At the outset of the section in which he speaks of the Egyptian, Josephus tells us that "impostors and deceitful men persuaded the crowd to follow them into the wilderness. For they said that they would show them unmistakable wonders and signs according to God's foreknowledge." They and many of their following "were brought before (Governor) Felix" and "were punished" (*Ant.* 20.8.6 §168). Felix's response suggests that the proclamations and activities of these men were not viewed as politically innocent. Indeed, Josephus tells us that these "madmen" promised their followers "signs of freedom" (*J.W.* 2.13.4 §259). Felix himself regarded these actions as "preliminary to insurrection" (*J.W.* 2.13.4 §260). In this the governor was probably correct. As to the Egyptian, Josephus reports: "At this time [ca. 56 C.E.] there came to Jerusalem from Egypt a man who said that he was a prophet [*prophētēs*] and advised the masses of the common people to go out with him to the mountain called the Mount of Olives, which lies opposite the city. . . . For he asserted that he wished to demonstrate from there that at his command Jerusalem's walls would fall down, through which he promised to provide them an entrance into the city" (*Ant.* 20.8.6 §§169–170). Felix promptly dispatched the cavalry, which routed and dispersed the following. However, the Egyptian himself escaped.

In the parallel account in *Jewish War* Josephus calls the Egyptian a "false prophet" and "impostor" who, with a following of thirty thousand, "proposed to force an entrance into Jerusalem and, after overpowering the Roman garrison, to set himself up as tyrant [*tyrannein*] over the people" (*J.W.* 2.13.5 §§261–263). The hoped-for sign of the walls falling down was probably inspired by the story of Israel's conquest of Jericho, led by Joshua the successor of Moses (Josh 6:20). This Egyptian is mentioned in other sources as well. According to Acts 21:38 a Roman tribune asked Paul: "Are you not the Egyptian, then, who recently stirred up a revolt and led the four thousand men of the Assassins out into the wilderness?"

It is possible that the rabbis may have confused Jesus, also thought to have spent time in Egypt where he acquired knowledge of magic (*b. Sanh.* 107b; cf. Origen, *Cels.* 1.38), with the Egyptian. It is interesting to note that according to the accounts in Acts and in *Jewish War,* the Egyptian summoned people "out into the wilderness." This wilderness summons, as well as the Joshua-like sign of the walls falling down, is very likely part of the prophet-like-Moses theme, or some variation of it, that evidently lay behind much of the messianic speculation of the first century. Moreover, the fact that this Jewish man was known as the man from Egypt might also have had to do with some sort of association with Moses.

Anonymous "Impostor." In a context in which he described the troubles brought on by the *sicarii,* Josephus reports that "Festus [ca. 61 C.E.] also sent a force of cavalry and infantry against those deceived by a certain impostor who had promised them salvation [*sōtērian*] and rest [*paula*] from troubles, if they chose to follow him into the wilderness [*erēmias*]. Those whom Festus sent destroyed that deceiver and those who had followed him" (*Ant.* 20.8.10 §188). It is likely that this "impostor" was another messianic prophet, probably in keeping with the prophet-like-Moses theme (as the wilderness summons would seem to indicate). The impostor's promise of rest, moreover, may have had something to do with Ps 95:7b–11, a passage warning Israelites not to put God to the test, as they did at Meribah and Massah "in the wilderness [*erēmo*]," and consequently fail to enter God's "rest [*katapausin*]" (cf. Exod 17:1–7; Num 20:1–13). Although the parallel is not precise, it is worth noting that this passage is cited and commented upon in Hebrews (3:7–4:13), a writing in which Jewish Christians are exhorted not to neglect their "salvation [*sōtērias*]" (2:3) but to "strive to enter that rest [*katapausin*]" (4:11).

Jonathan the refugee. Following the Roman victory over Israel, one Jonathan fled to Cyrene. According to Josephus, this man, by trade a weaver, was one of the sicarii. He persuaded many of the poorer Jews to follow him out into the desert, "promising to show them signs and apparitions" (*J.W.* 7.11.1 §§437–438; *Life* 76 §§424–425). Catullus the Roman governor dispatched troops who routed Jonathan's following and eventually captured the leader himself (*J.W.* 7.11.1 §§439–442). Although Josephus does not describe Jonathan as a (false) prophet, it is likely that this is how the man viewed himself, as the desert summons would imply.

Messianic Priests

Although there were eschatological ideas that envisioned the appearance of messianic priests, some based on the Hasmonean model (*T. Reu.* 6:10–12; *T. Jud.* 21:2–3), others based on Melchizedek (Heb 5, 7–8; perhaps 11QMelch), there are no clear examples of messianic priestly claimants in the period under consideration. It is possible that the Samaritan (see §3 above), who hoped to find the sacred vessels of the Samaritan temple, had some priestly ideas. And possibly the zealots thought that they were installing an anointed high priest (one "Phanni," possibly of Zadokite lineage) on the threshold of the restoration of the kingdom (Josephus, *J.W.* 4.3.8 §§155–157). But this is doubtful, since Phanni, described by Josephus as clownish, incompetent, and reluctant, was probably no more than a pawn in the hands of the rebels. Thus, it would appear that although there were many who made kingly and prophetic claims, evidently none attempted to fulfill the restorative ideas associated with the anointed high priest.

Later Messianic Claimants

Following the defeat of Simon in 135 C.E. it would be three centuries before the reappearance of messianic fervor. Based on various calculations it was believed that Messiah would come either in 440 C.E. (cf. *b. Sanh.* 97b) or in 471 C.E. (cf. *b. ʿAbod. Zar.* 9b). (Other dates were suggested.) Answering this expectation, one "Moses of Crete" (ca. 448 C.E.) promised to lead the Jewish people through the sea, dry-shod, from Crete to Palestine. At his command many of his followers threw themselves into the Mediterranean. Some drowned; others were rescued. Moses himself disappeared (cf. Socrates Scholasticus, *Historia ecclesiastica* 7.38; 12.33). Evidently Moses typology had continued to play an important role in shaping restoration hopes.

A variety of other pseudo-messiahs appeared in the Islamic period (especially in the eighth century), during the later crusades (especially in the twelfth and thirteenth centuries), and even as late as the sixteenth, seventeenth, and eighteenth centuries (cf. *JE* 10:252–55).

General Bibliography

E. BAMMEL and C. F. D. MOULE, eds., *Jesus and the Politics of His Day* (Cambridge: Cambridge University Press, 1984); O. BETZ, *Jesus und das Danielbuch* (Frankfurt am Main: Peter Lang, 1985); M. BLACK, "Judas of Galilee and Josephus' 'Fourth Philosophy,'" in *Josephus Studien* (ed. O. Betz, K. Haacker, and M. Hengel; Göttingen: Vandenhoeck & Ruprecht, 1974), 45–54; S. G. F. BRANDON, *Jesus and the Zealots* (Manchester, Eng.: Manchester University Press, 1967); J. D. CROSSAN, *Jesus and the Revolutionaries* (New York: Harper & Row, 1970); S. FREYNE, *Galilee from Alexander the Great to Hadrian* (Notre Dame, Ind.: University of Notre Dame Press, 1980); A. FUKS, "Aspects of the Jewish Revolt in A.D. 115–117," *JRS* 15 (1961): 98–104; M. HENGEL, *Die Zeloten* (2d ed.; Leiden: Brill, 1976); D. HILL, "Jesus and Josephus' 'Messianic Prophets,'" in *Text and Interpretation* (ed. E. Best and R. McL. Wilson; M. Black FS; New York: Cambridge University Press, 1979), 143–54; R. A. HORSLEY and J. S. HANSON, *Bandits, Prophets, and Messiahs: Popular Movements at the Time of Jesus* (Minneapolis: Winston, 1985); M. DE JONGE, "The Use of the Word 'Anointed' in the Time of Jesus," *NovT* 8 (1966): 132–48; H. P. KINGDON, "Who Were the Zealots and Their Leaders in A.D. 66?" *NTS* 17 (1970–1971): 68–72; W. KLASSEN, "Jesus and Phineas: A Rejected Role Model," *SBLSP* 25 (1986): 490–500; J. KLAUSNER, *The Messianic Idea in Israel* (New York: Macmillan, 1955); W. A. MEEKS, *The Prophet-King: Moses Traditions and the Johannine Christology* (NovTSup 14; Leiden: Brill, 1967); J. NEUSNER, *Messiah in Context* (Philadelphia: Fortress, 1984); J. NEUSNER, W. S. GREEN, and E. FRERICHS, eds., *Judaisms and Their Messiahs at the Turn of the Christian Era* (Cambridge: Cambridge University Press, 1987); J. REILING, "The Use of ψευδοπροφήτης in the Septuagint, Philo, and Josephus," *NovT* 13 (1971): 147–56; D. M. RHOADS, *Israel in Revolution* (Philadelphia: Fortress, 1976); A. J. SALDARINI, "Political and Social Roles of the Pharisees and the Scribes in Galilee," *SBLSP* 27 (1988): 200–209; E. SCHÜRER, *The History of the Jewish People in the Age of Jesus Christ* (rev. and ed. G. Vermes, F. Millar, and M. Black; 3 vols. in 4; Edinburgh: T&T Clark, 1973–1987), vol. 1; E. M. SMALLWOOD, *The Jews under Roman Rule from Pompey to Diocletian* (Leiden: Brill, 1976); M. SMITH, "Zealots and Sicarii, Their Origins and Relation," *HTR* 64 (1971): 1–19; B. WITHERINGTON, *The Christology of Jesus* (Minneapolis: Fortress, 1990), 81–96.

Index of Modern Authors

Index of Ancient Writings and Writers

This index enables the reader to find quickly the name of an ancient author or title. Titles are listed according to the normal form (e.g., *Testament of Levi*) and also according to the name of the ancient worthy (e.g., *Levi, Testament of*). The chapter(s) where the author or title is discussed in the present volume is noted in parentheses.

Testament of Simeon (2)
Testament of Solomon (2)
Testament of Zebulon (2)
Testaments of the Three Patriarchs (2)
Testaments of the Twelve Patriarchs (2)
Testamentum Domini ("Testament of the
    Lord") (8)
Testimony of Truth (10)
Thaddeus, Acts of (8)
Thallus the Samaritan (11)
Themistius (11)
Theocritus (11)
Theodotion (4)
Theodotus (2)
Theognis (11)
Theophilus of Antioch (9)
Theophrastus (11)
Thomas, Acts of (8)
Thomas, Apocalypse of (8)
Thomas, Consumption of (8)
Thomas, Gospel of (8, 10)
Thomas, Infancy Gospel of (8)
Thomas, Martyrdom of (8)
Thomas, Minor Acts of (8)
Thomas the Contender, Book of (10)
Thought of Norea (10)
Three Patriarchs, Testaments of the (2)
Three Steles of Seth (10)
Thucydides (11)
Thunder, Perfect Mind (10)
Tiberius, Pilate's Letter to (8)
Tiberius' Letter to Pilate (8)
Timothy and Aquila, The Dialogue of (8)
Titus' Epistle (8)
Tobit (1)
Tosepta (or Tosefta) (7)
Translation of Philip (8)
Treasures, Cave of (2)
Treatise of Shem (2)
Treatise on the Resurrection (10)
Trimorphic Protennoia (10)
Tripartite Tractate (10)

Truth, Gospel of (10)
Trypho the Jew (9)
Twelve Apostles, Gospel of the (8)
Twelve Patriarchs, Testaments of the (2)

Valentian Exposition (10)
Valerius Harpocration of Alexandria (11)
Valerius Maximus (11)
Velleius Paterculus (11)
Vettius Valens (11)
Virgil (or Publius Vergilius Maro) (11)
Virgin, Apocalypse of (8)
Virgin, Assumption of (8)
Virgin, Coptic Lives of (8)
Virtutibus (On the Virtues) (5)
Vision of Daniel (2)
Vision of Ezra (2)
Vision of Paul (8)
Vita Contemplativa (On the Contemplative
    Life) (5)
Vita Mosis (On the Life of Moses) (5)
Vulgate (4)

Wadi Ed-Daliyeh (3)
Wadi Sdeir (3)
Wadi Seiyâl (3)
Wisdom of Solomon (1)
Writings, Targums to the (6)

Xanthippe and Polyxena, Acts of (8)
Xenophon (11)

Yalqut Shimeoni (7)
Yerushalmi I, II (6)
Yosippon (or Josippon) (5)

Zebulon, Testament of (2)
Zechariah, Apocalypse of (8)
Zephaniah, Apocalypse of (2)
Zizith (7)
Zosimus (11)
Zostrianos (10)

Index of Ancient Sources

32:11   350, 365
32:17   385
32:20   335
32:21   382
32:25   212, 351 (LXX)
32:35   382
32:35–36   397
32:40   406
32:43   359, 383, 395 (LXX)
32:45   346, 347
33:2   404
33:4   365
33:8–11   100, 148
33:12   393
33:17–34:6   136
33:19–21   100

Joshua
1:5   399
2:4   400
2:11–12   398
2:15   400
3:14–17   375
6:12–21   398
6:17   400
6:21–25   398
6:26   148
10:13   24
10:18   352
18:1   375
22:4   396
23:9   375
23:20–21   366
24:14   362
24:18   375

Judges
4:4–22   13
5:4   399
13:2–21   361
13:4   361
13:5–7   343
14:6–7   398
21:23   108

Ruth
1:17   356, 368
3:3   345
4   357

1 Samuel
1:11   361 (LXX)
2:1–10   361
2:4   361

2:5   361
2:26   362
10:1–5   359
11   99
12:22   382
15:22   357
15:29   396
17:28   365
17:34–36   398
21:1–6   348, 353
22:2   349
24:13   348
25:6   364

2 Samuel
1:16   352
1:18   24
3:39   394
5:8   208
7   50, 100, 106, 305
7:2–16   375
7:8   388
7:10–14   100, 148
7:11–16   353
7:12–13   374
7:12–16   5
7:14   395, 398, 408
8:10   365
14–15   99
17:13   358, 367
17:23   352
20:9–10   359
22:3   395 (LXX)
22:14   377
22:18   361
22:50   383
23:7   133

1 Kings
1:32–40   357
1:32–48   357
2:31   364 (LXX)
4:32   354
6:1   375
8:17–18   375
8:19–20   375
9:7   345
10:1–13   348
11:41   24
13:21–22   352
14:19   24
14:29   24
15:7   24
17   50

17:1   401
17:8–16   362
17:17–24   363, 398
18:26–29   344
18:42–45   401
18:44   365
19:10   382
19:14   382
19:18   382
19:19–21   364
22:17   346, 355
22:19   405, 406, 407, 408
22:26–27   398

2 Kings
1–2   50
1:10   363 (LXX)
2   50, 118
2:9–16   363
3:27   367
4–6   50
4:8–37   363
4:25–37   398
4:42–44   355
5:1–14   362
5:13   353
5:27   353
6:15–17   368
8:12   367
9:12–13   357
13   50
17:1–6   12
19:26   354
19:30   354
20:17   367, 368

1 Chronicles
17:13   395
28:2   349 (LXX)
29:15   398
29:29   24

2 Chronicles
6:18   408
9:22   345
9:29   24
12:15   24
13:9   389
15:6   358
18:25–26   398
19:7   401
19:17   391
20:7   400
20:34   24

24:20–21   350
24:20–22   350
24:21   398
26:22   24
28:8–15   364
29:31   399
33:11–13   20
33:18   24
33:18–20   20
35:1–19   10
35:1–36:23   10
35:20–36:21   10
35:25   24
36:22–23   10

Ezra
1:1–3a   10
1:3b–11   10
2:1–4:5   10
4:7–24   10
5:1   346
5:1–10:44   10
9:7   367 (LXX)

Nehemiah
7:73–8:13a   10
9:15   371
10:37   382
12:44   358

Esther
1:1–3:13   14
3:6   367
3:14–4:17   14
5:1–2   14
5:3–8:12   14
8:13–10:3   14
11:1   13

Job
1:1   393
1:6–7   368
1:20   359
1:21   394
2:3   393
4:9   393
4:19   387
5:11   400
5:13   384
8:15   353
9:8   355 (LXX)
12:14   405
13:16   391
14:2   399 (LXX)

15:8   382
16:10   363
17:14–42:11   133
21:9   364
22:9   361
22:29   402
23:10   401
27:17   205
31:36   365
32:19   204
33:30b   369
34:19   400
39:30   351
41:11   382

Psalms
1:1   100, 218
2:1   100, 148
2:1–2   374
2:2   93, 214
2:2–7   359
2:7   213, 353, 355, 359,
      376 (LXX), 395 (LXX),
      396 (LXX)
2:8   345
2:9   407, 408
2:11   391
4:5   390 (LXX)
5:9–10   379 (LXX)
6:3   357 (LXX)
6:8   346
6:9   365 (LXX)
7:14   391 (LXX)
8:3   350 (LXX)
8:5–7   395 (LXX)
8:6   390, 395 (LXX)
8:7   386 (LXX)
9:8   377
9:14   357 (LXX)
9:28   379 (LXX)
11:1   148
11:4   344
11:6   407, 408
12:8   356
13:2–3   379 (LXX)
13:7   382 (LXX)
14:7   374
15:5   331
15:8–11   374 (LXX)
15:10   376 (LXX)
16:4   374
16:8–11   374
16:9–10   374
16:10   386

17:5–9   132
17:21   358
17:50   383 (LXX)
18:2   361
18:5   382 (LXX)
18:6   401
18:6–13   132
18:71   361
21:4   345
21:7   248, 358
21:9   401
21:23   395 (LXX)
22   401
22:1   360
22:7   360
22:8   352
22:18   360
22:21   394
23:1   349, 385 (LXX), 406
23:2   406
23:5   359
24:3–4   343
25:1   368
25:11   403
26:6   352
27:4   345
28:3   348
28:4   394, 401, 408
31:5   368, 402
32:1–2   380
32:6   398 (LXX)
32:9   398 (LXX)
33:9   401 (LXX)
33:13–17   402 (LXX)
33:15   398 (LXX)
34:7   343 (LXX)
34:8   382, 395
34:13   400
34:19   394
34:20   373
35:19   373
36:9   408
36:19   375 (LXX)
37:2–39   148
37:11   343
38:11   352
38:13   398 (LXX)
39:1   400
39:7   390 (LXX)
39:7–9   397 (LXX)
39:12   401
41:3   361
41:9   359, 372
43:23   381 (LXX)

27:2 344
27:3 407
37–71 29, 69, 71
37:7 355
38:2 352, 359
39:4 366
39:4–8 211
40:1 406
42:1–3 369, 370, 373
45:3 373
46:3 392
47:3 364
48:4 362
48:7 400
48:10 355, 404
51:1 408
51:2 367
51:3 248
51:4 357
51:5 355
52:4 355
54:6 348, 407
58:5–6 392
60:7 359
60:8 404
61:5 408
61:7 396
61:8 351
61:12 345
62:2–3 351
62:4 393
62:5 71
62:13–14 358
62:14 359
62:15 355
63:1 348
63:10 366
66:2 407
67:5–7 30
67:13 343, 362
69:27 351, 352, 371
69:28 354
70:1–4 398
72–82 29, 389
72–107 144
72:2 403
72:3 408
80:2–8 30
80:4–7 367
81:2–3 406
83–90 29
83:3–5 403
86:1 406
89 364

89–90 364
89:8 392
89:42–49 29
91–107 29
91:7 378
91:15 403
93:3 404
94:8 363, 401
96:7 343
97:6–104 29
97:8–10 364, 401
98:4 399
99:6–9 71
99:8 378
100:1–2 358
100:12 132
102:5 392
103:3–4 132
103:4 351
103:7–8 132
103:8 354
103:15 132
104:1 349, 364
104:4 357
105:1 132
106–107 97
106:9–10 91

2 Enoch
1:5 405, 407, 408
1:7 349, 378
3:1 373
3:3 405, 407
4:1 405
7:1 403, 404
8:1 388
8:3 405
9:1 351, 361
10:2 408
10:4 351, 379
14:8 349
19:4 407
20:1 392, 405
20:3 405, 406, 407, 408
20:4 391
22:8 387
22:9 405, 406
22:10 348
23:5 30, 351
24:2 30, 398
24:3 401
25:1 398
29:1 395
29:4 390

29:5 71, 364
30:2–3 30
30:15 346
30:16 380
30:17 393
31:4 364
31:6 388
33:4 368, 382, 399, 403
34:1 347, 387, 390
39:2 405
39:3–4 372
40:13 404
41:2 359
42:1 406, 408
42:3 351, 388
42:5 365
42:11 389
42:12 390
42:14 346
44:1 400
44:4 363
44:5 345
45:3 343
46:1 344
46:3 369, 370, 371
47:4 403
48:5 398
49:1 344, 401
50:2 367
50:3–4 394, 397, 399, 402
50:4 382, 397
50:5 363, 365
51:3 402
51:5 374, 376
52:9 343
53:3 396
54:1 374
60:1 392
61:2 346, 372
61:5 388
64:5 369
65:8 348
65:9 408
66:2 391
66:6 381, 388
67:2 392
70:16 352
70:23 351

3 Enoch
1–2 31
3–16 31
4:6–9 381
10:3–11:3 370

17–40   31
41–48   31
45:1   397

4 Ezra
3:6–8   380
3:17–18   381
3:20   354
3:21–22   380
4:8   370, 381
4:26–37   346
4:33–37   406
4:35–36   382
4:42   345
4:51–52   359
5:2   351
5:5   367
5:41–42   393
5:42   356
6:13–15   358
6:20   408
6:21   358
6:23   386, 393
6:25   358
6:26   349, 355, 363
6:38   369
6:52   359
6:56   359
6:58   343
7:11   381
7:11–14   365
7:15   383
7:26–44   408
7:33–34   386
7:36   366, 406
7:47–61   381
7:61   407
7:72   380
7:75   350
7:77   345
7:97   348, 355
7:98   343, 409
7:99   384, 409
7:118–19   380
8:3   350
8:22   395
8:41   353, 354
8:47b–50   367
8:51–55   408
8:52   405, 409
8:59   366
8:60   378
9:3   358
9:15   350

9:31   354
9:31–32   354
9:37   343, 380
10:7   389
10:9   381
10:27   398, 408
10:30   405
11   407
11:1   407
12:31–33   406
12:43   402
13:3–8   382
13:16–24   393
13:31   351, 358
13:34   407
13:35–37   382
13:43   408
14:15   387
14:20   369
14:23–26   394
14:37–48   394
15:15   351

Hellenistic Synagogal Prayers
1:8   59
4:22   59
5:20   59
6:2   59
6:13   59

History of the Rechabites
1–2   53
1:4   53, 390
3–15   53
16   53
19–23   53

Jannes and Jambres
394

Joseph and Aseneth
4:9   368
8:5   72, 359, 371
8:10–11   370, 371
8:11   359
14:3   352
15:8   365
16:14   371
16:16   359
19:8   359
21:21   353
28:12   48
29:4   352
29:9   54

Jubilees
1:23   379
1:28   375, 389
1:29   403
2:1   368
2:14   119
2:19   381
3:7–8   145
3:25   354
4:7–11   145
4:16–25   404
4:30   403
5:1–2   145
5:3–4   370
6:12   145
7:1   373
7:6   369
7:35   403
7:39   404
8:2   362
8:14   404
8:28   379
9:5   379
10:3   393
10:7   353
11:11   354
12:15–17   145
13:17   347
13:29   119
15:8   379
16:19   401, 406
17:1   379
17:21   371
19:9   400
19:21   380
21:11   356
21:22   404
21:22–24   145
22:11   391
22:16   388
23:6–7   145
23:21–23   101, 145
23:24   388
24:15   354
25:14   372
26:2   391
26:23–24   391
27:19–21   145
31:12–25   380
32:20–22   406
32:24–26   373
33:16   380
35:8–10   145
36:12   145

Ecclesiastes
1:1   201
1:4   201
1:11   201, 203
3:11   201
4:15   201
7:24   201, 203
9:7   201
10:6   200

Song of Songs
1:8   203
1:17   203
4:5   203
7:4   203
7:12–14   203
8:1   210
8:1–4   203
8:5   359

Lamentations
2:22   200, 203
4:22   200, 203

Esther (I)
1:1   201, 203
7:9   251

Cairo (Genizah) Targum

Genesis
2:17–3:6 (MS B)   191
4:4–16 (MS B)   191
6:18–7:15 (MS E)   191
7:17 (MS D)   191
8:8 (MS D)   191
9:5–23 (MS E)   191
15:1–4 (MS H)   191
28:17–31:34 (MS E)   191
31:38–54 (MS C)   191
32:13–29 (MS C)   191
34:9–25 (MS C)   191
34:23 (MS C)   345
35:6–15 (MS C)   191
36:8–9, 24 (MS D)   191
37:15–44 (MS E)   191
37:19–34 (MS D)   191
38:16–26 (MS D)   191
38:16–39:10 (MS E)   191
38:26 (MS D)   345
40:5–18 (MS E)   191
40:43–53 (MS E)   191
41:6–26 (MS C)   191
41:32–41 (MS E)   191
41:43–57 (MS E)   191
42:34–43:10 (MS E)   191

43:7–44:23 (MS D)   191
43:23–44:4 (MS E)   191
44:16–20 (MS Z)   191
46:26– 47:5 (MS D)   191
47:27–49:17 (MS Z)   191
47:29–48:21 (MS D)   191
49:18 (MS F)   397

Exodus
4:7–11 (MS A)   191
5:20–6:10 (MS D)   191
7:10–22 (MS D)   191
9:21–33 (MS D)   191
20:24–23:14 (MS A)   191
39:23– 37 (MS D)   191
40:9–27 (MS D)   191

Deuteronomy
5:19–26 (MS D)   191
26:18–27:11 (MS D)   191
28:15–18 (MS D)   191
28:26–29 (MS D)   191

DEAD SEA SCROLLS

**Cairo Damascus
Document (CD)**
1:7   144
2:4b–13   390
2:18   144
3:14–20   364
3:20   386
4:12–19   368
4:19   334, 357
4:19–5:2   350
4:20–5:2   150, 356
5:17–19   72, 394
6:1–2   346
6:7   218
6:15   205
6:17   150
7:13–21   377
7:18–21   247, 343
8:12   334, 357
8:18   334
9:6–8   349
9:7–10   129
9:16–10   349
10:14   353
11:13–14   348, 365
11:21–22   344
12:10–11   395
14:3–4   107

19:5–11   359
19:12–13   406, 407
19:33 [B]   152
19:33–34   370
20:12 [B]   152

1QpHab
2:1–2   150
2:3   152
3:8–12   351
7:17–8:3   378
8:8   150
8:8–13   87
8:11–12   150
9:4–5   150
9:9–12   87
9:14–10:1   367
10:1   150
10:9   150
11:2–8   90

1QapGen
2:5   4
20:28–29   355
22:27   4, 374

1Q27
frg. 1 i 2–8   393
5–6   369, 403

1Q28a
2:11–12   93

1Q28b
5   93

1QS
1:3   361
1:5   370, 403
1:9   366
1:21   152
2   129
2:4–10   384
2:16   366
3:7   371
3:13   366
3:13–15   393
3:18–19   372, 373, 404
3:20–21   393
3:21   371, 372
3:24–4:1   372
4:2–11   389
4:4   371
4:4–5   369